CODE OF VIRGINIA
1950

2023 Cumulative Supplement

ANNOTATED

Prepared under the Supervision of

The Virginia Code Commission

BY

The Editorial Staff of the Publishers

D1548684

VOLUME 9

2019 REPLACEMENT

[REPRINT]

*Current through the 2023 Regular Session
of the General Assembly*

**Place in Pocket of Corresponding Volume of Main Set.
This Supersedes Previous Supplement, Which
May Be Retained for Reference Purposes.**

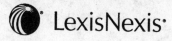 LexisNexis·

ISBN 978-0-327-11171-9 (set)
ISBN 978-1-5221-7081-5 (Vol. 9)

www.lexisnexis.com

Customer Service: 1-800-833-9844

(Pub. 49005)

PREFACE

A complete explanation of the supplements to the Code of Virginia is contained in the Foreword appearing in Volume 1.

Under Article IV, § 13, of the Constitution, the acts adopted at the 2023 Regular Session of the General Assembly are effective July 1, 2023, except where an act has an emergency clause or specifies some other effective date. Effective dates other than the constitutional effective date are stated in notes.

SCOPE OF LEGISLATION

This 2023 Supplement is current through the 2023 Regular Session of the General Assembly.

SCOPE OF ANNOTATIONS

To better serve our customers, by making our annotations more current, LexisNexis has changed the sources that are read to create annotations for this publication. Rather than waiting for cases to appear in printed reporters, we now read court decisions as they are released by the courts. A consequence of this more current reading of cases, as they are posted online on LEXIS, is that the most recent cases annotated may not yet have print reporter citations. These will be provided, as they become available, through later publications.

This publication contains annotations taken from decisions of the Virginia Supreme Court, Virginia Court of Appeals, selected Virginia Circuit Court opinions, and selected federal decisions posted on LEXIS as of April 30, 2023. Additionally, annotations have been taken from Opinions of the Attorney General through December 2022.

UNPUBLISHED OPINIONS OF COURT OF APPEALS

Some of the annotations contained in this supplement are derived from unpublished opinions of the Court of Appeals of Virginia. These opinions will not appear in the Court of Appeals Reports or any other court reporter.

The Court of Appeals has placed the following footnote on all unpublished opinions: "Pursuant to Code § 17.1-413, recodifying § 17-116.010, this opinion is not designated for publication."

"Although an unpublished opinion of the Court has no precedential value, a court or commission does not err by considering the rationale and adopting it to the extent it is persuasive." Fairfax County School Board v. Rose, 29 Va. App. 32, 509 S.E.2d 525 (1999).

A copy of the full text of any unpublished opinion can be obtained by contacting: Court of Appeals of Virginia, Attention: Clerk's Assistant (Opinions), 109 North Eighth Street, Richmond, Virginia 23219.

USER'S GUIDE

In order to assist both the legal profession and the lay person in obtaining the maximum benefit from the Code of Virginia, a User's Guide has been included in Volume 1. This guide contains comments and information on the many features found within the Code of Virginia intended to increase the usefulness of this set of laws to the user. See Volume 1 for the complete User's Guide.

Suggestions, comments, or questions about the Code of Virginia or this Cumulative Supplement are welcome. You may call us toll free 1-800-833-9844, or e-mail us at customer.support@bender.com. Direct written inquiries to the following address: 9443 Springboro Pike, Miamisburg, OH 45342.

For an online bookstore, technical and customer support, and other company information, visit our Internet home page at **http://www.lexisnexis.com**.

TABLE OF TITLES

TABLE OF TITLES

CODE OF VIRGINIA

2023 CUMULATIVE SUPPLEMENT

TITLE 59.1.

TRADE AND COMMERCE.

Chapter
54. Fair Food Delivery Act, §§ 59.1-586 through 59.1-588.
55. Benefits Consortium, §§ 59.1-589 through 59.1-592.
56. Genetic Data Privacy, §§ 59.1-593 through 59.1-602.

CHAPTER 1.1.

VIRGINIA ANTITRUST ACT.

Section
59.1-9.3. Definitions.
59.1-9.7. Discriminatory practices unlawful; proof; payment or acceptance of certain commissions, etc., unlawful.
59.1-9.11. Penalty for flagrant violations.
59.1-9.12. Personal suit for injunction or actual damages.
59.1-9.13. Effect of conviction in other proceedings.
59.1-9.14. Limitation of actions.
59.1-9.15. Actions on behalf of Commonwealth or localities; injunctive and other equitable relief; damages.

§ 59.1-9.3. Definitions.

When used in this chapter, unless the context requires a different meaning:
"*Commodity*" includes any kind of real or personal property.
"*Person*" includes any natural person; any trust or association of persons, formal or otherwise; or any corporation, partnership, company, or other legal or commercial entity.
"*Service*" includes any activity that is performed in whole or in part for the purpose of financial gain, including personal service, rental, leasing, or licensing for use.
"*Trade or commerce*," "*trade,*" or "*commerce*"includes all economic activity involving or relating to any commodity, service, or business activity.

History.
1974, c. 545; 2023, c. 522.

The 2023 amendments.
The 2023 amendment by c. 522, rewrote the section.

§ 59.1-9.7. Discriminatory practices unlawful; proof; payment or acceptance of certain commissions, etc., unlawful.

A. It is unlawful for any person engaged in commerce, in the course of such commerce, either directly or indirectly, to discriminate in price between different purchasers of commodities or services of like grade and quality, where either or any of the purchasers involved in such commerce are in competition, where such commodities or services are sold for use, consumption or resale within the Commonwealth and where the effect of such discrimination may be substantially to lessen competition or tend to create a monopoly in any line of commerce, or to injure, destroy or prevent competition with any person who either grants or knowingly receives the benefit of such discrimination, or with customers of either of them; provided, that nothing herein contained shall prevent differentials which make only due allowance for differences in the cost of manufacture, sale or delivery resulting from the different methods or quantities in which such commodities or services are to such purchasers sold or delivered; and provided further, that nothing herein contained shall prevent persons engaged in selling commodities or services in commerce from selecting their own customers in bona fide transactions and not in restraint of trade; and provided further, that nothing herein contained shall prevent price changes from time to time where in response to changing conditions affecting the market for or the marketability of the goods concerned, such as, but not limited to, actual or imminent deterioration of perishable goods, obsolescence of seasonal goods, distress sales under court process, or sales in good faith in discontinuance of business in the goods concerned.

B. Upon proof being made, at any suit on a complaint under this section, that there has been discrimination in price or services or facilities furnished or in payment for services or facilities to be rendered, the burden of rebutting the prima facie case thus made by showing justification shall be upon the person charged with a violation of this section; provided, however, that nothing herein contained shall prevent a seller rebutting the prima facie case thus made by showing that his lower price or the furnishing of services or facilities to any purchaser or purchasers was made in good faith to meet an equally low price of a competitor, or the services or facilities furnished by a competitor.

C. It is unlawful for any person engaged in commerce, in the course of such commerce, to pay or grant, or to receive or accept, anything of value as a commission, brokerage, or other compensation, or any allowance or discount in lieu thereof, except for and not exceeding the actual cost of such services rendered in connection with the sale or purchase of goods, wares or merchandise.

D. It is unlawful for any person engaged in commerce to pay or contract for the payment of anything of value to or for the benefit of a customer of such person in the course of such commerce as compensation or in consideration for any services or facilities furnished by or through such customer in connection with the processing, handling, sale or offering for sale of any products, commodities or services manufactured, sold or offered for sale by such person, unless such payment or consideration is available on proportionally equal terms to all other customers competing in the distribution of such products, commodities or services.

E. It is unlawful for any person to discriminate in favor of one purchaser against another purchaser or purchasers of a commodity bought for resale with or without processing, by contracting to furnish or furnishing, or by contributing to the furnishing of, any services or facilities connected with the processing, handling, sale or offering for sale of such commodity so purchased upon terms not accorded to all purchasers on proportionally equal terms.

F. It is unlawful for any person engaged in commerce, in the course of such commerce, knowingly to induce or receive a discrimination in price that is prohibited by this section.

History.
1974, c. 545; 2023, c. 522.

The 2023 amendments.
The 2023 amendment by c. 522, made stylistic changes.

§ 59.1-9.10. Investigation by Attorney General of suspected violations; civil investigative demand to witnesses; access to business records, etc.

CIRCUIT COURT OPINIONS

Construction. — Attorney General has a statutorily imposed duty under subsection N of § 59.1-9.10 to maintain the secrecy of all evidence obtained, but the statute also clearly gives the Attorney General discretion to share any such information with any federal or state law-enforcement authority that has restrictions governing confidentiality similar to those contained in this subsection. Commonwealth v. Nexus Servs., 102 Va. Cir. 458, 2018 Va. Cir. LEXIS 2473 (Richmond Aug. 7, 2018).

Subsection N permits the Attorney General to forward the collected information in his discretion, the court has no authority to override or limit that statute, and the law clearly provided the Attorney General the right to seek the information sought in the civil investigative demand in this case; the Attorney General needed the information to conduct its investigation and names and contact information of individuals who dealt with the business and/or are connected to the bond holders, was pertinent. Commonwealth v. Nexus Servs., 102 Va. Cir. 458, 2018 Va. Cir. LEXIS 2473 (Richmond Aug. 7, 2018).

§ 59.1-9.11. Penalty for flagrant violations.

In any action or proceeding brought under subsection A of § 59.1-9.15 the court may assess for the benefit of the Commonwealth a civil penalty of not more than $100,000 for each willful or flagrant violation of this chapter. No civil penalty shall be imposed in connection with any violation for which any fine or penalty is imposed pursuant to federal law.

History.
1974, c. 545; 2023, c. 522.

The 2023 amendments.
The 2023 amendment by c. 522, substituted "subsection A of § 59.1-9.15" for "§ 59.1-9.15(a)" in the first sentence.

§ 59.1-9.12. Personal suit for injunction or actual damages.

A. Any person threatened with injury or damage to his business or property by reason of a violation of this chapter may institute an action or proceeding for injunctive relief, disgorgement, and other forms of equitable monetary relief as the court deems appropriate when and under the same conditions and principles as injunctive relief is granted in other cases.

B. Any person injured in his business or property by reason of a violation of this chapter may recover the actual damages sustained, and, as determined by the court, the costs of suit and reasonable attorney fees. If the trier of facts finds that the violation is willful or flagrant, it may increase damages to an amount not in excess of three times the actual damages sustained.

History.
1974, c. 545; 2023, c. 522.

The 2023 amendments.
The 2023 amendment by c. 522, added "disgorgement, and other forms of equitable monetary relief as the court deems appropriate" in subsection A; substituted "attorney" for "attorney's" in the first sentence of subsection B: and made stylistic changes.

§ 59.1-9.13. Effect of conviction in other proceedings.

A final judgment or decree to the effect that a defendant has violated this chapter, other than a consent judgment or decree entered before any testimony has been taken, in an action or proceeding brought under subsection A of § 59.1-9.15 is prima facie evidence against that defendant in any other action or proceeding against him brought under § 59.1-9.12 or subsection B of § 59.1-9.15 as to all matters with respect to which the judgment or decree would be an estoppel between the parties thereto.

History.
  1974, c. 545; 2023, c. 522.

The 2023 amendments.
  The 2023 amendment by c. 522, substituted

"subsection A of § 59.1-9.15" for "§ 59.1-9.15(a)" and "subsection B of § 59.1-9.15" for "§ 59.1-9.15(b)".

§ 59.1-9.14. Limitation of actions.

A. An action under subsection A of § 59.1-9.15 to recover a civil penalty is barred if it is not commenced within four years after the cause of action accrues.

B. An action under subsection B of § 59.1-9.12 or subsection B of § 59.1-9.15 to recover damages is barred if it is not commenced within four years after the cause of action accrues, or within one year after the conclusion of any action or proceeding under subsection A of § 59.1-9.15 commenced within or before that time based in whole or in part on any matter complained of in the action for damages, whichever is later.

History.
  1974, c. 545; 2023, c. 522.

The 2023 amendments.
  The 2023 amendment by c. 522, substituted "subsection A of § 59.1-9.1" for "§ 59.1-9.15(a)" in subsection A; in subsection B, substituted "subsection B of § 59.1-9.12(b) or subsection B of § 59.1-9.15(b)" for "§ 59.1-9.12(b) or § 59.1-9.15(b)" in subsection B: and made stylistic changes.

§ 59.1-9.15. Actions on behalf of Commonwealth or localities; injunctive and other equitable relief; damages.

A. The Attorney General on behalf of the Commonwealth, or the attorney for the Commonwealth or county attorney on behalf of a county, or the city attorney on behalf of a city, or the town attorney on behalf of a town may institute actions and proceedings for injunctive relief, disgorgement, and other forms of equitable monetary relief as the court deems appropriate, and civil penalties for violations of this chapter. In any such action or proceeding in which the plaintiff substantially prevails, the court may award the cost of suit, including reasonable attorney fees, to such plaintiff.

B. The Commonwealth, a political subdivision thereof, or any public agency injured in its business or property by reason of a violation of this chapter, may recover the actual damages sustained, reasonable attorney fees and the costs of suit. If the trier of facts finds that the violation is willful or flagrant, it may increase damages to an amount not in excess of three times the actual damages sustained.

C. The Attorney General in acting under subsection (a) or (b) of this section may also bring such action on behalf of any political subdivision of the Commonwealth, provided that the Attorney General shall notify each such subdivision of the pendency of the action and give such subdivision the option of exclusion from the action.

D. The Attorney General may bring a civil action to recover damages and secure other relief as provided by this chapter as parens patriae respecting injury to the general economy of the Commonwealth.

History.
  1974, c. 545; 1982, c. 60; 1988, c. 589; 2023, c. 522.

The 2023 amendments.
  The 2023 amendment by c. 522, in subsection A, added "disgorgement, and other forms of equitable monetary relief as the court deems appropriate" in the first sentence, and substituted "including reasonable attorney fees" for "including a reasonable attorney's fee" in the second sentence; substituted "attorney" for "at-

torney's" in the first sentence of subsection B:
and made stylistic changes.

CHAPTER 2.1.

VIRGINIA HOME SOLICITATION SALES ACT.

Section
59.1-21.2. Definitions.

§ 59.1-21.2. Definitions.

A. As used in this chapter, *"home solicitation sale"* means:

1. A consumer sale or lease of goods or services in which the seller or a person acting for him engages (i) in a personal solicitation of the sale or lease or (ii) in a solicitation of the sale or lease by telephone or electronic means at any residence other than that of the seller without prior invitation or appointment; and

2. The buyer's agreement or offer to purchase or lease is there given to the seller or a person acting for him.

B. As used in this chapter:

1. *"Home solicitation sale"* does not mean a consumer sale or lease of farm equipment or a consumer sale made by an entity regulated by the State Corporation Commission's Bureau of Insurance, an affiliate of any such entity, or a dealer licensed by the Motor Vehicle Dealer Board.

2. *"Home solicitation sale"* does not include cash sales of less than $25, a sale or lease made pursuant to a preexisting revolving charge account, or a sale or lease made pursuant to prior negotiations between the parties.

3. *"Home solicitation sale"* does not include sales made entirely by telephone or electronic means at the initiation of the buyer and without any other contact between the buyer and the seller or its representative prior to the delivery of goods or performance of services.

C. As used in this chapter, *"goods"* means tangible personal property and also includes a merchandise certificate whereby a writing is issued by the seller which is not redeemable in cash and is usable in lieu of cash in exchange for goods or services; "seller" means seller or lessor and "buyer" means buyer or lessee.

History.
1970, c. 668; 1972, c. 448; 1975, c. 217; 1986, c. 577; 2023, cc. 301, 302.

The 2023 amendments.
The 2023 amendment by cc. 301 and 302 are identical, and added "As used in this chapter" in the introductory language of subsection A; in subdivision A 1, substituted "telephone or electronic" and added "without prior invitation or appointment"; added the introductory language of subsection B; rewrote subdivision B 1, which formerly read: "1. 'Home solicitation sale' shall does not mean a consumer sale or lease of farm equipment"; added "'Home solicitation sale'" in subdivision B 2; added subdivision B 3; and made a stylistic change.

CIRCUIT COURT OPINIONS

"Home Solicitation Sale." — Defendant's demurrer was sustained because plaintiff did not state sufficient facts to support a violation of the Virginia Home Solicitation Sales Act because she failed to sufficiently allege a home solicitation sale as defendant came to plaintiff's residence at her request to conduct home repair services; and her complaint failed to allege that she agreed to purchase services from defendant when its representative first visited her at her home because the contract for specific services was typed, indicating that it likely was not completed at the time of the initial visit, and the contract was dated almost two months before plaintiff's dated signature, further proof that she probably did not execute the agreement during the home visit. Theuer v. Norfolk Air Heating & Cooling, Inc., 106 Va. Cir. 113, 2020 Va. Cir. LEXIS 190 (Norfolk Oct. 7, 2020).

CHAPTER 9.
SECONDHAND ARTICLES.

Article 4. Scrap Metal Purchasers.

Section
59.1-136.3. Purchases of nonferrous scrap, metal articles, and proprietary articles.

ARTICLE 4.
SCRAP METAL PURCHASERS.

§ 59.1-136.3. Purchases of nonferrous scrap, metal articles, and proprietary articles.

A. Except as provided in § 59.1-136.4, scrap metal purchasers may purchase nonferrous scrap, metal articles, and proprietary articles from any person who is not an authorized scrap seller or the authorized agent and employee of an authorized scrap seller only in accordance with the following requirements and procedures:

1. At the time of sale, the seller of any nonferrous scrap, metal article, or proprietary article shall provide a driver's license or other government-issued current photographic identification including the seller's full name, current address, date of birth, and social security or other recognized identification number; and

2. The scrap metal purchaser shall record the seller's identification information, as well as the time and date of the transaction, the license number of the seller's vehicle, and a description of the items received from the seller, in a permanent ledger maintained at the scrap metal purchaser's place of business. The ledger shall be made available upon request to any law-enforcement official, conservator of the peace, or special conservator of the peace appointed pursuant to § 19.2-13, in the performance of his duties who presents his credentials at the scrap metal purchaser's normal business location during regular business hours. Records required by this subdivision shall be maintained by the scrap metal dealer at its normal place of business or at another readily accessible and secure location for at least five years.

B. Upon compliance with the other requirements of this section and § 59.1-136.4, a scrap metal purchaser may purchase proprietary articles from a person who is not an authorized scrap seller or the authorized agent and employee of an authorized scrap seller if the scrap metal purchaser complies with one of the following:

1. The scrap metal purchaser receives from the person seeking to sell the proprietary articles documentation, such as a bill of sale, receipt, letter of authorization, or similar evidence, establishing that the person lawfully possesses the proprietary articles to be sold; or

2. The scrap metal purchaser shall document a diligent inquiry into whether the person selling or delivering the same has a legal right to do so, and, after purchasing a proprietary article from a person without obtaining the documentation described in subdivision 1, shall submit a report to the local sheriff's department or the chief of police of the locality, by the close of the following business day, describing the proprietary article and including a copy

of the seller's identifying information, and hold the proprietary article for not less than 15 days following purchase.

C. The scrap metal purchaser shall take a photographic or video image of all proprietary articles purchased from anyone other than an authorized scrap seller. Such image shall be of sufficient quality so as to reasonably identify the subject of the image and shall be maintained by the scrap metal purchaser no less than 30 days from the date the image is taken. Any image taken and maintained in accordance with this subdivision shall be made available upon the request of any law-enforcement officer conducting official law-enforcement business.

D. The scrap metal purchaser may purchase nonferrous scrap, metal articles, and proprietary articles directly from an authorized scrap seller and from the authorized agent or employee of an authorized scrap seller.

E. For purchases of a catalytic converter or the parts thereof, a scrap metal purchaser shall adhere to the compliance provisions of subdivisions B 1 and 2. Copies of the documentation required under subdivisions B 1 and 2 shall (i) establish that the person from whom the scrap metal purchaser purchased the catalytic converter or the parts thereof had the lawful possession of such catalytic converter or the parts thereof at the time of sale or delivery and (ii) detail the scrap metal purchaser's diligent inquiry into whether such person selling or delivering the catalytic converter or the parts thereof had a legal right to do so. Such documentation shall be maintained by the scrap metal purchaser at his normal place of business or at another readily accessible and secure location for at least two years after the purchase. Such copies shall be made available upon request to any law-enforcement officer, conservator of the peace, or special conservator of the peace appointed pursuant to § 19.2-13 in the performance of his duties who presents his credentials at the scrap metal purchaser's normal business location during normal business hours.

History.
2007, c. 917; 2013, c. 414; 2022, cc. 664, 665.

The 2022 amendments.
The 2022 amendments by cc. 664 and 665 are identical, and added subsection E.

CHAPTER 11.1.

FIREARMS.

§ 59.1-148.3. Purchase of handguns or other weapons of certain officers.

A. The Department of State Police, the Department of Wildlife Resources, the Virginia Alcoholic Beverage Control Authority, the Virginia Lottery, the Marine Resources Commission, the Capitol Police, the Department of Conservation and Recreation, the Department of Forestry, any sheriff, any regional jail board or authority, and any local police department may allow any sworn law-enforcement officer, deputy, or regional jail officer, a local fire department may allow any full-time sworn fire marshal, the Department of Motor Vehicles may allow any law-enforcement officer, any institution of higher education named in § 23.1-1100 may allow any campus police officer appointed pursuant to Article 3 (§ 23.1-809 et seq.) of Chapter 8 of Title 23.1, retiring on or after

July 1, 1991, and the Department of Corrections may allow any employee with internal investigations authority designated by the Department of Corrections pursuant to subdivision 11 of § 53.1-10 who retires (i) after at least 10 years of service, (ii) at 70 years of age or older, or (iii) as a result of a service-incurred disability or who is receiving long-term disability payments for a service-incurred disability with no expectation of returning to the employment where he incurred the disability to purchase the service handgun issued or previously issued to him by the agency or institution at a price of $1. If the previously issued weapon is no longer available, a weapon of like kind may be substituted for that weapon. This privilege shall also extend to any former Superintendent of State Police who leaves service after a minimum of five years. This privilege shall also extend to any person listed in this subsection who is eligible for retirement with at least 10 years of service who resigns on or after July 1, 1991, in good standing from one of the agencies listed in this section to accept a position covered by the Virginia Retirement System. Other weapons issued by the agencies listed in this subsection for personal duty use of an officer may, with approval of the agency head, be sold to the officer subject to the qualifications of this section at a fair market price determined as in subsection B, so long as the weapon is a type and configuration that can be purchased at a regular hardware or sporting goods store by a private citizen without restrictions other than the instant background check.

B. The agencies listed in subsection A may allow any sworn law-enforcement officer who retires with five or more years of service, but less than 10, to purchase the service handgun issued to him by the agency at a price equivalent to the weapon's fair market value on the date of the officer's retirement. Any sworn law-enforcement officer employed by any of the agencies listed in subsection A who is retired for disability as a result of a nonservice-incurred disability may purchase the service handgun issued to him by the agency at a price equivalent to the weapon's fair market value on the date of the officer's retirement. Determinations of fair market value may be made by reference to a recognized pricing guide.

C. The agencies listed in subsection A may allow the immediate survivor of any sworn law-enforcement officer (i) who is killed in the line of duty or (ii) who dies in service and has at least 10 years of service to purchase the service handgun issued to the officer by the agency at a price of $1.

D. The governing board of any institution of higher learning named in § 23.1-1100 may allow any campus police officer appointed pursuant to Article 3 (§ 23.1-809 et seq.) of Chapter 8 of Title 23.1 who retires on or after July 1, 1991, to purchase the service handgun issued to him at a price equivalent to the weapon's fair market value on the date of the officer's retirement. Determinations of fair market value may be made by reference to a recognized pricing guide.

E. Any officer who at the time of his retirement is a sworn law-enforcement officer with a state agency listed in subsection A, when the agency allows purchases of service handguns, and who retires after 10 years of state service, even if a portion of his service was with another state agency, may purchase the service handgun issued to him by the agency from which he retires at a price of $1.

F. The sheriff of Hanover County may allow any auxiliary or volunteer deputy sheriff with a minimum of 10 years of service, upon leaving office, to purchase for $1 the service handgun issued to him.

G. Any sheriff or local police department may allow any auxiliary law-enforcement officer with more than 10 years of service to purchase the service handgun issued to him by the agency at a price that is equivalent to or less than the weapon's fair market value on the date of purchase by the officer.

17

H. The agencies listed in subsection A may allow any full-time sworn law-enforcement officer currently employed by the agency to purchase his service handgun, with the approval of the chief law-enforcement officer of the agency, at a fair market price. This subsection shall only apply when the agency has purchased new service handguns for its officers, and the handgun subject to the sale is no longer used by the agency or officer in the course of duty.

I. The Department of State Police may allow any law-enforcement officer formerly employed by the Department who had at least 10 years of service with the Department and has been elected to a constitutional office to purchase his service handgun, with the approval of the Superintendent of State Police, at a fair market price.

History.
1989, c. 175; 1990, c. 359; 1991, c. 389; 1992, cc. 63, 83, 195; 1996, c. 50; 1998, c. 173; 1999, c. 312; 2000, c. 391; 2002, c. 25; 2003, c. 106; 2004, c. 136; 2005, c. 168; 2006, c. 185; 2007, c. 813; 2009, cc. 289, 412; 2010, cc. 590, 864; 2011, c. 628; 2012, c. 218; 2013, c. 62; 2014, c. 225; 2015, cc. 38, 730; 2016, cc. 196, 210, 215; 2019, c. 608; 2020, c. 958; 2022, cc. 245, 246; 2023, c. 203.

The 2020 amendments.
The 2020 amendment by c. 958 substituted "Department of Wildlife Resources" for "Department of Game and Inland Fisheries" in subsection A in the first sentence.

The 2022 amendments.
The 2022 amendments by cc. 245 and 246 are identical, and in subsections A through C, and E, deleted "full-time" preceding "sworn law-enforcement officer" throughout; and substituted "education" for "learning" in subsection A in the first sentence.

The 2023 amendments.
The 2023 amendment by c. 203, deleted "of the Department" following "Superintendent" in the third sentence of subsection A; and added subsection I.

CHAPTER 17.

VIRGINIA CONSUMER PROTECTION ACT.

§ 59.1-196. Title.

CIRCUIT COURT OPINIONS

Particularity of claim. — Virginia Consumer Protection Act (VCPA) claim does not need to be alleged with the same particularity as common-law fraud because a VCPA claim need only be proven to the ordinary preponderance of the evidence standard; a cause of action for fraud had different elements of proof from a VCPA claim; and increasing the burden on a consumer to bring a VCPA claim by imposing a common-law pleading requirement would be contrary to the statutory purpose to expand the remedies afforded to consumers and to relax the restrictions imposed upon them by the common law. West v. Christopher Consultants,

106 Va. Cir. 6, 2020 Va. Cir. LEXIS 82 (Loudoun County June 10, 2020).
Pleading insufficient to state cause of action. — Court sustained the demurrer to Count IX alleging a violation of the Virginia Consumer Protection Act (VCPA) as the VCPA did not apply to the engineering work of the engineering firm and the engineers because a consumer had to be an actual party to a transaction; and plaintiffs never bought goods or services from the engineering firm and the engineers or any person downstream of their engineering work performed for the homeowners association. West v. Christopher Consul-

tants, 106 Va. Cir. 6, 2020 Va. Cir. LEXIS 82 (Loudoun County June 10, 2020).

Pleading sufficient to state cause of action. — Defendants' demurrer to plaintiff's claim under the Virginia Consumer Protection Act (VCPA) for damages was overruled; complaint contains sufficient allegations to withstand demurrer as to whether sales brochure for assisted living facility contained fraudulent misrepresentations or was just "sales trade talk or puffery." Henderson v. Hickory Hill Ret. Cmty., LLC, 103 Va. Cir. 190, 2019 Va. Cir. LEXIS 466 (Nottoway County Oct. 2, 2019), aff'd, 106 Va. Cir. 506, 2019 Va. Cir. LEXIS 1580 (Nottoway County Dec. 3, 2019).

Commonwealth's complaint against two pharmaceutical companies for violations of the Virginia Consumer Protection Act was sufficient to overcome their demurrers because the Commonwealth sufficiently alleged the misrepresentations it relied on, how those misrepresentations were disseminated, to whom the misrepresentations were made, and how they allegedly caused harm to Virginia citizens, and, although the FDA approved the the companies' drugs and allowed the advertisement and promotion thereof, the FDA did not authorize the companies to make misrepresentations while doing so. Commonwealth ex rel. Herring v. Teva Pharms. USA, Inc., 107 Va. Cir. 44, 2020 Va. Cir. LEXIS 670 (Richmond Nov. 13, 2020).

§ 59.1-197. Intent.

CIRCUIT COURT OPINIONS

Particularity of claim. — Virginia Consumer Protection Act (VCPA) claim does not need to be alleged with the same particularity as common-law fraud because a VCPA claim need only be proven to the ordinary preponderance of the evidence standard; a cause of action for fraud had different elements of proof from a VCPA claim; and increasing the burden on a consumer to bring a VCPA claim by imposing a common law pleading requirement would be contrary to the statutory purpose to expand the remedies afforded to consumers and to relax the restrictions imposed upon them by the common law. West v. Christopher Consultants, 106 Va. Cir. 6, 2020 Va. Cir. LEXIS 82 (Loudoun County June 10, 2020).

Pleading insufficient to state cause of action. — Court sustained the demurrer to Count IX alleging a violation of the Virginia Consumer Protection Act (VCPA) as the VCPA did not apply to the engineering work of the engineering firm and the engineers because a consumer had to be an actual party to a transaction; and plaintiffs never bought goods or services from the engineering firm and the engineers or any person downstream of their engineering work performed for the homeowners association. West v. Christopher Consultants, 106 Va. Cir. 6, 2020 Va. Cir. LEXIS 82 (Loudoun County June 10, 2020).

§ 59.1-198. Definitions.

CIRCUIT COURT OPINIONS

Applicability. — Court sustained the demurrer to Count IX alleging a violation of the Virginia Consumer Protection Act (VCPA) as the VCPA did not apply to the engineering work of the engineering firm and the engineers because a consumer had to be an actual party to a transaction; and plaintiffs never bought goods or services from the engineering firm and the engineers or any person downstream of their engineering work performed for the homeowners association. West v. Christopher Consultants, 106 Va. Cir. 6, 2020 Va. Cir. LEXIS 82 (Loudoun County June 10, 2020).

Definition of supplier. — Plaintiff alleged that defendants were suppliers within the meaning of the VCPA in that they offered for sale and did sell real property for residential use, and that plaintiff entered into a contract to purchase the residence from defendants and closed on the acquisition of the home; thus, the court overruled the demurrer to plaintiff's Consumer Protection Act claim. DeLeon v. McGaha, 109 Va. Cir. 264, 2022 Va. Cir. LEXIS 24 (Loudoun County Feb. 1, 2022).

§ 59.1-199. Exclusions.

Nothing in this chapter shall apply to:

1. Any aspect of a consumer transaction which aspect is authorized under laws or regulations of the Commonwealth or the United States, or the formal advisory opinions of any regulatory body or official of the Commonwealth or the United States.

2. Acts done by the publisher, owner, agent, or employee of a newspaper, periodical, or radio or television station, or other advertising media such as outdoor advertising and advertising agencies, in the publication or dissemination of an advertisement in violation of § 59.1-200, unless it be proved that such person knew that the advertisement was of a character prohibited by § 59.1-200.

3. Those aspects of a consumer transaction that are regulated by the Federal Consumer Credit Protection Act, 15 U.S.C. § 1601 et seq.

4. Banks, savings institutions, credit unions, small loan companies, public service corporations, mortgage lenders as defined in § 6.2-1600, broker-dealers as defined in § 13.1-501, gas suppliers as defined in subsection E of § 56-235.8, and insurance companies regulated and supervised by the State Corporation Commission or a comparable federal regulating body.

5. Any aspect of a consumer transaction that is subject to the Virginia Residential Landlord and Tenant Act (§ 55.1-1200 et seq.) or Chapter 14 (§ 55.1-1400 et seq.) of Title 55.1, unless the act or practice of a landlord constitutes a misrepresentation or fraudulent act or practice under § 59.1-200.

6. Real estate licensees who are licensed under Chapter 21 (§ 54.1-2100 et seq.) of Title 54.1.

7. Residential home sales between natural persons involving the seller's private residence.

History.
1977, c. 635; 1987, c. 464; 1994, c. 400; 1995, c. 703; 1996, cc. 61, 77, 179; 1999, c. 494; 2000, cc. 691, 706; 2023, c. 452.

The 2023 amendments.
The 2023 amendment by c. 452, redesignated former subsections A through F as subdivisions 1 through 6; substituted "the Commonwealth" for "this Commonwealth" twice in subdivision 1; added subdivision 7; and made related and stylistic changes.

CIRCUIT COURT OPINIONS

Federal Consumer Credit Protection Act. — Denial of seller's demurrer as to home buyer's claim that the seller violated the Virginia Consumer Protection Act, § 59.1-196 et seq., was appropriate because the buyers sufficiently pleaded that the action involved a consumer transaction and that the seller was a supplier in that the buyers pleaded that the seller sold the buyers a property which the buyers used for residential purposes. Furthermore, regulation of the transaction was not preempted by the Federal Consumer Credit Protection Act, 15 U.S.C.S. § 1601 et seq. Nazar v. Balderson, 104 Va. Cir. 173, 2020 Va. Cir. LEXIS 10 (Chesterfield County Jan. 29, 2020).

Tenant action. — Tenant's allegations that the landlord failed to provide habitable conditions at the time of leasing the unit was sufficient to state a cause of action for misrepresentation of the characteristics of the service being provided, the quality of that service, the advertisement of the service with the intent not to provide the service advertised, and fundamentally misrepresenting the landlord's obligation because the tenant sufficiently alleged that the landlord acted willfully when he did not adequately remedy the interior mold conditions. Stith v. Liberty Pointe LP, 110 Va. Cir. 141, 2022 Va. Cir. LEXIS 78 (Petersburg June 28, 2022).

No exemption for entire industries. — Defendants' demurrer to plaintiff's claim under the Virginia Consumer Protection Act (VCPA) for damages was overruled; in the absence of controlling precedent as to whether the VCPA applies to assisted living facilities, the court found persuasive the rationale of other state cases, which held that the statute did not exempt entire industries from the VCPA. Henderson v. Hickory Hill Ret. Cmty., LLC, 103 Va. Cir. 190, 2019 Va. Cir. LEXIS 466 (Nottoway

County Oct. 2, 2019), aff'd, 106 Va. Cir. 506,
2019 Va. Cir. LEXIS 1580 (Nottoway County
Dec. 3, 2019).

§ 59.1-200. (Effective until January 1, 2024) Prohibited practices.

A. The following fraudulent acts or practices committed by a supplier in connection with a consumer transaction are hereby declared unlawful:

1. Misrepresenting goods or services as those of another;

2. Misrepresenting the source, sponsorship, approval, or certification of goods or services;

3. Misrepresenting the affiliation, connection, or association of the supplier, or of the goods or services, with another;

4. Misrepresenting geographic origin in connection with goods or services;

5. Misrepresenting that goods or services have certain quantities, characteristics, ingredients, uses, or benefits;

6. Misrepresenting that goods or services are of a particular standard, quality, grade, style, or model;

7. Advertising or offering for sale goods that are used, secondhand, repossessed, defective, blemished, deteriorated, or reconditioned, or that are "seconds," irregulars, imperfects, or "not first class," without clearly and unequivocally indicating in the advertisement or offer for sale that the goods are used, secondhand, repossessed, defective, blemished, deteriorated, reconditioned, or are "seconds," irregulars, imperfects or "not first class";

8. Advertising goods or services with intent not to sell them as advertised, or with intent not to sell at the price or upon the terms advertised.

In any action brought under this subdivision, the refusal by any person, or any employee, agent, or servant thereof, to sell any goods or services advertised or offered for sale at the price or upon the terms advertised or offered, shall be prima facie evidence of a violation of this subdivision. This paragraph shall not apply when it is clearly and conspicuously stated in the advertisement or offer by which such goods or services are advertised or offered for sale, that the supplier or offeror has a limited quantity or amount of such goods or services for sale, and the supplier or offeror at the time of such advertisement or offer did in fact have or reasonably expected to have at least such quantity or amount for sale;

9. Making false or misleading statements of fact concerning the reasons for, existence of, or amounts of price reductions;

10. Misrepresenting that repairs, alterations, modifications, or services have been performed or parts installed;

11. Misrepresenting by the use of any written or documentary material that appears to be an invoice or bill for merchandise or services previously ordered;

12. Notwithstanding any other provision of law, using in any manner the words "wholesale," "wholesaler," "factory," or "manufacturer" in the supplier's name, or to describe the nature of the supplier's business, unless the supplier is actually engaged primarily in selling at wholesale or in manufacturing the goods or services advertised or offered for sale;

13. Using in any contract or lease any liquidated damage clause, penalty clause, or waiver of defense, or attempting to collect any liquidated damages or penalties under any clause, waiver, damages, or penalties that are void or unenforceable under any otherwise applicable laws of the Commonwealth, or under federal statutes or regulations;

13a. Failing to provide to a consumer, or failing to use or include in any written document or material provided to or executed by a consumer, in connection with a consumer transaction any statement, disclosure, notice, or other information however characterized when the supplier is required by 16

C.F.R. Part 433 to so provide, use, or include the statement, disclosure, notice, or other information in connection with the consumer transaction;

14. Using any other deception, fraud, false pretense, false promise, or misrepresentation in connection with a consumer transaction;

15. Violating any provision of § 3.2-6509, 3.2-6512, 3.2-6513, 3.2-6513.1, 3.2-6514, 3.2-6515, 3.2-6516, or 3.2-6519 is a violation of this chapter;

16. Failing to disclose all conditions, charges, or fees relating to:

a. The return of goods for refund, exchange, or credit. Such disclosure shall be by means of a sign attached to the goods, or placed in a conspicuous public area of the premises of the supplier, so as to be readily noticeable and readable by the person obtaining the goods from the supplier. If the supplier does not permit a refund, exchange, or credit for return, he shall so state on a similar sign. The provisions of this subdivision shall not apply to any retail merchant who has a policy of providing, for a period of not less than 20 days after date of purchase, a cash refund or credit to the purchaser's credit card account for the return of defective, unused, or undamaged merchandise upon presentation of proof of purchase. In the case of merchandise paid for by check, the purchase shall be treated as a cash purchase and any refund may be delayed for a period of 10 banking days to allow for the check to clear. This subdivision does not apply to sale merchandise that is obviously distressed, out of date, post season, or otherwise reduced for clearance; nor does this subdivision apply to special order purchases where the purchaser has requested the supplier to order merchandise of a specific or unusual size, color, or brand not ordinarily carried in the store or the store's catalog; nor shall this subdivision apply in connection with a transaction for the sale or lease of motor vehicles, farm tractors, or motorcycles as defined in § 46.2-100;

b. A layaway agreement. Such disclosure shall be furnished to the consumer (i) in writing at the time of the layaway agreement, or (ii) by means of a sign placed in a conspicuous public area of the premises of the supplier, so as to be readily noticeable and readable by the consumer, or (iii) on the bill of sale. Disclosure shall include the conditions, charges, or fees in the event that a consumer breaches the agreement;

16a. Failing to provide written notice to a consumer of an existing open-end credit balance in excess of $5 (i) on an account maintained by the supplier and (ii) resulting from such consumer's overpayment on such account. Suppliers shall give consumers written notice of such credit balances within 60 days of receiving overpayments. If the credit balance information is incorporated into statements of account furnished consumers by suppliers within such 60-day period, no separate or additional notice is required;

17. If a supplier enters into a written agreement with a consumer to resolve a dispute that arises in connection with a consumer transaction, failing to adhere to the terms and conditions of such an agreement;

18. Violating any provision of the Virginia Health Club Act, Chapter 24 (§ 59.1-294 et seq.);

19. Violating any provision of the Virginia Home Solicitation Sales Act, Chapter 2.1 (§ 59.1-21.1 et seq.);

20. Violating any provision of the Automobile Repair Facilities Act, Chapter 17.1 (§ 59.1-207.1 et seq.);

21. Violating any provision of the Virginia Lease-Purchase Agreement Act, Chapter 17.4 (§ 59.1-207.17 et seq.);

22. Violating any provision of the Prizes and Gifts Act, Chapter 31 (§ 59.1-415 et seq.);

23. Violating any provision of the Virginia Public Telephone Information Act, Chapter 32 (§ 59.1-424 et seq.);

24. Violating any provision of § 54.1-1505;

25. Violating any provision of the Motor Vehicle Manufacturers' Warranty Adjustment Act, Chapter 17.6 (§ 59.1-207.34 et seq.);

26. Violating any provision of § 3.2-5627, relating to the pricing of merchandise;

27. Violating any provision of the Pay-Per-Call Services Act, Chapter 33 (§ 59.1-429 et seq.);

28. Violating any provision of the Extended Service Contract Act, Chapter 34 (§ 59.1-435 et seq.);

29. Violating any provision of the Virginia Membership Camping Act, Chapter 25 (§ 59.1-311 et seq.);

30. Violating any provision of the Comparison Price Advertising Act, Chapter 17.7 (§ 59.1-207.40 et seq.);

31. Violating any provision of the Virginia Travel Club Act, Chapter 36 (§ 59.1-445 et seq.);

32. Violating any provision of §§ 46.2-1231 and 46.2-1233.1;

33. Violating any provision of Chapter 40 (§ 54.1-4000 et seq.) of Title 54.1;

34. Violating any provision of Chapter 10.1 (§ 58.1-1031 et seq.) of Title 58.1;

35. Using the consumer's social security number as the consumer's account number with the supplier, if the consumer has requested in writing that the supplier use an alternate number not associated with the consumer's social security number;

36. Violating any provision of Chapter 18 (§ 6.2-1800 et seq.) of Title 6.2;

37. Violating any provision of § 8.01-40.2;

38. Violating any provision of Article 7 (§ 32.1-212 et seq.) of Chapter 6 of Title 32.1;

39. Violating any provision of Chapter 34.1 (§ 59.1-441.1 et seq.);

40. Violating any provision of Chapter 20 (§ 6.2-2000 et seq.) of Title 6.2;

41. Violating any provision of the Virginia Post-Disaster Anti-Price Gouging Act, Chapter 46 (§ 59.1-525 et seq.);

42. Violating any provision of Chapter 47 (§ 59.1-530 et seq.);

43. Violating any provision of § 59.1-443.2;

44. Violating any provision of Chapter 48 (§ 59.1-533 et seq.);

45. Violating any provision of Chapter 25 (§ 6.2-2500 et seq.) of Title 6.2;

46. Violating the provisions of clause (i) of subsection B of § 54.1-1115;

47. Violating any provision of § 18.2-239;

48. Violating any provision of Chapter 26 (§ 59.1-336 et seq.);

49. Selling, offering for sale, or manufacturing for sale a children's product the supplier knows or has reason to know was recalled by the U.S. Consumer Product Safety Commission. There is a rebuttable presumption that a supplier has reason to know a children's product was recalled if notice of the recall has been posted continuously at least 30 days before the sale, offer for sale, or manufacturing for sale on the website of the U.S. Consumer Product Safety Commission. This prohibition does not apply to children's products that are used, secondhand or "seconds";

50. Violating any provision of Chapter 44.1 (§ 59.1-518.1 et seq.);

51. Violating any provision of Chapter 22 (§ 6.2-2200 et seq.) of Title 6.2;

52. Violating any provision of § 8.2-317.1;

53. Violating subsection A of § 9.1-149.1;

54. Selling, offering for sale, or using in the construction, remodeling, or repair of any residential dwelling in the Commonwealth, any drywall that the supplier knows or has reason to know is defective drywall. This subdivision shall not apply to the sale or offering for sale of any building or structure in which defective drywall has been permanently installed or affixed;

55. Engaging in fraudulent or improper or dishonest conduct as defined in § 54.1-1118 while engaged in a transaction that was initiated (i) during a

declared state of emergency as defined in § 44-146.16 or (ii) to repair damage resulting from the event that prompted the declaration of a state of emergency, regardless of whether the supplier is licensed as a contractor in the Commonwealth pursuant to Chapter 11 (§ 54.1-1100 et seq.) of Title 54.1;

56. Violating any provision of Chapter 33.1 (§ 59.1-434.1 et seq.);

57. Violating any provision of § 18.2-178, 18.2-178.1, or 18.2-200.1;

58. Violating any provision of Chapter 17.8 (§ 59.1-207.45 et seq.);

59. Violating any provision of subsection E of § 32.1-126;

60. Violating any provision of § 54.1-111 relating to the unlicensed practice of a profession licensed under Chapter 11 (§ 54.1-1100 et seq.) or Chapter 21 (§ 54.1-2100 et seq.) of Title 54.1;

61. Violating any provision of § 2.2-2001.5;

62. Violating any provision of Chapter 5.2 (§ 54.1-526 et seq.) of Title 54.1;

63. Violating any provision of § 6.2-312;

64. Violating any provision of Chapter 20.1 (§ 6.2-2026 et seq.) of Title 6.2;

65. Violating any provision of Chapter 26 (§ 6.2-2600 et seq.) of Title 6.2;

66. Violating any provision of Chapter 54 (§ 59.1-586 et seq.);

67. Knowingly violating any provision of § 8.01-27.5;

68. Failing to, in accordance with § 59.1-207.46, (i) make available a conspicuous online option to cancel a recurring purchase of a good or service or (ii) with respect to a free trial lasting more than 30 days, notify a consumer of his option to cancel such free trial within 30 days of the end of the trial period to avoid an obligation to pay for the goods or services;

69. Selling or offering for sale any substance intended for human consumption, orally or by inhalation, that contains a synthetic derivative of tetrahydrocannabinol. As used in this subdivision, "synthetic derivative" means a chemical compound produced by man through a chemical transformation to turn a compound into a different compound by adding or subtracting molecules to or from the original compound. This subdivision shall not (i) apply to products that are approved for marketing by the U.S. Food and Drug Administration and scheduled in the Drug Control Act (§ 54.1-3400 et seq.) or (ii) be construed to prohibit any conduct permitted under Article 4.2 (§ 54.1-3442.5 et seq.) of Chapter 34 of Title 54.1;

70. Selling or offering for sale to a person younger than 21 years of age any substance intended for human consumption, orally or by inhalation, that contains tetrahydrocannabinol. This subdivision shall not (i) apply to products that are approved for marketing by the U.S. Food and Drug Administration and scheduled in the Drug Control Act (§ 54.1-3400 et seq.) or (ii) be construed to prohibit any conduct permitted under Article 4.2 (§ 54.1-3442.5 et seq.) of Chapter 34 of Title 54.1;

71. Selling or offering for sale any substance intended for human consumption, orally or by inhalation, that contains tetrahydrocannabinol, unless such substance is (i) contained in child-resistant packaging, as defined in § 4.1-600; (ii) equipped with a label that states, in English and in a font no less than 1/16 of an inch, (a) that the substance contains tetrahydrocannabinol and may not be sold to persons younger than 21 years of age, (b) all ingredients contained in the substance, (c) the amount of such substance that constitutes a single serving, and (d) the total percentage and milligrams of tetrahydrocannabinol included in the substance and the number of milligrams of tetrahydrocannabinol that are contained in each serving; and (iii) accompanied by a certificate of analysis, produced by an independent laboratory that is accredited pursuant to standard ISO/IEC 17025 of the International Organization of Standardization by a third-party accrediting body, that states the tetrahydrocannabinol concentration of the substance or the tetrahydrocannabinol concentration of the batch from which the substance originates. This subdivision shall not (i) apply

to products that are approved for marketing by the U.S. Food and Drug Administration and scheduled in the Drug Control Act (§ 54.1-3400 et seq.) or (ii) be construed to prohibit any conduct permitted under Article 4.2 (§ 54.1-3442.5 et seq.) of Chapter 34 of Title 54.1;

72. Manufacturing, offering for sale at retail, or selling at retail an industrial hemp extract, as defined in § 3.2-5145.1, a food containing an industrial hemp extract, or a substance containing tetrahydrocannabinol that depicts or is in the shape of a human, animal, vehicle, or fruit;

73. Selling or offering for sale any substance intended for human consumption, orally or by inhalation, that contains tetrahydrocannabinol and, without authorization, bears, is packaged in a container or wrapper that bears, or is otherwise labeled to bear the trademark, trade name, famous mark as defined in 15 U.S.C. § 1125, or other identifying mark, imprint, or device, or any likeness thereof, of a manufacturer, processor, packer, or distributor of a product intended for human consumption other than the manufacturer, processor, packer, or distributor that did in fact so manufacture, process, pack, or distribute such substance;

74. Selling or offering for sale a topical hemp product, as defined in § 3.2-4112, that does not include a label stating that the product is not intended for human consumption. This subdivision shall not (i) apply to products that are approved for marketing by the U.S. Food and Drug Administration and scheduled in the Drug Control Act (§ 54.1-3400 et seq.), (ii) be construed to prohibit any conduct permitted under Article 4.2 (§ 54.1-3442.5 et seq.) of Chapter 34 of Title 54.1, or (iii) apply to topical hemp products that were manufactured prior to July 1, 2023, provided that the person provides documentation of the date of manufacture if requested;

75. Violating any provision of § 59.1-466.8.

76. Violating subsection F of § 36-96.3:1;

77. Selling or offering for sale (i) any kratom product to a person younger than 21 years of age or (ii) any kratom product that does not include a label listing all ingredients and with the following guidance: "This product may be harmful to your health, has not been evaluated by the FDA, and is not intended to diagnose, treat, cure, or prevent any disease." As used in this subdivision, "kratom" means any part of the leaf of the plant Mitragyna speciosa or any extract thereof; and

78. Failing to disclose the total cost of a good or continuous service, as defined in § 59.1-207.45, to a consumer, including any mandatory fees or charges, prior to entering into an agreement for the sale of any such good or provision of any such continuous service.

B. Nothing in this section shall be construed to invalidate or make unenforceable any contract or lease solely by reason of the failure of such contract or lease to comply with any other law of the Commonwealth or any federal statute or regulation, to the extent such other law, statute, or regulation provides that a violation of such law, statute, or regulation shall not invalidate or make unenforceable such contract or lease.

History.

1977, c. 635; 1979, c. 304; 1981, c. 205; 1983, c. 173; 1986, c. 432; 1987, cc. 462 to 464; 1988, cc. 24, 534; 1989, cc. 689, 703; 1990, c. 584; 1991, cc. 300, 605, 608, 630, 654; 1992, cc. 278, 545, 768; 1993, cc. 455, 760; 1994, cc. 261, 400, 655; 1995, c. 10; 1998, c. 848; 2000, cc. 880, 901; 2002, cc. 217, 897; 2003, cc. 800, 1003; 2004, cc. 784, 790, 798, 817; 2005, cc. 269, 303, 640, 861; 2006, c. 399; 2008, cc. 294, 791, 842; 2009, cc. 321, 359, 376, 699, 700; 2010, cc. 477, 713; 2011, c. 615; 2014, cc. 396, 459; 2016, c. 591; 2017, cc. 11, 16, 727; 2018, cc. 299, 704; 2019, cc. 291, 292, 521; 2020, cc. 412, 438, 481, 785, 1198, 1215, 1250, 1258; 2021, Sp. Sess. I, c. 485; 2022, cc. 351, 557; 2022, Sp. Sess. I, c. 2; 2023, cc. 304, 305, 439, 596, 688, 744, 794.

Cross references.

As to investigating and restraining prohibited acts, related to qualified education loans, see §§ 6.2-2620, 6.2-2621.

Editor's note.

At the direction of the Virginia Code Commission, "(§ 54.1-526 et seq.)" was substituted for "(§ 54.1-519 et seq.)" in subdivision A 62 to conform to the renumbering of §§ 54.1-519 through 54.1-525, as added by Acts 2020, c. 481, to §§ 54.1-526 through 54.1-542.

Acts 2020, c. 481, cl. 2 provides: "That the provisions of this act may result in a net increase in periods of imprisonment or commitment. Pursuant to § 30-19.1:4 of the Code of Virginia, the estimated amount of the necessary appropriation cannot be determined for periods of imprisonment in state adult correctional facilities; therefore, Chapter 854 of the Acts of Assembly of 2019 requires the Virginia Criminal Sentencing Commission to assign a minimum fiscal impact of $50,000. Pursuant to § 30-19.1:4 of the Code of Virginia, the estimated amount of the necessary appropriation cannot be determined for periods of commitment to the custody of the Department of Juvenile Justice."

Acts 2020, c. 785, cl. 2 provides: "That the provisions of the first enactment of this act shall become effective on July 1, 2021."

Acts 2020, c. 785, cl. 3 provides: "That the State Corporation Commission shall establish a procedure, to be in effect by March 1, 2021, for any person to apply, prior to July 1, 2021, for a license to be issued pursuant to Chapter 20.1 (§ 6.2-2026 et seq.) of Title 6.2 of the Code of Virginia, as created by this act, when such chapter becomes effective. In addition, upon the effective date of the first enactment of this act, July 1, 2021, the State Corporation Commission shall monitor settlements by all licensees, specifically looking at the number of settlements made pursuant to this act, the fees charged pursuant to § 6.2-2041 of the Code of Virginia, as created by this act, and the principal amount to be paid by the consumer to satisfy the debt, and shall report to the Chairs of the House Committee on Labor and Commerce and the Senate Committee on Commerce and Labor by December 1 of each year 2023, 2024, 2025."

Acts 2020, c. 785, cl. 4 provides: "That the provisions of this act may result in a net increase in periods of imprisonment or commitment. Pursuant to § 30-19.1:4 of the Code of Virginia, the estimated amount of the necessary appropriation cannot be determined for periods of imprisonment in state adult correctional facilities; therefore, Chapter 854 of the Acts of Assembly of 2019 requires the Virginia Criminal Sentencing Commission to assign a minimum fiscal impact of $50,000. Pursuant to

§ 30-19.1:4 of the Code of Virginia, the estimated amount of the necessary appropriation cannot be determined for periods of commitment to the custody of the Department of Juvenile Justice."

Acts 2020, cc. 1198 and 1250, cl. 2 provides: "That the provisions of the first enactment of this act shall become effective on July 1, 2021."

Acts 2020, cc. 1215 and 1258, cl. 5 provides: "That the provisions of the first and second enactments of this act shall become effective on January 1, 2021, except that the database required by § 6.2-1810 of the Code of Virginia, as amended by this act, shall be modified to accommodate the provisions of this first enactment of this act by January 1, 2022."

Acts 2023, c. 740, cl. 3 provides: "That the provisions of the first and second enactments of this act shall become effective on January 1, 2024."

Acts 2023, c. 773, cl. 3 provides: "That the provisions of the first and second enactments of this act shall become effective on January 1, 2024."

The 2020 amendments.

The 2020 amendment by c. 412 rewrote subdivision A 15, which read: "Violating any provision of § 3.2-6512, 3.2-6513, or 3.2-6516, relating to the sale of certain animals by pet dealers which is described in such sections, is a violation of this chapter."

The 2020 amendment by c. 438 added subdivision A 61 and made stylistic changes.

The 2020 amendment by c. 481 added subdivision A 61, which was subsequently redesignated as A 62 by the Virginia Code Commission, and made related changes.

The 2020 amendment by c. 785, effective July 1, 2021, added subdivision A 61, which was subsequently redesignated as A 64 by the Virginia Code Commission, and made related changes.

The 2020 amendments by cc. 1198 and 1250, effective July 1, 2021, are identical, and added subdivision A 61, which was subsequently redesignated as A 65 by the Virginia Code Commission, and made related changes.

The 2020 amendments by cc. 1215 and 1258, effective January 1, 2021, are identical, and added subdivision A 61, which was subsequently redesignated as A 63 by the Virginia Code Commission, and made related changes.

The 2021 Sp. Sess. I amendments.

The 2021 amendment by Sp. Sess. I, c. 485, effective July 1, 2021, added subdivision A 66 and made stylistic changes.

The 2022 amendments.

The 2022 amendment by c. 351 added subdivision A 67; and made stylistic changes.

The 2022 amendment by c. 557, added subdivision A 67, renumbered subdivision A 68 at the direction of the Virginia Code Commission, and made stylistic changes.

The 2022 Sp. Sess. I amendments.

The 2022 amendment by Sp. Sess. I, c. 2 added subdivisions A 67 through 70 and was renumbered as subdivisions 69 through 72 at the direction of the Virginia Code Commission.

The 2023 amendments.

The 2023 amendment by cc. 304 and 305 are identical, and added subdivision A 73; and made a related change. Redesignated as subdivision A 75 at the direction of the Virginia Code Commission.

The 2023 amendment by c. 439, substituted "Article 4.2 (§ 54.1-3442.5 et seq.) of Chapter 34 of Title 54.1" for "Article 4.2 of Chapter 34 of Title 54.1 of the Code of Virginia" in A 70; added subdivision A 73; and made a related change.

Redesignated as subdivision A 76 at the direction of the Virginia Code Commission.

The 2023 amendment by c. 596, added subdivision A 73. Redesignated as subdivision A 77 at the direction of the Virginia Code Commission.

The 2023 amendment by c. 688, rewrote subdivision A 68, which formerly read: "68. Failing to make available a conspicuous online option to cancel a recurring purchase of a good or service as required by § 59.1-207.46"; added subdivision A 73; and made a related change.

The 2023 amendment by cc. 744 and 794 are identical, and added subdivision A 69; redesignated former subdivisions A 69 through A 72 as subdivisions A 70 through A 73; substituted "Article 4.2 (§ 54.1-3442.5 et seq.) of Chapter 34 of Title 54.1" for "Article 4.2 of Chapter 34 of Title 54.1 of the Code of Virginia" in subdivisions A 70 and A 71; added A 74; and made a related change. The subdivisions in subsection A were redesignated at the direction of the Virginia Code Commission.

CIRCUIT COURT OPINIONS

Particularity of claim. — Virginia Consumer Protection Act (VCPA) claim does not need to be alleged with the same particularity as common-law fraud because a VCPA claim need only be proven to the ordinary preponderance of the evidence standard; a cause of action for fraud had different elements of proof from a VCPA claim; and increasing the burden on a consumer to bring a VCPA claim by imposing a common-law pleading requirement would be contrary to the statutory purpose to expand the remedies afforded to consumers and to relax the restrictions imposed upon them by the common law. West v. Christopher Consultants, 106 Va. Cir. 6, 2020 Va. Cir. LEXIS 82 (Loudoun County June 10, 2020).

Allegations sufficient. — Individual's demurrer to the Attorney General's Virginia Consumer Protection Act, § 59.1-198 et seq., claims was denied as actions brought on behalf of the Commonwealth were intended to be broader in scope and remedy than private causes of action, and the complaint adequately alleged that the actions of the corporation were those of the individual, both directly and as an active participant in the corporation. Commonwealth ex rel. Herring v. Serv. Dogs by Warren Retrievers, Inc., 107 Va. Cir. 333, 2021 Va. Cir. LEXIS 104 (Madison County Mar. 9, 2021).

Plaintiff alleged that defendants were suppliers within the meaning of the VCPA in that they offered for sale and did sell real property for residential use, and that plaintiff entered into a contract to purchase the residence from defendants and closed on the acquisition of the home; thus, the court overruled the demurrer to plaintiff's Consumer Protection Act claim. DeLeon v. McGaha, 109 Va. Cir. 264, 2022 Va. Cir. LEXIS 24 (Loudoun County Feb. 1, 2022).

Virginia Consumer Protection Act inapplicable. — Court sustained the demurrer to Count IX alleging a violation of the Virginia Consumer Protection Act (VCPA) as the VCPA did not apply to the engineering work of the engineering firm and the engineers because a consumer had to be an actual party to a transaction; and plaintiffs never bought goods or services from the engineering firm and the engineers or any person downstream of their engineering work performed for the homeowners association. West v. Christopher Consultants, 106 Va. Cir. 6, 2020 Va. Cir. LEXIS 82 (Loudoun County June 10, 2020).

§ 59.1-200. (Effective January 1, 2024) Prohibited practices.

A. The following fraudulent acts or practices committed by a supplier in connection with a consumer transaction are hereby declared unlawful:

1. Misrepresenting goods or services as those of another;

2. Misrepresenting the source, sponsorship, approval, or certification of goods or services;

3. Misrepresenting the affiliation, connection, or association of the supplier, or of the goods or services, with another;

4. Misrepresenting geographic origin in connection with goods or services;

5. Misrepresenting that goods or services have certain quantities, characteristics, ingredients, uses, or benefits;

6. Misrepresenting that goods or services are of a particular standard, quality, grade, style, or model;

7. Advertising or offering for sale goods that are used, secondhand, repossessed, defective, blemished, deteriorated, or reconditioned, or that are "seconds," irregulars, imperfects, or "not first class," without clearly and unequivocally indicating in the advertisement or offer for sale that the goods are used, secondhand, repossessed, defective, blemished, deteriorated, reconditioned, or are "seconds," irregulars, imperfects or "not first class";

8. Advertising goods or services with intent not to sell them as advertised, or with intent not to sell at the price or upon the terms advertised.

In any action brought under this subdivision, the refusal by any person, or any employee, agent, or servant thereof, to sell any goods or services advertised or offered for sale at the price or upon the terms advertised or offered, shall be prima facie evidence of a violation of this subdivision. This paragraph shall not apply when it is clearly and conspicuously stated in the advertisement or offer by which such goods or services are advertised or offered for sale, that the supplier or offeror has a limited quantity or amount of such goods or services for sale, and the supplier or offeror at the time of such advertisement or offer did in fact have or reasonably expected to have at least such quantity or amount for sale;

9. Making false or misleading statements of fact concerning the reasons for, existence of, or amounts of price reductions;

10. Misrepresenting that repairs, alterations, modifications, or services have been performed or parts installed;

11. Misrepresenting by the use of any written or documentary material that appears to be an invoice or bill for merchandise or services previously ordered;

12. Notwithstanding any other provision of law, using in any manner the words "wholesale," "wholesaler," "factory," or "manufacturer" in the supplier's name, or to describe the nature of the supplier's business, unless the supplier is actually engaged primarily in selling at wholesale or in manufacturing the goods or services advertised or offered for sale;

13. Using in any contract or lease any liquidated damage clause, penalty clause, or waiver of defense, or attempting to collect any liquidated damages or penalties under any clause, waiver, damages, or penalties that are void or unenforceable under any otherwise applicable laws of the Commonwealth, or under federal statutes or regulations;

13a. Failing to provide to a consumer, or failing to use or include in any written document or material provided to or executed by a consumer, in connection with a consumer transaction any statement, disclosure, notice, or other information however characterized when the supplier is required by 16 C.F.R. Part 433 to so provide, use, or include the statement, disclosure, notice, or other information in connection with the consumer transaction;

14. Using any other deception, fraud, false pretense, false promise, or misrepresentation in connection with a consumer transaction;

15. Violating any provision of § 3.2-6509, 3.2-6512, 3.2-6513, 3.2-6513.1, 3.2-6514, 3.2-6515, 3.2-6516, or 3.2-6519 is a violation of this chapter;

16. Failing to disclose all conditions, charges, or fees relating to:

a. The return of goods for refund, exchange, or credit. Such disclosure shall be by means of a sign attached to the goods, or placed in a conspicuous public area of the premises of the supplier, so as to be readily noticeable and readable by the person obtaining the goods from the supplier. If the supplier does not permit a refund, exchange, or credit for return, he shall so state on a similar sign. The provisions of this subdivision shall not apply to any retail merchant who has a policy of providing, for a period of not less than 20 days after date of purchase, a cash refund or credit to the purchaser's credit card account for the return of defective, unused, or undamaged merchandise upon presentation of proof of purchase. In the case of merchandise paid for by check, the purchase shall be treated as a cash purchase and any refund may be delayed for a period of 10 banking days to allow for the check to clear. This subdivision does not apply to sale merchandise that is obviously distressed, out of date, post season, or otherwise reduced for clearance; nor does this subdivision apply to special order purchases where the purchaser has requested the supplier to order merchandise of a specific or unusual size, color, or brand not ordinarily carried in the store or the store's catalog; nor shall this subdivision apply in connection with a transaction for the sale or lease of motor vehicles, farm tractors, or motorcycles as defined in § 46.2-100;

b. A layaway agreement. Such disclosure shall be furnished to the consumer (i) in writing at the time of the layaway agreement, or (ii) by means of a sign placed in a conspicuous public area of the premises of the supplier, so as to be readily noticeable and readable by the consumer, or (iii) on the bill of sale. Disclosure shall include the conditions, charges, or fees in the event that a consumer breaches the agreement;

16a. Failing to provide written notice to a consumer of an existing open-end credit balance in excess of $5 (i) on an account maintained by the supplier and (ii) resulting from such consumer's overpayment on such account. Suppliers shall give consumers written notice of such credit balances within 60 days of receiving overpayments. If the credit balance information is incorporated into statements of account furnished consumers by suppliers within such 60-day period, no separate or additional notice is required;

17. If a supplier enters into a written agreement with a consumer to resolve a dispute that arises in connection with a consumer transaction, failing to adhere to the terms and conditions of such an agreement;

18. Violating any provision of the Virginia Health Club Act, Chapter 24 (§ 59.1-294 et seq.);

19. Violating any provision of the Virginia Home Solicitation Sales Act, Chapter 2.1 (§ 59.1-21.1 et seq.);

20. Violating any provision of the Automobile Repair Facilities Act, Chapter 17.1 (§ 59.1-207.1 et seq.);

21. Violating any provision of the Virginia Lease-Purchase Agreement Act, Chapter 17.4 (§ 59.1-207.17 et seq.);

22. Violating any provision of the Prizes and Gifts Act, Chapter 31 (§ 59.1-415 et seq.);

23. Violating any provision of the Virginia Public Telephone Information Act, Chapter 32 (§ 59.1-424 et seq.);

24. Violating any provision of § 54.1-1505;

25. Violating any provision of the Motor Vehicle Manufacturers' Warranty Adjustment Act, Chapter 17.6 (§ 59.1-207.34 et seq.);

26. Violating any provision of § 3.2-5627, relating to the pricing of merchandise;

27. Violating any provision of the Pay-Per-Call Services Act, Chapter 33 (§ 59.1-429 et seq.);

28. Violating any provision of the Extended Service Contract Act, Chapter 34 (§ 59.1-435 et seq.);

29. Violating any provision of the Virginia Membership Camping Act, Chapter 25 (§ 59.1-311 et seq.);

30. Violating any provision of the Comparison Price Advertising Act, Chapter 17.7 (§ 59.1-207.40 et seq.);

31. Violating any provision of the Virginia Travel Club Act, Chapter 36 (§ 59.1-445 et seq.);

32. Violating any provision of §§ 46.2-1231 and 46.2-1233.1;

33. Violating any provision of Chapter 40 (§ 54.1-4000 et seq.) of Title 54.1;

34. Violating any provision of Chapter 10.1 (§ 58.1-1031 et seq.) of Title 58.1;

35. Using the consumer's social security number as the consumer's account number with the supplier, if the consumer has requested in writing that the supplier use an alternate number not associated with the consumer's social security number;

36. Violating any provision of Chapter 18 (§ 6.2-1800 et seq.) of Title 6.2;

37. Violating any provision of § 8.01-40.2;

38. Violating any provision of Article 7 (§ 32.1-212 et seq.) of Chapter 6 of Title 32.1;

39. Violating any provision of Chapter 34.1 (§ 59.1-441.1 et seq.);

40. Violating any provision of Chapter 20 (§ 6.2-2000 et seq.) of Title 6.2;

41. Violating any provision of the Virginia Post-Disaster Anti-Price Gouging Act, Chapter 46 (§ 59.1-525 et seq.);

42. Violating any provision of Chapter 47 (§ 59.1-530 et seq.);

43. Violating any provision of § 59.1-443.2;

44. Violating any provision of Chapter 48 (§ 59.1-533 et seq.);

45. Violating any provision of Chapter 25 (§ 6.2-2500 et seq.) of Title 6.2;

46. Violating the provisions of clause (i) of subsection B of § 54.1-1115;

47. Violating any provision of § 18.2-239;

48. Violating any provision of Chapter 26 (§ 59.1-336 et seq.);

49. Selling, offering for sale, or manufacturing for sale a children's product the supplier knows or has reason to know was recalled by the U.S. Consumer Product Safety Commission. There is a rebuttable presumption that a supplier has reason to know a children's product was recalled if notice of the recall has been posted continuously at least 30 days before the sale, offer for sale, or manufacturing for sale on the website of the U.S. Consumer Product Safety Commission. This prohibition does not apply to children's products that are used, secondhand or "seconds";

50. Violating any provision of Chapter 44.1 (§ 59.1-518.1 et seq.);

51. Violating any provision of Chapter 22 (§ 6.2-2200 et seq.) of Title 6.2;

52. Violating any provision of § 8.2-317.1;

53. Violating subsection A of § 9.1-149.1;

54. Selling, offering for sale, or using in the construction, remodeling, or repair of any residential dwelling in the Commonwealth, any drywall that the supplier knows or has reason to know is defective drywall. This subdivision shall not apply to the sale or offering for sale of any building or structure in which defective drywall has been permanently installed or affixed;

55. Engaging in fraudulent or improper or dishonest conduct as defined in § 54.1-1118 while engaged in a transaction that was initiated (i) during a declared state of emergency as defined in § 44-146.16 or (ii) to repair damage resulting from the event that prompted the declaration of a state of emergency, regardless of whether the supplier is licensed as a contractor in the Commonwealth pursuant to Chapter 11 (§ 54.1-1100 et seq.) of Title 54.1;

56. Violating any provision of Chapter 33.1 (§ 59.1-434.1 et seq.);

57. Violating any provision of § 18.2-178, 18.2-178.1, or 18.2-200.1;

58. Violating any provision of Chapter 17.8 (§ 59.1-207.45 et seq.);

59. Violating any provision of subsection E of § 32.1-126;

60. Violating any provision of § 54.1-111 relating to the unlicensed practice of a profession licensed under Chapter 11 (§ 54.1-1100 et seq.) or Chapter 21 (§ 54.1-2100 et seq.) of Title 54.1;

61. Violating any provision of § 2.2-2001.5;

62. Violating any provision of Chapter 5.2 (§ 54.1-526 et seq.) of Title 54.1;

63. Violating any provision of § 6.2-312;

64. Violating any provision of Chapter 20.1 (§ 6.2-2026 et seq.) of Title 6.2;

65. Violating any provision of Chapter 26 (§ 6.2-2600 et seq.) of Title 6.2;

66. Violating any provision of Chapter 54 (§ 59.1-586 et seq.);

67. Knowingly violating any provision of § 8.01-27.5;

68. Failing to, in accordance with § 59.1-207.46, (i) make available a conspicuous online option to cancel a recurring purchase of a good or service or (ii) with respect to a free trial lasting more than 30 days, notify a consumer of his option to cancel such free trial within 30 days of the end of the trial period to avoid an obligation to pay for the goods or services;

69. Selling or offering for sale any substance intended for human consumption, orally or by inhalation, that contains a synthetic derivative of tetrahydrocannabinol. As used in this subdivision, "synthetic derivative" means a chemical compound produced by man through a chemical transformation to turn a compound into a different compound by adding or subtracting molecules to or from the original compound. This subdivision shall not (i) apply to products that are approved for marketing by the U.S. Food and Drug Administration and scheduled in the Drug Control Act (§ 54.1-3400 et seq.) or (ii) be construed to prohibit any conduct permitted under Chapter 16 (§ 4.1-1600 et seq.) of Title 4.1;

70. Selling or offering for sale to a person younger than 21 years of age any substance intended for human consumption, orally or by inhalation, that contains tetrahydrocannabinol. This subdivision shall not (i) apply to products that are approved for marketing by the U.S. Food and Drug Administration and scheduled in the Drug Control Act (§ 54.1-3400 et seq.) or (ii) be construed to prohibit any conduct permitted under Chapter 16 (§ 4.1-1600 et seq.) of Title 4.1;

71. Selling or offering for sale any substance intended for human consumption, orally or by inhalation, that contains tetrahydrocannabinol, unless such substance is (i) contained in child-resistant packaging, as defined in § 4.1-600; (ii) equipped with a label that states, in English and in a font no less than 1/16 of an inch, (a) that the substance contains tetrahydrocannabinol and may not be sold to persons younger than 21 years of age, (b) all ingredients contained in the substance, (c) the amount of such substance that constitutes a single serving, and (d) the total percentage and milligrams of tetrahydrocannabinol included in the substance and the number of milligrams of tetrahydrocannabinol that are contained in each serving; and (iii) accompanied by a certificate of analysis, produced by an independent laboratory that is accredited pursuant to standard ISO/IEC 17025 of the International Organization of Standardization by a third-party accrediting body, that states the tetrahydrocannabinol concentration of the substance or the tetrahydrocannabinol concentration of the batch from which the substance originates. This subdivision shall not (i) apply to products that are approved for marketing by the U.S. Food and Drug Administration and scheduled in the Drug Control Act (§ 54.1-3400 et seq.) or (ii) be construed to prohibit any conduct permitted under Chapter 16 (§ 4.1-1600 et seq.) of Title 4.1;

72. Manufacturing, offering for sale at retail, or selling at retail an industrial hemp extract, as defined in § 3.2-5145.1, a food containing an industrial hemp extract, or a substance containing tetrahydrocannabinol that depicts or is in the shape of a human, animal, vehicle, or fruit;

73. Selling or offering for sale any substance intended for human consumption, orally or by inhalation, that contains tetrahydrocannabinol and, without authorization, bears, is packaged in a container or wrapper that bears, or is

otherwise labeled to bear the trademark, trade name, famous mark as defined in 15 U.S.C. § 1125, or other identifying mark, imprint, or device, or any likeness thereof, of a manufacturer, processor, packer, or distributor of a product intended for human consumption other than the manufacturer, processor, packer, or distributor that did in fact so manufacture, process, pack, or distribute such substance;

74. Selling or offering for sale a topical hemp product, as defined in § 3.2-4112, that does not include a label stating that the product is not intended for human consumption. This subdivision shall not (i) apply to products that are approved for marketing by the U.S. Food and Drug Administration and scheduled in the Drug Control Act (§ 54.1-3400 et seq.), (ii) be construed to prohibit any conduct permitted under Chapter 16 (§ 4.1-1600 et seq.) of Title 4.1, or (iii) apply to topical hemp products that were manufactured prior to July 1, 2023, provided that the person provides documentation of the date of manufacture if requested;

75. Violating any provision of § 59.1-466.8.

76. Violating subsection F of § 36-96.3:1;

77. Selling or offering for sale (i) any kratom product to a person younger than 21 years of age or (ii) any kratom product that does not include a label listing all ingredients and with the following guidance: "This product may be harmful to your health, has not been evaluated by the FDA, and is not intended to diagnose, treat, cure, or prevent any disease." As used in this subdivision, "kratom" means any part of the leaf of the plant Mitragyna speciosa or any extract thereof; and

78. Failing to disclose the total cost of a good or continuous service, as defined in § 59.1-207.45, to a consumer, including any mandatory fees or charges, prior to entering into an agreement for the sale of any such good or provision of any such continuous service.

B. Nothing in this section shall be construed to invalidate or make unenforceable any contract or lease solely by reason of the failure of such contract or lease to comply with any other law of the Commonwealth or any federal statute or regulation, to the extent such other law, statute, or regulation provides that a violation of such law, statute, or regulation shall not invalidate or make unenforceable such contract or lease.

History.
1977, c. 635; 1979, c. 304; 1981, c. 205; 1983, c. 173; 1986, c. 432; 1987, cc. 462 to 464; 1988, cc. 24, 534; 1989, cc. 689, 703; 1990, c. 584; 1991, cc. 300, 605, 608, 630, 654; 1992, cc. 278, 545, 768; 1993, cc. 455, 760; 1994, cc. 261, 400, 655; 1995, c. 10; 1998, c. 848; 2000, cc. 880, 901; 2002, cc. 217, 897; 2003, cc. 800, 1003; 2004, cc. 784, 790, 798, 817; 2005, cc. 269, 303, 640, 861; 2006, c. 399; 2008, cc. 294, 791, 842; 2009, cc. 321, 359, 376, 699, 700; 2010, cc. 477, 713; 2011, c. 615; 2014, cc. 396, 459; 2016, c. 591; 2017, cc. 11, 16, 727; 2018, cc. 299, 704; 2019, cc. 291, 292, 521; 2020, cc. 412, 438, 481, 785, 1198, 1215, 1250, 1258; 2021, Sp. Sess. I, c. 485; 2022, cc. 351, 557; 2022, Sp. Sess. I, c. 2; 2023, cc. 304, 305, 439, 596, 688, 744, 773, 794.

The 2023 amendments.
The 2023 amendment by cc. 740 and 773 are identical, and substituted "Chapter 16 (§ 4.1-1600 et seq.) of Title 4.1" for "Article 4.2 of Chapter 34 of Title 54.1 of the Code of Virginia" in subdivisions A 69 and A 70. The subdivisions in subsection A were redesignated at the direction of the Virginia Code Commission.

§ 59.1-200.1. Prohibited practices; foreclosure rescue.

CIRCUIT COURT OPINIONS

Allegations sufficient. —Individual's demurrer to the Attorney General's Virginia Consumer Protection Act, § 59.1-198 et seq., claims was denied as actions brought on behalf of the Commonwealth were intended to be broader in scope and remedy than private causes of action, and the complaint adequately alleged that the actions of the corporation were those of the individual, both directly and as an active participant in the corporation. Commonwealth ex rel. Herring v. Serv. Dogs by Warren Retrievers, Inc., 107 Va. Cir. 333, 2021 Va. Cir. LEXIS 104 (Madison County Mar. 9, 2021).

§ 59.1-203. Restraining prohibited acts.

A. Notwithstanding any other provisions of law to the contrary, the Attorney General, any attorney for the Commonwealth, or the attorney for any city, county, or town may cause an action to be brought in the appropriate circuit court in the name of the Commonwealth, or of the county, city, or town to enjoin any violation of § 59.1-200 or 59.1-200.1. The circuit court having jurisdiction may enjoin such violations notwithstanding the existence of an adequate remedy at law. In any action under this section, it shall not be necessary that damages be proved.

B. Unless the Attorney General, any attorney for the Commonwealth, or the attorney for any county, city, or town determines that a person subject to the provisions of this chapter intends to depart from this Commonwealth or to remove his property herefrom, or to conceal himself or his property herein, or on a reasonable determination that irreparable harm may occur if immediate action is not taken, he shall, before initiating any legal proceedings as provided in this section, give notice in writing that such proceedings are contemplated, and allow such person a reasonable opportunity to appear before said attorney and show that a violation did not occur or execute an assurance of voluntary compliance, as provided in § 59.1-202.

C. The circuit courts are authorized to issue temporary or permanent injunctions to restrain and prevent violations of § 59.1-200 or 59.1-200.1.

D. The Commissioner of the Department of Agriculture and Consumer Services, or his duly authorized representative, shall have the power to inquire into possible violations of subdivisions A 18, 28, 29, 31, 39, 41, as it relates to motor fuels, 69, 70, 71, 72, 73, and 74 of § 59.1-200 and § 59.1-335.12, and, if necessary, to request, but not to require, an appropriate legal official to bring an action to enjoin such violation.

E. The Board of Directors of the Virginia Cannabis Control Authority, or its duly authorized representative, shall, upon the referral or request of the Attorney General or the Department of Agriculture and Consumer Services, have the power to inquire into possible violations of subdivisions A 69, 70, 71, 72, 73, and 74 of § 59.1-200 and, if necessary, to request, but not require, an appropriate legal official to bring an action to enjoin such violation.

History.

1977, c. 635; 1982, c. 13; 1988, c. 485; 2008, c. 485; 2012, cc. 803, 835; 2023, cc. 744, 794.

The 2023 amendments.

The 2023 amendment by cc. 744 and 794 are identical, and added "69, 70, 71, 72, 73, and 74" in subsection D; added subsection E; and made a related change.

CASE NOTES

Restitution. — When § § 59.1-203 and 59.1-205 of the Virginia Consumer Protection Act (VCPA) are read together, the statutes implicitly authorize the Attorney General to request an award of restitution when pursuing a VCPA enforcement action on behalf of the Commonwealth. NC Fin. Sols. of Utah, LLC v. Commonwealth ex rel Herring, 299 Va. 452, 854 S.E.2d 642, cert. denied, 142 S. Ct. 582, 211 L. Ed. 2d 363 (2021).

§ 59.1-204. Individual action for damages or penalty.

CIRCUIT COURT OPINIONS

Allegations insufficient. — Court sustained the demurrer to Count IX alleging a violation of the Virginia Consumer Protection Act (VCPA) as the VCPA did not apply to the engineering work of the engineering firm and the engineers because a consumer had to be an actual party to a transaction; and plaintiffs never bought goods or services from the engineering firm and the engineers or any person downstream of their engineering work performed for the homeowners association. West v. Christopher Consultants, 106 Va. Cir. 6, 2020 Va. Cir. LEXIS 82 (Loudoun County June 10, 2020).

§ 59.1-205. Additional relief.

CASE NOTES

Restitution. — When § § 59.1-203 and 59.1-205 of the Virginia Consumer Protection Act (VCPA) are read together, the statutes implicitly authorize the Attorney General to request an award of restitution when pursuing a VCPA enforcement action on behalf of the Commonwealth. NC Fin. Sols. of Utah, LLC v. Commonwealth ex rel Herring, 299 Va. 452, 854 S.E.2d 642, cert. denied, 142 S. Ct. 582, 211 L. Ed. 2d 363 (2021).

Section 59.1-205 refers to the remedy of restitution, even though it fails to expressly use that particular term. NC Fin. Sols. of Utah, LLC v. Commonwealth ex rel Herring, 299 Va. 452, 854 S.E.2d 642, cert. denied, 142 S. Ct. 582, 211 L. Ed. 2d 363 (2021).

§ 59.1-206. Civil penalties; attorney fees.

A. In any action brought under this chapter, if the court finds that a person has willfully engaged in an act or practice in violation of § 59.1-200 or 59.1-200.1, the Attorney General, the attorney for the Commonwealth, or the attorney for the county, city, or town may recover for the Literary Fund, upon petition to the court, a civil penalty of not more than $2,500 per violation. If the court finds that a person has willfully committed a second or subsequent violation of subdivision A 69, 70, 71, 72, 73, or 74 of § 59.1-200, the Attorney General, the attorney for the Commonwealth, or the attorney for the county, city, or town may recover for the Literary Fund, upon petition to the court, a civil penalty of not more than $5,000 per violation.

B. For purposes of this section, prima facie evidence of a willful violation may be shown when the Attorney General, the attorney for the Commonwealth, or the attorney for the county, city, or town notifies the alleged violator by certified mail that an act or practice is a violation of § 59.1-200 or 59.1-200.1, and the alleged violator, after receipt of said notice, continues to engage in the act or practice.

C. Any person who willfully violates the terms of an assurance of voluntary compliance or an injunction issued under § 59.1-203 shall forfeit and pay to the Literary Fund a civil penalty of not more than $5,000 per violation. For purposes of this section, the circuit court issuing an injunction shall retain jurisdiction, and the cause shall be continued, and in such cases the Attorney General, the attorney for the Commonwealth, or the attorney for the county, city, or town may petition for recovery of civil penalties.

D. In any action pursuant to subsection A, B, or C and in addition to any other amount awarded, the Attorney General, the attorney for the Commonwealth, or the attorney for the county, city, or town may recover any applicable civil penalty or penalties, costs, reasonable expenses incurred by the state or local agency in investigating and preparing the case not to exceed $1,000 per violation, and attorney's fees. Such civil penalty or penalties, costs, reasonable expenses, and attorney's fees shall be paid into the general fund of the Commonwealth or of the county, city, or town which such attorney represented.

E. Nothing in this section shall be construed as limiting the power of the court to punish as contempt the violation of any order issued by the court, or as limiting the power of the court to enter other orders under § 59.1-203 or 59.1-205.

F. The right of trial by jury as provided by law shall be preserved in actions brought under this section.

History.
1977, c. 635; 1980, c. 171; 1982, c. 13; 1991, c. 156; 1995, c. 703; 2008, c. 485; 2023, cc. 744, 794.

The 2023 amendments.
The 2023 amendment by cc. 744 and 794 are identical, and added the last sentence of subsection A; redesignated the former second paragraph of subsection A as subsection B; redesignated former subsections B through E as subsections C through F; and substituted "subsection A, B, or C" for "subsection A or B" in the first sentence of subsection D.

CIRCUIT COURT OPINIONS

Scope. — Individual's demurrer to the Attorney General's Virginia Consumer Protection Act, § 59.1-198 et seq., claims was denied as actions brought on behalf of the Commonwealth were intended to be broader in scope and remedy than private causes of action, and the complaint adequately alleged that the actions of the corporation were those of the individual, both directly and as an active participant in the corporation. Commonwealth ex rel. Herring v. Serv. Dogs by Warren Retrievers, Inc., 107 Va. Cir. 333, 2021 Va. Cir. LEXIS 104 (Madison County Mar. 9, 2021).

CHAPTER 17.3.

MOTOR VEHICLE WARRANTY ENFORCEMENT ACT.

§ 59.1-207.9. Short title.

CASE NOTES

Attorney's fees. — Because pre-litigation attorney's fees are not a component of collateral or incidental damages under the Lemon Law, when a manufacturer provides a refund, it is not required to pay pre-litigation attorney's fees to satisfy its obligations under the Lemon Law. Accordingly, because the the only dispute here was whether a proper refund included pre-litigation attorney's fees, the manufacturer was entitled to summary judgment. Ranger v. Hyundai Motor Am., 885 S.E.2d 156 (Va. 2023).

§ 59.1-207.11. Definitions.

As used in this chapter, the following terms shall have the following meanings:

"Collateral charges" means any sales-related or lease-related charges including but not limited to sales tax, license fees, registration fees, title fees, finance charges and interest, transportation charges, dealer preparation charges or any other charges for service contracts, undercoating, rust proofing or installed options, not recoverable from a third party. If a refund involves a lease, "collateral charges" means, in addition to any of the above, capitalized cost

reductions, credits and allowances for any trade-in vehicles, fees to another to obtain the lease, and insurance or other costs expended by the lessor for the benefit of the lessee.

"Comparable motor vehicle" means a motor vehicle that is identical or reasonably equivalent to the motor vehicle to be replaced, as the motor vehicle to be replaced existed at the time of purchase or lease with an offset from this value for a reasonable allowance for its use.

"Consumer" means the purchaser, other than for purposes of resale, or the lessee, of a motor vehicle used in substantial part for personal, family, or household purposes, and any person to whom such motor vehicle is transferred for the same purposes during the duration of any warranty applicable to such motor vehicle, and any other person entitled by the terms of such warranty to enforce the obligations of the warranty.

"Incidental damages" shall have the same meaning as provided in § 8.2-715.

"Lemon law rights period" means the period ending 18 months after the date of the original delivery to the consumer of a new motor vehicle. This shall be the period during which the consumer can report any nonconformity to the manufacturer and pursue any rights provided for under this chapter.

"Lien" means a security interest in a motor vehicle.

"Lienholder" means a person, partnership, association, corporation or entity with a security interest in a motor vehicle pursuant to a lien.

"Manufacturer" means a person, partnership, association, corporation or entity engaged in the business of manufacturing or assembling motor vehicles, or of distributing motor vehicles to motor vehicle dealers.

"Manufacturer's express warranty" means the written warranty, so labeled, of the manufacturer of a new automobile, including any terms or conditions precedent to the enforcement of obligations under that warranty.

"Motor vehicle" means only passenger cars, pickup or panel trucks, motorcycles, autocycles, self-propelled motorized chassis of motor homes and mopeds as those terms are defined in § 46.2-100 and demonstrators or leased vehicles with which a warranty was issued.

"Motor vehicle dealer" shall have the same meaning as provided in § 46.2-1500.

"Nonconformity" means a failure to conform with a warranty, a defect or a condition, including those that do not affect the driveability of the vehicle, which significantly impairs the use, market value, or safety of a motor vehicle.

"Notify" or *"notification"* means that the manufacturer shall be deemed to have been notified under this chapter if a written complaint of the defect or defects has been mailed to it or it has responded to the consumer in writing regarding a complaint, or a factory representative has either inspected the vehicle or met with the consumer or an authorized dealer regarding the nonconformity.

"Reasonable allowance for use" shall not exceed one-half of the amount allowed per mile by the Internal Revenue Service, as provided by regulation, revenue procedure, or revenue ruling promulgated pursuant to § 162 of the Internal Revenue Code, for use of a personal vehicle for business purposes, plus an amount to account for any loss to the fair market value of the vehicle resulting from damage beyond normal wear and tear, unless the damage resulted from nonconformity to any warranty.

"Serious safety defect" means a life-threatening malfunction or nonconformity that impedes the consumer's ability to control or operate the new motor vehicle for ordinary use or reasonable intended purposes or creates a risk of fire or explosion.

"Significant impairment" means to render the new motor vehicle unfit, unreliable or unsafe for ordinary use or reasonable intended purposes.

"Warranty" means any implied warranty or any written warranty of the manufacturer, or any affirmations of fact or promise made by the manufacturer in connection with the sale or lease of a motor vehicle that become part of the basis of the bargain. The term "warranty" pertains to the obligations of the manufacturer in relation to materials, workmanship, and fitness of a motor vehicle for ordinary use or reasonable intended purposes throughout the duration of the lemon law rights period as defined under this section.

History.

1984, c. 773; 1988, c. 603; 1990, c. 772; 1998, c. 671; 2022, c. 411.

The 2022 amendments.

The 2022 amendment by c. 411 inserted "au-tocycles" in the definition of motor vehicle and made a stylistic change.

CIRCUIT COURT OPINIONS

"Manufacturer." — Dealership's demurrer was sustained because a purchaser's attorney stipulated that the dealership was not a "manufacturer"; the attorney ave no satisfac-tory reason for naming the dealership in the complaint or the amended complaint. Nikolov v. Ford Motor Co., 104 Va. Cir. 327, 2020 Va. Cir. LEXIS 67 (Norfolk Mar. 12, 2020).

§ 59.1-207.13. Nonconformity of motor vehicles.

A. If the manufacturer, its agents or authorized dealers do not conform the motor vehicle to any applicable warranty by repairing or correcting any defect or condition, including those that do not affect the driveability of the vehicle, which significantly impairs the use, market value, or safety of the motor vehicle to the consumer after a reasonable number of attempts during the lemon law rights period, the manufacturer shall:

1. Replace the motor vehicle with a comparable motor vehicle acceptable to the consumer, or

2. Accept return of the motor vehicle and refund to the consumer, lessor, and any lienholder as their interest may appear the full contract price, including all collateral charges, incidental damages, less a reasonable allowance for the consumer's use of the vehicle up to the date of the first notice of nonconformity that is given to the manufacturer, its agents or authorized dealer. Refunds or replacements shall be made to the consumer, lessor or lienholder, if any, as their interests may appear. The consumer shall have the unconditional right to choose a refund rather than a replacement vehicle and to drive the motor vehicle until he receives either the replacement vehicle or the refund. The subtraction of a reasonable allowance for use shall apply to either a replace-ment or refund of the motor vehicle. Mileage, expenses, and reasonable loss of use necessitated by attempts to conform such motor vehicle to the express warranty may be recovered by the consumer.

A1. In the case of a replacement of or refund for a leased vehicle, in addition to any other damages provided in this chapter, the motor vehicle shall be returned to the manufacturer and the consumer's written lease shall be terminated by the lessor without penalty to the consumer. The lessor shall transfer title to the manufacturer as necessary to effectuate the consumer's rights pursuant to this chapter, whether the consumer chooses vehicle replace-ment or a refund.

B. It shall be presumed that a reasonable number of attempts have been undertaken to conform a motor vehicle to any warranty and that the motor vehicle is significantly impaired if during the lemon law rights period either:

1. The same nonconformity has been subject to repair three or more times

by the manufacturer, its agents or its authorized dealers and the same nonconformity continues to exist;

2. The nonconformity is a serious safety defect and has been subject to repair one or more times by the manufacturer, its agent or its authorized dealer and the same nonconformity continues to exist; or

3. The motor vehicle is out of service due to repair for a cumulative total of 30 calendar days, unless such repairs could not be performed because of conditions beyond the control of the manufacturer, its agents or authorized dealers, including war, invasion, strike, fire, flood or other natural disasters.

C. The lemon law rights period shall be extended if the manufacturer has been notified but the nonconformity has not been effectively repaired by the manufacturer, or its agent, by the expiration of the lemon law rights period.

D. The manufacturer shall clearly and conspicuously disclose to the consumer, in the warranty or owner's manual, that written notification of the nonconformity to the manufacturer is required before the consumer may be eligible for a refund or replacement of the vehicle under this chapter. The manufacturer shall include with the warranty or owner's manual the name and address to which the consumer shall send such written notification.

E. It shall be the responsibility of the consumer, or his representative, prior to availing himself of the provisions of this section, to notify the manufacturer of the need for the correction or repair of the nonconformity, unless the manufacturer has been notified as defined in § 59.1-207.11. If the manufacturer or factory representative has not been notified of the conditions set forth in subsection B and any of the conditions set forth in subsection B already exists, the manufacturer shall be given an additional opportunity, not to exceed 15 days, to correct or repair the nonconformity. If notification shall be mailed to an authorized dealer, the authorized dealer shall upon receipt forward such notification to the manufacturer.

F. Nothing in this chapter shall be construed to limit or impair the rights and remedies of a consumer under any other law.

G. It is an affirmative defense to any claim under this chapter that:

1. An alleged nonconformity does not significantly impair the use, market value, or safety of the motor vehicle; or

2. A nonconformity is the result of abuse, neglect or unauthorized modification or alteration of a motor vehicle by a consumer.

History.
1984, c. 773; 1987, c. 607; 1988, c. 603; 1990, c. 772; 1998, c. 671; 2022, c. 411.

The 2022 amendments.
The 2022 amendment by c. 411 substituted "lemon law rights period" for "period of eigh-teen months following the date of original delivery of the motor vehicle to the consumer" in subsection B in the introductory language; in subsection E, deleted "of this section" following "subsection B" twice; and made stylistic changes.

§ 59.1-207.15. Informal dispute settlement procedure.

CIRCUIT COURT OPINIONS

Dispurte settlement procedure. — Company's plea in bar was sustained because a purchaser was advised of its "Dispute Settlement Board," but the letter the purchaser's attorney sent the company did not seek a resolution through that Board; rather, it was a notice of non-conformity, a claim for a full refund less an allowance for use, and a notice of intent to file suit if the company did not respond in ten days. Nikolov v. Ford Motor Co., 104 Va. Cir. 327, 2020 Va. Cir. LEXIS 67 (Norfolk Mar. 12, 2020).

Informal dispute settlement procedure under Virginia law need not be as detailed as 16 C.F.R. Part 703; however, at a minimum, it must have some agreed upon submission to the decision of a neutral person selected by the manufacturer. Nikolov v. Ford Motor Co., 104 Va. Cir. 327, 2020 Va. Cir. LEXIS 67 (Norfolk Mar. 12, 2020).

§ 59.1-207.16. Action to be brought within certain time.

Any action brought under this chapter shall be commenced within the lemon law rights period. However, any consumer whose good faith attempts to settle the dispute pursuant to the informal dispute settlement provisions of § 59.1-207.15 have not resulted in the satisfactory resolution of the matter shall have (i) 12 months from the date of the final action taken by the manufacturer in its dispute settlement procedure, if such procedure was resorted to within the lemon law rights period, or (ii) the original lemon law rights period, whichever is longer, to file an action in the proper court.

History.
1988, c. 603; 1990, c. 772; 1999, c. 387; 2022, c. 411.

The 2022 amendments.
The 2022 amendment by c. 411 substituted "the lemon law rights period" for "eighteen months following the date of original delivery of the motor vehicle to the consumer" in the first sentence; in the second sentence, substituted "lemon law rights period" for "eighteen months of delivery" in clause (i) and "lemon law rights period" for "eighteen-month period" in clause (ii); and made a stylistic change.

CHAPTER 17.5.

COLLISION DAMAGE WAIVER ACT.

§ 59.1-207.29. Scope.

This chapter shall apply (i) to all persons in the business of leasing rental motor vehicles from locations in the Commonwealth under an agreement that imposes upon the lessee an obligation to pay for any damages caused to the leased vehicle and (ii) to all peer-to-peer vehicle sharing platforms in the Commonwealth facilitating peer-to-peer vehicle sharing under a vehicle sharing platform agreement that imposes upon the shared vehicle driver an obligation to pay for any damages caused to the shared vehicle. The provisions of this chapter apply solely to the collision damage waiver portion of the rental agreement or vehicle sharing platform agreement. The definitions in § 46.2-1408 apply, mutatis mutandis, to this section.

History.
1988, c. 349; 2020, c. 1266.

The 2020 amendments.
The 2020 amendment by c. 1266, in the first sentence, added clause (ii); in the second sentence, added "or vehicle sharing platform agreement"; added the last sentence; and made a stylistic change.

§ 59.1-207.31. Required notice.

A. The definitions in § 46.2-1408 apply, mutatis mutandis, to this section.

B. No lessor or peer-to-peer vehicle sharing platform shall sell or offer to sell to a lessee a collision damage waiver as a part of a rental agreement or vehicle sharing platform agreement unless the lessor or peer-to-peer vehicle sharing platform first provides the lessee or shared vehicle driver the following written notice:

NOTICE: THIS CONTRACT OFFERS, FOR AN ADDITIONAL CHARGE, A COLLISION DAMAGE WAIVER TO COVER YOUR RESPONSIBILITY FOR DAMAGE TO THE VEHICLE. BEFORE DECIDING WHETHER TO PURCHASE THE COLLISION DAMAGE WAIVER, YOU MAY WISH TO DETERMINE WHETHER YOUR OWN VEHICLE INSURANCE AFFORDS YOU COVERAGE FOR DAMAGE TO THE RENTAL VEHICLE AND THE AMOUNT OF THE DEDUCTIBLE UNDER YOUR OWN INSURANCE COVERAGE. THE PURCHASE OF THIS COLLISION DAMAGE WAIVER IS NOT MANDATORY AND MAY BE WAIVED.

C. Such notice shall be made on the face of the rental agreement or vehicle sharing platform agreement either by stamp, label, or as part of the written contract, shall be set apart in boldface type and in no smaller print than 10-point type, and shall include a space for the lessee or shared vehicle driver, as defined in § 46.2-1408, to acknowledge his receipt of the notice.

History.
1988, c. 349; 2020, c. 1266.

The 2020 amendments.
The 2020 amendment by c. 1266 added subsection A and redesignated accordingly; in subsection B, inserted "or peer-to-peer vehicle sharing platform" twice, "or vehicle sharing platform agreement" and "or shared vehicle driver"; in subsection C, inserted "or vehicle sharing platform agreement" and "or shared vehicle driver, as defined in § 46.2-1408" and made stylistic changes.

§ 59.1-207.32. Prohibited exclusion.

No collision damage waiver subject to this chapter shall contain an exclusion from the waiver for damages caused by the ordinary negligence of the lessee or shared vehicle driver, as defined in § 46.2-1408. Any such exclusion in violation of this section shall be void. This section shall not be deemed to prohibit an exclusion from the waiver for damages caused intentionally by the lessee or shared vehicle driver or as a result of his willful or wanton misconduct or gross negligence, driving while intoxicated or under the influence of any drug or alcohol, or damages caused while engaging in any speed contest.

History.
1988, c. 349; 2020, c. 1266.

The 2020 amendments.
The 2020 amendment by c. 1266, in the first sentence, added "or shared vehicle driver, as defined in § 46.2-1408" at the end; and in the last sentence, inserted "or shared vehicle driver."

CHAPTER 17.8.
AUTOMATIC RENEWAL OFFERS AND CONTINUOUS SERVICE OFFERS.

§ 59.1-207.45. Definitions.

As used in this chapter, unless the context requires a different meaning:

"Automatic renewal" means a plan or arrangement in which a paid subscription or purchasing agreement is automatically renewed at the end of a definite term for a subsequent term of more than one month.

"Automatic renewal offer terms" means the following clear and conspicuous disclosures:

1. That the subscription or purchasing agreement will continue until the consumer cancels;

2. The description of the cancellation policy that applies to the offer;

3. The recurring charges that will be charged to the consumer's credit or debit card or payment account with a third party as part of the automatic renewal plan or arrangement and that the amount of the charge may change, if that is the case, and the amount to which the charge will change, if known;

4. The length of the automatic renewal term or that the service is continuous, unless the length of the term is chosen by the consumer; and

5. The minimum purchase obligation, if any.

"Clear and conspicuous" or *"clearly and conspicuously"* means in larger type than the surrounding text, or in contrasting type, font, or color to the surrounding text of the same size, or set off from the surrounding text of the same size by symbols or other marks, in a manner that clearly calls attention to the language. In the case of an audio disclosure, "clear and conspicuous" or "clearly and conspicuously" means in a volume and cadence sufficient to be readily audible and understandable.

"Consumer" means any individual who seeks or acquires, by purchase or lease, any goods, services, money, or credit for personal, family, or household purposes.

"Continuous service" means a plan or arrangement in which a subscription or purchasing agreement continues until the consumer cancels the service.

"Supplier" has the same meaning ascribed thereto in § 59.1-198.

History.
2018, c. 704; 2023, c. 288.

The 2023 amendments.
The 2023 amendment by c. 288, added "of more than one month" in the definition of "Automatic renewal."

§ 59.1-207.46. Making automatic renewal or continuous service offer to consumer; affirmative consent required; disclosures; prohibited conduct.

A. No supplier making an automatic renewal or continuous service offer to a consumer in the Commonwealth shall do any of the following:

1. Fail to present the automatic renewal offer terms or continuous service offer terms in a clear and conspicuous manner before the consumer becomes obligated on the automatic renewal or continuous service offer and in visual proximity, or in the case of an offer conveyed by voice, in temporal proximity, to the request for consent to the offer.

2. Charge the consumer's credit or debit card or the consumer's account with a third party for an automatic renewal or continuous service without first obtaining the consumer's affirmative consent to the agreement containing the automatic renewal offer terms or continuous service offer terms.

3. Fail to provide an acknowledgment that includes the automatic renewal or continuous service offer terms, cancellation policy, and information regarding how to cancel in a manner that is capable of being retained by the consumer. If the offer includes a free trial, the supplier shall also disclose in the acknowledgment how to cancel the free trial before the consumer pays or becomes obligated to pay for the goods or services.

B. A supplier making automatic renewal or continuous service offers shall provide a toll-free telephone number, an electronic mail address, a postal address only when the supplier directly bills the consumer, or another cost-effective, timely, and easy-to-use mechanism for cancellation that shall be described in the acknowledgment specified in subdivision A 3. Each supplier making automatic renewal or continuous service offers through an online website shall make available a conspicuous online option to cancel a recurring purchase of a good or service.

C. In the case of a material change in the terms of the automatic renewal or continuous service offer that has been accepted by a consumer in the Commonwealth, the supplier shall provide the consumer with a clear and conspicuous notice of the material change and provide information regarding how to cancel in a manner that is capable of being retained by the consumer.

D. A supplier making automatic renewal or continuous service offers that include a free trial lasting more than 30 days shall, within 30 days of the end of any such free trial, notify the consumer of his option to cancel the free trial before the end of the trial period to avoid an obligation to pay for the goods or services.

E. The requirements of this section shall apply only prior to the completion of the initial order for the automatic renewal or continuous service, except:

1. The requirement in subdivision A 3 may be fulfilled after completion of the initial order; and

2. The requirement in subsection C shall be fulfilled prior to implementation of the material change.

History.
2018, c. 704; 2022, c. 557; 2023, c. 688.

The 2022 amendments.
The 2022 amendment by c. 557, substituted "cancel the free trial" for "cancel and allow the consumer to cancel" in subdivision A 3; and added the last sentence of subsection B.

The 2023 amendments.
The 2023 amendment by c. 688, added subsection D; and redesignated former subsection D as subsection E.

§ 59.1-207.48. Exemptions.

This chapter shall not apply to:

1. Any service provided by a supplier or its affiliate where either the supplier or its affiliate is doing business pursuant to a franchise issued by a political subdivision of the Commonwealth or a license, franchise, certificate, or other authorization issued by the State Corporation Commission to a public service company or public utility pursuant to Title 56;

2. Any service provided by a supplier or its affiliate where either the supplier or its affiliate is regulated by the State Corporation Commission, the Federal Communications Commission, or the Federal Energy Regulatory Commission;

3. Alarm company operators that are regulated pursuant to § 15.2-911;

4. A bank, bank holding company, or the subsidiary or affiliate of either, or a credit union or other financial institution, licensed under federal or state law;

5. Any home protection company regulated by the State Corporation Commission pursuant to Chapter 26 (§ 38.2-2600 et seq.) of Title 38.2;

6. Any home service contract provider regulated by the Department of Agriculture and Consumer Services pursuant to Chapter 33.1 (§ 59.1-434.1 et seq.);

7. Any extended service contract provider regulated by the Department of Agriculture and Consumer Services pursuant to Chapter 34 (§ 59.1-435 et seq.) or its affiliates;

8. Any insurer or entity regulated under Title 38.2 or an affiliate of such insurer or entity; or

9. Any health club registered pursuant to the Virginia Health Club Act (59.1-294 et seq.).

History.
2018, c. 704; 2023, c. 288.

The 2023 amendments.
The 2023 amendment by c. 288, added sub-

sections 7 and 8; redesignated former subsection 7 as subsection 9; and made a related change.

CHAPTER 21.
BUSINESS OPPORTUNITY SALES ACT.

§ 59.1-263. Definitions.

Editor's note.
At the direction of the Virginia Code Commission, "franchise as defined in subsection A of § 13.1-559" should be substituted for "franchise as defined by §§ 13.1-559 (b)" in subdivision B 2, as it appears in the bound volume.

CHAPTER 22.14.
TRUCK MANUFACTURING GRANT FUND.

Section
59.1-284.33. Truck Manufacturing Grant Fund.

§ 59.1-284.33. Truck Manufacturing Grant Fund.

A. As used in this section, unless the context requires a different meaning:

"Capital investment" means an expenditure or an asset transfer from a site of a qualified company located outside of an eligible county to the facility, by or on behalf of the qualified company, on or after October 1, 2018, in real property, tangible personal property, or both, at a facility located in an eligible county that is properly chargeable to a capital account or would be so chargeable with a proper election. The purchase or lease of furniture; fixtures; business personal property; machinery and tools, including under an operating lease; and expected building expansion and up-fit by or on behalf of a qualified company shall qualify as a capital investment.

"Eligible county" means the County of Pulaski.

"Facility" means a truck manufacturing facility to be expanded, equipped, improved, or operated by a qualified company in an eligible county.

"Fund" means the Truck Manufacturing Grant Fund.

"Grants" means grants from the Fund awarded to a qualified company, in an aggregate not to exceed $16.5 million, intended to be used to pay or reimburse a qualified company for costs related to construction and renovation of a facility. A qualified company may use the grant payment for any lawful purpose.

"Memorandum of understanding" means a performance agreement or related document entered into on or before August 1, 2020, by a qualified company, the Commonwealth, and VEDP that sets forth the requirements for capital investments and the creation of new full-time jobs by a qualified company in order for a qualified company to be eligible for grants from the Fund.

"New full-time job" means a job position, in which position the employee of a qualified company works at a facility, for which the average annual wage is at least equal to the wage required by the memorandum of understanding, and for which a qualified company provides standard fringe benefits. Such position shall require a minimum of either (i) 35 hours of an employee's time per week for the entire normal year of a qualified company's operations, which "normal year" shall consist of at least 48 weeks, or (ii) 1,680 hours per year. Seasonal or temporary positions, and positions created when a job function is shifted from an existing location in the Commonwealth, shall not qualify as new full-time jobs. Other positions, including employees of affiliates and certain suppliers, may be considered new full-time jobs if designated as such in a memorandum of understanding. New full-time jobs shall be in addition to the baseline of 3,219 full-time employees at a facility. The Commonwealth may gauge compliance with the new full-time job requirements for a qualified company by reference to the new payroll generated by a qualified company, as set forth in a memorandum of understanding.

"Qualified company" means a truck manufacturer, including its affiliates, that engages in truck manufacturing in an eligible county, that between October 1, 2018, and September 30, 2029, is expected to (i) make or cause to be made a capital investment at a facility of at least $397 million, which shall include at least $93.6 million of investments related to the construction or renovation of real property at a facility, and (ii) create at least 777 new full-time jobs related to, or supportive of, its business.

"Secretary" means the Secretary of Commerce and Trade or his designee.

"VEDP" means the Virginia Economic Development Partnership Authority.

B. There is hereby created in the state treasury a special nonreverting fund to be known as the Truck Manufacturing Grant Fund. The Fund shall be established on the books of the Comptroller. All funds appropriated to the Fund shall be paid into the state treasury and credited to it. Interest earned on moneys in the Fund shall remain in the Fund and be credited to it. Any moneys remaining in the Fund, including interest thereon, at the end of each fiscal year shall not revert to the general fund but shall remain in the Fund. Moneys in the Fund shall be used to pay grants pursuant to this section. Expenditures and disbursements from the Fund shall be made by the State Treasurer on warrants issued by the Comptroller pursuant to subsection F.

C. A qualified company shall be eligible to receive grants each fiscal year beginning with the Commonwealth's fiscal year starting on July 1, 2020, and ending with the Commonwealth's fiscal year starting on July 1, 2029, unless such timeframe is extended in accordance with a memorandum of understanding. Grants paid pursuant to this chapter shall be subject to appropriation by the General Assembly during each such fiscal year, and contingent on a qualified company meeting the requirements set forth in this chapter and the memorandum of understanding for the number of new full-time jobs created and maintained and the amount of capital investment made related to the construction or renovation of a facility. The first grant installment of $2 million shall not be awarded until a qualified company has made a capital investment related to the construction and renovation of a facility of at least $46.8 million and has retained at least 2,700 full-time positions at the facility.

D. The aggregate amount of grants payable under this section shall not exceed $16.5 million. Grants are expected to be paid in 10 annual installments, calculated in accordance with a memorandum of understanding, with the grants that may be awarded in a particular fiscal year not to exceed the following:

1. $2,000,000 for the Commonwealth's fiscal year beginning July 1, 2020;

2. $4,000,000, less the total amount of grants previously awarded pursuant to this subsection, for the Commonwealth's fiscal year beginning July 1, 2021;

3. $4,300,000, less the total amount of grants previously awarded pursuant to this subsection, for the Commonwealth's fiscal year beginning July 1, 2022;

4. $6,042,857, less the total amount of grants previously awarded pursuant to this subsection, for the Commonwealth's fiscal year beginning July 1, 2023;

5. $7,785,714, less the total amount of grants previously awarded pursuant to this subsection, for the Commonwealth's fiscal year beginning July 1, 2024;

6. $9,528,571, less the total amount of grants previously awarded pursuant to this subsection, for the Commonwealth's fiscal year beginning July 1, 2025;

7. $11,271,428, less the total amount of grants previously awarded pursuant to this subsection, for the Commonwealth's fiscal year beginning July 1, 2026;

8. $13,014,285, less the total amount of grants previously awarded pursuant to this subsection, for the Commonwealth's fiscal year beginning July 1, 2027;

9. $14,757,142, less the total amount of grants previously awarded pursuant to this subsection, for the Commonwealth's fiscal year beginning July 1, 2028; and

10. $16,500,000, less the total amount of grants previously awarded pursuant to this subsection, for the Commonwealth's fiscal year beginning July 1, 2029.

E. A qualified company applying for a grant installment under this section shall provide evidence, satisfactory to the Secretary, of (i) the aggregate number of new full-time jobs in place in the grant year that immediately precedes the expected date on which the grant installment is to be paid and (ii) the aggregate amount of capital investment, and the capital investment related to the construction and renovation of a facility, made as of the last day of the grant year that immediately precedes the expected date on which the grant installment is to be paid. The application and evidence shall be filed with the Secretary in person, by mail, or as otherwise agreed upon in a memorandum of understanding, by no later than October 31 of each year reflecting performance in and through the prior grant year. Failure to meet the filing deadline shall result in a deferral of a scheduled grant installment payment. For filings by mail, the postmark cancellation shall govern the date of the filing determination.

F. Within 30 days of receiving an application and evidence pursuant to subsection E, the Secretary shall certify to the Comptroller and the qualified company the amount of grants to which such qualified company is entitled for payment. Payment of such grant shall be made by check issued by the State Treasurer on warrant of the Comptroller by the end of the calendar year of the submission of the application and evidence. The Comptroller shall not draw any warrant to issue checks for grants under this chapter without a specific appropriation for the same.

G. As a condition of receipt of grants, a qualified company shall make available to the Secretary for inspection, upon request, of all documents relevant and applicable to determining whether a qualified company has met the requirements for receipt of grants as set forth in this chapter and subject to a memorandum of understanding. All such documents appropriately identified by a qualified company shall be considered confidential and proprietary.

History.
2020, cc. 265, 604.

CHAPTER 22.15.

ADVANCED PRODUCTION GRANT PROGRAM AND FUND.

Section
59.1-284.34. Advanced Production Grant Program and Fund.

§ 59.1-284.34. Advanced Production Grant Program and Fund.

A. As used in this section:

"Capital investment" means an expenditure by or on behalf of a qualified company on or after October 1, 2019, in real property, tangible personal property, or both, at a facility within an eligible county that is properly chargeable to capital account or would be so chargeable with a proper election. The purchase or lease of furniture, fixtures, business personal property, machinery, and equipment, including under an operating lease, and expected building up-fit and improvements by or on behalf of a qualified company shall qualify as capital investment.

"Eligible county" means the County of Pittsylvania.

"Facility" means an advanced production and development facility to be purchased, equipped, improved, and operated by the qualified company in the eligible county.

"Fund" means the Advanced Production Grant Fund created under subsection B.

"Grants" means grants from the Advanced Production Grant Fund awarded to a qualified company in an aggregate amount not to exceed $7.0 million. A qualified company may use the proceeds of the grants for any lawful purpose.

"Memorandum of understanding" means a performance agreement or related document entered into on or before August 1, 2020, among a qualified company, the Commonwealth, and VEDP that sets forth the requirements for capital investment and the creation of new full-time jobs for the qualified company to be eligible for grants from the Fund.

"New full-time job" means a job position in which the employee of the qualified company works at the facility and for which the average annual wage is at least equal to $34,274, the qualified company provides standard fringe benefits, and the position requires a minimum of either (i) 35 hours of an employee's time per week for the entire normal year of the qualified company's operations, which "normal year" must consist of at least 48 weeks, or (ii) 1,680 hours per year. Seasonal or temporary positions, positions created when a job function is shifted from an existing location in the Commonwealth, and positions with construction contractors, vendors, suppliers, and similar multiplier or spin-off jobs shall not qualify as new full-time jobs. The Commonwealth may gauge compliance with the new full-time jobs requirements for a qualified company by reference to the new payroll generated by a qualified company, as indicated in a memorandum of understanding.

"Qualified company" means a business transportation manufacturer and producer, including its affiliates, that engages in the production of business trucks in the eligible county, that between October 1, 2019, and December 31, 2027, is expected (i) to make or cause to be made a capital investment at a facility of at least $57,837,356 and (ii) to create at least 703 new full-time jobs at the facility related to, or supportive of, its business.

"Secretary" means the Secretary of Commerce and Trade or his designee.

"VEDP" means the Virginia Economic Development Partnership Authority.

B. There is hereby created in the state treasury a special nonreverting fund to be known as the Advanced Production Grant Fund, referred to in this section as "the Fund." The Fund shall be established on the books of the Comptroller. All funds appropriated for the Fund shall be paid into the state treasury and credited to it. Interest earned on moneys in the Fund shall remain in the Fund and be credited to it. Any moneys remaining in the Fund, including interest thereon, at the end of each fiscal year shall not revert to the general fund but shall remain in the Fund. Moneys in the Fund shall be used for the purpose to pay grants pursuant to this chapter. Expenditures and disbursements from the Fund shall be made by the State Treasurer on warrants issued by the Comptroller pursuant to subsection F.

C. A qualified company shall be eligible to receive grants each fiscal year beginning with the Commonwealth's fiscal year starting on July 1, 2021, and ending with the Commonwealth's fiscal year starting on July 1, 2026, unless such time frame is extended in accordance with the memorandum of understanding. The grants under this section shall be paid to a qualified company from the Fund, subject to appropriation by the General Assembly, during each such fiscal year, contingent upon the qualified company's meeting the requirements set forth in the memorandum of understanding for the number of new full-time jobs created and maintained and the amount of capital investment made and retained. The first grant installment of $500,000 shall not be awarded until the qualified company has made a capital investment of at least $40,800,000 and has created at least 373 new full-time jobs at the facility.

D. The aggregate amount of grants payable under this section shall not exceed $7.0 million, and grants are expected to be paid in six annual installments, calculated in accordance with the memorandum of understanding, with the grants that may be awarded in a particular fiscal year not exceeding the following:

1. $500,000 for the Commonwealth's fiscal year beginning July 1, 2021;
2. $1,800,000, less the total amount of grants previously awarded pursuant to this subsection, for the Commonwealth's fiscal year beginning July 1, 2022;
3. $3,100,000, less the total amount of grants previously awarded pursuant to this subsection, for the Commonwealth's fiscal year beginning July 1, 2023;
4. $4,400,000, less the total amount of grants previously awarded pursuant to this subsection, for the Commonwealth's fiscal year beginning July 1, 2024;
5. $5,700,000, less the total amount of grants previously awarded pursuant to this subsection, for the Commonwealth's fiscal year beginning July 1, 2025; and
6. $7,000,000, less the total amount of grants previously awarded pursuant to this subsection, for the Commonwealth's fiscal year beginning July 1, 2026.

E. A qualified company applying for a grant installment under this section shall provide evidence, satisfactory to the Secretary, of (i) the aggregate number of new full-time jobs in place in the calendar year that immediately precedes the expected date on which the grant installment is to be paid and (ii) the aggregate amount of the capital investment made as of the last day of the calendar year that immediately precedes the expected date on which the grant installment is to be paid. The application and evidence shall be filed with the Secretary in person, by mail, or as otherwise agreed upon in the memorandum of understanding by no later than April 1 each year reflecting performance in and through the prior calendar year. Failure to meet the filing deadline shall result in a deferral of a scheduled grant installment payment set forth in subsection D. For filings by mail, the postmark cancellation shall govern the date of the filing determination.

F. Within 60 days of receiving the application and evidence pursuant to subsection E, the Secretary shall certify to the Comptroller and the qualified company the amount of grants to which such qualified company is entitled for payment. Payment of such grants shall be made by check issued by the State Treasurer on warrant of the Comptroller by the September 1 succeeding the submission of such timely filed application. The Comptroller shall not draw any warrants to issue checks for the grants under this section without a specific appropriation for the same.

G. As a condition of receipt of the grants, a qualified company shall make available to the Secretary for inspection, upon request, all documents relevant and applicable to determining whether the qualified company has met the requirements for the receipt of grants as set forth in this section and subject to the memorandum of understanding. All such documents appropriately identified by the qualified company shall be considered confidential and proprietary.

History.
2020, cc. 267, 763.

The number of this chapter was assigned by the Virginia Code Commission, the chapter in Acts 2020, cc. 267 and 763 having been enacted as Chapter 22.14.

The number of this section was assigned by the Virginia Code Commission, the number in Acts 2020, cc. 267 and 763 having been § 59.1-284.33.

CHAPTER 22.16.

PHARMACEUTICAL MANUFACTURING GRANT PROGRAM.

Section
59.1-284.35. Definitions.
59.1-284.36. Pharmaceutical Manufacturing Grant Fund created.
59.1-284.37. Resources for public institutions of higher education.

§ 59.1-284.35. Definitions.

A. As used in this section, unless the context requires a different meaning:

"Capital investment" means an expenditure by or on behalf of a qualified company on or after March 1, 2019, in real property, tangible personal property, or both, at a facility in an eligible county that is properly chargeable to a capital account or would be so chargeable with a proper election. The purchase or lease of furniture; fixtures; business personal property; machinery and tools, including under an operating lease; and expected building expansion and up-fit by or on behalf of a qualified company shall qualify as capital investment.

"Eligible county" means Rockingham County.

"Facility" means the building, group of buildings, or corporate campus, including any related machinery and tools, furniture, fixtures, and business personal property, that is located at or near a qualified company's existing operations in an eligible county and is owned, leased, licensed, occupied, or otherwise operated by a qualified company for use in the administration, management, and operation of its business.

"Fund" means the Pharmaceutical Manufacturing Grant Fund.

"Grants" means grants from the Fund awarded to a qualified company in an aggregate not to exceed $7.5 million, intended to be used to pay or reimburse a qualified company for the costs of workforce recruitment, development, and training, and for stormwater management. A qualified company may use the grant payment for any lawful purpose.

"Memorandum of understanding" means a performance agreement or related document entered into on or before August 1, 2020, by a qualified company, the Commonwealth, and VEDP, that sets forth the requirements for capital investment and the creation of new full-time jobs by a qualified company in order for a qualified company to be eligible for grants from the Fund.

"New full-time job" means a job position, in which the employee of a qualified company works at a facility, for which the average annual wage is at least $100,000 and the qualified company provides standard fringe benefits. Such position shall require a minimum of either (i) 35 hours of an employee's time per week for the entire normal year of the qualified company's operations, which "normal year" shall consist of at least 48 weeks, or (ii) 1,680 hours per year. Seasonal or temporary positions, and positions created when a job function is shifted from an existing location in the Commonwealth, shall not qualify as new full-time jobs. "New full-time job" shall not include any existing full-time positions at the facility as of March 1, 2019. The Commonwealth may gauge compliance with the new full-time job requirements for a qualified company by reference to the new payroll generated by a qualified company, as indicated in the memorandum of understanding.

"Qualified company" means a company, including its affiliates, that engages in pharmaceutical manufacturing in an eligible county and that, between March 1, 2019, and February 28, 2025, is expected to make (i) a capital investment of at least $1 billion and (ii) create at least 152 new full-time jobs related to, or supportive of, its business.

"Secretary" means the Secretary of Commerce and Trade or his designee.

"VEDP" means the Virginia Economic Development Partnership Authority.

History.
2020, cc. 275, 758.

The number of this chapter was assigned by the Virginia Code Commission, the chapter in Acts 2020, cc. 275 and 758 having been enacted as Chapter 22.14.

The number of this section was assigned by the Virginia Code Commission, the number in Acts 2020, cc. 275 and 758 having been § 59.1-284.33.

§ 59.1-284.36. Pharmaceutical Manufacturing Grant Fund created.

A. There is hereby created in the state treasury a special nonreverting fund to be known as the Pharmaceutical Manufacturing Grant Fund. The Fund shall be established on the books of the Comptroller. All funds appropriated to the Fund shall be paid into the state treasury and credited to the Fund. Interest earned on moneys in the Fund shall remain in the Fund and be credited to it. Any moneys remaining in the Fund, including interest thereon, at the end of each fiscal year shall not revert to the general fund but shall remain in the Fund. Moneys in the Fund shall be used to pay grants pursuant to this section. Expenditures and disbursements from the Fund shall be made by the State Treasurer on warrants issued by the Comptroller pursuant to subsection E.

B. A qualified company shall be eligible to receive grants each fiscal year beginning with the Commonwealth's fiscal year starting on July 1, 2020, and ending with the Commonwealth's fiscal year starting on July 1, 2022, unless such timeframe is extended in accordance with a memorandum of understanding. Grants paid pursuant to this section shall be subject to appropriation by the General Assembly during each such fiscal year and are contingent on a qualified company meeting the requirements set forth in this chapter and the memorandum of understanding for the number of new full-time jobs created and maintained and the amount of capital investment made. The first grant payment of $2.5 million shall not be awarded until a qualified company has made a capital investment of at least $420 million and has created at least 85 new full-time jobs.

C. The aggregate amount of grants payable under this section shall not exceed $7.5 million and such grants are expected to be paid in three annual installments of $2.5 million each, calculated in accordance with a memorandum of understanding as follows:

1. $2.5 million for the Commonwealth's fiscal year beginning July 1, 2020;

2. $2.5 million for the Commonwealth's fiscal year beginning July 1, 2021; and

3. $2.5 million for the Commonwealth's fiscal year beginning July 1, 2022.

D. A qualified company applying for a grant installment under this section shall provide evidence, satisfactory to the Secretary, of (i) the aggregate number of new full-time jobs created and maintained as of the last day of February in the fiscal year that immediately precedes the fiscal year in which the grant installment is to be paid and (ii) the aggregate amount of capital investment made as of the last day of February in the fiscal year that immediately precedes the fiscal year in which the grant installment is to be paid. The application and evidence shall be filed with the Secretary in person, by mail, or as otherwise agreed upon in a memorandum of understanding no later than June 1 each year reflecting performance through the last day of the prior February. Failure to meet the filing deadline shall result in a deferral of a scheduled grant installment payment set forth in subsection C. For filings by mail, the postmark cancellation shall govern the date of the filing determination.

E. Within 60 days of receiving an application and evidence pursuant to subsection D, the Secretary shall certify to the Comptroller and the qualified company the amount of grants to which such qualified company is entitled for payment. Payment of such grants shall be made by check issued by the State Treasurer on warrant of the Comptroller in the Commonwealth's fiscal year following the submission of an application. The Comptroller shall not draw any warrant to issue checks for grants without a specific appropriation for the same.

F. As a condition of receipt of grants under this section, a qualified company shall make available to the Secretary for inspection, upon request, all documents relevant and applicable to determining whether the qualified company has met the requirements for receipt of a grant as set forth in this section and subject to a memorandum of understanding. All such documents appropriately identified by a qualified company shall be considered confidential and proprietary.

History.
2020, cc. 275, 758.

The number of this section was assigned by the Virginia Code Commission, the number in Acts 2020, cc. 275 and 758 having been § 59.1-284.34.

§ 59.1-284.37. Resources for public institutions of higher education.

A. To support the needs of a qualified company, and other manufacturers and companies engaged in research and development in and near a qualified county, up to $2,525,000 shall be made available to a comprehensive community college and a baccalaureate public institution of higher education in or near an eligible county. Subject to appropriation, such funds are expected to be available in the Commonwealth's fiscal years beginning July 1, 2020, through July 1, 2024, as follows:

1. $730,000 for the Commonwealth's fiscal year beginning July 1, 2020;
2. $493,750 for the Commonwealth's fiscal year beginning July 1, 2021;
3. $493,750 for the Commonwealth's fiscal year beginning July 1, 2022;
4. $493,750 for the Commonwealth's fiscal year beginning July 1, 2023; and
5. $313,750 for the Commonwealth's fiscal year beginning July 1, 2024.

B. Funds awarded pursuant to this section shall be used for (i) enhanced soft-skilled training; (ii) collaboration to ensure an effective workforce development program; (iii) equipment, maintenance, and personnel needs for bioscience training and education; and (iv) increased educational opportunities in science, technology, engineering, and math.

C. Decisions regarding the application and awarding of funds shall be determined annually by the Secretary of Commerce and Trade, upon the recommendation of the President and Chief Executive Officer of VEDP, the Chancellor of the Virginia Community College System or his designee, and the Director of the State Council of Higher Education for Virginia or his designee. Such officials may request from applicant institutions, and base decisions upon, annual reports from such institutions setting forth proposals regarding how such funds would be spent and reviewing how awarded funds have been spent.

History.
2020, cc. 275, 758.

The number of this section was assigned

by the Virginia Code Commission, the number in Acts 2020, cc. 275 and 758 having been § 59.1-284.35.

CHAPTER 22.17.

TECHNOLOGY DEVELOPMENT GRANT FUND.

§ 59.1-284.38. Technology Development Grant Fund.

A. As used in this chapter, unless the context requires a different meaning:

"Capital investment" means an expenditure by or on behalf of a qualified company on or after January 1, 2020, in real property, tangible personal property, or both, at a facility located in an eligible county that is properly chargeable to a capital account or would be so chargeable with a proper election. The purchase or lease of machinery and tools, furniture, fixtures, and business personal property, including under an operating lease, and expected building expansion and up-fit by or on behalf of the qualified company shall qualify as capital investment.

"Eligible county" means Fairfax County.

"Facility" means the building, group of buildings, or corporate campus, including any related machinery and tools, furniture, fixtures, and business personal property, located in an eligible county, that is owned, leased, licensed, occupied, or otherwise operated by a qualified company for use in the administration, management, and operation of its business, including software development and technology research and development.

"Fund" means the Technology Development Grant Fund.

"Grants" means grants from the Fund awarded to a qualified company in an aggregate amount not to exceed $22.5 million.

"Memorandum of understanding" means a performance agreement or related document entered into on or before August 1, 2020, among a qualified

company, the Commonwealth, and VEDP that sets forth the requirements for capital investment and the creation of new full-time jobs for the qualified company to be eligible for grants from the Fund.

"New full-time job" means a job position, in which the employee of the qualified company works at the facility, for which the standard fringe benefits are provided by the company and for which the average annual wage is at least $112,215. Each such position shall require a minimum of either (i) 35 hours of an employee's time per week for the entire normal year of the qualified company's operations, which "normal year" shall consist of at least 48 weeks, or (ii) 1,680 hours per year. Seasonal or temporary positions, positions created when a job function is shifted from an existing location in the Commonwealth, unless the position in the existing location is backfilled, and positions with construction contractors, vendors, suppliers, and similar multiplier or spin-off jobs shall not qualify as new full-time jobs. The Commonwealth may gauge compliance with the new full-time jobs requirement for a qualified company by reference to the new payroll generated by the qualified company, as indicated in the memorandum of understanding.

"Qualified company" means a technology company, including its affiliates, that between January 1, 2020, and June 30, 2025, is expected to (i) make a capital investment at a facility of at least $64 million and (ii) create at least 1,500 new full-time jobs at the facility related to, or supportive of, its business.

"Secretary" means the Secretary of Commerce and Trade.

"VEDP" means the Virginia Economic Development Partnership Authority.

B. There is hereby created in the state treasury a special nonreverting fund to be known as the Technology Development Grant Fund. The Fund shall be established on the books of the Comptroller. All funds appropriated for such Fund shall be paid into the state treasury and credited to the Fund. Interest earned on moneys in the Fund shall remain in the Fund and be credited to it. Any moneys remaining in the Fund, including interest thereon, at the end of each fiscal year shall not revert to the general fund but shall remain in the Fund. Moneys in the Fund shall be used solely to pay grants pursuant to this chapter. Expenditures and disbursements from the Fund shall be made by the State Treasurer on warrants issued by the Comptroller pursuant to subsection F.

C. A qualified company shall be eligible to receive grants each fiscal year beginning with the Commonwealth's fiscal year starting on July 1, 2021, and ending with the Commonwealth's fiscal year starting on July 1, 2026, unless such timeframe is extended in accordance with the memorandum of understanding. Grants shall be paid to the qualified company from the Fund, subject to appropriation by the General Assembly, during each such fiscal year, contingent upon the qualified company's meeting the requirements set forth in the memorandum of understanding for the number of new full-time jobs created and maintained and the amount of capital investment made. The first grant installment of $5,625,000 shall not be awarded until the qualified company has made a capital investment of at least $19,260,000 and has created at least 500 new full-time jobs.

D. The aggregate amount of grants payable under this section shall not exceed $22.5 million, and grants are expected to be paid in four annual installments of $5,625,000 each, calculated in accordance with the memorandum of understanding as follows:

1. $5,625,000 for the Commonwealth's fiscal year beginning July 1, 2021;
2. $5,625,000 for the Commonwealth's fiscal year beginning July 1, 2022;
3. $5,625,000 for the Commonwealth's fiscal year beginning July 1, 2023; and
4. $5,625,000 for the Commonwealth's fiscal year beginning July 1, 2024.

E. A qualified company applying for a grant installment pursuant to this chapter shall provide evidence, satisfactory to the Secretary, of (i) the aggregate number of new full-time jobs created and maintained in the calendar year that immediately precedes the beginning of the fiscal year in which the grant installment is to be paid; (ii) the aggregate number of existing jobs maintained in certain other facilities operated by the qualified company in the calendar year that immediately precedes the beginning of the fiscal year in which the grant installment is to be paid; and (iii) the aggregate amount of the capital investment made through the calendar year that immediately precedes the beginning of the fiscal year in which the grant installment is to be paid. The application and evidence shall be filed with the Secretary in person, by mail, or as otherwise agreed upon in the memorandum of understanding, by no later than April 1 of each year, reflecting performance through the prior December 31. Failure to meet the filing deadline shall result in a deferral of a scheduled grant installment set forth in subsection D. For filings by mail, the postmark cancellation shall govern the date of the filing determination.

F. Within 60 days of receiving the application and evidence pursuant to subsection E, the Secretary shall certify to the Comptroller and the qualified company the amount of grants to which the qualified company is entitled for payment. Such grants shall be paid by the State Treasurer on warrant of the Comptroller in the Commonwealth's fiscal year following submission of such application. The Comptroller shall not draw any warrants for payment of grants pursuant to this chapter without a specific appropriation for the same.

G. As a condition of receipt of the grants, a qualified company shall make available to the Secretary for inspection, upon request, all documents relevant and applicable to determining whether the qualified company has met the requirements for receipt of grants as set forth in this chapter and subject to the memorandum of understanding. All such documents appropriately identified by the qualified company shall be considered confidential and proprietary.

History.
2021, Sp. Sess. I, c. 271.

Effective date.
This section is effective July 1, 2021.

CHAPTER 22.18.

SHIPPING AND LOGISTICS HEADQUARTERS GRANT PROGRAM.

Section
59.1-284.39. Shipping and Logistics Headquarters Grant Program.

§ 59.1-284.39. Shipping and Logistics Headquarters Grant Program.

A. As used in this chapter, unless the context requires a different meaning:

"Capital investment" means an expenditure within an eligible locality, by or on behalf of a qualified company on or after January 1, 2021, in real property, tangible personal property, or both, at one of the facilities within an eligible locality that has been capitalized or is subject to being capitalized. "Capital investment" may include (i) the purchase of land and buildings and the cost of infrastructure development and land improvements; (ii) a capital expenditure related to a leasehold interest in real property; and (iii) the purchase or lease of furniture, fixtures, machinery, and equipment, including under an operating lease.

"Eligible locality" means the City of Norfolk or the County of Arlington.

"Facilities" means the buildings, group of buildings, or campus, including

any related furniture, fixtures, equipment, and business personal property, in an eligible locality that is owned, leased, licensed, occupied, or otherwise operated by or on behalf of a qualified company for use as a headquarters facility, a customer care center, or a research and development innovation center in the furtherance of its shipping and logistics business.

"Fund" means the Shipping and Logistics Headquarters Grant Fund.

"Grant" means a grant from the Fund awarded to a qualified company in an aggregate amount of up to $9,042,875. Grant proceeds are intended to be used by the qualified company to pay or reimburse costs associated with constructing, renovating, acquiring, and staffing the facilities.

"Memorandum of understanding" means a performance agreement or related document entered into on or before August 1, 2022, between a qualified company and the Commonwealth that sets forth the requirements for capital investment and the creation of new jobs for the qualified company.

"New job" means full-time employment at or associated with any of the facilities measured at any time after January 1, 2021, for which the annual average wage is at least $56,713 for a position in the City of Norfolk or at least $99,385 for a position in the County of Arlington, that requires a minimum of 38 hours of an employee's time per week for the entire normal year, consisting of at least 48 weeks, of the qualified company's operations. Seasonal or temporary positions and positions created when a job function is shifted from an existing location in the Commonwealth shall not qualify as new jobs. Any new job shall be in addition to the baseline number of existing full-time positions at the qualified company's facilities, to be set forth in the memorandum of understanding.

"Qualified company" means a shipping and logistics company, and its affiliates, that between January 1, 2021, and September 30, 2030, is expected to (i) retain its North American headquarters operations in the City of Norfolk; (ii) make or cause to be made a capital investment at one or more of the facilities of at least $36 million; (iii) create and maintain at least 415 new jobs at or associated with the facilities related to, or supportive of, its shipping and logistics business functions; and (iv) establish and operate a research and development innovation center.

"Secretary" means the Secretary of Commerce and Trade or his designee.

B. There is hereby created in the state treasury a nonreverting fund to be known as the Shipping and Logistics Headquarters Grant Fund. The Fund shall be established on the books of the Comptroller. All funds appropriated to the Fund shall be paid into the state treasury and credited to it. Any moneys remaining in the Fund, including interest thereon, at the end of each fiscal year shall not revert to the general fund but shall remain in the Fund. Moneys in the Fund shall be used solely for the purpose to pay grant installments pursuant to this chapter. Payment of such grant installments shall be made by check issued by the State Treasurer on warrant of the Comptroller. The Comptroller shall not draw any warrants to issue checks for grant installments under this section without a specific appropriation for the same.

C. Subject to appropriation by the General Assembly, the aggregate amount of grants payable under this section to a qualified company shall not exceed $9,042,875. Grants shall be paid in nine annual installments, calculated in accordance with the memorandum of understanding, with grants that may be awarded in a particular fiscal year not to exceed the following:

1. $1,359,500 for the Commonwealth's fiscal year beginning July 1, 2022;

2. $2,514,000, less the total amount of grants previously awarded pursuant to this subsection, for the Commonwealth's fiscal year beginning July 1, 2023;

3. $3,468,500, less the total amount of grants previously awarded pursuant to this subsection, for the Commonwealth's fiscal year beginning July 1, 2024;

4. $4,423,000, less the total amount of grants previously awarded pursuant to this subsection, for the Commonwealth's fiscal year beginning July 1, 2025;

5. $5,377,500, less the total amount of grants previously awarded pursuant to this subsection, for the Commonwealth's fiscal year beginning July 1, 2026;

6. $6,332,000, less the total amount of grants previously awarded pursuant to this subsection, for the Commonwealth's fiscal year beginning July 1, 2027;

7. $7,286,500, less the total amount of grants previously awarded pursuant to this subsection, for the Commonwealth's fiscal year beginning July 1, 2028;

8. $8,241,000, less the total amount of grants previously awarded pursuant to this subsection, for the Commonwealth's fiscal year beginning July 1, 2029; and

9. $9,042,875, less the total amount of grants previously awarded pursuant to this subsection, for the Commonwealth's fiscal year beginning July 1, 2030.

D. A qualified company receiving a grant installment pursuant to this section shall provide evidence, satisfactory to the Secretary, annually of, for each facility: (i) the aggregate number of new jobs created and maintained as of the last day of the prior grant year as determined in the memorandum of understanding, the payroll paid by the qualified company during the grant year, and the average annual wage of the new jobs in the grant year and (ii) the aggregate amount of the capital investment made during the grant year, including the extent to which such capital investment was or was not subject to the Virginia Retail Sales and Use Tax Act (§ 58.1-600 et seq.). The report and evidence shall be filed with the Secretary in person, by mail, or as otherwise agreed upon in the memorandum of understanding, by no later than 90 days following the end of the prior grant year upon which the evidence is based.

E. The memorandum of understanding shall provide that if any annual report and evidence provided pursuant to subsection D indicates that the qualified company failed to meet certain targets for capital investment that is or is not subject to the Virginia Retail Sales and Use Tax Act (§ 58.1-600 et seq.), the average annual wage for new jobs, or the number of new jobs, the qualified company may qualify for a reduced grant installment for the grant year in an amount that reflects the value of the shortfall in the applicable target.

F. As a condition of receipt of the grant, a qualified company shall make available to the Secretary for inspection all documents relevant and applicable to determining whether the qualified company has met the requirements for the receipt of the grant as set forth herein and subject to the memorandum of understanding. All such documents appropriately identified by the qualified company shall be considered confidential and proprietary and shall not be subject to disclosure pursuant to the Virginia Freedom of Information Act (§ 2.2-3700 et seq.).

History.

2021, Sp. Sess. I, c. 434; 2022, cc. 10, 76.

The number of this chapter and section were assigned by the Virginia Code Commission, the numbers in the 2021 Sp. Sess. act having been Chapter 22.17 (§ 59.1-284.38).

Effective date.

This section is effective July 1, 2021.

The 2022 amendments.

The 2022 amendments by cc. 10 and 76 are identical, and in subsection A, deleted "the City of Chesapeake" following "means" in the definition of "Eligible locality," substituted "$9,042,875" for "$9.5 million" in the definition of "Grant," substituted "2022" for "2021" in the definition of "Memorandum of understanding," deleted "or the City of Chesapeake" following "City of Norfolk" in the definition of "New job," and substituted "September 30" for "December 31" in the definition of "Qualified company"; rewrote subsection C, which read: "Subject to appropriation by the General Assembly, a qualified company shall be eligible to receive grant installments of $6.33 million in fiscal year 2022 and $3.17 million in fiscal year 2023. Such grant installments shall be paid to the qualified company from the Fund during each such fiscal year, contingent upon the qualified company's meeting the requirements set forth in the memorandum of understanding to provide security for any potential repayment of the grant, including a cash escrow"; in subsection D, substituted "prior grant" or "grant" for "calendar" throughout, inserted "as determined in the memorandum of understanding", and substituted "90 days" for "April 1 each year"; substituted "qualify for a reduced grant installment for the grant year" for "be required to repay the Commonwealth a portion of the grant" in subsection E; deleted "and retention" following "receipt" twice in subsection F; and made stylistic changes.

CHAPTER 22.19.

NITRILE GLOVE MANUFACTURING TRAINING PROGRAM.

Section
59.1-284.40. Nitrile Glove Manufacturing Training Program.

§ 59.1-284.40. Nitrile Glove Manufacturing Training Program.

A. In order to support the recruiting and training needs of companies with facilities located in the Mount Rogers Planning District that manufacture nitrile gloves for personal protective equipment, or manufacture the inputs used to manufacture such gloves, up to $4,601,000 shall be made available to the Virginia Economic Development Partnership Authority through the Virginia Talent Accelerator Program to provide services to such companies. Subject to appropriation, funding for such services shall be awarded as follows:

1. $1,427,000 for the Commonwealth's fiscal year beginning July 1, 2021;

2. $1,987,000 less the total amount of funds previously awarded pursuant to this subsection for the Commonwealth's fiscal year beginning July 1, 2022;

3. $2,722,000 less the total amount of funds previously awarded pursuant to this subsection for the Commonwealth's fiscal year beginning July 1, 2023;

4. $3,574,000 less the total amount of funds previously awarded pursuant to this subsection for the Commonwealth's fiscal year beginning July 1, 2024; and

5. $4,601,000 less the total amount of funds previously awarded pursuant to this subsection for the Commonwealth's fiscal year beginning July 1, 2025.

B. Companies shall be eligible for services funded under this section only if they enter into a memorandum of understanding with the Virginia Economic Development Partnership Authority to:

1. Create at least 2,464 new jobs that are for full-time employees and that pay an annual wage of at least $37,321;

2. Make a capital investment of at least $714.1 million in the Commonwealth; and

3. Agree to meet the performance targets in subdivisions 1 and 2 on or before January 1, 2027, subject to an extension of no more than two years, as provided in the memorandum of understanding, where such extension may also extend the award dates described in subsection A.

C. Any company receiving services pursuant to this section shall annually provide evidence satisfactory to the Virginia Economic Development Partnership Authority of (i) the aggregate number of new jobs created and maintained as of the last month of the calendar year as determined in the memorandum of understanding, the payroll paid by the company during the calendar year, and the average annual wage of the new jobs in the calendar year and (ii) the aggregate amount of the capital investment made during the calendar year, including the extent to which such capital investment was or was not subject to the Virginia Retail Sales and Use Tax Act (§ 58.1-600 et seq.). The report and evidence shall be filed with the Virginia Economic Development Partnership

Authority in person, by mail, or as otherwise agreed upon in the memorandum of understanding by no later than April 1 each year following the end of the prior calendar year upon which the evidence is based.

D. Any memorandum of understanding entered into pursuant to this section shall provide that if any annual report and evidence provided pursuant to subsection C indicates that a company failed to meet the targets specified in subsection B, the company may be required to repay the Commonwealth a portion of the costs for services delivered pursuant to this section in an amount that reflects the value of the shortfall in the applicable target.

E. As a condition of receipt of the services funded under this section, a company receiving services pursuant to this section shall make available to the Virginia Economic Development Partnership Authority for inspection all documents relevant and applicable to determining whether the company has met the requirements for the receipt of the services as set forth in this section and subject to the memorandum of understanding. All such documents appropriately identified by the company shall be considered confidential and proprietary, and shall not be subject to disclosure pursuant to the Virginia Freedom of Information Act (§ 2.2-3700 et seq.).

F. Funding made available pursuant to this section shall be used to provide recruitment and training services for employees of companies that meet the eligibility requirements of this section. Services shall be coordinated by the Virginia Economic Development Partnership Authority through the Virginia Talent Accelerator Program.

History.
2022, cc. 746, 731.

CHAPTER 22.20.

PRECISION PLASTIC MANUFACTURING GRANT FUND.

Section
59.1-284.41. Precision Plastic Manufacturing Grant Fund.

§ 59.1-284.41. Precision Plastic Manufacturing Grant Fund.

A. As used in this chapter, unless the context requires a different meaning:

"Capital investment" means an expenditure by or on behalf of a qualified company on or after June 1, 2022, in real property, tangible personal property, or both, at a facility in an eligible county that is properly chargeable to a capital account or would be so chargeable with a proper election. The purchase or lease of furniture, fixtures, business personal property, machinery and tools, including under an operating lease, and expected building construction and up-fit by or on behalf of a qualified company shall qualify as capital investment.

"Eligible county" means Chesterfield County.

"Facility" means the building, group of buildings, or corporate campus, including any related machinery and tools, furniture, fixtures, and business personal property, that is located at or near a qualified company's operations in an eligible county and is owned, leased, licensed, occupied, or otherwise operated by a qualified company as a temporary or permanent manufacturing and distribution facility for use in the administration, management, and operation of its business.

"Fund" means the Precision Plastic Manufacturing Grant Fund.

"*Grants*" means the grant payments from the Fund awarded to a qualified company in an aggregate not to exceed $56 million. The proceeds of the grants may be used by the qualified company for payment or reimbursement of the costs of workforce development, costs of construction and development of the facility, or any other lawful purpose.

"*Memorandum of understanding*" means a performance agreement or related documents entered into on or before June 1, 2022, by a qualified company, the Commonwealth, and VEDP that sets forth the requirements for capital investment and the creation of new full-time jobs by a qualified company in order for a qualified company to be eligible for grants from the Fund.

"*New full-time job*" means a job position, in which the employee of a qualified company is principally located at a facility, for which the average annual wage for the applicable year is at least equal to the average annual wage for that year required by the memorandum of understanding and the qualified company provides standard fringe benefits. Such position shall require a minimum of either (i) 35 hours of an employee's time per week for the entire normal year of the qualified company's operations, which "normal year" shall consist of at least 48 weeks, or (ii) 1,680 hours per year. Seasonal or temporary positions and positions with construction contractors, vendors, suppliers, and similar multiplier or spin-off jobs shall not qualify as new full-time jobs. The Commonwealth may gauge compliance with the new full-time job requirements for a qualified company by reference to the new payroll generated by a qualified company, if so indicated in the memorandum of understanding.

"*Qualified company*" means a company, including its affiliates, that engages in the manufacture and distribution of precision plastic products in an eligible county and that between June 1, 2022, and December 31, 2035, is expected to (i) make a capital investment of at least $1 billion and (ii) create at least 1,761 new full-time jobs related to or supportive of its business. A qualified company shall be deemed to be engaged in manufacturing for purposes of Chapter 35 (§ 58.1-3500 et seq.) of Title 58.1.

"*Secretary*" means the Secretary of Commerce and Trade or his designee.

"*VEDP*" means the Virginia Economic Development Partnership Authority.

B. There is hereby created in the state treasury a special nonreverting fund to be known as the Precision Plastic Manufacturing Grant Fund. The Fund shall be established on the books of the Comptroller. All funds appropriated to the Fund shall be paid into the state treasury and credited to the Fund. Interest earned on moneys in the Fund shall remain in the Fund and be credited to it. Any moneys remaining in the Fund, including interest thereon, at the end of each fiscal year shall not revert to the general fund but shall remain in the Fund. Moneys in the Fund shall be used to pay grants pursuant to this chapter. Expenditures and disbursements from the Fund shall be made by the State Treasurer on warrants issued by the Comptroller pursuant to subsection F.

C. A qualified company shall be eligible to receive grants each fiscal year expected to begin with the Commonwealth's fiscal year starting on July 1, 2027, and ending with the Commonwealth's fiscal year starting on July 1, 2035, unless such timeframe is extended in accordance with a memorandum of understanding. Grants paid pursuant to this section shall be subject to appropriation by the General Assembly during each such fiscal year and are contingent on a qualified company meeting the requirements set forth in this chapter and the memorandum of understanding for the number of new full-time jobs created and maintained and the amount of capital investment made. The first grant payment shall not be awarded until a qualified company has created at least 500 new full-time jobs.

D. The aggregate amount of grants payable under this section shall not exceed $56 million. Grants are anticipated to be paid in nine annual installments, calculated in accordance with a memorandum of understanding as follows:

1. $5,939,900 for the Commonwealth's fiscal year beginning July 1, 2027;

2. $13,422,500, less the total amount of grants previously awarded pursuant to this subsection, for the Commonwealth's fiscal year beginning July 1, 2028;

3. $19,582,100, less the total amount of grants previously awarded pursuant to this subsection, for the Commonwealth's fiscal year beginning July 1, 2029;

4. $25,876,700, less the total amount of grants previously awarded pursuant to this subsection, for the Commonwealth's fiscal year beginning July 1, 2030;

5. $32,774,300, less the total amount of grants previously awarded pursuant to this subsection, for the Commonwealth's fiscal year beginning July 1, 2031;

6. $40,103,900, less the total amount of grants previously awarded pursuant to this subsection, for the Commonwealth's fiscal year beginning July 1, 2032;

7. $46,443,500, less the total amount of grants previously awarded pursuant to this subsection for the Commonwealth's fiscal year beginning July 1, 2033;

8. $52,783,100, less the total amount of grants previously awarded pursuant to this subsection for the Commonwealth's fiscal year beginning July 1, 2034; and

9. $56 million, less the total amount of grants previously awarded pursuant to this subsection for the Commonwealth's fiscal year beginning July 1, 2035.

In accordance with a memorandum of understanding, actual payment amounts and fiscal years may differ from the schedule above and may be extended beyond the fiscal year beginning July 1, 2035, but the aggregate amount of grant payments shall not exceed $56 million.

E. A qualified company applying for a grant installment under this section shall provide evidence satisfactory to the Secretary of (i) the aggregate number of new full-time jobs created and maintained as of the last day of the calendar year preceding the application and (ii) the amount of capital investment made in the calendar year preceding the application. The application and evidence shall be filed with the Secretary in person, by mail, or as otherwise agreed upon in a memorandum of understanding no later than April 1 each year reflecting performance through the last day of the prior calendar year. Failure to meet the filing deadline shall result in a deferral of a scheduled grant installment payment set forth in subsection D. For filings by mail, the postmark cancellation shall govern the date of the filing determination.

F. Within 60 days of receiving an application and evidence pursuant to subsection E, the Secretary shall certify to the Comptroller and the qualified company the amount of grants to which such qualified company is entitled for payment. Payment of such grants shall be made by check issued by the State Treasurer on warrant of the Comptroller in the Commonwealth's fiscal year following the submission of an application. The Comptroller shall not draw any warrant to issue checks for grants without a specific appropriation for the same.

G. As a condition of receipt of grants under this section, a qualified company shall make available to the Secretary for inspection, upon request, all documents relevant and applicable to determining whether the qualified company has met the requirements for receipt of a grant as set forth in this section and subject to the memorandum of understanding. All such documents appropriately identified by a qualified company shall be considered confidential and proprietary.

History.
  2023, cc. 155, 154.

Editor's note.
  Acts 2023, c. 671, cl. 2 provides: "That upon the signing of a memorandum of understanding, as defined in § 59.1-284.41 of the Code of Virginia, as created by this act, the Virginia Economic Development Partnership Authority (VEDP) shall hire a full-time project coordinator to assist each qualified company, as defined in § 59.1-284.41 of the Code of Virginia, as created by this act, with managing projects with the Commonwealth and its agencies and local government entities. Prior to the payment of any grants from the Cloud Computing Cluster Infrastructure Grant Fund, established pursuant to § 59.1-284.41 of the Code of Virginia, as created by this act, to a qualified company, VEDP shall be credited $200,000 annually to reimburse VEDP for the cost of such coordinator. The costs for the coordinator shall

count toward the aggregate cap of grants that may be paid to the qualified company."
  Acts 2023, c. 678, cl. 2 provides: "That upon the signing of a memorandum of understanding, as defined in § 59.1-284.41 of the Code of Virginia, as created by this act, the Virginia Economic Development Partnership Authority (VEDP) shall hire a full-time project coordinator to assist each qualified company, as defined in § 59.1-284.41 of the Code of Virginia, as created by this act, with managing projects with the Commonwealth and its agencies and local government entities. Prior to the payment of any grants from the Cloud Computing Cluster Infrastructure Grant Fund, established pursuant to § 59.1-284.41 of the Code of Virginia, as created by this act, to a qualified company, VEDP shall be credited $200,000 annually to reimburse VEDP for the cost of such coordinator. The costs for the coordinator shall count toward the aggregate cap of grants that may be paid to the qualified company."

CHAPTER 22.21.
CLOUD COMPUTING CLUSTER INFRASTRUCTURE GRANT FUND.

Section
59.1-284.42. Cloud Computing Cluster Infrastructure Grant Fund.

§ 59.1-284.42. Cloud Computing Cluster Infrastructure Grant Fund.

A. As used in this chapter, unless the context requires a different meaning:
  "Affiliate" means an entity that directly or indirectly through one or more intermediaries controls, is controlled by, or is under common control with a qualified company.
  "Capital investment" means an investment by or on behalf of a qualified company on or after January 1, 2023, but prior to July 1, 2040, in real property, tangible personal property, or both, at a facility that is properly chargeable to a capital account or would be so chargeable with a proper election.
  "Construction cost" means any capital investment, except for the purchase of land, by a qualified company on or after January 1, 2023, in real or tangible personal property to develop or support a data center in a locality identified in a memorandum of understanding. "Construction cost" includes infrastructure costs.
  "Facility" means the one or more buildings, group of buildings, and ancillary facilities and equipment that are located in a locality or localities identified in a memorandum of understanding and that are owned, occupied, or otherwise operated by or for the qualified company for data center and cloud computing cluster operations.
  "Fund" means the Cloud Computing Cluster Infrastructure Grant Fund.
  "Grant" means a grant from the Fund awarded to a qualified company that is intended to pay or reimburse the qualified company for (i) infrastructure costs related to the construction and support of facilities and (ii) costs for workforce development, recruiting, and training.
  "Infrastructure costs" includes the costs related to fiber, water, wastewater, and stormwater facilities; gas pipelines; electrical transmission and distribu-

tion lines; and site clearing, grading, and other improvements to support the construction and development of a facility.

"*Locality*" means a county or city in the Commonwealth in which a company makes an eligible investment in a facility and creates new full-time jobs, that is identified in a memorandum of understanding, and that has entered into a performance agreement.

"*Local match*" means the funds committed by a locality identified in a memorandum of understanding to a qualified company related to the construction and operation of a facility. The local match shall be at least twice the amount provided from the Fund to the qualified company related to the construction of, and creation of new full-time jobs at, the facility in such locality, as set forth in a performance agreement. Expenditures by a locality that the Secretary has certified as infrastructure costs incurred by the locality at the request of the qualified company may be counted toward the local match obligation.

"*MEI Commission*" means the MEI Project Approval Commission established pursuant to Chapter 47 (§ 30-309 et seq.) of Title 30.

"*Memorandum of understanding*" means a memorandum of understanding entered into on or after January 1, 2023, between a qualified company, the Commonwealth, and VEDP that sets forth (i) the grant amount that the qualified company shall be eligible to receive for each new full-time job created and each $1 million of capital investment in construction costs made; (ii) the total aggregate amount of grants that the qualified company shall be eligible to receive; (iii) the performance date; (iv) the requirements and timing for capital investment and new full-time job creation by the qualified company; (v) the identification of the locality or localities in which such investment and job creation shall take place; and (vi) any other terms and conditions deemed necessary or appropriate to be eligible for grant payments from the Fund.

"*New full-time jobs*" means job positions created on or after January 1, 2023, but prior to July 1, 2040, in which the employee of a qualified company works at a facility, for which the average annual wage is at least one and one-half times the prevailing wage of the locality where the job is located, and for which the qualified company provides standard fringe benefits. Such position shall require a minimum of either (i) 35 hours of an employee's time per week for the entire normal year of the employer's operations, which normal year shall consist of at least 48 weeks, or (ii) 1,680 hours per year. Seasonal or temporary positions shall not qualify as new full-time jobs. Positions created after January 1, 2023, by contractors that are dedicated full-time to providing operational services after the opening of a facility may constitute new full-time jobs of the qualified company but shall not exceed 20 percent of the number used to meet any performance criteria for the creation of new full-time jobs. A position created when a job function is shifted from an existing location in the Commonwealth to a new facility shall qualify as a new full-time job if the qualified company certifies that it has hired a new employee or contractor to fill substantially the same job at the existing location as that performed by the transferred position. Such jobs shall be in addition to any full-time jobs that a qualified company had in the Commonwealth as of January 1, 2023.

"*Performance agreement*" means an agreement entered into on or after January 1, 2023, between a qualified company, a locality identified in a memorandum of understanding, and VEDP that commits the locality to provide local funds, either as annual cash grants or via the expenditure of local funds, for infrastructure costs related to the qualified company. The local commitment shall equal at least twice the amount of grants from the Fund committed by the Commonwealth for capital investment and the creation of new full-time jobs in such locality. Such performance agreement may also include commitments related to accelerated permitting, property tax classifications, and other such issues to which the parties agree.

"*Performance date*" means the date set forth in a memorandum of understanding by which capital investment and new full-time job creation targets shall be met in order to qualify for grants from the Fund.

"*Qualification*" means the process by which a company becomes a qualified company eligible to enter into a memorandum of understanding and receive grants from the Fund. Qualification shall require:

1. An endorsement by the MEI Commission that the company be approved by the General Assembly to receive grants from the Fund. Such endorsement shall include a recommendation by the MEI Commission as to the grant amount that the company shall receive for each new full-time job created and each $1 million of capital investment in construction costs made, as well as a recommendation as to the total, aggregate amount of grants from the Fund that the company shall be eligible to receive. The recommendation regarding the amount of the grants shall be based upon information provided by VEDP to the MEI Commission based upon a return-on-investment analysis; and

2. Approval by the General Assembly in a general appropriation act, including approval of the specific grant amount that the company shall receive for each new full-time job created and each $1 million of capital investment in construction costs made, as well as the total, aggregate amount of grants from the Fund that the company shall be eligible to receive and the date of endorsement by the MEI Commission.

If the MEI Commission endorses a company to receive grants from the Fund, and legislation to implement the MEI Commission's recommendation is introduced in a subsequent session of the General Assembly, the specific grant amount recommended and any other recommended legislative changes shall become public at such time as the company publicly declares its intention to make or cause to be made a capital investment at facilities of at least $50 billion and to create at least 1,500 new full-time jobs that pay an average annual wage of at least one and one-half times the prevailing wage of the locality where the job is located, but in no case later than the first day of the session of the General Assembly in which approval is sought.

"*Qualified company*" means a company, including its affiliates, that, after qualification, enters into a memorandum of understanding and is expected by the performance date to (i) make or cause to be made a capital investment at facilities in localities identified in the memorandum of understanding of at least $50 billion and (ii) create at least 1,500 new full-time jobs that pay an average annual wage of at least one and one-half times the prevailing wage of the locality where the job is located.

"*Secretary*" means the Secretary of Commerce and Trade or his designee.

"*VEDP*" means the Virginia Economic Development Partnership Authority.

B. There is hereby created in the state treasury a special nonreverting fund to be known as the Cloud Computing Cluster Infrastructure Grant Fund. The Fund shall be established on the books of the Comptroller. All funds appropriated for the Fund shall be paid into the state treasury and credited to the Fund. Interest earned on moneys in the Fund shall remain in the Fund and be credited to it. Any moneys remaining in the Fund, including interest thereon, at the end of each fiscal year shall not revert to the general fund but shall remain in the Fund. Moneys in the Fund shall be used solely for the purpose of making grant payments pursuant to this chapter. Expenditures and disbursements from the Fund shall be made by the State Treasurer on warrants issued by the Comptroller pursuant to subsection F.

C. A qualified company shall be eligible to receive grant payments for each fiscal year beginning with the Commonwealth's fiscal year starting on July 1,

2025, and ending no later than the Commonwealth's fiscal year starting on July 1, 2044, based upon its actual investments and the number of new full-time jobs created prior to the performance date in localities that have entered into a performance agreement. The grant payments under this section shall be paid to the qualified company from the Fund, subject to appropriation by the General Assembly, during each such fiscal year, contingent upon the qualified company meeting the requirements for receiving grant payments set forth in this section and in the memorandum of understanding. The amount of the grant payment in each fiscal year shall be calculated based upon the grant amount approved for the qualified company for each new full-time job created by the qualified company in the prior calendar year and each $1 million of capital investment in construction costs by the qualified company in the prior calendar year, as approved by the General Assembly and included in the memorandum of understanding. The total aggregate amount of all grants paid to a qualified company shall not exceed the amount approved by the General Assembly and included in the memorandum of understanding.

D. Capital investments made by a qualified company and new full-time jobs created in a locality that (i) was not identified in the memorandum of understanding and (ii) did not enter into a performance agreement shall not qualify for grant payments pursuant to this chapter.

E. A qualified company applying for a grant payment pursuant to this chapter shall provide evidence, satisfactory to the Secretary, of (i) the capital investment in construction costs as of the last day of the calendar year that immediately precedes the application date; (ii) the aggregate number of new full-time jobs created and maintained as of the last day of the calendar year that immediately precedes the date of the application; and (iii) an average annual wage of the new full-time jobs of at least one and one-half times the prevailing wage of the locality where the job is located. The application and evidence shall be filed with the Secretary in person, by mail, or as otherwise agreed upon in the memorandum of understanding, by no later than April 1 of each year following the end of the calendar year upon which the evidence set forth is based. Failure to meet the filing deadline shall result in a deferral of a scheduled grant payment. For filings by mail, the postmark cancellation shall govern the date of the filing determination.

F. Within 60 days of receiving the application and evidence pursuant to subsection E, the Secretary shall certify to the Comptroller and the qualified company the verification of the information contained in the application and the resulting amount of the grant payments to which the grant-eligible company may be entitled for payment. Such grant payments shall be made annually by check or electronic payment issued by the State Treasurer on warrant of the Comptroller in each fiscal year following the submission of such application, as provided in the memorandum of understanding. The Comptroller shall not draw any warrants to issue checks or electronic payments for grant payments under this chapter without a specific appropriation for the same.

G. As a condition for the receipt of a grant payment, a qualified company shall make available for inspection to the Secretary, upon request, documents relevant and applicable to determining whether the qualified company has met the requirements for the receipt of a grant payment as set forth in this chapter and subject to the memorandum of understanding. Copies of the performance agreement and a certification by each locality subject to a performance agreement and the qualified company that the provisions of such agreement have been fulfilled shall also be provided to the Secretary.

History.
2023, cc. 678, 671.

Editor's note.
As enacted, this chapter and section were designated as Chapter 22.20 and Section 59.1-284.41. The chapter and section were redesignated at the direction of the Virginia Code Commission.

CHAPTER 24.

VIRGINIA HEALTH CLUB ACT.

§ 59.1-296. Definitions.

As used in this chapter, unless the context requires a different meaning:

"*Automated external defibrillator*" means a device that combines a heart monitor and defibrillator and (i) has been approved by the U.S. Food and Drug Administration; (ii) is capable of recognizing the presence or absence of ventricular fibrillation or rapid ventricular tachycardia; (iii) is capable of determining, without intervention by an operator, whether defibrillation should be performed; and (iv) automatically charges and requests delivery of an electrical impulse to an individual's heart upon determining that defibrillation should be performed.

"*Business day*" means any day except a Sunday or a legal holiday.

"*Buyer*" means a natural person who enters into a health club contract.

"*Commissioner*" means the Commissioner of Agriculture and Consumer Services, or a member of his staff to whom he may delegate his duties under this chapter.

"*Comparable alternate facility*" means a health club facility that is reasonably of like kind, in nature and quality, to the health club facility originally contracted, whether such facility is in the same location but owned or operated by a different health club or is at another location of the same health club.

"*Contract price*" means the sum of the initiation fee, if any, and all monthly fees except interest required by the health club contract.

"*Facility*" means a location where health club services are offered as designated in a health club contract.

"*Health club*" means any person, firm, corporation, organization, club or association whose primary purpose is to engage in the sale of memberships in a program consisting primarily of physical exercise with exercise machines or devices, or whose primary purpose is to engage in the sale of the right or privilege to use exercise machines or devices. The term "health club" shall not include the following: (i) bona fide nonprofit organizations, including, but not limited to, the Young Men's Christian Association, Young Women's Christian Association, or similar organizations whose functions as health clubs are only incidental to their overall functions and purposes; (ii) any private club owned and operated by its members; (iii) any organization primarily operated for the purpose of teaching a particular form of self-defense such as judo or karate; (iv) any facility owned or operated by the United States; (v) any facility owned or operated by the Commonwealth of Virginia or any of its political subdivisions; (vi) any nonprofit public or private school or institution of higher education; (vii) any club providing tennis or swimming facilities located in a residential planned community or subdivision, developed in conjunction with the development of such community or subdivision, and deriving at least 80 percent of its membership from residents of such community or subdivision; and (viii) any facility owned and operated by a private employer exclusively for the benefit of its employees, retirees, and family members and which facility is only incidental to the overall functions and purposes of the employer's business and is operated on a nonprofit basis.

"*Health club contract*" means an agreement whereby the buyer of health club services purchases, or becomes obligated to purchase, health club services.

"*Health club services*" means and includes services, privileges, or rights offered for sale or provided by a health club.

"*Initiation fee*" means a nonrecurring fee charged at or near the beginning of a health club membership, and includes all fees or charges not part of the monthly fee.

"*Monthly fee*" means the total consideration, including but not limited to, equipment or locker rental, credit check, finance, medical and dietary evaluation, class and training fees, and all other similar fees or charges and interest, but excluding any initiation fee, to be paid by a buyer, divided by the total number of months of health club service use allowed by the buyer's contract, including months or time periods called "free" or "bonus" months or time periods and such months or time periods that are described in any other terms suggesting that they are provided free of charge, which months or time periods are given or contemplated when the contract is initially executed.

"*Out of business*" means the status of a facility that is permanently closed and for which there is no comparable alternate facility.

"*Prepayment*" means payment of any consideration for services or the use of facilities made prior to the day on which the services or facilities of the health club are fully open and available for regular use by the members.

"*Relocation*" means the provision of health club services by the health club that entered into the membership contract at a location other than that designated in the member's contract.

History.
1984, c. 738; 1985, c. 585; 1986, c. 187; 1990, cc. 392, 433; 1991, c. 149; 1992, c. 102; 2003, c. 344; 2007, c. 683; 2010, c. 439; 2014, c. 459; 2020, c. 628.

The 2020 amendments.
The 2020 amendment by c. 628, in the intro-ductory language, added "unless the context requires a different meaning"; and added the definition for "Automated external defibrillator."

§ 59.1-296.2:2. Automated external defibrillator required.

Each health club location shall have a working automated external defibrillator.

History.
2020, c. 628.

§ 59.1-297. Right of cancellation.

A. Every health club contract for the sale of health club services may be cancelled under the following circumstances:

1. A buyer may cancel the contract without penalty within three business days of its making and, upon notice to the health club of the buyer's intent to cancel, shall be entitled to receive a refund of all moneys paid under the contract.

2. A buyer may cancel the contract if the facility relocates or goes out of

business and the health club fails to provide comparable alternate facilities within five driving miles of the location designated in the health club contract. Upon receipt of notice of the buyer's intent to cancel, the health club shall refund to the buyer funds paid or accepted in payment of the contract in an amount computed as prescribed in § 59.1-297.1.

3. The contract may be cancelled if the buyer dies or becomes physically unable to use a substantial portion of the services for 30 or more consecutive days. If the buyer becomes physically unable to use a substantial portion of the services for 30 or more consecutive days and wishes to cancel his contract, he must provide the health club with a signed statement from his doctor, physician assistant, or advanced practice registered nurse verifying that he is physically unable to use a substantial portion of the health club services for 30 or more consecutive days. Upon receipt of notice of the buyer's intent to cancel, the health club shall refund to the buyer funds paid or accepted in payment of the contract in an amount computed as prescribed in § 59.1-297.1. In the case of disability, the health club may require the buyer to submit to a physical examination by a doctor, a physician assistant, or an advanced practice registered nurse agreeable to the buyer and the health club within 30 days of receipt of notice of the buyer's intent to cancel. The cost of the examination shall be borne by the health club.

B. The buyer shall notify the health club of cancellation in writing, by certified mail, return receipt requested, or personal delivery, to the address of the health club as specified in the health club contract.

C. If the customer has executed any credit or lien agreement with the health club or its representatives or agents to pay for all or part of health club services, any such negotiable instrument executed by the buyer shall be returned to the buyer within 30 days after such cancellation.

D. If the club agrees to allow a consumer to cancel for any other reason not outlined in this section, upon receipt of notice of cancellation by the buyer, the health club shall refund to the buyer funds paid or accepted in payment of the contract in an amount computed as prescribed in § 59.1-297.1.

History.
1984, c. 738; 1990, cc. 392, 433; 2003, c. 344; 2004, c. 855; 2006, c. 396; 2010, c. 439; 2014, c. 459; 2023, c. 183.

The 2023 amendments.
The 2023 amendment by c. 183, in subdivision A 3, substituted "advanced practice registered nurse" for "nurse practitioner" in the second sentence, and substituted "a physician assistant, or an advanced practice registered nurse" for "physician assistant, or nurse practitioner" in the fourth sentence.

§ 59.1-298. Notice to buyer.

A copy of the executed health club contract shall be delivered to the buyer at the time the contract is executed. All health club contracts shall (i) be in writing, (ii) state the name and physical address of the health club, (iii) be signed by the buyer, (iv) designate the date on which the buyer actually signed the contract, (v) state the starting and expiration dates of the initial membership period, (vi) separately identify any initiation fee, (vii) either in the contract itself or in a separate notice provided to the buyer at the time the contract is executed, notify each buyer that the buyer should attempt to resolve with the health club any complaint the buyer has with the health club, and that the Virginia Department of Agriculture and Consumer Services regulates health clubs in the Commonwealth pursuant to the provisions of the Virginia Health Club Act, and (viii) contain the provisions set forth in § 59.1-297 under a conspicuous caption: "BUYER'S RIGHT TO CANCEL" that shall read substantially as follows:

If you wish to cancel this contract, you may cancel by making or delivering written notice to this health club. The notice must say that you do not wish to be bound by the contract and must be delivered or mailed before midnight of the third business day after you sign this contract. The notice must be delivered or mailed to _____ (Health club shall insert its name and mailing address).

If canceled within three business days, you will be entitled to a refund of all moneys paid. You may also cancel this contract if this club goes out of business or relocates and fails to provide comparable alternate facilities within five driving miles of the facility designated in this contract. You may also cancel if you become physically unable to use a substantial portion of the health club services for 30 or more consecutive days, and your estate may cancel in the event of your death. You must prove you are unable to use a substantial portion of the health club services by a doctor's, a physician assistant's, or an advanced practice registered nurse's certificate, and the health club may also require that you submit to a physical examination, within 30 days of the notice of cancellation, by a doctor, a physician assistant, or an advanced practice registered nurse agreeable to you and the health club. If you cancel after the three business days, the health club may retain or collect a portion of the contract price equal to the proportionate value of the services or use of facilities you have already received. Any refund due to you shall be paid within 30 days of the effective date of cancellation.

History.
1984, c. 738; 1990, cc. 392, 433; 2003, c. 344; 2004, c. 855; 2006, c. 396; 2010, c. 439; 2013, c. 24; 2014, c. 459; 2023, c. 183.

The 2023 amendments.
The 2023 amendment by c. 183, rewrote the fourth sentence in the third paragraph.

CHAPTER 24.1.

TANNING FACILITIES.

§ 59.1-310.3. Notice to customers; liability.

A. A tanning facility shall give each customer a written statement warning that:

1. Failure to use the eye protection provided to the customer by the tanning facility may result in damage to the eyes;

2. Overexposure to ultraviolet light causes burns;

3. Repeated exposure may result in premature aging of the skin and skin cancer;

4. Abnormal skin sensitivity or burning may be caused by reactions of ultraviolet light to certain (i) foods; (ii) cosmetics; or (iii) medications, including tranquilizers, diuretics, antibiotics, high blood pressure medicines, or birth control pills; and

5. Any person taking a prescription or over-the-counter drug should consult a physician prior to using a tanning device.

B. Prior to allowing a prospective customer to use a tanning device, the owner or his designee shall obtain on the written statement the signature of each customer on a duplicate of the written statement provided to the customer under subsection A.

C. Compliance with the notice requirements does not affect the liability of a tanning facility owner or a manufacturer of a tanning device.

D. The signed duplicates of the written statements provided under subsection A may be retained at a location other than the tanning facility if an electronic or facsimile image of the original is readily available at each of an owner's tanning facilities.

History.
1990, c. 776; 2007, c. 575; 2020, c. 387.

The 2020 amendments.
The 2020 amendment by c. 387 deleted the last sentence of subsection B, which read: "In addition, the owner or his designee shall obtain, every six months, the signature of the parent or legal guardian of a prospective customer who is under the age of 15 and is not emancipated under Virginia law."

§ 59.1-310.4. Warning signs.

A. A tanning facility shall post a warning sign in a conspicuous location where it is readily readable by persons entering the establishment. The sign shall contain the following warning:
DANGER: ULTRAVIOLET RADIATION
Repeated exposure to ultraviolet radiation may cause chronic sun damage to the skin characterized by wrinkling, dryness, fragility, and bruising of the skin, and skin cancer.
Failure to use protective eyewear may result in severe burns or permanent injury to the eyes.
Medications or cosmetics may increase your sensitivity to ultraviolet radiation. Consult a physician or an advanced practice registered nurse before using a sunlamp if you are using medications, have a history of skin problems, or believe you are especially sensitive to sunlight. Pregnant women or women taking oral contraceptives who use this product may develop discolored skin.
IF YOU DO NOT TAN IN THE SUN, YOU WILL NOT TAN FROM USE OF AN ULTRAVIOLET SUNLAMP.
B. A tanning facility shall post a warning sign, one sign for each tanning device, in a conspicuous location that is readily readable to a person about to use the device. The sign shall contain the following:
DANGER: ULTRAVIOLET RADIATION
1. Follow the manufacturer's instructions for use of this device.
2. Avoid too frequent or lengthy exposure. As with natural sunlight, exposure can cause serious eye and skin injuries and allergic reactions. Repeated exposure may cause skin cancer.
3. Wear protective eyewear. Failure to use protective eyewear may result in severe burns or permanent damage to the eyes.
4. Do not sunbathe before or after exposure to ultraviolet radiation from sunlamps.
5. Medications or cosmetics may increase your sensitivity to ultraviolet radiation. Consult a physician or an advanced practice registered nurse before using a sunlamp if you are using medication, have a history of skin problems, or believe you are especially sensitive to sunlight. Pregnant women or women using oral contraceptives who use this product may develop discolored skin.
IF YOU DO NOT TAN IN THE SUN, YOU WILL NOT TAN FROM USE OF THIS DEVICE.

History.
1990, c. 776; 2004, c. 855; 2023, c. 183.

The 2023 amendments.
The 2023 amendment by c. 183, substituted

"an advanced practice registered nurse" for "nurse practitioner" in the fourth paragraph of subsection A; and substituted "an advanced practice registered nurse" for "nurse practitioner" in subdivision B 5.

§ 59.1-310.5. Operational requirements.

A. A tanning facility shall have an operator present during operating hours. The operator shall be sufficiently knowledgeable in the correct operation of the tanning devices used at the facility and shall inform and assist each customer in the proper use of the tanning device.

B. The owner or his designee shall identify the skin type of the customer based on the Fitzpatrick scale, document the skin type of the customer, and advise the customer of the customer's maximum time of recommended exposure in the tanning device.

C. Before each use of a tanning device, the operator shall provide the customer with properly sanitized protective eyewear that protects the eyes from ultraviolet radiation and allows adequate vision to maintain balance. The operator shall not allow a person to use a tanning device if that person has not been provided protective eyewear. The operator shall also instruct each customer how to use suitable physical aids, such as handrails and markings on the floor, to maintain proper exposure distance as recommended by the manufacturer of the tanning device.

D. After each use of a tanning device, the owner or his designee shall clean the device with a cleaner or sanitizer capable of killing bacteria from any previous use.

E. The tanning facility shall use a timer with an accuracy of at least plus or minus ten percent of any selected time interval. The facility shall limit the exposure time of a customer on a tanning device to the maximum exposure time recommended by the manufacturer. The facility shall control the interior temperature of a tanning device so that it may not exceed 100 degrees Fahrenheit.

F. Either each time a customer uses a tanning facility or each time a person executes or renews a contract to use a tanning facility, the person shall sign a written statement acknowledging that the person has read and understood the required warnings before using the device and agrees to use the protective eyewear that the tanning facility provides.

G. No individual under the age of 18 shall be allowed to use any tanning device, other than a spray tanning device that does not emit ultraviolet light, at a tanning facility. The owner shall be responsible for ensuring that each customer using the tanning facility is of legal age to do so.

H. A tanning facility shall not claim, or distribute promotional material that claims that the use of a tanning device is safe, is without risk, or will result in medical or health benefits.

I. The provisions of subsection G shall not prohibit any person licensed by the Board of Medicine to practice medicine or osteopathic medicine from prescribing or using a phototherapy device for any patient, regardless of age. For the purposes of this section, "phototherapy device" means a device that emits ultraviolet radiation and is used in the diagnosis or treatment of disease or injury.

History.
1990, c. 776; 2007, c. 575; 2020, c. 387.

The 2020 amendments.
The 2020 amendment by c. 387, in subsection G, added the first sentence; and added subsection I.

CHAPTER 24.2.
SEPTIC SYSTEM INSPECTORS.

§ 59.1-310.9. Requirements for accredited septic system inspectors and performance of septic system inspections.

A. In order to use the title of "accredited septic system inspector" in connection with any real estate transaction, including refinancings, an applicant shall be accredited by the National Sanitation Foundation or an equivalent national accrediting organization, which accreditation shall include the passage of both a written and practical examination on the principles and practice of septic system inspections.

In addition, the applicant shall satisfy the following requirements:

1. Hold a high school diploma or equivalent; and

2. Have evidence of at least one year of active field experience conducting onsite septic systems inspections or completion of a nationally approved training course.

B. Any individual who holds a valid onsite sewage system operator, onsite sewage system installer, or onsite soil evaluator license pursuant to Chapter 23 (§ 54.1-2300 et seq.) of Title 54.1 shall be authorized to perform a septic system inspection in connection with any real estate transaction, including refinancings.

History.
2001, c. 52; 2020, c. 521.

The 2020 amendments.
The 2020 amendment by c. 521 added subsection B.

§ 59.1-310.10. Penalty for violation.

No person shall use the title "accredited septic system inspector" or perform a septic system inspection in connection with any real estate transaction unless he meets the requirements of this chapter. Any person who violates the provisions of this chapter is guilty of a Class 3 misdemeanor.

History.
2001, c. 52; 2020, c. 521.

The 2020 amendments.
The 2020 amendment by c. 521, in the first sentence, inserted "or perform a septic system inspection in connection with any real estate transaction," and in the last sentence, substituted "is" for "shall be."

CHAPTER 25.
VIRGINIA MEMBERSHIP CAMPING ACT.

Article 3. Protection of Purchasers.

ARTICLE 3.

PROTECTION OF PURCHASERS.

§ 59.1-332. Conditions on offering items as an inducement to execute.

A. It is unlawful for any person by any means, as part of an advertising program, to offer any item of value as an inducement to the recipient to visit a membership camping operator's campground, attend a sales presentation, or contact a salesperson, unless the person clearly discloses in writing in the offer in readily understandable language each of the following:

1. The name and campground address of the membership camping operator.

2. A general statement that the advertising program is being conducted by a membership camping operator and the purpose of any requested visit.

3. A statement of odds, in Arabic numerals, of receiving each item offered.

4. The approximate retail value of each item offered.

5. The number of campgrounds that are participating in such advertising program.

6. The restrictions, qualifications, and other conditions that must be satisfied before the recipient is entitled to receive the item, including:

a. Any deadline, if any, by which the recipient must visit the campground, attend the sales presentation, or contact a salesperson in order to receive the item.

b. The approximate duration of any visit and sales presentation.

c. The date upon which the offer shall terminate and the final date upon which the gifts or prizes are to be awarded.

d. Any other conditions, such as minimum age qualification, a financial qualification, or a requirement that if the recipient is married both spouses must be present in order to receive the item.

7. A statement that the membership camping operator reserves the right to provide a rain check or a substitute or like item, if these rights are reserved.

8. All other material rules, terms, and conditions of the offer or program.

B. It is unlawful for any person making an offer subject to subsection A, or any employee or agent of the person, to offer any item if the person knows or has reason to know that the offered item will not be available in a sufficient quantity based on the reasonably anticipated response to the offer.

C. It is unlawful for any person making an offer subject to subsection A, or any employee or agent of the person, to fail to provide any offered item that any recipient who has responded to the offer in the manner specified in the offer, has performed the requirements disclosed in the offer, and has met the qualifications described in the offer is entitled to receive, unless the offered item is not reasonably available and the offer discloses the reservation of a right to provide a rain check or a like or substitute item if the offered item is unavailable.

D. If the person making an offer subject to subsection A is unable to provide an offered item because of limitations of supply, quantity, or quality not reasonably foreseeable or controllable by the person making the offer, the person making the offer shall inform the recipient of the recipient's right to receive a rain check for the item offered, unless the person making the offer knows or has a reasonable basis for knowing that the item will not be reasonably available at approximately the same price to the person making the offer, and shall inform the recipient of the recipient's right to at least one of the following additional options:

1. The person making the offer will provide a like item of equivalent or greater retail value or a rain check for the item. This option must be offered if the offered item is not reasonably available.

2. The person making the offer will provide a substitute item of equivalent or greater retail value.

3. The person making the offer will provide a rain check for a like or substitute item.

E. If a rain check is provided, the person making an offer subject to subsection A shall, within a reasonable time, and in any event not more than 90 days after the rain check is provided, deliver the agreed item to the recipient's address without additional cost or obligation to the recipient, unless the item for which the rain check is provided remains unavailable because of limitations of supply, quantity, or quality not reasonably foreseeable or controllable by the person making the offer. If the item is unavailable for these reasons, the person shall, not more than 30 days after the expiration of the aforesaid 90-day period, deliver a like item of equal or greater retail value or, if the item is not reasonably available to the person at approximately the same price, a substitute item of equal or greater retail value.

F. On the written request of a recipient who has received or claims a right to receive any offered item, the person making an offer subject to subsection A shall furnish to the recipient sufficient evidence showing that the item provided matches the item randomly or otherwise selected for distribution to that recipient.

G. It is unlawful for any person making an offer subject to subsection A, or any employee or agent of the person, to:

1. Misrepresent the size, quantity, identity, or quality of any prize, gift, money, or other item of value offered.

2. Misrepresent in any manner the odds of receiving any particular gift, prize, amount of money, or other item of value.

3. Label any offer a "notice of termination" or "notice of cancellation."

4. Materially misrepresent, in any manner, the offer or program.

H. If any provision of this section is in conflict with the provisions of the Prizes and Gifts Act (§ 59.1-415 et seq.), the provisions of the Prizes and Gifts Act shall control.

History.
1985, c. 409; 1992, c. 545; 2020, c. 900.

The 2020 amendments.
The 2020 amendment by c. 900, in subdivi-sion A 6 d, substituted "spouses" for "husband and wife"; and made stylistic changes throughout the section.

CHAPTER 25.1.

VIRGINIA CREDIT SERVICES BUSINESSES ACT.

§ 59.1-335.2. Definitions.

In this chapter the following words have the following meanings:

"Attorney General" means the Office of the Attorney General of Virginia.

"Commissioner" means the Commissioner of Agriculture and Consumer Services, or a member of his staff to whom he may delegate his duties under this chapter.

"Consumer" means any individual who is solicited to purchase or who purchases the services of a credit services business.

§ 59.1-335.2   VIRGINIA CREDIT SERVICES BUSINESSES ACT   § 59.1-335.2

"Consumer report" means any written, oral, or other communication of any information by a consumer reporting agency bearing on a consumer's credit-worthiness, credit standing, credit capacity, character, general reputation, personal characteristics, or mode of living which (i) is furnished or (ii) is used or expected to be used or collected in whole or in part for the purpose of serving as a factor in establishing the consumer's eligibility for:

1. Credit or insurance to be used primarily for personal, family, or household purposes; or

2. Employment purposes; or

3. Other purposes which shall be limited to the following circumstances:

a. In response to the order of a court having jurisdiction to issue the order.

b. In accordance with the written instructions of the consumer to whom the report relates.

c. To a person which the agency has reason to believe:

(i) Intends to use the information in connection with a credit transaction involving the consumer on whom the information is to be furnished and involving the extension of credit to or review or collection of an account of, the consumer; or

(ii) Intends to use the information for employment purposes; or

(iii) Intends to use the information in connection with the underwriting of insurance involving the consumer; or

(iv) Intends to use the information in connection with a determination of the consumer's eligibility for a license or other benefit granted by a governmental instrumentality required by law to consider an applicant's financial responsibility or status; or

(v) Otherwise has a legitimate business need for the information in connection with a business transaction involving the consumer.

The term "consumer report" does not include:

1. Any report containing information solely as to transactions or experiences between the consumer and the person making the report;

2. Any authorization or approval of a specific extension of credit directly or indirectly by the issuer of a credit card or similar device; or

3. Any report in which a person who has been requested by a third party to make a specific extension of credit directly or indirectly to a consumer conveys his decision with respect to the request, if the third party advises the consumer of the name and address of the person to whom the request was made and the person makes the disclosures to the consumer as to the exact nature of the request and the effect of the report on its decision to extend credit.

"Consumer reporting agency" means any person that, for monetary fees, dues, or on a cooperative nonprofit basis, regularly engages in whole or in part in the practice of assembling or evaluating consumer credit information or other information on consumers for the purpose of furnishing consumer reports to third parties and that uses any means or facility of commerce for the purpose of preparing or furnishing consumer reports. "Consumer reporting agency" does not include a private investigator registered under the provisions of Article 4 (§ 9.1-138 et seq.) of Chapter 1 of Title 9.1.

"Credit services business" means any person that, with respect to the extension of credit by others, sells, provides, or performs, or represents that such person can or will sell, provide, or perform, any of the following services in return for the payment of money or other valuable consideration:

1. Improving a consumer's credit record, history, or rating;

2. Obtaining an extension of credit for a consumer; or

3. Providing advice or assistance to a consumer with regard to either subdivision 1 or 2.

"Credit services business" does not include:

(i) Any person authorized to make, arrange, or negotiate loans or extensions of credit under the laws of the Commonwealth or the United States;

(ii) Any bank, trust company, savings bank, or savings institution whose deposits or accounts are eligible for insurance by the Federal Deposit Insurance Corporation or other federal insurance agency, or any credit union organized and chartered under the laws of the Commonwealth or the United States;

(iii) Any nonprofit organization exempt from taxation under § 501(c) (3) of the Internal Revenue Code (26 U.S.C. § 501(c) (3));

(iv) Any person licensed as a real estate broker by the Commonwealth where the person is acting within the course and scope of that license;

(v) Any person licensed to practice law in the Commonwealth where the person renders services within the course and scope of that person's practice as a lawyer;

(vi) Any broker-dealer registered with the Securities and Exchange Commission or the Commodity Futures Trading Commission where the broker-dealer is acting within the course and scope of that regulation;

(vii) Any consumer reporting agency as defined in the Federal Fair Credit Reporting Act (15 U.S.C. § 1681 et seq.); or

(viii) Any person selling personal, family, or household goods to a consumer who, in connection with the seller's sale of its goods to the consumer, assists the consumer in obtaining a loan or extension of credit or extends credit to the consumer.

"Extension of credit" means the right to defer payment of debt or to incur debt and defer its payment, offered or granted primarily for personal, family, or household purposes.

"File" when used in connection with information on any consumer, means all of the information on that consumer recorded and retained by a consumer reporting agency regardless of how the information is stored.

"Investigative consumer report" means a consumer report or portion of it in which information on a consumer's character, general reputation, personal characteristics, or mode of living is obtained through personal interviews with neighbors, friends, or associates of the consumer reported on or with others with whom he is acquainted or who may have knowledge concerning any items of information. However, the information does not include specific factual information on a consumer's credit record obtained directly from a creditor of the consumer or from a consumer reporting agency when the information was obtained directly from a creditor of the consumer or from the consumer.

"Person" includes an individual, corporation, government or governmental subdivision or agency, business trust, estate, trust, partnership, association, two or more persons having a joint or common interest, and any other legal or commercial entity.

History.

1989, cc. 651, 655; 1990, c. 3; 2003, c. 359; 2023, c. 110.

The 2023 amendments.

The 2023 amendment by c. 110, in the definition of "Consumer reporting agency," substituted "that" for which" twice and "private investigator registered" for "private detective or investigator licensed"; in the definition of "Credit services business," substituted "that, with" for "who, with" in the introductory language and deleted "herein" at the end of subdivision 3; and in the definition of "Credit services business," substituted "Any person authorized to make, arrange, or negotiate loans or extensions of credit under the laws of the" for "The making, arranging, or negotiating for a loan or extension of credit under the laws of this" in clause (i), substituted "the Commonwealth" for "this Commonwealth" in clause (ii), (iv), and (v), and substituted "§ 1681 et seq." for "§§ 1681 -1681v" in clause (vii).

§ 59.1-335.5. Prohibited practices.

A credit services business, and its salespersons, agents and representatives, and independent contractors who sell or attempt to sell the services of a credit services business, shall not do any of the following:

1. Charge or receive any money or other valuable consideration prior to full and complete performance of the services that the credit services business has agreed to perform for or on behalf of the consumer, unless the consumer has agreed to pay for such services during the term of a written subscription agreement that provides for the consumer to make periodic payments during the agreement's term in consideration for the credit services business's ongoing performance of services for or on behalf of the consumer, provided that such subscription agreement may be cancelled at any time by the consumer;

2. Charge or receive any money or other valuable consideration solely for referral of the consumer to a retail seller or to any other credit grantor who will or may extend to the consumer, if the credit that is or will be extended to the consumer is upon substantially the same terms as those available to the general public;

3. Make, or counsel or advise any consumer to make, any statement that is untrue or misleading and which is known, or which by the exercise of reasonable care should be known, to be untrue or misleading, to a consumer reporting agency or to any person who has extended credit to a consumer or to whom a consumer is applying for an extension of credit, with respect to a consumer's creditworthiness, credit standing, or credit capacity;

4. Make or use any untrue or misleading representations in the offer or sale of the services of a credit services business or engage, directly or indirectly, in any act, practice, or course of business which operates or would operate as a fraud or deception upon any person in connection with the offer or sale of the services of a credit services business; or

5. Advertise, offer, sell, provide, or perform any of the services of a credit services business in connection with an extension of credit that meets any of the following conditions:

a. The amount of credit is less than $5,000;

b. The repayment term is one year or less;

c. The credit is provided under an open-end credit plan; or

d. The annual percentage rate exceeds 36 percent. For purposes of this section, "annual percentage rate" has the same meaning as in the federal Truth in Lending Act (15 U.S.C. § 1601 et seq.) and its implementing regulations, as they may be amended from time to time.

History.

1989, cc. 651, 655; 2010, c. 421; 2020, cc. 1215, 1258.

Editor's note.

Acts 2020, cc. 1215 and 1258, cl. 5 provide: "That the provisions of the first and second enactments of this act shall become effective on January 1, 2021, except that the database re-quired by § 6.2-1810 of the Code of Virginia, as amended by this act, shall be modified to accommodate the provisions of this first enactment of this act by January 1, 2022."

The 2020 amendments.

The 2020 amendments by cc. 1215 and 1258, effective January 1, 2021, are identical, and added subdivision 5 and made a related stylistic change.

§ 59.1-335.7. Contents of information statement.

The information statement required under § 59.1-335.6 shall include all of the following:

1. a. A complete and accurate statement of the consumer's right to review any file on the consumer maintained by any consumer reporting agency, and the right of the consumer to receive a copy of a consumer report containing all

information in that file as provided under the Federal Fair Credit Reporting Act (15 U.S.C. § 1681g);

b. A complete and accurate statement of the consumer's right to receive a free copy of the consumer's credit report every 12 months from each of the three nationwide consumer reporting agencies, including identification of the website and toll-free telephone number through which the free report may be obtained, as provided under the Federal Fair Credit Reporting Act (15 U.S.C. § 1681j);

c. A complete and accurate statement that a copy of the consumer report containing all information in the consumer's file will be furnished free of charge by the consumer reporting agency if requested by the consumer within 60 days of receiving a notice of a denial of credit as provided under the Federal Fair Credit Reporting Act (15 U.S.C. § 1681j); and

d. A complete and accurate statement that a nominal charge may be imposed on the consumer by the consumer reporting agency for a copy of the consumer report containing all information in the consumer's file, if the consumer has already obtained the free credit report to which the consumer is entitled on an annual basis and the consumer has not been denied credit within 60 days from receipt of the consumer's request;

2. A complete and accurate statement of the consumer's right to dispute the completeness or accuracy of any item contained in any file on the consumer that is maintained by any consumer reporting agency, as provided under the Federal Fair Credit Reporting Act (15 U.S.C. § 1681i);

3. A complete and detailed description of the services to be performed by the credit services business for or on behalf of the consumer, and the total amount the consumer will have to pay, or become obligated to pay, for the services. Such statement shall include the following notice in at least 10-point bold type: IMPORTANT NOTICE:
YOU HAVE NO OBLIGATION TO PAY ANY FEES OR CHARGES UNTIL ALL SERVICES HAVE BEEN PERFORMED COMPLETELY FOR YOU, UNLESS YOU ENTER INTO A SUBSCRIPTION AGREEMENT REQUIRING PERIODIC PAYMENTS IN CONSIDERATION FOR ONGOING SERVICES; and

4. The notice prescribed by subdivision 3 shall also be posted by means of a conspicuous sign so as to be readily noticeable and readable at the location within the premises of the credit services business where consumers are interviewed by personnel of the business.

History.
1989, cc. 651, 655; 2010, c. 421; 2023, c. 110.

The 2023 amendments.
The 2023 amendment by c. 110, deleted "of this chapter" following "59.1-335.6" in the introductory language; redesignated and rewrote former subdivision 1 b as 1 b and 1 c; redesignated former subdivision 1 c as 1 d; in subdivision 1 d, added "complete and accurate" and "has already obtained the free credit report to which the consumer is entitled on an annual basis and the consumer" and substituted "60" for "30"; and deleted "of this section" following "subdivision" in subdivision 4.

CHAPTER 26.

UNIFORM TRADE SECRETS ACT.

§ 59.1-336. Short title and definitions.

CASE NOTES

Analysis

II. Definitions.
   C. "Trade secrets.".

II. DEFINITIONS.

C. "Trade secrets.".

Insufficient allegations of trade secrets. — Where plaintiff and defendant were engaged in the business of identifying vulnerabilities in the source code of software and shared information about those vulnerabilities, plaintiff was properly granted a declaration that it had not misappropriated defendant's trade secrets as defendant had not shown that any of its alleged trade secrets satisfied the statutory definition since it failed to put forward admissible evidence showing that alleged trade secrets had independent economic value. Synopsys, Inc. v. Risk Based Sec., Inc., 70 F.4th 759 (4th Cir. 2023).

CIRCUIT COURT OPINIONS

Acquisition by improper means. — Virginia Uniform Trade Secrets Act, § 59.1-336 et seq., prohibits acquisition of trade secrets by improper means. It does not prohibit maintenance of those secrets after the initial proper acquisition unless one can prove an actual or threatened disclosure or use of those secrets. Knowesis, Inc. v. Herrera, 103 Va. Cir. 175, 2019 Va. Cir. LEXIS 459 (Fairfax County Oct. 2, 2019).

Virginia Uniform Trade Secrets Act (VUTSA), § 59.1-336 et seq., does not prohibit mere maintenance of trade secrets initially acquired through proper means. Rather, the VUTSA prohibits acquisition by improper means of the trade secrets or the actual or threatened disclosure or use of them. Knowesis, Inc. v. Herrera, 103 Va. Cir. 175, 2019 Va. Cir. LEXIS 459 (Fairfax County Oct. 2, 2019).

Former employee. — Virginia Uniform Trade Secrets Act, § 59.1-336 et seq., does not affect a former employee who properly acquires trade secrets and merely holds them post-employment with no actual or threatened disclosure or use. This statutory principle applies even if the retention is against the will of the employer. Knowesis, Inc. v. Herrera, 103 Va. Cir. 175, 2019 Va. Cir. LEXIS 459 (Fairfax County Oct. 2, 2019).

Material from public sources. — Materials did not derive independent value and were largely available through the government, and thus plaintiff's claim for misappropriation of trade secrets failed; many of the materials, regardless of how they were ultimately acquired, were developed in support of plaintiff's prior government contract, thereby making them government property. As property not in plaintiff's exclusive dominion, the materials remained readily ascertainable by proper means by other persons who could obtain economic value from their disclosure. Futrend Tech., Inc. v. MicroHealth LLC, 2020 Va. Cir. LEXIS 128 (Fairfax County Aug. 21, 2020).

Independent economic value. — To the extent that any of the materials were exclusively owned by plaintiff, they could not be considered trade secrets as plaintiff had not established a basis for independent economic value. Futrend Tech., Inc. v. MicroHealth LLC, 2020 Va. Cir. LEXIS 128 (Fairfax County Aug. 21, 2020).

Violation not found. — Employer was not entitled to prevail on its VUTSA claim against a former employee where it alleged that the employee properly acquired the trade secrets in furtherance of her employment and did not allege that she threatened to disclose or use, or in fact disclosed or used, those secrets in any way after she left employment. Her passive maintenance of the secrets was not a violation of the Virginia Uniform Trade Secrets Act, § 59.1-336 et seq. Knowesis, Inc. v. Herrera, 103 Va. Cir. 175, 2019 Va. Cir. LEXIS 459 (Fairfax County Oct. 2, 2019).

§ 59.1-337. Injunctive relief.

CIRCUIT COURT OPINIONS

Generally. — Virginia Uniform Trade Secrets Act (VUTSA), § 59.1-336 et seq., does not prohibit mere maintenance of trade secrets initially acquired through proper means. Rather, the VUTSA prohibits acquisition by improper means of the trade secrets or the actual or threatened disclosure or use of them. Knowesis, Inc. v. Herrera, 103 Va. Cir. 175, 2019 Va. Cir. LEXIS 459 (Fairfax County Oct. 2, 2019).

§ 59.1-338. Damages.

CIRCUIT COURT OPINIONS

No exclusive dominion. — Materials did not derive independent value and were largely available through the government, and thus plaintiff's claim for misappropriation of trade secrets failed; many of the materials, regardless of how they were ultimately acquired, were developed in support of plaintiff's prior government contract, thereby making them government property. As property not in plaintiff's exclusive dominion, the materials remained readily ascertainable by proper means by other persons who could obtain economic value from their disclosure. Futrend Tech., Inc. v. MicroHealth LLC, 2020 Va. Cir. LEXIS 128 (Fairfax County Aug. 21, 2020).

Generally. — Virginia Uniform Trade Secrets Act, § 59.1-336 et seq., prohibits acquisition of trade secrets by improper means. It does not prohibit maintenance of those secrets after the initial proper acquisition unless one can prove an actual or threatened disclosure or use of those secrets. Knowesis, Inc. v. Herrera, 103 Va. Cir. 175, 2019 Va. Cir. LEXIS 459 (Fairfax County Oct. 2, 2019).

CHAPTER 29.

HORSE RACING AND PARI-MUTUEL WAGERING.

Article 1. Virginia Racing Commission.

ARTICLE 1.

VIRGINIA RACING COMMISSION.

§ 59.1-364. Control of racing with pari-mutuel wagering.

A. Horse racing with pari-mutuel wagering as licensed herein shall be permitted in the Commonwealth for the promotion, sustenance and growth of a native industry, in a manner consistent with the health, safety and welfare of the people. The Virginia Racing Commission is vested with control of all horse racing with pari-mutuel wagering in the Commonwealth, with plenary power to prescribe regulations and conditions under which such racing and wagering shall be conducted, so as to maintain horse racing in the Commonwealth of the highest quality and free of any corrupt, incompetent, dishonest or unprincipled practices and to maintain in such racing complete honesty and integrity. The Virginia Racing Commission shall encourage participation by local individuals and businesses in those activities associated with horse racing.

B. The conduct of any horse racing with pari-mutuel wagering participation in such racing or wagering and entrance to any place where such racing or wagering is conducted is a privilege which may be granted or denied by the Commission or its duly authorized representatives in its discretion in order to effectuate the purposes set forth in this chapter.

C. The award of any prize money for any pari-mutuel wager placed at a racetrack or satellite facility licensed by the Commission shall not be deemed to be a part of any gaming contract within the purview of § 11-14.

D. This section shall not apply to any sports betting or related activity that is lawful under Chapter 41 (§ 58.1-4100 et seq.) of Title 58.1.

E. This section shall not apply to any sports betting or related activity that is lawful under Article 2 (§ 58.1-4030 et seq.) of Chapter 40 of Title 58.1, which shall be regulated pursuant to such chapter.

History.
1988, c. 855; 1992, c. 820; 1998, c. 619; 2020, cc. 1197, 1218, 1248, 1256.

Editor's note.
Acts 2020, cc. 1197 and 1248, cl. 2 provides: "That the provisions of this act may result in a net increase in periods of imprisonment or commitment. Pursuant to § 30-19.1:4 of the Code of Virginia, the estimated amount of the necessary appropriation cannot be determined for periods of imprisonment in state adult correctional facilities; therefore, Chapter 854 of the Acts of Assembly of 2019 requires the Virginia Criminal Sentencing Commission to assign a minimum fiscal impact of $50,000. Pursuant to § 30-19.1:4 of the Code of Virginia, the estimated amount of the necessary appropriation cannot be determined for periods of commitment to the custody of the Department of Juvenile Justice."

Acts 2020, cc. 1197 and 1248, cl. 3 provides: "That the Virginia Lottery Board shall promul-

gate regulations to implement the provisions of this act to be effective within 280 days of its enactment."

Acts 2020, cc. 1218 and 1256, cl. 2 provides: "That the Virginia Lottery Board (the Board) shall promulgate regulations implementing the provisions of this act. The Board's initial adoption of regulations shall be exempt from the Administrative Process Act (§ 2.2-4000 et seq. of the Code of Virginia), except that the Board shall provide an opportunity for public comment on the regulations prior to adoption. The Board shall complete work on such regulations no later than September 15, 2020."

The 2020 amendments.
The 2020 amendments by cc. 1197 and 1248 are identical, and added subsection D.

The 2020 amendments by cc. 1218 and 1256 are identical, and added subsection D, which was subsequently redesignated as subsection E at the direction of the Virginia Code Commission.

§ 59.1-365. Definitions.

Editor's note.
Acts 2020, c. 1289, as amended by Acts 2021, Sp. Sess. I, c. 552, Item 110 F 5, effective for the biennium ending June 30, 2022, provides: "For any local referendum passed pursuant to § 59.1-391 after July 1, 2020, the Virginia

Racing Commission shall not authorize any additional satellite facilities as defined in § 59.1-365 of the Code of Virginia, or additional simulcast wagering terminals pursuant to 11 VAC 10-47-180, during a period of two years after the effective date of this act."

§ 59.1-369. (Effective until July 1, 2024) Powers and duties of the Commission.

The Commission shall have all powers and duties necessary to carry out the provisions of this chapter and to exercise the control of horse racing as set forth in § 59.1-364. Such powers and duties shall include but not be limited to the following:

1. The Commission is vested with jurisdiction and supervision over all horse racing licensed under the provisions of this chapter including all persons conducting, participating in, or attending any race meeting. It shall employ such persons to be present at race meetings as are necessary to ensure that they are conducted with order and the highest degree of integrity. It may eject or exclude from the enclosure or from any part thereof any person, whether or not he possesses a license or permit, whose conduct or reputation is such that his presence may, in the opinion of the Commission, reflect on the honesty and integrity of horse racing or interfere with the orderly conduct of horse racing.

2. The Commission, its representatives, and employees shall visit, investigate, and have free access to the office, track, facilities, satellite facilities or other places of business of any license or permit holder, and may compel the production of any of the books, documents, records, or memoranda of any license or permit holder for the purpose of satisfying itself that this chapter and its regulations are strictly complied with. In addition, the Commission may require any person granted a permit by the Commission and shall require any person licensed by the Commission, the recognized majority horsemen's group, and the nonprofit industry stakeholder organization recognized by the Commission under this chapter to produce an annual balance sheet and operating statement prepared by a certified public accountant approved by the Commission. The Commission may require the production of any contract to which such person is or may be a party.

3. The Commission shall promulgate regulations and conditions under which horse racing with pari-mutuel wagering shall be conducted in the Commonwealth, and all such other regulations it deems necessary and appropriate to effect the purposes of this chapter, including a requirement that licensees post, in a conspicuous place in every place where pari-mutuel wagering is conducted, a sign which bears a toll-free telephone number for "Gamblers Anonymous" or other organization which provides assistance to compulsive gamblers. Such regulations shall include provisions for affirmative action to assure participation by minority persons in contracts granted by the Commission and its licensees. Nothing in this subdivision shall be deemed to preclude private local ownership or participation in any horse racetrack. Such regulations may include penalties for violations. The regulations shall be subject to the Administrative Process Act (§ 2.2-4000 et seq.).

4. The Commission shall promulgate regulations and conditions under which simulcast horse racing shall be conducted at a licensed horse racetrack or satellite facility in the Commonwealth and all such other regulations it deems necessary and appropriate to effect the purposes of this chapter. Such regulations shall include provisions that all simulcast horse racing shall comply with the Interstate Horse Racing Act of 1978 (15 U.S.C. § 3001 et seq.) and shall require the holder of a license to schedule no more than 125 live racing days in the Commonwealth each calendar year; however, the Commission shall have the authority to alter the required number of live racing days based on what the Commission deems to be in the best interest of the Virginia horse industry. Such regulations shall authorize up to 10 satellite facilities and restrict majority ownership of satellite facilities to an entity licensed by the Commission that is a significant infrastructure limited licensee, or if by August 1, 2015, there is no such licensee or a pending application for such license, then the nonprofit industry stakeholder organization recognized by the Commission may be granted licenses to own or operate satellite facilities. If, however, after the issuance of a license to own or operate a satellite facility to such nonprofit industry stakeholder organization, the Commission grants a license to a

significant infrastructure limited licensee pursuant to § 59.1-376, then such limited licensee may own or operate the remaining available satellite facilities authorized in accordance with this subdivision. In no event shall the Commission authorize any such entities to own or operate more than a combined total of 10 satellite facilities. Nothing in this subdivision shall be deemed to preclude private local ownership or participation in any satellite facility. Except as authorized pursuant to subdivision 5, wagering on simulcast horse racing shall take place only at a licensed horse racetrack or satellite facility.

5. The Commission shall promulgate regulations and conditions regulating and controlling advance deposit account wagering. Such regulations shall include, but not be limited to, (i) standards, qualifications, and procedures for the issuance of a license to an entity for the operation of pari-mutuel wagering in the Commonwealth; except that the Commission shall not issue a license to, and shall revoke the license of, an entity that, either directly or through an entity under common control with it, withholds the sale at fair market value to a licensee of simulcast horse racing signals that such entity or an entity under common control with it sells to other racetracks, satellite facilities, or advance deposit account wagering providers located in or outside of the Commonwealth; (ii) provisions regarding access to books, records, and memoranda, and submission to investigations and audits, as authorized by subdivisions 2 and 10; and (iii) provisions regarding the collection of all revenues due to the Commonwealth from the placing of such wagers. No pari-mutuel wager may be made on or with any computer owned or leased by the Commonwealth, or any of its subdivisions, or at any public elementary or secondary school or institution of higher education. The Commission also shall ensure that, except for this method of pari-mutuel wagering, all wagering on simulcast horse racing shall take place only at a licensed horse racetrack or satellite facility.

Nothing in this subdivision shall be construed to limit the Commission's authority as set forth elsewhere in this section.

6. The Commission may issue subpoenas for the attendance of witnesses before it, administer oaths, and compel production of records or other documents and testimony of such witnesses whenever, in the judgment of the Commission, it is necessary to do so for the effectual discharge of its duties.

7. The Commission may compel any person holding a license or permit to file with the Commission such data as shall appear to the Commission to be necessary for the performance of its duties including but not limited to financial statements and information relative to stockholders and all others with any pecuniary interest in such person. It may prescribe the manner in which books and records of such persons shall be kept.

8. The Commission may enter into arrangements with any foreign or domestic government or governmental agency, for the purposes of exchanging information or performing any other act to better ensure the proper conduct of horse racing.

9. The Commission shall report annually on or before March 1 to the Governor and the General Assembly, which report shall include a financial statement of the operation of the Commission.

10. The Commission may order such audits, in addition to those required by § 59.1-394, as it deems necessary and desirable.

11. The Commission shall upon the receipt of a complaint of an alleged criminal violation of this chapter immediately report the complaint to the Attorney General of the Commonwealth and the State Police for appropriate action.

12. The Commission shall provide for the withholding of the applicable amount of state and federal income tax of persons claiming a prize or pay-off for a winning wager and shall establish the thresholds for such withholdings.

13. The Commission, its representatives and employees may, within the enclosure, stable, or other facility related to the conduct of racing, and during regular or usual business hours, subject any (i) permit holder to personal inspections, including alcohol and drug testing for illegal drugs, inspections of personal property, and inspections of other property or premises under the control of such permit holder and (ii) horse eligible to race at a race meeting licensed by the Commission to testing for substances foreign to the natural horse within the racetrack enclosure or other place where such horse is kept. Any item, document or record indicative of a violation of any provision of this chapter or Commission regulations may be seized as evidence of such violation. All permit holders consent to the searches and seizures authorized by this subdivision, including breath, blood and urine sampling for alcohol and illegal drugs, by accepting the permit issued by the Commission. The Commission may revoke or suspend the permit of any person who fails or refuses to comply with this subdivision or any rules of the Commission. Commission regulations in effect on July 1, 1998, shall continue in full force and effect until modified by the Commission in accordance with law.

14. The Commission shall require the existence of a contract between each licensee and the recognized majority horsemen's group for that licensee. Such contract shall be subject to the approval of the Commission, which shall have the power to approve or disapprove any of its items, including but not limited to the provisions regarding purses and prizes. Such contracts shall provide that on pools generated by wagering on simulcast horse racing from outside the Commonwealth, (i) for the first $75 million of the total pari-mutuel handle for each breed, the licensee shall deposit funds at the minimum rate of five percent in the horsemen's purse account, (ii) for any amount in excess of $75 million but less than $150 million of the total pari-mutuel handle for each breed, the licensee shall deposit funds at the minimum rate of six percent in the horsemen's purse account, (iii) for amounts in excess of $150 million for each breed, the licensee shall deposit funds at the minimum rate of seven percent in the horsemen's purse account. Such deposits shall be made in the horsemen's purse accounts of the breed that generated the pools and such deposits shall be made within five days from the date on which the licensee receives wagers. In the absence of the required contract between the licensee and the recognized majority horsemen's group, the Commission may permit wagering to proceed on simulcast horse racing from outside of the Commonwealth, provided that the licensee deposits into the State Racing Operations Fund created pursuant to § 59.1-370.1 an amount equal to the minimum percentage of the total pari-mutuel handles as required in clauses (i), (ii), and (iii) or such lesser amount as the Commission may approve. The deposits shall be made within five days from the date on which the licensee receives wagers. Once a contract between the licensee and the recognized majority horsemen's group is executed and approved by the Commission, the Commission shall transfer these funds to the licensee and the horsemen's purse accounts.

15. Notwithstanding the provisions of § 59.1-391, the Commission may grant provisional limited licenses or provisional unlimited licenses to own or operate racetracks or satellite facilities to an applicant prior to the applicant securing the approval through the local referendum required by § 59.1-391. The provisional licenses issued by the Commission shall only become effective upon the approval of the racetrack or satellite wagering facilities in a referendum conducted pursuant to § 59.1-391 in the jurisdiction in which the racetrack or satellite wagering facility is to be located.

16. The Commission or its representatives shall participate in the Problem Gambling Treatment and Support Advisory Committee established pursuant to § 37.2-304 by the Department of Behavioral Health and Developmental

Services to enable collaboration among prevention and treatment providers and operators of legal gaming in the Commonwealth on efforts to reduce the negative effects of problem gambling.

History.
1988, c. 855; 1990, c. 271; 1991, c. 591; 1992, c. 820; 1993, c. 430; 1998, cc. 619, 845; 2000, cc. 99, 1031; 2003, c. 682; 2004, c. 774; 2005, cc. 633, 700; 2007, c. 757; 2009, c. 142; 2011, c. 732; 2015, cc. 731, 751; 2023, cc. 588, 589.

The 2023 amendments.
The 2023 amendment by cc. 588 and 589 are i.e. identical, and added subdivision 16.

§ 59.1-369. (Effective July 1, 2024) Powers and duties of the Commission.

The Commission shall have all powers and duties necessary to carry out the provisions of this chapter and to exercise the control of horse racing as set forth in § 59.1-364. Such powers and duties shall include but not be limited to the following:

1. The Commission is vested with jurisdiction and supervision over all horse racing licensed under the provisions of this chapter including all persons conducting, participating in, or attending any race meeting. It shall employ such persons to be present at race meetings as are necessary to ensure that they are conducted with order and the highest degree of integrity. It may eject or exclude from the enclosure or from any part thereof any person, whether or not he possesses a license or permit, whose conduct or reputation is such that his presence may, in the opinion of the Commission, reflect on the honesty and integrity of horse racing or interfere with the orderly conduct of horse racing.

2. The Commission, its representatives, and employees shall visit, investigate, and have free access to the office, track, facilities, satellite facilities or other places of business of any license or permit holder, and may compel the production of any of the books, documents, records, or memoranda of any license or permit holder for the purpose of satisfying itself that this chapter and its regulations are strictly complied with. In addition, the Commission may require any person granted a permit by the Commission and shall require any person licensed by the Commission, the recognized majority horsemen's group, and the nonprofit industry stakeholder organization recognized by the Commission under this chapter to produce an annual balance sheet and operating statement prepared by a certified public accountant approved by the Commission. The Commission may require the production of any contract to which such person is or may be a party.

3. The Commission shall promulgate regulations and conditions under which horse racing with pari-mutuel wagering shall be conducted in the Commonwealth, and all such other regulations it deems necessary and appropriate to effect the purposes of this chapter, including a requirement that licensees post, in a conspicuous place in every place where pari-mutuel wagering is conducted, a sign which bears a toll-free telephone number for "Gamblers Anonymous" or other organization which provides assistance to compulsive gamblers. Such regulations shall include provisions for affirmative action to assure participation by minority persons in contracts granted by the Commission and its licensees. Nothing in this subdivision shall be deemed to preclude private local ownership or participation in any horse racetrack. Such regulations may include penalties for violations. The regulations shall be subject to the Administrative Process Act (§ 2.2-4000 et seq.).

4. The Commission shall promulgate regulations and conditions under which simulcast horse racing shall be conducted at a licensed horse racetrack or satellite facility in the Commonwealth and all such other regulations it

deems necessary and appropriate to effect the purposes of this chapter. Such regulations shall include provisions that all simulcast horse racing shall comply with the Interstate Horse Racing Act of 1978 (15 U.S.C. § 3001 et seq.) and shall require the holder of a license to schedule no more than 125 live racing days in the Commonwealth each calendar year; however, the Commission shall have the authority to alter the required number of live racing days in the event of force majeure. Such regulations shall authorize up to 10 satellite facilities and restrict majority ownership of satellite facilities to an entity licensed by the Commission that is a significant infrastructure limited licensee, or if by August 1, 2015, there is no such licensee or a pending application for such license, then the nonprofit industry stakeholder organization recognized by the Commission may be granted licenses to own or operate satellite facilities. If, however, after the issuance of a license to own or operate a satellite facility to such nonprofit industry stakeholder organization, the Commission grants a license to a significant infrastructure limited licensee pursuant to § 59.1-376, then such limited licensee may own or operate the remaining available satellite facilities authorized in accordance with this subdivision. In no event shall the Commission authorize any such entities to own or operate more than a combined total of 10 satellite facilities. Nothing in this subdivision shall be deemed to preclude private local ownership or participation in any satellite facility. Except as authorized pursuant to subdivision 5, wagering on simulcast horse racing shall take place only at a licensed horse racetrack or satellite facility. For purposes of this subdivision, "force majeure" means an event or events reasonably beyond the ability of the Commission to anticipate and control. "Force majeure" includes acts of God, incidences of terrorism, war or riots, labor strikes or civil disturbances, floods, earthquakes, fire, explosions, epidemics, hurricanes, tornadoes, and governmental actions and restrictions.

5. The Commission shall promulgate regulations and conditions regulating and controlling advance deposit account wagering. Such regulations shall include, but not be limited to, (i) standards, qualifications, and procedures for the issuance of a license to an entity for the operation of pari-mutuel wagering in the Commonwealth; except that the Commission shall not issue a license to, and shall revoke the license of, an entity that, either directly or through an entity under common control with it, withholds the sale at fair market value to a licensee of simulcast horse racing signals that such entity or an entity under common control with it sells to other racetracks, satellite facilities, or advance deposit account wagering providers located in or outside of the Commonwealth; (ii) provisions regarding access to books, records, and memoranda, and submission to investigations and audits, as authorized by subdivisions 2 and 10; and (iii) provisions regarding the collection of all revenues due to the Commonwealth from the placing of such wagers. No pari-mutuel wager may be made on or with any computer owned or leased by the Commonwealth, or any of its subdivisions, or at any public elementary or secondary school or institution of higher education. The Commission also shall ensure that, except for this method of pari-mutuel wagering, all wagering on simulcast horse racing shall take place only at a licensed horse racetrack or satellite facility.

Nothing in this subdivision shall be construed to limit the Commission's authority as set forth elsewhere in this section.

6. The Commission may issue subpoenas for the attendance of witnesses before it, administer oaths, and compel production of records or other documents and testimony of such witnesses whenever, in the judgment of the Commission, it is necessary to do so for the effectual discharge of its duties.

7. The Commission may compel any person holding a license or permit to file with the Commission such data as shall appear to the Commission to be

necessary for the performance of its duties including but not limited to financial statements and information relative to stockholders and all others with any pecuniary interest in such person. It may prescribe the manner in which books and records of such persons shall be kept.

8. The Commission may enter into arrangements with any foreign or domestic government or governmental agency, for the purposes of exchanging information or performing any other act to better ensure the proper conduct of horse racing.

9. The Commission shall report annually on or before March 1 to the Governor and the General Assembly, which report shall include a financial statement of the operation of the Commission.

10. The Commission may order such audits, in addition to those required by § 59.1-394, as it deems necessary and desirable.

11. The Commission shall upon the receipt of a complaint of an alleged criminal violation of this chapter immediately report the complaint to the Attorney General of the Commonwealth and the State Police for appropriate action.

12. The Commission shall provide for the withholding of the applicable amount of state and federal income tax of persons claiming a prize or pay-off for a winning wager and shall establish the thresholds for such withholdings.

13. The Commission, its representatives and employees may, within the enclosure, stable, or other facility related to the conduct of racing, and during regular or usual business hours, subject any (i) permit holder to personal inspections, including alcohol and drug testing for illegal drugs, inspections of personal property, and inspections of other property or premises under the control of such permit holder and (ii) horse eligible to race at a race meeting licensed by the Commission to testing for substances foreign to the natural horse within the racetrack enclosure or other place where such horse is kept. Any item, document or record indicative of a violation of any provision of this chapter or Commission regulations may be seized as evidence of such violation. All permit holders consent to the searches and seizures authorized by this subdivision, including breath, blood and urine sampling for alcohol and illegal drugs, by accepting the permit issued by the Commission. The Commission may revoke or suspend the permit of any person who fails or refuses to comply with this subdivision or any rules of the Commission. Commission regulations in effect on July 1, 1998, shall continue in full force and effect until modified by the Commission in accordance with law.

14. The Commission shall require the existence of a contract between each licensee and the recognized majority horsemen's group for that licensee. Such contract shall be subject to the approval of the Commission, which shall have the power to approve or disapprove any of its items, including but not limited to the provisions regarding purses and prizes. Such contracts shall provide that on pools generated by wagering on simulcast horse racing from outside the Commonwealth, (i) for the first $75 million of the total pari-mutuel handle for each breed, the licensee shall deposit funds at the minimum rate of five percent in the horsemen's purse account, (ii) for any amount in excess of $75 million but less than $150 million of the total pari-mutuel handle for each breed, the licensee shall deposit funds at the minimum rate of six percent in the horsemen's purse account, (iii) for amounts in excess of $150 million for each breed, the licensee shall deposit funds at the minimum rate of seven percent in the horsemen's purse account. Such deposits shall be made in the horsemen's purse accounts of the breed that generated the pools and such deposits shall be made within five days from the date on which the licensee receives wagers. In the absence of the required contract between the licensee and the recognized majority horsemen's group, the Commission may permit

wagering to proceed on simulcast horse racing from outside of the Commonwealth, provided that the licensee deposits into the State Racing Operations
Fund created pursuant to § 59.1-370.1 an amount equal to the minimum
percentage of the total pari-mutuel handles as required in clauses (i), (ii), and
(iii) or such lesser amount as the Commission may approve. The deposits shall
be made within five days from the date on which the licensee receives wagers.
Once a contract between the licensee and the recognized majority horsemen's
group is executed and approved by the Commission, the Commission shall
transfer these funds to the licensee and the horsemen's purse accounts.

15. Notwithstanding the provisions of § 59.1-391, the Commission may
grant provisional limited licenses or provisional unlimited licenses to own or
operate racetracks or satellite facilities to an applicant prior to the applicant
securing the approval through the local referendum required by § 59.1-391.
The provisional licenses issued by the Commission shall only become effective
upon the approval of the racetrack or satellite wagering facilities in a
referendum conducted pursuant to § 59.1-391 in the jurisdiction in which the
racetrack or satellite wagering facility is to be located.

16. The Commission or its representatives shall participate in the Problem
Gambling Treatment and Support Advisory Committee established pursuant
to § 37.2-304 by the Department of Behavioral Health and Developmental
Services to enable collaboration among prevention and treatment providers
and operators of legal gaming in the Commonwealth on efforts to reduce the
negative effects of problem gambling.

17. The Commission shall promulgate regulations requiring, for each calendar year, any significant infrastructure limited licensee that offers pari-
mutuel wagering on historical horse racing to hold at least one live Thoroughbred horse racing day, consisting of not less than eight races per day, for every
100 historical horse racing terminals installed at its significant infrastructure
facility together with any satellite facility owned, operated, controlled, managed, or otherwise directly or indirectly affiliated with such licensee. The
regulations shall require any such significant infrastructure limited licensee
that holds more than one live Thoroughbred horse racing day in accordance
with the provisions of this subdivision to hold at least one of those racing days
on a weekend. The number of historical horse racing terminals installed at a
significant infrastructure facility shall be calculated as of December 31 of the
calendar year in question; however, only historical horse racing terminals that
are fully operational shall be included in such calculation.

History.
  1988, c. 855; 1990, c. 271; 1991, c. 591; 1992,
c. 820; 1993, c. 430; 1998, cc. 619, 845; 2000, cc.
99, 1031; 2003, c. 682; 2004, c. 774; 2005, cc.
633, 700; 2007, c. 757; 2009, c. 142; 2011, c. 732;
2015, cc. 731, 751; 2023, cc. 588, 589, 590, 591.

Editor's note.
  Acts 2023, cc. 590 and 591, cl. 2 provides:
"That the provisions of this act shall become
effective on July 1, 2024."

The 2023 amendments.
  The 2023 amendment by cc. 590 and 591 are
identical, and in subdivision 4, substituted "in
the event of force majeure" for "based on what
the Commission deems to be in the best interest
of the Virginia horse industry" in the second
sentence, and added the last two sentences; and
added subdivision 16. Redesignated as subdivision 17 at the direction of the Virginia Code
Commission.

§ 59.1-372. Virginia Breeders Fund.

There is hereby created within the State Treasury the Virginia Breeders
Fund, which Fund, together with the interest thereon, shall be administered in
whole or in part by the Commission or by an entity designated by the
Commission. The cost of administering and promoting the Fund shall be

deducted from the Fund, and the balance shall be disbursed by the Commission or designated entity to the breeders of Virginia-bred horses that finish first, second, or third in races at race meetings designated by the Commission, to the owners of Virginia sires of Virginia-bred horses that finish first, second, or third in races at race meetings designated by the Commission, to the owners of Virginia-bred horses that win or earn purse money in nonrestricted races at racetracks in Virginia licensed by the Commission, to the owners of Virginia-bred horses that win races at race meetings designated by the Commission and for purses for races restricted to Virginia-bred or Virginia-sired horses or both at race meetings designated by the Commission. To assist it in establishing this awards and incentive program to foster the industry of breeding race-horses in Virginia, the Commission shall appoint an advisory committee composed of two members from each of the registered breed associations representing each breed of horse participating in the Fund program, one member representing the owners and operators of racetracks and one member representing all of the meets sanctioned by the National Steeplechase Association.

History.
1988, c. 855; 1993, c. 146; 1997, c. 798; 2002, c. 852; 2023, c. 356.

The 2023 amendments.
The 2023 amendment by c. 356, substituted

"finish first, second, or third in" for "win" twice in the second sentence.

ARTICLE 4.
LOCAL REFERENDUM.

§ 59.1-391. Local referendum required.

Editor's note.
Acts 2020, cc. 1197 and 1248, cl. 7 provide: "That the Virginia Racing Commission (the Commission) shall authorize an additional 600 historical racing terminals each time a local referendum required by § 58.1-4123 of the Code of Virginia, as created by this act, is approved, provided that the total number of additional machines authorized in this enactment shall not exceed 2,000 statewide. The tax rate for any machine added pursuant to this enactment clause shall be 20 percent as calculated and distributed pursuant to the method used to calculate and distribute such rate in effect for machines in existence as of January 1, 2020. For every 100 additional machines authorized pursuant to this enactment clause, the total number of live horse racing days shall be increased by one day. Excluding machines installed as of March 1, 2020, each location operating historical racing terminals shall be prohibited from having more than forty percent of its terminals manufactured by any single manufacturer. The increase in historical racing terminals shall not apply with respect to any city where a significant infrastructure limited licensee, as defined in § 59.1-365 of the Code of Virginia, or the affiliate of such licensee is awarded a casino operator's license pursuant to this act. Notwithstanding the provisions of 11VAC10-47-180 and subject to the local referendum requirements of § 59.1-391 of the Code of Virginia, for the machines specifically authorized in this enactment, the Commission shall authorize up to 1,650 machines in a satellite facility in a metropolitan area with a population in excess of 2.5 million located in a jurisdiction that has passed a referendum pursuant to the requirements of § 59.1-391 of the Code of Virginia prior to January 1, 2020, and 500 machines in a metropolitan area with a population in excess of 300,000, provided that no additional machines authorized in this enactment shall be located within 35 miles of an eligible host city as described in § 58.1-4107 of the Code of Virginia, as created by this act. No satellite facility shall be authorized in any locality that is included in the Regional Improvement Commission established in the fifth enactment of this act. Population determinations pursuant to this enactment shall be based on the 2018 population estimates from the Weldon Cooper Center for Public Service of the University of Virginia. Except as provided

herein, the Commission shall not be authorized to promulgate regulations to allow or grant a license to authorize historical horse racing terminals in excess of those permitted by the emergency regulations that became effective on October 5, 2018."

Acts 2020, c. 1289, as amended by Acts 2021, Sp. Sess. I, c. 552, Item 110 F 5, effective for the biennium ending June 30, 2022, provides: "For any local referendum passed pursuant to § 59.1-391 after July 1, 2020, the Virginia Racing Commission shall not authorize any additional satellite facilities as defined in § 59.1-365 of the Code of Virginia, or additional simulcast wagering terminals pursuant to 11 VAC 10-47-180, during a period of two years after the effective date of this act."

ARTICLE 5.

TAXATION AND AUDIT.

§ 59.1-392. Percentage retained; tax.

A. Any person holding an operator's license to operate a horse racetrack or satellite facility in the Commonwealth pursuant to this chapter shall be authorized to conduct pari-mutuel wagering on horse racing subject to the provisions of this chapter and the conditions and regulations of the Commission.

B. On pari-mutuel pools generated by wagering at the racetrack on live horse racing conducted within the Commonwealth, involving win, place and show wagering, the licensee shall retain a percentage amount approved by the Commission as jointly requested by a recognized majority horsemen's group and a licensee and the legitimate breakage, out of which shall be paid one and one-quarter percent to be distributed as follows: one percent to the Commonwealth as a license tax and one-quarter percent to the locality in which the racetrack is located. The remainder of the retainage shall be paid as provided in subsection D, provided, however, that if the percentage amount approved by the Commission is other than 18 percent, the amounts provided in subdivisions D 1, 2 and 3 shall be adjusted by the proportion that the approved percentage amount bears to 18 percent.

C. On pari-mutuel pools generated by wagering at each Virginia satellite facility on live horse racing conducted within the Commonwealth, involving win, place and show wagering, the licensee shall retain a percentage amount approved by the Commission as jointly requested by a recognized majority horsemen's group and a licensee and the legitimate breakage, out of which shall be paid one and one-quarter percent to be distributed as follows: three-quarters percent to the Commonwealth as a license tax, one-quarter percent to the locality in which the satellite facility is located, and one-quarter percent to the locality in which the racetrack is located. The remainder of the retainage shall be paid as provided in subsection D; provided, however, that if the percentage amount approved by the Commission is other than 18 percent, the amounts provided in subdivisions D 1, 2 and 3 shall be adjusted by the proportion that the approved percentage amount bears to 18 percent.

D. On pari-mutuel pools generated by wagering at the racetrack and each Virginia satellite facility on live horse racing conducted within the Commonwealth, involving win, place and show wagering, the licensee shall retain a percentage amount approved by the Commission as jointly requested by a recognized majority horsemen's group and a licensee and the legitimate breakage, out of which shall be paid:

1. Eight percent as purses or prizes to the participants in such race meeting;

2. Seven and one-half percent, and all of the breakage and the proceeds of pari-mutuel tickets unredeemed 180 days from the date on which the race was conducted, to the operator;

3. One percent to the Virginia Breeders Fund;

4. Fifteen one-hundredths percent to the Virginia-Maryland Regional College of Veterinary Medicine;

5. Five one-hundredths percent to the Virginia Horse Center Foundation;

6. Five one-hundredths percent to the Virginia Horse Industry Board; and

7. The remainder of the retainage shall be paid as appropriate under subsection B or C.

E. On pari-mutuel pools generated by wagering at the racetrack on live horse racing conducted within the Commonwealth involving wagering other than win, place and show wagering, the licensee shall retain a percentage amount approved by the Commission as jointly requested by a recognized majority horsemen's group and a licensee and the legitimate breakage, out of which shall be paid two and three-quarters percent to be distributed as follows: two and one-quarter percent to the Commonwealth as a license tax, and one-half percent to the locality in which the racetrack is located. The remainder of the retainage shall be paid as provided in subsection G; provided, however, that if the percentage amount approved by the Commission is other than 22 percent, the amounts provided in subdivisions G 1, 2 and 3 shall be adjusted by the proportion that the approved percentage amount bears to 22 percent.

F. On pari-mutuel pools generated by wagering at each Virginia satellite facility on live horse racing conducted within the Commonwealth involving wagering other than win, place and show wagering, the licensee shall retain a percentage amount approved by the Commission as jointly requested by a recognized majority horsemen's group and a licensee and the legitimate breakage, out of which shall be paid two and three-quarters percent to be distributed as follows: one and three-quarters percent to the Commonwealth as a license tax, one-half percent to the locality in which the satellite facility is located, and one-half percent to the locality in which the racetrack is located. The remainder of the retainage shall be paid as provided in subsection G; provided, however, that if the percentage amount approved by the Commission is other than 22 percent, the amounts provided in subdivisions G 1, 2 and 3 shall be adjusted by the proportion that the approved percentage amount bears to 22 percent.

G. On pari-mutuel pools generated by wagering at the racetrack and each Virginia satellite facility on live horse racing conducted within the Commonwealth involving wagering other than win, place and show wagering, the licensee shall retain a percentage amount approved by the Commission as jointly requested by a recognized majority horsemen's group and a licensee and the legitimate breakage, out of which shall be paid:

1. Nine percent as purses or prizes to the participants in such race meeting;

2. Nine percent, and the proceeds of the pari-mutuel tickets unredeemed 180 days from the date on which the race was conducted, to the operator;

3. One percent to the Virginia Breeders Fund;

4. Fifteen one-hundredths percent to the Virginia-Maryland Regional College of Veterinary Medicine;

5. Five one-hundredths percent to the Virginia Horse Center Foundation;

6. Five one-hundredths percent to the Virginia Horse Industry Board; and

7. The remainder of the retainage shall be paid as appropriate under subsection E or F.

H. On pari-mutuel wagering generated by simulcast horse racing transmitted from jurisdictions outside the Commonwealth, the licensee may, with the approval of the Commission, commingle pools with the racetrack where the transmission emanates or establish separate pools for wagering within the Commonwealth. All simulcast horse racing in this subsection must comply with the Interstate Horse Racing Act of 1978 (15 U.S.C. § 3001 et seq.).

I. On pari-mutuel pools generated by wagering at the racetrack on simulcast horse racing transmitted from jurisdictions outside the Commonwealth, involving win, place and show wagering, the licensee shall retain one and one-quarter percent of such pool to be distributed as follows: three-quarters percent to the Commonwealth as a license tax, and one-half percent to the Virginia locality in which the racetrack is located.

J. On pari-mutuel pools generated by wagering at each Virginia satellite facility on simulcast horse racing transmitted from jurisdictions outside the Commonwealth, involving win, place and show wagering, the licensee shall retain one and one-quarter percent of such pool to be distributed as follows: three-quarters percent to the Commonwealth as a license tax, one-quarter percent to the locality in which the satellite facility is located, and one-quarter percent to the Virginia locality in which the racetrack is located.

K. On pari-mutuel pools generated by wagering at the racetrack and each Virginia satellite facility on simulcast horse racing transmitted from jurisdictions outside the Commonwealth, involving win, place and show wagering, the licensee shall retain one and thirty one-hundredths percent of such pool to be distributed as follows:

1. One percent of the pool to the Virginia Breeders Fund;

2. Fifteen one-hundredths percent to the Virginia-Maryland Regional College of Veterinary Medicine;

3. Five one-hundredths percent to the Virginia Horse Center Foundation;

4. Five one-hundredths percent to the Virginia Horse Industry Board; and

5. Five one-hundredths percent to the Virginia Thoroughbred Association for the promotion of breeding in the Commonwealth.

L. On pari-mutuel pools generated by wagering at the racetrack on simulcast horse racing transmitted from jurisdictions outside the Commonwealth, involving wagering other than win, place and show wagering, the licensee shall retain two and three-quarters percent of such pool to be distributed as follows: one and three-quarters percent to the Commonwealth as a license tax, and one percent to the Virginia locality in which the racetrack is located.

M. On pari-mutuel pools generated by wagering at each Virginia satellite facility on simulcast horse racing transmitted from jurisdictions outside the Commonwealth, involving wagering other than win, place and show wagering, the licensee shall retain two and three-quarters percent of such pool to be distributed as follows: one and three-quarters percent to the Commonwealth as a license tax, one-half percent to the locality in which the satellite facility is located, and one-half percent to the Virginia locality in which the racetrack is located.

N. On pari-mutuel pools generated by wagering at the racetrack and each Virginia satellite facility on simulcast horse racing transmitted from jurisdictions outside the Commonwealth, involving wagering other than win, place and show wagering, the licensee shall retain one and thirty one-hundredths percent of such pool to be distributed as follows:

1. One percent of the pool to the Virginia Breeders Fund;

2. Fifteen one-hundredths percent to the Virginia-Maryland Regional College of Veterinary Medicine;

3. Five one-hundredths percent to the Virginia Horse Center Foundation;

4. Five one-hundredths percent to the Virginia Horse Industry Board; and

5. Five one-hundredths percent to the Virginia Thoroughbred Association for the promotion of breeding in the Commonwealth.

O. Moneys payable to the Commonwealth shall be deposited in the general fund. Gross receipts for license tax purposes under Chapter 37 (§ 58.1-3700 et seq.) of Title 58.1 shall not include pari-mutuel wagering pools and license taxes authorized by this section.

P. All payments by the licensee to the Commonwealth or any locality shall be made within five days from the date on which such wagers are received by the licensee. All payments by the licensee to the Virginia Breeders Fund shall be made to the Commission within five days from the date on which such wagers are received by the licensee. All payments by the licensee to the Virginia-Maryland Regional College of Veterinary Medicine, the Virginia Horse Center Foundation, the Virginia Horse Industry Board, and the Virginia Thoroughbred Association shall be made by the first day of each quarter of the calendar year. All payments made under this section shall be used in support of the policy of the Commonwealth to sustain and promote the growth of a native industry.

Q. If a satellite facility is located in more than one locality, any amount a licensee is required to pay under this section to the locality in which the satellite facility is located shall be prorated in equal shares among those localities.

R. Any contractual agreement between a licensee and other entities concerning the distribution of the remaining portion of the retainage under subsections I through N and subsections U and V shall be subject to the approval of the Commission.

S. The recognized majority horsemen's group racing at a licensed race meeting may, subject to the approval of the Commission, withdraw for administrative costs associated with serving the interests of the horsemen an amount not to exceed two percent of the amount in the horsemen's account.

T. The legitimate breakage from each pari-mutuel pool for live, historical, and simulcast horse racing shall be distributed as follows:

1. Seventy percent to be retained by the licensee to be used for capital improvements that are subject to approval of the Commission; and

2. Thirty percent to be deposited in the Racing Benevolence Fund, administered jointly by the licensee and the recognized majority horsemen's group racing at a licensed race meeting, to be disbursed with the approval of the Commission for gambling addiction and substance abuse counseling, recreational, educational or other related programs.

U. On pari-mutuel pools generated by wagering on historical horse racing on the first 3,000 terminals authorized, the licensee shall retain 1.25 percent of such pool to be distributed as follows:

1. Seventy-four hundredths percent to the Commonwealth as a license tax and 0.01 percent to the Problem Gambling Treatment and Support Fund established pursuant to § 37.2-314.2; and

2. a. If generated at a racetrack, 0.5 percent to the locality in which the racetrack is located; or

b. If generated at a satellite facility, 0.25 percent to the locality in which the satellite facility is located and 0.25 percent to the Virginia locality in which the racetrack is located.

V. On pari-mutuel pools generated by wagering on historical racing on the 2,000 terminals authorized by the seventh enactment of Chapters 1197 and 1248 of the Acts of Assembly of 2020, the licensee shall retain 1.6 percent of such pool to be distributed as follows:

1. Ninety-five hundredths percent to the Commonwealth as a license tax and 0.01 percent to the Problem Gambling Treatment and Support Fund established pursuant to § 37.2-314.2; and

2. a. If generated at a racetrack, 0.64 percent to the locality in which the racetrack is located; or

b. If generated at a satellite facility, 0.32 percent to the locality in which the satellite facility is located and 0.32 percent to the Virginia locality in which the racetrack is located.

History.

1988, c. 855; 1991, c. 591; 1992, c. 820; 1995, c. 217; 1998, cc. 608, 619; 2000, c. 1031; 2007, c. 61; 2011, c. 732; 2015, cc. 731, 751; 2018, c. 811; 2022, c. 511.

Editor's note.

Acts 2020, c. 1289, as amended by Acts 2021, Sp. Sess. I, c. 552, Item 110 B, effective for the biennium ending June 30, 2022 and 2022, Sp. Sess. I, c. 2, Item 111 B, effective for the biennium ending June 30, 2023, provides: "Notwithstanding the provisions of § 59.1-392, Code of Virginia, up to $255,000 the first year and $255,000 the second year shall be transferred to Virginia Polytechnic Institute and State University to support the Virginia-Maryland Regional College of Veterinary Medicine."

The 2022 amendments.

The 2022 amendment by c. 511, substituted "subsections U and V" for "subsection U" in subsection R; in subsection U, inserted "on the first 3,000 terminals authorized" and substituted "retain 1.25 percent" for "retain one and one-quarter percent"; rewrote subdivision U 1, which read: "Three-quarters percent to the Commonwealth as a license tax; and"; substituted "0.5 percent" for "one-half percent" in subdivision U 2 a; substituted "0.25 percent" for "one-quarter percent" twice in subdivision U 2 b; and added subsection V.

ARTICLE 6.
CRIMINAL PENALTIES.

§ 59.1-403. Prohibition on persons under 21 years of age; penalty.

No person shall wager on or conduct any wagering on the outcome of a horse race pursuant to the provisions of this chapter unless such person is 18 years of age or older. No person shall accept any wager from a minor. No person shall be admitted into a satellite facility if such person is under 18 years of age unless accompanied by one of his parents or his legal guardian. No person under 21 years of age shall use any electronic gaming terminal or other electronic device in a satellite facility to wager on or conduct any wagering on historical horse racing. Violation of this section shall be a Class 1 misdemeanor.

History.

1988, c. 855; 1996, cc. 915, 1025; 2022, cc. 502, 503.

The 2022 amendments.

The 2022 amendments by cc. 502 and 503 are identical, and substituted "18 years" for "eighteen years" twice; and added the fourth sentence.

CHAPTER 34.1.
LEGAL SERVICES CONTRACTS.

Section
59.1-441.2. Registration; fees.

§ 59.1-441.2. Registration; fees.

A. It is unlawful for any legal services plan seller to offer, advertise, or execute, or cause to be executed by the subscriber, any subscription contract in the Commonwealth unless the legal services plan seller at the time of the offer, advertisement, sale, or execution of a subscription contract has been properly registered with the Commissioner or the legal services plan seller has submitted the registration information and fee required by this section to the legal services organization for which the seller will offer subscription contracts. The registration shall (i) disclose the address, ownership, and affiliation with the legal services organization and such other information as the Commissioner may require consistent with the purposes of this chapter, (ii) be renewed annually on July 1, and (iii) be accompanied by the appropriate registration fee of $50 per each annual registration. Further, the registration shall be accompanied by a late fee of $25 if the registration renewal is neither postmarked nor received on or before July 1. A legal services plan seller's initial or renewal registration may be accomplished either by the legal services plan seller or on behalf of such seller by the legal services organization for which the seller offers subscription contracts, and the Commissioner shall accept any registration information or fee required to be submitted pursuant to this chapter that is submitted to the Commissioner. A legal services organization shall submit the registration information and fees received pursuant to this section to the Commissioner, in a form and manner prescribed by the Commissioner, no later than 30 days after the information and fees are received by the organization.

B. Any legal services plan seller or legal services organization that violates the provisions of subsection A shall pay a late filing fee of $100 for each 30-day period the registration is late. This fee shall be in addition to all other penalties allowed by law.

C. A registration shall be amended within 21 days if there is a change in the information included in the registration. If the legal services plan seller has submitted such changes to the legal services organization for which the seller will offer subscription contracts, the legal services organization shall submit the amended registration, in the form and manner prescribed by the Commissioner, no later than 30 days after such information is received by the organization.

D. Any matter subject to the insurance regulatory authority of the State Corporation Commission pursuant to Title 38.2 shall not be subject to the provisions of this chapter.

E. All fees shall be remitted to the State Treasurer and shall be placed to the credit and special fund of the Virginia Department of Agriculture and Consumer Services to be used in the administration of this chapter.

F. All insurance agent licenses issued by the State Corporation Commission including authority to sell legal services plan subscription contracts shall continue in effect for a period of 90 days following the effective date of this chapter, during which time those holding such authority from the State Corporation Commission shall apply for registration with the Department. At the end of the 90-day period, no insurance agent license shall include the authority to sell legal services plan subscription contracts.

History.
2004, c. 784; 2020, c. 408; 2021, Sp. Sess. I, c. 180.

The 2020 amendments.
The 2020 amendment by c. 408 added the last sentence to subsection A.

The 2021 Sp. Sess. I amendments.
The 2021 amendment by Sp. Sess. I, c. 180, effective July 1, 2021, in subsection A, substituted "It is unlawful" for "It shall be unlawful" and inserted "or the legal services plan seller has submitted the registration information and fee required by this section to the legal services organization for which the seller will offer subscription contracts" in the first sentence, deleted "on a monthly basis by the organization on behalf of such a legal services plan seller" from the end of the fourth sentence, and added the last sentence; in subsection B, substituted "or legal services organization that violates the provisions of subsection A" for "that sells a subscription contract prior to registering pursuant to this section"; and added the second sentence in subsection C.

CHAPTER 35.

PERSONAL INFORMATION PRIVACY ACT.

§ 59.1-442. Sale of purchaser information; notice required.

A. No merchant, without giving notice to the purchaser, shall sell to any third person information that concerns the purchaser and that is gathered in connection with the sale, rental, or exchange of tangible personal property to the purchaser at the merchant's place of business. Notice required by this section may be by the posting of a sign or any other reasonable method. If requested by a purchaser not to sell such information, the merchant shall not do so. No merchant shall sell any information gathered solely as the result of any customer payment by personal check, credit card, or where the merchant records the number of the customer's driver's license or other document issued under Chapter 3 (§ 46.2-300 et seq.) of Title 46.2 or the comparable law of another jurisdiction. This subsection shall not be construed as authorizing a merchant to sell to a third person any information concerning a purchaser if the sale or dissemination of the information is prohibited pursuant to § 59.1-443.3.

B. For the purposes of this section and § 59.1-443.3, "merchant" means any person or entity engaged in the sale of goods from a fixed retail location in Virginia.

History.
1992, c. 807; 2014, cc. 789, 795; 2020, cc. 1227, 1246.

Editor's note.
Acts 2020, cc. 1227 and 1246, cl. 2 provides: "That the provisions of this act shall become effective on January 1, 2021."

Acts 2020, cc. 1227 and 1246, cl. 4 provides: "That the provisions of this act may result in a net increase in periods of imprisonment or commitment. Pursuant to § 30-19.1:4 of the Code of Virginia, the estimated amount of the necessary appropriation cannot be determined for periods of imprisonment in state adult correctional facilities; therefore, Chapter 854 of the Acts of Assembly of 2019 requires the Virginia Criminal Sentencing Commission to assign a minimum fiscal impact of $50,000. Pursuant to § 30-19.1:4 of the Code of Virginia, the estimated amount of the necessary appropriation cannot be determined for periods of commitment to the custody of the Department of Juvenile Justice."

The 2020 amendments.
The 2020 amendments by cc. 1227 and 1246, effective January 1, 2021, are identical and substituted "records the number of the customer's driver's license or other document issued under Chapter 3 (§ 46.2-300 et seq.) of Title 46.2 or the comparable law of another jurisdiction" for "records the customer's driver's license number" in the next-to-last sentence of subsection A; and made stylistic changes.

§ 59.1-443.3. Scanning information from driver's license or other document; retention, sale, or dissemination of information.

A. No merchant may scan the machine-readable zone of a driver's license or other document issued by the Department of Motor Vehicles under Chapter 3 (§ 46.2-300 et seq.) of Title 46.2 or the comparable law of another jurisdiction, except for the following purposes:

1. To verify authenticity of the driver's license or other document or to verify the identity of the individual if the individual requests a service pursuant to a

membership or a service agreement, pays for goods or services with a method other than cash, returns an item, or requests a refund or an exchange;

2. To verify the individual's age when providing age-restricted goods or services to the individual if there is a reasonable doubt of the individual having reached 18 years of age or older;

3. To prevent fraud or other criminal activity if the individual returns an item or requests a refund or an exchange and the merchant uses a fraud prevention service company or system. Information collected by scanning an individual's driver's license or other document pursuant to this subdivision shall be limited to the individual's name, address, and date of birth and the number of the driver's license or other document;

4. To comply with a requirement imposed on the merchant by the laws of the Commonwealth or federal law;

5. To provide to a check services company regulated by the federal Fair Credit Reporting Act, (15 U.S.C. § 1681 et seq.), that receives information obtained from an individual's driver's license or other document to administer or enforce a transaction or to prevent fraud or other criminal activity; or

6. To complete a transaction permitted under the federal Gramm-Leach-Bliley Act, (15 U.S.C. § 6801 et seq.), or the federal Fair Credit Reporting Act, (15 U.S.C. § 1681 et seq.).

B. No merchant shall retain any information obtained from a scan of the machine-readable zone of an individual's driver's license or other document except as permitted in subdivision A 1, 3, 4, 5, or 6. The merchant shall destroy the retained information when the purpose for which it was provided and retained under this section has been satisfied.

C. No merchant shall sell or disseminate to a third party any information obtained from a scan of the machine-readable zone of an individual's driver's license or other document for any marketing, advertising, or promotional purpose. This subsection shall not prohibit a merchant from disseminating to a third party any such information for a purpose described in subdivision A 3, 4, 5, or 6.

D. Any waiver of a provision of this section is contrary to public policy and is void and unenforceable.

History.

2014, cc. 789, 795; 2020, cc. 542, 1227, 1246.

Editor's note.

Acts 2020, cc. 1227 and 1246, cl. 2 provides: "That the provisions of this act shall become effective on January 1, 2021."

Acts 2020, cc. 1227 and 1246, cl. 4 provides: "That the provisions of this act may result in a net increase in periods of imprisonment or commitment. Pursuant to § 30-19.1:4 of the Code of Virginia, the estimated amount of the necessary appropriation cannot be determined for periods of imprisonment in state adult correctional facilities; therefore, Chapter 854 of the Acts of Assembly of 2019 requires the Virginia Criminal Sentencing Commission to assign a minimum fiscal impact of $50,000. Pursuant to § 30-19.1:4 of the Code of Virginia, the estimated amount of the necessary appropriation cannot be determined for periods of commitment to the custody of the Department of Juvenile Justice."

The 2020 amendments.

The 2020 amendment by c. 542, in subdivision A 1, inserted "requests a service pursuant to a membership or a service agreement"; and in subsection B, substituted "A 1, 3, 4, 5, or 6" for "A 3, 4, 5, or 6" in the first sentence and added the second sentence.

The 2020 amendments by cc. 1227 and 1246, effective January 1, 2021, are identical, and rewrote the introductory language of subsection A, which formerly read: "No merchant may scan the machine-readable zone of a Department of Motor Vehicles-issued identification card or driver's license, except for the following purposes"; substituted "driver's license or other document" for "identification card or driver's license" or similar language throughout the section; substituted "the laws of the Commonwealth" for "state" in subdivision A 4; and inserted the first occurrence of "federal" in subdivision A 6.

CHAPTER 35.1.

SECURITY FREEZES.

§ 59.1-444.2. Security freezes.

A. As used in this section, "security freeze" means a notice placed in a consumer's credit report, at the request of the consumer and subject to certain exceptions, that prohibits the consumer reporting agency from releasing the consumer's credit report or score relating to the extension of credit.

B. A consumer may request that a security freeze be placed on his or her credit report by sending a request in writing by certified mail, or such other secure method authorized by a consumer reporting agency, to a consumer reporting agency at an address designated by the consumer reporting agency to receive such requests. This subsection does not prevent a consumer reporting agency from advising a third party that a security freeze is in effect with respect to the consumer's credit report.

C. A consumer reporting agency shall place a security freeze on a consumer's credit report no later than three business days after receiving from the consumer:

1. A written request described in subsection B; and

2. Proper identification.

A consumer reporting agency shall place a security freeze on a consumer's credit report no later than one business day after receiving such a request, if such request is made electronically at an address designated by the consumer reporting agency to receive such requests.

D. The consumer reporting agency shall send a written confirmation of the placement of the security freeze to the consumer within 10 business days. Upon placing the security freeze on the consumer's credit report, the consumer reporting agency shall provide the consumer with a unique personal identification number or password, or similar device to be used by the consumer when providing authorization for the release of his credit report for a specific period of time or for a specific party.

E. If the consumer wishes to allow his credit report to be accessed for a specific period of time or for a specific party while a freeze is in place, he shall contact the consumer reporting agency using a point of contact designated by the consumer reporting agency, request that the freeze be temporarily lifted, and provide the following:

1. Proper identification;

2. The unique personal identification number or password provided by the consumer reporting agency pursuant to subsection D; and

3. The proper information regarding the time period or the specific party for which the report shall be available to users of the credit report.

F. A consumer reporting agency:

1. Shall comply with a request made under subsection E:

a. Within three business days after receiving the request if the request is made at a postal address designated by the agency to receive such requests; or

b. Within 15 minutes after the consumer's request is received by the consumer reporting agency through the electronic contact method chosen by the consumer reporting agency in accordance with this section;

2. Is not required to temporarily lift a security freeze within the time provided in subdivision 1 b if:

a. The consumer fails to meet the requirements of subsection E; or

b. The consumer reporting agency's ability to temporarily lift the security freeze within 15 minutes is prevented by:

(1) An act of God, including fire, earthquakes, hurricanes, storms, or similar natural disaster or phenomena;

(2) Unauthorized or illegal acts by a third party, including terrorism, sabotage, riot, vandalism, labor strikes or disputes disrupting operations, or similar occurrence;

(3) Operational interruption, including electrical failure, unanticipated delay in equipment or replacement part delivery, computer hardware or software failures inhibiting response time, or similar disruption;

(4) Governmental action, including emergency orders or regulations, judicial or law-enforcement action, or similar directives;

(5) Regularly scheduled maintenance, during other than normal business hours, of, or updates to, the consumer reporting agency's systems; or

(6) Commercially reasonable maintenance of, or repair to, the consumer reporting agency's systems that is unexpected or unscheduled; and

3. May develop procedures involving the use of telephone, fax, the Internet, or other electronic media to receive and process a request from a consumer to temporarily lift a freeze on a credit report pursuant to subsection E in an expedited manner.

G. A consumer reporting agency shall remove or temporarily lift a freeze placed on a consumer's credit report only in the following cases:

1. Upon a consumer request, pursuant to subsection E or subsection J; or

2. If the consumer's credit report was frozen due to a material misrepresentation of fact by the consumer. If a consumer reporting agency intends to remove a freeze upon a consumer's credit report pursuant to this subdivision, the consumer reporting agency shall notify the consumer in writing prior to removing the freeze on the consumer's credit report.

H. If a third party requests access to a consumer credit report on which a security freeze is in effect, and this request is in connection with an application for credit or any other use, and the consumer does not allow his or her credit report to be accessed for that period of time, the third party may treat the application as incomplete.

I. If a consumer requests a security freeze, the consumer reporting agency shall disclose the process of placing and temporarily lifting a freeze and the process for allowing access to information from the consumer's credit report for a period of time while the freeze is in place.

J. A security freeze shall remain in place until the consumer requests, using a point of contact designated by the consumer reporting agency, that the security freeze be removed. A consumer reporting agency shall remove a security freeze within three business days of receiving a request for removal from the consumer, who provides:

1. Proper identification; and

2. The unique personal identification number or password or similar device provided by the consumer reporting agency pursuant to subsection D.

K. A consumer reporting agency shall require proper identification of the person making a request to place or remove a security freeze.

L. The provisions of this section do not apply to the use of a consumer credit report by any of the following:

1. A person or entity, or a subsidiary, affiliate, or agent of that person or entity, or an assignee of a financial obligation owing by the consumer to that person or entity, or a prospective assignee of a financial obligation owing by the consumer to that person or entity in conjunction with the proposed purchase of the financial obligation, with which the consumer has or had prior to

assignment an account or contract, including a demand deposit account, or to whom the consumer issued a negotiable instrument, for the purposes of reviewing the account or collecting the financial obligation owing for the account, contract, or negotiable instrument. For purposes of this paragraph, "reviewing the account" includes activities related to account maintenance, monitoring, credit line increases, and account upgrades and enhancements;

2. A subsidiary, affiliate, agent, assignee, or prospective assignee of a person to whom access has been granted for purposes of facilitating the extension of credit or other permissible use;

3. Any state or local agency, law-enforcement agency, trial court, or private collection agency acting pursuant to a court order, warrant, or subpoena;

4. A child support agency acting pursuant to Title IV-D of the Social Security Act (42 U.S.C. § 654 et seq.);

5. The Commonwealth or its agents or assigns acting to investigate fraud or acting to investigate or collect delinquent taxes or unpaid court orders or to fulfill any of its other statutory responsibilities provided such responsibilities are consistent with a permissible purpose under 15 U.S.C. § 1681b;

6. The use of credit information for the purposes of prescreening or post-screening as provided for by the federal Fair Credit Reporting Act;

7. Any person or entity administering a credit file monitoring subscription or similar service to which the consumer has subscribed;

8. Any person or entity for the purpose of providing a consumer with a copy of his credit report or score upon the consumer's request;

9. Any person or entity for use in setting or adjusting a rate, adjusting a claim, or underwriting for insurance purposes; or

10. Any employer in connection with any application for employment with the employer.

M. A consumer reporting agency shall not charge a fee for any service performed under this section.

N. If a security freeze is in place, a consumer reporting agency shall not change any of the following official information in a consumer credit report without sending a written confirmation of the change to the consumer within 30 days of the change being posted to the consumer's file: name, date of birth, social security number, and address. Written confirmation is not required for technical modifications of a consumer's official information, including name and street abbreviations, complete spellings, or transposition of numbers or letters. In the case of an address change, the written confirmation shall be sent to both the new address and to the former address.

O. The following entities are not required to place a security freeze on a credit report:

1. A consumer reporting agency that acts only as a reseller of credit information by assembling and merging information contained in the database of another consumer reporting agency or multiple consumer credit reporting agencies, and does not maintain a permanent database of credit information from which new consumer credit reports are produced. However, a consumer reporting agency acting as a reseller shall honor any security freeze placed on a consumer credit report by another consumer reporting agency;

2. A check services or fraud prevention services company, which issues reports on incidents of fraud or authorizations for the purpose of approving or processing negotiable instruments, electronic funds transfers, or similar methods of payments;

3. A deposit account information service company, which issues reports regarding account closures due to fraud, substantial overdrafts, ATM abuse, or similar negative information regarding a consumer, to inquiring banks or other financial institutions for use only in reviewing a consumer request for a deposit account at the inquiring bank or financial institution; and

4. A consumer reporting agency's database or file that consists of information concerning, and used for, one or more of the following: criminal record information, fraud prevention or detection, personal loss history information, and employment, tenant, or background screening.

P. At any time a consumer is required to receive a summary of rights required under 15 U.S.C. § 1681g(d), the following notice shall be included:

"Virginia Consumers Have the Right to Obtain a Security Freeze.

You have a right to place a "security freeze" on your credit report, which will prohibit a consumer reporting agency from releasing information in your credit report without your express authorization. A security freeze must be requested in writing by certified mail. The security freeze is designed to prevent credit, loans, and services from being approved in your name without your consent. However, you should be aware that using a security freeze to take control over who gets access to the personal and financial information in your credit report may delay, interfere with, or prohibit the timely approval of any subsequent request or application you make regarding a new loan, credit, mortgage, government services or payments, rental housing, employment, investment, license, cellular phone, utilities, digital signature, Internet credit card transaction, or other services, including an extension of credit at point of sale. When you place a security freeze on your credit report, you will be provided a personal identification number or password to use if you choose to remove the freeze on your credit report or authorize the release of your credit report for a period of time or for a specific party after the freeze is in place. To provide that authorization you must contact the consumer reporting agency and provide all of the following:

1. The personal identification number or password;

2. Proper identification to verify your identity; and

3. The proper information regarding the period of time or the specific party for which the report shall be available.

A consumer reporting agency must authorize the release of your credit report no later than three business days after receiving the above information. A consumer credit reporting agency must authorize the release of your credit report no later than 15 minutes after receiving the request.

A security freeze does not apply to a person or entity, or its affiliates, or collection agencies acting on behalf of the person or entity, with which you have an existing account, that requests information in your credit report for the purposes of reviewing or collecting the account. Reviewing the account includes activities related to account maintenance, monitoring, credit line increases, and account upgrades and enhancements.

You have a right to bring civil action against anyone, including a consumer reporting agency, who improperly obtains access to a file, knowingly or willfully misuses file data, or fails to correct inaccurate file data.

A consumer reporting agency does not have the right to charge you a fee to place a freeze on your credit report."

Q. Any person who willfully fails to comply with any requirement imposed under this section or § 59.1-444.3 with respect to any consumer is liable to that consumer in an amount equal to the sum of:

1. Any actual damages sustained by the consumer as a result of the failure or damages of not less than $100 and not more than $1,000;

2. Such amount of punitive damages as the court may allow; and

3. In the case of any successful action to enforce any liability under this section, the costs of the action together with reasonable attorney fees as determined by the court.

R. Any person who obtains a consumer report, requests a security freeze, requests the temporary lift of a freeze, or requests the removal of a security freeze from a consumer reporting agency under false pretenses or in an attempt to violate federal or state law shall be liable to the consumer reporting agency for actual damages sustained by the consumer reporting agency or $1,000, whichever is greater.

S. Any person who is negligent in failing to comply with any requirement imposed under this section with respect to any consumer is liable to that consumer in an amount equal to the sum of:

1. Any actual damages sustained by the consumer as a result of the failure; and

2. In the case of any successful action to enforce any liability under this section, the costs of the action together with reasonable attorney fees as determined by the court.

T. Upon a finding by the court that an unsuccessful pleading, motion, or other paper filed in connection with an action under this section was filed in bad faith or for purposes of harassment, the court shall award to the prevailing party attorney fees reasonable in relation to the work expended in responding to the pleading, motion, or other paper.

U. Notwithstanding any other provision of law:

1. The exclusive authority to bring an action for any violation of subdivision F 1 b shall be with the Attorney General. In any action brought under this subsection, the Attorney General may cause an action to be brought in the name of the Commonwealth to enjoin the violation and to recover damages for aggrieved consumers consistent with the limits stated in subsections Q and S for such violations.

2. In any action brought under this subsection, if the court finds a willful violation, the court may, in its discretion, also award a civil penalty of not more than $1,000 per violation, to be deposited in the Literary Fund of the Commonwealth.

3. In any action brought under this subsection, the Attorney General may recover any costs, the reasonable expenses incurred in investigating and preparing the case, and attorney fees.

History.

2008, cc. 480, 496; 2009, c. 406; 2014, c. 570; 2018, cc. 264, 303; 2020, c. 243.

The 2020 amendments.

The 2020 amendment by c. 243 deleted subdivision C 3, which read: "Payment of a fee not to exceed $5, if applicable"; rewrote subsection M, which formerly read: "This section does not prevent a consumer reporting agency from charging a fee of no more than $5 to a consumer to place each freeze, except that a consumer reporting agency may not charge a fee to a victim of identity theft who has submitted a valid police report to the consumer reporting agency"; rewrote the last paragraph of subsection P, which read: "Unless you are a victim of identity theft with a police report to verify the crimes, a consumer reporting agency has the right to charge you up to $5 to place a freeze on your credit report"; and in subsection R, inserted "requests" preceding "the removal of."

§ 59.1-444.3. Security freezes for protected consumers.

A. As used in this section, unless the context requires a different meaning:

"*Protected consumer*" means a consumer who is either:

1. Under the age of 16 years at the time a request for the placement of a security freeze is made; or

2. An incapacitated person for whom a guardian or conservator has been appointed in accordance with Chapter 20 (§ 64.2-2000 et seq.) of Title 64.2.

"*Record*" means a compilation of information regarding a specific identified protected consumer, which compilation is created by a consumer reporting agency solely for the purpose of complying with the requirement for a record's establishment set forth in subsection D.

"Representative" means a person who provides to a consumer reporting agency sufficient proof of authority to act on behalf of a protected consumer.

"Security freeze" means:

1. If a consumer reporting agency does not have a file pertaining to a protected consumer, a restriction that (i) is placed on the protected consumer's record in accordance with this section and (ii) prohibits the consumer reporting agency from releasing the protected consumer's record except as provided in this section; or

2. If a consumer reporting agency has a file pertaining to the protected consumer, a restriction that (i) is placed on the protected consumer's credit report in accordance with this section and (ii) prohibits the consumer reporting agency from releasing the protected consumer's credit report or any information derived from the protected consumer's credit report except as provided in this section.

"Sufficient proof of authority" means documentation that shows a representative has authority to act on behalf of a protected consumer. "Sufficient proof of authority" includes (i) an order issued by a court of law, (ii) a lawfully executed and valid power of attorney, (iii) a birth certification; or (iv) a written, notarized statement signed by a representative that expressly describes the authority of the representative to act on behalf of the protected consumer.

"Sufficient proof of identification" means information or documentation that identifies a protected consumer or a representative of a protected consumer. "Sufficient proof of identification" includes (i) a social security number or a copy of a social security card issued by the U.S. Social Security Administration; (ii) a certified or official copy of a birth certificate issued by the entity authorized to issue the birth certificate; (iii) a copy of a driver's license, an identification card issued by the Department of Motor Vehicles, or any other government-issued identification; or (iv) a copy of a bill, including a bill for telephone, sewer, septic tank, water, electric, oil, or natural gas services, that shows a name and home address.

B. This section does not apply to the use of a protected consumer's credit report or record by:

1. A person administering a credit file monitoring subscription service to which the protected consumer has subscribed or the representative of the protected consumer has subscribed on behalf of the protected consumer;

2. A person providing the protected consumer or the protected consumer's representative with a copy of the protected consumer's credit report on request of the protected consumer or the protected consumer's representative; or

3. An entity listed in subsection O of § 59.1-444.2.

C. A consumer reporting agency shall place a security freeze for a protected consumer if:

1. The consumer reporting agency receives a request from the protected consumer's representative for the placement of the security freeze under this section; and

2. The protected consumer's representative:

a. Submits the request to the consumer reporting agency at the address or other point of contact and in the manner specified by the consumer reporting agency;

b. Provides to the consumer reporting agency sufficient proof of identification of the protected consumer and the representative; and

c. Provides to the consumer reporting agency sufficient proof of authority to act on behalf of the protected consumer.

D. If a consumer reporting agency does not have a file pertaining to a protected consumer when the consumer reporting agency receives a request under subsection C from the protected consumer's representative for the placement of a security freeze, the consumer reporting agency shall create a record for the protected consumer. A record may not be created or used to consider the protected consumer's creditworthiness, credit standing, credit capacity, character, general reputation, personal characteristics, or mode of living for the purpose of serving as a factor in establishing the consumer's eligibility for (i) credit or insurance to be used primarily for personal, family, or household purposes or (ii) employment.

E. Within 30 days after receiving a request that meets the requirements of subsection C, a consumer reporting agency shall place a security freeze for the protected consumer.

F. Unless a security freeze for a protected consumer is removed in accordance with subsection H or K, a consumer reporting agency may not release the protected consumer's credit report, any information derived from the protected consumer's credit report, or any record created for the protected consumer.

G. A security freeze for a protected consumer placed under subsection E shall remain in effect until:

1. The protected consumer or the protected consumer's representative requests the consumer reporting agency to remove the security freeze in accordance with subsection H; or

2. The security freeze is removed in accordance with subsection K.

H. If a protected consumer or a protected consumer's representative wishes to remove a security freeze for the protected consumer, the protected consumer or the protected consumer's representative shall:

1. Submit a request for the removal of the security freeze to the consumer reporting agency at the address or other point of contact and in the manner specified by the consumer reporting agency; and

2. Provide to the consumer reporting agency:

a. In the case of a request by the protected consumer:

(1) Proof that the sufficient proof of authority for the protected consumer's representative to act on behalf of the protected consumer is no longer valid; and

(2) Sufficient proof of identification of the protected consumer; or

b. In the case of a request by the representative of a protected consumer:

(1) Sufficient proof of identification of the protected consumer and the representative; and

(2) Sufficient proof of authority to act on behalf of the protected consumer.

I. Within 30 days after receiving a request that meets the requirements of subsection H, the consumer reporting agency shall remove the security freeze for the protected consumer.

J. A consumer reporting agency shall not charge a fee for any service performed under this section.

K. A consumer reporting agency may remove a security freeze for a protected consumer or delete a record of a protected consumer if the security freeze was placed or the record was created based on a material misrepresentation of fact by the protected consumer or the protected consumer's representative.

L. Any person who obtains a consumer report, requests a security freeze, requests the temporary lift of a freeze, or requests the removal of a security freeze from a consumer reporting agency under false pretenses or in an attempt to violate federal or state law shall be liable to the consumer reporting agency for damages sustained by the consumer reporting agency as provided in subsection R of § 59.1-444.2.

M. Notwithstanding any other provision of law:

1. The exclusive authority to bring an action for any violation of subsection E shall be with the Attorney General. In any action brought under this

subsection, the Attorney General may cause an action to be brought in the name of the Commonwealth to enjoin the violation and to recover damages for aggrieved protected consumers.

2. In any action brought under this subsection, if the court finds a willful violation, the court may, in its discretion, also award a civil penalty of not more than $1,000 per violation, to be deposited in the Literary Fund.

3. In any action brought under this subsection, the Attorney General may recover any costs, the reasonable expenses incurred in investigating and preparing the case, and attorney fees.

History.
2014, c. 570; 2018, cc. 264, 303, 480; 2020, c. 243.

The 2020 amendments.
The 2020 amendment by c. 243 deleted subdivision C 2 d, which read: "Pays to the consumer reporting agency a fee as provided in subsection J"; deleted subdivision H 3, which read: "Pays to the consumer reporting agency a fee as provided in subsection J"; and in subsection J, substituted "shall" for "may" and deleted "except for a reasonable fee, not exceeding $5, for each placement or removal of a security freeze for a protected consumer. Notwithstanding the foregoing, a consumer reporting agency shall not charge any fee for the placement or removal of a security freeze for a protected consumer if" and deleted subdivisions J 1 and J 2.

CHAPTER 38.2.

TICKET RESALE RIGHTS ACT.

§ 59.1-466.5. Definitions.

As used in this chapter, unless the context requires a different meaning:

"Event" means any professional concert, live entertainment event, professional sporting or athletic event, or professional theatrical production open to the public for which tickets are ordinarily sold.

"Internet ticketing platform" means a marketplace or exchange that enables consumers to purchase and sell tickets to events.

"Operator" means a person or subsidiary thereof that owns, operates, or controls a place of entertainment.

"Primary ticket provider" means a provider of ticketing services, or an agent of such provider, that engages in the original sale of tickets for an event.

"Purchaser" means an individual who purchases a ticket to an event.

"Resale" means the sale of a ticket other than the original sale of a ticket by a primary ticket provider.

"Reseller" means a person that sells or offers to sell tickets for resale.

"Rights holder" means any person or entity that has the initial ownership rights to sell a ticket to an event for which tickets for entry by the public are required and does not include a primary ticket provider unless the primary ticket provider is also the rights holder.

"URL" means the Uniform Resource Locator associated with an online website.

History.
2017, cc. 261, 268; 2023, cc. 304, 305.

The 2023 amendments.
The 2023 amendment by cc. 304 and 305 are identical, and rewrote the section, which for-merly read, "As used in this chapter, 'event' means any professional concert, professional sporting event, or professional theatrical production, open to the public for which tickets are ordinarily sold."

§ 59.1-466.8. Ticket resale; deceptive trade practices prohibited.

No Internet ticketing platform or reseller shall (i) use or display any trademarked or copyrighted URL, title, designation, image, mark, or any other symbol of an operator, rights holder, or primary ticket provider without the consent of such operator, rights holder, or primary ticket provider or (ii) use or display any combination of text, images, website graphics, website display, or website addresses that is substantially similar to the website of an operator in a manner that could reasonably be expected to mislead a potential purchaser.

History.
2023, cc. 305, 304.

CHAPTER 42.1.

UNIFORM ELECTRONIC TRANSACTIONS ACT.

Section
59.1-497. Interoperability.

§ 59.1-497. Interoperability.

A public body of the Commonwealth that adopts standards pursuant to § 59.1-496 and the Secretary of Administration may encourage and promote consistency and interoperability with similar requirements adopted by other public bodies of the Commonwealth, other states and the federal government and nongovernmental persons interacting with public bodies of the Commonwealth. If appropriate, those standards may specify differing levels of standards from which public bodies of the Commonwealth may choose in implementing the most appropriate standard for a particular application.

History.
2000, c. 995; 2020, c. 738.

The 2020 amendments.
The 2020 amendment by c. 738 substituted "that" for "which" and "Administration" for "Technology" in the first sentence.

CHAPTER 43.

UNIFORM COMPUTER INFORMATION TRANSACTIONS ACT.

Article 9. Miscellaneous Provisions.

Section
59.1-509.1. [Repealed.]

ARTICLE 1.

GENERAL PROVISIONS.

§ 59.1-501.1. Title.

Editor's note.
At the direction of the Code Commission, Parts have been changed to Articles in this chapter to correct the 2000 acts.

ARTICLE 2.

FORMATION AND TERMS.

§ 59.1-502.1. Formal requirements.

Editor's note.
At the direction of the Code Commission, Parts have been changed to Articles in this chapter to correct the 2000 acts.

ARTICLE 3.

CONSTRUCTION.

§ 59.1-503.1. Parol or extrinsic evidence.

Editor's note.
At the direction of the Code Commission, Parts have been changed to Articles in this chapter to correct the 2000 acts.

ARTICLE 4.

WARRANTIES.

§ 59.1-504.1. Warranty and obligations concerning noninterference and noninfringement.

Editor's note.
At the direction of the Code Commission, Parts have been changed to Articles in this chapter to correct the 2000 acts.

ARTICLE 5.
TRANSFER OF INTERESTS AND RIGHTS.

§ 59.1-505.1. Ownership of informational rights.

Editor's note.
At the direction of the Code Commission, Parts have been changed to Articles in this chapter to correct the 2000 acts.

ARTICLE 6.
PERFORMANCE.

§ 59.1-506.1. Performance of contract in general.

Editor's note.
At the direction of the Code Commission, Parts have been changed to Articles in this chapter to correct the 2000 acts.

ARTICLE 7.
BREACH OF CONTRACT.

§ 59.1-507.1. Breach of contract; material breach.

Editor's note.
At the direction of the Code Commission, Parts have been changed to Articles in this chapter to correct the 2000 acts.

ARTICLE 8.
REMEDIES.

§ 59.1-508.1. Remedies in general.

Editor's note.
At the direction of the Code Commission, Parts have been changed to Articles in this chapter to correct the 2000 acts.

ARTICLE 9.
MISCELLANEOUS PROVISIONS.

§ 59.1-509.1. Repealed by Acts 2015, c. 709, cl. 2.

Editor's note.
At the direction of the Code Commission, Parts have been changed to Articles in this chapter to correct the 2000 acts.

CHAPTER 44.
VIRGINIA TELEPHONE PRIVACY PROTECTION ACT.

Section
59.1-518.01. Communication with state agencies.

§ 59.1-510. Definitions; rule of construction.

As used in this chapter:

"Established business relationship" means a relationship between the called person and the person on whose behalf the telephone solicitation call is being made or initiated based on (i) the called person's purchase from, or transaction with, the person on whose behalf the telephone solicitation call is being made or initiated within the 18 months immediately preceding the date of the call or (ii) the called person's inquiry or application regarding any property, good, or service offered by the person on whose behalf the telephone solicitation call is being made or initiated within the three months immediately preceding the date of the call.

"Personal relationship" means the relationship between a telephone solicitor making or initiating a telephone solicitation call and any family member, friend, or acquaintance of that telephone solicitor.

"Responsible person" means either or both of (i) a telephone solicitor or (ii) a seller if the telephone solicitation call offering or advertising the seller's property, goods, or services is presumed to have been made or initiated on behalf of or for the benefit of the seller and the presumption is not rebutted as provided in subsection B of § 59.1-514.1.

"Seller" means any person on whose behalf or for whose benefit a telephone solicitation call offering or advertising the person's property, goods, or services is made or initiated.

"Telephone solicitation call" means (i) any telephone call made or initiated to any natural person's residence in the Commonwealth, to any landline or wireless telephone with a Virginia area code, or to a landline or wireless telephone registered to any natural person who is a resident of the Commonwealth or (ii) any text message sent to any wireless telephone with a Virginia area code or to a wireless telephone registered to any natural person who is a resident of the Commonwealth, for the purpose of offering or advertising any property, goods, or services for sale, lease, license, or investment, including offering or advertising an extension of credit or for the purpose of fraudulent activity, including engaging in any conduct that results in the display of false or misleading caller identification information on the called person's telephone.

"Telephone solicitor" means any person who makes or initiates, or causes another person to make or initiate, a telephone solicitation call on its own behalf or for its own benefit or on behalf of or for the benefit of a seller.

History.
2001, cc. 528, 553; 2004, cc. 202, 224; 2019, cc. 256, 264; 2020, cc. 263, 607.

The 2020 amendments.
The 2020 amendments by cc. 263 and 607 are identical, and in the definition for "Telephone solicitation call," inserted "(i)," "landline or" twice, and "or (ii) any text message sent to any wireless telephone with a Virginia area code or to a wireless telephone registered to any natural person who is a resident of the Commonwealth," added "or for the purpose of fraudulent activity, including engaging in any conduct that results in the display of false or misleading caller identification information on the called person's telephone" and made a stylistic change.

§ 59.1-513. Transmission of caller identification information required.

A. A telephone solicitor who makes a telephone solicitation call shall transmit the telephone number, and, when available by the telephone solicitor's carrier, the name of the telephone solicitor. The number so provided must permit, during regular business hours, any individual to make a request not to receive telephone solicitation calls.

B. No telephone solicitor shall take any intentional action to prevent the transmission of the telephone solicitor's name or telephone number to any person receiving a telephone solicitation call or engage in any conduct that results in the display of false or misleading caller identification information on the called person's telephone.

C. It shall not be a violation of this section to substitute for the name and telephone number used in, or billed for, making the call the name of the person on whose behalf the telephone solicitation call is being made and that person's customer service telephone number.

History.
2001, cc. 528, 553; 2004, cc. 202, 224; 2020, cc. 263, 607.

The 2020 amendments.
The 2020 amendments by cc. 263 and 607 are identical, and in subsection A, deleted the second sentence, which read: "It shall not be a violation of this section to substitute (for the name and telephone number used in, or billed for, making the call) the name of the person on whose behalf the telephone solicitation call is being made and that person's customer service telephone number"; in subsection B, added "or engage in any conduct that results in the display of false or misleading caller identification information on the called person's telephone"; and added subsection C.

§ 59.1-515. Individual action for damages.

A. Any natural person who is aggrieved by a violation of this chapter shall be entitled to initiate an action against any responsible person to enjoin such violation and to recover from any responsible person damages in the amount of $500 for a first violation, $1,000 for a second violation, and $5,000 for each subsequent violation.

B. If the court finds a willful violation, the court may, in its discretion, increase the amount of any damages awarded for a first or second violation under subsection A to an amount not exceeding $5,000.

C. Notwithstanding any other provision of law to the contrary, in addition to any damages awarded, such person may be awarded under subsection A or B reasonable attorney fees and court costs.

D. An action for damages, attorney fees, and costs brought under this section may be filed in an appropriate general district court or small claims court against any responsible person so long as the amount claimed does not exceed the jurisdictional limits set forth in § 16.1-77 or 16.1-122.2, as applicable. Any action brought under this section that includes a request for an injunction shall be filed in an appropriate circuit court.

History.
2001, cc. 528, 553; 2019, cc. 256, 264; 2020, cc. 263, 607.

The 2020 amendments.
The 2020 amendments by cc. 263 and 607 are identical, and in subsection A, substituted "for a first violation, $1,000 for a second violation, and $5,000 for each subsequent violation" for "for each such violation"; and in subsection B, inserted "for a first or second violation" and substituted "$5,000" for "$1,500."

§ 59.1-517. Enforcement; civil penalties.

A. The Attorney General, an attorney for the Commonwealth, or the attorney for any locality may cause an action to be brought in the name of the Commonwealth or of the locality, as applicable, to enjoin any violation of this chapter by any responsible person and to recover from any responsible person damages for aggrieved persons in the amount of $500 for a first violation, $1,000 for a second violation, and $5,000 for each subsequent violation.

B. If the court finds a willful violation, the court may, in its discretion, also assess against any responsible person a civil penalty of not more than $5,000 for each such violation.

C. In any action brought under this section, the Attorney General, the attorney for the Commonwealth, or the attorney for the locality may recover reasonable expenses incurred by the state or local agency in investigating and preparing the case, and attorney fees.

D. Any civil penalties assessed under subsection B in an action brought in the name of the Commonwealth shall be paid into the Literary Fund. Any civil penalties assessed under subsection B in an action brought in the name of a locality shall be paid into the general fund of the locality.

History.
  2001, cc. 528, 553; 2019, cc. 256, 264; 2020, cc. 263, 607.

The 2020 amendments.
  The 2020 amendments by cc. 263 and 607 are identical, and in subsection A, substituted "for a first violation, $1,000 for a second violation, and $5,000 for each subsequent violation" for "for each such violation"; and in subsection B, substituted "$5,000" for "$1,000."

§ 59.1-518.01. Communication with state agencies.

The Attorney General shall establish ongoing communication with the Department for Aging and Rehabilitative Services to ensure that adults, as defined in § 63.2-1603, have access to information regarding the prevention of potential patterns of financial exploitation. The Attorney General shall coordinate with the Commissioner of the Department for Aging and Rehabilitative Services to determine an effective and efficient manner of communicating such information, while also ensuring that confidential or privileged information is not exchanged.

History.
  2020, c. 939.

CHAPTER 46.

VIRGINIA POST-DISASTER ANTI-PRICE GOUGING ACT.

Section
59.1-526. Definitions.
59.1-527. Prohibitions.

§ 59.1-526. Definitions.

As used in this chapter:

"Consumer transaction," "goods," and *"services,"* have the same meanings as are set forth for those terms in § 59.1-198.

"Disaster" means any *"disaster," "emergency,"* or *"major disaster,"* as those terms are used and defined in § 44-146.16, that results in the declaration of a state of emergency by the Governor or the President of the United States.

"Necessary goods and services" means any necessary good or service for which consumer demand does, or is likely to, increase as a consequence of the disaster, and includes water, ice, consumer food items or supplies, property or services for emergency cleanup, emergency supplies, communication supplies and services, medical supplies and services, home heating fuel, building

materials and services, tree removal supplies and services, freight, storage services, housing, lodging, transportation, and motor fuels.

"*Supplier*" means a seller, lessor, licensor, or professional who advertises, solicits, or engages in consumer transactions, or a manufacturer, distributor, or licensor who sells, leases, or licenses goods or services to be resold, leased, or sublicensed by other persons in consumer transactions. However, a manufacturer, distributor, or licensor who sells, leases, or licenses agricultural goods or services to be resold, leased, or sublicensed by other persons in consumer transactions shall not be considered a "supplier" unless such manufacturer, distributor, or licensor advertises such agricultural goods or services.

"*Time of disaster*" means the shorter of (i) the period of time when a state of emergency declared by the Governor or the President of the United States as the result of a disaster, emergency, or major disaster, as those terms are used and defined in § 44-146.16, is in effect or (ii) 30 days after the occurrence of the disaster, emergency, or major disaster that resulted in the declaration of the state of emergency; however, if the state of emergency is extended or renewed within 30 days after such an occurrence, then such period shall be extended to include the 30 days following the date the state of emergency was extended or renewed.

History.

2004, cc. 798, 817; 2006, c. 362; 2008, cc. 121, 157; 2020, Sp. Sess. I, c. 16.

The 2020 Sp. Sess. I amendments.

The 2020 amendment by Sp. Sess. I, c. 16, effective March 1, 2021, substituted the definition "Consumer transaction," "goods," and "services," for "Goods," "services," and "supplier," deleted "but is not limited to" following "and includes" in the definition of "Necessary goods and services" and added the definition of "Supplier."

§ 59.1-527. Prohibitions.

During any time of disaster, it shall be unlawful for any supplier to sell, lease, or license, or to offer to sell, lease, or license, any necessary goods and services at an unconscionable price within the area for which the state of emergency is declared. Actual sales at the increased price shall not be required for the increase to be considered unconscionable. In determining whether a price increase is unconscionable, the following shall be considered:

1. Whether the price charged by the supplier grossly exceeded the price charged by the supplier for the same or similar goods or services during the 10 days immediately prior to the time of disaster, provided that, with respect to any supplier who was offering a good or service at a reduced price immediately prior to the time of disaster, the price at which the supplier usually offers the good or service shall be used as the benchmark for these purposes;

2. Whether the price charged by the supplier grossly exceeded the price at which the same or similar goods or services were readily obtainable by purchasers in the trade area during the 10 days immediately prior to the time of disaster;

3. Whether the increase in the amount charged by the supplier was attributable solely to additional costs incurred by the supplier in connection with the sale of the goods or services, including additional costs imposed by the supplier's source. Proof that the supplier incurred such additional costs during the time of disaster shall be prima facie evidence that the price increase by that supplier was not unconscionable; and

4. Whether the increase in the amount charged by the supplier was attributable solely to a regular seasonal or holiday adjustment in the price charged for the good or service. Proof that the supplier regularly increased the price for a particular good or service during portions of the period covered by

the time of disaster would be prima facie evidence that the price increase was not unconscionable during those periods.

History.

2004, cc. 798, 817; 2020, Sp. Sess. I, c. 16.

The 2020 Sp. Sess. I amendments.
The 2020 amendment by Sp. Sess. I, c. 16,

effective March 1, 2021, substituted "purchasers" for "consumers" in subdivision 2 and inserted "by that supplier" in subdivision 3.

CHAPTER 49.

ENTERPRISE ZONE GRANT PROGRAM.

§ 59.1-546. Review and termination of enterprise zones.

A. If the local governing body is unable or unwilling to provide the specified local incentives as proposed in its application for zone designation or as approved by the Department in an amendment, the zone designation shall terminate. Qualified business firms located in such enterprise zone shall be eligible to receive the incentives provided by this chapter even though the zone designation has terminated. No business firm may become a qualified business firm after the date of zone termination.

B. If no business firms have qualified for incentives as provided for in this chapter within a five-year period, the Department shall terminate that enterprise zone designation.

C. The Department shall review the effectiveness in creating jobs and capital investment and activity occurring within designated enterprise zones and shall annually report its findings to the Senate Committee on Finance and Appropriations, the Senate Committee on Commerce and Labor, the House Committee on Appropriations, and the House Committee on Labor and Commerce.

History.
2005, cc. 863, 884.

Editor's note.
The Virginia Code Commission authorized the substitution of "Senate Committee on Finance and Appropriations, the Senate Committee on Commerce and Labor, the House Committee on Appropriations, and the House Committee on Labor and Commerce" for "Senate Finance Committee, the Senate Committee on Commerce and Labor, the House Appropriations Committee, and the House Committee on Commerce and Labor." March 10, 2021.

§ 59.1-547. Enterprise zone job creation grants.

A. As used in this section:

"Base year" means either of the two calendar years immediately preceding a qualified business firm's first year of grant eligibility, at the choice of the business firm.

"Federal minimum wage" means the minimum wage standard as currently defined by the United States Department of Labor in the Fair Labor Standards Act, 29 U.S.C. § 201 et seq. Such definition applies to permanent full-time employees paid on an hourly or wage basis. For those permanent full-time employees filling permanent full-time, salaried positions, the minimum wage is defined as the employee's annual salary divided by 52 weeks per year divided by 35 hours per week.

"Full month" means the number of days that a permanent full-time position must be filled in order to count in the calculation of the job creation grant amount. A full month is calculated by dividing the total number of days in the calendar year by 12. A full month for the purpose of calculating job creation grants is equivalent to 30.416666 days.

"Grant eligible position" means a new permanent full-time position created above the threshold number at an eligible business firm. Positions in retail, personal service or food and beverage service shall not be considered grant eligible positions.

"Minimum wage" means the federal minimum wage or the Virginia minimum wage, whichever is higher. The Department shall determine whichever is higher for the current calendar year as of December 1 of the prior calendar year, and its determination shall be continuously in effect throughout the calendar year, regardless of changes to the federal minimum wage or the Virginia minimum wage during that year.

"Permanent full-time position" means a job of indefinite duration at a business firm located within an enterprise zone requiring the employee to report for work within the enterprise zone; and requiring (i) a minimum of 35 hours of an employee's time per week for the entire normal year of the business firm's operation, which "normal year" must consist of at least 48 weeks, (ii) a minimum of 35 hours of an employee's time per week for the portion of the calendar year in which the employee was initially hired for or transferred to the business firm, or (iii) a minimum of 1,680 hours per year. Such position shall not include (i) seasonal, temporary or contract positions, (ii) a position created when a job function is shifted from an existing location in the Commonwealth to a business firm located within an enterprise zone, (iii) any position that previously existed in the Commonwealth, or (iv) positions created by a business that is simultaneously closing facilities in other areas of the Commonwealth.

"Qualified business firm" means a business firm designated as a qualified business firm by the Department pursuant to § 59.1-542.

"Report to work" means that the employee filling a permanent full-time position reports to the business' zone establishment on a regular basis.

"Subsequent base year" means the base year for calculating the number of grant eligible positions in a second or subsequent five consecutive calendar year grant period. If a second or subsequent five-year grant period is requested within two years after the previous five-year grant period, the subsequent base year will be the last grant year. The calculation of this subsequent base year employment will be determined by the number of permanent full-time positions in the preceding base year, plus the number of threshold positions, plus the number of grant eligible positions in the final year of the previous grant period. If a business firm applies for subsequent five consecutive calendar year grant periods beyond the two years immediately following the completion of the previous five-year grant period, the business firm shall use one of the two preceding calendar years as the subsequent base year, at the choice of the business firm.

"Threshold number" means an increase of four permanent full-time positions over the number of permanent full-time positions in the base year or subsequent base year.

"Virginia minimum wage" means the applicable minimum wage as determined pursuant to the Virginia Minimum Wage Act (§ 40.1-28.8 et seq.).

B. A business firm shall be eligible to receive enterprise zone job creation grants for any and all years in which the business firm qualifies in the five consecutive calendar years period commencing with the first year of grant eligibility. A business firm may be eligible for subsequent five consecutive calendar year grant periods if it creates new grant eligible positions above the threshold for its subsequent base year.

C. The amount of the grant for which a business firm is eligible shall be calculated as follows:

1. Either (i) $800 per year for up to five consecutive years for each grant eligible position that during such year is paid a minimum of 175 percent of the minimum wage and that is provided with health benefits, or (ii) $500 per year for up to five years for each grant eligible position that during such year is paid less than 175 percent of the minimum wage, but at least 150 percent of the minimum wage, and that is provided with health benefits. In areas with an unemployment rate that is one and one-half times or more the state average, or for businesses that are certified under regulations adopted by the Director of the Department of Small Business and Supplier Diversity pursuant to subdivision 8 of § 2.2-1606, the business firm will receive $500 per year for up to five years for each grant eligible position that during such year is paid at least 125 percent of the minimum wage and that is provided with health benefits. Unemployment rates used to determine eligibility for the reduced wage rate threshold shall be based on the most recent annualized unemployment data published by the Virginia Employment Commission. A business firm may receive grants for up to a maximum of 350 grant eligible jobs annually.

2. Positions paying less than 150 percent of the minimum wage or that are not provided with health benefits shall not be eligible for enterprise zone job creation grants.

D. Job creation grants shall be based on a calendar year. The amount of the grant for which a qualified business firm is eligible with respect to any permanent full-time position that is filled for less than a full calendar year shall be prorated based on the number of full months worked.

E. The amount of the job creation grant for which a qualified business firm is eligible in any year shall not include amounts for grant eligible positions in any year other than the preceding calendar year. Job creation grants shall not be available for any calendar year prior to 2005.

F. Permanent full-time positions that have been used to qualify for any other enterprise zone incentive pursuant to the Enterprise Zone Act (former § 59.1-270 et seq.) shall not be eligible for job creation grants and shall not be counted as a part of the minimum threshold of four new positions.

G. Any qualified business firm receiving a major business facility job tax credit pursuant to § 58.1-439 shall not be eligible to receive an enterprise zone job creation grant under this section for any job used to qualify for the major business facility job tax credit.

History.
2005, cc. 863, 884; 2006, c. 668; 2010, c. 328; 2012, c. 445; 2021, Sp. Sess. I, c. 402.

Editor's note.
Acts 2020, c. 1289, as amended by Acts 2021, Sp. Sess. I, c. 552, Item 115, effective for the biennium ending June 30, 2022, provides: "Out of the amounts in this Item, $14,500,000 the first year and $14,750,000 the second year from the general fund shall be provided to carry out the provisions of §§ 59.1-547 and 59.1-548, Code of Virginia, related to the Enterprise Zone Grant Act. Notwithstanding the provisions of §§ 59.1-547 and 59.1-548, Code of Virginia, the department is authorized to prorate, with no payment of the unpaid portion of the grant necessary in the next fiscal year, the amount of awards each business receives to match the appropriation for this Item. Should actual grants awarded in each fiscal year be less than the amounts provided in this Item, the excess shall not revert to the general fund but shall be deposited to the Virginia Removal or Rehabilitation of Derelict Structures Fund for revitalization purposes. Consistent with the provisions of § 59.1-548, Code of Virginia, beginning on January 1, 2019, the installation of solar panels shall be considered eligible investments for the purposes of the real property improvement grants, provided that such solar installation investment is in an amount of at least $50,000 and the grant shall be calculated at a rate of 20 percent of the amount of qualified

real property investments in excess of $450,000 in the case of the construction of a new building or facility. Grants shall be calculated at a rate of 20 percent of the amount of qualified real property investment in excess of $50,000 in the case of the rehabilitation or expansion of an existing building or facility. In the case where a grant is awarded based solely on a solar investment, the grant shall be calculated at a rate of 20 percent of the amount of total qualified real property investments made in solar installation. For such properties eligible for real property improvement grants made solely on the basis of solar installation investments of at least $50,000 but not more than $100,000, awards shall not exceed $1,000,000 in aggregate in any fiscal year."

Acts 2021, Sp. Sess. I, c. 402, cl. 2 provides: "That the provisions of this act shall become effective on January 1, 2022."

The 2020 Sp. Sess. I amendments.

The 2021 amendment by Sp. Sess. I, c. 402, effective January 1, 2022, in subsection A, inserted the definitions for "Minimum wage" and "Virginia minimum wage"; and in subsection C, deleted "federal" preceding "minimum wage" throughout and substituted "175" for "200" twice, "150" for "175" twice, and "125" for "150"; and inserted "or for businesses that are certified under regulations adopted by the Director of the Department of Small Business and Supplier Diversity pursuant to subdivision 8 of § 2.2-1606" in subdivision C 1.

§ 59.1-548. Enterprise zone real property investment grants.

Editor's note.

Acts 2020, c. 1289, as amended by Acts 2021, Sp. Sess. I, c. 552, Item 115, effective for the biennium ending June 30, 2022, provides: "Out of the amounts in this Item, $14,500,000 the first year and $14,750,000 the second year from the general fund shall be provided to carry out the provisions of §§ 59.1-547 and 59.1-548, Code of Virginia, related to the Enterprise Zone Grant Act. Notwithstanding the provisions of §§ 59.1-547 and 59.1-548, Code of Virginia, the department is authorized to prorate, with no payment of the unpaid portion of the grant necessary in the next fiscal year, the amount of awards each business receives to match the appropriation for this Item. Should actual grants awarded in each fiscal year be less than the amounts provided in this Item, the excess shall not revert to the general fund but shall be deposited to the Virginia Removal or Rehabilitation of Derelict Structures Fund for revitalization purposes. Consistent with the provisions of § 59.1-548, Code of Virginia, beginning

on January 1, 2019, the installation of solar panels shall be considered eligible investments for the purposes of the real property improvement grants, provided that such solar installation investment is in an amount of at least $50,000 and the grant shall be calculated at a rate of 20 percent of the amount of qualified real property investments in excess of $450,000 in the case of the construction of a new building or facility. Grants shall be calculated at a rate of 20 percent of the amount of qualified real property investment in excess of $50,000 in the case of the rehabilitation or expansion of an existing building or facility. In the case where a grant is awarded based solely on a solar investment, the grant shall be calculated at a rate of 20 percent of the amount of total qualified real property investments made in solar installation. For such properties eligible for real property improvement grants made solely on the basis of solar installation investments of at least $50,000 but not more than $100,000, awards shall not exceed $1,000,000 in aggregate in any fiscal year."

CHAPTER 50.

ELECTRONIC IDENTITY MANAGEMENT ACT.

§ 59.1-550. Definitions.

As used in this chapter, unless the context requires a different meaning:

"Attribute provider" means an entity, or a supplier, employee, or agent

thereof, that acts as the authoritative record of identifying information about an identity credential holder.

"Commonwealth identity management standards" means the minimum specifications and standards that must be included in an identity trust framework so as to define liability pursuant to this chapter that are set forth in guidance documents approved by the Secretary of Administration pursuant to Chapter 4.3 (§ 2.2-436 et seq.) of Title 2.2.

"Federated digital identity system" or *"federation"* means a digital identity system that (i) utilizes federated identity management to enable the portability of identity information across otherwise autonomous security domains; (ii) is compliant with the Commonwealth's identity management standards and with the provisions of the governing identity trust framework; (iii) has established identity, security, privacy, technology, and enforcement rules and policies adhered to by certified identity providers that are members of the federated digital identity system; (iv) includes as members federation administrators, federation operators, identity trust framework operators, and identity providers; and (v) allows, but does not require, relying parties to be members of the federated digital identity system in order to accept an identity credential issued by a certified identity provider to verify an identity credential holder's identity.

"Federated identity management" means a process that allows the conveyance of identity credentials and authentication information across digital identity systems through the use of a common set of policies, practices, and protocols for managing the identity of users and devices across security domains.

"Federation administrator" means a person or entity that certifies compliance with the Commonwealth's identity management standards by either a federation operator or an identity trust framework operator at the time of issuance of identity credentials, identity and entitlement attributes, or trustmarks.

"Federation operator" means the entity that (i) defines rule and policies for member parties to a federation; (ii) certifies identity and entitlement attribute providers to be members of and issue identity credentials pursuant to the federation; and (iii) evaluates participation in the federation to ensure compliance by members of the federation with its rules and policies, including the ability to request audits of participants for verification of compliance.

"Identity attribute" means identifying information associated with an identity credential holder.

"Identity credential" means the data, or the physical object upon which the data may reside, that an identity credential holder may present to verify or authenticate his identity in a digital or online transaction.

"Identity credential holder" means a person bound to or in possession of an identity credential who has agreed to the terms and conditions of the identity provider.

"Identity proofer" means a person or entity authorized to act as a representative of an identity provider in the confirmation of a potential identity credential holder's identification and identity attributes prior to issuing an identity credential to a person.

"Identity provider" means an entity, or a supplier, employee, or agent thereof, certified by an identity trust framework operator to provide identity credentials that may be used by an identity credential holder to assert his identity, or any related attributes, in a digital or online transaction. For purposes of this chapter, "identity provider" includes an attribute provider, an identity proofer, and any suppliers, employees, or agents thereof.

"Identity trust framework" means a digital identity system with established identity, security, privacy, technology, and enforcement rules and policies

adhered to by certified identity providers that are members of the identity trust framework. Members of an identity trust framework include identity trust framework operators and identity providers. Relying parties may be, but are not required to be, a member of an identity trust framework in order to accept an identity credential issued by a certified identity provider to verify an identity credential holder's identity.

"Identity trust framework operator" means the entity that (i) defines rules and policies for member parties to an identity trust framework, (ii) certifies identity providers to be members of and issue identity credentials pursuant to the identity trust framework, and (iii) evaluates participation in the identity trust framework to ensure compliance by members of the identity trust framework with its rules and policies, including the ability to request audits of participants for verification of compliance.

"Relying party" is an individual or entity that relies on the validity of an identity credential or an associated trustmark.

"Trustmark" means a machine-readable official seal, authentication feature, certification, license, or logo that may be provided by an identity trust framework operator to certified identity providers within its identity trust framework or federation to signify that the identity provider complies with the written rules and policies of the identity trust framework or federation.

History.
2015, cc. 482, 483; 2020, cc. 736, 738.

The 2020 amendments.
The 2020 amendment by c. 736 inserted the definitions for "Federated digital identity system" or "federation," "Federated identity management," "Federation administrator," and "Federation operator" and in the definition for "Trustmark," inserted "or federation" twice.

The 2020 amendment by c. 738 substituted "Administration" for "Technology" in the definition for "Commonwealth identity management standards."

§ 59.1-551. Trustmark; warranty.

The use of a trustmark on an identity credential provides a warranty by the identity provider that the written rules and policies of the identity trust framework or federation of which it is a member have been adhered to in asserting the identity and any related attributes contained on the identity credential. No other warranties are applicable unless expressly provided by the identity provider.

History.
2015, cc. 482, 483; 2020, c. 736.

The 2020 amendments.
The 2020 amendment by c. 736 inserted "or federation" in the first sentence.

§ 59.1-552. Establishment of liability; limitation of liability.

A. An identity trust framework operator, identity provider, federation administrator, or federation operator shall be liable if the issuance of an identity credential or assignment of an identity attribute, or a trustmark, is not in compliance with the Commonwealth's identity management standards in place at the time of issuance. Further, the identity trust framework operator or identity provider shall be liable for noncompliance with applicable terms of any contractual agreement with a contracting party and any written rules and policies of the identity trust framework or federation of which it is a member.

B. An identity trust framework operator, identity provider, federation administrator, or federation operator shall not be liable if the issuance of the identity credential or assignment of an identity attribute or a trustmark was in compliance with (i) the Commonwealth's identity management standards in place at the time of issuance or assignment, (ii) applicable terms of any contractual agreement with a contracting party, and (iii) any written rules and policies of the identity trust framework or federation of which it is a member, provided such identity trust framework operator or identity provider did not commit an act or omission that constitutes gross negligence or willful misconduct. An identity trust framework operator or identity provider shall not be liable for misuse of an identity credential by the identity credential holder or by any other person who misuses an identity credential.

History.
2015, cc. 482, 483; 2020, c. 736.

The 2020 amendments.
The 2020 amendment by c. 736, in subsection A, inserted "federation administrator, or federation operator" in the first sentence and "or federation" in the last sentence; in subsection B, inserted "federation administrator, or federation operator" in the introductory wording and "or federation" in clause (iii) in the first sentence; and made stylistic changes.

§ 59.1-553. Commercially reasonable security procedures for electronic fund transfers.

Use of an identity credential or identity attribute shall satisfy any requirement for a commercially reasonable security or attribution procedure in Title 8.4A, the Uniform Electronic Transactions Act (§ 59.1-479 et seq.), and the Uniform Computer Information Transactions Act (§ 59.1-501.1 et seq.), provided that the identity credential or identity attribute was issued or assigned in accordance with (i) the Commonwealth's identity management standards in place at the time of issuance or assignment, (ii) the terms of any contractual agreement, and (iii) any written rules and policies of the identity trust framework or federation of which the issuer is a member.

History.
2015, cc. 482, 483; 2020, c. 736.

The 2020 amendments.
The 2020 amendment by c. 736 inserted "or federation" in clause (iii).

§ 59.1-555. Sovereign immunity.

No provisions of this chapter nor any act or omission of a state, regional, or local governmental entity related to the issuance of electronic identity credentials or attributes or the administration or participation in an identity trust framework or federation related to the issuance of electronic identity credentials or attributes shall be deemed a waiver of sovereign immunity to which the governmental entity or its officers, employees, or agents are otherwise entitled.

History.
2015, cc. 482, 483; 2020, c. 736.

The 2020 amendments.
The 2020 amendment by c. 736 inserted "or federation."

CHAPTER 51.

FANTASY CONTESTS ACT.

§ 59.1-569. Fantasy contests conducted under this chapter not illegal gambling.

A. Nothing contained in Article 1 (§ 18.2-325 et seq.) of Chapter 8 of Title 18.2 shall be applicable to a fantasy contest conducted in accordance with this chapter. The award of any prize money for any fantasy contest shall not be deemed to be part of any gaming contract within the purview of § 11-14.

B. This section shall not apply to any sports betting or related activity that is lawful under Article 2 (§ 58.1-4030 et seq.) of Chapter 40 of Title 58.1, which shall be regulated pursuant to such chapter.

History.
2016, cc. 318, 703; 2020, cc. 1218, 1256.

Editor's note.
Acts 2020, cc. 1218 and 1256, cl. 2 provides: "That the Virginia Lottery Board (the Board) shall promulgate regulations implementing the provisions of this act. The Board's initial adoption of regulations shall be exempt from the Administrative Process Act (§ 2.2-4000 et seq. of the Code of Virginia), except that the Board shall provide an opportunity for public comment on the regulations prior to adoption. The Board shall complete work on such regulations no later than September 15, 2020."

The 2020 amendments.
The 2020 amendments by cc. 1218 and 1256 are identical, and added subsection B.

CHAPTER 52.

HUMANE COSMETICS ACT.

§ 59.1-571. Definitions.

As used in this chapter, unless the context requires a different meaning:

"Cosmetic" means any article intended to be rubbed, poured, sprinkled, or sprayed on, introduced into, or otherwise applied to the human body or any part thereof for cleansing, beautifying, promoting attractiveness, or altering the appearance, including, without limitation, personal hygiene products such as deodorant, shampoo, or conditioner.

"Cosmetic animal testing" means the internal or external application of a cosmetic, either in its final form or any ingredient thereof, to the skin, eyes, or other body part of a live, nonhuman vertebrate. Merely reviewing, assessing, or retaining evidence from a cosmetic animal test shall not constitute developing or manufacturing using cosmetic animal testing for purposes of this chapter.

"Cosmetics manufacturer" means any person whose name appears on the label of a cosmetic product pursuant to the requirements of 21 C.F.R. § 701.12.

"Ingredient" has the meaning ascribed to it in 21 C.F.R. § 700.3(e).

118

History.
2021, Sp. Sess. I, cc. 113, 114.

Effective date.
This chapter is effective July 1, 2021.

§ 59.1-572. Prohibited conduct.

A. Except as provided in subsection B, no cosmetics manufacturer shall:

1. Conduct or contract for cosmetic animal testing that occurs in the Commonwealth on or after January 1, 2022;

2. Manufacture or import for profit into the Commonwealth any cosmetic or ingredient thereof, if the cosmetics manufacturer knew or reasonably should have known that the cosmetic or any component thereof was developed or manufactured using cosmetic animal testing that was conducted on or after January 1, 2022; or

3. Beginning July 1, 2022, sell or offer for sale within the Commonwealth any cosmetic, if the cosmetics manufacturer knows or reasonably should know that the cosmetic or any component thereof was developed or manufactured using cosmetic animal testing that was conducted on or after January 1, 2022.

B. The prohibitions in subsection A shall not apply to cosmetic animal testing or a cosmetic for which cosmetic animal testing was conducted, if the cosmetic animal testing was conducted:

1. To comply with a requirement of a federal or state regulatory agency and (i) the tested ingredient is in wide use and cannot be replaced by another ingredient capable of performing a similar function; (ii) a specific human health problem related to the cosmetic or ingredient is substantiated that justifies the need to conduct the cosmetic animal testing, and such testing is supported by a detailed research protocol proposed as the basis for the evaluation of the cosmetic or ingredient; and (iii) there does not exist a method of testing other than cosmetic animal testing that is accepted for the relevant purpose by the federal or state regulatory agency;

2. To comply with a requirement of a regulatory agency of a foreign jurisdiction, so long as no evidence derived from such testing was relied upon to substantiate the safety of a cosmetic sold within Virginia by the cosmetics manufacturer;

3. On any cosmetic or cosmetic ingredient subject to the requirements of Subchapter V of the Federal Food, Drug, and Cosmetic Act (21 U.S.C. § 351 et seq.); or

4. Pursuant to a requirement of a federal, state, or foreign regulatory agency for a purpose unrelated to cosmetics, provided that either no evidence derived from such testing was relied upon to substantiate the safety of the cosmetic or there is (i) documented evidence of a noncosmetic intent of the test and (ii) a history of use of the ingredient outside of cosmetics for at least 12 months prior to such reliance.

History.
2021, Sp. Sess. I, cc. 113, 114.

Effective date.
This section is effective July 1, 2021.

§ 59.1-573. Civil penalties.

Any person who violates any provision of this chapter is subject to a civil penalty of $5,000 and an additional $1,000 for each day the violation continues. Such penalty shall be collected by the Attorney General and the proceeds shall be deposited into the Literary Fund.

History.
2021, Sp. Sess. I, cc. 113, 114.

Effective date.
This section is effective July 1, 2021.

§ 59.1-574. Local regulation prohibited unless identical.

No locality may establish or continue any regulation relating to cosmetic animal testing that is not identical to the provisions set forth in this chapter.

History.
2021, Sp. Sess. I, cc. 113, 114.

Effective date.
This section is effective July 1, 2021.

CHAPTER 53.

CONSUMER DATA PROTECTION ACT.

§ 59.1-575. Definitions.

As used in this chapter, unless the context requires a different meaning:

"Affiliate" means a legal entity that controls, is controlled by, or is under common control with another legal entity or shares common branding with another legal entity. For the purposes of this definition, "control" or "controlled" means (i) ownership of, or the power to vote, more than 50 percent of the outstanding shares of any class of voting security of a company; (ii) control in any manner over the election of a majority of the directors or of individuals exercising similar functions; or (iii) the power to exercise controlling influence over the management of a company.

"Authenticate" means verifying through reasonable means that the consumer, entitled to exercise his consumer rights in § 59.1-577, is the same consumer exercising such consumer rights with respect to the personal data at issue.

"Biometric data" means data generated by automatic measurements of an individual's biological characteristics, such as a fingerprint, voiceprint, eye retinas, irises, or other unique biological patterns or characteristics that is used to identify a specific individual. "Biometric data" does not include a physical or digital photograph, a video or audio recording or data generated therefrom, or information collected, used, or stored for health care treatment, payment, or operations under HIPAA.

"Business associate" means the same meaning as the term established by HIPAA.

"Child" means any natural person younger than 13 years of age.

"Consent" means a clear affirmative act signifying a consumer's freely given, specific, informed, and unambiguous agreement to process personal data relating to the consumer. Consent may include a written statement, including a statement written by electronic means, or any other unambiguous affirmative action.

"Consumer" means a natural person who is a resident of the Commonwealth acting only in an individual or household context. It does not include a natural person acting in a commercial or employment context.

120

"Controller" means the natural or legal person that, alone or jointly with others, determines the purpose and means of processing personal data.

"Covered entity" means the same as the term is established by HIPAA.

"Decisions that produce legal or similarly significant effects concerning a consumer" means a decision made by the controller that results in the provision or denial by the controller of financial and lending services, housing, insurance, education enrollment, criminal justice, employment opportunities, health care services, or access to basic necessities, such as food and water.

"De-identified data" means data that cannot reasonably be linked to an identified or identifiable natural person, or a device linked to such person. A controller that possesses "de-identified data" shall comply with the requirements of subsection A of § 59.1-581.

"Health record" means the same as that term is defined in § 32.1-127.1:03.

"Health care provider" means the same as that term is defined in § 32.1-276.3.

"HIPAA" means the federal Health Insurance Portability and Accountability Act of 1996 (42 U.S.C. § 1320d et seq.).

"Identified or identifiable natural person" means a person who can be readily identified, directly or indirectly.

"Institution of higher education" means a public institution and private institution of higher education, as those terms are defined in § 23.1-100.

"Nonprofit organization" means any corporation organized under the Virginia Nonstock Corporation Act (§ 13.1-801 et seq.) or any organization exempt from taxation under § 501(c)(3), 501(c)(6), or 501(c)(12) of the Internal Revenue Code, any political organization, any organization exempt from taxation under § 501(c)(4) of the Internal Revenue Code that is identified in § 52-41, and any subsidiary or affiliate of entities organized pursuant to Chapter 9.1 (§ 56-231.15 et seq.) of Title 56.

"Personal data" means any information that is linked or reasonably linkable to an identified or identifiable natural person. "Personal data" does not include de-identified data or publicly available information.

"Political organization" means a party, committee, association, fund, or other organization, whether or not incorporated, organized and operated primarily for the purpose of influencing or attempting to influence the selection, nomination, election, or appointment of any individual to any federal, state, or local public office or office in a political organization or the election of a presidential/vice-presidential elector, whether or not such individual or elector is selected, nominated, elected, or appointed.

"Precise geolocation data" means information derived from technology, including but not limited to global positioning system level latitude and longitude coordinates or other mechanisms, that directly identifies the specific location of a natural person with precision and accuracy within a radius of 1,750 feet. "Precise geolocation data" does not include the content of communications or any data generated by or connected to advanced utility metering infrastructure systems or equipment for use by a utility.

"Process" or *"processing"* means any operation or set of operations performed, whether by manual or automated means, on personal data or on sets of personal data, such as the collection, use, storage, disclosure, analysis, deletion, or modification of personal data.

"Processor" means a natural or legal entity that processes personal data on behalf of a controller.

"Profiling" means any form of automated processing performed on personal data to evaluate, analyze, or predict personal aspects related to an identified or identifiable natural person's economic situation, health, personal preferences, interests, reliability, behavior, location, or movements.

"Protected health information" means the same as the term is established by HIPAA.

"Pseudonymous data" means personal data that cannot be attributed to a specific natural person without the use of additional information, provided that such additional information is kept separately and is subject to appropriate technical and organizational measures to ensure that the personal data is not attributed to an identified or identifiable natural person.

"Publicly available information" means information that is lawfully made available through federal, state, or local government records, or information that a business has a reasonable basis to believe is lawfully made available to the general public through widely distributed media, by the consumer, or by a person to whom the consumer has disclosed the information, unless the consumer has restricted the information to a specific audience.

"Sale of personal data" means the exchange of personal data for monetary consideration by the controller to a third party. "Sale of personal data" does not include:

1. The disclosure of personal data to a processor that processes the personal data on behalf of the controller;

2. The disclosure of personal data to a third party for purposes of providing a product or service requested by the consumer;

3. The disclosure or transfer of personal data to an affiliate of the controller;

4. The disclosure of information that the consumer (i) intentionally made available to the general public via a channel of mass media and (ii) did not restrict to a specific audience; or

5. The disclosure or transfer of personal data to a third party as an asset that is part of a merger, acquisition, bankruptcy, or other transaction in which the third party assumes control of all or part of the controller's assets.

"Sensitive data" means a category of personal data that includes:

1. Personal data revealing racial or ethnic origin, religious beliefs, mental or physical health diagnosis, sexual orientation, or citizenship or immigration status;

2. The processing of genetic or biometric data for the purpose of uniquely identifying a natural person;

3. The personal data collected from a known child; or

4. Precise geolocation data.

"State agency" means the same as that term is defined in § 2.2-307.

"Targeted advertising" means displaying advertisements to a consumer where the advertisement is selected based on personal data obtained from that consumer's activities over time and across nonaffiliated websites or online applications to predict such consumer's preferences or interests. "Targeted advertising" does not include:

1. Advertisements based on activities within a controller's own websites or online applications;

2. Advertisements based on the context of a consumer's current search query, visit to a website, or online application;

3. Advertisements directed to a consumer in response to the consumer's request for information or feedback; or

4. Processing personal data processed solely for measuring or reporting advertising performance, reach, or frequency.

"Third party" means a natural or legal person, public authority, agency, or body other than the consumer, controller, processor, or an affiliate of the processor or the controller.

History.
2021, Sp. Sess. I, cc. 35, 36; 2022, cc. 451, 452.

The numbers of this chapter and section were assigned by the Virginia Code Commission, the numbers in the 2021 Sp. Sess. I acts having been Chapter 52 (§ 59.1-571 et seq.).

Editor's note.

Acts 2021, Sp. Sess. I, cc. 35 and 36, cl. 2 provides: "The Chairman of the Joint Commission on Technology and Science shall create a work group composed of the Secretary of Commerce and Trade, the Secretary of Administration, the Attorney General, the Chairman of the Senate Committee on Transportation, representatives of businesses who control or process personal data of at least 100,000 persons, and consumer rights advocates. The work group shall review the provisions of this act and issues related to its implementation. The Chairman of the Joint Commission on Technology and Science shall submit the work group's findings, best practices, and recommendations regarding the implementation of this act to the Chairmen of the Senate Committee on General Laws and Technology and the House Committee on Communications, Technology and Innovation no later than November 1, 2021."

Acts 2021, Sp. Sess. I, cc. 35 and 36, cl. 3 provides: "That any reference to federal law or statute in this act shall be deemed to include any accompanying rules or regulations or exemptions thereto. Further, this enactment is declaratory of existing law."

Acts 2021, Sp. Sess. I, cc. 35 and 36, cl. 4 provides: "That the provisions of the first and third enactments of this act shall become effective on January 1, 2023."

The 2022 amendments.

The 2022 amendments by cc. 451 and 452 are identical, and deleted the definition of "Fund," which read: "'Fund' means the Consumer Privacy Fund established pursuant to § 59.1-585"; in the definition of "Nonprofit organization," inserted "any political organization, any organization exempt from taxation under § 501(c)(4) of the Internal Revenue Code that is identified in § 52-41" and substituted "subsidiary or affiliate" for "subsidiaries and affiliates"; added the definition of "Political organization"; and made a stylistic change.

§ 59.1-576. Scope; exemptions.

A. This chapter applies to persons that conduct business in the Commonwealth or produce products or services that are targeted to residents of the Commonwealth and that (i) during a calendar year, control or process personal data of at least 100,000 consumers or (ii) control or process personal data of at least 25,000 consumers and derive over 50 percent of gross revenue from the sale of personal data.

B. This chapter shall not apply to any (i) body, authority, board, bureau, commission, district, or agency of the Commonwealth or of any political subdivision of the Commonwealth; (ii) financial institution or data subject to Title V of the federal Gramm-Leach-Bliley Act (15 U.S.C. § 6801 et seq.); (iii) covered entity or business associate governed by the privacy, security, and breach notification rules issued by the U.S. Department of Health and Human Services, 45 C.F.R. Parts 160 and 164 established pursuant to HIPAA, and the Health Information Technology for Economic and Clinical Health Act (P.L. 111-5); (iv) nonprofit organization; or (v) institution of higher education.

C. The following information and data is exempt from this chapter:

1. Protected health information under HIPAA;

2. Health records for purposes of Title 32.1;

3. Patient identifying information for purposes of 42 U.S.C. § 290dd-2;

4. Identifiable private information for purposes of the federal policy for the protection of human subjects under 45 C.F.R. Part 46; identifiable private information that is otherwise information collected as part of human subjects research pursuant to the good clinical practice guidelines issued by The International Council for Harmonisation of Technical Requirements for Pharmaceuticals for Human Use; the protection of human subjects under 21 C.F.R. Parts 6, 50, and 56, or personal data used or shared in research conducted in accordance with the requirements set forth in this chapter, or other research conducted in accordance with applicable law;

5. Information and documents created for purposes of the federal Health Care Quality Improvement Act of 1986 (42 U.S.C. § 11101 et seq.);

6. Patient safety work product for purposes of the federal Patient Safety and Quality Improvement Act (42 U.S.C. § 299b-21 et seq.);

7. Information derived from any of the health care-related information listed in this subsection that is de-identified in accordance with the requirements for de-identification pursuant to HIPAA;

8. Information originating from, and intermingled to be indistinguishable with, or information treated in the same manner as information exempt under this subsection that is maintained by a covered entity or business associate as defined by HIPAA or a program or a qualified service organization as defined by 42 U.S.C. § 290dd-2;

9. Information used only for public health activities and purposes as authorized by HIPAA;

10. The collection, maintenance, disclosure, sale, communication, or use of any personal information bearing on a consumer's credit worthiness, credit standing, credit capacity, character, general reputation, personal characteristics, or mode of living by a consumer reporting agency or furnisher that provides information for use in a consumer report, and by a user of a consumer report, but only to the extent that such activity is regulated by and authorized under the federal Fair Credit Reporting Act (15 U.S.C. § 1681 et seq.);

11. Personal data collected, processed, sold, or disclosed in compliance with the federal Driver's Privacy Protection Act of 1994 (18 U.S.C. § 2721 et seq.);

12. Personal data regulated by the federal Family Educational Rights and Privacy Act (20 U.S.C. § 1232g et seq.);

13. Personal data collected, processed, sold, or disclosed in compliance with the federal Farm Credit Act (12 U.S.C. § 2001 et seq.); and

14. Data processed or maintained (i) in the course of an individual applying to, employed by, or acting as an agent or independent contractor of a controller, processor, or third party, to the extent that the data is collected and used within the context of that role; (ii) as the emergency contact information of an individual under this chapter used for emergency contact purposes; or (iii) that is necessary to retain to administer benefits for another individual relating to the individual under clause (i) and used for the purposes of administering those benefits.

D. Controllers and processors that comply with the verifiable parental consent requirements of the Children's Online Privacy Protection Act (15 U.S.C. § 6501 et seq.) shall be deemed compliant with any obligation to obtain parental consent under this chapter.

History.
2021, Sp. Sess. I, cc. 35, 36.

The number of this section was assigned by the Virginia Code Commission, the number in the 2021 Sp. Sess. I act having been § 59.1-572.

Editor's note.
Acts 2021, Sp. Sess. I, cc. 35 and 36, cl. 3 provides: "That any reference to federal law or statute in this act shall be deemed to include any accompanying rules or regulations or exemptions thereto. Further, this enactment is declaratory of existing law."

Acts 2021, Sp. Sess. I, cc. 35 and 36, cl. 4 provides: "That the provisions of the first and third enactments of this act shall become effective on January 1, 2023."

§ 59.1-577. Personal data rights; consumers.

A. A consumer may invoke the consumer rights authorized pursuant to this subsection at any time by submitting a request to a controller specifying the consumer rights the consumer wishes to invoke. A known child's parent or legal guardian may invoke such consumer rights on behalf of the child regarding processing personal data belonging to the known child. A controller shall comply with an authenticated consumer request to exercise the right:

1. To confirm whether or not a controller is processing the consumer's personal data and to access such personal data;

2. To correct inaccuracies in the consumer's personal data, taking into account the nature of the personal data and the purposes of the processing of the consumer's personal data;

3. To delete personal data provided by or obtained about the consumer;

4. To obtain a copy of the consumer's personal data that the consumer previously provided to the controller in a portable and, to the extent technically feasible, readily usable format that allows the consumer to transmit the data to another controller without hindrance, where the processing is carried out by automated means; and

5. To opt out of the processing of the personal data for purposes of (i) targeted advertising, (ii) the sale of personal data, or (iii) profiling in further-ance of decisions that produce legal or similarly significant effects concerning the consumer.

B. Except as otherwise provided in this chapter, a controller shall comply with a request by a consumer to exercise the consumer rights authorized pursuant to subsection A as follows:

1. A controller shall respond to the consumer without undue delay, but in all cases within 45 days of receipt of the request submitted pursuant to the methods described in subsection A. The response period may be extended once by 45 additional days when reasonably necessary, taking into account the complexity and number of the consumer's requests, so long as the controller informs the consumer of any such extension within the initial 45-day response period, together with the reason for the extension.

2. If a controller declines to take action regarding the consumer's request, the controller shall inform the consumer without undue delay, but in all cases and at the latest within 45 days of receipt of the request, of the justification for declining to take action and instructions for how to appeal the decision pursuant to subsection C.

3. Information provided in response to a consumer request shall be provided by a controller free of charge, up to twice annually per consumer. If requests from a consumer are manifestly unfounded, excessive, or repetitive, the controller may charge the consumer a reasonable fee to cover the administra-tive costs of complying with the request or decline to act on the request. The controller bears the burden of demonstrating the manifestly unfounded, excessive, or repetitive nature of the request.

4. If a controller is unable to authenticate the request using commercially reasonable efforts, the controller shall not be required to comply with a request to initiate an action under subsection A and may request that the consumer provide additional information reasonably necessary to authenticate the consumer and the consumer's request.

5. A controller that has obtained personal data about a consumer from a source other than the consumer shall be deemed in compliance with a consumer's request to delete such data pursuant to subdivision A 3 by either (i) retaining a record of the deletion request and the minimum data necessary for the purpose of ensuring the consumer's personal data remains deleted from the business's records and not using such retained data for any other purpose pursuant to the provisions of this chapter or (ii) opting the consumer out of the processing of such personal data for any purpose except for those exempted pursuant to the provisions of this chapter.

C. A controller shall establish a process for a consumer to appeal the controller's refusal to take action on a request within a reasonable period of time after the consumer's receipt of the decision pursuant to subdivision B 2. The appeal process shall be conspicuously available and similar to the process for submitting requests to initiate action pursuant to subsection A. Within 60 days of receipt of an appeal, a controller shall inform the consumer in writing of any action taken or not taken in response to the appeal, including a written explanation of the reasons for the decisions. If the appeal is denied, the controller shall also provide the consumer with an online mechanism, if available, or other method through which the consumer may contact the Attorney General to submit a complaint.

History.
2021, Sp. Sess. I, cc. 35, 36; 2022, c. 423.

The number of this section was assigned by the Virginia Code Commission, the number in the 2021 Sp. Sess. I act having been § 59.1-573.

Editor's note.
Acts 2021, Sp. Sess. I, cc. 35 and 36, cl. 4

provides: "That the provisions of the first and third enactments of this act shall become effective on January 1, 2023."

The 2022 amendments.
The 2022 amendments by c. 423 added subdivision B 5.

§ 59.1-578. Data controller responsibilities; transparency.

A. A controller shall:

1. Limit the collection of personal data to what is adequate, relevant, and reasonably necessary in relation to the purposes for which such data is processed, as disclosed to the consumer;

2. Except as otherwise provided in this chapter, not process personal data for purposes that are neither reasonably necessary to nor compatible with the disclosed purposes for which such personal data is processed, as disclosed to the consumer, unless the controller obtains the consumer's consent;

3. Establish, implement, and maintain reasonable administrative, technical, and physical data security practices to protect the confidentiality, integrity, and accessibility of personal data. Such data security practices shall be appropriate to the volume and nature of the personal data at issue;

4. Not process personal data in violation of state and federal laws that prohibit unlawful discrimination against consumers. A controller shall not discriminate against a consumer for exercising any of the consumer rights contained in this chapter, including denying goods or services, charging different prices or rates for goods or services, or providing a different level of quality of goods and services to the consumer. However, nothing in this subdivision shall be construed to require a controller to provide a product or service that requires the personal data of a consumer that the controller does not collect or maintain or to prohibit a controller from offering a different price, rate, level, quality, or selection of goods or services to a consumer, including offering goods or services for no fee, if the consumer has exercised his right to opt out pursuant to § 59.1-577 or the offer is related to a consumer's voluntary participation in a bona fide loyalty, rewards, premium features, discounts, or club card program; and

5. Not process sensitive data concerning a consumer without obtaining the consumer's consent, or, in the case of the processing of sensitive data concerning a known child, without processing such data in accordance with the federal Children's Online Privacy Protection Act (15 U.S.C. § 6501 et seq.).

B. Any provision of a contract or agreement of any kind that purports to waive or limit in any way consumer rights pursuant to § 59.1-577 shall be deemed contrary to public policy and shall be void and unenforceable.

C. Controllers shall provide consumers with a reasonably accessible, clear, and meaningful privacy notice that includes:

1. The categories of personal data processed by the controller;

2. The purpose for processing personal data;

3. How consumers may exercise their consumer rights pursuant § 59.1-577, including how a consumer may appeal a controller's decision with regard to the consumer's request;

4. The categories of personal data that the controller shares with third parties, if any; and

5. The categories of third parties, if any, with whom the controller shares personal data.

D. If a controller sells personal data to third parties or processes personal data for targeted advertising, the controller shall clearly and conspicuously disclose such processing, as well as the manner in which a consumer may exercise the right to opt out of such processing.

E. A controller shall establish, and shall describe in a privacy notice, one or more secure and reliable means for consumers to submit a request to exercise their consumer rights under this chapter. Such means shall take into account the ways in which consumers normally interact with the controller, the need for secure and reliable communication of such requests, and the ability of the controller to authenticate the identity of the consumer making the request. Controllers shall not require a consumer to create a new account in order to exercise consumer rights pursuant to § 59.1-577 but may require a consumer to use an existing account.

History.
2021, Sp. Sess. I, cc. 35, 36.

The number of this section was assigned by the Virginia Code Commission, the number in the 2021 Sp. Sess. I act having been § 59.1-574.

Editor's note.
Acts 2021, Sp. Sess. I, cc. 35 and 36, cl. 3 provides: "That any reference to federal law or statute in this act shall be deemed to include any accompanying rules or regulations or exemptions thereto. Further, this enactment is declaratory of existing law."

Acts 2021, Sp. Sess. I, cc. 35 and 36, cl. 4 provides: "That the provisions of the first and third enactments of this act shall become effective on January 1, 2023."

§ 59.1-579. Responsibility according to role; controller and processor.

A. A processor shall adhere to the instructions of a controller and shall assist the controller in meeting its obligations under this chapter. Such assistance shall include:

1. Taking into account the nature of processing and the information available to the processor, by appropriate technical and organizational measures, insofar as this is reasonably practicable, to fulfill the controller's obligation to respond to consumer rights requests pursuant to § 59.1-577.

2. Taking into account the nature of processing and the information available to the processor, by assisting the controller in meeting the controller's obligations in relation to the security of processing the personal data and in relation to the notification of a breach of security of the system of the processor pursuant to § 18.2-186.6 in order to meet the controller's obligations.

3. Providing necessary information to enable the controller to conduct and document data protection assessments pursuant to § 59.1-580.

B. A contract between a controller and a processor shall govern the processor's data processing procedures with respect to processing performed on behalf of the controller. The contract shall be binding and clearly set forth instructions for processing data, the nature and purpose of processing, the type of data subject to processing, the duration of processing, and the rights and obligations of both parties. The contract shall also include requirements that the processor shall:

1. Ensure that each person processing personal data is subject to a duty of confidentiality with respect to the data;

2. At the controller's direction, delete or return all personal data to the controller as requested at the end of the provision of services, unless retention of the personal data is required by law;

3. Upon the reasonable request of the controller, make available to the controller all information in its possession necessary to demonstrate the processor's compliance with the obligations in this chapter;

4. Allow, and cooperate with, reasonable assessments by the controller or the controller's designated assessor; alternatively, the processor may arrange for a qualified and independent assessor to conduct an assessment of the processor's policies and technical and organizational measures in support of the obligations under this chapter using an appropriate and accepted control standard or framework and assessment procedure for such assessments. The processor shall provide a report of such assessment to the controller upon request; and

5. Engage any subcontractor pursuant to a written contract in accordance with subsection C that requires the subcontractor to meet the obligations of the processor with respect to the personal data.

C. Nothing in this section shall be construed to relieve a controller or a processor from the liabilities imposed on it by virtue of its role in the processing relationship as defined by this chapter.

D. Determining whether a person is acting as a controller or processor with respect to a specific processing of data is a fact-based determination that depends upon the context in which personal data is to be processed. A processor that continues to adhere to a controller's instructions with respect to a specific processing of personal data remains a processor.

History.

2021, Sp. Sess. I, cc. 35, 36.

The number of this section was assigned by the Virginia Code Commission, the number in the 2021 Sp. Sess. I act having been § 59.1-575.

Editor's note.

Acts 2021, Sp. Sess. I, cc. 35 and 36, cl. 4 provides: "That the provisions of the first and third enactments of this act shall become effective on January 1, 2023."

§ 59.1-580. Data protection assessments.

A. A controller shall conduct and document a data protection assessment of each of the following processing activities involving personal data:

1. The processing of personal data for purposes of targeted advertising;

2. The sale of personal data;

3. The processing of personal data for purposes of profiling, where such profiling presents a reasonably foreseeable risk of (i) unfair or deceptive treatment of, or unlawful disparate impact on, consumers; (ii) financial, physical, or reputational injury to consumers; (iii) a physical or other intrusion upon the solitude or seclusion, or the private affairs or concerns, of consumers, where such intrusion would be offensive to a reasonable person; or (iv) other substantial injury to consumers;

4. The processing of sensitive data; and

5. Any processing activities involving personal data that present a heightened risk of harm to consumers.

B. Data protection assessments conducted pursuant to subsection A shall identify and weigh the benefits that may flow, directly and indirectly, from the processing to the controller, the consumer, other stakeholders, and the public against the potential risks to the rights of the consumer associated with such processing, as mitigated by safeguards that can be employed by the controller to reduce such risks. The use of de-identified data and the reasonable expectations of consumers, as well as the context of the processing and the relationship between the controller and the consumer whose personal data will be processed, shall be factored into this assessment by the controller.

C. The Attorney General may request, pursuant to a civil investigative demand, that a controller disclose any data protection assessment that is relevant to an investigation conducted by the Attorney General, and the controller shall make the data protection assessment available to the Attorney General. The Attorney General may evaluate the data protection assessment for compliance with the responsibilities set forth in § 59.1-578. Data protection assessments shall be confidential and exempt from public inspection and copying under the Virginia Freedom of Information Act (§ 2.2-3700 et seq.). The disclosure of a data protection assessment pursuant to a request from the Attorney General shall not constitute a waiver of attorney-client privilege or work product protection with respect to the assessment and any information contained in the assessment.

D. A single data protection assessment may address a comparable set of processing operations that include similar activities.

E. Data protection assessments conducted by a controller for the purpose of compliance with other laws or regulations may comply under this section if the assessments have a reasonably comparable scope and effect.

F. Data protection assessment requirements shall apply to processing activities created or generated after January 1, 2023, and are not retroactive.

History.
2021, Sp. Sess. I, cc. 35, 36.

The number of this section was assigned by the Virginia Code Commission, the number in the 2021 Sp. Sess. I act having been § 59.1-576.

Editor's note.
Acts 2021, Sp. Sess. I, cc. 35 and 36, cl. 4 provides: "That the provisions of the first and third enactments of this act shall become effective on January 1, 2023."

§ 59.1-581. Processing de-identified data; exemptions.

A. The controller in possession of de-identified data shall:

1. Take reasonable measures to ensure that the data cannot be associated with a natural person;

2. Publicly commit to maintaining and using de-identified data without attempting to re-identify the data; and

3. Contractually obligate any recipients of the de-identified data to comply with all provisions of this chapter.

B. Nothing in this chapter shall be construed to (i) require a controller or processor to re-identify de-identified data or pseudonymous data or (ii) maintain data in identifiable form, or collect, obtain, retain, or access any data or technology, in order to be capable of associating an authenticated consumer request with personal data.

C. Nothing in this chapter shall be construed to require a controller or processor to comply with an authenticated consumer rights request, pursuant to § 59.1-577, if all of the following are true:

1. The controller is not reasonably capable of associating the request with the personal data or it would be unreasonably burdensome for the controller to associate the request with the personal data;

2. The controller does not use the personal data to recognize or respond to the specific consumer who is the subject of the personal data, or associate the personal data with other personal data about the same specific consumer; and

3. The controller does not sell the personal data to any third party or otherwise voluntarily disclose the personal data to any third party other than a processor, except as otherwise permitted in this section.

D. The consumer rights contained in subdivisions A 1 through 4 of § 59.1-577 and § 59.1-578 shall not apply to pseudonymous data in cases where the controller is able to demonstrate any information necessary to identify the consumer is kept separately and is subject to effective technical and organizational controls that prevent the controller from accessing such information.

E. A controller that discloses pseudonymous data or de-identified data shall exercise reasonable oversight to monitor compliance with any contractual commitments to which the pseudonymous data or de-identified data is subject and shall take appropriate steps to address any breaches of those contractual commitments.

History.
2021, Sp. Sess. I, cc. 35, 36.

The number of this section was assigned by the Virginia Code Commission, the number in the 2021 Sp. Sess. I act having been § 59.1-577.

Editor's note.
Acts 2021, Sp. Sess. I, cc. 35 and 36, cl. 4 provides: "That the provisions of the first and third enactments of this act shall become effective on January 1, 2023."

§ 59.1-582. Limitations.

A. Nothing in this chapter shall be construed to restrict a controller's or processor's ability to:

1. Comply with federal, state, or local laws, rules, or regulations;

2. Comply with a civil, criminal, or regulatory inquiry, investigation, subpoena, or summons by federal, state, local, or other governmental authorities;

3. Cooperate with law-enforcement agencies concerning conduct or activity that the controller or processor reasonably and in good faith believes may violate federal, state, or local laws, rules, or regulations;

4. Investigate, establish, exercise, prepare for, or defend legal claims;

5. Provide a product or service specifically requested by a consumer, perform a contract to which the consumer is a party, including fulfilling the terms of a written warranty, or take steps at the request of the consumer prior to entering into a contract;

6. Take immediate steps to protect an interest that is essential for the life or physical safety of the consumer or of another natural person, and where the processing cannot be manifestly based on another legal basis;

7. Prevent, detect, protect against, or respond to security incidents, identity theft, fraud, harassment, malicious or deceptive activities, or any illegal activity; preserve the integrity or security of systems; or investigate, report, or prosecute those responsible for any such action;

8. Engage in public or peer-reviewed scientific or statistical research in the public interest that adheres to all other applicable ethics and privacy laws and is approved, monitored, and governed by an institutional review board, or similar independent oversight entities that determine: (i) if the deletion of the information is likely to provide substantial benefits that do not exclusively accrue to the controller; (ii) the expected benefits of the research outweigh the privacy risks; and (iii) if the controller has implemented reasonable safeguards to mitigate privacy risks associated with research, including any risks associated with reidentification; or

9. Assist another controller, processor, or third party with any of the obligations under this subsection.

B. The obligations imposed on controllers or processors under this chapter shall not restrict a controller's or processor's ability to collect, use, or retain data to:

1. Conduct internal research to develop, improve, or repair products, services, or technology;

2. Effectuate a product recall;

3. Identify and repair technical errors that impair existing or intended functionality; or

4. Perform internal operations that are reasonably aligned with the expectations of the consumer or reasonably anticipated based on the consumer's existing relationship with the controller or are otherwise compatible with processing data in furtherance of the provision of a product or service specifically requested by a consumer or the performance of a contract to which the consumer is a party.

C. The obligations imposed on controllers or processors under this chapter shall not apply where compliance by the controller or processor with this chapter would violate an evidentiary privilege under the laws of the Commonwealth. Nothing in this chapter shall be construed to prevent a controller or processor from providing personal data concerning a consumer to a person covered by an evidentiary privilege under the laws of the Commonwealth as part of a privileged communication.

D. A controller or processor that discloses personal data to a third-party controller or processor, in compliance with the requirements of this chapter, is not in violation of this chapter if the third-party controller or processor that receives and processes such personal data is in violation of this chapter, provided that, at the time of disclosing the personal data, the disclosing controller or processor did not have actual knowledge that the recipient intended to commit a violation. A third-party controller or processor receiving personal data from a controller or processor in compliance with the requirements of this chapter is likewise not in violation of this chapter for the transgressions of the controller or processor from which it receives such personal data.

E. Nothing in this chapter shall be construed as an obligation imposed on controllers and processors that adversely affects the rights or freedoms of any persons, such as exercising the right of free speech pursuant to the First Amendment to the United States Constitution, or applies to the processing of personal data by a person in the course of a purely personal or household activity.

F. Personal data processed by a controller pursuant to this section shall not be processed for any purpose other than those expressly listed in this section unless otherwise allowed by this chapter. Personal data processed by a controller pursuant to this section may be processed to the extent that such processing is:

1. Reasonably necessary and proportionate to the purposes listed in this section; and

2. Adequate, relevant, and limited to what is necessary in relation to the specific purposes listed in this section. Personal data collected, used, or retained pursuant to subsection B shall, where applicable, take into account the nature and purpose or purposes of such collection, use, or retention. Such data shall be subject to reasonable administrative, technical, and physical measures to protect the confidentiality, integrity, and accessibility of the personal data and to reduce reasonably foreseeable risks of harm to consumers relating to such collection, use, or retention of personal data.

G. If a controller processes personal data pursuant to an exemption in this section, the controller bears the burden of demonstrating that such processing qualifies for the exemption and complies with the requirements in subsection F.

H. Processing personal data for the purposes expressly identified in subdivisions A 1 through 9 shall not solely make an entity a controller with respect to such processing.

History.
2021, Sp. Sess. I, cc. 35, 36.

The number of this section was assigned by the Virginia Code Commission, the number in the 2021 Sp. Sess. I act having been § 59.1-578.

Editor's note.
Acts 2021, Sp. Sess. I, cc. 35 and 36, cl. 4 provides: "That the provisions of the first and third enactments of this act shall become effective on January 1, 2023."

§ 59.1-583. Investigative authority.

Whenever the Attorney General has reasonable cause to believe that any person has engaged in, is engaging in, or is about to engage in any violation of this chapter, the Attorney General is empowered to issue a civil investigative demand. The provisions of § 59.1-9.10 shall apply mutatis mutandis to civil investigative demands issued under this section.

History.
2021, Sp. Sess. I, cc. 35, 36.

The number of this section was assigned by the Virginia Code Commission, the number in the 2021 Sp. Sess. I act having been § 59.1-579.

Editor's note.
Acts 2021, Sp. Sess. I, cc. 35 and 36, cl. 4 provides: "That the provisions of the first and third enactments of this act shall become effective on January 1, 2023."

§ 59.1-584. Enforcement; civil penalty; expenses.

A. The Attorney General shall have exclusive authority to enforce the provisions of this chapter.

B. Prior to initiating any action under this chapter, the Attorney General shall provide a controller or processor 30 days' written notice identifying the specific provisions of this chapter the Attorney General alleges have been or are being violated. If within the 30-day period the controller or processor cures the noticed violation and provides the Attorney General an express written statement that the alleged violations have been cured and that no further violations shall occur, no action shall be initiated against the controller or processor.

C. If a controller or processor continues to violate this chapter following the cure period in subsection B or breaches an express written statement provided to the Attorney General under that subsection, the Attorney General may initiate an action in the name of the Commonwealth and may seek an injunction to restrain any violations of this chapter and civil penalties of up to $7,500 for each violation under this chapter. All civil penalties, expenses, and attorney fees collected pursuant to this chapter shall be paid into the state treasury and credited to the Regulatory, Consumer Advocacy, Litigation, and Enforcement Revolving Trust Fund.

D. The Attorney General may recover reasonable expenses incurred in investigating and preparing the case, including attorney fees, in any action initiated under this chapter.

E. Nothing in this chapter shall be construed as providing the basis for, or be subject to, a private right of action for violations of this chapter or under any other law.

History.
2021, Sp. Sess. I, cc. 35, 36; 2022, cc. 451, 452.

The number of this section was assigned by the Virginia Code Commission, the number in the 2021 Sp. Sess. I act having been § 59.1-580.

Editor's note.
Acts 2021, Sp. Sess. I, cc. 35 and 36, cl. 4

provides: "That the provisions of the first and third enactments of this act shall become effective on January 1, 2023."

The 2022 amendments.

The 2022 amendments by cc. 451 and 452 are identical, and added the second sentence in subsection C.

§ 59.1-585. Repealed by Acts 2022, cc. 451 and 452, cl. 2.

CHAPTER 54.

FAIR FOOD DELIVERY ACT.

Section
59.1-586. Definitions.
59.1-587. Food delivery platform; agreements required.
59.1-588. Enforcement; penalties.

§ 59.1-586. Definitions.

As used in this chapter, unless the context requires a different meaning:

"Food delivery platform" means a person that operates a mobile application or other online service to act as an intermediary between consumers and multiple restaurants to submit food orders on behalf of a consumer to a participating restaurant and to arrange for the delivery of the order from the restaurant to the consumer.

"Restaurant" has the same meaning as provided in § 35.1-1 and excludes establishments listed in § 35.1-25.

History.
2021, Sp. Sess. I, c. 485.

The number of this chapter and section were assigned by the Virginia Code Commission, the numbers in the 2021 Sp. Sess. I act having been Chapter 52 (§ 59.1-571 et seq.).

Effective date.
This chapter is effective July 1, 2021.

§ 59.1-587. Food delivery platform; agreements required.

No food delivery platform shall submit an order on behalf of a consumer to a restaurant or arrange for the delivery of an order from a restaurant without first obtaining an agreement with the restaurant expressly authorizing the food delivery platform to submit orders to and deliver food prepared by the restaurant.

History.
2021, Sp. Sess. I, c. 485.

The number of this section was assigned by the Virginia Code Commission, the number in the 2021 Sp. Sess. I act having been 59.1-572.

Effective date.
This section is effective July 1, 2021.

§ 59.1-588. Enforcement; penalties.

Any violation of this chapter shall constitute a prohibited practice under the provisions of § 59.1-200 and shall be subject to any and all of the enforcement provisions of Chapter 17 (§ 59.1-196 et seq.).

History.
2021, Sp. Sess. I, c. 485.

The number of this section was assigned by the Virginia Code Commission, the number in the 2021 Sp. Sess. I act having been 59.1-573.

Effective date.
This section is effective July 1, 2021.

CHAPTER 55.

BENEFITS CONSORTIUM.

Section
59.1-589. Definitions.
59.1-590. Conditions for a benefits consortium.
59.1-591. Additional requirements.
59.1-592. Exemptions; license tax.

§ 59.1-589. Definitions.

As used in this chapter, unless the context requires a different meaning:

"Benefits consortium" means a trust that is a self-funded MEWA, as defined in § 38.2-3420, and that complies with the conditions set forth in § 59.1-590.

"ERISA" means the federal Employee Retirement Income Security Act of 1974, P.L. 93-406, 88 Stat. 829, as amended.

"Health benefit plan" has the same meaning as in § 38.2-3431.

"Member" means a person that is part of a sponsoring association, that conducts business operations within the Commonwealth, and that employs individuals who reside in the Commonwealth.

"Sponsoring association" has the same meaning as in § 38.2-3431 and includes any wholly owned subsidiary of a sponsoring association.

"Trust" means a trust that (i) is established to accept and hold assets of a health benefit plan in trust in accordance with the terms of the written trust document for the sole purposes of providing medical, prescription drug, dental, and vision benefits and defraying reasonable administrative costs of providing health benefits under a health benefit plan and (ii) complies with the conditions set forth in § 59.1-590.

History.
2022, cc. 404, 405.

§ 59.1-590. Conditions for a benefits consortium.

A. This section does not apply to a multiple employer welfare arrangement (MEWA) that offers or provides health benefit plans that are fully insured by an insurer authorized to transact the business of health insurance in the Commonwealth.

B. A trust shall constitute a benefits consortium and shall be authorized to sell or offer to sell health benefit plans to members of a sponsoring association in accordance with the provisions of this chapter if all of the following conditions are satisfied:

1. The trust shall be subject to (i) ERISA and U.S. Department of Labor regulations applicable to multiple employer welfare arrangements and (ii) the authority of the U.S. Department of Labor to enforce such law and regulations;

2. A Form M-1, Report for Multiple Employer Welfare Arrangements (MEWAs), for the applicable plan year shall be filed with the U.S. Department of Labor identifying the arrangement among the trust, sponsoring association, and health benefit plans offered through the trust as a multiple employer welfare arrangement;

3. The trust's organizational documents shall:

a. Provide that the trust is sponsored by the sponsoring association;

b. State that the purpose of the trust is to provide medical, prescription drug, dental, and vision benefits to participating employees of the sponsoring association or its members, and the dependents of those employees, through health benefit plans;

c. Provide that the funds of the trust are to be used for the benefit of participating employees, and the dependents of those employees, through self-funding of claims, the purchase of reinsurance, or a combination thereof, as determined by the trustee, and for defraying reasonable expenses of administering and operating the trust and any health benefit plan;

d. Limit participation in health benefit plans to participating employees of the sponsoring association and its members;

e. Provide for a board of trustees, composed of no fewer than five trustees, that has complete fiscal control over the arrangement and is responsible for all operations of the arrangement. The trustees selected for the board shall be owners, partners, officers, directors, or employees of one or more employers in the arrangement. A trustee or director may not be an owner, officer, or employee of the administrator or service company of the arrangement. The board shall have the authority to approve applications of association members for participation in the arrangement and to contract with a licensed administrator or service company to administer the day-to-day affairs of the arrangement;

f. Provide for the election of trustees to the board of trustees; and

g. Require the trustees to discharge their duties with respect to the trust in accordance with the fiduciary duties defined in ERISA;

4. Five or more members shall participate in one or more health benefit plans;

5. The trust shall establish and maintain reserves determined in accordance with sound actuarial principles and in compliance with all financial and solvency requirements imposed upon domestic self-funded MEWAs;

6. The trust shall purchase and maintain policies of specific, aggregate, and terminal excess insurance with retention levels determined in accordance with sound actuarial principles from insurers licensed to transact the business of insurance in the Commonwealth;

7. The trust shall secure one or more guarantees or standby letters of credit that:

a. Guarantee the payment of claims under the health benefit plan in an aggregate amount not less than the amount of the trust's annual aggregate excess insurance retention level minus (i) the annual premium assessments for the health benefit plans and (ii) the trust's net assets, which amount shall be the net of the trust's reasonable estimate of incurred but not reported claims; and

b. Have been issued by a qualified United States financial institution, as such term is used in subdivision 2 c of § 38.2-1316.4;

8. The trust shall purchase and maintain commercially reasonable fiduciary liability insurance;

9. The trust shall purchase and maintain a bond that satisfies the requirements of ERISA;

10. The trust is audited annually by an independent certified public accountant; and

11. The trust does not include in its name the words "insurance," "insurer," "underwriter," "mutual," or any other word or term or combination of words or terms that is uniquely descriptive of an insurance company or insurance business unless the context of the remaining words or terms clearly indicates that the entity is not an insurance company and is not transacting the business of insurance.

History.
2022, cc. 404, 405.

§ 59.1-591. Additional requirements.

A. The board of trustees established pursuant to subsection B of § 59.1-590 shall (i) operate any health benefit plans in accordance with the fiduciary duties defined in ERISA and (ii) have the power to make and collect special assessments against members and, if any assessment is not timely paid, to enforce collection of such assessment.

B. Each member shall be liable for his allocated share of the liabilities of the sponsoring association under a health benefit plan as determined by the board of trustees.

C. Health benefit plan documents shall have the following statement printed on the first page in size 14-point boldface type:

"This coverage is not insurance and is not offered through an insurance company. This coverage is not required to comply with certain federal market requirements for health insurance, nor is it required to comply with certain state laws for health insurance. Each member shall be liable for his allocated share of the liabilities of the sponsoring association under the health benefit plan as determined by the board of trustees. This means that each member may be responsible for paying an additional sum if the annual premiums present a deficit of funds for the trust. The trust's financial documents shall be available for public inspection at (insert website of where sponsoring association trust documents are posted)."

History.
2022, cc. 404, 405.

§ 59.1-592. Exemptions; license tax.

Notwithstanding any other provision of law, a benefits consortium or sponsoring association, by virtue of its sponsorship of a benefits consortium or any health benefit plan, shall not be subject to the following: (i) the provisions of Chapter 17 (§ 38.2-1700 et seq.) of Title 38.2 or any regulations adopted thereunder or (ii) any annual license tax levied pursuant to § 58.1-2501.

History.
2022, cc. 404, 405.

CHAPTER 56.

GENETIC DATA PRIVACY.

§ 59.1-593. Definitions.

As used in this chapter, unless the context requires a different meaning:

"Affirmative authorization" means an action that demonstrates an intentional decision by a consumer.

"Biological sample" means any material part of the human, discharge therefrom, or derivative thereof, such as tissue, blood, urine, or saliva, known to contain deoxyribonucleic acid (DNA).

"Consumer" means a natural person who is a resident of the Commonwealth.

"Deidentified data" means data that cannot be used to infer information about, or otherwise be linked to, a particular individual, provided that the direct-to-consumer genetic testing company (i) takes reasonable measures to ensure that such information cannot be associated with a consumer or household; (ii) publicly commits to maintain and use such information only in deidentified form and not to attempt to reidentify the information, except that the direct-to-consumer genetic testing company may attempt to reidentify the information solely for the purpose of determining whether its deidentification processes satisfy the requirements of this clause, provided that the direct-to-consumer genetic testing company does not use or disclose any information reidentified in this process and destroys the reidentified information upon completion of that assessment; and (iii) contractually obligates any recipients of the information to take reasonable measures to ensure that the information cannot be associated with a consumer or household and to commit to maintaining and using the information only in deidentified form and not to reidentify the information.

"Direct-to-consumer genetic testing company" means an entity that (i) offers consumer-initiated genetic testing products or services directly to a consumer or (ii) collects, uses, or analyzes genetic data that is collected or derived from a direct-to-consumer genetic testing product or service and is directly provided by a consumer. "Direct-to-consumer genetic testing company" does not include an entity when such entity is only engaged in collecting, using, or analyzing genetic data or biological samples in the context of research conducted in accordance with the (a) federal Common Rule, 45 C.F.R. Part 46; (b) International Conference on Harmonization Good Clinical Practice Guideline; or (c) U.S. Food and Drug Administration Policy for the Protection of Human Subjects, 21 C.F.R. Parts 50 and 56.

"Express consent" means a consumer's affirmative authorization to grant permission in response to a clear, meaningful, and prominent notice regarding the collection, use, maintenance, or disclosure of genetic data for a specific purpose.

"Genetic data" means any data, regardless of its format, that results from the analysis of a biological sample from a consumer, or from another element enabling equivalent information to be obtained, and concerns genetic material. Genetic material includes deoxyribonucleic acids (DNA), ribonucleic acids (RNA), genes, chromosomes, alleles, genomes, alterations, or modifications to DNA or RNA, and single nucleotide polymorphisms (SNPs). "Genetic data" includes uninterpreted data that results from the analysis of the biological sample and any information extrapolated, derived, or inferred therefrom. "Genetic data" does not include (i) deidentified data or (ii) data or a biological sample to the extent that data or a biological sample is collected, used, maintained, and disclosed exclusively for scientific research conducted by an investigator with an institution that holds an assurance with the U.S. Department of Health and Human Services pursuant to 45 C.F.R. Part 46, in compliance with all applicable federal and state laws and regulations for the protection of human subjects in research, including the Common Rule pursu-

137

ant to 45 C.F.R. Part 46, U.S. Food and Drug Administration regulations pursuant to 21 C.F.R. Parts 50 and 56, and the federal Family Educational Rights and Privacy Act, 20 U.S.C. § 1232g.

"Genetic testing" means any laboratory test of a biological sample from a consumer for the purpose of determining information concerning genetic material contained within the biological sample, or any information extrapolated, derived, or inferred therefrom.

"Service provider" means a sole proprietorship, partnership, limited liability company, corporation, association, or other legal entity that is organized or operated for the profit or financial benefit of its shareholders or other owners that is involved in (i) the collection, transportation, and analysis of the consumer's biological sample or extracted genetic material (a) on behalf of the direct-to-consumer genetic testing company or (b) on behalf of any other company that collects, uses, maintains, or discloses genetic data collected or derived from a direct-to-consumer genetic testing product or service or directly provided by a consumer or (ii) the delivery of the results of the analysis of the biological sample or genetic material.

History.
2023, c. 526.

§ 59.1-594. Exclusions.

This chapter shall not apply to any of the following:

1. Protected health information that is collected, maintained, used, or disclosed by a covered entity or business associate governed by the privacy, security, and data breach notification rules issued by the U.S. Department of Health and Human Services, 45 C.F.R. Parts 160 and 164, established pursuant to the federal Health Insurance Portability and Accountability Act of 1996, P.L. 104-191, and the federal Health Information Technology for Economic and Clinical Health Act, Title XIII of the federal American Recovery and Reinvestment Act of 2009, P.L. 111-5;

2. A covered entity governed by the privacy, security, and data breach notification rules issued by the U.S. Department of Health and Human Services, 45 C.F.R. Parts 160 and 164, established pursuant to the Health Insurance Portability and Accountability Act of 1996, P.L. 104-191, and the federal Health Information Technology for Economic and Clinical Health Act, Title XIII of the federal American Recovery and Reinvestment Act of 2009, P.L. 111-5, to the extent that the covered entity maintains, uses, and discloses genetic data in the same manner as protected health information, as described in subdivision 1;

3. A business associate of a covered entity governed by the privacy, security, and data breach notification rules issued by the U.S. Department of Health and Human Services, 45 C.F.R. Parts 160 and 164, established pursuant to the federal Health Insurance Portability and Accountability Act of 1996, P.L. 104-191, and the federal Health Information Technology for Economic and Clinical Health Act, Title XIII of the federal American Recovery and Reinvestment Act of 2009, P.L. 111-5, to the extent that the business associate maintains, uses, and discloses genetic data in the same manner as protected health information, as described in subdivision 1;

4. Scientific research or educational activities conducted by a public or private nonprofit institution of higher education that holds an assurance with the U.S. Department of Health and Human Services pursuant to 45 C.F.R. Part 46, to the extent that such scientific research and educational activities comply with all applicable federal and state laws and regulations for the

protection of human subjects in research, including the Common Rule pursuant to 45 C.F.R. Part 46, U.S. Food and Drug Administration regulations pursuant to 21 C.F.R. Parts 50 and 56, and the federal Family Educational Rights and Privacy Act, 20 U.S.C. § 1232g;

5. The newborn screening program established pursuant to Article 7 (§ 32.1-65 et seq.) of Chapter 2 of Title 32.1;

6. Tests conducted exclusively to diagnose whether an individual has a specific disease, to the extent that all persons involved in the conduct of the test maintain, use, and disclose genetic data in the same manner as protected health information, as described in subdivision 1; or

7. Genetic data used or maintained by an employer, or disclosed by an employee to an employer, to the extent that the use, maintenance, or disclosure of such data is necessary to comply with a local, state, or federal workplace health and safety ordinance, law, or regulation.

History.
2023, c. 526.

§ 59.1-595. Information to be made available to consumers.

A. Every direct-to-consumer genetic testing company shall provide to consumers:

1. A summary of the company's (i) policies and procedures related to the collection, use, maintenance, retention, disclosure, transfer, deletion, and security of and access to genetic data and (ii) privacy practices;

2. Information regarding the requirement for express consent for the collection, use, and disclosure of genetic data and the process for revoking express consent pursuant to § 59.1-596;

3. Notice that a consumer's deidentified genetic or phenotypic data may be shared with or disclosed to third parties for research purposes in accordance with 45 C.F.R. Part 46; and

4. Information about the process by which a consumer may file a complaint alleging a violation of this chapter.

B. Information required to be made available pursuant to subsection A shall be written in plain language and shall be provided to consumers together with any genetic testing product provided to consumers. Such information shall also be included on any website maintained by the direct-to-consumer genetic testing company in a manner that is easily accessible by the public.

History.
2023, c. 526.

§ 59.1-596. Express consent required; revocation of express consent.

A. Express consent required pursuant to this chapter requires a statement of the nature of the data collection, use, maintenance, or disclosure for which express consent is sought in plain and prominent language that an ordinary consumer would notice and understand and an affirmative authorization by the consumer granting permission in response to such statement. Express consent shall not be inferred from inaction.

B. Every direct-to-consumer genetic testing company shall obtain a consumer's express consent for the collection, use, and disclosure of the consumer's genetic data, including, at a minimum, separate and express consent for each of the following:

1. The use of genetic data collected through the genetic testing product or service offered to the consumer. Express consent for such use of genetic data

139

shall include a statement describing who will receive access to the genetic data, how such genetic data will be shared, and the purposes for which such data shall be collected, used, and disclosed;

2. The storage of a consumer's biological sample after the initial testing required by the consumer has been completed;

3. Each use of genetic data or the biological sample beyond the primary purpose of the genetic testing or service and inherent contextual uses;

4. Each transfer or disclosure of the consumer's genetic data or biological sample to a third party other than a service provider, including the name of the third party to which the consumer's genetic data or biological sample will be transferred or disclosed; and

5. Any marketing or facilitation of marketing to a consumer based on the consumer's genetic data or marketing or facilitation of marketing by a third party based on the consumer's having ordered, purchased, received, or used a genetic testing product or service, except that a direct-to-consumer genetic testing company shall not be required to obtain a consumer's express consent to marketing to the consumer on the company's own website or mobile application based on the consumer having ordered, purchased, received, or used a genetic testing product or service from that company if (i) the advertisement does not depend on any information specific to that consumer other than information regarding the product or service that the consumer ordered, purchased, received, or used; (ii) the placement of the advertisement does not result in disparate exposure to advertising content on the basis of the sex, race, color, religion, ancestry, national origin, disability, medical condition, genetic data, marital status, sexual orientation, citizenship, primary language, or immigration status of the consumer; and (iii) the advertisement of a third-party product or service is clearly labeled as advertising content, is accompanied by the name of the third party that has contributed to the placement of the advertisement, and, if applicable, indicates that the advertised product or service and claims regarding the product or service have not been vetted or endorsed by the direct-to-consumer genetic testing company.

C. Every direct-to-consumer genetic testing company shall provide a mechanism by which a consumer may revoke the express consent required pursuant to subsection B, which shall include an option for revocation of express consent through the primary medium through which the company communicates with consumers.

D. Upon revocation of the express consent required pursuant to subsection B by a consumer, a direct-to-consumer genetic testing company shall (i) honor such revocation of express consent as soon as is practicable but in all cases within 30 days of receipt of such revocation and (ii) destroy the consumer's biological sample within 30 days of receipt of revocation of the consumer's express consent to store such sample.

History.
2023, c. 526.

§ 59.1-597. Other requirements applicable to direct-to-consumer genetic testing companies.

Every direct-to-consumer genetic testing company shall:

1. Implement and maintain reasonable security procedures and practices to protect a consumer's genetic data against unauthorized access, destruction, use, modification, or disclosure; and

2. Develop procedures and practices to allow a consumer to easily (i) access the consumer's genetic data; (ii) delete the consumer's genetic data, except any data required by state or federal law to be retained by the direct-to-consumer

genetic testing company and any account the consumer may have created with the direct-to-consumer genetic testing company; and (iii) revoke express consent to storage of the consumer's biological sample and request destruction of such biological sample.

History.
2023, c. 526.

§ 59.1-598. Contracts with service providers.

A. Every direct-to-consumer genetic testing company that enters into a contract with a service provider shall prohibit the service provider from retaining, using, or disclosing the biological sample, extracted genetic material, genetic data, or any information regarding the identity of the consumer, including whether the consumer has solicited or received genetic testing, as applicable, for any purpose other than for the specific purpose of performing the services specified in the contract with the service provider for the business.

B. Every contract between a direct-to-consumer genetic testing company and a service provider shall include:

1. A provision prohibiting the service provider from retaining, using, or disclosing the biological sample, extracted genetic material, genetic data, or any information regarding the identity of the consumer, including whether the consumer has solicited or received genetic testing, as applicable, for a commercial purpose other than providing the services specified in the contract with the service provider with the business; and

2. A provision prohibiting the service provider from associating or combining the biological sample, extracted genetic material, genetic data, or any information regarding the identity of the consumer, including whether the consumer has solicited or received genetic testing, as applicable, with information the service provider has received from or on behalf of another person or has collected from its own interaction with consumers or as required by law.

History.
2023, c. 526.

§ 59.1-599. Certain disclosures of genetic data prohibited.

No direct-to-consumer genetic testing company shall disclose a consumer's genetic data to any entity that is responsible for administering or making decisions regarding health insurance, life insurance, long-term care insurance, disability insurance, or employment or any entity that provides advice to such an entity without the consumer's express consent.

History.
2023, c. 526.

§ 59.1-600. Discrimination prohibited.

No person or public entity shall discriminate against a consumer on the grounds that the consumer has exercised any of the rights granted by this chapter with regard to:

1. Providing or denying any good, service, or benefit to the consumer;

2. Charging any different price or rate for any good or service provided to the consumer, including through the use of discounts or other incentives or imposition of penalties;

3. Providing a different level or quality of goods, services, or benefits to the consumer;

4. Suggesting that the consumer will receive a different price or rate for goods, services, or benefits or a different level or quality of goods, services, or benefits; or

5. Considering the consumer's exercise of rights pursuant to this chapter as a basis or suspicion of criminal wrongdoing or unlawful conduct.

History.
  2023, c. 526.

§ 59.1-601. Enforcement; civil penalty.

A. The Attorney General shall have exclusive authority to enforce the provisions of this chapter.

B. Whenever the Attorney General has reasonable cause to believe that any person has engaged in, is engaging in, or is about to engage in any violation of this chapter, the Attorney General is empowered to issue a civil investigative demand. The provisions of § 59.1-9.10 shall apply mutatis mutandis to civil investigative demands issued pursuant to this subsection.

C. Notwithstanding any contrary provision of law, the Attorney General may cause an action to be brought in the appropriate circuit court in the name of the Commonwealth to enjoin any violation of this chapter. The circuit court having jurisdiction may enjoin such violation notwithstanding the existence of an adequate remedy at law. In any action brought pursuant to this subsection, it shall not be necessary that damages be proved.

D. Any person who violates the provisions of this chapter shall be subject to a civil penalty in an amount not to exceed $1,000 plus reasonable attorney fees, expenses, and court costs, as determined by the court. Any person who willfully violates the provisions of this chapter shall be subject to a civil penalty in an amount not less than $1,000 and not more than $10,000 plus reasonable attorney fees, expenses, and court costs, as determined by the court. Such civil penalties shall be paid into the Literary Fund.

E. Each violation of this chapter shall constitute a separate violation and shall be subject to any civil penalties imposed under this section.

History.
  2023, c. 526.

§ 59.1-602. Limitations.

A. The provisions of this chapter shall not reduce a direct-to-consumer genetic testing company's duties, obligations, requirements, or standards under any applicable state and federal laws for the protection of privacy and security.

B. In the event of a conflict between the provisions of this chapter and any other provision of law, the provisions of the law that afford the greatest protection for the right of privacy for consumers shall control.

C. Nothing in this chapter shall be construed to affect access to information made available to the public by the consumer.

History.
  2023, c. 526.

TITLE 60.2.

UNEMPLOYMENT COMPENSATION.

CHAPTER 1.

GENERAL PROVISIONS AND ADMINISTRATION.

Article 1. General Provisions.

Article 2. Administration.

ARTICLE 1.

GENERAL PROVISIONS.

§ 60.2-105. Publication and distribution of law, regulations, etc.

The Commission shall cause to be readily available for distribution to the public the text of this title, the Commission's regulations and general rules, its annual reports to the Governor, and any other material the Commission deems relevant and suitable. The Commission shall furnish these materials to any person upon request.

History.
Code 1950, § 60-31; 1968, c. 738, § 60.1-36; 1986, c. 480; 2023, cc. 624, 625.

The 2023 amendments.
The 2023 amendment by cc. 624 and 625 are identical, and substituted "readily available" for "printed".

ARTICLE 2.

ADMINISTRATION.

§ 60.2-109. Bond of Commissioner.

The Commissioner shall be bonded in accordance with § 2.2-1840, conditioned upon the faithful discharge of his duties.

History.
Code 1950, § 60-27; 1968, c. 738, § 60.1-32; 1986, c. 480; 2021, Sp. Sess. I, c. 152.

The 2021 Sp. Sess. I amendments.
The 2021 amendment by Sp. Sess. I, c. 152, effective July 1, 2021, rewrote the section, which formerly read: "The Commissioner shall, before entering upon the discharge of his duties, give bond payable to the Commonwealth, in a form approved by the Attorney General, in such penalty as shall be fixed by the Governor, with some surety or guaranty company duly authorized to do business in this Commonwealth. The bond shall be approved by the Governor as security and conditioned upon the faithful discharge of his duties. The premium of such bond shall be paid by the Commission, and the bond shall be filed with and preserved by the Comptroller."

§ 60.2-110. Repealed by Acts 2023, cc. 624 and 625, cl. 2, effective July 1, 2023.

Editor's note.
Former § 60.2-110, relating to State Job Service and Unemployment Insurance Services Division, was derived from Code 1950, § 60-28; 1968, c. 738, § 60.1-33; 1986, c. 480; 2022, c. 668.

§ 60.2-111. Duties and powers of Commission; reporting requirements.

A. It shall be the duty of the Commission to administer this title. The Commission may establish separate divisions as necessary to carry out the duties and powers prescribed by this section. It shall have power and authority to adopt, amend, or rescind such rules and regulations, to employ such persons, make such expenditures, require such reports, make such investigations, and take such other action, including the appointment of advisory groups, as it deems necessary or suitable to that end. Such rules and regulations shall be subject to the provisions of Chapter 40 (§ 2.2-4000 et seq.) of Title 2.2, except as to the subject matter of subdivisions 2 and 3 of § 60.2-515, which shall become effective in the manner prescribed by § 2.2-4103. The Commission shall determine its own organization and methods of procedure in accordance with provisions of this title, and shall have an official seal which shall be judicially noticed. In the discharge of the duties imposed by this title, the Commissioner shall have the authority to authorize any attorney employed by the Commission to have the power to issue subpoenas to compel the attendance of witnesses and the production of books, papers, correspondence, memoranda, and other records deemed necessary as evidence in connection with the investigation or adjudication of any disputed claim or the administration of this title. Any party who disputes such subpoena may file a motion to quash any subpoena issued pursuant to this section prior to the date production is required in a miscellaneous action in a circuit court for which such motion shall be given priority on the docket.

B. The Commission shall take all necessary steps to maintain a solvent trust fund financed through equitable employer taxes that provides temporary partial income replacement to involuntarily unemployed covered workers.

C. The Commission shall prepare an annual balance sheet of the moneys in the fund and in the Unemployment Trust Fund to the credit of the Commonwealth in which there shall be provided, if possible, a reserve against the liability in future years to pay benefits in excess of the then-current taxes. That reserve shall be set up by the Commission in accordance with accepted actuarial principles on the basis of statistics of employment, business activity, and other relevant factors for the longest possible period. Whenever the Commission believes that a change in tax or benefit rates is necessary to protect the solvency of the Fund, it shall promptly so inform the Governor and the General Assembly and make recommendations with respect thereto.

D. In preparing the annual balance sheet required by subsection C, the Commission shall regularly track metrics related to unemployment insurance benefits, establish a mechanism to help assess the adequacy of benefits, and examine metrics related to recipiency, average benefit levels, and benefit income replacement ratios. The annual balance sheet shall include the following calculations: (i) the average unemployment insurance benefit levels, (ii) the average income replacement of unemployment insurance benefits, and (iii) the recipiency rate for unemployment insurance benefits in the Commonwealth.

E. The Commission, as part of its biennial strategic plan submitted to the Department of Planning and Budget, shall develop and maintain a comprehensive unemployment insurance Resiliency Plan that describes specific actions the Commission will take, depending on the level of increase in unemployment insurance (UI) claims, to address staffing, communications, and other relevant aspects of operations to ensure continued efficient and effective administration of the UI program. The Resiliency Plan shall include proposed actions consistent with the following objectives to effectively prepare for periods of high unemployment:

1. Develop specific strategies or steps the Commission will take to modify staffing levels in response to incidents that increase UI program demand. These strategies or steps shall (i) include a staffing plan for varying levels of UI workload volume, (ii) cover several scenarios that may affect UI assistance services, (iii) explain how existing staff would be reallocated to high-priority functions in response to high demand, and (iv) describe how the Commission's hiring process will be streamlined to fill key vacant positions such as adjudication and appeals staff.

2. Develop specific strategies or steps the Commission will take to modify policies, procedures, or processes in response to high demands on its services.

3. Outline a strategy for clearly communicating key UI program changes to customers. This strategy shall indicate which staff will be responsible for different types of communications and include several communications goals, such as clearly conveying UI program and policy changes.

4. Outline a strategy for clearly communicating important UI information to Commission staff, the public, and the General Assembly.

5. Formalize a policy for prioritizing and assigning claims for adjudication during periods of high claims volume. This policy shall detail how prioritization may change in response to claims volume and state that the policy of the Commission is to generally prioritize resolving older claims before newer claims.

6. Identify other tactical actions to be taken to ensure the continuity of UI claims processing and customer service.

History.

Code 1950, § 60-29; 1968, c. 738, § 60.1-34; 1977, c. 445; 1984, c. 734; 1986, c. 480; 2022, cc. 716, 754; 2023, cc. 102, 103, 624, 625.

The 2022 amendments.

The 2022 amendment by cc. 716 and 754, effective April 27, 2022, are identical, and substituted "then-current taxes" for "then current taxes" in the first sentence of subsection B; and added subsections C and D.

The 2023 amendments.
The 2023 amendment by cc. 102 and 103 are identical, and added the last two sentences of subsection A.

The 2023 amendment by cc. 624 and 625 are identical, added the second sentence in subsection A; added subsection B; redesignated former subsections B and C as subsection C and D; substituted "subsection C" for "subsection D" in the first sentence of subsection D; and redesignated former subsection D as subsection E.

§ 60.2-113. Repealed by Acts 2023, cc. 624 and 625, cl. 2, effective July 1, 2023.

Editor's note.
Former § 60.2-113, relating to employment stabilization, was derived from Code 1950, § 60-34; 1968, c. 738, § 60.1-39; 1986, c. 480;

1989, c. 108; 1999, c. 357; 2004, cc.14, 154, 592; 2008, cc. 98, 222; 2011, cc. 594, 681; 2014, c. 815; 2015, cc. 275, 292; 2017, c. 20; 2018, c. 225.

§ 60.2-113.1. Repealed by Acts 2023, cc. 624 and 625, cl. 2, effective July 1, 2023.

Editor's note.
Former § 60.2-113.1, relating to veterans skills database, was derived from 2010, c. 277.

§ 60.2-114. Records and reports.

A. Each employing unit shall keep true and accurate work records, containing such information as the Commission may prescribe. Such records shall be open to inspection and be subject to being copied by the Commission or its authorized representatives at any reasonable time and as often as may be necessary. The Commission may require from any employing unit any sworn or unsworn reports, with respect to persons employed by it, which the Commission deems necessary for the effective administration of this title. Information thus obtained shall not be published or be open to public inspection, other than to public employees in the performance of their public duties, in any manner revealing the employing unit's identity, except as the Commissioner or his delegates deem appropriate, nor shall such information be used in any judicial or administrative proceeding other than one arising out of the provisions of this title; however, the Commission shall make its records about a claimant available to the Workers' Compensation Commission if it requests such records. However, any claimant at a hearing before an appeal tribunal or the Commission shall be supplied with information from such records to the extent necessary for the proper presentation of his claim. Notwithstanding other provisions of this section, the Commissioner, or his delegate, may, in his discretion, reveal information when such communication is not inconsistent with the proper administration of this title.

B. Notwithstanding the provisions of subsection A, the Commission shall, on a reimbursable basis, furnish wage and unemployment compensation information contained in its records to the Secretary of Health and Human Services and the Division of Child Support Enforcement of the Department of Social Services for their use as necessary for the purposes of the National Directory of New Hires established under § 453(i) of the Social Security Act.

C. Notwithstanding the provisions of subsection A, the Commission shall, upon written request, furnish:

1. Any agency or political subdivision of the Commonwealth, or its designated agent, such information as it may require for the purpose of collecting fines, penalties, and costs owed to the Commonwealth or its political subdivi-

sions. Such information shall not be published or used in any administrative or judicial proceeding, except in matters arising out of the collection of fines, penalties, and costs owed to the Commonwealth or its political subdivisions;

2. The Virginia Economic Development Partnership Authority such information as it may require to facilitate the administration and enforcement by the Authority of performance agreements with businesses that have received incentive awards. Any information provided to the Authority under this subdivision shall be confidential pursuant to 20 C.F.R. Part 603 and shall only be disclosed to members of the Authority who are public officials or employees of the Authority for the performance of their official duties. No public official or employee shall redisclose any confidential information obtained pursuant to this subdivision to nonlegislative citizen members of the Authority or to the public. Any information so provided shall be used by the Authority solely for the purpose of verifying employment and wage claims of those businesses that have received incentive awards; and

3. **(Expires January 1, 2027)** An arresting official such information as he may require to comply with the provisions of § 19.2-83.1. Such information shall not be published or used in any administrative or judicial proceeding.

D. Each employing unit shall report to the Virginia New Hire Reporting Center the employment of any newly hired employee in compliance with § 63.2-1946.

E. Any member or employee of the Commission and any member, employee, or agent of any agency or political subdivision of the Commonwealth who violates any provision of this section shall be guilty of a Class 2 misdemeanor.

History.
   Code 1950, § 60-35; 1968, c. 738, § 60.1-40; 1972, c. 764; 1986, c. 480; 1988, c. 766; 1993, cc. 246, 806; 1996, c. 220; 1997, c. 385; 1998, cc. 91, 108, 745; 2003, c. 721; 2013, c. 329; 2017, cc. 804, 824; 2023, cc. 282, 283.

Editor's note.
   Acts 2023, cc. 282 and 283, cl. 2 provides:

"That the provisions of subsection C of § 19.2-83.1 and § 60.2-114 of the Code of Virginia, as amended by this act, shall expire on July 1, 2027."

The 2023 amendments.
   The 2023 amendment by cc. 282 and 283 are identical, and added subdivision C 3; and made stylistic changes.

§ 60.2-116. Reciprocal agreements.

A. Subject to the approval of the Governor, the Commission is hereby authorized to enter into arrangements with the appropriate agencies of other states or the federal government whereby individuals performing services in this and other states for a single employing unit under circumstances not specifically provided for in §§ 60.2-212 through 60.2-219, or under similar provisions in the unemployment compensation laws of such other states, shall be deemed to be engaged in employment performed entirely within this Commonwealth or within one of such other states. Such arrangements may set forth terms whereby the potential right to benefits accumulated under the unemployment compensation laws of one or more states or under such a law of the federal government, or both, may constitute the basis for the payment of benefits through a single appropriate agency of any state under terms which the Commission finds will be fair and reasonable as to all affected interests and will not result in any substantial loss to the fund.

B. Subject to the approval of the Governor, the Commission is also authorized to enter into arrangements with the appropriate agencies of other states or of the federal government:

1. a. Whereby wages or services, upon the basis of which an individual may become entitled to benefits under the unemployment compensation law of

another state or of the federal government, shall be deemed to be wages for employment by employers for the purposes of §§ 60.2-602, 60.2-606, 60.2-607, 60.2-609, 60.2-610, 60.2-611, subdivision A 1 of § 60.2-612 and §§ 60.2-614 through 60.2-617, provided such other state agency or agency of the federal government has agreed to reimburse the fund for such portion of benefits paid under this title upon the basis of such wages or services as the Commission finds will be fair and reasonable as to all affected interests; and

b. Whereby the Commission will reimburse other state or federal agencies charged with the administration of unemployment compensation laws with such reasonable portion of benefits, paid under the law of any such other states or of the federal government upon the basis of employment or wages for employment by employers, as the Commission finds will be fair and reasonable as to all affected interests.

2. Reimbursements so payable under subdivision 1 b of this subsection shall be deemed to be benefits for the purposes of §§ 60.2-300 through 60.2-304, but no reimbursement so payable shall be charged against any employer's account for the purposes of §§ 60.2-526 through 60.2-531. The Commission is hereby authorized to make to other state or federal agencies and receive from such other state or federal agencies, reimbursements from or to the fund, in accordance with arrangements pursuant to this section.

C. Subject to the approval of the Governor, the Commission is also authorized to enter into arrangements with the appropriate agencies of other states or of the federal government:

1. Whereby the Commission may deduct, in accordance with the provisions of § 60.2-633, from unemployment benefits otherwise payable to an individual an amount equal to any overpayment made to such individual under an unemployment benefit program of the United States or of any other state, and not previously recovered. The amount so deducted shall be paid to the jurisdiction under whose program such overpayment was made and in accordance with the arrangement between the Commission and the jurisdiction.

2. Whereby the United States agrees to allow the Commission to recover from unemployment benefits otherwise payable to an individual under an unemployment benefit program of the United States any overpayments made by the Commission to such individual under this title and not previously recovered, in accordance with the same procedures that apply under subdivision 1 of this subsection.

3. The amendments made by this subsection shall apply to recoveries made on or after July 1, 1987, and shall apply with respect to overpayments made before, on, or after such date.

History.
Code 1950, § 60-40; 1968, c. 738, § 60.1-45; 1986, c. 480; 1987, c. 113; 2022, c. 668.

The 2022 amendments.
The 2022 amendment by c. 668, inserted "A" following "subdivision" in subdivision B 1 a.

§ 60.2-119. Criminal cases.

All criminal actions for violation of any provision of this title, or of any rules or regulations issued pursuant to this title, shall be prosecuted by the attorney for the Commonwealth of the county or city in which the offense, or a part thereof, was committed, except that the offense set out in § 60.2-518 or 60.2-632 shall be deemed to be committed and venue for the prosecution shall lie in the county or city wherein the statement, representation, or nondisclosure originates or, alternatively, is received by the Commission. However, if a defendant resides in this Commonwealth and the courthouse of the county or city in which he resides is more than 100 miles from the City of Richmond, venue for such prosecution shall lie in the city or county where he resides, and the offense shall be prosecuted by the attorney for the Commonwealth for the city or county where the defendant resides. If, in the opinion of the Commission, the prosecution should be conducted by the Office of the Attorney General, that office, upon the request of the Commission, shall have authority to conduct or supervise such prosecution.

History.
Code 1950, § 60-110; 1968, c. 738, § 60.1-127; 1972, c. 764; 1980, c. 674; 1986, c. 480; 2005, c. 105; 2023, cc. 82, 83.

The 2023 amendments.
The 2023 amendment by cc. 82 and 83 are identical, and added "originates or, alternatively" in the first sentence.

§ 60.2-121.1. Communications with parties.

In any action commenced under this title, the Commission may, if the party elects, send notices and other communications to such party through email or other electronic means. The Commission shall allow any party to change its election regarding receiving communications through electronic means. If an electronic notice is not successfully transmitted through electronic means, the Commission shall send a new notice by first-class mail to the party's alternative address on record.

History.
2021, Sp. Sess. I, c. 290.

Editor's note.
Acts 2021, Sp. Sess. I, c. 290, cl. 2 provides: "That the Virginia Employment Commission (Commission) shall report to the Commission on Unemployment Compensation and the Chairs of the House Committee on Labor and Commerce and the Senate Committee on Commerce and Labor (i) the number of unemployment insurance claimants who elect to receive their communications by email or other electronic means pursuant to § 60.2-121.1 of the Code of Virginia, as created by this act, and (ii) how such use of electronic communications impacts the Commission's operations no later than December 31, 2022."

Effective date.
This section is effective July 1, 2021.

§ 60.2-121.2. Electronic submission of information; payments.

A. Each employer subject to the provisions of this title shall submit claim-related forms, including separation information, using an electronic format as prescribed by the Commission, unless the employer has been granted a waiver by the Commission. An employer shall submit any other information related to a claim, as defined in § 60.2-528.1, at any time when requested by the Commission, to the Commission by electronic means, unless the employer has been granted a waiver by the Commission. The Commission may also require, at any time, that an employer submit unemployment insurance tax payments electronically, unless the employer has been granted a waiver by the Commission.

B. The Commission may grant a waiver to an employer from providing information or payments electronically pursuant to this section at any time. The Commission may grant a waiver only if the Commission finds that the electronic submission requirement creates an unreasonable burden on the employer. All requests for a waiver shall be submitted in writing.

History.
2022, cc. 716, 754.

§ 60.2-121.3. Unemployment Compensation Ombudsman; established; responsibilities.

A. The Commission shall create the Office of the Unemployment Compensation Ombudsman (the Office) and shall appoint an Unemployment Compensation Ombudsman to head the Office. The Unemployment Compensation Ombudsman shall provide neutral educational information and assistance to, shall protect the interests of, and shall ensure that due process is afforded to all persons seeking assistance in (i) appeals proceedings brought pursuant to Chapter 6 (§ 60.2-600 et seq.) and (ii) any other matter related to unemployment compensation under this title. Subject to annual appropriations, the Unemployment Compensation Ombudsman shall employ sufficient personnel to carry out the duties and powers prescribed by this section. The Unemployment Compensation Ombudsman and personnel of the Office shall carry out their duties with impartiality and shall not serve as an advocate for any person or provide legal advice.

B. The Unemployment Compensation Ombudsman shall maintain data on inquiries received related to the unemployment compensation process, the types of assistance requested, and actions taken and the disposition of each such matter. The Unemployment Compensation Ombudsman shall report information summarizing this data, including outcomes of individual cases, without disclosing individual-level identifying data, to the Commission at least once annually. The Unemployment Compensation Ombudsman shall carry out any additional activities as the Commission determines to be appropriate.

C. All memoranda, work products, and other materials contained in the case files of the Unemployment Compensation Ombudsman and personnel of the Office shall be confidential. Any communication between the Unemployment Compensation Ombudsman and personnel of the Office and a person receiving assistance that is made during or in connection with the provision of services of the Unemployment Compensation Ombudsman and personnel of the Office shall be confidential. Confidential materials and communications shall not be subject to disclosure and shall not be admissible in any judicial or administrative proceeding except where (i) a threat to inflict bodily injury is made; (ii) communications are intentionally used to plan, attempt to commit, or commit a crime or conceal an ongoing crime; (iii) a complaint is made against the Unemployment Compensation Ombudsman or personnel of the Office by a person receiving assistance to the extent necessary for the complainant to prove misconduct or the Unemployment Compensation Ombudsman or personnel of the Office to defend against such complaint; or (iv) communications are sought or offered to prove or disprove a claim or complaint of misconduct or malpractice filed against the legal representative of a person who received assistance from the Unemployment Compensation Ombudsman or personnel of the Office. Confidential materials and communications as described in this section are not subject to mandatory disclosure under the Virginia Freedom of Information Act (§ 2.2-3700 et seq.).

D. The Unemployment Compensation Ombudsman and personnel of the Office shall be immune from civil liability in their performance of the duties specified in this section.

History.
2022, cc. 716, 754.

CHAPTER 2.
DEFINITIONS.

Section
60.2-212. Employment.
60.2-229. Wages.

§ 60.2-210. Employer.

Cross references.
As to worker misclassification, see § 58.1-1900 et seq.

§ 60.2-212. Employment.

A. "Employment" means:

1. Any service including service in interstate commerce, performed for remuneration or under any contract of hire, written or oral, express or implied; and

2. Any service, of whatever nature, performed by an individual for any employing unit, for remuneration or under any contract of hire, written or oral, and irrespective of citizenship or residence of either,

a. Within the United States, or

b. On or in connection with an American vessel or American aircraft under a contract of service which is entered into within the United States or during the performance of which and while the individual is employed on the vessel or aircraft it touches at a port in the United States, if such individual performs such services on or in connection with such vessel or aircraft when outside the United States, provided that the operating office, from which the operations of the vessel or aircraft are ordinarily and regularly supervised, managed, directed or controlled, is within the Commonwealth.

B. Notwithstanding subdivision 2 b of subsection A of this section, "employment" means all service performed by an officer or member of the crew of an American vessel on or in connection with such vessel, if the operating office from which the operations of such vessel operating on navigable waters within, or within and without, the United States are ordinarily and regularly supervised, managed, directed and controlled is within the Commonwealth.

C. Services performed by an individual for remuneration shall be deemed to be employment subject to this title unless the Commission determines that such individual is not an employee for purposes of the Federal Insurance Contributions Act and the Federal Unemployment Tax Act, based upon an application of the standard used by the Internal Revenue Service for such determinations.

D. Notwithstanding the provisions of subsection C, an individual who performs services as a real estate salesperson, under direction of a real estate broker under Chapter 21 (§ 54.1-2100 et seq.) of Title 54.1, or as a real estate appraiser under Chapter 20.1 (§ 54.1-2009 et seq.) of Title 54.1 pursuant to an executed independent contractor agreement and for remuneration solely by way of commission or fee, shall not be an employee for purposes of this chapter.

E. Notwithstanding the provisions of subsection C, a hiring party providing an individual with personal protective equipment in response to a disaster caused by a communicable disease of public health threat for which a state of emergency has been declared pursuant to § 44-146.17 shall not be considered in any determination regarding whether such individual is an employee or

151

independent contractor. For the purposes of this subsection, the terms "communicable disease of public health threat," "disaster," and "state of emergency" have the same meaning as provided in § 44-146.16.

History.

Code 1950, § 60-14; 1952, cc. 30, 184; 1956, c. 440; 1962, c. 71; 1968, c. 738, § 60.1-14; 1971, Ex. Sess., c. 235; 1972, c. 824; 1974, cc. 466, 660; 1976, c. 304; 1977, c. 330; 1979, c. 637; 1980, cc. 520, 522; 1981, cc. 28, 369, 374, 375; 1982, c. 25; 1983, c. 14; 1984, cc. 120, 139, 204; 1985, cc. 152, 254; 1986, c. 480; 1996, c. 244; 2005, c. 892; 2020, c. 1261; 2021, Sp. Sess. I, c. 448.

Editor's note.

Acts 2020, c. 1261, cl. 2 provides: "That the provisions of § 30-19.03:1.2 of the Code of Virginia shall not apply to this act."

Acts 2020, c. 1261, cl. 3 provides: "That the provisions of this act shall expire on January 1, 2021, if the Virginia Employment Commission has not, on or before such date, received adequate funding from the U.S. Department of Labor that covers the costs of information technology upgrades, training, publicity, and marketing that are incurred by the Virginia Employment Commission in connection with establishing the short-time compensation pro-gram pursuant to the first enactment of this act." Acts 2020 Sp. Sess. I, c. 8, cl. 2, effective October 21, 2020, repealed clauses 3 and 4 of Acts 2020, c. 1261. The amendments by Acts 2020, c. 1261 will not expire.

Acts 2020, c. 1261, cl. 4 provides: "That, if not sooner expired pursuant to the provisions of the third enactment of this act, this act shall expire on July 1, 2022." Acts 2020 Sp. Sess. I, c. 8, cl. 2, effective October 21, 2020, repealed clauses 3 and 4 of Acts 2020, c. 1261. The amendments by Acts 2020, c. 1261 will not expire.

The 2020 amendments.

The 2020 amendment by c. 1261, substituted "standard used by the Internal Revenue Service for such determinations" for "20 factors set forth in Internal Revenue Service Revenue Ruling 87-41, issued pursuant to 26 C.F.R. 31.3306(i)-1 and 26 C.F.R. 31.3121(d)-1" in subsection C at the end.

The 2021 Sp. Sess. I amendments.

The 2021 amendment by Sp. Sess. I, c. 448, effective July 1, 2021, added subsection E.

§ 60.2-229. Wages.

A. "Wages" means all remuneration paid, or which should have been paid, for personal services, including commissions, bonuses, tips, back pay, dismissal pay, severance pay and any other payments made by an employer to an employee during his employment and thereafter and the cash value of all remuneration payable in any medium other than cash. Notwithstanding the other provisions of this subsection, wages paid in back pay awards shall be allocated to, and reported as being paid during, the calendar quarter or quarters in which such back pay would have been earned. Severance pay paid at the time of, or subsequent to, separation from employment shall be allocated to the last day of work unless otherwise allocated by the employer. If otherwise allocated, severance pay shall be allocated at a rate not less than the average weekly wage of such employee during the last calendar quarter, and reported as such. Severance pay shall be deducted from any benefits payable after the Commission's receipt of notification of severance pay by the employer pursuant to § 60.2-603. The reasonable cash value of remuneration payable in any medium other than cash shall be estimated and determined in accordance with rules prescribed by the Commission.

B. The term "wages" shall not include:

1. Subsequent to December 31, 1990, for purposes of taxes only, that part of the remuneration, other than remuneration referred to in the succeeding subdivisions of this subsection, that is greater than $8,000 and is payable during any calendar year to an individual by any employer with respect to employment in this Commonwealth or any other state. If an employer, hereinafter referred to as "successor employer," during any calendar year acquires substantially all of the property used in a trade or business of another employer, hereinafter referred to as a "predecessor," or used in a separate unit

of a trade or business of a predecessor, and immediately after the acquisition employs in his trade or business an individual who immediately prior to the acquisition was employed in the trade or business of such predecessor, then, for the purpose of determining whether remuneration, other than remuneration referred to in the succeeding subdivisions of this subsection, with respect to employment equal to $8,000 is payable by the successor to such individual during such calendar year, any remuneration, other than remuneration referred to in the succeeding subdivisions of this subsection, with respect to employment payable, or considered under this subdivision as payable, to such individual by such predecessor during such calendar year and prior to such acquisition shall be considered as payable by such successor employer;

2. The amount of any payment, including any amount paid by an employer for insurance or annuities, or into a fund, to provide for any such payment, made to, or on behalf of, an employee or any of his dependents under a plan or system established by an employer which makes provisions for (i) his employees generally, (ii) for his employees generally and their dependents, (iii) for a class or classes of his employees, or (iv) for a class or classes of his employees and their dependents, on account of:

a. Retirement;

b. Sickness or accident disability payments which are received under a workers' compensation law;

c. Medical or hospitalization expenses in connection with sickness or accident disability;

d. Death; or

e. Unemployment benefits under any private plan financed in whole or in part by an employer;

3. The payment by an employer, without deduction from the remuneration of the employee, of the tax imposed upon an employer under § 3101 of the Federal Internal Revenue Code;

4. Any payment on account of sickness or accident disability, or medical or hospitalization expenses in connection with the sickness or accident disability, made by an employer to, or on behalf of, an employee after the expiration of six calendar months following the last calendar month in which the employee worked for such employer;

5. Remuneration paid in any medium other than cash to an employee for service not in the course of the employer's trade or business;

6. Any payment, other than vacation or sick pay, made to an employee after the month in which he attains the age of sixty-five, if he did not work for the employer in the period for which such payment is made; or

7. Any payment made to, or on behalf of, an employee or his beneficiary under a cafeteria plan, as defined in § 125 of the Internal Revenue Code, if such payment would not be treated as wages under the Internal Revenue Code.

History.

Code 1950, § 60-22; 1952, c. 184; 1954, c. 203; 1956, c. 440; 1968, c. 9; 1968, c. 738, § 60.1-26; 1971, Ex. Sess., c. 235; 1974, c. 466; 1976, c. 591; 1977, c. 330; 1979, cc. 629, 637; 1982, c. 363; 1983, c. 14; 1984, cc. 204, 408; 1986, c. 480; 1990, c. 908; 1993, c. 576; 1995, c. 515; 2020, c. 1261.

Editor's note.

Acts 2020, c. 1261, cl. 2 provides: "That the provisions of § 30-19.03:1.2 of the Code of Virginia shall not apply to this act."

Acts 2020, c. 1261, cl. 3 provides: "That the provisions of this act shall expire on January 1, 2021, if the Virginia Employment Commission has not, on or before such date, received adequate funding from the U.S. Department of Labor that covers the costs of information technology upgrades, training, publicity, and marketing that are incurred by the Virginia Employment Commission in connection with establishing the short-time compensation program pursuant to the first enactment of this act." Acts 2020 Sp. Sess. I, c. 8, cl. 2, effective October 21, 2020, repealed clauses 3 and 4 of Acts 2020, c. 1261. The amendments by Acts 2020, c. 1261 will not expire.

Acts 2020, c. 1261, cl. 4 provides: "That, if not sooner expired pursuant to the provisions of the third enactment of this act, this act shall expire on July 1, 2022." Acts 2020 Sp. Sess. I, c. 8, cl. 2, effective October 21, 2020, repealed clauses 3 and 4 of Acts 2020, c. 1261. The amendments by Acts 2020, c. 1261 will not expire.

The 2020 amendments.
The 2020 amendment by c. 1261 added subdivision B 7 and made related changes.

CHAPTER 3.

FUNDS.

ARTICLE 2.

UNEMPLOYMENT COMPENSATION ADMINISTRATION FUND.

§ 60.2-309. Repealed by Acts 2023, cc. 624 and 625, cl. 2, effective July 1, 2023.

Editor's note.
Former § 60.2-309, relating to special employment service account, was derived from

Code 1950, § 60-99; 1968, c. 738, § 60.1-116; 1986, c. 480.

§ 60.2-310. Repealed by Acts 2023, cc. 624 and 625, cl. 2, effective July 1, 2023.

Editor's note.
Former § 60.2-310, relating to financing, was

derived from Code 1950, § 60-88; 1968, c. 738, § 60.1-104; 1986, c. 480.

CHAPTER 4.

JOB SERVICE.

§ 60.2-400. Repealed by Acts 2023, cc. 624 and 625, cl. 2, effective July 1, 2023.

Editor's note.
Former § 60.2-400, relating to Virginia State Job Service; cooperation with U.S. Employment

Service agencies, was derived from Code 1950, §§ 60-85, 60-87, 60-89; 1968, c. 738, §§ 60.1-101, 60.1-103, 60.1-105; 1986, c. 480.

§ 60.2-400.1. Repealed by Acts 2023, cc. 624 and 625, cl. 2, effective July 1, 2023.

Editor's note.
Former § 60.2-400.1, relating to human traf-

ficking hotline; posted notice required, was derived from 2019, c. 388.

§ 60.2-401. Repealed by Acts 2023, cc. 624 and 625, cl. 2, effective July 1, 2023.

Editor's note.
Former § 60.2-401, relating to financial literacy courses, was derived from 2014, c. 449.

CHAPTER 5.
TAXATION.

Article 1. Employer Taxation.

Article 2. Employer Reporting Requirements.

Article 4. Computation of Tax Rate.

ARTICLE 1.
EMPLOYER TAXATION.

§ 60.2-500. Determination with respect to whether employing unit is employer; whether services constitute employment; or whether business transfer is illegal.

CASE NOTES

Employee status finding upheld. — In finding that a claimant was an employee and not an independent contractor, the Virginia Employment Commission made factual findings on each of the factors comprising the twenty-factor test and found that the over- whelming majority of those factors weighed in favor of employee status; those factual findings were conclusive in this appeal according to the plain language of § 60.2-500(C). Career Dev. Ctr. v. Va. Emp. Comm'n, 2021 Va. App. LEXIS 233 (Va. Ct. App. Dec. 14, 2021).

§ 60.2-508. Period of coverage generally; account required.

Any employing unit which is or becomes an employer subject to this title within any calendar year shall be subject to this title during the whole of such calendar year. Any such employing unit shall establish an account with the Commission by the end of the calendar quarter in which it becomes subject to this title.

History.
Code 1950, § 60-82; 1968, c. 738, § 60.1-98; 1986, c. 480; 2020, c. 1261.

Editor's note.
Acts 2020, c. 1261, cl. 2 provides: "That the provisions of § 30-19.03:1.2 of the Code of Virginia shall not apply to this act."
Acts 2020, c. 1261, cl. 3 provides: "That the provisions of this act shall expire on January 1, 2021, if the Virginia Employment Commission has not, on or before such date, received adequate funding from the U.S. Department of Labor that covers the costs of information technology upgrades, training, publicity, and marketing that are incurred by the Virginia Employment Commission in connection with establishing the short-time compensation program pursuant to the first enactment of this act." Acts 2020 Sp. Sess. I, c. 8, cl. 2, effective October 21, 2020, repealed clauses 3 and 4 of Acts 2020, c. 1261. The amendments by Acts 2020, c. 1261 will not expire.
Acts 2020, c. 1261, cl. 4 provides: "That, if not sooner expired pursuant to the provisions of the third enactment of this act, this act shall expire on July 1, 2022." Acts 2020 Sp. Sess. I, c. 8, cl. 2, effective October 21, 2020, repealed clauses 3 and 4 of Acts 2020, c. 1261. The amendments by Acts 2020, c. 1261 will not expire.

The 2020 amendments.
The 2020 amendment by c. 1261 added the second sentence.

ARTICLE 2.

EMPLOYER REPORTING REQUIREMENTS.

§ 60.2-512. Requiring payroll and tax reports and payment of taxes.

A. The Commission is hereby expressly authorized to require the filing of payroll and tax reports, and the payment of the taxes required by § 60.2-511 in monthly, quarterly, semiannual or annual payments as shall be determined by the Commission; however, if the due date for filing of reports or payment of taxes falls on a Saturday, Sunday or legal holiday, the due date shall be extended to the next business day that is not a Saturday, Sunday or legal holiday. Beginning January 1, 2013, employers may file payroll and tax reports, and pay the taxes required by § 60.2-511, annually, in the time, form and manner prescribed by the Commission, if the employment that is the subject of the report of taxes due under this chapter consists exclusively of domestic service in a private home of the employer, as defined in §§ 31.3121 (a)(7)-1, 31.3306 (c)(2)-1, and 31.3401 (a)(3)-1 of the Employment Tax Regulations promulgated pursuant to §§ 3121, 3306, and 3401 of the Internal Revenue Code, as amended. The aggregate amount of taxes shall be fully paid to the Commission on or before January 31 of each year next succeeding the year with respect to employment during which year such taxes are imposed, or in the event the time is extended for filing the return of the taxes imposed by Title IX of the Social Security Act for the year for which such taxes are imposed, then before the expiration of such extension. Taxes due and payable in an amount less than five dollars shall be deemed to be fully paid; however, this does not relieve an employer from filing payroll and tax reports as herein required.

B. Beginning January 1, 2021, all employers shall file quarterly reports on an electronic medium using a format prescribed by the Commission. Waivers will be granted only if the Commission finds this requirement creates an unreasonable burden on the employer. All requests for waiver must be submitted in writing. Beginning January 1, 2021, if any employer who has not obtained a waiver by the date the employer's quarterly report is due, fails, without good cause shown, to file electronically, the Commission shall assess upon the employer a penalty of $75, which penalty shall be in addition to the taxes due and payable with respect to such report and to any penalty assessed under subsection B of § 60.2-513. Penalties collected pursuant to this section shall be paid into the Special Unemployment Compensation Administration Fund established pursuant to § 60.2-314.

C. Notwithstanding the provisions of subsection A, no payroll and tax reports shall be filed with respect to an employee of a state or local agency performing intelligence or counterintelligence functions, if the head of such agency has determined that filing such a report could endanger the safety of the employee or compromise an ongoing investigation or intelligence mission.

History.

Code 1950, § 60-61; 1968, c. 738, § 60.1-73; 1981, c. 99; 1984, c. 458; 1986, c. 480; 1993, c. 249; 1996, c. 264; 1997, c. 385; 2007, cc. 426, 638; 2012, c. 316; 2020, c. 1261.

Editor's note.

Acts 2020, c. 1261, cl. 2 provides: "That the provisions of § 30-19.03:1.2 of the Code of Virginia shall not apply to this act."

Acts 2020, c. 1261, cl. 3 provides: "That the provisions of this act shall expire on January 1, 2021, if the Virginia Employment Commission has not, on or before such date, received adequate funding from the U.S. Department of Labor that covers the costs of information technology upgrades, training, publicity, and marketing that are incurred by the Virginia Employment Commission in connection with establishing the short-time compensation program pursuant to the first enactment of this act." Acts 2020 Sp. Sess. I, c. 8, cl. 2, effective October 21, 2020, repealed clauses 3 and 4 of Acts 2020, c. 1261. The amendments by Acts 2020, c. 1261 will not expire.

Acts 2020, c. 1261, cl. 4 provides: "That, if not sooner expired pursuant to the provisions of the third enactment of this act, this act shall expire on July 1, 2022." Acts 2020 Sp. Sess. I, c. 8, cl. 2, effective October 21, 2020, repealed clauses 3 and 4 of Acts 2020, c. 1261. The amendments by Acts 2020, c. 1261 will not expire.

The 2020 amendments.
The 2020 amendment by c. 1261, in subsec-

tion B, deleted the first sentence, which read: "Beginning January 1, 1994, through December 31, 2008, employers who report 250 or more employees in any calendar quarter shall file quarterly reports on a magnetic medium using a format prescribed by the Commission"; in the second sentence, substituted "2021, all employers" for "2009, employers who report 100 or more employees in any calendar quarter in 2009, or thereafter" and in the fourth sentence, substituted "2021, if any employer who" for "2009, if any employer who reports 100 or more employees in any calendar quarter in 2009, or thereafter, and who."

§ 60.2-513. Failure of employing unit to file reports; assessment and amount of penalty.

A. If any employing unit fails to file with the Commission any report which the Commission deems necessary for the effective administration of this title within 30 days after the Commission requires the same by written notice mailed to the last known address of such employing unit, the Commission may determine on the basis of such information as it may have whether such employing unit is an employer, unless such determination has already been made. Also, on the basis of such information, the Commission may assess the amount of tax due from such employer and shall give written notice of such determination and assessment to such employer. Such determination and assessment shall be final (i) unless such employer, within 30 days after the mailing to the employer at his last known address or other service of the notice of such determination or assessment, applies to the Commission for a review of such determination and assessment or (ii) unless the Commission, on its own motion, sets aside, reduces or increases the same.

B. If any employer had wages payable for a calendar quarter and fails, without good cause shown, to file any report as required of him under this title with respect to wages or taxes, the Commission shall assess upon the employer a penalty of $100, which shall be in addition to the taxes due and payable with respect to such report.

C. For the purposes of this subsection, "newly covered" refers to the time at which an employer initially becomes subject to liability under the provisions of this title. A newly covered employer shall file by the due date of the calendar quarter in which such employer becomes subject to liability under the provisions of this title. If such employer's report is not filed by that date, and in the absence of good cause shown for the failure to so file, a $100 penalty shall be assessed for each report. Penalties collected pursuant to this section shall be paid into the Special Unemployment Compensation Administration Fund.

History.
Code 1950, § 60-62; 1968, c. 738, § 60.1-74; 1974, c. 466; 1976, c. 708; 1977, c. 445; 1978, c. 238; 1984, c. 458; 1986, c. 480; 1999, c. 79; 2004, c. 495; 2018, c. 227; 2020, c. 1261.

Editor's note.
Acts 2020, c. 1261, cl. 2 provides: "That the provisions of § 30-19.03:1.2 of the Code of Virginia shall not apply to this act."
Acts 2020, c. 1261, cl. 3 provides: "That the

provisions of this act shall expire on January 1, 2021, if the Virginia Employment Commission has not, on or before such date, received adequate funding from the U.S. Department of Labor that covers the costs of information technology upgrades, training, publicity, and marketing that are incurred by the Virginia Employment Commission in connection with establishing the short-time compensation program pursuant to the first enactment of this act." Acts 2020 Sp. Sess. I, c. 8, cl. 2, effective

October 21, 2020, repealed clauses 3 and 4 of Acts 2020, c. 1261. The amendments by Acts 2020, c. 1261 will not expire.

Acts 2020, c. 1261, cl. 4 provides: "That, if not sooner expired pursuant to the provisions of the third enactment of this act, this act shall expire on July 1, 2022." Acts 2020 Sp. Sess. I, c. 8, cl. 2, effective October 21, 2020, repealed clauses 3 and 4 of Acts 2020, c. 1261. The amendments by Acts 2020, c. 1261 will not expire.

The 2020 amendments.
The 2020 amendment by c. 1261 divided subsection B into subsections B and C by moving the former second, third and fourth sentences of subsection B to C; and in subsection C, added the first sentence, and rewrote the second sentence, which read: "A newly covered employer may file by the due date of the quarter in which his account number is assigned by the Commission, without penalty."

ARTICLE 3.
COLLECTION OF TAXES.

§ 60.2-521. Collection by civil action; persons subject to civil actions; other remedies; compromise and adjustment.

Editor's note.
Acts 2022, Sp. Sess. I, c. 2, Item 370 D, effective for the biennium ending June 30, 2023, provides: "Notwithstanding any other provision of law, all fees incurred by the Virginia Employment Commission with respect to the collection of debts authorized to be collected under § 2.2- 4806 of the Code of Virginia, using the Treasury Offset Program of the United States, shall become part of the debt owed the Commission and may be recovered accordingly."

ARTICLE 4.
COMPUTATION OF TAX RATE.

§ 60.2-528. Individual benefit charges.

A. An individual's "benefit charges" shall be computed in the following manner:

1. For each week benefits are received, a claimant's "benefit charges" shall be equal to his benefits received for such week.

2. For each week extended benefits are received, pursuant to § 60.2-610 or 60.2-611, a claimant's "benefit charges" shall be equal to one-half his benefits received for such week. However, a claimant's "benefit charges" for extended benefits attributable to service in the employ of a governmental entity referred to in subdivisions 1 through 3 of subsection A of § 60.2-213 shall be equal to the full amount of such extended benefit.

3. For each week partial benefits are received, the claimant's "benefit charges" shall be computed (i) in the case of regular benefits as in subdivision 1 of this subsection, or (ii) in the case of extended benefits as in subdivision 2 of this subsection.

B. 1. The employing unit from whom such individual was separated, resulting in the current period of unemployment, shall be the most recent employing unit for whom such individual has performed services for remuneration (i) during 30 days, whether or not such days are consecutive, or (ii) during 240 hours. If such individual's unemployment is caused by separation from an employer, such individual's "benefit charges" for such period of unemployment shall be deemed the responsibility of the last employer for (i) 30 days or (ii) 240 hours prior to such period of unemployment.

2. Any employer charged with benefits paid shall be notified of the charges quarterly by the Commission. The amount specified shall be conclusive on the employer unless, not later than 30 days after the notice of benefit charges was

mailed to its last known address or otherwise delivered to it, the employer files an appeal with the Commission, setting forth the grounds for such an appeal. Proceedings on appeal to the Commission regarding the amount of benefit charges under this subsection or a redetermination of such amount shall be in accordance with the provisions of § 60.2-500. The decision of the Commission shall be subject to the provisions of § 60.2-500. Any appeal perfected pursuant to the provisions of this section shall not address any issue involving the merits or conditions of a claimant's separation from employment.

C. No "benefit charges" shall be deemed the responsibility of an employer of:

1. An individual whose separation from the work of such employer arose as a result of a violation of the law by such individual, which violation led to confinement in any jail or prison;

2. An individual who voluntarily left employment in order to accept other employment, genuinely believing such employment to be permanent;

3. An individual with respect to any weeks in which benefits are claimed and received after such date as that individual refused to accept an offer of rehire by the employer because such individual was in training with approval of the Commission pursuant to § 60.2-613;

4. An individual who voluntarily left employment to enter training approved under § 236 of the Trade Act of 1974 (19 U.S.C. § 2296 et seq.);

5. An individual hired to replace a member of the Reserve of the United States Armed Forces or the National Guard called into active duty in connection with an international conflict and whose employment is terminated concurrent with and because of that member's return from active duty;

6. An individual who left employment voluntarily with good cause due to a personal bona fide medical reason caused by a non-job-related injury or medical condition;

7. An individual participating as an inmate in (i) state or local work release programs pursuant to § 53.1-60 or 53.1-131; (ii) community residential programs pursuant to §§ 53.1-177, 53.1-178, and 53.1-179; or (iii) any similar work release program, whose separation from work arose from conditions of release or parole from such program;

8. An individual who was unable to work at his regular employment due to a disaster for which the Governor, by executive order, has declared a state of emergency, if such disaster forced the closure of the employer's business. In no case shall more than four weeks of benefit charges be waived; or

9. An individual who leaves employment to accompany his spouse to the location of the spouse's new duty assignment if (i) the spouse is on active duty in the military or naval services of the United States; (ii) the spouse's relocation to a new military-related assignment is pursuant to a permanent change of station order; (iii) the location of the spouse's new duty assignment is not readily accessible from the individual's place of employment; and (iv) the spouse's new duty assignment is located in a state that, pursuant to statute, does not deem a person accompanying a military spouse as a person leaving work voluntarily without good cause.

History.

Code 1950, § 60-68; 1952, c. 184; 1954, c. 203; 1956, c. 440; 1958, c. 36; 1960, c. 136; 1962, cc. 12, 83; 1964, c. 3; 1966, c. 30; 1968, c. 9; 1968, c. 738, § 60.1-80; 1970, c. 104; 1972, c. 764; 1974, c. 466; 1976, c. 708; 1977, c. 330; 1978, c. 493; 1979, c. 634; 1980, c. 463; 1981, cc. 250, 606; 1986, c. 480; 1989, c. 104; 1991, c. 249; 1991, Sp. Sess., c. 9; 1997, c. 202; 2001, c. 721;

2004, cc. 583, 977; 2005, cc. 44, 105; 2009, c. 878; 2014, c. 442.

Editor's note.

Acts 2014, c. 442, cl. 4, which would have made subdivision C 9 expire on December 31, 2020, was repealed by Acts 2020, c. 261, cl. 1.

Acts 2020, c. 261, cl. 2 provides: "That the provisions of this act enhance the benefits payable to an individual pursuant to Title 60.2 of the Code of Virginia. Pursuant to § 30-19.03:1.2 of the Code of Virginia, the Virginia Employment Commission, in consultation with the Department of Planning and Budget, estimates that over the ensuing eight years (i) the provisions of this act are projected to reduce the solvency level of the Unemployment Trust Fund by an average of 0.1 percent in each of the eight years and (ii) the projected average annual increase in state unemployment tax liability of employers on a per-employee basis that would result from the provisions of this act is $0."

§ 60.2-528.1. Charging of benefits relating to certain overpayments; penalty for pattern of failure to respond to requests for information.

Editor's note.

Acts 2021, Sp. Sess. I, c. 539, cl. 5, which expires on July 1, 2022, provides: "That all costs to the Unemployment Compensation Fund (the Fund) resulting from the provisions of this act for overpayments of benefits under Chapter 6 (§ 60.2-600 et seq.) of Title 60.2 of the Code of Virginia shall be reimbursed to the Fund from the general fund in the general appropriation act. For an overpayment waived pursuant to this act, no employer shall be responsible for (i) reimbursing benefits or (ii) benefits charges, except as provided in § 60.2-528.1 of the Code of Virginia."

§ 60.2-533. Fund balance factor.

Editor's note.

Acts 2022, Sp. Sess. I, c. 2, Item 370 I, effective for the biennium ending June 30, 2023, provides: "Notwithstanding § 60.2-533, Code of Virginia, the fund building rate shall be set for Calendar Year 2023 at a rate not to exceed the rate in effect for Calendar Year 2020."

At the direction of the Virginia Code Commission, in subsection C as set out in the bound volume, the phrase "fund balance factor determined pursuant to subsection B of this section" should read: "fund balance factor determined pursuant to subsection A of this section."

CHAPTER 6.
BENEFITS.

Article 4. Eligibility Criteria.

ARTICLE 4.
ELIGIBILITY CRITERIA.

§ 60.2-612. Benefit eligibility conditions.

A. An unemployed individual shall be eligible to receive benefits for any week only if the Commission finds that:

1. He has, in the highest two quarters of earnings within his base period, been paid wages in employment for employers that are equal to not less than the lowest amount appearing in Column A of the "Benefit Table" appearing in § 60.2-602 on the line which extends through Division C and on which in Column B of the "Benefit Table" appears his weekly benefit amount. Such wages shall be earned in not less than two quarters.

2. a. His total or partial unemployment is not due to a labor dispute in active progress or to shutdown or start-up operations caused by such dispute which exists (i) at the factory, establishment, or other premises, including a vessel, at which he is or was last employed, or (ii) at a factory, establishment or other premises, including a vessel, either within or without this Commonwealth, which (a) is owned or operated by the same employing unit which owns or operates the premises at which he is or was last employed and (b) supplies materials or services necessary to the continued and usual operation of the premises at which he is or was last employed. This subdivision shall not apply if it is shown to the satisfaction of the Commission that:

(1) He is not participating in or financing or directly interested in the labor dispute; and

(2) He does not belong to a grade or class of workers of which, immediately before the commencement of the labor dispute, there were members employed at the premises, including a vessel, at which the labor dispute occurs, any of whom are participating in or financing or directly interested in the dispute.

b. If separate branches of work which are commonly conducted as separate businesses at separate premises are conducted in separate departments of the same premises, each such department shall, for the purposes of this subdivision, be deemed to be a separate factory, establishment or other premises. Membership in a union, or the payment of regular dues to a bona fide labor organization, however, shall not alone constitute financing a labor dispute.

3. He is not receiving, has not received or is not seeking unemployment benefits under an unemployment compensation law of any other state or of the United States; however, if the appropriate agency of such other state or of the United States finally determines that he is not entitled to such unemployment benefits, this subdivision shall not apply.

4. He is not on a bona fide paid vacation. If an individual is paid vacation pay for any week in an amount less than the individual's weekly benefit amount his eligibility for benefits shall be computed under the provisions of § 60.2-603.

5. He has registered for work and thereafter has continued to report at an employment office in accordance with such regulations as the Commission may prescribe. The Commission may, by regulation, waive or alter either or both of the requirements of this subdivision for certain types of cases when it finds that compliance with such requirements would be oppressive, or would be inconsistent with the purposes of this title.

6. He has made a claim for benefits in accordance with regulations the Commission may prescribe.

7. a. He is able to work, is available for work, and is actively seeking and unable to obtain suitable work. Every claimant who is totally unemployed shall report to the Commission the names of employers contacted each week in his effort to obtain work. This information may be subject to employer verification by the Commission through a program designed for that purpose. The Commission may determine that registration by a claimant with the Virginia State Job Service may constitute a valid employer contact and satisfy the search for work requirement of this subsection in labor market areas where job opportunities are limited. The Commission may determine that an individual, whose usual and customary means of soliciting work in his occupation

is through contact with a single hiring hall which makes contacts with multiple employers on behalf of the claimant, meets the requirement that he be actively seeking and unable to obtain suitable work by contacting that hiring hall alone. In areas of high unemployment, as determined by the Commission, the Commission has the authority to adjust the requirement that he be actively seeking and unable to obtain suitable work.

b. An individual who leaves the normal labor market area of the individual for the major portion of any week is presumed to be unavailable for work within the meaning of this section. This presumption may be overcome if the individual establishes to the satisfaction of the Commission that the individual has conducted a bona fide search for work and has been reasonably accessible to suitable work in the labor market area in which the individual spent the major portion of the week to which the presumption applies.

c. An individual whose type of work is such that it is performed by individuals working two or more shifts in a 24-hour period shall not be deemed unavailable for work if the individual is currently enrolled in one or more classes of education related to employment or is continuing in a certificate or degree program at an institution of higher education, provided that the enrollment would only limit the individual's availability for one shift and the individual is otherwise available to work any of the other shifts.

8. He has given notice of resignation to his employer and the employer subsequently made the termination of employment effective prior to the date of termination as given in the notice, but in no case shall unemployment compensation benefits awarded under this subdivision exceed two weeks; provided, that the claimant could not establish good cause for leaving work pursuant to § 60.2-618 and was not discharged for misconduct as provided in § 60.2-618.

9. Beginning January 6, 1991, he has served a waiting period of one week during which he was eligible for benefits under this section in all other respects and has not received benefits, except that only one waiting week shall be required of such individual within any benefit year. For claims filed effective November 28, 1999, and after, this requirement shall be waived for any individual whose unemployment was caused by his employer terminating operations, closing its business or declaring bankruptcy without paying the final wages earned as required by § 40.1-29 of the Code of Virginia. Notwithstanding any other provision of this title, if an employer who terminates operations, closes its business or declares bankruptcy pays an individual his final wages after the period of time prescribed by § 40.1-29 of the Code of Virginia, such payment shall not be offset against the benefits the individual was otherwise entitled to receive and shall not, under any circumstances, cause such individual to be declared overpaid benefits.

10. He is not imprisoned or confined in jail.

11. He participates in reemployment services, such as job search assistance services, if he has been determined to be likely to exhaust regular benefits and need reemployment services pursuant to a profiling system established by the Commission, unless the Commission determines that (i) such claimant has completed such services or (ii) there is good cause for such claimant's failure to participate in such services.

B. Prior to any individual receiving benefits under this chapter, the Commission shall conduct an incarceration check and an employment identification check to verify the status of the unemployed individual seeking a claim for benefits.

History.
Code 1950, § 60-46; 1954, c. 203; 1956, c.　　440; 1962, c. 270; 1966, c. 30; 1968, c. 9; 1968, c.
738, § 60.1-52; 1970, c. 104; 1974, c. 264; 1976,

c. 708; 1977, c. 445; 1980, c. 463; 1981, c. 606; 1982, c. 265; 1983, c. 359; 1984, c. 458; 1985, c. 563; 1986, c. 480; 1988, c. 521; 1990, c. 908; 1993, c. 249; 1995, c. 436; 2000, c. 573; 2004, c. 496; 2022, c. 668.

The 2022 amendments.

The 2022 amendment by c. 668, added the subsection A designation; and added subsection B.

§ 60.2-612.1. Program integrity.

A. In order to verify that an individual is eligible to receive benefits, the Commission shall conduct all mandatory and recommended program integrity activities as identified by the U.S. Department of Labor Employment and Training Administration and the U.S. Department of Labor Office of Inspector General.

B. The Commission shall perform a full eligibility review of suspicious or potentially improper claims. In determining if a claim is suspicious or potentially improper, the Commission shall consider the factors utilized by the Integrity Data Hub and any additional factors that may be appropriate, including commonalities in physical addresses, mailing addresses, internet protocol addresses, email addresses, multi-factor authentication, and bank accounts.

C. The Commission shall recover any improper overpayment of benefits to the fullest extent authorized by this title and federal law.

D. The Department of Social Services, the Department of Medical Assistance Services, and the Department of Housing and Community Development, upon receipt of notification that an individual enrolled in any of such department's public assistance programs has become employed, shall notify the Commission of such fact in order for the Commission to determine the individual's eligibility for benefits.

E. The Commission may enter into a memorandum of understanding with any state agency necessary to implement the provisions of this section.

F. The Commission shall report by December 1 of each year to the Commission on Unemployment Compensation addressing the implementation and enforcement of the provisions of this section. The report shall include:

1. The Commission's general program integrity processes, including tools, resources, and databases utilized, to the extent that sharing the information does not jeopardize program integrity measures;

2. A description of efforts to identify, prevent, and recover improper overpayments of benefits and fraudulent payments and measures being taken to improve such efforts;

3. The type and amount of improper payments detected retroactively;

4. The type and amount of improper payments prevented;

5. Moneys saved in preventing improper overpayments and, if any, in recouping improper overpayments; and

6. An explanation for the nonrecovery of overpayments, including the application of any allowable recovery exceptions.

History.
2022, c. 740.

Editor's note.
Acts 2022, c. 740, cl. 2 provides: "That the

provisions of this act shall become effective on January 1, 2023."

§ 60.2-613. Benefits not denied to individuals in training with approval of Commission.

A. No otherwise eligible individual shall be denied benefits for any week because he is in training with the approval of the Commission, including training under § 134 of the Workforce Investment Act, nor shall such individual be denied benefits for any week in which he is in training with the approval of the Commission, including training under § 134 of the Workforce Investment Act, by reason of the application of the provisions in subdivision A 7 of § 60.2-612 relating to availability for work, or the provisions of subdivision 3 of § 60.2-618 relating to failure to apply for, or a refusal to accept, suitable work.

B. Notwithstanding any other provisions of this chapter, no otherwise eligible individual shall be denied benefits for any week because he is in training approved under § 2296 of the Trade Act (19 U.S.C. § 2101 et seq.), nor shall such individual be denied benefits by reason of leaving work to enter such training, provided the work left is not suitable employment, or because of the application to any such week in training of provisions in this law (or any applicable federal unemployment compensation law), relating to availability for work, active search for work, or refusal to accept work.

C. For purposes of this section, "suitable employment" means, with respect to an individual, work of a substantially equal or higher skill level than the individual's past adversely affected employment, as defined for purposes of the Trade Act, and wages for such work at not less than eighty percent of the individual's average weekly wage as determined for the purposes of the Trade Act.

History.
1971, Ex. Sess., c. 235, § 60.1-52.1; 1982, c. 237; 1984, c. 204; 1985, c. 152; 1986, c. 480; 1995, c. 436; 2000, c. 687; 2022, c. 668.

The 2022 amendments.
The 2022 amendment by c. 668, substituted "subdivision A 7 of § 60.2-612" for "subdivision 7 of § 60.2-612" in subsection A.

§ 60.2-618. Disqualification for benefits.

An individual shall be disqualified for benefits upon separation from the last employing unit for whom he has worked 30 days or 240 hours or from any subsequent employing unit:

1. For any week benefits are claimed until he has performed services for an employer (i) during 30 days, whether or not such days are consecutive, or (ii) for 240 hours, and subsequently becomes totally or partially separated from such employment, if the Commission finds such individual is unemployed because he left work voluntarily without good cause.

If (a) at the time of commencing employment with such employing unit an individual is enrolled in an accredited academic program of study provided by an institution of higher education for students that have been awarded a baccalaureate degree, which academic program culminates in the awarding of a master's, doctoral, or professional degree; (b) the individual's employment with such employing unit commenced and ended during the period between spring and fall semesters of the academic program in which the individual is enrolled; and (c) the individual returned to such academic program following his separation from such employing unit, there shall be a rebuttable presumption that the individual left work voluntarily.

As used in this chapter, "good cause" shall not include (1) voluntarily leaving work with an employer to become self-employed or (2) voluntarily leaving work with an employer to accompany or to join his or her spouse in a new locality, except where an individual leaves employment to accompany a spouse to the location of the spouse's new duty assignment if (A) the spouse is on active duty in the military or naval services of the United States; (B) the spouse's relocation to a new military-related assignment is pursuant to a permanent change of station order; (C) the location of the spouse's new duty assignment is not readily accessible from the individual's place of employment; and (D) except for members of the Virginia National Guard relocating to a new assignment within the Commonwealth, the spouse's new duty assignment is located in a state that, pursuant to statute, does not deem a person accompanying a military spouse as a person leaving work voluntarily without good cause. An individual shall not be deemed to have voluntarily left work solely because the separation was in accordance with a seniority-based policy.

2. a. For any week benefits are claimed until he has performed services for an employer (i) during 30 days, whether or not such days are consecutive, or (ii) for 240 hours, and subsequently becomes totally or partially separated from such employment, if the Commission finds such individual is unemployed because he has been discharged for misconduct connected with his work.

b. For the purpose of this subdivision, "misconduct" includes, but shall not be limited to:

(1) An employee's confirmed positive test for a nonprescribed controlled substance, identified as such in Chapter 34 (§ 54.1-3400 et seq.) of Title 54.1, where such test was conducted at the direction of his employer in conjunction with the employer's administration and enforcement of a known workplace drug policy. Such test shall have been performed, and a sample collected, in accordance with scientifically recognized standards by a laboratory accredited by the United States Department of Health and Human Services, or the College of American Pathology, or the American Association for Clinical Chemistry, or the equivalent, or shall have been a United States Department of Transportation-qualified drug screen conducted in accordance with the employer's bona fide drug policy. The Commission may consider evidence of mitigating circumstances in determining whether misconduct occurred.

(2) An employee's intentionally false or misleading statement of a material nature concerning past criminal convictions made in a written job application furnished to the employer, where such statement was a basis for the termination and the employer terminated the employee promptly upon the discovery thereof. The Commission may consider evidence of mitigating circumstances in determining whether misconduct occurred.

(3) A willful and deliberate violation of a standard or regulation of the Commonwealth, by an employee of an employer licensed or certified by the Commonwealth, which violation would cause the employer to be sanctioned or have its license or certification suspended by the Commonwealth. The Commission may consider evidence of mitigating circumstances in determining whether misconduct occurred.

(4) Chronic absenteeism or tardiness in deliberate violation of a known policy of the employer or one or more unapproved absences following a written reprimand or warning relating to more than one unapproved absence. The Commission may consider evidence of mitigating circumstances in determining whether misconduct occurred.

(5) An employee's loss of or failure to renew a license or certification that is a requisite of the position held by the employee, provided the employer is not at fault for the employee's loss of or failure to renew the license or certification. The Commission may consider evidence of mitigating circumstances in determining whether misconduct occurred.

3. a. If it is determined by the Commission that such individual has failed, without good cause, either to apply for available, suitable work when so directed by the employment office or the Commission or to accept suitable work when offered him. The disqualification shall commence with the week in which such failure occurred, and shall continue for the period of unemployment next ensuing until he has performed services for an employer (i) during 30 days, whether or not such days are consecutive, or (ii) for 240 hours, and subsequently becomes totally or partially separated from such employment.

b. In determining whether or not any work is suitable for an individual, the Commission shall consider the degree of risk involved to his health, safety and morals, his physical fitness and prior training, his experience, his length of unemployment and the accessibility of the available work from his residence.

c. No work shall be deemed suitable and benefits shall not be denied under this title to any otherwise eligible individual for refusing to accept new work under any of the following conditions:

(1) If the position offered is vacant due directly to a strike, lockout, or other labor dispute;

(2) If the wages, hours, or other conditions of the work offered are substantially less favorable to the individual than those prevailing for similar work in the locality; or

(3) If as a condition of being employed the individual would be required to join a company union or to resign from or refrain from joining any bona fide labor organization.

d. No individual shall be qualified for benefits during any week that such individual, in connection with an offer of suitable work, has a confirmed positive test for a nonprescribed controlled substance, identified as such in Chapter 34 (§ 54.1-3400 et seq.) of Title 54.1, if the test is required as a condition of employment and (i) performed, and a sample is collected, in accordance with scientifically recognized standards by a laboratory accredited by the United States Department of Health and Human Services, or the College of American Pathology, or the American Association for Clinical Chemistry, or the equivalent, or (ii) a United States Department of Transportation-qualified drug screen conducted in accordance with the employer's bona fide drug policy. The disqualification shall commence with the week in which such a test was conducted, and shall continue for the period of unemployment next ensuing until he has performed services for an employer (i) during 30 days, whether or not such days are consecutive, or (ii) for 240 hours, and subsequently becomes totally or partially separated from such employment.

4. For 52 weeks, beginning with the date of the determination or decision, if the Commission finds that such individual, within 36 calendar months immediately preceding such determination or decision, has made a false statement or representation knowing it to be false, or has knowingly failed to disclose a material fact, to obtain or increase any benefit or payment under this title, the unemployment compensation of any other state, or any other program of the federal government which is administered in any way under this title, either for himself or any other person. Overpayments that have been fraudulently obtained and any penalty assessed against the individual pursuant to § 60.2-636 shall be recoverable as provided in § 60.2-633.

5. If such separation arose as a result of an unlawful act which resulted in a conviction and after his release from prison or jail until he has performed services for an employer for (i) 30 days, whether or not such days are consecutive, or (ii) 240 hours, and subsequently becomes totally or partially separated from such employment.

6. If such separation arose as a condition of the individual's parole or release from a custodial or penal institution and such individual was participating in the community corrections alternative program pursuant to § 19.2-316.4.

History.

Code 1950, § 60-47; 1952, c. 184; 1954, c. 203; 1956, c. 440; 1960, c. 136; 1962, c. 12; 1966, c. 30; 1968, c. 738, § 60.1-58; 1972, c. 764; 1974, c. 466; 1977, c. 286; 1979, cc. 675, 681; 1981, c. 251; 1982, cc. 319, 363; 1983, c. 559; 1984, c. 458; 1986, c. 480; 1991, c. 296; 1993, c. 249;

1996, cc. 175, 182, 194, 199; 1997, c. 202; 1998, c. 241; 1999, c. 919; 2004, cc. 525, 977; 2005, c. 464; 2008, c. 719; 2009, c. 878; 2013, cc. 175, 771; 2014, cc. 201, 442; 2019, c. 618.

Editor's note.

Acts 2014, c. 442, cl. 4, which would have

made the 2014 amendments to this section expire on December 31, 2020, was repealed by Acts 2020, c. 261, cl. 1.

Acts 2020, c. 261, cl. 2 provides: "That the provisions of this act enhance the benefits payable to an individual pursuant to Title 60.2 of the Code of Virginia. Pursuant to § 30-19.03:1.2 of the Code of Virginia, the Virginia Employment Commission, in consultation with the Department of Planning and Budget, esti-mates that over the ensuing eight years (i) the provisions of this act are projected to reduce the solvency level of the Unemployment Trust Fund by an average of 0.1 percent in each of the eight years and (ii) the projected average annual increase in state unemployment tax liability of employers on a per-employee basis that would result from the provisions of this act is $0."

CIRCUIT COURT OPINIONS

Misconduct not found. — Employment Commission erred in disqualifying an employee from receiving unemployment benefits for "misconduct connected with his work" because, while the employee's conduct in falling asleep at work on at least one occasion was "clearly inappropriate," it did not rise to the level of "misconduct" where the employer had no written policy regarding sleeping, the employee's uncontroverted testimony explained that his conduct was caused by recent symptoms of his previously diagnosed sleep apnea, he provided medical documents to the Commission substantiating that he suffered from sleep apnea, and his explanation was corroborated by the fact that, prior to his discharge, he had scheduled a medical appointment to discuss his recent symptoms. Peart v. Va. Empl. Comm'n, 103 Va. Cir. 109, 2019 Va. Cir. LEXIS 456 (Campbell County Sept. 16, 2019).

ARTICLE 5.

CLAIMS ADJUDICATION.

§ 60.2-619. Determinations and decisions by deputy; appeals therefrom.

A. 1. A representative designated by the Commission as a deputy, shall promptly examine the claim. On the basis of the facts found by him, the deputy shall either:

a. Determine whether or not such claim is valid, and if valid, the week with respect to which benefits shall commence, the weekly benefit amount payable and the maximum duration thereof; or

b. Refer such claim or any question involved therein to any appeal tribunal or to the Commission, which tribunal or Commission shall make its determination in accordance with the procedure described in § 60.2-620.

2. When the payment or denial of benefits will be determined by the provisions of subdivision A 2 of § 60.2-612, the deputy shall promptly transmit his full finding of fact with respect to that subdivision to any appeal tribunal, which shall make its determination in accordance with the procedure described in § 60.2-620.

B. Upon the filing of an initial claim for benefits, the Commission shall cause an informatory notice of such filing to be mailed to the most recent 30-day or 240-hour employing unit of the claimant and all subsequent employing units, and any reimbursable employing units which may be liable for reimbursement to the Commission for any benefits paid. However, the failure to furnish such notice shall not have any effect upon the claim for benefits. If a claimant has had a determination of initial eligibility for benefits under this chapter, as evidenced by the issuance of compensation or waiting-week credit, payments shall continue, subject to a presumption of continued eligibility and in accordance with the terms of this subsection, until a determination is made that provides the claimant notice and an opportunity to be heard. When a question concerning continued eligibility for benefits arises, a determination shall be made as to whether it affects future weeks of benefits or only past weeks. With respect to future weeks, presumptive payment shall not be made until but no later than the end of the week following the week in which such issue arises, regardless of the type of issue. With respect to past weeks, presumptive payment shall be issued immediately, regardless of the type of issue. Notice shall be given to individuals who receive payments under such presumption that pending eligibility may affect their entitlement to the payment and may result in an overpayment that requires repayment.

C. Notice of determination upon a claim shall be promptly given to the claimant by delivering or by mailing such notice to the claimant's last known address. In addition, notice of any determination which involves the application of the provisions of § 60.2-618, together with the reasons therefor, shall be promptly given in the same manner to the most recent 30-day or 240-hour employing unit by whom the claimant was last employed and any subsequent employing unit which is a party. The Commission may dispense with the giving of notice of any determination to any employing unit, and such employing unit shall not be entitled to such notice if it has failed to respond timely or adequately to a written request of the Commission for information, as required by § 60.2-528.1, from which the deputy may have determined that the claimant may be ineligible or disqualified under any provision of this title. The deputy shall promptly notify the claimant of any decision made by him at any time which in any manner denies benefits to the claimant for one or more weeks.

D. Such determination or decision shall be final unless the claimant or any such employing unit files an appeal from such determination or decision (i) within 30 calendar days after the delivery of such notification, (ii) within 30 calendar days after such notification was mailed to his last known address, or (iii) within 30 days after such notification was mailed to the last known address of an interstate claimant. For good cause shown, the 30-day period may be extended. A claim that the Commission has determined to be invalid because of monetary ineligibility shall first be subject to review only upon a request for redetermination pursuant to § 60.2-629. The Commission shall issue a new monetary determination as a result of such review, and such monetary determination shall become final unless appealed by the claimant within 30 days of the date of mailing. The Commission shall clearly set out the process for requesting a redetermination and the process for filing an appeal on each monetary determination issued. Monetary ineligibility does not include an appeal on the effective date of the claim, unless the claimant has requested and received a redetermination of the monetary determination pursuant to § 60.2-629.

E. Benefits shall be paid promptly in accordance with a determination or redetermination under this chapter, or decision of an appeal tribunal, the Commission, the Board of Review or a reviewing court under §§ 60.2-625 and 60.2-631 upon the issuance of such determination, redetermination or decision, regardless of the pendency of the period to file an appeal or petition for judicial review that is provided in this chapter, or the pendency of any such appeal or review. Such benefits shall be paid unless or until such determination, redetermination or decision has been modified or reversed by a subsequent redetermination or decision, in which event benefits shall be paid or denied for weeks of unemployment thereafter in accordance with such modifying or reversing redetermination or decision. If a decision of an appeal tribunal allowing benefits is affirmed in any amount by the Commission, benefits shall continue to be paid until such time as a court decision has become final so that no further appeal can be taken. If an appeal is taken from the Commission's decision, benefits paid shall result in a benefit charge to the account of the employer under § 60.2-530 only when, and as of the date on which, as the result of an appeal, the courts finally determine that the Commission should have awarded benefits to the claimant or claimants involved in such appeal.

History.
Code 1950, § 60-49; 1954, c. 203; 1966, c. 30; 1968, c. 738, § 60.1-61; 1970, c. 104; 1972, c. 692; 1974, c. 466; 1976, c. 708; 1980, cc. 408, 426; 1982, c. 363; 1986, c. 480; 1995, c. 515; 1997, c. 202; 1999, c. 79; 2013, c. 771; 2021, Sp. Sess. I, c. 539; 2022, cc. 668, 716, 754.

The 2022 amendments.
The 2022 amendment by c. 668, substituted

"subdivision A 2 of § 60.2-612" for "subdivision 2 of § 60.2-612" in subdivision A 2.

The 2022 amendment by cc. 716 and 754, effective April 27, 2022, are identical, and added the third through sixth sentences of subsection D.

§ 60.2-623. Procedure generally; confidentiality of information.

CASE NOTES

Absolute privilege. — Supreme Court held that subsection B of § 60.2-623 grants absolute privilege to statements made during proceedings before the Virginia Employment Commis- sion. Bryant-Shannon v. Hampton Rds. Cmty. Action Program, Inc., 299 Va. 579, 856 S.E.2d 575 (2021).

§ 60.2-625. Judicial review.

CASE NOTES

No evidence of fraud. — Circuit court did not err by affirming the Virginia Employment Commission's decision denying the employee unemployment benefits after concluding that he had been discharged for misconduct, be- cause he did not allege that the Commission's decision was procured by extrinsic fraud com- mitted by the employer for purposes of Va. Code Ann. § 60.2-625(A); nor did he make a proffer of proof. The record was sufficient to demonstrate that the employee refused to obey a reasonable directive of his employer, because he received a text message from his employer's HR supervi- sor instructing him to complete his time sheet but repeatedly failed to do so in a timely man- ner. Doe v. Va. Empl. Comm'n, 2022 Va. App. LEXIS 319 (Va. Ct. App. July 26, 2022).

CIRCUIT COURT OPINIONS

Error in finding employee discharged for misconduct. — Employment Commission erred in disqualifying an employee from receiv- ing unemployment benefits for "misconduct connected with his work" because, while the employee did fall asleep at work on at least one occasion, it did not rise to the level of "miscon- duct" where the employer had no written policy regarding sleeping, and because the Commis- sion made no factual findings as to the exis- tence or substance of any such company policy, the Court could look to the record for evidence of such company policy or rule. Peart v. Va. Empl. Comm'n, 103 Va. Cir. 109, 2019 Va. Cir. LEXIS 456 (Campbell County Sept. 16, 2019).

§ 60.2-627. Failure to obey subpoenas; orders of court; penalty.

A. In case of contumacy by, or refusal to obey a subpoena issued to any person, any court of this Commonwealth within the jurisdiction of which the inquiry is carried on or within the jurisdiction of which such person guilty of contumacy or refusal to obey is found or resides or transacts business, upon application by the Commission or its duly authorized representative, shall have jurisdiction to issue to such person an order requiring such person to appear before an appeal tribunal, a commissioner, the Commission, or its duly authorized representative, in order to produce evidence or to give testimony concerning the matter under investigation or in question. Any failure to obey such court order may be punished by the court as contempt.

B. Any person subpoenaed by the Commission who, without just cause, fails or refuses to attend and testify or to answer to any lawful inquiry or to produce books, papers, correspondence, memoranda and other records, when it is within his power to do so, shall be guilty of a Class 1 misdemeanor.

C. Each day any violation of such court-issued subpoena, court order, or Commission-issued subpoena continues shall be deemed to be a separate offense.

History.
Code 1950, § 60-37; 1968, c. 738, § 60.1-42; 1986, c. 480; 2020, c. 1261.

Editor's note.
Acts 2020, c. 1261, cl. 2 provides: "That the provisions of § 30-19.03:1.2 of the Code of Virginia shall not apply to this act."

Acts 2020, c. 1261, cl. 3 provides: "That the provisions of this act shall expire on January 1, 2021, if the Virginia Employment Commission has not, on or before such date, received adequate funding from the U.S. Department of Labor that covers the costs of information technology upgrades, training, publicity, and marketing that are incurred by the Virginia Employment Commission in connection with establishing the short-time compensation program pursuant to the first enactment of this act." Acts 2020 Sp. Sess. I, c. 8, cl. 2, effective

October 21, 2020, repealed clauses 3 and 4 of Acts 2020, c. 1261. The amendments by Acts 2020, c. 1261 will not expire.

Acts 2020, c. 1261, cl. 4 provides: "That, if not sooner expired pursuant to the provisions of the third enactment of this act, this act shall expire on July 1, 2022." Acts 2020 Sp. Sess. I, c. 8, cl. 2, effective October 21, 2020, repealed clauses 3 and 4 of Acts 2020, c. 1261. The amendments by Acts 2020, c. 1261 will not expire.

The 2020 amendments.
The 2020 amendment by c. 1261 designated the former first and second sentences of the section as subsection A and the former third sentence of the section as subsection B; and rewrote the former last sentence of the section, which read: "Each day such violation continues shall be deemed to be a separate offense" and designated it as subsection C.

§ 60.2-631. Board of Review.

A. The Commissioner, in his discretion, is hereby authorized to appoint a Board of Review consisting of three members, one of whom shall be designated chairman for a term of six years. The terms of the members first taking office shall be two, four, and six years, respectively, as designated by the Commissioner at the time of the appointment. Vacancies shall be filled by appointment by the Commissioner for the unexpired term. During his term of membership on the Board no member shall serve as an officer or committee member of any political organization. The members of the Board shall be compensated in a manner determined by the Commission. The Commission shall furnish the Board such stenographic and clerical assistance as the Board may require. All compensation of the members of the Board and all necessary expenses for the operation thereof shall be paid out of the administrative fund provided for in §§ 60.2-306, 60.2-307, and 60.2-308 and §§ 60.2-311, 60.2-312, and 60.2-313. The Commissioner may at any time, after notice and hearing, remove any member for cause. The Commissioner may, after thirty days' notice to the members of the Board and upon a finding that the Board is no longer needed, abolish the same.

B. 1. The Board shall meet upon the call of the chairman. It shall have the same powers and perform the same functions vested in the Commission in this title for review of decisions by an appeal tribunal, including the power to administer oaths and affirmations, take depositions, certify to official acts, and issue subpoenas to compel the attendance of witnesses and the production of books, papers, correspondence, memoranda and other records deemed necessary as evidence in connection with disputed claims.

2. The Board may hold its hearings in the county or city where the claimant was last employed, except that hearings involving the provisions of subdivision A 2 of § 60.2-612 shall be held in the county or city where the claimant was last employed. When the same or substantially similar evidence is relevant and material to matters in issue in claims by more than one individual or in claims by a single individual with respect to two or more weeks of unemployment, the same time and place for considering each such claim may be fixed, hearings thereon jointly conducted, and a single record of the proceedings made.

C. The Commission may issue such regulations as it deems necessary for the procedure of the Board in the conduct of its hearings. During the time the Board is organized under authority of the Commissioner, the Commission shall have no jurisdiction under § 60.2-622. Any decision of the Board shall become final ten days after the date of notification or mailing and judicial review shall be permitted the claimant, the Commission or any interested party claiming to be aggrieved. In any judicial action involving any such decision the Commission shall be represented by the Office of the Attorney General. Any decision of the Board from which no judicial review is sought within the time prescribed in § 60.2-625 shall be conclusive against any party to the hearing before the Board and the Commission in any subsequent judicial proceedings involving liability for taxes under this title.

D. Within the time specified in § 60.2-625 the Commission, or any party to the proceedings before the Board, may obtain judicial review by filing in the circuit court of the county or city in which the individual who filed the claim was last employed, in the Commonwealth, a petition for review of such decision. In any such proceeding any other party to the proceeding shall be made a party respondent. The Commission shall be deemed to be a party to any such proceeding. The petition need not be verified. A copy of such petition shall be served upon the Commission and each party to the proceeding held before the Board at least thirty days prior to the placing of the petition upon the docket. The mailing of a copy of such petition to each party at his last known address shall be sufficient service. The Commission shall file along with its petition or answer a certified copy of the record of the case, including all documents and papers and a transcript of all testimony taken in the matter, together with the Board's findings, conclusions and decision therein.

E. In any proceeding under this section the Board's findings of facts, if supported by the evidence and in the absence of fraud, shall be conclusive and the jurisdiction of the court shall be confined to questions of law. The court may order additional evidence to be taken by the Board, which such additional evidence, findings of fact or conclusions, together with the additional transcript of the record, shall be certified by the chairman of the Board and filed by him with the court. Such petition for review shall be heard in a summary manner and shall have preference over all other cases on the docket, except cases in which the Commonwealth is a party.

F. An appeal may be taken from the decision of such court to the Court of Appeals in conformity with Part Five A of the Rules of Supreme Court and other applicable laws. From any such decision involving (i) the provisions of § 60.2-612 or § 60.2-618, (ii) whether an employing unit constitutes an employer or (iii) whether services performed for or in connection with the business of an employing unit constitute employment for such employing unit, the Court of Appeals shall have jurisdiction to review such decision regardless of the amount involved in any claim for benefits. It shall not be necessary, in any proceeding before the Board, to enter exceptions to its ruling, and no bond shall be required upon any appeal to any court. Upon the final determination of such judicial proceeding, the Board shall enter an order in accordance with such determination.

History.
  Code 1950, § 60-57; 1966, c. 30; 1968, c. 738, § 60.1-69; 1974, c. 466; 1984, c. 703; 1986, c. 480; 2022, c. 668; 2023, cc. 624, 625.

The 2022 amendments.
  The 2022 amendment by c. 668, substituted "subdivision A 2 of § 60.2-612" for "subdivision 2 of § 60.2-612" in subdivision B 2.

The 2023 amendments.
  The 2023 amendment by cc. 624 and 625 are identical, and substituted "§§ 60.2-306, 60.2-307, and 60.2-308 and §§ 60.2-311, 60.2-312, and 60.2-313" for "§§ 60.2-306 through 60.2-309 and §§ 60.2-311 through 60.2-313" in the sixth sentence of subsection A.

ARTICLE 6.

VIOLATIONS, PENALTIES, AND LIABILITIES.

§ 60.2-633. Receiving benefits to which not entitled.

A. Any person who has received any sum as benefits under this title to which he was not entitled shall be liable to repay such sum to the Commission. For purposes of this section, "benefits under this title" includes benefits under an unemployment benefit program of the United States or of any other state. In the event the claimant does not refund the overpayment, the Commission shall deduct from any future benefits such sum payable to him under this title. However, if an overpayment of benefits under this chapter, but not under an unemployment benefit program of the United States or of any other state, occurred due to administrative error, the Commission shall have the authority to negotiate the terms of repayment, which shall include (i) deducting up to 50 percent of the payable amount for any future week of benefits claimed, rounded down to the next lowest dollar until the overpayment is satisfied; (ii) forgoing collection of the payable amount until the recipient has found employment as defined in § 60.2-212; or (iii) determining and instituting an individualized repayment plan. The Commission shall collect an overpayment of benefits under this chapter caused by administrative error only by offset against future benefits or a negotiated repayment plan; however, the Commission may institute any other method of collection if the individual fails to enter into or comply with the terms of the repayment plan. Administrative error shall not include decisions reversed in the appeals process. In addition, the overpayment may be collectible by civil action in the name of the Commission. Amounts collected in this manner may be subject to an interest charge as prescribed in § 58.1-15 from the date of judgment and may be subject to fees and costs. Collection activities for any benefit overpayment established of five dollars or less may be suspended. The Commission may, for good cause, determine as uncollectible and discharge from its records any benefit overpayment which remains unpaid after the expiration of seven years from the date such overpayment was determined, or immediately upon the death of such person or upon his discharge in bankruptcy occurring subsequently to the determination of overpayment. Any existing overpayment balance not equal to an even dollar amount shall be rounded to the next lowest even dollar amount.

B. The Commission is authorized to accept repayment of benefit overpayments by use of a credit card. The Virginia Employment Commission shall add to such payment a service charge for the acceptance of such card. Such service charge shall not exceed the percentage charged to the Virginia Employment Commission for use of such card.

C. Final orders of the Commission with respect to benefit overpayments may be recorded, enforced and satisfied as orders or decrees of a circuit court upon certification of such orders by the Commissioner as may be appropriate.

History.
   Code 1950, § 60-115; 1962, c. 138; 1968, c. 738, § 60.1-132; 1974, c. 466; 1979, c. 675; 1980, c. 751; 1981, c. 251; 1984, c. 458; 1985, c. 151; 1986, c. 480; 1988, c. 544; 1990, c. 687; 1996, c. 95; 2008, c. 492; 2010, c. 327; 2013, c. 683; 2021, Sp. Sess. I, c. 539.

CHAPTER 7.

SHORT-TIME COMPENSATION PROGRAM.

§ 60.2-711. Definitions.

As used in this chapter, unless the context requires a different meaning:

"Affected unit" means a specific plant, department, shift, or other definable unit of an employing unit that has at least two employees to which an approved short-time compensation plan applies.

"Health and retirement benefits" means employer-provided health benefits and retirement benefits under a defined benefit pension plan as defined in § 414(j) of the Internal Revenue Code or contributions under a defined contribution plan as defined in § 414(i) of the Internal Revenue Code that are incidents of employment in addition to the cash remuneration earned.

"Program" means the short-time compensation program established pursuant to this chapter.

"Short-time compensation" means the unemployment benefits payable to employees in an affected unit under an approved short-time compensation plan, as distinguished from the unemployment benefits otherwise payable under the unemployment compensation provisions of this title.

"Work sharing plan" or *"plan"* means a plan submitted by an employer to the Commission for approval to participate in the Program.

History.
   2020, c. 1261.

Editor's note.
   Acts 2020, c. 1261, cl. 2 provides: "That the provisions of § 30-19.03:1.2 of the Code of Virginia shall not apply to this act."
   Acts 2020, c. 1261, cl. 3 provides: "That the provisions of this act shall expire on January 1, 2021, if the Virginia Employment Commission has not, on or before such date, received adequate funding from the U.S. Department of Labor that covers the costs of information technology upgrades, training, publicity, and marketing that are incurred by the Virginia Employment Commission in connection with establishing the short-time compensation program pursuant to the first enactment of this act." Acts 2020 Sp. Sess. I, c. 8, cl. 2, effective October 21, 2020, repealed clauses 3 and 4 of Acts 2020, c. 1261. This section as enacted by Acts 2020, c. 1261 will not expire.
   Acts 2020, c. 1261, cl. 4 provides: "That, if not sooner expired pursuant to the provisions of the third enactment of this act, this act shall expire on July 1, 2022." Acts 2020 Sp. Sess. I, c. 8, cl. 2, effective October 21, 2020, repealed clauses 3 and 4 of Acts 2020, c. 1261. This section as enacted by Acts 2020, c. 1261 will not expire.

§ 60.2-712. Application to participate in short-time compensation program.

A. The Commission shall establish and implement a short-time compensation program by January 1, 2022. The Program shall meet the requirements of 22 U.S.C. § 3306(v) and all other applicable federal and state laws.

B. An employer that wishes to participate in the Program shall submit to the Commission a signed, written work sharing plan for approval. The Commission shall develop an application form to request approval of a plan and an approval process. The application shall include:

1. The affected unit covered by the plan, including the number of employees in the unit; the percentage of employees in the affected unit covered by the plan; identification of each individual employee in the affected unit by name, social security number, and the employer's unemployment tax account number; and any other information required by the Commission to identify plan participants.

2. A description of how employees in the affected unit will be notified of the employer's participation in the plan if such application is approved, including how the employer will notify those employees in a collective bargaining unit as well as any employees in the affected unit who are not in a collective bargaining unit. If the employer does not intend to provide advance notice to employees in the affected unit, the employer shall explain in a statement in the application why it is not feasible to provide such notice.

3. A requirement that the employer identify, in the application, the usual weekly hours of work for employees in the affected unit and the specific percentage by which their hours will be reduced during all weeks covered by the plan. The percentage of reduction for which a work sharing plan application may be approved shall be not less than 10 percent and not more than 60 percent. If the plan includes any week for which the employer regularly does not provide work, including incidences due to a holiday or other plant closing, then such week shall be identified in the application.

4. Certification by the employer that, if the employer provides health benefits and retirement benefits to any employee whose usual weekly hours of work are reduced under the Program, such benefits will continue to be provided to employees participating in the Program under the same terms and conditions as though the usual weekly hours of work of such employee had not been reduced or to the same extent as other employees not participating in the Program. For defined benefit retirement plans, the hours that are reduced under the plan shall be credited for purposes of participation, vesting, and accrual of benefits as though the usual weekly hours of work had not been reduced. The dollar amount of employer contributions to a defined contribution plan that are based on a percentage of compensation may be less due to the reduction in the employee's compensation.

5. Certification by the employer that the aggregate reduction in work hours is in lieu of layoffs, whether temporary or permanent layoffs or both. The application shall include an estimate of the number of employees who would have been laid off in the absence of the plan. The employer shall also certify that new employees will not be hired in or transferred to an affected unit for the duration of the plan.

6. Certification by the employer that participation in the plan and its implementation is consistent with the employer's obligations under applicable federal and state laws.

7. Agreement by the employer to (i) furnish reports to the Commission relating to the proper conduct of the plan; (ii) allow the Commission access to all records necessary to approve or disapprove the plan application and, after approval of a plan, monitor and evaluate the plan; and (iii) follow any other directives the Commission deems necessary to implement the plan and that are consistent with the requirements for plan applications.

8. Any other provision added to the application by the Commission that the

U.S. Secretary of Labor determines to be appropriate for purposes of a work sharing plan.

History.
2020, c. 1261; 2020, Sp. Sess. I, c. 8.

Editor's note.
Acts 2020, c. 1261, cl. 2 provides: "That the provisions of § 30-19.03:1.2 of the Code of Virginia shall not apply to this act."
Acts 2020, c. 1261, cl. 3 provides: "That the provisions of this act shall expire on January 1, 2021, if the Virginia Employment Commission has not, on or before such date, received adequate funding from the U.S. Department of Labor that covers the costs of information technology upgrades, training, publicity, and marketing that are incurred by the Virginia Employment Commission in connection with establishing the short-time compensation program pursuant to the first enactment of this

act." Acts 2020 Sp. Sess. I, c. 8, cl. 2, effective October 21, 2020, repealed clauses 3 and 4 of Acts 2020, c. 1261. This section as enacted by Acts 2020, c. 1261 will not expire.
Acts 2020, c. 1261, cl. 4 provides: "That, if not sooner expired pursuant to the provisions of the third enactment of this act, this act shall expire on July 1, 2022." Acts 2020 Sp. Sess. I, c. 8, cl. 2, effective October 21, 2020, repealed clauses 3 and 4 of Acts 2020, c. 1261. This section as enacted by Acts 2020, c. 1261 will not expire.

The 2020 Sp. Sess. I amendments.
The 2020 amendment by Sp. Sess. I, c. 8, effective October 21, 2020, "substituted "January 1, 2022" for "January 1, 2021" in subsection A.

§ 60.2-713. Approval and disapproval of plan.

The Commission shall approve or disapprove a work sharing plan in writing within 10 working days of its receipt and promptly communicate the decision to the employer. A decision disapproving the plan shall clearly identify the reasons for the disapproval. If a plan is disapproved, the employer may submit a different work sharing plan for approval.

History.
2020, c. 1261.

Editor's note.
Acts 2020, c. 1261, cl. 2 provides: "That the provisions of § 30-19.03:1.2 of the Code of Virginia shall not apply to this act."
Acts 2020, c. 1261, cl. 3 provides: "That the provisions of this act shall expire on January 1, 2021, if the Virginia Employment Commission has not, on or before such date, received adequate funding from the U.S. Department of Labor that covers the costs of information technology upgrades, training, publicity, and marketing that are incurred by the Virginia Em-

ployment Commission in connection with establishing the short-time compensation program pursuant to the first enactment of this act." Acts 2020 Sp. Sess. I, c. 8, cl. 2, effective October 21, 2020, repealed clauses 3 and 4 of Acts 2020, c. 1261. This section as enacted by Acts 2020, c. 1261 will not expire.
Acts 2020, c. 1261, cl. 4 provides: "That, if not sooner expired pursuant to the provisions of the third enactment of this act, this act shall expire on July 1, 2022." Acts 2020 Sp. Sess. I, c. 8, cl. 2, effective October 21, 2020, repealed clauses 3 and 4 of Acts 2020, c. 1261. This section as enacted by Acts 2020, c. 1261 will not expire.

§ 60.2-714. Effective date, duration, and modification of plan.

A. A work sharing plan shall be effective on the date that is mutually agreed upon by the employer and the Commission, which shall be specified in the notice of approval to the employer. The plan shall expire on the date specified in the notice of approval, which shall be either the date at the end of the twelfth full calendar month after its effective date or an earlier date mutually agreed upon by the employer and the Commission. However, if a work sharing plan is revoked by the Commission under subsection B, the plan shall terminate on the date specified in the Commission's written order of revocation. An employer may terminate a plan at any time upon written notice to the Commission. Upon receipt of such notice from the employer, the Commission shall promptly notify each member of the affected unit of the termination date. An employer may submit a new application to participate in another plan at any time after the expiration or termination date.

B. The Commission may revoke approval of a work sharing plan for good cause at any time, including upon the request of any of the affected unit's employees. The revocation order shall be in writing and shall specify the reasons for the revocation and the date the revocation is effective. The Commission may periodically review the operation of each employer's plan to assure that no good cause exists for revocation of the approval of the plan. Good cause shall include failure to comply with the assurances given in the plan, unreasonable revision of productivity standards for the affected unit, conduct or occurrences tending to defeat the intent and effective operation of the plan, and violation of any criteria on which approval of the plan was based.

C. An employer may request a modification of an approved plan by filing a written request to the Commission. The request shall identify the specific provisions proposed to be modified and provide an explanation of why the proposed modification is appropriate for the plan. The Commission shall approve or disapprove the proposed modification in writing within 10 working days and promptly communicate the decision to the employer. An employer is not required to request approval of a plan modification from the Commission if the change is not substantial, but the employer shall report every change to the plan to the Commission promptly and in writing.

History.
2020, c. 1261.

Editor's note.
Acts 2020, c. 1261, cl. 2 provides: "That the provisions of § 30-19.03:1.2 of the Code of Virginia shall not apply to this act."
Acts 2020, c. 1261, cl. 3 provides: "That the provisions of this act shall expire on January 1, 2021, if the Virginia Employment Commission has not, on or before such date, received adequate funding from the U.S. Department of Labor that covers the costs of information technology upgrades, training, publicity, and marketing that are incurred by the Virginia Employment Commission in connection with establishing the short-time compensation program pursuant to the first enactment of this act." Acts 2020 Sp. Sess. I, c. 8, cl. 2, effective October 21, 2020, repealed clauses 3 and 4 of Acts 2020, c. 1261. This section as enacted by Acts 2020, c. 1261 will not expire.
Acts 2020, c. 1261, cl. 4 provides: "That, if not sooner expired pursuant to the provisions of the third enactment of this act, this act shall expire on July 1, 2022." Acts 2020 Sp. Sess. I, c. 8, cl. 2, effective October 21, 2020, repealed clauses 3 and 4 of Acts 2020, c. 1261. This section as enacted by Acts 2020, c. 1261 will not expire.

§ 60.2-715. Eligibility for short-time compensation.

A. An employee is eligible to receive short-time compensation under a work sharing plan with respect to any week only if the employee is monetarily eligible for unemployment compensation, not otherwise disqualified for unemployment compensation, and:

1. During the week, the employee is employed as a member of an affected unit under an approved work sharing plan that was approved prior to that week, and the plan is in effect with respect to the week for which short-time compensation is claimed; and

2. Notwithstanding any other provisions of this title relating to availability for work and actively seeking work, the employee is available for the employee's usual hours of work with the short-time compensation employer, which may include, for purposes of this section, participating in training, including employer-sponsored training or training funded under the federal Workforce Innovation and Opportunity Act of 2014, to enhance job skills that is approved by the Commission.

B. Notwithstanding any other provision of law, an employee covered by a work sharing plan is deemed unemployed in any week during the duration of that plan if the employee's remuneration as an employee in an affected unit is reduced based on a reduction of the employee's usual weekly hours of work under an approved work sharing plan.

C. The short-term compensation program shall not serve as a subsidy of seasonal employment during the off-season, nor as a subsidy of temporary part-time or intermittent employment.

History.
2020, c. 1261.

Editor's note.
Acts 2020, c. 1261, cl. 2 provides: "That the provisions of § 30-19.03:1.2 of the Code of Virginia shall not apply to this act."

Acts 2020, c. 1261, cl. 3 provides: "That the provisions of this act shall expire on January 1, 2021, if the Virginia Employment Commission has not, on or before such date, received adequate funding from the U.S. Department of Labor that covers the costs of information technology upgrades, training, publicity, and marketing that are incurred by the Virginia Employment Commission in connection with establishing the short-time compensation program pursuant to the first enactment of this act." Acts 2020 Sp. Sess. I, c. 8, cl. 2, effective October 21, 2020, repealed clauses 3 and 4 of Acts 2020, c. 1261. This section as enacted by Acts 2020, c. 1261 will not expire.

Acts 2020, c. 1261, cl. 4 provides: "That, if not sooner expired pursuant to the provisions of the third enactment of this act, this act shall expire on July 1, 2022." Acts 2020 Sp. Sess. I, c. 8, cl. 2, effective October 21, 2020, repealed clauses 3 and 4 of Acts 2020, c. 1261. This section as enacted by Acts 2020, c. 1261 will not expire.

§ 60.2-716. Benefits.

A. The short-time compensation weekly benefit amount shall be the product of the regular weekly unemployment compensation amount for a week of total unemployment multiplied by the percentage of reduction in the individual's usual weekly hours of work.

B. An individual may be eligible for short-time compensation or unemployment compensation, as appropriate, except that (i) no individual shall be eligible for combined benefits in any benefit year in an amount more than the maximum entitlement established for regular unemployment compensation and (ii) no individual shall be paid short-time compensation benefits for more than 26 weeks under a plan.

C. Provisions applicable to unemployment compensation claimants shall apply to short-time compensation claimants to the extent that they are not inconsistent with the Program's provisions. An individual who files an initial claim for short-time compensation benefits shall receive a monetary determination.

D. An employee who is not provided any work during a week by the short-time compensation employer, or any other employer, and who is otherwise eligible for unemployment compensation shall be eligible for the amount of regular unemployment compensation to which he would otherwise be eligible.

E. An employee who is not provided any work by the short-time compensation employer during a week, but who works for another employer and is otherwise eligible, may be paid unemployment compensation for that week subject to the disqualifying income and other provisions applicable to claims for regular compensation.

F. An employee who has received all of the short-time compensation or combined unemployment compensation and short-time compensation available in a benefit year shall be considered an exhaustee for purposes of extended benefits and, if otherwise eligible under those provisions, shall be eligible to receive extended benefits.

History.

2020, c. 1261.

Editor's note.

Acts 2020, c. 1261, cl. 2 provides: "That the provisions of § 30-19.03:1.2 of the Code of Virginia shall not apply to this act."

Acts 2020, c. 1261, cl. 3 provides: "That the provisions of this act shall expire on January 1, 2021, if the Virginia Employment Commission has not, on or before such date, received adequate funding from the U.S. Department of Labor that covers the costs of information technology upgrades, training, publicity, and marketing that are incurred by the Virginia Employment Commission in connection with establishing the short-time compensation program pursuant to the first enactment of this act." Acts 2020 Sp. Sess. I, c. 8, cl. 2, effective October 21, 2020, repealed clauses 3 and 4 of Acts 2020, c. 1261. This section as enacted by Acts 2020, c. 1261 will not expire.

Acts 2020, c. 1261, cl. 4 provides: "That, if not sooner expired pursuant to the provisions of the third enactment of this act, this act shall expire on July 1, 2022." Acts 2020 Sp. Sess. I, c. 8, cl. 2, effective October 21, 2020, repealed clauses 3 and 4 of Acts 2020, c. 1261. This section as enacted by Acts 2020, c. 1261 will not expire.

TITLE 62.1.

WATERS OF THE STATE, PORTS AND HARBORS.

CHAPTER 3.1.

STATE WATER CONTROL LAW.

Article 1. General Provisions.

Article 2. Control Board Generally.

Article 2.1. Permit Fees.

Article 2.2. Virginia Water Resources and Wetlands Protection Program.

ARTICLE 1.
GENERAL PROVISIONS.

§ 62.1-44.3. (Effective until July 1, 2024) Definitions.

Unless a different meaning is required by the context, the following terms as used in this chapter shall have the meanings hereinafter respectively ascribed to them:

"Beneficial use" means both instream and offstream uses. Instream beneficial uses include, but are not limited to, the protection of fish and wildlife resources and habitat, maintenance of waste assimilation, recreation, navigation, and cultural and aesthetic values. The preservation of instream flows for purposes of the protection of navigation, maintenance of waste assimilation capacity, the protection of fish and wildlife resources and habitat, recreation, cultural and aesthetic values is an instream beneficial use of Virginia's waters. Offstream beneficial uses include, but are not limited to, domestic (including public water supply), agricultural uses, electric power generation, commercial, and industrial uses.

"Board" means the State Water Control Board. However, when used outside the context of the promulgation of regulations, including regulations to establish general permits, pursuant to this chapter, "Board" means the Department of Environmental Quality.

"Certificate" means any certificate issued by the Department.

"Department" means the Department of Environmental Quality.

"Director" means the Director of the Department of Environmental Quality.

"Establishment" means any industrial establishment, mill, factory, tannery, paper or pulp mill, mine, coal mine, colliery, breaker or coal-processing operations, quarry, oil refinery, boat, vessel, and every other industry or plant or works the operation of which produces industrial wastes or other wastes or which may otherwise alter the physical, chemical or biological properties of any state waters.

"Excavate" or "excavation" means ditching, dredging, or mechanized removal of earth, soil or rock.

"Industrial wastes" means liquid or other wastes resulting from any process of industry, manufacture, trade, or business or from the development of any natural resources.

"The law" or "this law" means the law contained in this chapter as now existing or hereafter amended.

181

"Member" means a member of the Board.

"Normal agricultural activities" means those activities defined as an agricultural operation in § 3.2-300 and any activity that is conducted as part of or in furtherance of such agricultural operation but shall not include any activity for which a permit would have been required as of January 1, 1997, under 33 U.S.C. § 1344 or any regulations promulgated pursuant thereto.

"Normal silvicultural activities" means any silvicultural activity as defined in § 10.1-1181.1 and any activity that is conducted as part of or in furtherance of such silvicultural activity but shall not include any activity for which a permit would have been required as of January 1, 1997, under 33 U.S.C. § 1344 or any regulations promulgated pursuant thereto.

"Other wastes" means decayed wood, sawdust, shavings, bark, lime, garbage, refuse, ashes, offal, tar, oil, chemicals, and all other substances except industrial wastes and sewage which may cause pollution in any state waters.

"Owner" means the Commonwealth or any of its political subdivisions, including but not limited to sanitation district commissions and authorities and any public or private institution, corporation, association, firm, or company organized or existing under the laws of this or any other state or country, or any officer or agency of the United States, or any person or group of persons acting individually or as a group that owns, operates, charters, rents, or otherwise exercises control over or is responsible for any actual or potential discharge of sewage, industrial wastes, or other wastes to state waters, or any facility or operation that has the capability to alter the physical, chemical, or biological properties of state waters in contravention of § 62.1-44.5.

"Person" means an individual, corporation, partnership, association, governmental body, municipal corporation, or any other legal entity.

"Policies" means policies established under subdivisions (3a) and (3b) of § 62.1-44.15.

"Pollution" means such alteration of the physical, chemical, or biological properties of any state waters as will or is likely to create a nuisance or render such waters (a) harmful or detrimental or injurious to the public health, safety, or welfare or to the health of animals, fish, or aquatic life; (b) unsuitable with reasonable treatment for use as present or possible future sources of public water supply; or (c) unsuitable for recreational, commercial, industrial, agricultural, or other reasonable uses, provided that (i) an alteration of the physical, chemical, or biological property of state waters or a discharge or deposit of sewage, industrial wastes or other wastes to state waters by any owner which by itself is not sufficient to cause pollution but which, in combination with such alteration of or discharge or deposit to state waters by other owners, is sufficient to cause pollution; (ii) the discharge of untreated sewage by any owner into state waters; and (iii) contributing to the contravention of standards of water quality duly established by the Board, are "pollution" for the terms and purposes of this chapter.

"Pretreatment requirements" means any requirements arising under the Board's pretreatment regulations including the duty to allow or carry out inspections, entry, or monitoring activities; any rules, regulations, or orders issued by the owner of a publicly owned treatment works; or any reporting requirements imposed by the owner of a publicly owned treatment works or by the regulations of the Board.

"Pretreatment standards" means any standards of performance or other requirements imposed by regulation of the Board upon an industrial user of a publicly owned treatment works.

"Reclaimed water" means water resulting from the treatment of domestic, municipal, or industrial wastewater that is suitable for a direct beneficial or controlled use that would not otherwise occur. Specifically excluded from this definition is "gray water."

"Reclamation" means the treatment of domestic, municipal, or industrial wastewater or sewage to produce reclaimed water for a direct beneficial or controlled use that would not otherwise occur.

"Regulation" means a regulation issued under § 62.1-44.15 (10).

"Reuse" means the use of reclaimed water for a direct beneficial use or a controlled use that is in accordance with the requirements of the Board.

"Rule" means a rule adopted by the Board to regulate the procedure of the Board pursuant to § 62.1-44.15 (7).

"Ruling" means a ruling issued under § 62.1-44.15 (9).

"Sewage" means the water-carried human wastes from residences, buildings, industrial establishments or other places together with such industrial wastes and underground, surface, storm, or other water as may be present.

"Sewage treatment works" or "treatment works" means any device or system used in the storage, treatment, disposal, or reclamation of sewage or combinations of sewage and industrial wastes, including but not limited to pumping, power, and other equipment, and appurtenances, and any works, including land, that are or will be (i) an integral part of the treatment process or (ii) used for the ultimate disposal of residues or effluent resulting from such treatment. These terms shall not include onsite sewage systems or alternative discharging sewage systems.

"Sewerage system" means pipelines or conduits, pumping stations, and force mains, and all other construction, devices, and appliances appurtenant thereto, used for conducting sewage or industrial wastes or other wastes to a point of ultimate disposal.

"Special order" means a special order issued under subdivisions (8a), (8b), and (8c) of § 62.1-44.15.

"Standards" means standards established under subdivisions (3a) and (3b) of § 62.1-44.15.

"State waters" means all water, on the surface and under the ground, wholly or partially within or bordering the Commonwealth or within its jurisdiction, including wetlands.

"Wetlands" means those areas that are inundated or saturated by surface or groundwater at a frequency and duration sufficient to support, and that under normal circumstances do support, a prevalence of vegetation typically adapted for life in saturated soil conditions. Wetlands generally include swamps, marshes, bogs and similar areas.

History.
Code 1950, § 62.1-15; 1968, c. 659; 1970, c. 638; 1988, c. 167; 1990, c. 717; 1991, c. 702; 2000, cc. 972, 1032, 1054; 2003, c. 614; 2007, c. 659; 2015, cc. 104, 677; 2016, cc. 68, 758; 2022, c. 356.

Section set out twice.
The section above is effective until July 1, 2024. For this section as in effect on July 1, 2024, see the following section, also numbered 62.1-44.3.

The 2022 amendments.
The 2022 amendment by c. 356 added the second sentence in the definition of "Board"; and substituted "Department" for "Board" in the definition of "Certificate."

§ 62.1-44.3. (Effective July 1, 2024) Definitions.

Unless a different meaning is required by the context, the following terms as used in this chapter shall have the meanings hereinafter respectively ascribed to them:

"Beneficial use" means both instream and offstream uses. Instream beneficial uses include, but are not limited to, the protection of fish and wildlife resources and habitat, maintenance of waste assimilation, recreation, navigation, and cultural and aesthetic values. The preservation of instream flows for

purposes of the protection of navigation, maintenance of waste assimilation capacity, the protection of fish and wildlife resources and habitat, recreation, cultural and aesthetic values is an instream beneficial use of Virginia's waters. Offstream beneficial uses include, but are not limited to, domestic (including public water supply), agricultural uses, electric power generation, commercial, and industrial uses.

"*Board*" means the State Water Control Board. However, when used outside the context of the promulgation of regulations, including regulations to establish general permits, pursuant to this chapter, "*Board*" means the Department of Environmental Quality.

"*Certificate*" means any certificate or permit issued by the Department.

"*Department*" means the Department of Environmental Quality.

"*Director*" means the Director of the Department of Environmental Quality.

"*Establishment*" means any industrial establishment, mill, factory, tannery, paper or pulp mill, mine, coal mine, colliery, breaker or coal-processing operations, quarry, oil refinery, boat, vessel, and every other industry or plant or works the operation of which produces industrial wastes or other wastes or which may otherwise alter the physical, chemical or biological properties of any state waters.

"*Excavate*" or "excavation" means ditching, dredging, or mechanized removal of earth, soil or rock.

"*Industrial wastes*" means liquid or other wastes resulting from any process of industry, manufacture, trade, or business or from the development of any natural resources.

"*Land-disturbance approval*" means an approval allowing a land-disturbing activity to commence issued by (i) a Virginia Erosion and Stormwater Management Program authority after the requirements of § 62.1-44.15:34 have been met or (ii) a Virginia Erosion and Sediment Control Program authority after the requirements of § 62.1-44.15:55 have been met.

"*The law*" or "*this law*" means the law contained in this chapter as now existing or hereafter amended.

"*Member*" means a member of the Board.

"*Municipal separate storm sewer*" means a conveyance or system of conveyances otherwise known as a municipal separate storm sewer system or "MS4," including roads with drainage systems, municipal streets, catch basins, curbs, gutters, ditches, man-made channels, or storm drains, that is:

1. Owned or operated by a federal entity, state, city, town, county, district, association, or other public body, created by or pursuant to state law, having jurisdiction over disposal of sewage, industrial wastes, stormwater, or other wastes, including a special district under state law such as a sewer district, flood control district, drainage district or similar entity, or a designated and approved management agency under § 208 of the federal Clean Water Act (33 U.S.C. § 1251 et seq.) that discharges to surface waters;

2. Designed or used for collecting or conveying stormwater;

3. Not a combined sewer; and

4. Not part of a publicly owned treatment works.

"*Normal agricultural activities*" means those activities defined as an agricultural operation in § 3.2-300 and any activity that is conducted as part of or in furtherance of such agricultural operation but shall not include any activity for which a permit would have been required as of January 1, 1997, under 33 U.S.C. § 1344 or any regulations promulgated pursuant thereto.

"*Normal silvicultural activities*" means any silvicultural activity as defined in § 10.1-1181.1 and any activity that is conducted as part of or in furtherance of such silvicultural activity but shall not include any activity for which a permit would have been required as of January 1, 1997, under 33 U.S.C. § 1344 or any regulations promulgated pursuant thereto.

"Other wastes" means decayed wood, sawdust, shavings, bark, lime, garbage, refuse, ashes, offal, tar, oil, chemicals, and all other substances except industrial wastes and sewage which may cause pollution in any state waters.

"Owner" means the Commonwealth or any of its political subdivisions, including but not limited to sanitation district commissions and authorities and any public or private institution, corporation, association, firm, or company organized or existing under the laws of this or any other state or country, or any officer or agency of the United States, or any person or group of persons acting individually or as a group that owns, operates, charters, rents, or otherwise exercises control over or is responsible for any actual or potential discharge of sewage, industrial wastes, or other wastes to state waters, or any facility or operation that has the capability to alter the physical, chemical, or biological properties of state waters in contravention of § 62.1-44.5.

"Person" means an individual, corporation, partnership, association, governmental body, municipal corporation, or any other legal entity.

"Policies" means policies established under subdivisions (3a) and (3b) of § 62.1-44.15.

"Pollution" means such alteration of the physical, chemical, or biological properties of any state waters as will or is likely to create a nuisance or render such waters (a) harmful or detrimental or injurious to the public health, safety, or welfare or to the health of animals, fish, or aquatic life; (b) unsuitable with reasonable treatment for use as present or possible future sources of public water supply; or (c) unsuitable for recreational, commercial, industrial, agricultural, or other reasonable uses, provided that (i) an alteration of the physical, chemical, or biological property of state waters or a discharge or deposit of sewage, industrial wastes or other wastes to state waters by any owner which by itself is not sufficient to cause pollution but which, in combination with such alteration of or discharge or deposit to state waters by other owners, is sufficient to cause pollution; (ii) the discharge of untreated sewage by any owner into state waters; and (iii) contributing to the contravention of standards of water quality duly established by the Board, are "pollution" for the terms and purposes of this chapter.

"Pretreatment requirements" means any requirements arising under the Board's pretreatment regulations including the duty to allow or carry out inspections, entry, or monitoring activities; any rules, regulations, or orders issued by the owner of a publicly owned treatment works; or any reporting requirements imposed by the owner of a publicly owned treatment works or by the regulations of the Board.

"Pretreatment standards" means any standards of performance or other requirements imposed by regulation of the Board upon an industrial user of a publicly owned treatment works.

"Reclaimed water" means water resulting from the treatment of domestic, municipal, or industrial wastewater that is suitable for a direct beneficial or controlled use that would not otherwise occur. Specifically excluded from this definition is "gray water."

"Reclamation" means the treatment of domestic, municipal, or industrial wastewater or sewage to produce reclaimed water for a direct beneficial or controlled use that would not otherwise occur.

"Regulation" means a regulation issued under subdivision (10) of § 62.1-44.15.

"Reuse" means the use of reclaimed water for a direct beneficial use or a controlled use that is in accordance with the requirements of the Board.

"Rule" means a rule adopted by the Board to regulate the procedure of the Board pursuant to subdivision (7) of § 62.1-44.15.

"Ruling" means a ruling issued under subdivision (9) of § 62.1-44.15.

"*Sewage*" means the water-carried human wastes from residences, buildings, industrial establishments or other places together with such industrial wastes and underground, surface, storm, or other water as may be present.

"*Sewage treatment works*" or "treatment works" means any device or system used in the storage, treatment, disposal, or reclamation of sewage or combinations of sewage and industrial wastes, including but not limited to pumping, power, and other equipment, and appurtenances, and any works, including land, that are or will be (i) an integral part of the treatment process or (ii) used for the ultimate disposal of residues or effluent resulting from such treatment. These terms shall not include onsite sewage systems or alternative discharging sewage systems.

"*Sewerage system*" means pipelines or conduits, pumping stations, and force mains, and all other construction, devices, and appliances appurtenant thereto, used for conducting sewage or industrial wastes or other wastes to a point of ultimate disposal.

"*Special order*" means a special order issued under subdivisions (8a), (8b), and (8c) of § 62.1-44.15.

"*Standards*" means standards established under subdivisions (3a) and (3b) of § 62.1-44.15.

"*State waters*" means all water, on the surface and under the ground, wholly or partially within or bordering the Commonwealth or within its jurisdiction, including wetlands.

"*Wetlands*" means those areas that are inundated or saturated by surface or groundwater at a frequency and duration sufficient to support, and that under normal circumstances do support, a prevalence of vegetation typically adapted for life in saturated soil conditions. Wetlands generally include swamps, marshes, bogs and similar areas.

History.
Code 1950, § 62.1-15; 1968, c. 659; 1970, c. 638; 1988, c. 167; 1990, c. 717; 1991, c. 702; 2000, cc. 972, 1032, 1054; 2003, c. 614; 2007, c. 659; 2015, cc. 104, 677; 2016, cc. 68, 758; 2022, c. 356.

Section set out twice.
The section above is effective July 1, 2024. For this section as in effect until July 1, 2024, see the preceding section, also numbered 62.1-44.3.

§ 62.1-44.6:1. Permit rationale.

In granting a permit pursuant to this chapter, the Department shall provide in writing a clear and concise statement of the legal basis, scientific rationale, and justification for the decision reached. When the decision of the Department is to deny a permit pursuant to this chapter, the Department shall, in consultation with legal counsel, provide a clear and concise statement explaining the reason for the denial, the scientific justification for the same, and how the Department's decision is in compliance with applicable laws and regulations. Copies of the decision, certified by the Director, shall be mailed by certified mail to the permittee or applicant.

History.
2022, c. 356.

ARTICLE 2.
CONTROL BOARD GENERALLY.

§ 62.1-44.14. Chairman; Executive Director; employment of personnel; supervision; budget preparation.

The Board shall elect its chairman, and the Executive Director shall be appointed as set forth in § 2.2-106. The Executive Director shall serve as executive officer and devote his whole time to the performance of his duties, and he shall have such administrative powers as are conferred upon him by the Board; and, further, the Board may delegate to its Executive Director any of the powers and duties invested in it by this chapter except the adoption and promulgation of standards, rules and regulations; and the revocation of certificates. The Executive Director is authorized to issue, modify or revoke orders in cases of emergency as described in §§ 62.1-44.15 (8b) and 62.1-44.34:20 of this chapter. The Executive Director is further authorized to employ such consultants and full-time technical and clerical workers as are necessary and within the available funds to carry out the purposes of this chapter.

It shall be the duty of the Executive Director to exercise general supervision and control over the quality and management of all state waters and to administer and enforce this chapter, and all certificates, standards, policies, rules, regulations, rulings and special orders promulgated by the Board. The Executive Director shall prepare, approve, and submit all requests for appropriations and be responsible for all expenditures pursuant to appropriations. The Executive Director shall be vested with all the authority of the Board when it is not in session, except for the Board's authority to issue special orders pursuant to subdivisions (8a) and (8b) of § 62.1-44.15 and subject to such regulations as may be prescribed by the Board. In no event shall the Executive Director have the authority to adopt or promulgate any regulation.

History.
Code 1950, § 62.1-26; 1968, c. 659; 1970, c. 638; 1981, c. 620; 1984, c. 444; 1985, c. 397; 1992, c. 456; 2005, c. 706; 2013, cc. 756, 793; 2022, c. 356.

The 2022 amendments.
The 2022 amendment by c. 356 deleted "to consider permits pursuant to § 62.1-44.15:02" following "the Board's authority" in the second paragraph in the penultimate sentence.

§ 62.1-44.15. (Effective until July 1, 2024) Powers and duties; civil penalties.

It shall be the duty of the Board and it shall have the authority:

(1) [Repealed.]

(2) To study and investigate all problems concerned with the quality of state waters and to make reports and recommendations.

(2a) To study and investigate methods, procedures, devices, appliances, and technologies that could assist in water conservation or water consumption reduction.

(2b) To coordinate its efforts toward water conservation with other persons or groups, within or without the Commonwealth.

(2c) To make reports concerning, and formulate recommendations based upon, any such water conservation studies to ensure that present and future water needs of the citizens of the Commonwealth are met.

(3a) To establish such standards of quality and policies for any state waters consistent with the general policy set forth in this chapter, and to modify, amend or cancel any such standards or policies established and to take all appropriate steps to prevent quality alteration contrary to the public interest or to standards or policies thus established, except that a description of provisions of any proposed standard or policy adopted by regulation which are more restrictive than applicable federal requirements, together with the reason why the more restrictive provisions are needed, shall be provided to the standing committee of each house of the General Assembly to which matters relating to the content of the standard or policy are most properly referable. The Board shall, from time to time, but at least once every three years, hold public hearings pursuant to § 2.2-4007.01 but, upon the request of an affected person or upon its own motion, hold hearings pursuant to § 2.2-4009, for the purpose of reviewing the standards of quality, and, as appropriate, adopting, modifying, or canceling such standards. Whenever the Board considers the adoption, modification, amendment or cancellation of any standard, it shall give due consideration to, among other factors, the economic and social costs and benefits which can reasonably be expected to obtain as a consequence of the standards as adopted, modified, amended or cancelled. The Board shall also give due consideration to the public health standards issued by the Virginia Department of Health with respect to issues of public health policy and protection. If the Board does not follow the public health standards of the Virginia Department of Health, the Board's reason for any deviation shall be made in writing and published for any and all concerned parties.

(3b) Except as provided in subdivision (3a), such standards and policies are to be adopted or modified, amended or cancelled in the manner provided by the Administrative Process Act (§ 2.2-4000 et seq.).

(4) To conduct or have conducted scientific experiments, investigations, studies, and research to discover methods for maintaining water quality consistent with the purposes of this chapter. To this end the Board may cooperate with any public or private agency in the conduct of such experiments, investigations and research and may receive in behalf of the Commonwealth any moneys that any such agency may contribute as its share of the cost under any such cooperative agreement. Such moneys shall be used only for the purposes for which they are contributed and any balance remaining after the conclusion of the experiments, investigations, studies, and research, shall be returned to the contributors.

(5) To issue, revoke or amend certificates under prescribed conditions for: (a) the discharge of sewage, industrial wastes and other wastes into or adjacent to state waters; (b) the alteration otherwise of the physical, chemical or biological properties of state waters; (c) excavation in a wetland; or (d) on and after October 1, 2001, the conduct of the following activities in a wetland: (i) new activities to cause draining that significantly alters or degrades existing wetland acreage or functions, (ii) filling or dumping, (iii) permanent flooding or impounding, or (iv) new activities that cause significant alteration or degradation of existing wetland acreage or functions. However, to the extent allowed by federal law, any person holding a certificate issued by the Board that is intending to upgrade the permitted facility by installing technology, control equipment, or other apparatus that the permittee demonstrates to the satisfaction of the Director will result in improved energy efficiency, reduction in the amount of nutrients discharged, and improved water quality shall not be required to obtain a new, modified, or amended permit. The permit holder shall provide the demonstration anticipated by this subdivision to the Department no later than 30 days prior to commencing construction.

(5a) All certificates issued by the Board under this chapter shall have fixed terms. The term of a Virginia Pollution Discharge Elimination System permit shall not exceed five years. The term of a Virginia Water Protection Permit shall be based upon the projected duration of the project, the length of any required monitoring, or other project operations or permit conditions; however, the term shall not exceed 15 years. The term of a Virginia Pollution Abatement permit shall not exceed 10 years, except that the term of a Virginia Pollution Abatement permit for confined animal feeding operations shall be 10 years. The Department of Environmental Quality shall inspect all facilities for which a Virginia Pollution Abatement permit has been issued to ensure compliance with statutory, regulatory, and permit requirements. Department personnel performing inspections of confined animal feeding operations shall be certified under the voluntary nutrient management training and certification program established in § 10.1-104.2. The term of a certificate issued by the Board shall not be extended by modification beyond the maximum duration and the certificate shall expire at the end of the term unless an application for a new permit has been timely filed as required by the regulations of the Board and the Board is unable, through no fault of the permittee, to issue a new permit before the expiration date of the previous permit.

(5b) Any certificate issued by the Board under this chapter may, after notice and opportunity for a hearing, be amended or revoked on any of the following grounds or for good cause as may be provided by the regulations of the Board:

1. The owner has violated any regulation or order of the Board, any condition of a certificate, any provision of this chapter, or any order of a court, where such violation results in a release of harmful substances into the environment or poses a substantial threat of release of harmful substances into the environment or presents a hazard to human health or the violation is representative of a pattern of serious or repeated violations which, in the opinion of the Board, demonstrates the owner's disregard for or inability to comply with applicable laws, regulations, or requirements;

2. The owner has failed to disclose fully all relevant material facts or has misrepresented a material fact in applying for a certificate, or in any other report or document required under this law or under the regulations of the Board;

3. The activity for which the certificate was issued endangers human health or the environment and can be regulated to acceptable levels by amendment or revocation of the certificate; or

4. There exists a material change in the basis on which the permit was issued that requires either a temporary or a permanent reduction or elimination of any discharge controlled by the certificate necessary to protect human health or the environment.

(5c) Any certificate issued by the Board under this chapter relating to dredging projects governed under Chapter 12 (§ 28.2-1200 et seq.) or Chapter 13 (§ 28.2-1300 et seq.) of Title 28.2 may be conditioned upon a demonstration of financial responsibility for the completion of compensatory mitigation requirements. Financial responsibility may be demonstrated by a letter of credit, a certificate of deposit or a performance bond executed in a form approved by the Board. If the U.S. Army Corps of Engineers requires demonstration of financial responsibility for the completion of compensatory mitigation required for a particular project, then the mechanism and amount approved by the U.S. Army Corps of Engineers shall be used to meet this requirement.

(6) To make investigations and inspections, to ensure compliance with any certificates, standards, policies, rules, regulations, rulings and special orders which it may adopt, issue or establish and to furnish advice, recommendations, or instructions for the purpose of obtaining such compliance. In recognition of §§ 32.1-164 and 62.1-44.18, the Board and the State Department of Health shall enter into a memorandum of understanding establishing a common format to consolidate and simplify inspections of sewage treatment plants and

coordinate the scheduling of the inspections. The new format shall ensure that all sewage treatment plants are inspected at appropriate intervals in order to protect water quality and public health and at the same time avoid any unnecessary administrative burden on those being inspected.

(7) To adopt rules governing the procedure of the Board with respect to: (a) hearings; (b) the filing of reports; (c) the issuance of certificates and special orders; and (d) all other matters relating to procedure; and to amend or cancel any rule adopted. Public notice of every rule adopted under this section shall be by such means as the Board may prescribe.

(8a) Except as otherwise provided in Articles 2.4 (§ 62.1-44.15:51 et seq.) and 2.5 (§ 62.1-44.15:67 et seq.), to issue special orders to owners who (i) are permitting or causing the pollution, as defined by § 62.1-44.3, of state waters to cease and desist from such pollution, (ii) have failed to construct facilities in accordance with final approved plans and specifications to construct such facilities in accordance with final approved plans and specifications, (iii) have violated the terms and provisions of a certificate issued by the Board to comply with such terms and provisions, (iv) have failed to comply with a directive from the Board to comply with such directive, (v) have contravened duly adopted and promulgated water quality standards and policies to cease and desist from such contravention and to comply with such water quality standards and policies, (vi) have violated the terms and provisions of a pretreatment permit issued by the Board or by the owner of a publicly owned treatment works to comply with such terms and provisions or (vii) have contravened any applicable pretreatment standard or requirement to comply with such standard or requirement; and also to issue such orders to require any owner to comply with the provisions of this chapter and any decision of the Board. Except as otherwise provided by a separate article, orders issued pursuant to this subdivision may include civil penalties of up to $32,500 per violation, not to exceed $100,000 per order. The Board may assess penalties under this subdivision if (a) the person has been issued at least two written notices of alleged violation by the Department for the same or substantially related violations at the same site, (b) such violations have not been resolved by demonstration that there was no violation, by an order issued by the Board or the Director, or by other means, (c) at least 130 days have passed since the issuance of the first notice of alleged violation, and (d) there is a finding that such violations have occurred after a hearing conducted in accordance with subdivision (8b). The actual amount of any penalty assessed shall be based upon the severity of the violations, the extent of any potential or actual environmental harm, the compliance history of the facility or person, any economic benefit realized from the noncompliance, and the ability of the person to pay the penalty. The Board shall provide the person with the calculation for the proposed penalty prior to any hearing conducted for the issuance of an order that assesses penalties pursuant to this subdivision. The issuance of a notice of alleged violation by the Department shall not be considered a case decision as defined in § 2.2-4001. Any notice of alleged violation shall include a description of each violation, the specific provision of law violated, and information on the process for obtaining a final decision or fact finding from the Department on whether or not a violation has occurred, and nothing in this section shall preclude an owner from seeking such a determination. Such civil penalties shall be paid into the state treasury and deposited by the State Treasurer into the Virginia Environmental Emergency Response Fund (§ 10.1-2500 et seq.), except that civil penalties assessed for violations of Article 9 (§ 62.1-44.34:8 et seq.) or Article 11 (§ 62.1-44.34:14 et seq.) shall be paid into the Virginia Petroleum Storage Tank Fund in accordance with § 62.1-44.34:11, and except that civil penalties assessed for violations of

Article 2.3 (§ 62.1-44.15:24 et seq.) shall be paid in accordance with the provisions of § 62.1-44.15:48.

(8b) Such special orders are to be issued only after a hearing before a hearing officer appointed by the Supreme Court in accordance with § 2.2-4020 or, if requested by the person, before a quorum of the Board with at least 30 days' notice to the affected owners, of the time, place and purpose thereof, and they shall become effective not less than 15 days after service as provided in § 62.1-44.12; provided that if the Board finds that any such owner is grossly affecting or presents an imminent and substantial danger to (i) the public health, safety or welfare, or the health of animals, fish or aquatic life; (ii) a public water supply; or (iii) recreational, commercial, industrial, agricultural or other reasonable uses, it may issue, without advance notice or hearing, an emergency special order directing the owner to cease such pollution or discharge immediately, and shall provide an opportunity for a hearing, after reasonable notice as to the time and place thereof to the owner, to affirm, modify, amend or cancel such emergency special order. If an owner who has been issued such a special order or an emergency special order is not complying with the terms thereof, the Board may proceed in accordance with § 62.1-44.23, and where the order is based on a finding of an imminent and substantial danger, the court shall issue an injunction compelling compliance with the emergency special order pending a hearing by the Board. If an emergency special order requires cessation of a discharge, the Board shall provide an opportunity for a hearing within 48 hours of the issuance of the injunction.

(8c) The provisions of this section notwithstanding, the Board may proceed directly under § 62.1-44.32 for any past violation or violations of any provision of this chapter or any regulation duly promulgated hereunder.

(8d) With the consent of any owner who has violated or failed, neglected or refused to obey any regulation or order of the Board, any condition of a permit or any provision of this chapter, the Board may provide, in an order issued by the Board against such person, for the payment of civil charges for past violations in specific sums not to exceed the limit specified in § 62.1-44.32 (a). Such civil charges shall be instead of any appropriate civil penalty which could be imposed under § 62.1-44.32 (a) and shall not be subject to the provisions of § 2.2-514. Such civil charges shall be paid into the state treasury and deposited by the State Treasurer into the Virginia Environmental Emergency Response Fund (§ 10.1-2500 et seq.), excluding civil charges assessed for violations of Article 9 (§ 62.1-44.34:8 et seq.) or 10 (§ 62.1-44.34:10 et seq.) of Chapter 3.1, or a regulation, administrative or judicial order, or term or condition of approval relating to or issued under those articles, or civil charges assessed for violations of Article 2.3 (§ 62.1-44.15:24 et seq.), or a regulation, administrative or judicial order, or term or condition of approval relating to or issued under that article.

The amendments to this section adopted by the 1976 Session of the General Assembly shall not be construed as limiting or expanding any cause of action or any other remedy possessed by the Board prior to the effective date of said amendments.

(8e) The Board shall develop and provide an opportunity for public comment on guidelines and procedures that contain specific criteria for calculating the appropriate penalty for each violation based upon the severity of the violations, the extent of any potential or actual environmental harm, the compliance history of the facility or person, any economic benefit realized from the noncompliance, and the ability of the person to pay the penalty.

(8f) Before issuing a special order under subdivision (8a) or by consent under (8d), with or without an assessment of a civil penalty, to an owner of a

191

sewerage system requiring corrective action to prevent or minimize overflows of sewage from such system, the Board shall provide public notice of and reasonable opportunity to comment on the proposed order. Any such order under subdivision (8d) may impose civil penalties in amounts up to the maximum amount authorized in § 309(g) of the Clean Water Act. Any person who comments on the proposed order shall be given notice of any hearing to be held on the terms of the order. In any hearing held, such person shall have a reasonable opportunity to be heard and to present evidence. If no hearing is held before issuance of an order under subdivision (8d), any person who commented on the proposed order may file a petition, within 30 days after the issuance of such order, requesting the Board to set aside such order and provide a formal hearing thereon. If the evidence presented by the petitioner in support of the petition is material and was not considered in the issuance of the order, the Board shall immediately set aside the order, provide a formal hearing, and make such petitioner a party. If the Board denies the petition, the Board shall provide notice to the petitioner and make available to the public the reasons for such denial, and the petitioner shall have the right to judicial review of such decision under § 62.1-44.29 if he meets the requirements thereof.

(8g) To issue special orders for violations of this chapter to persons constructing or operating any natural gas transmission pipeline greater than 36 inches inside diameter. An order issued pursuant to this subdivision may include a civil penalty of up to $50,000 per violation, not to exceed $500,000 per order. The Board may assess a penalty under this subdivision if (i) the person has been issued at least two written notices of alleged violation by the Department for violations involving the same pipeline; (ii) such violations have not been resolved by a demonstration that there was no violation, by an order issued by the Board or the Director, including an order pursuant to subdivision (8d), or by other means; and (iii) there is a finding that such violation occurred after a hearing was conducted (a) before a hearing officer appointed by the Supreme Court, (b) in accordance with § 2.2-4020, and (c) with at least 30 days' notice to such person of the time, place, and purpose thereof. Such order shall become effective not less than 15 days after service as provided in § 62.1-44.12. The actual amount of any penalty assessed shall be based upon the severity of the violation, the extent of any potential or actual environmental harm, the compliance history of the person, any economic benefit realized from the noncompliance, and the ability of the person to pay the penalty. The Board shall provide the person with the calculation for the proposed penalty prior to any hearing conducted for the issuance of an order that assesses penalties pursuant to this subdivision. The issuance of a notice of alleged violation by the Department shall not be a case decision as defined in § 2.2-4001. Any notice of alleged violation shall include a description of each violation, the specific provision of law violated, and information on the process for obtaining a final decision or fact-finding from the Department on whether or not a violation has occurred, and nothing in this subdivision shall preclude a person from seeking such a determination. Such civil penalties shall be paid into the state treasury and deposited by the State Treasurer into the Virginia Environmental Emergency Response Fund (§ 10.1-2500 et seq.), except that civil penalties assessed for violations of Article 2.3 (§ 62.1-44.15:24 et seq.) or 2.4 (§ 62.1-44.15:51 et seq.) shall be paid into the state treasury and deposited by the State Treasurer into the Virginia Stormwater Management Fund (§ 62.1-44.15:29).

(9) To make such rulings under §§ 62.1-44.16, 62.1-44.17, and 62.1-44.19 as may be required upon requests or applications to the Board, the owner or owners affected to be notified by certified mail as soon as practicable after the Board makes them and such rulings to become effective upon such notification.

(10) To adopt such regulations as it deems necessary to enforce the general water quality management program of the Board in all or part of the Commonwealth, except that a description of provisions of any proposed regulation which are more restrictive than applicable federal requirements, together with the reason why the more restrictive provisions are needed, shall be provided to the standing committee of each house of the General Assembly to which matters relating to the content of the regulation are most properly referable.

(11) To investigate any large-scale killing of fish.

(a) Whenever the Board shall determine that any owner, whether or not he shall have been issued a certificate for discharge of waste, has discharged sewage, industrial waste, or other waste into state waters in such quantity, concentration or manner that fish are killed as a result thereof, it may effect such settlement with the owner as will cover the costs incurred by the Board and by the Department of Wildlife Resources in investigating such killing of fish, plus the replacement value of the fish destroyed, or as it deems proper, and if no such settlement is reached within a reasonable time, the Board shall authorize its executive secretary to bring a civil action in the name of the Board to recover from the owner such costs and value, plus any court or other legal costs incurred in connection with such action.

(b) If the owner is a political subdivision of the Commonwealth, the action may be brought in any circuit court within the territory embraced by such political subdivision. If the owner is an establishment, as defined in this chapter, the action shall be brought in the circuit court of the city or the circuit court of the county in which such establishment is located. If the owner is an individual or group of individuals, the action shall be brought in the circuit court of the city or circuit court of the county in which such person or any of them reside.

(c) For the purposes of this subdivision 11, the State Water Control Board shall be deemed the owner of the fish killed and the proceedings shall be as though the State Water Control Board were the owner of the fish. The fact that the owner has or held a certificate issued under this chapter shall not be raised as a defense in bar to any such action.

(d) The proceeds of any recovery had under this subdivision 11 shall, when received by the Board, be applied, first, to reimburse the Board for any expenses incurred in investigating such killing of fish. The balance shall be paid to the Board of Wildlife Resources to be used for the fisheries' management practices as in its judgment will best restore or replace the fisheries' values lost as a result of such discharge of waste, including, where appropriate, replacement of the fish killed with game fish or other appropriate species. Any such funds received are hereby appropriated for that purpose.

(e) Nothing in this subdivision 11 shall be construed in any way to limit or prevent any other action which is now authorized by law by the Board against any owner.

(f) Notwithstanding the foregoing, the provisions of this subdivision 11 shall not apply to any owner who adds or applies any chemicals or other substances that are recommended or approved by the State Department of Health to state waters in the course of processing or treating such waters for public water supply purposes, except where negligence is shown.

(12) To administer programs of financial assistance for planning, construction, operation, and maintenance of water quality control facilities for political subdivisions in the Commonwealth.

(13) To establish policies and programs for effective area-wide or basin-wide water quality control and management. The Board may develop comprehensive pollution abatement and water quality control plans on an area-wide or

basin-wide basis. In conjunction with this, the Board, when considering proposals for waste treatment facilities, is to consider the feasibility of combined or joint treatment facilities and is to ensure that the approval of waste treatment facilities is in accordance with the water quality management and pollution control plan in the watershed or basin as a whole. In making such determinations, the Board is to seek the advice of local, regional, or state planning authorities.

(14) To establish requirements for the treatment of sewage, industrial wastes and other wastes that are consistent with the purposes of this chapter; however, no treatment shall be less than secondary or its equivalent, unless the owner can demonstrate that a lesser degree of treatment is consistent with the purposes of this chapter.

(15) To promote and establish requirements for the reclamation and reuse of wastewater that are protective of state waters and public health as an alternative to directly discharging pollutants into waters of the state. The requirements shall address various potential categories of reuse and may include general permits and provide for greater flexibility and less stringent requirements commensurate with the quality of the reclaimed water and its intended use. The requirements shall be developed in consultation with the Department of Health and other appropriate state agencies. This authority shall not be construed as conferring upon the Board any power or duty duplicative of those of the State Board of Health.

(16) To establish and implement policies and programs to protect and enhance the Commonwealth's wetland resources. Regulatory programs shall be designed to achieve no net loss of existing wetland acreage and functions. Voluntary and incentive-based programs shall be developed to achieve a net resource gain in acreage and functions of wetlands. The Board shall seek and obtain advice and guidance from the Virginia Institute of Marine Science in implementing these policies and programs.

(17) To establish additional procedures for obtaining a Virginia Water Protection Permit pursuant to §§ 62.1-44.15:20 and 62.1-44.15:22 for a proposed water withdrawal involving the transfer of water resources between major river basins within the Commonwealth that may impact water basins in another state. Such additional procedures shall not apply to any water withdrawal in existence as of July 1, 2012, except where the expansion of such withdrawal requires a permit under §§ 62.1-44.15:20 and 62.1-44.15:22, in which event such additional procedures may apply to the extent of the expanded withdrawal only. The applicant shall provide as part of the application (i) an analysis of alternatives to such a transfer, (ii) a comprehensive analysis of the impacts that would occur in the source and receiving basins, (iii) a description of measures to mitigate any adverse impacts that may arise, (iv) a description of how notice shall be provided to interested parties, and (v) any other requirements that the Board may adopt that are consistent with the provisions of this section and §§ 62.1-44.15:20 and 62.1-44.15:22 or regulations adopted thereunder. This subdivision shall not be construed as limiting or expanding the Board's authority under §§ 62.1-44.15:20 and 62.1-44.15:22 to issue permits and impose conditions or limitations on the permitted activity.

(18) To be the lead agency for the Commonwealth's nonpoint source pollution management program, including coordination of the nonpoint source control elements of programs developed pursuant to certain state and federal laws, including § 319 of the federal Clean Water Act and § 6217 of the federal Coastal Zone Management Act. Further responsibilities include the adoption of regulations necessary to implement a nonpoint source pollution management program in the Commonwealth, the distribution of assigned funds, the identification and establishment of priorities to address nonpoint source

related water quality problems, the administration of the Statewide Nonpoint Source Advisory Committee, and the development of a program for the prevention and control of soil erosion, sediment deposition, and nonagricultural runoff to conserve Virginia's natural resources.

History.
Code 1950, § 62.1-27; 1968, c. 659; 1970, c. 638; 1972, c. 741; 1975, c. 335; 1976, c. 621; 1977, c. 32; 1978, c. 827; 1984, c. 11; 1985, cc. 249, 397; 1988, cc. 167, 328; 1989, c. 389; 1990, c. 717; 1991, cc. 239, 718; 1993, c. 456; 1994, c. 698; 1998, cc. 805, 863; 2000, cc. 972, 1032, 1054; 2002, cc. 49, 396; 2004, c. 431; 2005, c. 706; 2007, cc. 144, 633, 873, 916; 2011, cc. 52, 101; 2012, cc. 574, 581; 2013, cc. 756, 793; 2020, cc. 449, 958.

Section set out twice.
The section above is effective until July 1, 2024. For this section as in effect at that time, see the following section, also numbered 62.1-44.15.

The 2020 amendments.
The 2020 amendment by c. 449, in subdivi-sion (8a), in the first sentence, substituted "to issue special orders to owners who" for "issue special orders to owners" and deleted "who" following the (i) through (vii) designators, and substituted "this subdivision" for "this subsection" wherever it occurs; added subdivision (8g); and in subdivisions (11) (c) through (f), substituted "subdivision 11" for "subsection" wherever it occurs.

The 2020 amendment by c. 958, in subdivision (11) (a), substituted "by the Board and by the Department of Wildlife Resources" for "by the Board and by the Department of Game and Inland Fisheries" and in subdivision (11) (d), substituted "Board of Wildlife Resources" for "Board of Game and Inland Fisheries" in the second sentence.

§ 62.1-44.15. (Effective July 1, 2024) Powers and duties; civil penalties.

It shall be the duty of the Board and it shall have the authority:

(1) [Repealed.]

(2) To study and investigate all problems concerned with the quality of state waters and to make reports and recommendations.

(2a) To study and investigate methods, procedures, devices, appliances, and technologies that could assist in water conservation or water consumption reduction.

(2b) To coordinate its efforts toward water conservation with other persons or groups, within or without the Commonwealth.

(2c) To make reports concerning, and formulate recommendations based upon, any such water conservation studies to ensure that present and future water needs of the citizens of the Commonwealth are met.

(3a) To establish such standards of quality and policies for any state waters consistent with the general policy set forth in this chapter, and to modify, amend, or cancel any such standards or policies established and to take all appropriate steps to prevent quality alteration contrary to the public interest or to standards or policies thus established, except that a description of provisions of any proposed standard or policy adopted by regulation which are more restrictive than applicable federal requirements, together with the reason why the more restrictive provisions are needed, shall be provided to the standing committee of each house of the General Assembly to which matters relating to the content of the standard or policy are most properly referable. The Board shall, from time to time, but at least once every three years, hold public hearings pursuant to § 2.2-4007.01 but, upon the request of an affected person or upon its own motion, hold hearings pursuant to § 2.2-4009, for the purpose of reviewing the standards of quality, and, as appropriate, adopting, modifying, or canceling such standards. Whenever the Board considers the adoption, modification, amendment, or cancellation of any standard, it shall give due consideration to, among other factors, the economic and social costs and benefits which can reasonably be expected to obtain as a consequence of the standards as adopted, modified, amended, or cancelled. The Board shall also give due consideration to the public health standards issued by the Virginia Department of Health with respect to issues of public health policy and protection. If the Board does not follow the public health standards of the Virginia Department of Health, the Board's reason for any deviation shall be made in writing and published for any and all concerned parties.

(3b) Except as provided in subdivision (3a), such standards and policies are to be adopted or modified, amended, or cancelled in the manner provided by the Administrative Process Act (§ 2.2-4000 et seq.).

(4) To conduct or have conducted scientific experiments, investigations, studies, and research to discover methods for maintaining water quality consistent with the purposes of this chapter. To this end the Board may cooperate with any public or private agency in the conduct of such experiments, investigations, and research and may receive in behalf of the Commonwealth any moneys that any such agency may contribute as its share of the cost under any such cooperative agreement. Such moneys shall be used only for the purposes for which they are contributed and any balance remaining after the conclusion of the experiments, investigations, studies, and research, shall be returned to the contributors.

(5) To issue, revoke, or amend certificates and land-disturbance approvals under prescribed conditions for (a) the discharge of sewage, stormwater, industrial wastes, and other wastes into or adjacent to state waters; (b) the alteration otherwise of the physical, chemical, or biological properties of state waters; (c) excavation in a wetland; or (d) on and after October 1, 2001, the conduct of the following activities in a wetland: (i) new activities to cause draining that significantly alters or degrades existing wetland acreage or functions, (ii) filling or dumping, (iii) permanent flooding or impounding, or (iv) new activities that cause significant alteration or degradation of existing wetland acreage or functions. However, to the extent allowed by federal law, any person holding a certificate issued by the Board that is intending to upgrade the permitted facility by installing technology, control equipment, or other apparatus that the permittee demonstrates to the satisfaction of the Director will result in improved energy efficiency, reduction in the amount of nutrients discharged, and improved water quality shall not be required to obtain a new, modified, or amended permit. The permit holder shall provide the demonstration anticipated by this subdivision to the Department no later than 30 days prior to commencing construction.

(5a) All certificates issued by the Board under this chapter shall have fixed terms. The term of a Virginia Pollution Discharge Elimination System permit shall not exceed five years. The term of a Virginia Water Protection Permit shall be based upon the projected duration of the project, the length of any required monitoring, or other project operations or permit conditions; however, the term shall not exceed 15 years. The term of a Virginia Pollution Abatement permit shall not exceed 10 years, except that the term of a Virginia Pollution Abatement permit for confined animal feeding operations shall be 10 years. The Department of Environmental Quality shall inspect all facilities for which a Virginia Pollution Abatement permit has been issued to ensure compliance with statutory, regulatory, and permit requirements. Department personnel performing inspections of confined animal feeding operations shall be certified under the voluntary nutrient management training and certification program established in § 10.1-104.2. The term of a certificate issued by the Board shall not be extended by modification beyond the maximum duration and the certificate shall expire at the end of the term unless an application for a new permit has been timely filed as required by the regulations of the Board and the Board is unable, through no fault of the permittee, to issue a new permit before the expiration date of the previous permit.

(5b) Any certificate or land-disturbance approval issued by the Board under this chapter may, after notice and opportunity for a hearing, be amended or revoked on any of the following grounds or for good cause as may be provided by the regulations of the Board:

1. The owner has violated any regulation or order of the Board, any condition of a certificate or land-disturbance approval, any provision of this chapter, or any order of a court, where such violation results in a release of harmful substances into the environment, poses a substantial threat of release of harmful substances into the environment, causes unreasonable property degradation, or presents a hazard to human health or the violation is representative of a pattern of serious or repeated violations which, in the opinion of the Board, demonstrates the owner's disregard for or inability to comply with applicable laws, regulations, or requirements;

2. The owner has failed to disclose fully all relevant material facts or has misrepresented a material fact in applying for a certificate or land-disturbance approval, or in any other report or document required under this law or under the regulations of the Board;

3. The activity for which the certificate or land-disturbance approval was issued endangers human health or the environment or causes unreasonable property degradation and can be regulated to acceptable levels or practices by amendment or revocation of the certificate or land-disturbance approval; or

4. There exists a material change in the basis on which the certificate, land-disturbance approval, or permit was issued that requires either a temporary or a permanent reduction or elimination of any discharge or land-disturbing activity controlled by the certificate, land-disturbance approval, or permit necessary to protect human health or the environment or stop or prevent unreasonable degradation of property.

(5c) Any certificate issued by the Board under this chapter relating to dredging projects governed under Chapter 12 (§ 28.2-1200 et seq.) or Chapter 13 (§ 28.2-1300 et seq.) of Title 28.2 may be conditioned upon a demonstration of financial responsibility for the completion of compensatory mitigation requirements. Financial responsibility may be demonstrated by a letter of credit, a certificate of deposit, or a performance bond executed in a form approved by the Board. If the U.S. Army Corps of Engineers requires demonstration of financial responsibility for the completion of compensatory mitigation required for a particular project, then the mechanism and amount approved by the U.S. Army Corps of Engineers shall be used to meet this requirement.

(6) To make investigations and inspections, to ensure compliance with the conditions of any certificates, land-disturbance approvals, standards, policies, rules, regulations, rulings, and orders that it may adopt, issue, or establish, and to furnish advice, recommendations, or instructions for the purpose of obtaining such compliance. In recognition of §§ 32.1-164 and 62.1-44.18, the Board and the State Department of Health shall enter into a memorandum of understanding establishing a common format to consolidate and simplify inspections of sewage treatment plants and coordinate the scheduling of the inspections. The new format shall ensure that all sewage treatment plants are inspected at appropriate intervals in order to protect water quality and public health and at the same time avoid any unnecessary administrative burden on those being inspected.

(7) To adopt rules governing the procedure of the Board with respect to (a) hearings; (b) the filing of reports; (c) the issuance of certificates and orders; and (d) all other matters relating to procedure; and to amend or cancel any rule adopted. Public notice of every rule adopted under this section shall be by such means as the Board may prescribe.

(8a) Except as otherwise provided in subdivision (19) and Article 2.3 (§ 62.1-44.15:24 et seq.), to issue special orders to owners, including owners as defined in § 62.1-44.15:24, who (i) are permitting or causing the pollution, as defined by § 62.1-44.3, of state waters or the unreasonable degradation of property to cease and desist from such pollution or degradation, (ii) have failed to construct facilities in accordance with final approved plans and specifications to construct such facilities in accordance with final approved plans and specifications, (iii) have violated the terms and provisions of a certificate or land-disturbance approval issued by the Board to comply with such terms and provisions, (iv) have failed to comply with a directive from the Board to comply with such directive, (v) have contravened duly adopted and promulgated water quality standards and policies to cease and desist from such contravention and to comply with such water quality standards and policies, (vi) have violated the terms and provisions of a pretreatment permit issued by the Board or by the owner of a publicly owned treatment works to comply with such terms and provisions, or (vii) have contravened any applicable pretreatment standard or requirement to comply with such standard or requirement; and also to issue such orders to require any owner to comply with the provisions of this chapter and any decision of the Board. Except as otherwise provided by a separate article, orders issued pursuant to this subdivision may include civil penalties of up to $ 32,500 per violation, not to exceed $ 100,000 per order. The Board may assess penalties under this subdivision if (a) the person has been issued at least two written notices of alleged violation by the Department for the same or substantially related violations at the same site, (b) such violations have not been resolved by demonstration that there was no violation, by an order issued by the Board or the Director, or by other means, (c) at least 130 days have passed since the issuance of the first notice of alleged violation, and (d) there is a finding that such violations have occurred after a hearing conducted in accordance with subdivision (8b). The actual amount of any penalty assessed shall be based upon the severity of the violations, the extent of any potential or actual environmental harm, the compliance history of the facility or person, any economic benefit realized from the noncompliance, and the ability of the person to pay the penalty. The Board shall provide the person with the calculation for the proposed penalty prior to any hearing conducted for the issuance of an order that assesses penalties pursuant to this subdivision. The issuance of a notice of alleged violation by the Department shall not be considered a case decision as defined in § 2.2-4001. Any notice of alleged violation shall include a description of each violation, the specific provision of law violated, and information on the process for obtaining a final decision or fact finding from the Department on whether or not a violation has occurred, and nothing in this section shall preclude an owner from seeking such a determination. Such civil penalties shall be paid into the state treasury and deposited by the State Treasurer into the Virginia Environmental Emergency Response Fund (§ 10.1-2500 et seq.), except that civil penalties assessed for violations of Article 9 (§ 62.1-44.34:8 et seq.) or Article 11 (§ 62.1-44.34:14 et seq.) shall be paid into the Virginia Petroleum Storage Tank Fund in accordance with § 62.1-44.34:11, and except that civil penalties assessed for violations of subdivision (19) or Article 2.3 (§ 62.1-44.15:24 et seq.) shall be paid into the Stormwater Local Assistance Fund in accordance with § 62.1-44.15:29.1.

(8b) Such special orders are to be issued only after a hearing before a hearing officer appointed by the Supreme Court in accordance with § 2.2-4020 or, if requested by the person, before a quorum of the Board with at least 30 days' notice to the affected owners, of the time, place, and purpose thereof, and they shall become effective not less than 15 days after service as provided in

62.1-44.12, provided that if the Board finds that any such owner is grossly affecting or presents an imminent and substantial danger to (i) the public health, safety, or welfare, or the health of animals, fish, or aquatic life; (ii) a public water supply; or (iii) recreational, commercial, industrial, agricultural, or other reasonable uses, it may issue, without advance notice or hearing, an emergency special order directing the owner to cease such pollution or discharge immediately, and shall provide an opportunity for a hearing, after reasonable notice as to the time and place thereof to the owner, to affirm, modify, amend, or cancel such emergency special order. If an owner who has been issued such a special order or an emergency special order is not complying with the terms thereof, the Board may proceed in accordance with 62.1-44.23, and where the order is based on a finding of an imminent and substantial danger, the court shall issue an injunction compelling compliance with the emergency special order pending a hearing by the Board. If an emergency special order requires cessation of a discharge, the Board shall provide an opportunity for a hearing within 48 hours of the issuance of the injunction.

(8c) The provisions of this section notwithstanding, the Board may proceed directly under § 62.1-44.32 for any past violation or violations of any provision of this chapter or any regulation duly promulgated hereunder.

(8d) Except as otherwise provided in subdivision (19), subdivision 2 of § 62.1-44.15:25, or § 62.1-44.15:63, with the consent of any owner who has violated or failed, neglected, or refused to obey any regulation or order of the Board, any condition of a certificate, land-disturbance approval, or permit, or any provision of this chapter, the Board may provide, in an order issued by the Board against such person, for the payment of civil charges for past violations in specific sums not to exceed the limit specified in subsection (a) of § 62.1-44.32. Such civil charges shall be instead of any appropriate civil penalty which could be imposed under subsection (a) of § 62.1-44.32 and shall not be subject to the provisions of § 2.2-514. Such civil charges shall be paid into the state treasury and deposited by the State Treasurer into the Virginia Environmental Emergency Response Fund (§ 10.1-2500 et seq.), excluding civil charges assessed for violations of Article 9 (§ 62.1-44.34:8 et seq.) or 10 (§ 62.1-44.34:10 et seq.) of Chapter 3.1, or a regulation, administrative or judicial order, or term or condition of approval relating to or issued under those articles, or civil charges assessed for violations of Article 2.3 (§ 62.1-44.15:24 et seq.) or 2.5 (§ 62.1-44.15:67 et seq.) or a regulation, administrative or judicial order, or term or condition of approval relating to or issued under Article 2.3 or 2.5.

The amendments to this section adopted by the 1976 Session of the General Assembly shall not be construed as limiting or expanding any cause of action or any other remedy possessed by the Board prior to the effective date of said amendments.

(8e) The Board shall develop and provide an opportunity for public comment on guidelines and procedures that contain specific criteria for calculating the appropriate penalty for each violation based upon the severity of the violations, the extent of any potential or actual environmental harm, the compliance history of the facility or person, any economic benefit realized from the noncompliance, and the ability of the person to pay the penalty.

(8f) Before issuing a special order under subdivision (8a) or by consent under (8d), with or without an assessment of a civil penalty, to an owner of a sewerage system requiring corrective action to prevent or minimize overflows of sewage from such system, the Board shall provide public notice of and reasonable opportunity to comment on the proposed order. Any such order under subdivision (8d) may impose civil penalties in amounts up to the maximum amount authorized in § 309(g) of the Clean Water Act. Any person who comments on the proposed order shall be given notice of any hearing to be held on the terms of the order. In any hearing held, such person shall have a reasonable opportunity to be heard and to present evidence. If no hearing is held before issuance of an order under subdivision (8d), any person who commented on the proposed order may file a petition, within 30 days after the issuance of such order, requesting the Board to set aside such order and provide a formal hearing thereon. If the evidence presented by the petitioner in support of the petition is material and was not considered in the issuance of the order, the Board shall immediately set aside the order, provide a formal hearing, and make such petitioner a party. If the Board denies the petition, the Board shall provide notice to the petitioner and make available to the public the reasons for such denial, and the petitioner shall have the right to judicial review of such decision under § 62.1-44.29 if he meets the requirements thereof.

(8g) To issue special orders for violations of this chapter to persons constructing or operating any natural gas transmission pipeline greater than 36 inches inside diameter. An order issued pursuant to this subdivision may include a civil penalty of up to $50,000 per violation, not to exceed $500,000 per order. The Board may assess a penalty under this subdivision if (i) the person has been issued at least two written notices of alleged violation by the Department for violations involving the same pipeline; (ii) such violations have not been resolved by a demonstration that there was no violation, by an order issued by the Board or the Director, including an order pursuant to subdivision (8d), or by other means; and (iii) there is a finding that such violation occurred after a hearing was conducted (a) before a hearing officer appointed by the Supreme Court, (b) in accordance with § 2.2-4020, and (c) with at least 30 days' notice to such person of the time, place, and purpose thereof. Such order shall become effective not less than 15 days after service as provided in § 62.1-44.12. The actual amount of any penalty assessed shall be based upon the severity of the violation, the extent of any potential or actual environmental harm, the compliance history of the person, any economic benefit realized from the noncompliance, and the ability of the person to pay the penalty. The Board shall provide the person with the calculation for the proposed penalty prior to any hearing conducted for the issuance of an order that assesses penalties pursuant to this subdivision. The issuance of a notice of alleged violation by the Department shall not be a case decision as defined in § 2.2-4001. Any notice of alleged violation shall include a description of each violation, the specific provision of law violated, and information on the process for obtaining a final decision or fact-finding from the Department on whether or not a violation has occurred, and nothing in this subdivision shall preclude a person from seeking such a determination. Such civil penalties shall be paid into the state treasury and deposited by the State Treasurer into the Virginia Environmental Emergency Response Fund (§ 10.1-2500 et seq.), except that civil penalties assessed for violations of Article 2.3 (§ 62.1-44.15:24 et seq.) or 2.4 (§ 62.1-44.15:51 et seq.) shall be paid into the state treasury and deposited by the State Treasurer into the Virginia Stormwater Management Fund (§ 62.1-44.15:29).

(9) To make such rulings under §§ 62.1-44.16, 62.1-44.17, and 62.1-44.19 as may be required upon requests or applications to the Board, the owner or owners affected to be notified by certified mail as soon as practicable after the Board makes them and such rulings to become effective upon such notification.

(10) To adopt such regulations as it deems necessary to enforce the general soil erosion control and stormwater management program and water quality management program of the Board in all or part of the Commonwealth, except that a description of provisions of any proposed regulation which are more

restrictive than applicable federal requirements, together with the reason why the more restrictive provisions are needed, shall be provided to the standing committee of each house of the General Assembly to which matters relating to the content of the regulation are most properly referable.

(11) To investigate any large-scale killing of fish.

(a) Whenever the Board shall determine that any owner, whether or not he shall have been issued a certificate for discharge of waste, has discharged sewage, industrial waste, or other waste into state waters in such quantity, concentration, or manner that fish are killed as a result thereof, it may effect such settlement with the owner as will cover the costs incurred by the Board and by the Department of Wildlife Resources in investigating such killing of fish, plus the replacement value of the fish destroyed, or as it deems proper, and if no such settlement is reached within a reasonable time, the Board shall authorize its executive secretary to bring a civil action in the name of the Board to recover from the owner such costs and value, plus any court or other legal costs incurred in connection with such action.

(b) If the owner is a political subdivision of the Commonwealth, the action may be brought in any circuit court within the territory embraced by such political subdivision. If the owner is an establishment, as defined in this chapter, the action shall be brought in the circuit court of the city or the circuit court of the county in which such establishment is located. If the owner is an individual or group of individuals, the action shall be brought in the circuit court of the city or circuit court of the county in which such person or any of them reside.

(c) For the purposes of this subdivision 11, the State Water Control Board shall be deemed the owner of the fish killed and the proceedings shall be as though the State Water Control Board were the owner of the fish. The fact that the owner has or held a certificate issued under this chapter shall not be raised as a defense in bar to any such action.

(d) The proceeds of any recovery had under this subdivision 11 shall, when received by the Board, be applied, first, to reimburse the Board for any expenses incurred in investigating such killing of fish. The balance shall be paid to the Board of Wildlife Resources to be used for the fisheries' management practices as in its judgment will best restore or replace the fisheries' values lost as a result of such discharge of waste, including, where appropriate, replacement of the fish killed with game fish or other appropriate species. Any such funds received are hereby appropriated for that purpose.

(e) Nothing in this subdivision 11 shall be construed in any way to limit or prevent any other action which is now authorized by law by the Board against any owner.

(f) Notwithstanding the foregoing, the provisions of this subdivision 11 shall not apply to any owner who adds or applies any chemicals or other substances that are recommended or approved by the State Department of Health to state waters in the course of processing or treating such waters for public water supply purposes, except where negligence is shown.

(12) To administer programs of financial assistance for planning, construction, operation, and maintenance of water quality control facilities for political subdivisions in the Commonwealth.

(13) To establish policies and programs for effective area-wide or basin-wide water quality control and management. The Board may develop comprehensive pollution abatement and water quality control plans on an area-wide or basin-wide basis. In conjunction with this, the Board, when considering proposals for waste treatment facilities, is to consider the feasibility of combined or joint treatment facilities and is to ensure that the approval of waste treatment facilities is in accordance with the water quality management

and pollution control plan in the watershed or basin as a whole. In making such determinations, the Board is to seek the advice of local, regional, or state planning authorities.

(14) To establish requirements for the treatment of sewage, industrial wastes, and other wastes that are consistent with the purposes of this chapter; however, no treatment shall be less than secondary or its equivalent, unless the owner can demonstrate that a lesser degree of treatment is consistent with the purposes of this chapter.

(15) To promote and establish requirements for the reclamation and reuse of wastewater that are protective of state waters and public health as an alternative to directly discharging pollutants into waters of the state. The requirements shall address various potential categories of reuse and may include general permits and provide for greater flexibility and less stringent requirements commensurate with the quality of the reclaimed water and its intended use. The requirements shall be developed in consultation with the Department of Health and other appropriate state agencies. This authority shall not be construed as conferring upon the Board any power or duty duplicative of those of the State Board of Health.

(16) To establish and implement policies and programs to protect and enhance the Commonwealth's wetland resources. Regulatory programs shall be designed to achieve no net loss of existing wetland acreage and functions. Voluntary and incentive-based programs shall be developed to achieve a net resource gain in acreage and functions of wetlands. The Board shall seek and obtain advice and guidance from the Virginia Institute of Marine Science in implementing these policies and programs.

(17) To establish additional procedures for obtaining a Virginia Water Protection Permit pursuant to §§ 62.1-44.15:20 and 62.1-44.15:22 for a proposed water withdrawal involving the transfer of water resources between major river basins within the Commonwealth that may impact water basins in another state. Such additional procedures shall not apply to any water withdrawal in existence as of July 1, 2012, except where the expansion of such withdrawal requires a permit under §§ 62.1-44.15:20 and 62.1-44.15:22, in which event such additional procedures may apply to the extent of the expanded withdrawal only. The applicant shall provide as part of the application (i) an analysis of alternatives to such a transfer, (ii) a comprehensive analysis of the impacts that would occur in the source and receiving basins, (iii) a description of measures to mitigate any adverse impacts that may arise, (iv) a description of how notice shall be provided to interested parties, and (v) any other requirements that the Board may adopt that are consistent with the provisions of this section and §§ 62.1-44.15:20 and 62.1-44.15:22 or regulations adopted thereunder. This subdivision shall not be construed as limiting or expanding the Board's authority under §§ 62.1-44.15:20 and 62.1-44.15:22 to issue permits and impose conditions or limitations on the permitted activity.

(18) To be the lead agency for the Commonwealth's nonpoint source pollution management program, including coordination of the nonpoint source control elements of programs developed pursuant to certain state and federal laws, including § 319 of the federal Clean Water Act and § 6217 of the federal Coastal Zone Management Act. Further responsibilities include the adoption of regulations necessary to implement a nonpoint source pollution management program in the Commonwealth, the distribution of assigned funds, the identification and establishment of priorities to address nonpoint source related water quality problems, the administration of the Statewide Nonpoint Source Advisory Committee, and the development of a program for the prevention and control of soil erosion, sediment deposition, and nonagricultural runoff to conserve Virginia's natural resources.

(19) To review for compliance with the provisions of this chapter the Virginia Erosion and Stormwater Management Programs adopted by localities pursuant to § 62.1-44.15:27, the Virginia Erosion and Sediment Control Programs adopted by localities pursuant to subdivision B 3 of § 62.1-44.15:27, and the programs adopted by localities pursuant to the Chesapeake Bay Preservation Act (§ 62.1-44.15:67 et seq.). The Board shall develop and implement a schedule for conducting such program reviews as often as necessary but at least once every five years. Following the completion of a compliance review in which deficiencies are found, the Board shall establish a schedule for the locality to follow in correcting the deficiencies and bringing its program into compliance. If the locality fails to bring its program into compliance in accordance with the compliance schedule, then the Board is authorized to (i) issue a special order to any locality imposing a civil penalty not to exceed $ 5,000 per violation with the maximum amount not to exceed $ 50,000 per order for noncompliance with the state program, to be paid into the state treasury and deposited in the Stormwater Local Assistance Fund established in § 62.1-44.15:29.1 or (ii) with the consent of the locality, provide in an order issued against the locality for the payment of civil charges for violations in lieu of civil penalties, in specific sums not to exceed the limit stated in this subdivision. Such civil charges shall be in lieu of any appropriate civil penalty that could be imposed under subsection (a) of § 62.1-44.32 and shall not be subject to the provisions of § 2.2-514. The Board shall not delegate to the Department its authority to issue special orders pursuant to clause (i). In lieu of issuing an order, the Board is authorized to take legal action against a locality pursuant to § 62.1-44.23 to ensure compliance.

History.
Code 1950, § 62.1-27; 1968, c. 659; 1970, c. 638; 1972, c. 741; 1975, c. 335; 1976, c. 621; 1977, c. 32; 1978, c. 827; 1984, c. 11; 1985, cc. 249, 397; 1988, cc. 167, 328; 1989, c. 389; 1990, c. 717; 1991, cc. 239, 718; 1993, c. 456; 1994, c. 698; 1998, cc. 805, 863; 2000, cc. 972, 1032, 1054; 2002, cc. 49, 396; 2004, c. 431; 2005, c. 706; 2007, cc. 144, 633, 873, 916; 2011, cc. 52, 101; 2012, cc. 574, 581; 2013, cc. 756, 793; 2016, cc. 68, 758; 2020, cc. 449, 958.

Section set out twice.
The section above is effective July 1, 2018. For this section as in effect until that time, see the preceding section, also numbered 62.1-44.15.

§ 62.1-44.15:02. Repealed by Acts 2022, c. 356, effective July 1, 2022.

Editor's note.
This section was also amended in 2022 by Acts 2022, c. 597, but due to the repeal by Acts 2022, c. 256 the amendment is not set out.

§ 62.1-44.15:03. Disposal of fill; notice to locality.

The Department shall establish a process whereby any person that receives coverage under the General Virginia Pollutant Discharge Elimination System Permit for Discharges of Stormwater from Construction Activities and that will be transporting fill from a project site for disposal as part of its land-disturbing activities shall disclose to the Department the following information, which the Department shall disclose to every locality where such fill will be disposed of: (i) the source of the fill to be disposed of, (ii) the contents of the fill, and (iii) the location of the disposal.

History.
2020, c. 565.

Editor's note.
Acts 2020, c. 565 was codified as this section

at the direction of the Virginia Code Commission.

§ 62.1-44.15:5.01. Coordinated review of water resources projects.

A. Applications for water resources projects that require an individual Virginia Water Protection Permit and a Virginia Marine Resources permit under § 28.2-1205 shall be submitted and processed through a joint application and review process.

B. The Director and the Commissioner of the Virginia Marine Resources Commission, in consultation with the Virginia Institute of Marine Science, the Department of Wildlife Resources, the Department of Historic Resources, the Department of Health, the Department of Conservation and Recreation, the Virginia Department of Agriculture and Consumer Services, and any other appropriate or interested state agency, shall coordinate the joint review process to ensure the orderly evaluation of projects requiring both permits.

C. The joint review process shall include, but not be limited to, provisions to ensure that: (i) the initial application for the project shall be advertised simultaneously by the Department of Environmental Quality and the Virginia Marine Resources Commission; (ii) project reviews shall be completed by all state agencies that have been asked to review and provide comments within 45 days of project notification by the Department of Environmental Quality and the Virginia Marine Resources Commission; (iii) the Board and the Virginia Marine Resources Commission shall coordinate permit issuance and, to the extent practicable, shall take action on the permit application no later than one year after the agencies have received complete applications; (iv) to the extent practicable, the Board and the Virginia Marine Resources Commission shall take action concurrently, but no more than six months apart; and (v) upon taking its final action on each permit, the Board and the Virginia Marine Resources Commission shall provide each other with notification of their actions and any and all supporting information, including any background materials or exhibits used in the application. Any state agency asked to review and provide comments in accordance with clause (ii) shall provide such comments within 45 days of project notification by the Department of Environmental Quality and the Virginia Marine Resources Commission or be deemed to have waived its right to provide comment.

D. If requested by the applicant, the Department of Environmental Quality shall convene a preapplication review panel to assist applicants for water resources projects in the early identification of issues related to the protection of beneficial instream and offstream uses of state waters. The Virginia Marine Resources Commission, the Virginia Institute of Marine Science, the Department of Wildlife Resources, the Department of Conservation and Recreation, and the Department of Environmental Quality shall participate in the preapplication review panel by providing information and guidance on the potential natural resource impacts and regulatory implications of the options being considered by the applicant. However, the participation by these agencies in such a review process shall not limit any authority they may exercise pursuant to state and federal laws or regulations.

History.
    2005, c. 49; 2011, cc. 829, 842; 2020, c. 958.

The 2020 amendments.
    The 2020 amendment by c. 958, in subsection

B and in subsection D, substituted "Department of Wildlife Resources" for "Department of Game and Inland Fisheries."

§ 62.1-44.15:5.3. Requirements to test for PFAS chemicals; publicly owned treatment works.

A. As used in this section, "PFAS chemical" means (i) Perfluorooctanoic Acid (PFOA), (ii) Perfluorooctane Sulfonate (PFOS), (iii) hexafluoropropylene oxide dimer acid (HFPO-DA), (iv) perfluorobutane sulfonate (PFBS), or (v) any substance in a class of fluorinated organic chemicals containing at least two adjacent fluorinated carbon atoms, where one carbon atom is fully fluorinated and the other atom is at least partially fluorinated, excluding gases and volatile liquids, also referred to as perfluoroalkyl and polyfluoroalkyl substances, identified by a publicly owned treatment works in its pretreatment program for which there is an EPA approved testing method.

B. The pretreatment standards adopted by the Board shall require any industrial user of a publicly owned treatment works that receives and cleans, repairs, refurbishes, or processes any equipment, parts, or media used to treat any water or wastewater from any off-site manufacturing process that the industrial user knows or reasonably should know uses PFAS chemicals to test its wastestream for PFAS chemicals prior to and after cleaning, repairing, refurbishing, or processing such items. The results of such tests shall be transmitted to the receiving publicly owned treatment works within three days of receipt of the test results by the industrial user of the publicly owned treatment works.

History.
2023, c. 276.

ARTICLE 2.1.
PERMIT FEES.

§ 62.1-44.15:6. Permit fee regulations.

A. The Board shall promulgate regulations establishing a fee assessment and collection system to recover a portion of the State Water Control Board's, the Department of Wildlife Resources' and the Department of Conservation and Recreation's direct and indirect costs associated with the processing of an application to issue, reissue, amend or modify any permit or certificate, which the Board has authority to issue under this chapter and Chapters 24 (§ 62.1-242 et seq.) and 25 (§ 62.1-254 et seq.) of this title, from the applicant for such permit or certificate for the purpose of more efficiently and expeditiously processing permits. The fees shall be exempt from statewide indirect costs charged and collected by the Department of Accounts. The Board shall have no authority to charge such fees where the authority to issue such permits has been delegated to another agency that imposes permit fees.

B1. Permit fees charged an applicant for a Virginia Pollutant Discharge Elimination System permit or a Virginia Pollution Abatement permit shall reflect the average time and complexity of processing a permit in each of the various categories of permits and permit actions. However, notwithstanding any other provision of law, in no instance shall the Board charge a fee for a permit pertaining to a farming operation engaged in production for market or for a permit pertaining to maintenance dredging for federal navigation channels or other Corps of Engineers- or Department of the Navy-sponsored dredging projects or for the regularly scheduled renewal of an individual permit for an existing facility. Fees shall be charged for a major modification or reissuance of a permit initiated by the permittee that occurs between permit issuance and the stated expiration date. No fees shall be charged for a modification or amendment made at the Board's initiative. In no instance shall the Board exceed the following amounts for the processing of each type of permit/certificate category:

Type of Permit/Certificate Category	Maximum Amount
1. Virginia Pollutant Discharge Elimination System	
Major Industrial	$24,000
Major Municipal	$21,300
Minor Industrial with nonstandard limits	$10,300
Minor Industrial with standard limits	$ 6,600
Minor Municipal greater than 100,000 gallons per day	$ 7,500
Minor Municipal 10,001-100,000 gallons per day	$ 6,000
Minor Municipal 1,000-10,000 gallons per day	$ 5,400
Minor Municipal less than 1,000 gallons per day	$ 2,000
General-industrial stormwater management	$ 500
General-stormwater management-phase I land clearing	$ 500
General-stormwater management-phase II land clearing	$ 300
General-other	$ 600
2. Virginia Pollution Abatement	
Industrial/Wastewater 10 or more inches per year	$15,000
Industrial/Wastewater less than 10 inches per year	$10,500
Industrial/Sludge	$ 7,500
Municipal/Wastewater	$13,500
Municipal/Sludge	$ 7,500
General Permit	$ 600
Other	$ 750

The fee for the major modification of a permit or certificate that occurs between the permit issuance and expiration dates shall be 50 percent of the maximum amount established by this subsection. No fees shall be charged for minor modifications or minor amendments to such permits. For the purpose of this subdivision, "minor modifications" or "minor amendments" means specific types of changes defined by the Board that are made to keep the permit current with routine changes to the facility or its operation that do not require extensive review. A minor permit modification or amendment does not substantially alter permit conditions, increase the size of the operation, or reduce the capacity of the facility to protect human health or the environment.

B2. Each permitted facility shall pay a permit maintenance fee to the Board by October 1 of each year, not to exceed the following amounts:

Type of Permit/Certificate Category	Maximum Amount
1. Virginia Pollutant Discharge Elimination System	
Major Industrial	$ 4,800
Major Municipal greater than 10 million gallons per day	$ 4,750
Major Municipal 2-10 million gallons per day	$ 4,350
Major Municipal less than 2 million gallons per day	$ 3,850
Minor Industrial with nonstandard limits	$ 2,040
Minor Industrial with standard limits	$ 1,320
Minor Industrial water treatment system	$ 1,200
Minor Municipal greater than 100,000 gallons per day	$ 1,500
Minor Municipal 10,001-100,000 gallons per day	$ 1,200
Minor Municipal 1,000-10,000 gallons per day	$ 1,080
Minor Municipal less than 1,000 gallons per day	$ 400
2. Virginia Pollution Abatement	
Industrial/Wastewater 10 or more inches per year	$ 3,000
Industrial/Wastewater less than 10 inches per year	$ 2,100
Industrial/Sludge	$ 3,000

Municipal/Wastewater	$ 2,700
Municipal/Sludge	$ 1,500

An additional permit maintenance fee of $1,000 shall be collected from facilities in a toxics management program and an additional permit maintenance fee shall be collected from facilities that have more than five process wastewater discharge outfalls. Permit maintenance fees shall be collected annually and shall be remitted by October 1 of each year. For a local government or public service authority with permits for multiple facilities in a single jurisdiction, the permit maintenance fees for permits held as of April 1, 2004, shall not exceed $20,000 per year. No permit maintenance fee shall be assessed for facilities operating under a general permit or for permits pertaining to a farming operation engaged in production for market.

B3. Permit application fees charged for Virginia Water Protection Permits, ground water withdrawal permits, and surface water withdrawal permits shall reflect the average time and complexity of processing a permit in each of the various categories of permits and permit actions and the size of the proposed impact. Only one permit fee shall be assessed for a water protection permit involving elements of more than one category of permit fees under this section. The fee shall be assessed based upon the primary purpose of the proposed activity. In no instance shall the Board charge a fee for a permit pertaining to maintenance dredging for federal navigation channels or other U.S. Army Corps of Engineers- or Department of the Navy-sponsored dredging projects, and in no instance shall the Board exceed the following amounts for the processing of each type of permit/certificate category:

	Type of Permit	Maximum Amount
1.	Virginia Water Protection Individual-wetland impacts	$2,400 plus $220 per 1/10 acre of impact over two acres, not to exceed $60,000
	Individual-minimum instream flow	
	Individual-reservoir	$25,000
	Individual-nonmetallic mineral mining	
	General-less than 1/10 acre impact	$0
	General-1/10 to 1/2 acre impact	$600
	General-greater than 1/2 to one acre impact	$1,200
	General-greater than one acre to two acres of impact	$120 per 1/10 acre of impact
2.	Ground Water Withdrawal	$9,000
3.	Surface Water Withdrawal	$12,000

No fees shall be charged for minor modifications or minor amendments to such permits. For the purpose of this subdivision, "minor modifications" or "minor amendments" means specific types of changes defined by the Board that are made to keep the permit current with routine changes to the facility or its operation that do not require extensive review. A minor permit modification or amendment does not substantially alter permit conditions, increase the size of the operation, or reduce the capacity of the facility to protect human health or the environment.

C. When promulgating regulations establishing permit fees, the Board shall take into account the permit fees charged in neighboring states and the importance of not placing existing or prospective industries in the Commonwealth at a competitive disadvantage.

D. Beginning January 1, 1998, and January 1 of every even-numbered year thereafter, the Board shall make a report on the implementation of the water permit program to the Senate Committee on Agriculture, Conservation and Natural Resources, the Senate Committee on Finance and Appropriations, the House Committee on Appropriations, the House Committee on Agriculture, Chesapeake and Natural Resources and the House Committee on Finance. The report shall include the following: (i) the total costs, both direct and indirect, including the costs of overhead, water quality planning, water quality assessment, operations coordination, and surface water and ground water investigations, (ii) the total fees collected by permit category, (iii) the amount of general funds allocated to the Board, (iv) the amount of federal funds received, (v) the Board's use of the fees, the general funds, and the federal funds, (vi) the number of permit applications received by category, (vii) the number of permits issued by category, (viii) the progress in eliminating permit backlogs, (ix) the timeliness of permit processing, and (x) the direct and indirect costs to neighboring states of administering their water permit programs, including what activities each state categorizes as direct and indirect costs, and the fees charged to the permit holders and applicants.

E. Fees collected pursuant to this section shall not supplant or reduce in any way the general fund appropriation to the Board.

F. Permit fee schedules shall apply to permit programs in existence on July 1, 1992, any additional permits that may be required by the federal government and administered by the Board, or any new permit required pursuant to any law of the Commonwealth.

G. The Board is authorized to promulgate regulations establishing a schedule of reduced permit fees for facilities that have established a record of compliance with the terms and requirements of their permits and shall establish criteria by regulation to provide for reductions in the annual fee amount assessed for facilities accepted into the Department's programs to recognize excellent environmental performance.

History.
1992, cc. 621, 657; 1993, cc. 749, 756; 1995, c. 107; 1997, cc. 115, 154; 2002, c. 822; 2004, cc. 249, 324; 2011, cc. 87, 149; 2018, c. 424; 2020, c. 958.

Editor's note.
The Virginia Code Commission authorized the substitution of "Senate Committee on Finance and Appropriations" for "Senate Committee on Finance." March 10, 2021.

Acts 2021, Sp. Sess. I, c. 275, cl. 1, § 2 provides: "The Director of the Department of Environmental Quality (the Director), or his designee, shall convene a working group for the purpose of developing a schedule of annual maintenance fees for water withdrawal permits including (i) Virginia Water Protection Individual-minimum instream flow permits, (ii) Virginia Water Protection Individual-reservoir permits, (iii) Ground Water Withdrawal permits, and (iv) Surface Water Withdrawal permits. The working group shall include representatives of (a) ground water with withdrawal permittees, including at least one representa-

tive each from the municipal, commercial, and industrial sectors; (b) Virginia Water Protection surface water withdrawal permittees, including at least one representative each from the municipal, commercial, and power generation sectors; (c) environmental organizations; (d) agricultural organizations; and (e) any others whom the Director determines would assist the group in its deliberations. The working group shall convene no later than August 1, 2021, and shall meet as necessary thereafter. The Department of Environmental Quality shall submit to the Governor and the General Assembly by December 1, 2021, a summary of the working group's discussions and recommendations for a schedule of annual maintenance fees that shall, at a minimum, be sufficient to reflect no less than 40 percent of the direct costs required for the development, administration, compliance, and enforcement of such permits."

The 2020 amendments.
The 2020 amendment by c. 958 substituted "Department of Wildlife Resources' " for "Department of Game and Inland Fisheries' " in subsection A in the first sentence.

§ 62.1-44.15:8. Conformance with federal requirements.

Notwithstanding the provisions of this article, any fee system developed by the Board may be modified by regulation promulgated by the Board, as may be necessary to conform with the requirements of the federal Clean Water Act and any regulations promulgated thereunder. Any modification imposed under this section shall be submitted to the members of the Senate Committees on Agriculture, Conservation and Natural Resources, and on Finance and Appropriations; and the House Committees on Appropriations, Conservation and Natural Resources, and Finance.

History.
1992, cc. 621, 657.

Editor's note.
The Virginia Code Commission authorized the substitution of "the Senate Committees on Agriculture, Conservation and Natural Resources, and on Finance and Appropriations" for "Senate Committees on Agriculture, Conservation and Natural Resources, and Finance." March 10, 2021.

ARTICLE 2.2.

VIRGINIA WATER RESOURCES AND WETLANDS PROTECTION PROGRAM.

§ 62.1-44.15:20. Virginia Water Protection Permit.

A. Except in compliance with an individual or general Virginia Water Protection Permit issued in accordance with this article, it shall be unlawful to:
1. Excavate in a wetland;
2. On or after October 1, 2001, conduct the following in a wetland:
a. New activities to cause draining that significantly alters or degrades existing wetland acreage or functions;
b. Filling or dumping;
c. Permanent flooding or impounding; or
d. New activities that cause significant alteration or degradation of existing wetland acreage or functions; or
3. Alter the physical, chemical, or biological properties of state waters and make them detrimental to the public health, animal or aquatic life, or to the uses of such waters for domestic or industrial consumption, or for recreation, or for other uses unless authorized by a certificate issued by the Board.

B. The Board shall, after providing an opportunity for public comment, issue a Virginia Water Protection Permit if it has determined that the proposed activity is consistent with the provisions of the Clean Water Act and the State Water Control Law and will protect instream beneficial uses.

C. Prior to the issuance of a Virginia Water Protection Permit, the Board shall consult with and give full consideration to any relevant information contained in the state water supply plan described in subsection A of § 62.1-44.38:1 as well as to the written recommendations of the following agencies: the Department of Wildlife Resources, the Department of Conservation and Recreation, the Virginia Marine Resources Commission, the Department of Health, the Department of Agriculture and Consumer Services, and any other interested and affected agencies. When considering the state water supply plan, nothing shall be construed to limit the operation or expansion of an electric generation facility located on a man-made lake or impoundment built for the purpose of providing cooling water to such facility. Such consultation shall include the need for balancing instream uses with offstream uses. Agencies may submit written comments on proposed permits within 45 days after notification by the Board. If written comments are not submitted by an agency within this time period, the Board shall assume that the agency has no comments on the proposed permit and deem that the agency has waived its right to comment. After the expiration of the 45-day period, any such agency shall have no further opportunity to comment.

D. Issuance of a Virginia Water Protection Permit shall constitute the certification required under § 401 of the Clean Water Act, except for any applicant to the Federal Energy Regulatory Commission for a certificate of public convenience and necessity pursuant to § 7c of the federal Natural Gas Act (15 U.S.C. § 717f(c)) to construct any natural gas transmission pipeline greater than 36 inches inside diameter, in which case issuance of a Virginia Water Protection Permit pursuant to this article and a certification issued pursuant to Article 2.6 (§ 62.1-44.15:80 et seq.) shall together constitute the certification required under § 401 of the federal Clean Water Act.

E. No locality may impose wetlands permit requirements duplicating state or federal wetlands permit requirements. In addition, no locality shall impose or establish by ordinance, policy, plan, or any other means provisions related to the location of wetlands or stream mitigation in satisfaction of aquatic resource impacts regulated under a Virginia Water Protection Permit or under a permit issued by the U.S. Army Corps of Engineers pursuant to § 404 of the Clean Water Act. However, a locality's determination of allowed uses within zoning classifications or its approval of the siting or construction of wetlands or stream mitigation banks or other mitigation projects shall not be affected by the provisions of this subsection.

F. The Board shall assess compensation implementation, inventory permitted wetland impacts, and work to prevent unpermitted impacts to wetlands.

History.
 2007, c. 659; 2010, c. 233; 2011, cc. 829, 842; 2012, c. 628; 2018, c. 636; 2020, c. 958.

The 2020 amendments.
 The 2020 amendment by c. 958 substituted

"Department of Wildlife Resources" for "Department of Game and Inland Fisheries" in subsection C in the first sentence.

§ 62.1-44.15:21. Impacts to wetlands.

A. Permits shall address avoidance and minimization of wetland impacts to the maximum extent practicable. A permit shall be issued only if the Board finds that the effect of the impact, together with other existing or proposed impacts to wetlands, will not cause or contribute to a significant impairment of state waters or fish and wildlife resources.

B. Permits shall contain requirements for compensating impacts on wetlands. Such compensation requirements shall be sufficient to achieve no net loss of existing wetland acreage and functions and may be met through (i) wetland creation or restoration, (ii) purchase or use of mitigation bank credits pursuant to § 62.1-44.15:23, (iii) contribution to the Wetland and Stream Replacement Fund established pursuant to § 62.1-44.15:23.1 to provide compensation for impacts to wetlands, streams, or other state waters that occur in areas where neither mitigation bank credits nor credits from a Board-approved fund that have met the success criteria are available at the time of permit application, or (iv) contribution to a Board-approved fund dedicated to achieving no net loss of wetland acreage and functions. The Board shall evaluate the appropriate compensatory mitigation option on a case-by-case basis with consideration for which option is practicable and ecologically and environmentally preferable, including, in terms of replacement of acreage and functions, which option offers the greatest likelihood of success and avoidance of temporal loss of acreage and function. This evaluation shall be consistent with the U.S. Army Corps of Engineers Compensatory Mitigation for Losses of Aquatic Resources (33 C.F.R. Part 332). When utilized in conjunction with creation, restoration, or mitigation bank credits, compensation may incorporate (a) preservation or restoration of upland buffers adjacent to wetlands or other state waters or (b) preservation of wetlands.

C. The Board shall utilize the U.S. Army Corps of Engineers' "Wetlands Delineation Manual, Technical Report Y-87-1, January 1987, Final Report" as the approved method for delineating wetlands. The Board shall adopt appropriate guidance and regulations to ensure consistency with the U.S. Army Corps of Engineers' implementation of delineation practices. The Board shall also adopt guidance and regulations for review and approval of the geographic area of a delineated wetland. Any such approval of a delineation shall remain effective for a period of five years; however, if the Board issues a permit pursuant to this article for an activity in the delineated wetland within the five-year period, the approval shall remain effective for the term of the permit. Any delineation accepted by the U.S. Army Corps of Engineers as sufficient for its exercise of jurisdiction pursuant to § 404 of the Clean Water Act shall be determinative of the geographic area of that delineated wetland.

D. The Board shall develop general permits for such activities in wetlands as it deems appropriate. General permits shall include such terms and conditions as the Board deems necessary to protect state waters and fish and wildlife resources from significant impairment. The Board is authorized to waive the requirement for a general permit or deem an activity in compliance with a general permit when it determines that an isolated wetland is of minimal ecological value. The Board shall develop general permits for:

1. Activities causing wetland impacts of less than one-half of an acre;

2. Facilities and activities of utilities and public service companies regulated by the Federal Energy Regulatory Commission or State Corporation Commission, except for construction of any natural gas transmission pipeline that is greater than 36 inches inside diameter pursuant to a certificate of public convenience and necessity under § 7c of the federal Natural Gas Act (15 U.S.C. § 717f(c)). No Board action on an individual or general permit for such facilities shall alter the siting determination made through Federal Energy Regulatory Commission or State Corporation Commission approval. The Board and the State Corporation Commission shall develop a memorandum of agreement pursuant to §§ 56-46.1, 56-265.2, 56-265.2:1, and 56-580 to ensure that consultation on wetland impacts occurs prior to siting determinations;

3. Coal, natural gas, and coalbed methane gas mining activities authorized by the Department of Energy, and sand mining;

4. Virginia Department of Transportation or other linear transportation projects; and

5. Activities governed by nationwide or regional permits approved by the Board and issued by the U.S. Army Corps of Engineers. Conditions contained in the general permits shall include, but not be limited to, filing with the Board any copies of preconstruction notification, postconstruction report, and certificate of compliance required by the U.S. Army Corps of Engineers.

E. Within 15 days of receipt of an individual permit application, the Board shall review the application for completeness and either accept the application or request additional specific information from the applicant. Provided the application is not administratively withdrawn, the Board shall, within 120 days of receipt of a complete application, issue the permit, issue the permit with conditions, deny the permit, or decide to conduct a public meeting or hearing. If a public meeting or hearing is held, it shall be held within 60 days of the decision to conduct such a proceeding, and a final decision as to the permit shall be made within 90 days of completion of the public meeting or hearing. A permit application may be administratively withdrawn from processing by the Board if the application is incomplete or for failure by the applicant to provide the required information after 60 days from the date of the latest written information request made by the Board. Such administrative withdrawal shall occur after the Board has provided (i) notice to the applicant and (ii) an opportunity for an informal fact-finding proceeding pursuant to § 2.2-4019. An applicant may request a suspension of application review by the Board. A submission by the applicant making such a request shall not preclude the Board from administratively withdrawing an application. Resubmittal of a permit application for the same or similar project, after such time that the original permit application was administratively withdrawn, shall require submittal of an additional permit application fee and may be subject to additional notice requirements. In addition, for an individual permit application related to an application to the Federal Energy Regulatory Commission for a certificate of public convenience and necessity pursuant to § 7c of the federal Natural Gas Act (15 U.S.C. § 717f(c)) for construction of any natural gas transmission pipeline greater than 36 inches inside diameter, the Board shall complete its consideration within the one-year period established under 33 U.S.C. § 1341(a).

F. Within 15 days of receipt of a general permit coverage application, the Board shall review the application for completeness and either accept the application or request additional specific information from the applicant. Provided the application is not administratively withdrawn, the Board shall, within 45 days of receipt of a complete application, deny, approve, or approve with conditions any application for coverage under a general permit within 45 days of receipt of a complete preconstruction application. The application shall be deemed approved if the Board fails to act within 45 days. A permit coverage application may be administratively withdrawn from processing by the Board if the application is incomplete or for failure by the applicant to provide the required information after 60 days from the date of the latest written application request made by the Board. Such administrative withdrawal shall occur after the Board has provided (i) notice to the applicant and (ii) an opportunity for an informal fact-finding proceeding pursuant to § 2.2-4019. An applicant may request suspension of an application review by the Board. A submission by the applicant making such a request shall not preclude the Board from administratively withdrawing an application. Resubmittal of a permit coverage application for the same or similar project, after such time that the original permit application was administratively withdrawn, shall require submittal of an additional permit application fee and may be subject to additional notice requirements.

G. No Virginia Water Protection Permit shall be required for impacts to wetlands caused by activities governed under Chapter 13 (§ 28.2-1300 et seq.) of Title 28.2 or normal agricultural activities or normal silvicultural activities. This section shall also not apply to normal residential gardening, lawn and landscape maintenance, or other similar activities that are incidental to an occupant's ongoing residential use of property and of minimal ecological impact. The Board shall develop criteria governing this exemption and shall specifically identify the activities meeting these criteria in its regulations.

H. No Virginia Water Protection Permit shall be required for impacts caused by the construction or maintenance of farm or stock ponds, but other permits may be required pursuant to state and federal law. For purposes of this exclusion, farm or stock ponds shall include all ponds and impoundments that do not fall under the authority of the Virginia Soil and Water Conservation Board pursuant to Article 2 (§ 10.1-604 et seq.) of Chapter 6 pursuant to normal agricultural or silvicultural activities.

I. No Virginia Water Protection Permit shall be required for wetland and open water impacts to a stormwater management facility that was created on dry land for the purpose of conveying, treating, or storing stormwater, but other permits may be required pursuant to local, state, or federal law. The Department shall adopt guidance to ensure that projects claiming this exemption create no more than minimal ecological impact.

J. An individual Virginia Water Protection Permit shall be required for impacts to state waters for the construction of any natural gas transmission pipeline greater than 36 inches inside diameter pursuant to a certificate of public convenience and necessity under § 7c of the federal Natural Gas Act (15 U.S.C. § 717f(c)). For purposes of this subsection:

1. Each wetland and stream crossing shall be considered as a single and complete project; however, only one individual Virginia Water Protection Permit addressing all such crossings shall be required for any such pipeline. Notwithstanding the requirement for only one such individual permit addressing all such crossings, individual review of each proposed water body crossing with an upstream drainage area of five square miles or greater shall be performed.

2. All pipelines shall be constructed in a manner that minimizes temporary and permanent impacts to state waters and protects water quality to the maximum extent practicable, including by the use of applicable best management practices that the Board determines to be necessary to protect water quality.

3. The Department shall assess an administrative charge to any applicant for such project to cover the direct costs of services rendered associated with its responsibilities pursuant to this subsection. This administrative charge shall be in addition to any fee assessed pursuant to § 62.1-44.15:6.

History.
2007, c. 659; 2008, c. 244; 2013, c. 742; 2018, cc. 114, 636; 2019, c. 545; 2020, c. 622; 2021, Sp. Sess. I, c. 532.

Editor's note.
Acts 2021, Sp. Sess. I, c. 532, cl. 2 provides: "That the provisions of this act shall become effective on October 1, 2021."

The 2020 amendments.
The 2020 amendment by c. 622, in subsection E, substituted "Provided the application is not administratively withdrawn, the Board shall, within 120 days of receipt of a complete application, issue" for "Within 120 days of receipt of a complete application, the Board shall issue" in the second sentence and added the fourth through the eighth sentences; and in subsection F, inserted "coverage" in the first sentence, substituted "Provided the application is not administratively withdrawn, the Board shall, within 45 days of receipt of a complete application, deny" for "A determination that an application is complete shall not mean the Board will issue the permit but means only that the applicant has submitted sufficient information to process the application. The Board shall deny" and added the last five sentences.

The 2021 Sp. Sess. I amendments.
The 2021 amendment by Sp. Sess. I, c. 532, effective October 1, 2021, substituted "Department of Energy" for "Department of Mines, Minerals and Energy" in subdivision D 3.

CASE NOTES

Applicability. — Va. Code Ann. § 62.1-44.15:21(D)(2) applied to the permit process for a 42-inch diameter natural gas pipeline because it operates in two ways. First, it prohibits the State Water Control Board from developing general permits for pipelines greater than 36 inches in diameter. Second, it provides that regardless of the type of permit at issue — namely, individual, or general — the Board is prohibited from taking any action that would alter the Federal Energy Regulatory Commission's siting determinations. Sierra Club v. State Water Control Bd., 64 F.4th 187 (4th Cir. 2023).

§ 62.1-44.15:22. (For contingent effective date, see Acts 2021, Sp. Sess. I, c. 100) Water withdrawals and preservation of instream flow.

A. 1. Conditions contained in a Virginia Water Protection Permit may include the volume of water that may be withdrawn as a part of the permitted activity and conditions necessary to protect beneficial uses. Domestic and other existing beneficial uses shall be considered the highest priority uses.

2. Every application for a Virginia Water Protection Permit for a surface water withdrawal shall include a (i) water auditing plan and (ii) leak detection and repair plan. Both such plans shall comply with requirements established by the Board in regulations. The Board shall approve every water auditing plan and leak detection and repair plan that complies with such regulatory requirements. Once approved by the Board, such water auditing plan and leak detection and repair plan shall be incorporated by reference as a condition in the Virginia Water Protection Permit. The Board shall not issue a Virginia Water Protection Permit for a surface water withdrawal without an approved water auditing plan and an approved leak detection and repair plan.

B. Notwithstanding any other provision of law, no Virginia Water Protection Permit shall be required for any water withdrawal in existence on July 1, 1989; however, a permit shall be required if a new § 401 certification is required to increase a withdrawal. No Virginia Water Protection Permit shall be required for any water withdrawal not in existence on July 1, 1989, if the person proposing to make the withdrawal received a § 401 certification before January 1, 1989, with respect to installation of any necessary withdrawal structures to make such withdrawal; however, a permit shall be required before any such withdrawal is increased beyond the amount authorized by the certification.

C. The Board may issue an Emergency Virginia Water Protection Permit for a new or increased withdrawal when it finds that because of drought there is an insufficient public drinking water supply that may result in a substantial threat to human health or public safety. Such a permit may be issued to authorize the proposed activity only after conservation measures mandated by local or state authorities have failed to protect public health and safety and notification of the agencies designated in subsection C of § 62.1-44.15:20 and only for the amount of water necessary to protect public health and safety. Such agencies shall have five days to provide comments or written recommendations on the issuance of the permit. Notwithstanding the provisions of subsection B of § 62.1-44.15:20, no public comment shall be required prior to issuance of the emergency permit. Not later than 14 days after the issuance of the emergency permit, the permit holder shall apply for a Virginia Water Protection Permit authorized under other provisions of this section. The application for such Virginia Water Protection Permit shall be subject to public comment for a period established by the Board. Any Emergency Virginia Water Protection Permit issued under this section shall be valid until the Board approves or denies the subsequent request for a Virginia Water Protection Permit or for a period of one year, whichever occurs sooner. The fee for the emergency permit shall be 50 percent of the fee charged for a comparable Virginia Water Protection Permit.

History.
2007, c. 659; 2021, Sp. Sess. I, c. 100.

For this section as in effect until the amendments by Acts 2021, Sp. Sess. I, c. 100 become effective, see the bound volume.

Editor's note.
Acts 2021, Sp. Sess. I, c. 100, cl. 2 provides: "That the State Water Control Board (the Board) shall adopt regulations to implement the provisions of this act."

Acts 2021, Sp. Sess. I, c. 100, cl. 3 provides:

"That the provisions of the first enactment of this act shall become effective 30 days after the adoption by the State Water Control Board of the regulations required by the second enactment of this act."

The 2021 Sp. Sess. I amendments.
The 2021 amendment by Sp. Sess. I, c. 100, in subsection A, deleted "but are not limited to" following "Virginia Water Protection Permit may include" in subdivision A 1, and added subdivision A 2; in subsection B, inserted "of law" following "Notwithstanding any other provision"; and made stylistic changes. For contingent effective date, see Editor's note.

§ 62.1-44.15:23. Wetland and stream mitigation banks.

A. For purposes of this section:

"Physiographic province" means one of the five physiographic provinces of Virginia designated as the Appalachian Plateaus, Blue Ridge, Coastal Plain, Piedmont, and Ridge and Valley physiographic provinces as identified on Figure 2 in the Overview of the Physiography and Vegetation of Virginia prepared by the Department of Conservation and Recreation, Division of Natural Heritage and dated February 2016. The Department of Environmental Quality may adjust the boundaries of a physiographic province to reflect site-specific boundaries based on relative elevation, relief, geomorphology, and lithology provided by the bank sponsor.

"Primary service area" means the fourth order subbasin in which the bank is located, as defined by the hydrologic unit boundaries of the National Watershed Boundary Dataset or the hydrologic unit system or dataset utilized and depicted or described in the bank's approved mitigation banking instrument, and any adjacent fourth order subbasin within the same river watershed.

"River watershed" means the Potomac River Basin; Shenandoah River Basin; James River Basin; Rappahannock River Basin; Roanoke and Yadkin Rivers Basin; Chowan River Basin, including the Dismal Swamp and Albemarle Sound; Tennessee River Basin/Big Sandy River Basin Complex; Chesapeake Bay and its Small Coastal Basins; Atlantic Ocean; York River Basin; and New River Basin.

"Secondary service area" means the area outside the primary service area but within the same physiographic province in which the bank is located and any adjacent physiographic province within the same river watershed.

"Tree canopy" includes all of the area of canopy coverage by self-supporting and healthy woody plant material exceeding five feet in height.

B. When a Virginia Water Protection Permit is conditioned upon compensatory mitigation for adverse impacts to wetlands or streams, the applicant may be permitted to satisfy all or part of such mitigation requirements by the purchase or use of credits from any wetland or stream mitigation bank in the Commonwealth, or in Maryland on property wholly surrounded by and located in the Potomac River if the mitigation banking instrument provides that the Board shall have the right to enter and inspect the property and that the mitigation bank instrument and the contract for the purchase or use of such credits may be enforced in the courts of the Commonwealth, including any banks owned by the permit applicant, that has been approved and is operating in accordance with applicable federal and state guidance, laws, or regulations for the establishment, use, and operation of mitigation banks as long as (i) the impacted site is located in the bank's primary or secondary service area as provided in subsection C or it meets all the conditions found in clauses (a) through (d) and either clause (e) or (f); (ii) the bank is ecologically preferable to practicable onsite and offsite individual mitigation options as defined by federal wetland regulations; and (iii) the banking instrument, if approved after July 1, 1996, has been approved by a process that included public review and comment. When the impacted site is not located in the bank's primary or

215

secondary service area, the purchase or use of credits shall not be allowed unless the applicant demonstrates to the satisfaction of the Department of Environmental Quality that (a) the impacts will occur as a result of a Virginia Department of Transportation linear project or as the result of a locality project for a locality whose jurisdiction encompasses multiple river watersheds; (b) there is no practical same river watershed mitigation alternative; (c) the impacts are less than one acre in a single and complete project within a subbasin; (d) there is no significant harm to water quality or fish and wildlife resources within the river watershed of the impacted site; and either (e) impacts within the Chesapeake Bay watershed are mitigated within the Chesapeake Bay watershed as close as possible to the impacted site or (f) impacts within subbasins 02080108, 02080208, and 03010205, as defined by the National Watershed Boundary Dataset, are mitigated in-kind within those subbasins, as close as possible to the impacted site. For the purposes of this subsection, the hydrologic unit boundaries of the National Watershed Boundary Dataset or other hydrologic unit system may be adjusted by the Department of Environmental Quality to reflect site-specific geographic or hydrologic information provided by the bank sponsor.

C. For impacts to a site for which no credits are available to purchase (i) in the primary service area of any mitigation provider or (ii) at a price below 200 percent of the current price of credits applicable to that site from a Board-approved fund dedicated to achieving no net loss of wetland acreage and functions, a permit applicant may be permitted to purchase or use credits from the secondary service area of a mitigation provider to satisfy all or any part of such applicant's mitigation requirements. For purposes of this subsection, the permit applicant shall provide a determination of credit availability and credit price no later than the time such applicant submits to the Department (a) its proof of credit acquisition or (b) a later change to such proof.

If a permit applicant purchases or uses credits from a secondary service area, the permit applicant shall:

1. Acquire three times the credits it would have had to acquire from a bank in the primary service area for wetland impacts and two times the number of credits it would have had to acquire in the primary service area for stream impacts;

2. When submitting proof of acquisition of credits for a subdivision or development, provide to the Department a plan that the permit applicant will implement that is certified by a licensed professional engineer, surveyor, or landscape architect for the planting, preservation, or replacement of trees on the development site such that the minimum tree canopy percentage 20 years after development is projected to be as follows:

a. Ten percent tree canopy for a site zoned for business, commercial, or industrial use;

b. Ten percent tree canopy for a residential site zoned for 20 or more units per acre;

c. Fifteen percent tree canopy for a residential site zoned for more than eight but fewer than 20 units per acre;

d. Twenty percent tree canopy for a residential site zoned for more than four but not more than eight units per acre;

e. Twenty-five percent tree canopy for a residential site zoned for more than two but not more than four units per acre; and

f. Thirty percent tree canopy for a residential site zoned for two or fewer units per acre.

For a mixed-use development, the tree canopy percentage required pursuant to this subdivision shall be that which is applicable to the predominant use.

The tree canopy requirements established under this subsection shall not supersede any additional requirements imposed by a locality pursuant to § 15.2-961 or 15.2-961.1.

D. The Department is authorized to serve as a signatory to agreements governing the operation of mitigation banks. The Commonwealth and its officials, agencies, and employees shall not be liable for any action taken under any agreement developed pursuant to such authority.

E. State agencies and localities are authorized to purchase credits from mitigation banks.

F. A locality may establish, operate and sponsor wetland or stream single-user mitigation banks within the Commonwealth that have been approved and are operated in accordance with the requirements of subsection B, provided that such single-user banks may only be considered for compensatory mitigation for the sponsoring locality's municipal, joint municipal or governmental projects. For the purposes of this subsection, the term "sponsoring locality's municipal, joint municipal or governmental projects" means projects for which the locality is the named permittee, and for which there shall be no third-party leasing, sale, granting, transfer, or use of the projects or credits. Localities may enter into agreements with private third parties to facilitate the creation of privately sponsored wetland and stream mitigation banks having service areas developed through the procedures of subsection B.

G. Notwithstanding any provision of this section restricting the location of the source of credits, the Department may, for tidal wetland impacts, authorize the use of, including without the application of subsection C, a tidal wetland mitigation bank located in an adjacent river watershed when such bank contains the same plant community type and salinity regime as the impacted wetlands, which shall be the preferred form of compensation. This subsection shall apply only (i) to tidal wetland mitigation banks with a polyhaline salinity regime located in subbasins 02080102, 02080107, 02080108, and 02080208 and (ii) when a tidal wetland mitigation bank with the same plant community type and salinity regime as the impacted wetlands is not available in the same river watershed as the impacted wetland.

History.

2007, c. 659; 2008, c. 173; 2011, c. 253; 2012, c. 631; 2014, c. 332; 2021, Sp. Sess. I, c. 265; 2023, c. 245.

The 2021 Sp. Sess. I amendments.

The 2021 amendment by Sp. Sess. I, c. 265, effective July 1, 2021, added subsections A and C and redesignated former subsection A as subsection B; in subsection B, in the first paragraph, substituted "impacted site, is located in the bank's primary or secondary service area as provided in subsection C" for "bank is in the same fourth order subbasin, as defined by the hydrologic unit boundaries of the National Watershed Boundary Dataset or by the hydrologic unit system or dataset utilized and depicted or described in the bank's approved mitigation banking instrument, as the impacted site, or in an adjacent subbasin within the same river watershed as the impacted site" in the first sentence, and substituted "impacted site is not located in the bank's primary or secondary service area" for "bank is not located in the same subbasin or adjacent subbasin within the same river watershed as the impacted site" in the second sentence and deleted the second paragraph which defined "river watershed"; and made stylistic changes.

The 2023 amendments.

The 2023 amendment by c. 245, added subsection G.

§ 62.1-44.15:23.1. Wetland and Stream Replacement Fund established.

There is hereby created in the state treasury a special nonreverting fund to be known as the Wetland and Stream Replacement Fund, hereafter referred to as "the Fund." The Fund shall be established on the books of the Comptroller. All contributions to the Board pursuant to clause (iii) of subsection B of § 62.1-44.15:21 shall be paid into the state treasury and credited to the Fund. Interest earned on moneys in the Fund shall remain in the Fund and be credited to it. Any moneys remaining in the Fund, including interest thereon, at the end of each fiscal year shall not revert to the general fund but shall remain in the Fund. The Fund shall be administered and utilized by the Department. The Fund may be used as an additional mechanism for compensatory mitigation for impacts to aquatic resources (i) that result from activities authorized under (a) § 404 and 401 of the Clean Water Act (33 U.S.C. § 1251 et seq.), (b) the Virginia Water Protection Permit Regulation (9 VAC 25-210 et seq.), or (c) § 10 of the Rivers and Harbors Act (33 U.S.C. § 403); (ii) that result from unauthorized activities in waters of the United States or state waters; and (iii) in other cases, as the appropriate regulatory agencies deem acceptable. Moneys in the Fund shall be used for the purpose of purchasing mitigation bank credits in compliance with the provisions of subsection B of § 62.1-44.15:23 as soon as practicable after moneys are collected. If the Department determines within two years after the collection of moneys for a specific impact that credits will not be available within three years of the collection of moneys for such specific impact, then funds may be utilized either (1) to purchase credits from a Board-approved fund that have met the success criteria, if qualifying credits are available, (2) for the planning, construction, monitoring, and preservation of wetland and stream mitigation projects and preservation, enhancement, or restoration of upland buffers adjacent to wetlands or other state waters when used in conjunction with creation or restoration of wetlands and streams, or (3) for other water quality improvement projects as deemed acceptable by the Department. Such projects developed under clause (2) shall be developed in accordance with guidelines, responsibilities, and standards established by the Department for use, operation, and maintenance consistent with 33 CFR Part 332, governing compensatory mitigation for activities authorized by U.S. Army Corps of Engineer permits. Expenditures and disbursements from the Fund shall be made by the State Treasurer on warrants issued by the Comptroller upon written request signed by the Director of the Department. The Department may charge a reasonable fee to administer the Fund.

History.
2013, c. 742; 2021, Sp. Sess. I, c. 265; 2023, c. 206.

The 2021 Sp. Sess. I amendments.
The 2021 amendment by Sp. Sess. I, c. 265, effective July 1, 2021, substituted "subsection B of § 62.1-44.15:23" for "subsection A of § 62.1-44.15:23."

The 2023 amendments.
The 2023 amendment by c. 206, deleted "of Environmental Quality" throughout; substituted "after moneys are collected" for "if qualifying credits are available"; substituted "the Department determines within two years after the collection of moneys for a specific impact that" for "such"; and made related changes.

ARTICLE 2.3.

STORMWATER MANAGEMENT ACT.

§ 62.1-44.15:24. (Effective until July 1, 2024) Definitions.

As used in this article, unless the context requires a different meaning:
"Agreement in lieu of a stormwater management plan" means a contract between the VSMP authority and the owner or permittee that specifies methods that shall be implemented to comply with the requirements of a VSMP for the construction of a (i) single-family residence or (ii) farm building or structure on a parcel of land with a total impervious cover percentage, including the impervious cover from the farm building or structure to be

constructed, of less than five percent; such contract may be executed by the VSMP authority in lieu of a stormwater management plan.

"Chesapeake Bay Preservation Act land-disturbing activity" means a land-disturbing activity including clearing, grading, or excavation that results in a land disturbance equal to or greater than 2,500 square feet and less than one acre in all areas of jurisdictions designated as subject to the regulations adopted pursuant to the Chesapeake Bay Preservation provisions of this chapter.

"CWA" means the federal Clean Water Act (33 U.S.C. § 1251 et seq.), formerly referred to as the Federal Water Pollution Control Act or Federal Water Pollution Control Act Amendments of 1972, P.L. 92-500, as amended by P.L. 95-217, P.L. 95-576, P.L. 96-483, and P.L. 97-117, or any subsequent revisions thereto.

"Department" means the Department of Environmental Quality.

"Director" means the Director of the Department of Environmental Quality.

"Farm building or structure" means the same as that term is defined in § 36-97 and also includes any building or structure used for agritourism activity, as defined in § 3.2-6400, and any related impervious surfaces including roads, driveways, and parking areas.

"Flooding" means a volume of water that is too great to be confined within the banks or walls of the stream, water body, or conveyance system and that overflows onto adjacent lands, thereby causing or threatening damage.

"Land disturbance" or *"land-disturbing activity"* means a man-made change to the land surface that potentially changes its runoff characteristics including clearing, grading, or excavation, except that the term shall not include those exemptions specified in § 62.1-44.15:34.

"Municipal separate storm sewer" means a conveyance or system of conveyances otherwise known as a municipal separate storm sewer system or "MS4," including roads with drainage systems, municipal streets, catch basins, curbs, gutters, ditches, man-made channels, or storm drains:

1. Owned or operated by a federal, state, city, town, county, district, association, or other public body, created by or pursuant to state law, having jurisdiction or delegated authority for erosion and sediment control and stormwater management, or a designated and approved management agency under § 208 of the CWA that discharges to surface waters;

2. Designed or used for collecting or conveying stormwater;

3. That is not a combined sewer; and

4. That is not part of a publicly owned treatment works.

"Municipal Separate Storm Sewer System Management Program" means a management program covering the duration of a state permit for a municipal separate storm sewer system that includes a comprehensive planning process that involves public participation and intergovernmental coordination, to reduce the discharge of pollutants to the maximum extent practicable, to protect water quality, and to satisfy the appropriate water quality requirements of the CWA and regulations, and this article and its attendant regulations, using management practices, control techniques, and system, design, and engineering methods, and such other provisions that are appropriate.

"Nonpoint source pollution" means pollution such as sediment, nitrogen, phosphorus, hydrocarbons, heavy metals, and toxics whose sources cannot be pinpointed but rather are washed from the land surface in a diffuse manner by stormwater runoff.

"Peak flow rate" means the maximum instantaneous flow from a prescribed design storm at a particular location.

"Permit" or *"VSMP authority permit"* means an approval to conduct a land-disturbing activity issued by the VSMP authority for the initiation of a

land-disturbing activity after evidence of state VSMP general permit coverage has been provided where applicable.

"Permittee" means the person to which the permit or state permit is issued.

"Runoff volume" means the volume of water that runs off the land development project from a prescribed storm event.

"Rural Tidewater locality" means any locality that is (i) subject to the provisions of the Chesapeake Bay Preservation Act (§ 62.1-44.15:67 et seq.) and (ii) eligible to join the Rural Coastal Virginia Community Enhancement Authority established by Chapter 76 (§ 15.2-7600 et seq.) of Title 15.2.

"Small construction activity" means:

1. A construction activity, including clearing, grading, or excavating, that results in land disturbance of equal to or greater than one acre and less than five acres. "Small construction activity" also includes the disturbance of less than one acre of total land area that is part of a larger common plan of development or sale if the larger common plan will ultimately disturb an area equal to or greater than one acre and less than five acres. "Small construction activity" does not include routine maintenance that is performed to maintain the original line and grade, hydraulic capacity, or original purpose of the facility.

The Board may waive the otherwise applicable requirements in a general permit for a stormwater discharge from construction activities that disturb less than five acres where stormwater controls are not needed based on an approved total maximum daily load (TMDL) that addresses the pollutants of concern or, for nonimpaired waters that do not require TMDLs, an equivalent analysis that determines allocations for small construction sites for the pollutants of concern or that determines that such allocations are not needed to protect water quality based on consideration of existing in-stream concentrations, expected growth in pollutant contributions from all sources, and a margin of safety. For the purpose of this subdivision, the pollutants of concern include sediment or a parameter that addresses sediment, such as total suspended solids, turbidity, or siltation, and any other pollutant that has been identified as a cause of impairment of any water body that will receive a discharge from the construction activity. The operator shall certify to the Board that the construction activity will take place, and that stormwater discharges will occur, within the drainage area addressed by the TMDL or provide an equivalent analysis.

As of the start date in the table of start dates for electronic submissions of Virginia Pollutant Discharge Elimination System (VPDES) information within the regulation governing the implementation of electronic reporting requirements for certain VPDES permittees, facilities, and entities, all certifications submitted in support of such waiver shall be submitted electronically by the owner or operator to the Department in compliance with (i) this subdivision; (ii) 40 C.F.R. Part 3, including, in all cases, 40 C.F.R. Part 3 Subpart D; (iii) the regulation addressing signatories to state permit applications and reports; and (iv) regulations addressing the VPDES electronic reporting requirements. Such regulations addressing the VPDES electronic reporting requirements shall not undo existing requirements for electronic reporting. Prior to such date, and independent of the regulations addressing the VPDES electronic reporting requirements, a permittee shall be required to report electronically if specified by a particular permit.

2. Any other construction activity designated by either the Board or the Regional Administrator of the U.S. Environmental Protection Agency, based on the potential for contribution to a violation of a water quality standard or for significant contribution of pollutants to surface waters.

"State permit" means an approval to conduct a land-disturbing activity issued by the Board in the form of a state stormwater individual permit or

coverage issued under a state general permit or an approval issued by the Board for stormwater discharges from an MS4. Under these permits, the Commonwealth imposes and enforces requirements pursuant to the federal Clean Water Act and regulations and this article and its attendant regulations.

"Stormwater" means precipitation that is discharged across the land surface or through conveyances to one or more waterways and that may include stormwater runoff, snow melt runoff, and surface runoff and drainage.

"Stormwater management plan" means a document containing material describing methods for complying with the requirements of a VSMP.

"Subdivision" means the same as defined in § 15.2-2201.

"Virginia Stormwater Management Program" or *"VSMP"* means a program approved by the Soil and Water Conservation Board after September 13, 2011, and until June 30, 2013, or the State Water Control Board on and after June 30, 2013, that has been established by a VSMP authority to manage the quality and quantity of runoff resulting from land-disturbing activities and shall include such items as local ordinances, rules, permit requirements, annual standards and specifications, policies and guidelines, technical materials, and requirements for plan review, inspection, enforcement, where authorized in this article, and evaluation consistent with the requirements of this article and associated regulations.

"Virginia Stormwater Management Program authority" or *"VSMP authority"* means an authority approved by the Board after September 13, 2011, to operate a Virginia Stormwater Management Program or the Department. An authority may include a locality; state entity, including the Department; federal entity; or, for linear projects subject to annual standards and specifications in accordance with subsection B of § 62.1-44.15:31, electric, natural gas, and telephone utility companies, interstate and intrastate natural gas pipeline companies, railroad companies, or authorities created pursuant to § 15.2-5102.

"Water quality volume" means the volume equal to the first one-half inch of runoff multiplied by the impervious surface of the land development project.

"Water quantity technical criteria" means standards set forth in regulations adopted pursuant to this article that establish minimum design criteria for measures to control localized flooding and stream channel erosion.

"Watershed" means a defined land area drained by a river or stream, karst system, or system of connecting rivers or streams such that all surface water within the area flows through a single outlet. In karst areas, the karst feature to which water drains may be considered the single outlet for the watershed.

History.

1989, cc. 467, 499, § 10.1-603.2; 1991, c. 84; 1994, cc. 605, 898; 2004, c. 372; 2006, cc. 21, 171; 2012, cc. 785, 819; 2013, cc. 756, 793; 2014, cc. 303, 598; 2018, cc. 154, 155; 2023, cc. 48, 49.

Editor's note.

Acts 2016, cc. 68 and 758, cl. 9, as amended by Acts 2023, cc. 665 and 666, cl. 1, provides: "That the State Water Control Board (the Board) shall adopt regulations to implement the requirements of this act before July 1, 2024. The adoption of such regulations shall include the reduction of regulations through consolidation of duplicative requirements and be exempt from the requirements of Article 2 (§ 2.2-4006 et seq.) of the Administrative Process Act (§ 2.2-4000 et seq.) of the Code of Virginia. However, the Department shall (i) provide a Notice of Intended Regulatory Action, (ii) form a stakeholders advisory group, (iii) provide for a 60-day public comment period prior to the Board's adoption of the regulations, and (iv) provide the Board with a written summary of comments received and responses to comments prior to the Board's adoption of the regulations. This enactment shall become effective in due course. The regulations shall become effective on July 1, 2024, concurrent with the effective date of the remainder of this act."

Acts 2016, cc. 68 and 758, cl. 10, as amended by Acts 2017, c. 345, cl. 2 and Acts 2023, cc. 665 and 666, cl. 1, provides: "That the provisions of this act, except for the ninth enactment, shall become effective on July 1, 2024, concurrent with the effective date of the regulations required by the ninth enactment of this act."

The 2023 amendments.

The 2023 amendment by cc. 48 and 49, in the definition for "Agreement in lieu of a stormwater management plan" added "or (ii) farm build-ing or structure on a parcel of land with a total impervious cover percentage, including the impervious cover from the farm building or structure to be constructed, of less than five percent"; and added the definitions for "Farm building or structure" and "Small construction activity".

§ 62.1-44.15:24. (Effective July 1, 2024) Definitions.

As used in this article, unless the context requires a different meaning:

"Agreement in lieu of a stormwater management plan" means a contract between the VSMP authority and the owner or permittee that specifies methods that shall be implemented to comply with the requirements of a VSMP for the construction of a (i) single-family residence or (ii) farm building or structure on a parcel of land with a total impervious cover percentage, including the impervious cover from the farm building or structure to be constructed, of less than five percent; such contract may be executed by the VSMP authority in lieu of a stormwater management plan.

"Applicant" means any person submitting a soil erosion control and stormwater management plan to a VESMP authority, or a stormwater management plan to the Board when it is serving as a VSMP authority, for approval in order to obtain authorization to commence a land-disturbing activity.

"CWA" means the federal Clean Water Act (33 U.S.C. § 1251 et seq.), formerly referred to as the Federal Water Pollution Control Act or Federal Water Pollution Control Act Amendments of 1972, P.L. 92-500, as amended by P.L. 95-217, P.L. 95-576, P.L. 96-483, and P.L. 97-117, or any subsequent revisions thereto.

"Department" means the Department of Environmental Quality.

"Director" means the Director of the Department of Environmental Quality.

"Erosion impact area" means an area of land that is not associated with a current land-disturbing activity but is subject to persistent soil erosion resulting in the delivery of sediment onto neighboring properties or into state waters. This definition shall not apply to any lot or parcel of land of 10,000 square feet or less used for residential purposes or any shoreline where the erosion results from wave action or other coastal processes.

"Farm building or structure" means the same as that term is defined in § 36-97 and also includes any building or structure used for agritourism activity, as defined in § 3.2-6400, and any related impervious surfaces including roads, driveways, and parking areas.

"Flooding" means a volume of water that is too great to be confined within the banks or walls of the stream, water body, or conveyance system and that overflows onto adjacent lands, thereby causing or threatening damage.

"Land disturbance" or *"land-disturbing activity"* means a man-made change to the land surface that may result in soil erosion or has the potential to change its runoff characteristics, including construction activity such as the clearing, grading, excavating, or filling of land.

"Land-disturbance approval" means the same as that term is defined in § 62.1-44.3.

"Municipal separate storm sewer" or *"MS4"* means the same as that term is defined in § 62.1-44.3.

"Municipal Separate Storm Sewer System Management Program" means a management program covering the duration of a permit for a municipal separate storm sewer system that includes a comprehensive planning process that involves public participation and intergovernmental coordination, to

reduce the discharge of pollutants to the maximum extent practicable, to protect water quality, and to satisfy the appropriate water quality requirements of the CWA and regulations, and this article and its attendant regulations, using management practices, control techniques, and system, design, and engineering methods, and such other provisions that are appropriate.

"Natural channel design concepts" means the utilization of engineering analysis and fluvial geomorphic processes to create, rehabilitate, restore, or stabilize an open conveyance system for the purpose of creating or recreating a stream that conveys its bankfull storm event within its banks and allows larger flows to access its bankfull bench and its floodplain.

"Nonpoint source pollution" means pollution such as sediment, nitrogen, phosphorus, hydrocarbons, heavy metals, and toxics whose sources cannot be pinpointed but rather are washed from the land surface in a diffuse manner by stormwater.

"Owner" means the same as that term is defined in § 62.1-44.3. For a regulated land-disturbing activity that does not require a permit, "owner" also means the owner or owners of the freehold of the premises or lesser estate therein, mortgagee or vendee in possession, assignee of rents, receiver, executor, trustee, lessee, or other person, firm, or corporation in control of a property.

"Peak flow rate" means the maximum instantaneous flow from a prescribed design storm at a particular location.

"Permit" means a Virginia Pollutant Discharge Elimination System (VPDES) permit issued by the Board pursuant to § 62.1-44.15 for stormwater discharges from a land-disturbing activity or MS4.

"Permittee" means the person to whom the permit is issued.

"Runoff volume" means the volume of water that runs off the land development project from a prescribed storm event.

"Rural Tidewater locality" means any locality that is (i) subject to the provisions of the Chesapeake Bay Preservation Act (§ 62.1-44.15:67 et seq.) and (ii) eligible to join the Rural Coastal Virginia Community Enhancement Authority established by Chapter 76 (§ 15.2-7600 et seq.) of Title 15.2.

"Small construction activity" means:

1. A construction activity, including clearing, grading, or excavating, that results in land disturbance of equal to or greater than one acre and less than five acres. "Small construction activity" also includes the disturbance of less than one acre of total land area that is part of a larger common plan of development or sale if the larger common plan will ultimately disturb an area equal to or greater than one acre and less than five acres. "Small construction activity" does not include routine maintenance that is performed to maintain the original line and grade, hydraulic capacity, or original purpose of the facility.

The Board may waive the otherwise applicable requirements in a general permit for a stormwater discharge from construction activities that disturb less than five acres where stormwater controls are not needed based on an approved total maximum daily load (TMDL) that addresses the pollutants of concern or, for nonimpaired waters that do not require TMDLs, an equivalent analysis that determines allocations for small construction sites for the pollutants of concern or that determines that such allocations are not needed to protect water quality based on consideration of existing in-stream concentrations, expected growth in pollutant contributions from all sources, and a margin of safety. For the purpose of this subdivision, the pollutants of concern include sediment or a parameter that addresses sediment, such as total suspended solids, turbidity, or siltation, and any other pollutant that has been identified as a cause of impairment of any water body that will receive a discharge from the construction activity. The operator shall certify to the Board that the construction activity will take place, and that stormwater discharges will occur, within the drainage area addressed by the TMDL or provide an equivalent analysis.

As of the start date in the table of start dates for electronic submissions of Virginia Pollutant Discharge Elimination System (VPDES) information within the regulation governing the implementation of electronic reporting requirements for certain VPDES permittees, facilities, and entities, all certifications submitted in support of such waiver shall be submitted electronically by the owner or operator to the Department in compliance with (i) this subdivision; (ii) 40 C.F.R. Part 3, including, in all cases, 40 C.F.R. Part 3 Subpart D; (iii) the regulation addressing signatories to state permit applications and reports; and (iv) regulations addressing the VPDES electronic reporting requirements. Such regulations addressing the VPDES electronic reporting requirements shall not undo existing requirements for electronic reporting. Prior to such date, and independent of the regulations addressing the VPDES electronic reporting requirements, a permittee shall be required to report electronically if specified by a particular permit.

2. Any other construction activity designated by either the Board or the Regional Administrator of the U.S. Environmental Protection Agency, based on the potential for contribution to a violation of a water quality standard or for significant contribution of pollutants to surface waters.

"Soil erosion" means the movement of soil by wind or water into state waters or onto lands in the Commonwealth.

"Soil Erosion Control and Stormwater Management plan" or *"plan"* means a document describing methods for controlling soil erosion and managing stormwater in accordance with the requirements adopted pursuant to this article.

"Stormwater," for the purposes of this article, means precipitation that is discharged across the land surface or through conveyances to one or more waterways and that may include stormwater runoff, snow melt runoff, and surface runoff and drainage.

"Stormwater management plan" means a document containing material describing methods for complying with the requirements of a VSMP.

"Subdivision" means the same as that term is defined in § 15.2-2201.

"Virginia Erosion and Sediment Control Program" or *"VESCP"* means a program approved by the Board that is established by a VESCP authority pursuant to Article 2.4 (§ 62.1-44.15:51 et seq.) for the effective control of soil erosion, sediment deposition, and nonagricultural runoff associated with a land-disturbing activity to prevent the unreasonable degradation of properties, stream channels, waters, and other natural resources. The VESCP shall include, where applicable, such items as local ordinances, rules, policies and guidelines, technical materials, and requirements for plan review, inspection, and evaluation consistent with the requirements of Article 2.4 (§ 62.1-44.15:51 et seq.).

"Virginia Erosion and Sediment Control Program authority" or *"VESCP authority"* means a locality that is approved by the Board to operate a Virginia Erosion and Sediment Control Program in accordance with Article 2.4 (§ 62.1-44.15:51 et seq.). Only a locality for which the Department administered a Virginia Stormwater Management Program as of July 1, 2017, is authorized to choose to operate a VESCP pursuant to Article 2.4 (§ 62.1-44.15:51 et seq.).

"Virginia Erosion and Stormwater Management Program" or *"VESMP"* means a program established by a VESMP authority for the effective control of soil erosion and sediment deposition and the management of the quality and

quantity of runoff resulting from land-disturbing activities to prevent the unreasonable degradation of properties, stream channels, waters, and other natural resources. The program shall include such items as local ordinances, rules, requirements for permits and land-disturbance approvals, policies and guidelines, technical materials, and requirements for plan review, inspection, and enforcement consistent with the requirements of this article.

"Virginia Erosion and Stormwater Management Program authority" or *"VESMP authority"* means the Board or a locality approved by the Board to operate a Virginia Erosion and Stormwater Management Program. For state agency or federal entity land-disturbing activities and land-disturbing activities subject to approved standards and specifications, the Board shall serve as the VESMP authority.

"Virginia Stormwater Management Program" or *"VSMP"* means a program established by the Board pursuant to § 62.1-44.15:27.1 on behalf of a locality on or after July 1, 2014, to manage the quality and quantity of runoff resulting from any land-disturbing activity that (i) disturbs one acre or more of land or (ii) disturbs less than one acre of land and is part of a larger common plan of development or sale that results in one acre or more of land disturbance.

"Virginia Stormwater Management Program authority" or *"VSMP authority"* means the Board when administering a VSMP on behalf of a locality that, pursuant to subdivision B 3 of § 62.1-44.15:27, has chosen not to adopt and administer a VESMP.

"Water quality technical criteria" means standards set forth in regulations adopted pursuant to this article that establish minimum design criteria for measures to control nonpoint source pollution.

"Water quantity technical criteria" means standards set forth in regulations adopted pursuant to this article that establish minimum design criteria for measures to control localized flooding and stream channel erosion.

"Watershed" means a defined land area drained by a river or stream, karst system, or system of connecting rivers or streams such that all surface water within the area flows through a single outlet. In karst areas, the karst feature to which water drains may be considered the single outlet for the watershed.

History.
1989, cc. 467, 499, § 10.1-603.2; 1991, c. 84; 1994, cc. 605, 898; 2004, c. 372; 2006, cc. 21, 171; 2012, cc. 785, 819; 2013, cc. 756, 793; 2014, cc. 303, 598; 2016, cc. 68, 758; 2018, cc. 154, 155; 2023, cc. 48, 49.

§ 62.1-44.15:25. (Effective until July 1, 2024) Further powers and duties of the State Water Control Board.

Acts 2023, cc. 196 and 197, cl. 1 provides: "§ 1. As used in this act, "electric utility" means any person that generates, transmits, or distributes electric energy for use by retail customers in the Commonwealth, including any investor-owned electric utility, cooperative electric utility, or electric utility owned or operated by a municipality.

"§ 2. The Department of Environmental Quality (the Department) shall include specifications for stormwater management and erosion and sediment control for the installation of permanent gravel access roads by an electric utility for the purpose of construction and maintenance of electric transmission lines in the next publication of the Department's Virginia Stormwater Management Handbook (the Handbook). Such specifications shall be developed after seeking input from electric utility representatives. Any electric utility that complies with the Handbook's specifications for stormwater management and erosion and sediment control for the installation of a permanent gravel access road for the purpose of construction and maintenance of electric transmission lines shall be deemed to satisfy the water quantity technical criteria in the Stormwater Management Act pursuant to Article 2.3 (§ 62.1-44.15:24 et seq.) of Chapter 3.1 of Title 62.1 of the Code of Virginia.

"An electric utility may provide in its annual standards and specifications reasonable assurance that the specifications in the Handbook will be satisfied. The electric utility may achieve such reasonable assurance by incorporating the applicable specifications from the Handbook into a stormwater management plan and an erosion and sediment control plan developed for a project to install a permanent gravel access road under its annual standards and specifications.

"§ 3. Until the effective date of the next publication of the Handbook, any new permanent gravel access road associated with the construction and maintenance of electric transmission lines by an electric utility shall be deemed to have satisfied the required water quantity technical criteria if (i) the maximum width of the permanent gravel access road is no more than 14 feet with passing areas not more than 100 feet in length and 24 feet in width every 2,000 feet, on average; (ii) the permanent gravel access road follows the contour of the natural terrain to the extent possible and slopes should not exceed 10 percent; (iii) the permanent gravel access road is constructed using clean, open-graded, angular aggregate at a depth of no less than six inches; and (iv) the following conditions are met:

"1. The project is managed so that during construction of the permanent gravel access road the area of land-disturbing activity is less than one acre;

"2. The area where land-disturbing activity has been completed is adequately stabilized prior to initiating construction of the gravel access road on the next area subject to land-disturbing activity. "Adequately stabilized" means compliance with Standard and Specification 3.36 in the 1992 Virginia Erosion and Sediment Control Handbook;

"3. The environment is protected from erosion and sedimentation damage associated with the land-disturbing activity; and

"4. The project owner or construction activity operator designs, installs, implements, and maintains pollution prevention measures to (i) minimize the discharge of pollutants from equipment and vehicle wash water, wheel wash water, and other wash waters; (ii) minimize the exposure of building materials, building products, construction waste, trash, landscape materials, fertilizers, pesticides, herbicides, detergents, sanitary waste, and other materials present on site to precipitation and to stormwater; (iii) minimize the discharge of pollutants from spills and leaks and implement chemical spill and leak prevention and response procedures; (iv) prohibit the discharge of wastewater from the washout of concrete; (v) prohibit the discharge of wastewater from the washout and cleanout of stucco, paint, form release oils, curing compounds, and other construction materials; and (vi) prohibit the discharge of fuels, oils, or other pollutants used in vehicle and equipment operation and maintenance.

"The electric utility shall provide in its annual standards and specifications reasonable assurance that such conditions will be satisfied. The electric utility may achieve such reasonable assurance by incorporating the conditions of this section into an erosion and sediment control plan developed for the project under the utility's annual standards and specifications."

§ 62.1-44.15:27. (Effective until July 1, 2024) Establishment of Virginia Stormwater Management Programs.

A. Any locality that operates a regulated MS4 or that notifies the Department of its decision to participate in the establishment of a VSMP shall be required to adopt a VSMP for land-disturbing activities consistent with the provisions of this article according to a schedule set by the Department. Such schedule shall require implementation no later than July 1, 2014. Thereafter, the Department shall provide an annual schedule by which localities can submit applications to implement a VSMP. Localities subject to this subsection are authorized to coordinate plan review and inspections with other entities in accordance with subsection H.

The Department shall operate a VSMP on behalf of any locality that does not operate a regulated MS4 and that does not notify the Department, according to a schedule set by the Department, of its decision to participate in the establishment of a VSMP. A locality that decides not to establish a VSMP shall still comply with the requirements set forth in this article and attendant regulations as required to satisfy the stormwater flow rate capacity and velocity requirements set forth in the Erosion and Sediment Control Law (§ 62.1-44.15:51 et seq.). A locality that is subject to the provisions of the Chesapeake Bay Preservation Act (§ 62.1-44.15:67 et seq.) also shall adopt requirements set forth in this article and attendant regulations as required to regulate Chesapeake Bay Preservation Act land-disturbing activities in accordance with § 62.1-44.15:28. To comply with the water quantity technical criteria set forth in this article and attendant regulations, a rural Tidewater locality may adopt a tiered approach to water quantity management for Chesapeake Bay Preservation Act land-disturbing activities pursuant to § 62.1-44.15:27.2.

Notwithstanding any other provision of this subsection, any county that operates an MS4 that became a regulated MS4 on or after January 1, 2014 may elect, on a schedule set by the Department, to defer the implementation of the county's VSMP until no later than January 1, 2015. During this deferral period, when such county thus lacks the legal authority to operate a VSMP, the Department shall operate a VSMP on behalf of the county and address post-construction stormwater runoff and the required design criteria for stormwater runoff controls. Any such county electing to defer the establishment of its VSMP shall still comply with the requirements set forth in this article and attendant regulations as required to satisfy the stormwater flow rate capacity and velocity requirements set forth in the Erosion and Sediment Control Law (§ 62.1-44.15:51 et seq.).

B. Any town, including a town that operates a regulated MS4, lying within a county that has adopted a VSMP in accordance with subsection A may decide, but shall not be required, to become subject to the county's VSMP. Any town lying within a county that operates an MS4 that became a regulated MS4 on or after January 1, 2014 may elect to become subject to the county's VSMP according to the deferred schedule established in subsection A. During the county's deferral period, the Department shall operate a VSMP on behalf of the town and address post-construction stormwater runoff and the required design criteria for stormwater runoff controls for the town as provided in subsection A. If a town lies within the boundaries of more than one county, the town shall be considered to be wholly within the county in which the larger portion of the town lies. Towns shall inform the Department of their decision according to a schedule established by the Department. Thereafter, the Department shall provide an annual schedule by which towns can submit applications to adopt a VSMP.

C. In support of VSMP authorities, the Department shall:

1. Provide assistance grants to localities not currently operating a local stormwater management program to help the localities to establish their VSMP.

2. Provide technical assistance and training.

3. Provide qualified services in specified geographic areas to a VSMP to assist localities in the administration of components of their programs. The Department shall actively assist localities in the establishment of their programs and in the selection of a contractor or other entity that may provide support to the locality or regional support to several localities.

D. The Department shall develop a model ordinance for establishing a VSMP consistent with this article and its associated regulations, including the Virginia Stormwater Management Program (VSMP) General Permit for Discharges of Stormwater from Construction Activities.

E. Each locality that administers an approved VSMP shall, by ordinance, establish a VSMP that shall be administered in conjunction with a local MS4 program and a local erosion and sediment control program if required pursuant to the Erosion and Sediment Control Law (§ 62.1-44.15:51 et seq.), and which shall include the following:

1. Consistency with regulations adopted in accordance with provisions of this article;

2. Provisions for long-term responsibility for and maintenance of stormwater management control devices and other techniques specified to manage the quality and quantity of runoff; and

3. Provisions for the integration of the VSMP with local erosion and sediment control, flood insurance, flood plain management, and other programs requiring compliance prior to authorizing construction in order to make the submission and approval of plans, issuance of permits, payment of fees, and coordination of inspection and enforcement activities more convenient and efficient both for the local governments and those responsible for compliance with the programs.

F. The Board may approve a state entity, including the Department, federal entity, or, for linear projects subject to annual standards and specifications, electric, natural gas, and telephone utility companies, interstate and intrastate natural gas pipeline companies, railroad companies, or authorities created pursuant to § 15.2-5102 to operate a Virginia Stormwater Management Program consistent with the requirements of this article and its associated regulations and the VSMP authority's Department-approved annual standards and specifications. For these programs, enforcement shall be administered by the Department and the Board where applicable in accordance with the provisions of this article.

G. The Board shall approve a VSMP when it deems a program consistent with this article and associated regulations, including the Virginia Stormwater Management Program (VSMP) General Permit for Discharges of Stormwater from Construction Activities.

H. A VSMP authority may enter into agreements or contracts with soil and water conservation districts, adjacent localities, or other public or private entities to carry out or assist with the responsibilities of this article. A VSMP authority may enter into contracts with third-party professionals who hold certificates of competence in the appropriate subject areas, as provided in subsection A of § 62.1-44.15:30, to carry out any or all of the responsibilities that this article requires of a VSMP authority, including plan review and inspection but not including enforcement.

I. If a locality establishes a VSMP, it shall issue a consolidated stormwater management and erosion and sediment control permit that is consistent with the provisions of the Erosion and Sediment Control Law (§ 62.1-44.15:51 et seq.). When available in accordance with subsection J, such permit, where applicable, shall also include a copy of or reference to state VSMP permit coverage authorization to discharge.

J. Upon the development of an online reporting system by the Department, but no later than July 1, 2014, a VSMP authority shall then be required to obtain evidence of state VSMP permit coverage where it is required prior to providing approval to begin land disturbance.

K. Any VSMP adopted pursuant to and consistent with this article shall be considered to meet the stormwater management requirements under the Chesapeake Bay Preservation Act (§ 62.1-44.15:67 et seq.) and attendant regulations, and effective July 1, 2014, shall not be subject to local program review under the stormwater management provisions of the Chesapeake Bay Preservation Act.

L. All VSMP authorities shall comply with the provisions of this article and the stormwater management provisions of the Erosion and Sediment Control Law (§ 62.1-44.15:51 et seq.) and related regulations. The VSMP authority responsible for regulating the land-disturbing activity shall require compliance with the issued permit, permit conditions, and plan specifications. The state shall enforce state permits.

M. In the case of a land-disturbing activity located on property controlled by a regional industrial facility authority established pursuant to Chapter 64 (§ 15.2-6400 et seq.) of Title 15.2, if a participating local member of such an authority also administers a VSMP, such locality shall be authorized to administer the VSMP on authority property, in accordance with an agreement entered into with all relevant localities and the existing VSMP for the property.

History.
1989, cc. 467, 499, § 10.1-603.3; 2004, c. 372; 2006, c. 171; 2009, c. 18; 2012, cc. 785, 819; 2013, cc. 756, 793; 2014, cc. 303, 598; 2016, cc. 68, 758; 2017, c. 349; 2018, c. 154; 2022, c. 160.

Section set out twice.
The section above is effective until July 1, 2024. For this section as in effect at that time, see the following section, also numbered 62.1-44.15:27.

Editor's note.
Acts 2016, cc. 68 and 758, cl. 9, as amended by Acts 2023, cc. 665 and 666, cl. 1, provides: "That the State Water Control Board (the Board) shall adopt regulations to implement the requirements of this act before July 1, 2024. The adoption of such regulations shall include the reduction of regulations through consolidation of duplicative requirements and be exempt from the requirements of Article 2 (§ 2.2-4006 et seq.) of the Administrative Process Act (§

2.2-4000 et seq.) of the Code of Virginia. However, the Department shall (i) provide a Notice of Intended Regulatory Action, (ii) form a stakeholders advisory group, (iii) provide for a 60-day public comment period prior to the Board's adoption of the regulations, and (iv) provide the Board with a written summary of comments received and responses to comments prior to the Board's adoption of the regulations. This enactment shall become effective in due course. The regulations shall become effective on July 1, 2024, concurrent with the effective date of the remainder of this act."

Acts 2016, cc. 68 and 758, cl. 10, as amended by Acts 2017, c. 345, cl. 2 and Acts 2023, cc. 665 and 666, cl. 1, provides: "That the provisions of this act, except for the ninth enactment, shall become effective on July 1, 2024, concurrent with the effective date of the regulations required by the ninth enactment of this act."

The 2022 amendments.
The 2022 amendment by c. 160 added subsection M.

§ 62.1-44.15:27. (Effective July 1, 2024) Virginia Programs for Erosion Control and Stormwater Management.

A. Any locality that operates a regulated MS4 or that administers a Virginia Stormwater Management Program (VSMP) as of July 1, 2017, shall be required to adopt and administer a VESMP consistent with the provisions of this article that regulates any land-disturbing activity that (i) disturbs 10,000 square feet or more or (ii) disturbs 2,500 square feet or more in an area of a locality designated as a Chesapeake Bay Preservation Area pursuant to the Chesapeake Bay Preservation Act (§ 62.1-44.15:67 et seq.). The VESMP shall be adopted according to a process established by the Department.

B. Any locality that does not operate a regulated MS4 and for which the Department administers a VSMP as of July 1, 2017, shall choose one of the following options and shall notify the Department of its choice according to a process established by the Department:

1. Adopt and administer a VESMP consistent with the provisions of this article that regulates any land-disturbing activity that (i) disturbs 10,000 square feet or more or (ii) disturbs 2,500 square feet or more in an area of a locality designated as a Chesapeake Bay Preservation Area pursuant to the Chesapeake Bay Preservation Act (§ 62.1-44.15:67 et seq.);

2. Adopt and administer a VESMP consistent with the provisions of this article that regulates any land-disturbing activity that (i) disturbs 10,000 square feet or more or (ii) disturbs 2,500 square feet or more in an area of a locality designated as a Chesapeake Bay Preservation Area pursuant to the Chesapeake Bay Preservation Act (§ 62.1-44.15:67 et seq.), except that the Department shall provide the locality with review of the plan required by § 62.1-44.15:34 and provide a recommendation to the locality on the plan's compliance with the water quality and water quantity technical criteria; or

3. Adopt and administer a VESCP pursuant to Article 2.4 (§ 62.1-44.15:51 et seq.) that regulates any land-disturbing activity that (i) disturbs 10,000 square

feet or more or (ii) disturbs 2,500 square feet or more in an area of a locality designated as a Chesapeake Bay Preservation Area pursuant to the Chesapeake Bay Preservation Act (§ 62.1-44.15:67 et seq.). For such a land-disturbing activity in a Chesapeake Bay Preservation Area, the VESCP authority also shall adopt requirements set forth in this article and attendant regulations as required to regulate those activities in accordance with §§ 62.1-44.15:28 and 62.1-44.15:34.

The Board shall administer a VSMP on behalf of each VESCP authority for any land-disturbing activity that (a) disturbs one acre or more of land or (b) disturbs less than one acre of land and is part of a larger common plan of development or sale that results in one acre or greater of land disturbance.

C. Any town that is required to or elects to adopt and administer a VESMP or VESCP, as applicable, may choose one of the following options and shall notify the Department of its choice according to a process established by the Department:

1. Any town, including a town that operates a regulated MS4, lying within a county may enter into an agreement with the county to become subject to the county's VESMP. If a town lies within the boundaries of more than one county, it may enter into an agreement with any of those counties that operates a VESMP.

2. Any town that chooses not to adopt and administer a VESMP pursuant to subdivision B 3 and that lies within a county may enter into an agreement with the county to become subject to the county's VESMP or VESCP, as applicable. If a town lies within the boundaries of more than one county, it may enter into an agreement with any of those counties.

3. Any town that is subject to the provisions of the Chesapeake Bay Preservation Act (§ 62.1-44.15:67 et seq.) may enter into an agreement with a county pursuant to subdivision C 1 or 2 only if the county administers a VESMP for land-disturbing activities that disturb 2,500 square feet or more.

D. Any locality that chooses not to implement a VESMP pursuant to subdivision B 3 may notify the Department at any time that it has chosen to implement a VESMP pursuant to subdivision B 1 or 2. Any locality that chooses to implement a VESMP pursuant to subdivision B 2 may notify the Department at any time that it has chosen to implement a VESMP pursuant to subdivision B 1. A locality may petition the Board at any time for approval to change from fully administering a VESMP pursuant to subdivision B 1 to administering a VESMP in coordination with the Department pursuant to subdivision B 2 due to a significant change in economic conditions or other fiscal emergency in the locality. The provisions of the Administrative Process Act (§ 2.2-4000 et seq.) shall govern any appeal of the Board's decision.

E. To comply with the water quantity technical criteria set forth in this article and attendant regulations for land-disturbing activities that disturb an area of 2,500 square feet or more but less than one acre, any rural Tidewater locality may adopt a tiered approach to water quantity management pursuant to § 62.1-44.15:27.2.

F. In support of VESMP authorities, the Department shall provide technical assistance and training and general assistance to localities in the establishment and administration of their individual or regional programs.

G. The Department shall develop a model ordinance for establishing a VESMP consistent with this article.

H. Each locality that operates a regulated MS4 or that chooses to administer a VESMP shall, by ordinance, establish a VESMP that shall be administered in conjunction with a local MS4 management program, if applicable, and which shall include the following:

1. Ordinances, policies, and technical materials consistent with regulations adopted in accordance with this article;

2. Requirements for land-disturbance approvals;

3. Requirements for plan review, inspection, and enforcement consistent with the requirements of this article, including provisions requiring periodic inspections of the installation of stormwater management measures. A VESMP authority may require monitoring and reports from the person responsible for meeting the permit conditions to ensure compliance with the permit and to determine whether the measures required in the permit provide effective stormwater management;

4. Provisions charging each applicant a reasonable fee to defray the cost of program administration for a regulated land-disturbing activity that does not require permit coverage. Such fee may be in addition to any fee charged pursuant to the statewide fee schedule established in accordance with subdivision 9 of § 62.1-44.15:28, although payment of fees may be consolidated in order to provide greater convenience and efficiency for those responsible for compliance with the program. A VESMP authority shall hold a public hearing prior to establishing such fees. The fee shall not exceed an amount commensurate with the services rendered, taking into consideration the time, skill, and the VESMP authority's expense involved;

5. Provisions for long-term responsibility for and maintenance of stormwater management control devices and other techniques specified to manage the quality and quantity of runoff; and

6. Provisions for the coordination of the VESMP with flood insurance, flood plain management, and other programs requiring compliance prior to authorizing land disturbance in order to make the submission and approval of plans, issuance of land-disturbance approvals, payment of fees, and coordination of inspection and enforcement activities more convenient and efficient both for the local governments and those responsible for compliance with the programs.

I. The Board shall approve a VESMP when it deems a program consistent with this article and associated regulations.

J. A VESMP authority may enter into agreements or contracts with the Department, soil and water conservation districts, adjacent localities, planning district commissions, or other public or private entities to carry out or assist with plan review and inspections. A VESMP authority may enter into contracts with third-party professionals who hold certifications in the appropriate subject areas, as provided in subsection A of § 62.1-44.15:30, to carry out any or all of the responsibilities that this article requires of a VESMP authority, including plan review and inspection but not including enforcement.

K. A VESMP authority shall be required to obtain evidence of permit coverage from the Department's online reporting system, where such coverage is required, prior to providing land-disturbance approval.

L. The VESMP authority responsible for regulating the land-disturbing activity shall require compliance with its applicable ordinances and the conditions of its land-disturbance approval and plan specifications. The Board shall enforce permits and require compliance with its applicable regulations, including when serving as a VSMP authority in a locality that chose not to adopt a VESMP in accordance with subdivision B 3.

M. In the case of a land-disturbing activity located on property controlled by a regional industrial facility authority established pursuant to Chapter 64 (§ 15.2-6400 et seq.) of Title 15.2, if a participating local member of such an authority also administers a VESMP, such locality shall be authorized to administer the VESMP on authority property, in accordance with an agreement entered into with all relevant localities and the existing VSMP or VESMP for the property.

History.
1989, cc. 467, 499, § 10.1-603.3; 2004, c. 372; 2006, c. 171; 2009, c. 18; 2012, cc. 785, 819; 2013, cc. 756, 793; 2014, cc. 303, 598; 2016, cc. 68, 758; 2017, c. 349; 2018, c. 154; 2022, c. 160.

Section set out twice.
The section above is effective July 1, 2024. For this section as in effect until that time, see the preceding section, also numbered 62.1-44.15:27.

§ 62.1-44.15:27.4. Department acceptance of plans in lieu of plan review.

A. Notwithstanding any other provision of this article, the Board, when administering a VSMP or VESMP pursuant to Article 2.3 (§ 62.1-44.15:24 et seq.), may choose to accept a set of plans and supporting calculations for any land-disturbing activity determined to be de minimis using a risk-based approach established by the Board.

B. The Board is authorized to accept such plans and supporting calculations in satisfaction of the requirement of this article that it retain a certified plan reviewer or conduct a plan review. This section shall not excuse any applicable performance bond requirement pursuant to § 62.1-44.15:34 or § 62.1-44.15:57.

History.
2020, c. 812.

Editor's note.
At the direction of the Virginia Code Commission, "de minimis" was substituted for "de minimus" in subsection A.
Acts 2020, c. 812, cl. 2 provides: "That the State Water Control Board (the Board) shall adopt regulations to implement the requirements of §§ 62.1-44.15:27.4 and 62.1-44.15:56.1 of the Code of Virginia as created by

this act. The initial adoption of such regulations shall be exempt from the requirements of Article 2 (§ 2.2-4006 et seq.) of Chapter 40 of Title 2.2 of the Code of Virginia. However, the Board shall (i) provide a Notice of Intended Regulatory Action, (ii) form a stakeholder advisory group, (iii) provide a 60-day public comment period prior to the Board's adoption of the regulations, and (iv) provide a written summary of comments received and responses to comments prior to the Board's adoption of the regulations."

§ 62.1-44.15:28. (Effective until July 1, 2024) Development of regulations.

A. The Board is authorized to adopt regulations that specify minimum technical criteria and administrative procedures for Virginia Stormwater Management Programs. The regulations shall:

1. Establish standards and procedures for administering a VSMP;

2. Establish minimum design criteria for measures to control nonpoint source pollution and localized flooding, and incorporate the stormwater management regulations adopted pursuant to the Erosion and Sediment Control Law (§ 62.1-44.15:51 et seq.), as they relate to the prevention of stream channel erosion. These criteria shall be periodically modified as required in order to reflect current engineering methods;

3. Require the provision of long-term responsibility for and maintenance of stormwater management control devices and other techniques specified to manage the quality and quantity of runoff;

4. Require as a minimum the inclusion in VSMPs of certain administrative procedures that include, but are not limited to, specifying the time period within which a VSMP authority shall grant land-disturbing activity approval, the conditions and processes under which approval shall be granted, the procedures for communicating disapproval, the conditions under which an approval may be changed, and requirements for inspection of approved projects;

5. Establish by regulations a statewide permit fee schedule to cover all costs associated with the implementation of a VSMP related to land-disturbing

activities of one acre or greater. Such fee attributes include the costs associated with plan review, VSMP registration statement review, permit issuance, state-coverage verification, inspections, reporting, and compliance activities associated with the land-disturbing activities as well as program oversight costs. The fee schedule shall also include a provision for a reduced fee for land-disturbing activities between 2,500 square feet and up to one acre in Chesapeake Bay Preservation Act (§ 62.1-44.15:67 et seq.) localities. The fee schedule shall be governed by the following:

a. The revenue generated from the statewide stormwater permit fee shall be collected utilizing, where practicable, an online payment system, and the Department's portion shall be remitted to the State Treasurer for deposit in the Virginia Stormwater Management Fund established pursuant to § 62.1-44.15:29. However, whenever the Board has approved a VSMP, no more than 30 percent of the total revenue generated by the statewide stormwater permit fees collected shall be remitted to the State Treasurer for deposit in the Virginia Stormwater Management Fund, with the balance going to the VSMP authority.

b. Fees collected pursuant to this section shall be in addition to any general fund appropriation made to the Department or other supporting revenue from a VSMP; however, the fees shall be set at a level sufficient for the Department and the VSMP to fully carry out their responsibilities under this article and its attendant regulations and local ordinances or standards and specifications where applicable. When establishing a VSMP, the VSMP authority shall assess the statewide fee schedule and shall have the authority to reduce or increase such fees, and to consolidate such fees with other program-related charges, but in no case shall such fee changes affect the amount established in the regulations as available to the Department for program oversight responsibilities pursuant to subdivision 5 a. A VSMP's portion of the fees shall be used solely to carry out the VSMP's responsibilities under this article and its attendant regulations, ordinances, or annual standards and specifications.

c. Until July 1, 2014, the fee for coverage under the General Permit for Discharges of Stormwater from Construction Activities issued by the Board, or where the Board has issued an individual permit or coverage under the General Permit for Discharges of Stormwater from Construction Activities for an entity for which it has approved annual standards and specifications, shall be $750 for each large construction activity with sites or common plans of development equal to or greater than five acres and $450 for each small construction activity with sites or common plans of development equal to or greater than one acre and less than five acres. On and after July 1, 2014, such fees shall only apply where coverage has been issued under the Board's General Permit for Discharges of Stormwater from Construction Activities to a state agency or federal entity for which it has approved annual standards and specifications. After establishment, such fees may be modified in the future through regulatory actions.

d. Until July 1, 2014, the Department is authorized to assess a $125 reinspection fee for each visit to a project site that was necessary to check on the status of project site items noted to be in noncompliance and documented as such on a prior project inspection.

e. In establishing the fee schedule under this subdivision, the Department shall ensure that the VSMP authority portion of the statewide permit fee for coverage under the General Permit for Discharges of Stormwater from Construction Activities for small construction activity involving a single family detached residential structure with a site or area, within or outside a common plan of development or sale, that is equal to or greater than one acre but less than five acres shall be no greater than the VSMP authority portion of the fee for coverage of sites or areas with a land-disturbance acreage of less than one acre within a common plan of development or sale.

f. When any fees are collected pursuant to this section by credit cards, business transaction costs associated with processing such payments may be additionally assessed;

6. Establish statewide standards for stormwater management from land-disturbing activities of one acre or greater, except as specified otherwise within this article, and allow for the consolidation in the permit of a comprehensive approach to addressing stormwater management and erosion and sediment control, consistent with the provisions of the Erosion and Sediment Control Law (§ 62.1-44.15:51 et seq.) and this article. However, such standards shall also apply to land-disturbing activity exceeding an area of 2,500 square feet in all areas of the jurisdictions designated as subject to the Chesapeake Bay Preservation Area Designation and Management Regulations;

7. Establish a procedure by which a stormwater management plan that is approved for a residential, commercial, or industrial subdivision shall govern the development of the individual parcels, including those parcels developed under subsequent owners;

8. Notwithstanding the provisions of subdivision 5, establish a procedure by which payment of the Department's portion of the statewide permit fee established pursuant to that subdivision shall not be required for coverage under the General Permit for Discharges of Stormwater from Construction Activities for construction activity involving a single-family detached residential structure, within or outside a common plan of development or sale;

9. Provide for the certification and use of a proprietary best management practice only if another state, regional, or national program has verified its nutrient or sediment removal effectiveness and all of such program's established test protocol requirements were met or exceeded. As used in this subdivision and any regulations or guidance adopted pursuant to this subdivision, "certification" means a determination by the Department that a proprietary best management practice is approved for use in accordance with this article;

10. Require that VSMPs maintain after-development runoff rate of flow and characteristics that replicate, as nearly as practicable, the existing predevelopment runoff characteristics and site hydrology, or improve upon the contributing share of the existing predevelopment runoff characteristics and site hydrology if stream channel erosion or localized flooding is an existing predevelopment condition. Except where more stringent requirements are necessary to address total maximum daily load requirements or to protect exceptional state waters, any land-disturbing activity that provides for stormwater management shall satisfy the conditions of this subsection if the practices are designed to (i) detain the water quality volume and to release it over 48 hours; (ii) detain and release over a 24-hour period the expected rainfall resulting from the one year, 24-hour storm; and (iii) reduce the allowable peak flow rate resulting from the 1.5-year, two-year, and 10-year, 24-hour storms to a level that is less than or equal to the peak flow rate from the site assuming it was in a good forested condition, achieved through multiplication of the forested peak flow rate by a reduction factor that is equal to the runoff volume from the site when it was in a good forested condition divided by the runoff volume from the site in its proposed condition, and shall be exempt from any flow rate capacity and velocity requirements for natural or man-made channels as defined in any regulations promulgated pursuant to this section or any ordinances adopted pursuant to § 62.1-44.15:27 or 62.1-44.15:33;

11. Encourage low-impact development designs, regional and watershed approaches, and nonstructural means for controlling stormwater;

12. Promote the reclamation and reuse of stormwater for uses other than potable water in order to protect state waters and the public health and to minimize the direct discharge of pollutants into state waters;

13. Establish procedures to be followed when a locality that operates a VSMP wishes to transfer administration of the VSMP to the Department;

14. Establish a statewide permit fee schedule for stormwater management related to municipal separate storm sewer system permits;

15. Provide for the evaluation and potential inclusion of emerging or innovative nonproprietary stormwater control technologies that may prove effective in reducing nonpoint source pollution;

16. Require the owner of property that is zoned for residential use and on which is located a privately owned stormwater management facility serving one or more residential properties to record the long-term maintenance and inspection requirements for such facility with the deed for the owner's property;

17. Require that all final plan elements, specifications, or calculations whose preparation requires a license under Chapter 4 (§ 54.1-400 et seq.) or 22 (§ 54.1-2200 et seq.) of Title 54.1 be appropriately signed and sealed by a professional who is licensed to engage in practice in the Commonwealth. Nothing in this subdivision shall authorize any person to engage in practice outside his area of professional competence; and

18. Establish a procedure by which a registration statement shall not be required for coverage under the General Permit for Discharges of Stormwater from Construction Activities for a small construction activity involving a single-family detached residential structure, within or outside a common plan of development or sale.

B. The Board may integrate and consolidate components of the regulations implementing the Erosion and Sediment Control program and the Chesapeake Bay Preservation Area Designation and Management program with the regulations governing the Virginia Stormwater Management Program (VSMP) Permit program or repeal components so that these programs may be implemented in a consolidated manner that provides greater consistency, understanding, and efficiency for those regulated by and administering a VSMP.

History.
1989, cc. 467, 499, § 10.1-603.4; 1991, c. 84; 2004, c. 372; 2005, c. 102; 2006, c. 21; 2008, c. 405; 2009, c. 709; 2012, c. 785, 819; 2013, cc. 756, 793; 2014, cc. 303, 598; 2017, cc. 10, 163; 2020, cc. 313, 667; 2022, c. 32; 2023, cc. 48, 49.

Editor's note.
Acts 2016, cc. 68 and 758, cl. 9, as amended by Acts 2023, cc. 665 and 666, cl. 1, provides: "That the State Water Control Board (the Board) shall adopt regulations to implement the requirements of this act before July 1, 2024. The adoption of such regulations shall include the reduction of regulations through consolidation of duplicative requirements and be exempt from the requirements of Article 2 (§ 2.2-4006 et seq.) of the Administrative Process Act (§ 2.2-4000 et seq.) of the Code of Virginia. However, the Department shall (i) provide a Notice of Intended Regulatory Action, (ii) form a stakeholders advisory group, (iii) provide for a 60-day public comment period prior to the Board's adoption of the regulations, and (iv) provide the Board with a written summary of comments received and responses to comments prior to the Board's adoption of the regulations. This enactment shall become effective in due course. The regulations shall become effective on July 1, 2024, concurrent with the effective date of the remainder of this act."

Acts 2016, cc. 68 and 758, cl. 10, as amended by Acts 2017, c. 345, cl. 2 and Acts 2023, cc. 665 and 666, cl. 1, provides: "That the provisions of this act, except for the ninth enactment, shall become effective on July 1, 2024, concurrent with the effective date of the regulations required by the ninth enactment of this act."

Acts 2020, c. 667, cl. 2 provides: "That any proprietary best management practice (BMP) that is included by the Department of Environmental Quality (the Department) on the Virginia Stormwater BMP Clearinghouse website prior to July 1, 2020, shall by December 31, 2021, provide documentation to the Department showing that another state, regional, or national certification program has verified and certified its nutrient or sediment removal effectiveness."

Acts 2020, c. 667, cl. 3 provides: "That any proprietary best management practice (BMP) that fails to provide the Department of Environmental Quality (the Department) with the documentation required by the second enactment of this act shall not be approved for use in any stormwater management plan submitted on or after January 1, 2022, until such proprietary BMP provides the Department with such required documentation."

Acts 2020, c. 1289, as amended by Acts 2020, Sp. Sess. I, c. 56, Item 377 L 2, as amended by Acts 2021, Sp. Sess. I, c. 552 and Acts 2022, Sp. Sess. I, c. 2, Item 378 J 2, effective for the biennium ending June 30, 2023, provides: "Notwithstanding § 62.1-44.15:28, as it is currently effective and as it shall become effective, Code of Virginia, the permit fee regulations adopted by the State Water Control Board pursuant to § 62.1-44.15:28, as it is currently effective and as it shall become effective, Code of Virginia, for the Virginia Pollutant Discharge Elimination System Permit for Discharges of Stormwater from Construction Activities and municipal separate storm sewer system permits shall be set at an amount representing no less than 60 percent, not to exceed 62 percent, of the direct costs for the administration, compliance and enforcement of Virginia Pollutant Discharge Elimination System Permit for Discharges of Stormwater from Construction Activities and municipal separate storm sewer system permits. To the extent practicable, the Board shall solicit input from affected stakeholders when establishing the new fee structure."

Acts 2022, c. 32, effective April 1, 2022, provides: "That the Department of Environmental Quality shall prioritize review of any proprietary best management practice (BMP) that was on the Virginia Stormwater BMP Clearinghouse prior to December 31, 2021, and that submits documentation that another state, regional, or national program has verified its nutrient or sediment removal effectiveness and that it met or exceeded all of such program's established test protocol requirements."

The 2020 amendments.

The 2020 amendment by c. 313 inserted subdivision A 16 and renumbered former subdivision A 16 as subdivision A 17.

The 2020 amendment by c. 667, in subdivision A 8, substituted "subdivision 5" for "subdivision A 5"; rewrote subdivision A 9, which read: "Provide for reciprocity with programs in other states for the certification of proprietary best management practices"; and in subdivision A 15, inserted "nonproprietary."

The 2020 amendment by c. 313 inserted subdivision 19, renumbered former subdivision 19 as subdivision 20, and made stylistic changes.

The 2020 amendment by c. 667 rewrote subdivision 12, which read: "Provide for reciprocity with programs in other states for the certification of proprietary best management practices"; and in subdivision 18, inserted "nonproprietary."

The 2022 amendments.

¶The 2022 amendment by c. 32, effective April 1, 2022, in subdivision A 9, in the first sentence, inserted "certification and," substituted "national program has verified" for "national certification program has verified and certified" and added "and all of such program's established test protocol requirements were met or exceeded" at the end and added the last sentence.

The 2023 amendments.

The 2023 amendments by cc. 48 and 49 are identical, and added subdivision A 18.

§ 62.1-44.15:28. (Effective July 1, 2024) Development of regulations.

The Board is authorized to adopt regulations that establish requirements for the effective control of soil erosion, sediment deposition, and stormwater, including nonagricultural runoff, that shall be met in any VESMP to prevent the unreasonable degradation of properties, stream channels, waters, and other natural resources, and that specify minimum technical criteria and administrative procedures for VESMPs. The regulations shall:

1. Establish standards and procedures for administering a VESMP;

2. Establish minimum standards of effectiveness of the VESMP and criteria and procedures for reviewing and evaluating its effectiveness. The minimum standards of program effectiveness established by the Board shall provide that (i) no soil erosion control and stormwater management plan shall be approved until it is reviewed by a plan reviewer certified pursuant to § 62.1-44.15:30, (ii) each inspection of a land-disturbing activity shall be conducted by an inspector certified pursuant to § 62.1-44.15:30, and (iii) each VESMP shall contain a

program administrator, a plan reviewer, and an inspector, each of whom is certified pursuant to § 62.1-44.15:30 and all of whom may be the same person;

3. Be based upon relevant physical and developmental information concerning the watersheds and drainage basins of the Commonwealth, including data relating to land use, soils, hydrology, geology, size of land area being disturbed, proximate water bodies and their characteristics, transportation, and public facilities and services;

4. Include any survey of lands and waters as the Board deems appropriate or as any applicable law requires to identify areas, including multijurisdictional and watershed areas, with critical soil erosion and sediment problems;

5. Contain conservation standards for various types of soils and land uses, which shall include criteria, techniques, and methods for the control of soil erosion and sediment resulting from land-disturbing activities;

6. Establish water quality and water quantity technical criteria. These criteria shall be periodically modified as required in order to reflect current engineering methods;

7. Require the provision of long-term responsibility for and maintenance of stormwater management control devices and other techniques specified to manage the quality and quantity of runoff;

8. Require as a minimum the inclusion in VESMPs of certain administrative procedures that include, but are not limited to, specifying the time period within which a VESMP authority shall grant land-disturbance approval, the conditions and processes under which such approval shall be granted, the procedures for communicating disapproval, the conditions under which an approval may be changed, and requirements for inspection of approved projects;

9. Establish a statewide fee schedule to cover all costs associated with the implementation of a VESMP related to land-disturbing activities where permit coverage is required, and for land-disturbing activities where the Board serves as a VESMP authority or VSMP authority. Such fee attributes include the costs associated with plan review, permit registration statement review, permit issuance, permit coverage verification, inspections, reporting, and compliance activities associated with the land-disturbing activities as well as program oversight costs. The fee schedule shall also include a provision for a reduced fee for a land-disturbing activity that disturbs 2,500 square feet or more but less than one acre in an area of a locality designated as a Chesapeake Bay Preservation Area pursuant to the Chesapeake Bay Preservation Act (§ 62.1-44.15:67 et seq.). The fee schedule shall be governed by the following:

a. The revenue generated from the statewide fee shall be collected utilizing, where practicable, an online payment system, and the Department's portion shall be remitted to the State Treasurer for deposit in the Virginia Stormwater Management Fund established pursuant to § 62.1-44.15:29. However, whenever the Board has approved a VESMP, no more than 30 percent of the total revenue generated by the statewide fees collected shall be remitted to the State Treasurer for deposit in the Virginia Stormwater Management Fund, with the balance going to the VESMP authority;

b. Fees collected pursuant to this section shall be in addition to any general fund appropriation made to the Department or other supporting revenue from a VESMP; however, the fees shall be set at a level sufficient for the Department, the Board, and the VESMP to fully carry out their responsibilities under this article and local ordinances or standards and specifications where applicable. When establishing a VESMP, the VESMP authority shall assess the statewide fees pursuant to the schedule and shall have the authority to reduce or increase such fees, and to consolidate such fees with other program-related charges, but in no case shall such fee changes affect the amount established in the regulations as available to the Department for program oversight responsibilities pursuant to subdivision a. A VESMP's portion of the fees shall be used solely to carry out the VESMP's responsibilities under this article and associated ordinances;

c. In establishing the fee schedule under this subdivision, the Department shall ensure that the VESMP authority portion of the statewide fee for coverage under the General Permit for Discharges of Stormwater from Construction Activities for small construction activity involving a single-family detached residential structure with a site or area, within or outside a common plan of development or sale, that is equal to or greater than one acre but less than five acres shall be no greater than the VESMP authority portion of the fee for coverage of sites or areas with a land-disturbance acreage of less than one acre within a common plan of development or sale;

d. When any fees are collected pursuant to this section by credit cards, business transaction costs associated with processing such payments may be additionally assessed;

e. Notwithstanding the other provisions of this subdivision 9, establish a procedure by which payment of the Department's portion of the statewide fee established pursuant to this subdivision 9 shall not be required for coverage under the General Permit for Discharges of Stormwater from Construction Activities for construction activity involving a single-family detached residential structure, within or outside a common plan of development or sale;

f. Establish a procedure by which a registration statement shall not be required for coverage under the General Permit for Discharges of Stormwater from Construction Activities for a small construction activity involving a single-family detached residential structure, within or outside a common plan of development or sale;

10. Establish statewide standards for soil erosion control and stormwater management from land-disturbing activities;

11. Establish a procedure by which a soil erosion control and stormwater management plan or stormwater management plan that is approved for a residential, commercial, or industrial subdivision shall govern the development of the individual parcels, including those parcels developed under subsequent owners;

12. Provide for the certification and use of a proprietary best management practice only if another state, regional, or national program has verified its nutrient or sediment removal effectiveness and all of such program's established test protocol requirements were met or exceeded. As used in this subdivision and any regulations or guidance adopted pursuant to this subdivision, "certification" means a determination by the Department that a proprietary best management practice is approved for use in accordance with this article;

13. Require that VESMPs maintain after-development runoff rate of flow and characteristics that replicate, as nearly as practicable, the existing predevelopment runoff characteristics and site hydrology, or improve upon the contributing share of the existing predevelopment runoff characteristics and site hydrology if stream channel erosion or localized flooding is an existing predevelopment condition.

a. Except where more stringent requirements are necessary to address total maximum daily load requirements or to protect exceptional state waters, any land-disturbing activity that was subject to the water quantity requirements that were in effect pursuant to this article prior to July 1, 2014, shall be deemed to satisfy the conditions of this subsection if the practices are designed to (i) detain the water volume equal to the first one-half inch of runoff multiplied by the impervious surface of the land development project and to release it over 48 hours; (ii) detain and release over a 24-hour period the expected rainfall resulting from the one year, 24-hour storm; and (iii) reduce the allowable peak flow rate resulting from the 1.5-year, two-year, and 10-year, 24-hour storms to a level that is less than or equal to the peak flow rate from the site assuming it was in a good forested condition, achieved through multiplication of the forested peak flow rate by a reduction factor that is equal to the runoff volume from the site when it was in a good forested condition divided by the runoff volume from the site in its proposed condition. Any land-disturbing activity that complies with these requirements shall be exempt from any flow rate capacity and velocity requirements for natural or man-made channels as defined in any regulations promulgated pursuant to this section or any ordinances adopted pursuant to § 62.1-44.15:27 or 62.1-44.15:33;

b. Any stream restoration or relocation project that incorporates natural channel design concepts is not a man-made channel and shall be exempt from any flow rate capacity and velocity requirements for natural or man-made channels as defined in any regulations promulgated pursuant to this article;

14. Encourage low-impact development designs, regional and watershed approaches, and nonstructural means for controlling stormwater;

15. Promote the reclamation and reuse of stormwater for uses other than potable water in order to protect state waters and the public health and to minimize the direct discharge of pollutants into state waters;

16. Establish procedures to be followed when a locality chooses to change the type of program it administers pursuant to subsection D of § 62.1-44.15:27;

17. Establish a statewide permit fee schedule for stormwater management related to MS4 permits;

18. Provide for the evaluation and potential inclusion of emerging or innovative nonproprietary stormwater control technologies that may prove effective in reducing nonpoint source pollution;

19. Require the owner of property that is zoned for residential use and on which is located a privately owned stormwater management facility serving one or more residential properties to record the long-term maintenance and inspection requirements for such facility with the deed for the owner's property; and

20. Require that all final plan elements, specifications, or calculations whose preparation requires a license under Chapter 4 (§ 54.1-400 et seq.) or 22 (§ 54.1-2200 et seq.) of Title 54.1 be appropriately signed and sealed by a professional who is licensed to engage in practice in the Commonwealth. Nothing in this subdivision shall authorize any person to engage in practice outside his area of professional competence.

History.
1989, cc. 467, 499, § 10.1-603.4; 1991, c. 84; 2004, c. 372; 2005, c. 102; 2006, c. 21; 2008, c. 405; 2009, c. 709; 2012, cc. 785, 819; 2013, cc. 756, 793; 2014, cc. 303, 598; 2016, cc. 68, 758; 2017, cc. 10, 163; 2020, cc. 313, 667; 2022, c. 32; 2023, cc. 48, 49.

The 2023 amendments.
The 2023 amendments by cc. 48 and 49 are identical, and deleted "neither a registration statement nor" preceding "payment" and inserted "not" following "shall" in subdivision A 9 e and added subdivision A 9 f.

§ 62.1-44.15:29.1. (Effective July 1, 2024) Stormwater Local Assistance Fund.

A. The State Comptroller shall continue in the state treasury the Stormwater Local Assistance Fund (the Fund) established by Chapter 806 of the Acts of Assembly of 2013, which shall be administered by the Department. All civil penalties and civil charges collected by the Board pursuant to §§ 62.1-

44.15:25, 62.1-44.15:48, 62.1-44.15:63, and 62.1-44.15:74, subdivision (19) of § 62.1-44.15, and § 62.1-44.19:22 shall be paid into the state treasury and credited to the Fund, together with such other funds as may be made available to the Fund, which shall also receive bond proceeds from bonds authorized by the General Assembly, sums appropriated to it by the General Assembly, and other grants, gifts, and moneys as may be made available to it from any other source, public or private. Interest earned on moneys in the Fund shall remain in the Fund and be credited to it. Any moneys remaining in the Fund, including interest thereon, at the end of each fiscal year shall not revert to the general fund but shall remain in the Fund.

B. The purpose of the Fund is to provide matching grants to local governments for the planning, design, and implementation of stormwater best management practices that address cost efficiency and commitments related to reducing water quality pollutant loads. Moneys in the Fund shall be used to meet (i) obligations related to the Chesapeake Bay total maximum daily load (TMDL) requirements, (ii) requirements for local impaired stream TMDLs, (iii) water quality measures of the Chesapeake Bay Watershed Implementation Plan, and (iv) water quality requirements related to the permitting of small municipal separate storm sewer systems. The grants shall be used solely for stormwater capital projects, including (a) new stormwater best management practices, (b) stormwater best management practice retrofitting or maintenance, (c) stream restoration, (d) low-impact development projects, (e) buffer restoration, (f) pond retrofitting, and (g) wetlands restoration. Such grants shall be made in accordance with eligibility determinations made by the Department pursuant to criteria established by the Board. Grants awarded for projects related to Chesapeake Bay TMDL requirements may take into account total phosphorus reductions or total nitrogen reductions. Grants awarded for eligible projects in localities with high or above average fiscal stress as reported by the Commission on Local Government may account for more than 50 percent of the costs of a project.

C. Moneys in the Fund shall be used solely for the purpose set forth herein and disbursements from it shall be made by the State Treasurer on warrants issued by the Comptroller upon written request signed by the Director.

History.
2016, cc. 68, 758; 2021, Sp. Sess. I, c. 385.

The 2021 Sp. Sess. I amendments.
The 2021 amendment by Sp. Sess. I, c. 385,

effective July 1, 2021, added the last two sentences of subsection B.

§ 62.1-44.15:33. (Effective until July 1, 2024) Authorization for more stringent ordinances.

A. Localities that are VSMP authorities are authorized to adopt more stringent stormwater management ordinances than those necessary to ensure compliance with the Board's minimum regulations, provided that the more stringent ordinances are based upon factual findings of local or regional comprehensive watershed management studies or findings developed through the implementation of a MS4 permit or a locally adopted watershed management study and are determined by the locality to be necessary to prevent any further degradation to water resources, to address TMDL requirements, to protect exceptional state waters, or to address specific existing water pollution including nutrient and sediment loadings, stream channel erosion, depleted groundwater resources, or excessive localized flooding within the watershed and that prior to adopting more stringent ordinances a public hearing is held. Notice of such hearing shall be given by publication once a week for two consecutive weeks in a newspaper of general circulation in the locality seeking to adopt the ordinance, with the first publication appearing no more than 14 days before the hearing.

B. Localities that are VSMP authorities shall submit a letter report to the Department when more stringent stormwater management ordinances or more stringent requirements authorized by such ordinances, such as may be set forth in design manuals, policies, or guidance documents developed by the localities, are determined to be necessary pursuant to this section within 30 days after adoption thereof. Any such letter report shall include a summary explanation as to why the more stringent ordinance or requirement has been determined to be necessary pursuant to this section. Upon the request of an affected landowner or his agent submitted to the Department with a copy to be sent to the locality, within 90 days after adoption of any such ordinance or derivative requirement, localities shall submit the ordinance or requirement and all other supporting materials to the Department for a determination of whether the requirements of this section have been met and whether any determination made by the locality pursuant to this section is supported by the evidence. The Department shall issue a written determination setting forth its rationale within 90 days of submission. Such a determination, or a failure by the Department to make such a determination within the 90-day period, may be appealed to the Board.

C. Localities shall not prohibit or otherwise limit the use of any best management practice (BMP) approved for use by the Director or the Board except as follows:

1. When the Director or the Board approves the use of any BMP in accordance with its stated conditions, the locality serving as a VSMP authority shall have authority to preclude the onsite use of the approved BMP, or to require more stringent conditions upon its use, for a specific land-disturbing project based on a review of the stormwater management plan and project site conditions. Such limitations shall be based on site-specific concerns. Any project or site-specific determination purportedly authorized pursuant to this subsection may be appealed to the Department and the Department shall issue a written determination regarding compliance with this section to the requesting party within 90 days of submission. Any such determination, or a failure by the Department to make any such determination within the 90-day period, may be appealed to the Board.

2. When a locality is seeking to uniformly preclude jurisdiction-wide or otherwise limit geographically the use of a BMP approved by the Director or Board, or to apply more stringent conditions to the use of a BMP approved by the Director or Board, upon the request of an affected landowner or his agent submitted to the Department, with a copy submitted to the locality, within 90 days after adoption, such authorizing ordinances, design manuals, policies, or guidance documents developed by the locality that set forth the BMP use policy shall be provided to the Department in such manner as may be prescribed by the Department that includes a written justification and explanation as to why such more stringent limitation or conditions are determined to be necessary. The Department shall review all supporting materials provided by the locality to determine whether the requirements of this section have been met and that any determination made by the locality pursuant to this section is reasonable under the circumstances. The Department shall issue its determination to the locality in writing within 90 days of submission. Such a determination, or a failure by the Department to make such a determination within the 90-day period, may be appealed to the Board.

D. Based on a determination made in accordance with subsection B or C, any ordinance or other requirement enacted or established by a locality that is found to not comply with this section shall be null and void, replaced with state minimum standards, and remanded to the locality for revision to ensure compliance with this section. Any such ordinance or other requirement that has been proposed but neither enacted nor established shall be remanded to the locality for revision to ensure compliance with this section.

E. Any provisions of a local stormwater management program in existence before January 1, 2013, that contains more stringent provisions than this article shall be exempt from the requirements of this section. However, such provisions shall be reported to the Board at the time of the locality's VSMP approval package.

History.

1989, cc. 467, 499, § 10.1-603.7; 1991, c. 84; 2004, c. 372; 2011, cc. 341, 353; 2012, cc. 785, 819; 2013, cc. 591, 756, 793; 2014, cc. 303, 598; 2023, cc. 506, 507.

Editor's note.

Acts 2016, cc. 68 and 758, cl. 9, as amended by Acts 2023, cc. 665 and 666, cl. 1, provides: "That the State Water Control Board (the Board) shall adopt regulations to implement the requirements of this act before July 1, 2024. The adoption of such regulations shall include the reduction of regulations through consolidation of duplicative requirements and be exempt from the requirements of Article 2 (§ 2.2-4006 et seq.) of the Administrative Process Act (§ 2.2-4000 et seq.) of the Code of Virginia. However, the Department shall (i) provide a Notice of Intended Regulatory Action, (ii) form a stakeholders advisory group, (iii) provide for a 60-day public comment period prior to the Board's adoption of the regulations, and (iv) provide the Board with a written summary of comments received and responses to comments prior to the Board's adoption of the regulations. This enactment shall become effective in due course. The regulations shall become effective on July 1, 2024, concurrent with the effective date of the remainder of this act." ¶Acts 2016, cc. 68 and 758, cl. 10, as amended by Acts 2017, c. 345, cl. 2 and Acts 2023, cc. 665 and 666, cl. 1, provides: "That the provisions of this act, except for the ninth enactment, shall become effective on July 1, 2024, concurrent with the effective date of the regulations required by the ninth enactment of this act."

Effective October 1, 2021, "Title 45.2" was substituted for "Title 45.1" in subdivision F 5 to conform to the recodification of Title 45.1 by Acts 2021, Sp. Sess. I, c. 387, at the direction of the Virginia Code Commission.

Acts 2023, cc. 665 and 666, cl. 1 provides: "That the State Water Control Board (the Board) shall adopt regulations to implement the requirements of this act before July 1, 2024. The adoption of such regulations shall include the reduction of regulations through consolidation of duplicative requirements and be exempt from the requirements of Article 2 (§ 2.2-4006 et seq.) of the Administrative Process Act (§ 2.2-4000 et seq.) of the Code of Virginia. However, the Department shall (i) provide a Notice of Intended Regulatory Action, (ii) form a stakeholders advisory group, (iii) provide for a 60-day public comment period prior to the Board's adoption of the regulations, and (iv) provide the Board with a written summary of comments received and responses to comments prior to the Board's adoption of the regulations. This enactment shall become effective in due course. The regulations shall become effective on July 1, 2024, concurrent with the effective date of the remainder of this act."

The 2023 amendments.

The 2023 amendments by cc. 506 and 507 are identical, and deleted "after giving due notice" following "held" and added the present second sentence.

§ 62.1-44.15:33. (Effective July 1, 2024) Authorization for more stringent ordinances.

A. Localities that are serving as VESMP authorities are authorized to adopt more stringent soil erosion control or stormwater management ordinances than those necessary to ensure compliance with the Board's minimum regulations, provided that the more stringent ordinances are based upon factual findings of local or regional comprehensive watershed management studies or findings developed through the implementation of an MS4 permit or a locally adopted watershed management study and are determined by the locality to be necessary to prevent any further degradation to water resources, to address total maximum daily load requirements, to protect exceptional state waters, or to address specific existing water pollution including nutrient and sediment loadings, stream channel erosion, depleted groundwater resources, or excessive localized flooding within the watershed and that prior to adopting more stringent ordinances a public hearing is held. Notice of such hearing shall be given by publication once a week for two consecutive weeks in a newspaper of general circulation in the locality seeking to adopt the ordinance, with the first publication appearing no more than 14 days before the hearing. This process shall not be required when a VESMP authority chooses to reduce the threshold for regulating land-disturbing activities to a smaller area of disturbed land pursuant to § 62.1-44.15:34. However, this section shall not be construed to authorize a VESMP authority to impose a more stringent timeframe for land-disturbance review and approval than those provided in this article.

B. Localities that are serving as VESMP authorities shall submit a letter report to the Department when more stringent stormwater management ordinances or more stringent requirements authorized by such stormwater management ordinances, such as may be set forth in design manuals, policies, or guidance documents developed by the localities, are determined to be necessary pursuant to this section within 30 days after adoption thereof. Any such letter report shall include a summary explanation as to why the more stringent ordinance or requirement has been determined to be necessary pursuant to this section. Upon the request of an affected landowner or his agent submitted to the Department with a copy to be sent to the locality, within 90 days after adoption of any such ordinance or derivative requirement, localities shall submit the ordinance or requirement and all other supporting materials to the Department for a determination of whether the requirements of this section have been met and whether any determination made by the locality pursuant to this section is supported by the evidence. The Department shall issue a written determination setting forth its rationale within 90 days of submission. Such a determination, or a failure by the Department to make such a determination within the 90-day period, may be appealed to the Board.

C. Localities shall not prohibit or otherwise limit the use of any best management practice (BMP) approved for use by the Director or the Board except as follows:

1. When the Director or the Board approves the use of any BMP in accordance with its stated conditions, the locality serving as a VESMP authority shall have authority to preclude the onsite use of the approved BMP, or to require more stringent conditions upon its use, for a specific land-disturbing project based on a review of the stormwater management plan and project site conditions. Such limitations shall be based on site-specific concerns. Any project or site-specific determination purportedly authorized pursuant to this subsection may be appealed to the Department and the Department shall issue a written determination regarding compliance with this section to the requesting party within 90 days of submission. Any such determination, or a failure by the Department to make any such determination within the 90-day period, may be appealed to the Board.

2. When a locality is seeking to uniformly preclude jurisdiction-wide or otherwise limit geographically the use of a BMP approved by the Director or Board, or to apply more stringent conditions to the use of a BMP approved by the Director or Board, upon the request of an affected landowner or his agent submitted to the Department, with a copy submitted to the locality, within 90 days after adoption, such authorizing ordinances, design manuals, policies, or guidance documents developed by the locality that set forth the BMP use policy shall be provided to the Department in such manner as may be prescribed by the Department that includes a written justification and explanation as to why such more stringent limitation or conditions are determined to be necessary.

The Department shall review all supporting materials provided by the locality to determine whether the requirements of this section have been met and that any determination made by the locality pursuant to this section is reasonable under the circumstances. The Department shall issue its determination to the locality in writing within 90 days of submission. Such a determination, or a failure by the Department to make such a determination within the 90-day period, may be appealed to the Board.

D. Based on a determination made in accordance with subsection B or C, any ordinance or other requirement enacted or established by a locality that is found to not comply with this section shall be null and void, replaced with state minimum standards, and remanded to the locality for revision to ensure compliance with this section. Any such ordinance or other requirement that has been proposed but neither enacted nor established shall be remanded to the locality for revision to ensure compliance with this section.

E. Any provisions of a local erosion and sediment control or stormwater management program in existence before January 1, 2016, that contains more stringent provisions than this article shall be exempt from the requirements of this section if the locality chooses to retain such provisions when it becomes a VESMP authority. However, such provisions shall be reported to the Board at the time of submission of the locality's VESMP approval package.

History.
1989, cc. 467, 499, § 10.1-603.7; 1991, c. 84; 2004, c. 372; 2011, cc. 341, 353; 2012, cc. 785, 819; 2013, cc. 591, 756, 793; 2014, cc. 303, 598; 2016, cc. 68, 758; 2023, cc. 506, 507.

§ 62.1-44.15:34. (Effective until July 1, 2024) Regulated activities; submission and approval of a permit application; security for performance; exemptions.

A. A person shall not conduct any land-disturbing activity until he has submitted a permit application to the VSMP authority that includes a state VSMP permit registration statement, if such statement is required, and, after July 1, 2014, a stormwater management plan or an executed agreement in lieu of a stormwater management plan, and has obtained VSMP authority approval to begin land disturbance. A locality that is not a VSMP authority shall provide a general notice to applicants of the state permit coverage requirement and report all approvals pursuant to the Erosion and Sediment Control Law (§ 62.1-44.15:51 et seq.) to begin land disturbance of one acre or greater to the Department at least monthly. Upon the development of an online reporting system by the Department, but no later than July 1, 2014, a VSMP authority shall be required to obtain evidence of state VSMP permit coverage where it is required prior to providing approval to begin land disturbance. The VSMP authority shall act on any permit application within 60 days after it has been determined by the VSMP authority to be a complete application. The VSMP authority may either issue project approval or denial and shall provide written rationale for the denial. The VSMP authority shall act on any permit application that has been previously disapproved within 45 days after the application has been revised, resubmitted for approval, and deemed complete. Prior to issuance of any approval, the VSMP authority may also require an applicant, excluding state and federal entities, to submit a reasonable performance bond with surety, cash escrow, letter of credit, any combination thereof, or such other legal arrangement acceptable to the VSMP authority, to ensure that measures could be taken by the VSMP authority at the applicant's expense should he fail, after proper notice, within the time specified to initiate or maintain appropriate actions that may be required of him by the permit conditions as a result of his land-disturbing activity. If the VSMP authority takes such action upon such failure by the applicant, the VSMP authority may collect from the applicant the difference should the amount of the reasonable cost of such action exceed the amount of the security held. Within 60 days of the completion of the requirements of the permit conditions, such bond, cash escrow, letter of credit, or other legal arrangement, or the unexpended or unobligated portion thereof, shall be refunded to the applicant or terminated. These requirements are in addition to all other provisions of law relating to the issuance of permits and are not intended to otherwise affect the requirements for such permits.

B. A Chesapeake Bay Preservation Act Land-Disturbing Activity shall be subject to coverage under the Virginia Stormwater Management Program (VSMP) General Permit for Discharges of Stormwater from Construction Activities until July 1, 2014, at which time it shall no longer be considered a small construction activity but shall be then regulated under the requirements of this article.

C. Notwithstanding any other provisions of this article, the following activities are exempt, unless otherwise required by federal law:

1. Permitted surface or deep mining operations and projects, or oil and gas operations and projects conducted under the provisions of Title 45.2;

2. Clearing of lands specifically for agricultural purposes and the management, tilling, planting, or harvesting of agricultural, horticultural, or forest crops, livestock feedlot operations, or as additionally set forth by the Board in regulations, including engineering operations as follows: construction of terraces, terrace outlets, check dams, desilting basins, dikes, ponds, ditches, strip cropping, lister furrowing, contour cultivating, contour furrowing, land drainage, and land irrigation; however, this exception shall not apply to harvesting of forest crops unless the area on which harvesting occurs is reforested artificially or naturally in accordance with the provisions of Chapter 11 (§ 10.1-1100 et seq.) or is converted to bona fide agricultural or improved pasture use as described in subsection B of § 10.1-1163;

3. Single-family residences separately built and disturbing less than one acre and not part of a larger common plan of development or sale, including additions or modifications to existing single-family detached residential structures. However, localities subject to the provisions of the Chesapeake Bay Preservation Act (§ 62.1-44.15:67 et seq.) may regulate these single-family residences where land disturbance exceeds 2,500 square feet;

4. Land-disturbing activities that disturb less than one acre of land area except for land-disturbing activity exceeding an area of 2,500 square feet in all areas of the jurisdictions designated as subject to the Chesapeake Bay Preservation Area Designation and Management Regulations adopted pursuant to the provisions of the Chesapeake Bay Preservation Act (§ 62.1-44.15:67 et seq.) or activities that are part of a larger common plan of development or sale that is one acre or greater of disturbance; however, the governing body of any locality that administers a VSMP may reduce this exception to a smaller area of disturbed land or qualify the conditions under which this exception shall apply;

5. Discharges to a sanitary sewer or a combined sewer system;

6. Activities under a state or federal reclamation program to return an abandoned property to an agricultural or open land use;

7. Routine maintenance that is performed to maintain the original line and grade, hydraulic capacity, or original construction of the project. The paving of an existing road with a compacted or impervious surface and reestablishment of existing associated ditches and shoulders shall be deemed routine maintenance if performed in accordance with this subsection; and

8. Conducting land-disturbing activities in response to a public emergency where the related work requires immediate authorization to avoid imminent

endangerment to human health or the environment. In such situations, the VSMP authority shall be advised of the disturbance within seven days of commencing the land-disturbing activity, and compliance with the administrative requirements of subsection A is required within 30 days of commencing the land-disturbing activity.

History.
  1989, cc. 467, 499, § 10.1-603.8; 1994, cc. 605, 898; 2004, c. 372; 2011, c. 400; 2012, cc. 785, 819; 2013, cc. 756, 793; 2014, cc. 303, 598.

Section set out twice.
  The section above is effective until July 1, 2024. For this section as in effect at that time, see the following section, also numbered 62.1-44.15:34.

Editor's note.
  Effective October 1, 2021, "Title 45.2" was substituted for "Title 45.1" in subdivision F 5 to conform to the recodification of Title 45.1 by Acts 2021, Sp. Sess. I, c. 387, at the direction of the Virginia Code Commission.

The 2023 amendments.
  The 2023 amendment by cc. 48 and 49 are identical, and deleted "for construction of a single-family detached residential structure" and "for the single-family detached residential structure" in subsection A.

§ 62.1-44.15:34. (Effective July 1, 2024) Regulated activities; submission and approval of a permit application; security for performance; exemptions.

  A. A person shall not conduct any land-disturbing activity until (i) he has submitted to the appropriate VESMP authority an application that includes a permit registration statement, if required, a soil erosion control and stormwater management plan or an executed agreement in lieu of a plan, if required, and (ii) the VESMP authority has issued its land-disturbance approval. In addition, as a prerequisite to engaging in an approved land-disturbing activity, the name of the individual who will be assisting the owner in carrying out the activity and holds a Responsible Land Disturber certificate pursuant to § 62.1-44.15:30 shall be submitted to the VESMP authority. Any VESMP authority may waive the Responsible Land Disturber certificate requirement for an agreement in lieu of a plan; however, if a violation occurs during the land-disturbing activity, then the owner shall correct the violation and provide the name of the individual holding a Responsible Land Disturber certificate as provided by § 62.1-14:30. Failure to provide the name of an individual holding a Responsible Land Disturber certificate prior to engaging in land-disturbing activities may result in revocation of the land-disturbance approval and shall subject the owner to the penalties provided in this article.

  1. A VESMP authority that is implementing its program pursuant to subsection A of § 62.1-44.15:27 or subdivision B 1 of § 62.1-44.15:27 shall determine the completeness of any application within 15 days after receipt, and shall act on any application within 60 days after it has been determined by the VESMP authority to be complete. The VESMP authority shall issue either land-disturbance approval or denial and provide written rationale for any denial. Prior to issuing a land-disturbance approval, a VESMP authority shall be required to obtain evidence of permit coverage when such coverage is required. The VESMP authority also shall determine whether any resubmittal of a previously disapproved application is complete within 15 days after receipt and shall act on the resubmitted application within 45 days after receipt.

  2. A VESMP authority implementing its program in coordination with the Department pursuant to subdivision B 2 of § 62.1-44.15:27 shall determine the completeness of any application within 15 days after receipt, and shall act on any application within 60 days after it has been determined by the VESMP authority to be complete. The VESMP authority shall forward a soil erosion

control and stormwater management plan to the Department for review within five days of receipt. If the plan is incomplete, the Department shall return the plan to the locality immediately and the application process shall start over. If the plan is complete, the Department shall review it for compliance with the water quality and water quantity technical criteria and provide its recommendation to the VESMP authority. The VESMP authority shall either (i) issue the land-disturbance approval or (ii) issue a denial and provide a written rationale for the denial. In no case shall a locality have more than 60 days for its decision on an application after it has been determined to be complete. Prior to issuing a land-disturbance approval, a VESMP authority shall be required to obtain evidence of permit coverage when such coverage is required.

The VESMP authority also shall forward to the Department any resubmittal of a previously disapproved application within five days after receipt, and the VESMP authority shall determine whether the plan is complete within 15 days of its receipt of the plan. The Department shall review the plan for compliance with the water quality and water quantity technical criteria and provide its recommendation to the VESMP authority, and the VESMP authority shall act on the resubmitted application within 45 days after receipt.

3. When a state agency or federal entity submits a soil erosion control and stormwater management plan for a project, land disturbance shall not commence until the Board has reviewed and approved the plan and has issued permit coverage when it is required.

a. The Board shall not approve a soil erosion control and stormwater management plan submitted by a state agency or federal entity for a project involving a land-disturbing activity (i) in any locality that has not adopted a local program with more stringent ordinances than those of the state program or (ii) in multiple jurisdictions with separate local programs, unless the plan is consistent with the requirements of the state program.

b. The Board shall not approve a soil erosion control and stormwater management plan submitted by a state agency or federal entity for a project involving a land-disturbing activity in one locality with a local program with more stringent ordinances than those of the state program, unless the plan is consistent with the requirements of the local program.

c. If onsite changes occur, the state agency or federal entity shall submit an amended soil erosion control and stormwater management plan to the Department.

d. The state agency or federal entity responsible for the land-disturbing activity shall ensure compliance with the approved plan. As necessary, the Board shall provide project oversight and enforcement.

4. Prior to issuance of any land-disturbance approval, the VESMP authority may also require an applicant, excluding state agencies and federal entities, to submit a reasonable performance bond with surety, cash escrow, letter of credit, any combination thereof, or such other legal arrangement acceptable to the VESMP authority, to ensure that measures could be taken by the VESMP authority at the applicant's expense should he fail, after proper notice, within the time specified to comply with the conditions imposed by the VESMP authority as a result of his land-disturbing activity. If the VESMP authority takes such action upon such failure by the applicant, the VESMP authority may collect from the applicant the difference should the amount of the reasonable cost of such action exceed the amount of the security held. Within 60 days of the completion of the VESMP authority's conditions, such bond, cash escrow, letter of credit, or other legal arrangement, or the unexpended or unobligated portion thereof, shall be refunded to the applicant or terminated.

B. The VESMP authority may require changes to an approved soil erosion control and stormwater management plan in the following cases:

1. Where inspection has revealed that the plan is inadequate to satisfy applicable regulations or ordinances; or

2. Where the owner finds that because of changed circumstances or for other reasons the plan cannot be effectively carried out, and proposed amendments to the plan, consistent with the requirements of this article, are agreed to by the VESMP authority and the owner.

C. In order to prevent further erosion, a VESMP authority may require approval of a soil erosion control and stormwater management plan for any land identified as an erosion impact area by the VESMP authority.

D. A VESMP authority may enter into an agreement with an adjacent VESMP authority regarding the administration of multijurisdictional projects, specifying who shall be responsible for all or part of the administrative procedures. Should adjacent VESMP authorities fail to reach such an agreement, each shall be responsible for administering the area of the multijurisdictional project that lies within its jurisdiction.

E. The following requirements shall apply to land-disturbing activities in the Commonwealth:

1. Any land-disturbing activity that (i) disturbs one acre or more of land or (ii) disturbs less than one acre of land and is part of a larger common plan of development or sale that results in one acre or greater of land disturbance may, in accordance with regulations adopted by the Board, be required to obtain permit coverage.

2. For a land-disturbing activity occurring in an area not designated as a Chesapeake Bay Preservation Area subject to the Chesapeake Bay Preservation Act (§ 62.1-44.15:67 et seq.):

a. Soil erosion control requirements and water quantity technical criteria adopted pursuant to this article shall apply to any activity that disturbs 10,000 square feet or more, although the locality may reduce this regulatory threshold to a smaller area of disturbed land. A plan addressing these requirements shall be submitted to the VESMP authority in accordance with subsection A. This subdivision shall also apply to additions or modifications to existing single-family detached residential structures.

b. Soil erosion control requirements and water quantity and water quality technical criteria shall apply to any activity that (i) disturbs one acre or more of land or (ii) disturbs less than one acre of land and is part of a larger common plan of development or sale that results in one acre or greater of land disturbance, although the locality may reduce this regulatory threshold to a smaller area of disturbed land. A plan addressing these requirements shall be submitted to the VESMP authority in accordance with subsection A.

3. For a land-disturbing activity occurring in an area designated as a Chesapeake Bay Preservation Area subject to the Chesapeake Bay Preservation Act (§ 62.1-44.15:67 et seq.):

a. Soil erosion control and water quantity and water quality technical criteria shall apply to any land-disturbing activity that disturbs 2,500 square feet or more of land, other than a single-family detached residential structure. However, the governing body of any affected locality may reduce this regulatory threshold to a smaller area of disturbed land. A plan addressing these requirements shall be submitted to the VESMP authority in accordance with subsection A.

b. For land-disturbing activities for single-family detached residential structures, soil erosion control and water quantity technical criteria shall apply to any land-disturbing activity that disturbs 2,500 square feet or more of land, and the locality also may require compliance with the water quality technical criteria. A plan addressing these requirements shall be submitted to the VESMP authority in accordance with subsection A.

F. Notwithstanding any other provisions of this article, the following activities are not required to comply with the requirements of this article unless otherwise required by federal law:

1. Minor land-disturbing activities, including home gardens and individual home landscaping, repairs, and maintenance work;

2. Installation, maintenance, or repair of any individual service connection;

3. Installation, maintenance, or repair of any underground utility line when such activity occurs on an existing hard surfaced road, street, or sidewalk, provided the land-disturbing activity is confined to the area of the road, street, or sidewalk that is hard surfaced;

4. Installation, maintenance, or repair of any septic tank line or drainage field unless included in an overall plan for land-disturbing activity relating to construction of the building to be served by the septic tank system;

5. Permitted surface or deep mining operations and projects, or oil and gas operations and projects conducted pursuant to Title 45.2;

6. Clearing of lands specifically for bona fide agricultural purposes; the management, tilling, planting, or harvesting of agricultural, horticultural, or forest crops; livestock feedlot operations; agricultural engineering operations, including construction of terraces, terrace outlets, check dams, desilting basins, dikes, ponds, ditches, strip cropping, lister furrowing, contour cultivating, contour furrowing, land drainage, and land irrigation; or as additionally set forth by the Board in regulations. However, this exception shall not apply to harvesting of forest crops unless the area on which harvesting occurs is reforested artificially or naturally in accordance with the provisions of Chapter 11 (§ 10.1-1100 et seq.) or is converted to bona fide agricultural or improved pasture use as described in subsection B of § 10.1-1163;

7. Installation of fence and sign posts or telephone and electric poles and other kinds of posts or poles;

8. Shoreline erosion control projects on tidal waters when all of the land-disturbing activities are within the regulatory authority of and approved by local wetlands boards, the Marine Resources Commission, or the United States Army Corps of Engineers; however, any associated land that is disturbed outside of this exempted area shall remain subject to this article and the regulations adopted pursuant thereto;

9. Repair or rebuilding of the tracks, rights-of-way, bridges, communication facilities, and other related structures and facilities of a railroad company;

10. Land-disturbing activities in response to a public emergency where the related work requires immediate authorization to avoid imminent endangerment to human health or the environment. In such situations, the VESMP authority shall be advised of the disturbance within seven days of commencing the land-disturbing activity, and compliance with the administrative requirements of subsection A is required within 30 days of commencing the land-disturbing activity; and

11. Discharges to a sanitary sewer or a combined sewer system that are not from a land-disturbing activity.

G. Notwithstanding any other provision of this article, the following activities are required to comply with the soil erosion control requirements but are not required to comply with the water quantity and water quality technical criteria, unless otherwise required by federal law:

1. Activities under a state or federal reclamation program to return an abandoned property to an agricultural or open land use;

2. Routine maintenance that is performed to maintain the original line and grade, hydraulic capacity, or original construction of the project. The paving of an existing road with a compacted or impervious surface and reestablishment of existing associated ditches and shoulders shall be deemed routine maintenance if performed in accordance with this subsection; and

3. Discharges from a land-disturbing activity to a sanitary sewer or a combined sewer system.

History.
1989, cc. 467, 499, § 10.1-603.8; 1994, cc. 605, 898; 2004, c. 372; 2011, c. 400; 2012, cc. 785, 819; 2013, cc. 756, 793; 2014, cc. 303, 598; 2016, cc. 68, 758; 2023, cc. 48, 49.

§ 62.1-44.15:37.1. Inspections; land-disturbing activities of natural gas pipelines; stop work instructions.

A. The Department is authorized to conduct inspections of the land-disturbing activities of interstate and intrastate natural gas pipeline companies that have approved annual standards and specifications pursuant to § 62.1-44.15:31 as such land-disturbing activities relate to construction of any natural gas transmission pipeline equal to or greater than 24 inches inside diameter to determine (i) compliance with such annual standards and specifications, (ii) compliance with any site-specific plans, and (iii) if there have been or are likely to be adverse impacts to water quality as a result of such land-disturbing activities, including instances where (a) there has been a violation of any water quality standard adopted pursuant to the State Water Control Law (§ 62.1-44.2 et seq.), (b) sediment has been deposited in significant amounts in areas where those deposits are not contained by best management practices, (c) there are repeated instances of adverse impacts or likely adverse impacts within a 30-day period, or (d) there have been widespread and repeated instances of adverse impacts or likely impacts. When the Department determines that there has been a substantial adverse impact to water quality or that an imminent and substantial adverse impact to water quality is likely to occur as a result of such land-disturbing activities, the Department may issue a stop work instruction, without advance notice or hearing, requiring that all or part of such land-disturbing activities on the part of the site that caused the substantial adverse impacts to water quality or are likely to cause imminent and substantial adverse impacts to water quality be stopped until corrective measures specified in the stop work instruction have been completed and approved by the Department. Where substantial adverse impacts or likely adverse impacts are found on a repeated, frequent, and widespread basis, the Department may issue a stop work instruction for every work area in Virginia until the Department determines that any systemic cause that contributed to such occurrences has been corrected.

Such stop work instruction shall become effective upon service on the company by email or other technology agreed to in writing by the Department and the company, by mailing with confirmation of delivery to the address specified in the annual standards and specifications, if available, or by delivery at the site to a person previously identified to the Department by the company. Upon request by the company, the Director or his designee shall review such stop work instruction within 48 hours of issuance.

B. Within 10 business days of issuance of a stop work instruction, the Department shall promptly provide to such company an opportunity for an informal fact-finding proceeding concerning the stop work instruction and any review by the Director or his designee. Reasonable notice as to the time and place of the informal fact-finding proceeding shall be provided to such company. Within 10 business days of the informal fact-finding proceeding, the Department shall affirm, modify, amend, or cancel such stop work instruction. Upon written documentation from the company of the completion and approval by the Department in writing of the corrective measures specified in the stop work instruction, the instruction shall be immediately lifted.

C. The company may appeal such stop work instruction or preliminary decision rendered by the Director or his designee to the circuit court of the jurisdiction wherein the land-disturbing activities subject to the stop work instruction occurred, or to another appropriate court, in accordance with the requirements of the Administrative Process Act (§ 2.2-4000 et seq.). Any person violating or failing, neglecting, or refusing to obey a stop work instruction issued by the Department may be compelled in a proceeding instituted in the circuit court of the jurisdiction wherein the violation was alleged to have occurred or other appropriate court to obey same and to comply therewith by injunction, mandamus, or other appropriate remedy. Nothing in this section shall prevent the Board or the Department from taking any other action authorized by this chapter.

History.
2018, c. 298; 2021, Sp. Sess. I, c. 277.

The 2021 Sp. Sess. I amendments.
The 2021 amendment by Sp. Sess. I, c. 277, effective July 1, 2021, in subsection A, substituted "transmission pipeline equal to or greater than 24 inches" for "transmission pipeline greater than 36 inches," inserted "including instances where (a) there has been a violation of any water quality standard adopted pursu- ant to the State Water Control Law (§ 62.1-44.2 et seq.), (b) sediment has been deposited in significant amounts in areas where those deposits are not contained by best management practices, (c) there are repeated instances of adverse impacts or likely adverse impacts within a 30-day period, or (d) there have been widespread and repeated instances of adverse impacts or likely impacts" and added the last sentence in the first paragraph.

ARTICLE 2.4.
EROSION AND SEDIMENT CONTROL LAW.

§ 62.1-44.15:51. (Effective until July 1, 2024) Definitions.

As used in this article, unless the context requires a different meaning:

"Agreement in lieu of a plan" means a contract between the plan-approving authority and the owner that specifies conservation measures that must be implemented in the construction of a (i) single-family residence or (ii) farm building or structure on a parcel of land with a total impervious cover percentage, including the impervious cover from the farm building or structure to be constructed, of less than five percent; this contract may be executed by the plan-approving authority in lieu of a formal site plan.

"Applicant" means any person submitting an erosion and sediment control plan for approval or requesting the issuance of a permit, when required, authorizing land-disturbing activities to commence.

"Certified inspector" means an employee or agent of a VESCP authority who (i) holds a certificate of competence from the Board in the area of project inspection or (ii) is enrolled in the Board's training program for project inspection and successfully completes such program within one year after enrollment.

"Certified plan reviewer" means an employee or agent of a VESCP authority who (i) holds a certificate of competence from the Board in the area of plan review, (ii) is enrolled in the Board's training program for plan review and successfully completes such program within one year after enrollment, or (iii) is licensed as a professional engineer, architect, landscape architect, land surveyor pursuant to Article 1 (§ 54.1-400 et seq.) of Chapter 4 of Title 54.1, or professional soil scientist as defined in § 54.1-2200.

"Certified program administrator" means an employee or agent of a VESCP authority who (i) holds a certificate of competence from the Board in the area

of program administration or (ii) is enrolled in the Board's training program for program administration and successfully completes such program within one year after enrollment.

"Department" means the Department of Environmental Quality.

"Director" means the Director of the Department of Environmental Quality.

"District" or *"soil and water conservation district"* means a political subdivision of the Commonwealth organized in accordance with the provisions of Article 3 (§ 10.1-506 et seq.) of Chapter 5 of Title 10.1.

"Erosion and sediment control plan" or *"plan"* means a document containing material for the conservation of soil and water resources of a unit or group of units of land. It may include appropriate maps, an appropriate soil and water plan inventory and management information with needed interpretations, and a record of decisions contributing to conservation treatment. The plan shall contain all major conservation decisions to ensure that the entire unit or units of land will be so treated to achieve the conservation objectives.

"Erosion impact area" means an area of land not associated with current land-disturbing activity but subject to persistent soil erosion resulting in the delivery of sediment onto neighboring properties or into state waters. This definition shall not apply to any lot or parcel of land of 10,000 square feet or less used for residential purposes or to shorelines where the erosion results from wave action or other coastal processes.

"Farm building or structure" means the same as that term is defined in § 36-97 and also includes any building or structure used for agritourism activity, as defined in § 3.2-6400, and any related impervious surfaces including roads, driveways, and parking areas.

"Land-disturbing activity" means any man-made change to the land surface that may result in soil erosion from water or wind and the movement of sediments into state waters or onto lands in the Commonwealth, including, but not limited to, clearing, grading, excavating, transporting, and filling of land, except that the term shall not include:

1. Minor land-disturbing activities such as home gardens and individual home landscaping, repairs, and maintenance work;

2. Individual service connections;

3. Installation, maintenance, or repair of any underground public utility lines when such activity occurs on an existing hard surfaced road, street, or sidewalk, provided the land-disturbing activity is confined to the area of the road, street, or sidewalk that is hard surfaced;

4. Septic tank lines or drainage fields unless included in an overall plan for land-disturbing activity relating to construction of the building to be served by the septic tank system;

5. Permitted surface or deep mining operations and projects, or oil and gas operations and projects conducted pursuant to Title 45.2;

6. Tilling, planting, or harvesting of agricultural, horticultural, or forest crops, livestock feedlot operations, or as additionally set forth by the Board in regulation, including engineering operations as follows: construction of terraces, terrace outlets, check dams, desilting basins, dikes, ponds, ditches, strip cropping, lister furrowing, contour cultivating, contour furrowing, land drainage, and land irrigation; however, this exception shall not apply to harvesting of forest crops unless the area on which harvesting occurs is reforested artificially or naturally in accordance with the provisions of Chapter 11 (§ 10.1-1100 et seq.) of Title 10.1 or is converted to bona fide agricultural or improved pasture use as described in subsection B of § 10.1-1163;

7. Repair or rebuilding of the tracks, rights-of-way, bridges, communication facilities, and other related structures and facilities of a railroad company;

8. Agricultural engineering operations, including but not limited to the construction of terraces, terrace outlets, check dams, desilting basins, dikes,

ponds not required to comply with the provisions of the Dam Safety Act (§ 10.1-604 et seq.), ditches, strip cropping, lister furrowing, contour cultivating, contour furrowing, land drainage, and land irrigation;

9. Disturbed land areas of less than 10,000 square feet in size or 2,500 square feet in all areas of the jurisdictions designated as subject to the Chesapeake Bay Preservation Area Designation and Management Regulations; however, the governing body of the program authority may reduce this exception to a smaller area of disturbed land or qualify the conditions under which this exception shall apply;

10. Installation of fence and sign posts or telephone and electric poles and other kinds of posts or poles;

11. Shoreline erosion control projects on tidal waters when all of the land-disturbing activities are within the regulatory authority of and approved by local wetlands boards, the Marine Resources Commission, or the United States Army Corps of Engineers; however, any associated land that is disturbed outside of this exempted area shall remain subject to this article and the regulations adopted pursuant thereto; and

12. Emergency work to protect life, limb, or property, and emergency repairs; however, if the land-disturbing activity would have required an approved erosion and sediment control plan, if the activity were not an emergency, then the land area disturbed shall be shaped and stabilized in accordance with the requirements of the VESCP authority.

"Natural channel design concepts" means the utilization of engineering analysis and fluvial geomorphic processes to create, rehabilitate, restore, or stabilize an open conveyance system for the purpose of creating or recreating a stream that conveys its bankfull storm event within its banks and allows larger flows to access its bankfull bench and its floodplain.

"Owner" means the owner or owners of the freehold of the premises or lesser estate therein, mortgagee or vendee in possession, assignee of rents, receiver, executor, trustee, lessee, or other person, firm, or corporation in control of a property.

"Peak flow rate" means the maximum instantaneous flow from a given storm condition at a particular location.

"Permittee" means the person to whom the local permit authorizing land-disturbing activities is issued or the person who certifies that the approved erosion and sediment control plan will be followed.

"Person" means any individual, partnership, firm, association, joint venture, public or private corporation, trust, estate, commission, board, public or private institution, utility, cooperative, county, city, town, or other political subdivision of the Commonwealth, governmental body, including a federal or state entity as applicable, any interstate body, or any other legal entity.

"Runoff volume" means the volume of water that runs off the land development project from a prescribed storm event.

"Town" means an incorporated town.

"Virginia Erosion and Sediment Control Program" or "VESCP" means a program approved by the Board that has been established by a VESCP authority for the effective control of soil erosion, sediment deposition, and nonagricultural runoff associated with a land-disturbing activity to prevent the unreasonable degradation of properties, stream channels, waters, and other natural resources and shall include such items where applicable as local ordinances, rules, permit requirements, annual standards and specifications, policies and guidelines, technical materials, and requirements for plan review, inspection, enforcement where authorized in this article, and evaluation consistent with the requirements of this article and its associated regulations.

"Virginia Erosion and Sediment Control Program authority" or "VESCP authority" means an authority approved by the Board to operate a Virginia

Erosion and Sediment Control Program. An authority may include a state entity, including the Department; a federal entity; a district, county, city, or town; or for linear projects subject to annual standards and specifications, electric, natural gas, and telephone utility companies, interstate and intra-state natural gas pipeline companies, railroad companies, or authorities created pursuant to § 15.2-5102.

"Water quality volume" means the volume equal to the first one-half inch of runoff multiplied by the impervious surface of the land development project.

History.

1973, c. 486, § 21-89.3; 1974, c. 265; 1977, c. 149; 1980, c. 305; 1988, cc. 690, 732, 891, § 10.1-560; 1990, c. 491; 1991, c. 469; 1992, c. 184; 1993, c. 925; 1994, c. 703; 2003, c. 423; 2004, c. 476; 2005, c. 107; 2006, c. 21; 2009, c. 309; 2012, cc. 785, 819; 2013, cc. 756, 793; 2023, cc. 48, 49.

Editor's note.

Effective October 1, 2021, "Title 45.2" was substituted for "Title 45.1" to conform to the recodification of Title 45.1 by Acts 2021, Sp.

Sess. I, c. 387, at the direction of the Virginia Code Commission.

The 2023 amendments.

The 2023 amendments by cc. 48 and 49, in the definition for "Agreement in lieu of a plan" added "or (ii) farm building or structure on a parcel of land with a total impervious cover percentage, including the impervious cover from the farm building or structure to be constructed, of less than five percent"; and added the definition for "Farm building or structure".

§ 62.1-44.15:51. (Effective July 1, 2024) Definitions.

As used in this article, unless the context requires a different meaning:

"Agreement in lieu of a plan" means a contract between the VESCP authority and the owner that specifies conservation measures that must be implemented in the construction of a (i) single-family detached residential structure or (ii) farm building or structure on a parcel of land with a total impervious cover percentage, including the impervious cover from the farm building or structure to be constructed, of less than five percent; this contract may be executed by the VESCP authority in lieu of a formal site plan.

"Applicant" means any person submitting an erosion and sediment control plan for approval in order to obtain authorization for land-disturbing activities to commence.

"Certified inspector" means an employee or agent of a VESCP authority who (i) holds a certification from the Board in the area of project inspection or (ii) is enrolled in the Board's training program for project inspection and success-fully completes such program within one year after enrollment.

"Certified plan reviewer" means an employee or agent of a VESCP authority who (i) holds a certification from the Board in the area of plan review, (ii) is enrolled in the Board's training program for plan review and successfully completes such program within one year after enrollment, or (iii) is licensed as a professional engineer, architect, landscape architect, land surveyor pursuant to Article 1 (§ 54.1-400 et seq.) of Chapter 4 of Title 54.1, or professional soil scientist as defined in § 54.1-2200.

"Certified program administrator" means an employee or agent of a VESCP authority who (i) holds a certification from the Board in the area of program administration or (ii) is enrolled in the Board's training program for program administration and successfully completes such program within one year after enrollment.

"Department" means the Department of Environmental Quality.

"Director" means the Director of the Department of Environmental Quality.

"District" or *"soil and water conservation district"* means a political subdivi-sion of the Commonwealth organized in accordance with the provisions of Article 3 (§ 10.1-506 et seq.) of Chapter 5 of Title 10.1.

"Erosion and sediment control plan" or *"plan"* means a document containing material for the conservation of soil and water resources of a unit or group of units of land. It may include appropriate maps, an appropriate soil and water plan inventory and management information with needed interpretations, and a record of decisions contributing to conservation treatment. The plan shall contain all major conservation decisions to ensure that the entire unit or units of land will be so treated to achieve the conservation objectives.

"Erosion impact area" means an area of land that is not associated with a current land-disturbing activity but is subject to persistent soil erosion resulting in the delivery of sediment onto neighboring properties or into state waters. This definition shall not apply to any lot or parcel of land of 10,000 square feet or less used for residential purposes or to shorelines where the erosion results from wave action or other coastal processes.

"Farm building or structure" means the same as that term is defined in § 36-97 and also includes any building or structure used for agritourism activity, as defined in § 3.2-6400, and any related impervious surfaces including roads, driveways, and parking areas.

"Land disturbance" or *"land-disturbing activity"* means any man-made change to the land surface that may result in soil erosion or has the potential to change its runoff characteristics, including the clearing, grading, excavating, transporting, and filling of land.

"Natural channel design concepts" means the utilization of engineering analysis and fluvial geomorphic processes to create, rehabilitate, restore, or stabilize an open conveyance system for the purpose of creating or recreating a stream that conveys its bankfull storm event within its banks and allows larger flows to access its bankfull bench and its floodplain.

"Owner" means the same as provided in § 62.1-44.3. For a land-disturbing activity that is regulated under this article, "owner" also includes the owner or owners of the freehold of the premises or lesser estate therein, mortgagee or vendee in possession, assignee of rents, receiver, executor, trustee, lessee, or other person, firm, or corporation in control of a property.

"Peak flow rate" means the maximum instantaneous flow from a given storm condition at a particular location.

"Person" means any individual, partnership, firm, association, joint venture, public or private corporation, trust, estate, commission, board, public or private institution, utility, cooperative, county, city, town, or other political subdivision of the Commonwealth, governmental body, including a federal or state entity as applicable, any interstate body, or any other legal entity.

"Runoff volume" means the volume of water that runs off the land development project from a prescribed storm event.

"Soil erosion" means the movement of soil by wind or water into state waters or onto lands in the Commonwealth.

"Town" means an incorporated town.

"Virginia Erosion and Sediment Control Program" or *"VESCP"* means a program approved by the Board that has been established by a VESCP authority for the effective control of soil erosion, sediment deposition, and nonagricultural runoff associated with a land-disturbing activity to prevent the unreasonable degradation of properties, stream channels, waters, and other natural resources and shall include such items where applicable as local ordinances, rules, policies and guidelines, technical materials, and requirements for plan review, inspection, and evaluation consistent with the requirements of this article.

"Virginia Erosion and Sediment Control Program authority" or *"VESCP authority"* means a locality approved by the Board to operate a Virginia Erosion and Sediment Control Program. A locality that has chosen not to

255

establish a Virginia Erosion and Stormwater Management Program pursuant to subdivision B 3 of § 62.1-44.15:27 is required to become a VESCP authority in accordance with this article.

"Virginia Stormwater Management Program" or *"VSMP"* means a program established by the Board pursuant to § 62.1-44.15:27.1 on behalf of a locality on or after July 1, 2014, to manage the quality and quantity of runoff resulting from any land-disturbing activity that (i) disturbs one acre or more of land or (ii) disturbs less than one acre of land and is part of a larger common plan of development or sale that results in one acre or greater of land disturbance.

History.

1973, c. 486, § 21-89.3; 1974, c. 265; 1977, c. 149; 1980, c. 305; 1988, cc. 690, 732, 891, § 10.1-560; 1990, c. 491; 1991, c. 469; 1992, c. 184; 1993, c. 925; 1994, c. 703; 2003, c. 423; 2004, c. 476; 2005, c. 107; 2006, c. 21; 2009, c. 309; 2012, cc. 785, 819; 2013, cc. 756, 793; 2016, cc. 68, 758; 2023, cc. 48, 49.

§ 62.1-44.15:55. (Effective until July 1, 2024) Regulated land-disturbing activities; submission and approval of erosion and sediment control plan.

A. Except as provided in § 62.1-44.15:56 for state agency and federal entity land-disturbing activities, no person shall engage in any land-disturbing activity until he has submitted to the VESCP authority an erosion and sediment control plan for the land-disturbing activity and the plan has been reviewed and approved. Upon the development of an online reporting system by the Department, but no later than July 1, 2014, a VESCP authority shall then be required to obtain evidence of Virginia Stormwater Management Program permit coverage where it is required prior to providing approval to begin land disturbance. Where land-disturbing activities involve lands under the jurisdiction of more than one VESCP, an erosion and sediment control plan may, at the request of one or all of the VESCP authorities, be submitted to the Department for review and approval rather than to each jurisdiction concerned. The Department may charge the jurisdictions requesting the review a fee sufficient to cover the cost associated with conducting the review. A VESCP may enter into an agreement with an adjacent VESCP regarding the administration of multijurisdictional projects whereby the jurisdiction that contains the greater portion of the project shall be responsible for all or part of the administrative procedures. Where the land-disturbing activity results from the construction of a (i) single-family residence or (ii) farm building or structure on a parcel of land with a total impervious cover percentage, including the impervious cover from the farm building or structure to be constructed, of less than five percent, an agreement in lieu of a plan may be substituted for an erosion and sediment control plan if executed by the VESCP authority.

B. The VESCP authority shall review erosion and sediment control plans submitted to it and grant written approval within 60 days of the receipt of the plan if it determines that the plan meets the requirements of this article and the Board's regulations and if the person responsible for carrying out the plan certifies that he will properly perform the erosion and sediment control measures included in the plan and shall comply with the provisions of this article. In addition, as a prerequisite to engaging in the land-disturbing activities shown on the approved plan, the person responsible for carrying out the plan shall provide the name of an individual holding a certificate of competence to the VESCP authority, as provided by § 62.1-44.15:52, who will be in charge of and responsible for carrying out the land-disturbing activity. However, any VESCP authority may waive the certificate of competence requirement for an agreement in lieu of a plan. If a violation occurs during the land-disturbing activity, then the person responsible for carrying out the agreement in lieu of a plan shall correct the violation and provide the name of an individual holding a certificate of competence, as provided by § 62.1-44.15:52. Failure to provide the name of an individual holding a certificate of competence prior to engaging in land-disturbing activities may result in revocation of the approval of the plan and the person responsible for carrying out the plan shall be subject to the penalties provided in this article.

When a plan is determined to be inadequate, written notice of disapproval stating the specific reasons for disapproval shall be communicated to the applicant within 45 days. The notice shall specify the modifications, terms, and conditions that will permit approval of the plan. If no action is taken by the VESCP authority within the time specified in this subsection, the plan shall be deemed approved and the person authorized to proceed with the proposed activity. The VESCP authority shall act on any erosion and sediment control plan that has been previously disapproved within 45 days after the plan has been revised, resubmitted for approval, and deemed adequate.

C. The VESCP authority may require changes to an approved plan in the following cases:

1. Where inspection has revealed that the plan is inadequate to satisfy applicable regulations; or

2. Where the person responsible for carrying out the approved plan finds that because of changed circumstances or for other reasons the approved plan cannot be effectively carried out, and proposed amendments to the plan, consistent with the requirements of this article and associated regulations, are agreed to by the VESCP authority and the person responsible for carrying out the plan.

D. Electric, natural gas, and telephone utility companies, interstate and intrastate natural gas pipeline companies, and railroad companies shall, and authorities created pursuant to § 15.2-5102 may, file general erosion and sediment control standards and specifications annually with the Department for review and approval. Such standards and specifications shall be consistent with the requirements of this article and associated regulations and the Stormwater Management Act (§ 62.1-44.15:24 et seq.) and associated regulations where applicable. The specifications shall apply to:

1. Construction, installation, or maintenance of electric transmission, natural gas, and telephone utility lines and pipelines, and water and sewer lines; and

2. Construction of the tracks, rights-of-way, bridges, communication facilities, and other related structures and facilities of the railroad company.

The Department shall have 60 days in which to approve the standards and specifications. If no action is taken by the Department within 60 days, the standards and specifications shall be deemed approved. Individual approval of separate projects within subdivisions 1 and 2 is not necessary when approved specifications are followed. Projects not included in subdivisions 1 and 2 shall comply with the requirements of the appropriate VESCP. The Board shall have the authority to enforce approved specifications and charge fees equal to the lower of (i) $1,000 or (ii) an amount sufficient to cover the costs associated with standard and specification review and approval, project inspections, and compliance.

E. Any person engaging, in more than one jurisdiction, in the creation and operation of a wetland mitigation or stream restoration bank or banks, which have been approved and are operated in accordance with applicable federal and state guidance, laws, or regulations for the establishment, use, and operation of (i) wetlands mitigation or stream restoration banks, pursuant to a mitigation banking instrument signed by the Department of Environmental Quality, the Marine Resources Commission, or the U.S. Army Corps of Engineers, or (ii) a stream restoration project for purposes of reducing nutrients or sediment entering state waters may, at the option of that person, file general erosion and sediment control standards and specifications for wetland mitigation or stream restoration banks annually with the Department for review and approval consistent with guidelines established by the Board.

The Department shall have 60 days in which to approve the specifications. If no action is taken by the Department within 60 days, the specifications shall be deemed approved. Individual approval of separate projects under this subsection is not necessary when approved specifications are implemented through a project-specific erosion and sediment control plan. Projects not included in this subsection shall comply with the requirements of the appropriate local erosion and sediment control program. The Board shall have the authority to enforce approved specifications and charge fees equal to the lower of (i) $1,000 or (ii) an amount sufficient to cover the costs associated with standard and specification review and approval, projection inspections, and compliance. Approval of general erosion and sediment control specifications by the Department does not relieve the owner or operator from compliance with any other local ordinances and regulations including requirements to submit plans and obtain permits as may be required by such ordinances and regulations.

F. In order to prevent further erosion, a VESCP authority may require approval of an erosion and sediment control plan for any land identified by the VESCP authority as an erosion impact area.

G. For the purposes of subsections A and B, when land-disturbing activity will be required of a contractor performing construction work pursuant to a construction contract, the preparation, submission, and approval of an erosion and sediment control plan shall be the responsibility of the owner.

History.

1973, c. 486, § 21-89.6; 1979, c. 432; 1988, cc. 732, 891, § 10.1-563; 1993, c. 925; 1999, c. 555; 2001, c. 490; 2003, cc. 827, 966; 2006, c. 466; 2008, c. 23; 2011, cc. 720, 721; 2012, cc. 785, 819; 2013, cc. 756, 793; 2018, c. 627; 2023, cc. 48, 49.

Editor's note.

Acts 2016, cc. 68 and 758, cl. 9, as amended by Acts 2023, cc. 665 and 666, cl. 1, provides: "That the State Water Control Board (the Board) shall adopt regulations to implement the requirements of this act before July 1, 2024. The adoption of such regulations shall include the reduction of regulations through consolidation of duplicative requirements and be exempt from the requirements of Article 2 (§ 2.2-4006 et seq.) of the Administrative Process Act (§ 2.2-4000 et seq.) of the Code of Virginia. However, the Department shall (i) provide a Notice of Intended Regulatory Action, (ii) form a stakeholders advisory group, (iii) provide for a 60-day public comment period prior to the Board's adoption of the regulations, and (iv) provide the Board with a written summary of comments received and responses to comments prior to

the Board's adoption of the regulations. This enactment shall become effective in due course. The regulations shall become effective on July 1, 2024, concurrent with the effective date of the remainder of this act."

Acts 2016, cc. 68 and 758, cl. 10, as amended by Acts 2017, c. 345, cl. 2 and Acts 2023, cc. 665 and 666, cl. 1, provides: "That the provisions of this act, except for the ninth enactment, shall become effective on July 1, 2024, concurrent with the effective date of the regulations required by the ninth enactment of this act."

Effective October 1, 2021, "Title 45.2" was substituted for "Title 45.1" to conform to the recodification of Title 45.1 by Acts 2021, Sp. Sess. I, c. 387, at the direction of the Virginia Code Commission.

The 2023 amendments.

The 2023 amendments by cc. 48 and 49, in A added "or (ii) farm building or structure on a parcel of land with a total impervious cover percentage, including the impervious cover from the farm building or structure to be constructed, of less than five percent"; and in B deleted "for construction of a single-family residence".

§ 62.1-44.15:55. (Effective July 1, 2024) Regulated land-disturbing activities; submission and approval of erosion and sediment control plan.

A. Except as provided in § 62.1-44.15:31 for a land-disturbing activity conducted by a state agency, federal entity, or other specified entity, no person shall engage in any land-disturbing activity until he has submitted to the VESCP authority an erosion and sediment control plan for the land-disturbing activity and the plan has been reviewed and approved. Where Virginia Pollutant Discharge Elimination System permit coverage is required, a VESCP authority shall be required to obtain evidence of such coverage from the Department's online reporting system prior to approving the erosion and sediment control plan. A VESCP authority may enter into an agreement with an adjacent VESCP or VESMP authority regarding the administration of multijurisdictional projects specifying who shall be responsible for all or part of the administrative procedures. Should adjacent authorities fail to come to such an agreement, each shall be responsible for administering the area of the multijurisdictional project that lies within its jurisdiction. Where the land-disturbing activity results from the construction of a (i) single-family residence or (ii) farm building or structure on a parcel of land with a total impervious cover percentage, including the impervious cover from the farm building or structure to be constructed, of less than five percent, an agreement in lieu of a plan may be substituted for an erosion and sediment control plan if executed by the VESCP authority.

B. The VESCP authority shall review erosion and sediment control plans submitted to it and grant written approval within 60 days of the receipt of the plan if it determines that the plan meets the requirements of this article and the Board's regulations and if the person responsible for carrying out the plan certifies that he will properly perform the erosion and sediment control measures included in the plan and shall comply with the provisions of this article. In addition, as a prerequisite to engaging in the land-disturbing activities shown on the approved plan, the person responsible for carrying out the plan shall provide the name of an individual holding a certificate to the VESCP authority, as provided by § 62.1-44.15:52, who will be in charge of and responsible for carrying out the land-disturbing activity. However, any VESCP authority may waive the certificate requirement for an agreement in lieu of a plan. If a violation occurs during the land-disturbing activity, then the person responsible for carrying out the agreement in lieu of a plan shall correct the violation and provide the name of an individual holding a certificate, as provided by § 62.1-44.15:52. Failure to provide the name of an individual holding a certificate prior to engaging in land-disturbing activities may result in revocation of the approval of the plan and the person responsible for carrying out the plan shall be subject to the penalties provided in this article.

When a plan is determined to be inadequate, written notice of disapproval stating the specific reasons for disapproval shall be communicated to the applicant within 45 days. The notice shall specify the modifications, terms, and conditions that will permit approval of the plan. If no action is taken by the VESCP authority within the time specified in this subsection, the plan shall be deemed approved and the person authorized to proceed with the proposed activity. The VESCP authority shall act on any erosion and sediment control plan that has been previously disapproved within 45 days after the plan has been revised, resubmitted for approval, and deemed adequate.

C. The VESCP authority may require changes to an approved plan in the following cases:

1. Where inspection has revealed that the plan is inadequate to satisfy applicable regulations; or

2. Where the person responsible for carrying out the approved plan finds that because of changed circumstances or for other reasons the approved plan cannot be effectively carried out, and proposed amendments to the plan, consistent with the requirements of this article and associated regulations, are agreed to by the VESCP authority and the person responsible for carrying out the plan.

D. In order to prevent further erosion, a VESCP authority may require approval of an erosion and sediment control plan for any land identified by the VESCP authority as an erosion impact area.

E. For the purposes of subsections A and B, when land-disturbing activity will be required of a contractor performing construction work pursuant to a construction contract, the preparation, submission, and approval of an erosion and sediment control plan shall be the responsibility of the owner.

F. Notwithstanding any other provisions of this article, the following activities are not required to comply with the requirements of this article unless otherwise required by federal law:

1. Disturbance of a land area of less than 10,000 square feet in size or less than 2,500 square feet in an area designated as a Chesapeake Bay Preservation Area pursuant to the Chesapeake Bay Preservation Act (§ 62.1-44.15:67 et seq.). However, the governing body of the program authority may reduce this exception to a smaller area of disturbed land or qualify the conditions under which this exception shall apply;

2. Minor land-disturbing activities such as home gardens and individual home landscaping, repairs, and maintenance work;

3. Installation, maintenance, or repair of any individual service connection;

4. Installation, maintenance, or repair of any underground utility line when such activity occurs on an existing hard surfaced road, street, or sidewalk, provided the land-disturbing activity is confined to the area of the road, street, or sidewalk that is hard surfaced;

5. Installation, maintenance, or repair of any septic tank line or drainage field unless included in an overall plan for land-disturbing activity relating to construction of the building to be served by the septic tank system;

6. Permitted surface or deep mining operations and projects, or oil and gas operations and projects conducted pursuant to Title 45.2;

7. Clearing of lands specifically for bona fide agricultural purposes; the management, tilling, planting, or harvesting of agricultural, horticultural, or forest crops; livestock feedlot operations; agricultural engineering operations, including construction of terraces, terrace outlets, check dams, desilting basins, dikes, ponds, ditches, strip cropping, lister furrowing, contour cultivating, contour furrowing, land drainage, and land irrigation; or as additionally set forth by the Board in regulations. However, this exception shall not apply to harvesting of forest crops unless the area on which harvesting occurs is reforested artificially or naturally in accordance with the provisions of Chapter 11 (§ 10.1-1100 et seq.) of Title 10.1 or is converted to bona fide agricultural or improved pasture use as described in subsection B of § 10.1-1163;

8. Installation of fence and sign posts or telephone and electric poles and other kinds of posts or poles;

9. Shoreline erosion control projects on tidal waters when all of the land-disturbing activities are within the regulatory authority of and approved by local wetlands boards, the Marine Resources Commission, or the United States Army Corps of Engineers; however, any associated land that is disturbed outside of this exempted area shall remain subject to this article and the regulations adopted pursuant thereto;

10. Land-disturbing activities in response to a public emergency where the related work requires immediate authorization to avoid imminent endanger-

ment to human health or the environment. In such situations, the VESMP authority shall be advised of the disturbance within seven days of commencing the land-disturbing activity, and compliance with the administrative requirements of subsection A is required within 30 days of commencing the land-disturbing activity;

11. Discharges to a sanitary sewer or a combined sewer system that are not from a land-disturbing activity; and

12. Repair or rebuilding of the tracks, rights-of-way, bridges, communication facilities, and other related structures and facilities of a railroad company.

History.
1973, c. 486, § 21-89.6; 1979, c. 432; 1988, cc. 732, 891, § 10.1-563; 1993, c. 925; 1999, c. 555; 2001, c. 490; 2003, cc. 827, 966; 2006, c. 466; 2008, c. 23; 2011, cc. 720, 721; 2012, cc. 785, 819; 2013, cc. 756, 793; 2016, cc. 68, 758; 2023, cc. 48, 49.

§ 62.1-44.15:55.1. Department review of erosion and sediment control plans for solar projects.

A. Any locality that does not operate a regulated MS4 and for which the Department did not administer a VSMP as of July 1, 2020, shall notify the Department if it decides to have the Department provide the locality with (i) review of the erosion and sediment control plan required by subsection A of § 62.1-44.15:55 and (ii) a recommendation on the plan's compliance with the requirements of this article and the Board's regulations, for any solar project and its associated infrastructure with a rated electrical generation capacity exceeding five megawatts.

B. The VESCP authority for a locality that notifies the Department pursuant to subsection A shall, within five days of receiving an erosion and sediment control plan, forward such plan to the Department for review. If a plan forwarded to the Department is incomplete, the Department shall return the plan to the VESCP authority immediately and the application process shall start over. If a plan forwarded to the Department is complete, the Department shall review it for compliance with the requirements of this article and the Board's regulations and provide a recommendation to the VESCP authority. The VESCP authority shall then (i) grant written approval of the plan or (ii) provide written notice of disapproval of the plan in accordance with subsection B of § 62.1-44.15:55.

C. The VESCP authority for a locality that notifies the Department pursuant to subsection A shall, within five days of receiving any resubmittal of a previously disapproved erosion and sediment control plan, forward such resubmitted plan to the Department. The Department shall review a resubmittal of a previously disapproved erosion and sediment control plan for compliance with the requirements of this article and the Board's regulations and provide a recommendation to the VESCP authority. The VESCP authority shall then (i) grant written approval of the plan or (ii) provide written notice of disapproval of the plan in accordance with subsection B of § 62.1-44.15:55.

D. The Department shall adopt a fee schedule and charge fees for conducting reviews pursuant to this section. The fees shall be charged to applicants and not to any VESCP authority. Such fees shall be remitted to the State Treasurer for deposit in the Fund established by subsection E. The amount of the fees shall be set at an amount representing no less than 60 percent, but not to exceed 62 percent, of the administrative and other costs to the Department of conducting such reviews.

E. There is hereby created in the state treasury a special nonreverting fund to be known as the Virginia Erosion and Sediment Control Fund, referred to in this section as "the Fund." The Fund shall be established on the books of the Comptroller. All moneys collected by the Department pursuant to this section and all other funds appropriated for such purpose and any gifts, donations, grants, bequests, and other funds received on its behalf shall be paid into the state treasury and credited to the Fund. Interest earned on moneys in the Fund shall remain in the Fund and be credited to it. Any moneys remaining in the Fund, including interest thereon, at the end of each fiscal year shall not revert to the general fund but shall remain in the Fund. Moneys in the Fund shall be used solely for the purposes of carrying out the Department's responsibilities pursuant to this section. Expenditures and disbursements from the Fund shall be made by the State Treasurer on warrants issued by the Comptroller upon written request signed by the Director.

An accounting of moneys received by and distributed from the Fund shall be kept by the State Comptroller.

History.
2021, Sp. Sess. I, c. 497.

Effective date.
This section is effective July 1, 2021.

§ 62.1-44.15:56. (Repealed effective July 1, 2024) State agency and federal entity projects.

Editor's note.
Acts 2020, c. 1289, as amended by Acts 2021, Sp. Sess. I, c. 552, Item 377 D, and Acts 2022, Sp. Sess. I, c. 2, Item 378 D, effective for the biennium ending June 30, 2023, provides: "1. Notwithstanding § 62.1-44.15:56, Code of Virginia, public institutions of higher education, including community colleges, colleges, and universities, shall be subject to project review and compliance for state erosion and sediment control requirements by the local program authority of the locality within which the land disturbing activity is located, unless such institution submits annual specifications to the Department of Environmental Quality, in accordance with § 62.1-44.15:56 A (i), Code of Virginia.

"2. The State Water Control Board is authorized to amend the Erosion and Sediment Control Regulations (9 VAC 25-840 et seq.) to conform such regulations with this project review requirement and to clarify the process. These amendments shall be exempt from Article 2 (§ 2.2-4006 et seq.) of the Administrative Process Act."

§ 62.1-44.15:56.1. Department acceptance of plans in lieu of plan review.

A. Notwithstanding any other provision of this article, the Department, when administering a VESCP pursuant to Article 2.4 (§ 62.1-44.15:51 et seq.), may choose to accept a set of plans and supporting calculations for any land-disturbing activity determined to be de minimis using a risk-based approach established by the Board.

B. The Department is authorized to accept such plans and supporting calculations in satisfaction of the requirement of this article that it retain a certified plan reviewer or conduct a plan review. This section shall not excuse any applicable performance bond requirement pursuant to § 62.1-44.15:57.

History.
2020, c. 812.

Editor's note.
At the direction of the Virginia Code Commission, "de minimis" was substituted for "de minimus" in subsection A.

Acts 2020, c. 812, cl. 2 provides: "That the State Water Control Board (the Board) shall adopt regulations to implement the requirements of §§ 62.1-44.15:27.4 and 62.1-44.15:56.1 of the Code of Virginia as created by this act. The initial adoption of such regulations shall be exempt from the requirements of Article 2 (§ 2.2-4006 et seq.) of Chapter 40 of Title 2.2 of the Code of Virginia. However, the Board shall (i) provide a Notice of Intended Regulatory Action, (ii) form a stakeholder advisory group, (iii) provide a 60-day public comment period prior to the Board's adoption of the regulations, and (iv) provide a written summary of comments received and responses to comments prior to the Board's adoption of the regulations."

§ 62.1-44.15:58. (Effective until July 1, 2024) Monitoring, reports, and inspections.

A. The VESCP authority (i) shall provide for periodic inspections of the land-disturbing activity and require that an individual holding a certificate of competence, as provided by § 62.1-44.15:52, who will be in charge of and responsible for carrying out the land-disturbing activity and (ii) may require monitoring and reports from the person responsible for carrying out the erosion and sediment control plan, to ensure compliance with the approved plan and to determine whether the measures required in the plan are effective in controlling erosion and sediment. However, any VESCP authority may waive the certificate of competence requirement for an agreement in lieu of a plan. The owner, permittee, or person responsible for carrying out the plan shall be given notice of the inspection. If the VESCP authority, where authorized to enforce this article, or the Department determines that there is a failure to comply with the plan following an inspection, notice shall be served upon the permittee or person responsible for carrying out the plan by mailing with confirmation of delivery to the address specified in the permit application or in the plan certification, or by delivery at the site of the land-disturbing activities to the agent or employee supervising such activities. The notice shall specify the measures needed to comply with the plan and shall specify the time within which such measures shall be completed. Upon failure to comply within the time specified, the permit may be revoked and the VESCP authority, where authorized to enforce this article, the Department, or the Board may pursue enforcement as provided by § 62.1-44.15:63.

B. Notwithstanding the provisions of subsection A, a VESCP authority is authorized to enter into agreements or contracts with districts, adjacent localities, or other public or private entities to assist with the responsibilities of this article, including but not limited to the review and determination of adequacy of erosion and sediment control plans submitted for land-disturbing activities as well as monitoring, reports, inspections, and enforcement where an authority is granted such powers by this article.

C. Upon issuance of an inspection report denoting a violation of this section, § 62.1-44.15:55 or 62.1-44.15:56, in conjunction with or subsequent to a notice to comply as specified in subsection A, a VESCP authority, where authorized to enforce this article, or the Department may issue an order requiring that all or part of the land-disturbing activities permitted on the site be stopped until the specified corrective measures have been taken or, if land-disturbing activities have commenced without an approved plan as provided in § 62.1-44.15:55, requiring that all of the land-disturbing activities be stopped until an approved plan or any required permits are obtained. Where the alleged noncompliance is causing or is in imminent danger of causing harmful erosion of lands or sediment deposition in waters within the watersheds of the Commonwealth, or where the land-disturbing activities have commenced without an approved erosion and sediment control plan or any required permits, such an order may be issued whether or not the alleged violator has been issued a notice to comply as specified in subsection A. Otherwise, such an order may be issued only after the alleged violator has failed to comply with a notice to comply. The order for noncompliance with a plan shall be served in the same manner as a notice to comply, and shall remain in effect for seven days from the date of service pending application by the VESCP authority, the Department, or alleged violator for appropriate relief to the circuit court of the jurisdiction wherein the violation was alleged to have occurred or other appropriate court. The order for disturbance without an approved plan or permits shall be served upon the owner by mailing with confirmation of delivery to the address specified in the land records of the locality, shall be posted on the site where the disturbance is occurring, and shall remain in effect until such time as permits and plan approvals are secured, except in such situations where an agricultural exemption applies. If the alleged violator has not obtained an approved erosion and sediment control plan or any required permit within seven days from the date of service of the order, the Department or the chief administrative officer or his designee on behalf of the VESCP authority may issue a subsequent order to the owner requiring that all construction and other work on the site, other than corrective measures, be stopped until an approved erosion and sediment control plan and any required permits have been obtained. The subsequent order shall be served upon the owner by mailing with confirmation of delivery to the address specified in the permit application or the land records of the locality in which the site is located. The owner may appeal the issuance of any order to the circuit court of the jurisdiction wherein the violation was alleged to have occurred or other appropriate court. Any person violating or failing, neglecting, or refusing to obey an order issued by the Department or the chief administrative officer or his designee on behalf of the VESCP authority may be compelled in a proceeding instituted in the circuit court of the jurisdiction wherein the violation was alleged to have occurred or other appropriate court to obey same and to comply therewith by injunction, mandamus, or other appropriate remedy. Upon completion and approval of corrective action or obtaining an approved plan or any required permits, the order shall immediately be lifted. Nothing in this section shall prevent the Department, the Board, or the chief administrative officer or his designee on behalf of the VESCP authority from taking any other action specified in § 62.1-44.15:63.

History.
1973, c. 486, § 21-89.8; 1986, c. 328; 1988, cc. 694, 891, § 10.1-566; 1992, c. 298; 1993, c. 925; 2001, c. 490; 2003, c. 827; 2012, cc. 249, 785, 819; 2013, cc. 756, 793; 2023, cc. 48, 49.

Editor's note.
Acts 2016, cc. 68 and 758, cl. 9, as amended by Acts 2023, cc. 665 and 666, cl. 1, provides: "That the State Water Control Board (the Board) shall adopt regulations to implement the requirements of this act before July 1, 2024. The adoption of such regulations shall include the reduction of regulations through consolidation of duplicative requirements and be exempt from the requirements of Article 2 (§ 2.2-4006 et seq.) of the Administrative Process Act (§ 2.2-4000 et seq.) of the Code of Virginia. However, the Department shall (i) provide a Notice of Intended Regulatory Action, (ii) form a stakeholders advisory group, (iii) provide for a 60-day public comment period prior to the Board's adoption of the regulations, and (iv) provide the Board with a written summary of comments received and responses to comments prior to the Board's adoption of the regulations. This enactment shall become effective in due course. The regulations shall become effective on July 1, 2024, concurrent with the effective date of the remainder of this act."

Acts 2016, cc. 68 and 758, cl. 10, as amended by Acts 2017, c. 345, cl. 2 and Acts 2023, cc. 665 and 666, cl. 1, provides: "That the provisions of this act, except for the ninth enactment, shall become effective on July 1, 2024, concurrent with the effective date of the regulations required by the ninth enactment of this act."

The 2023 amendments.
The 2023 amendments by cc. 48 and 49 are identical, and deleted "for construction of a single-family residence" in subsection A.

§ 62.1-44.15:58. (Effective July 1, 2024) Monitoring, reports, and inspections.

A. The VESCP authority (i) shall provide for periodic inspections of the land-disturbing activity and require that an individual holding a certificate, as provided by § 62.1-44.15:52, will be in charge of and responsible for carrying out the land-disturbing activity and (ii) may require monitoring and reports from the person responsible for carrying out the erosion and sediment control plan, to ensure compliance with the approved plan and to determine whether the measures required in the plan are effective in controlling erosion and sediment. However, any VESCP authority may waive the certificate requirement for an agreement in lieu of a plan. The owner shall be given notice of the inspection. When the VESCP authority or the Board determines that there is a failure to comply with the conditions of land-disturbance approval or to obtain an approved plan or a land-disturbance approval prior to commencing land-disturbing activity, the VESCP authority or the Board may serve a notice to comply upon the owner or person responsible for carrying out the land-disturbing activity. Such notice to comply shall be served by delivery by facsimile, e-mail, or other technology; by mailing with confirmation of delivery to the address specified in the plan or land-disturbance application, if available, or in the land records of the locality; or by delivery at the site to a person previously identified to the VESCP authority by the owner. The notice to comply shall specify the measures needed to comply with the land-disturbance approval conditions or shall identify the plan approval or land-disturbance approval needed to comply with this article and shall specify a reasonable time within which such measures shall be completed. In any instance in which a required land-disturbance approval has not been obtained, the VESCP authority or the Board may require immediate compliance. In any other case, the VESCP authority or the Board may establish the time for compliance by taking into account the risk of damage to natural resources and other relevant factors. Notwithstanding any other provision in this subsection, a VESCP authority or the Board may count any days of noncompliance as days of violation should the VESCP authority or the Board take an enforcement action. The issuance of a notice to comply by the Board shall not be considered a case decision as defined in § 2.2-4001. Upon failure to comply within the time specified, any plan approval or land-disturbance approval may be revoked and the VESCP authority or the Board may pursue enforcement as provided by § 62.1-44.15:63.

B. Notwithstanding the provisions of subsection A, a VESCP authority is authorized to enter into agreements or contracts with districts, adjacent localities, or other public or private entities to assist with the responsibilities of this article, including but not limited to the review and determination of adequacy of erosion and sediment control plans submitted for land-disturbing activities as well as monitoring, reports, inspections, and enforcement.

C. Upon issuance of an inspection report denoting a violation of this section or § 62.1-44.15:55, in conjunction with or subsequent to a notice to comply as specified in subsection A, a VESCP authority or the Board may issue a stop work order requiring that all or part of the land-disturbing activities on the site be stopped until the specified corrective measures have been taken or, if land-disturbing activities have commenced without an approved plan as provided in § 62.1-44.15:55, requiring that all of the land-disturbing activities be stopped until an approved plan is obtained. When such an order is issued by the Board, it shall be issued in accordance with the procedures of the Administrative Process Act (§ 2.2-4000 et seq.). Where the alleged noncompliance is causing or is in imminent danger of causing harmful erosion of lands or sediment deposition in waters within the watersheds of the Commonwealth, or where the land-disturbing activities have commenced without an approved erosion and sediment control plan, such a stop work order may be issued whether or not the alleged violator has been issued a notice to comply as specified in subsection A. Otherwise, such an order may be issued only after the alleged violator has failed to comply with a notice to comply. The order for noncompliance with a plan shall be served in the same manner as a notice to comply, and shall remain in effect for seven days from the date of service pending application by the VESCP authority, the Board, or alleged violator for appropriate relief to the circuit court of the jurisdiction wherein the violation was alleged to have occurred or other appropriate court. The stop work order for disturbance without an approved plan shall be served upon the owner by mailing with confirmation of delivery to the address specified in the land records of the locality, shall be posted on the site where the disturbance is occurring, and shall remain in effect until such time as plan approvals are secured, except in such situations where an agricultural exemption applies. If the alleged violator has not obtained an approved erosion and sediment control plan within seven days from the date of service of the stop work order, the Board or the chief administrative officer or his designee on behalf of the VESCP authority may issue a subsequent order to the owner requiring that all construction and other work on the site, other than corrective measures, be stopped until an approved erosion and sediment control plan has been obtained. The subsequent order shall be served upon the owner by mailing with confirmation of delivery to the address specified in the plan or the land records of the locality in which the site is located. The owner may appeal the issuance of any order to the circuit court of the jurisdiction wherein the violation was alleged to have occurred or other appropriate court. Any person violating or failing, neglecting, or refusing to obey an order issued by the Board or the chief administrative officer or his designee on behalf of the VESCP authority may be compelled in a proceeding instituted in the circuit court of the jurisdiction wherein the violation was alleged to have occurred or other appropriate court to obey same and to comply therewith by injunction, mandamus, or other appropriate remedy. Upon completion and approval of corrective action or obtaining an approved plan, the order shall immediately be lifted. Nothing in this section shall prevent the Board or the chief administrative officer or his designee on behalf of the VESCP authority from taking any other action specified in § 62.1-44.15:63.

History.
1973, c. 486, § 21-89.8; 1986, c. 328; 1988, cc. 694, 891, § 10.1-566; 1992, c. 298; 1993, c. 925; 2001, c. 490; 2003, c. 827; 2012, cc. 249, 785, 819; 2013, cc. 756, 793; 2016, cc. 68, 758; 2023, cc. 48, 49.

§ 62.1-44.15:58.1. Inspections; land-disturbing activities of natural gas pipelines; stop work instructions.

A. The Department is authorized to conduct inspections of the land-disturbing activities of interstate and intrastate natural gas pipeline companies that have approved annual standards and specifications pursuant to § 62.1-44.15:55 as such land-disturbing activities relate to construction of any natural gas transmission pipeline equal to or greater than 24 inches inside diameter to determine (i) compliance with such annual standards and specifications, (ii) compliance with any site-specific plans, and (iii) if there have been or are likely to be adverse impacts to water quality as a result of such land-disturbing activities, including instances where (a) there has been a violation of any water quality standard adopted pursuant to the State Water Control Law (§ 62.1-44.2 et seq.), (b) sediment has been deposited in significant amounts in areas where those deposits are not contained by best management practices, (c) there are repeated instances of adverse impacts or likely adverse impacts within a 30-day period, or (d) there have been widespread and repeated instances of adverse impacts or likely impacts. When the Department determines that there has been a substantial adverse impact to water quality or that an imminent and substantial adverse impact to water quality is likely to occur as a result of such land-disturbing activities, the Department may issue a stop work instruction, without advance notice or hearing, requiring that all or part of such land-disturbing activities on the part of the site that caused the substantial adverse impacts to water quality or are likely to cause imminent and substantial adverse impacts to water quality be stopped until corrective measures specified in the stop work instruction have been completed and approved by the Department. Where substantial adverse impacts or likely adverse impacts are found on a repeated, frequent, and widespread basis, the Department may issue a stop work instruction for every work area in Virginia until the Department determines that any systemic cause that contributed to such occurrences has been corrected.

Such stop work instruction shall become effective upon service on the company by email or other technology agreed to in writing by the Department and the company, by mailing with confirmation of delivery to the address specified in the annual standards and specifications, if available, or by delivery at the site to a person previously identified to the Department by the company. Upon request by the company, the Director or his designee shall review such stop work instruction within 48 hours of issuance.

B. Within 10 business days of issuance of a stop work instruction, the Department shall promptly provide to such company an opportunity for an informal fact-finding proceeding concerning the stop work instruction and any review by the Director or his designee. Reasonable notice as to the time and place of the informal fact-finding proceeding shall be provided to such company. Within 10 business days of the informal fact-finding proceeding, the Department shall affirm, modify, amend, or cancel such stop work instruction. Upon written documentation from the company of the completion and approval by the Department in writing of the corrective measures specified in the stop work instruction, the instruction shall be immediately lifted.

C. The company may appeal such stop work instruction or preliminary decision rendered by the Director or his designee to the circuit court of the jurisdiction wherein the land-disturbing activities subject to the stop work instruction occurred, or to another appropriate court, in accordance with the requirements of the Administrative Process Act (§ 2.2-4000 et seq.). Any person violating or failing, neglecting, or refusing to obey a stop work instruction issued by the Department may be compelled in a proceeding instituted in the circuit court of the jurisdiction wherein the violation was alleged to have occurred or other appropriate court to obey same and to comply therewith by injunction, mandamus, or other appropriate remedy. Nothing in this section shall prevent the Board or the Department from taking any other action authorized by this chapter.

History.
2018, c. 297; 2021, Sp. Sess. I, c. 277.

The 2021 Sp. Sess. I amendments.
The 2021 amendment by Sp. Sess. I, c. 277, effective July 1, 2021, in subsection A, substituted "equal to or greater than 24 inches" for "greater than 36 inches" and inserted "including instances where (a) there has been a violation of any water quality standard adopted pursuant to the State Water Control Law (§ 62.1-44.2 et seq.), (b) sediment has been deposited in significant amounts in areas where those deposits are not contained by best management practices, (c) there are repeated instances of adverse impacts or likely adverse impacts within a 30-day period, or (d) there have been widespread and repeated instances of adverse impacts or likely impacts" in the first sentence and added the last sentence in the first paragraph.

§ 62.1-44.15:60. (Effective until July 1, 2024) Right of entry.

Editor's note.
Acts 2016, cc. 68 and 758, cl. 9, as amended by Acts 2023, cc. 665 and 666, cl. 1, provides: "That the State Water Control Board (the Board) shall adopt regulations to implement the requirements of this act before July 1, 2024.

The adoption of such regulations shall include the reduction of regulations through consolidation of duplicative requirements and be exempt from the requirements of Article 2 (§ 2.2-4006 et seq.) of the Administrative Process Act (§ 2.2-4000 et seq.) of the Code of Virginia. However, the Department shall (i) provide a Notice of Intended Regulatory Action, (ii) form a stakeholders advisory group, (iii) provide for a 60-day public comment period prior to the Board's adoption of the regulations, and (iv) provide the Board with a written summary of comments received and responses to comments prior to the Board's adoption of the regulations. This enactment shall become effective in due course. The regulations shall become effective on July 1, 2024, concurrent with the effective date of the remainder of this act."

Acts 2016, cc. 68 and 758, cl. 10, as amended by Acts 2017, c. 345, cl. 2 and Acts 2023, cc. 665 and 666, cl. 1, provides: "That the provisions of this act, except for the ninth enactment, shall become effective on July 1, 2024, concurrent with the effective date of the regulations required by the ninth enactment of this act."

CASE NOTES

Entry onto property not authorized. — Because the floodplain manager in the Planning Department was not in the Building Inspections/Permits Department, which was responsible for enforcing the Virginia Statewide Building Code and erosion and sediment control ordinances, the floodplain manager's entry onto plaintiff's property was not authorized by the Virginia Erosion and Sediment Control Program regulatory scheme. Mendes v. Wendling, No. 5:19-cv-00072, 2021 U.S. Dist. LEXIS 53819 (W.D. Va. Mar. 23, 2021).

§ 62.1-44.15:65. (Effective until July 1, 2024) Authorization for more stringent regulations.

A. As part of a VESCP, a district or locality is authorized to adopt more stringent soil erosion and sediment control regulations or ordinances than those necessary to ensure compliance with the Board's regulations, provided that the more stringent regulations or ordinances are based upon factual findings of local or regional comprehensive watershed management studies or findings developed through the implementation of an MS4 permit or a locally adopted watershed management study and are determined by the district or locality to be necessary to prevent any further degradation to water resources, to address total maximum daily load requirements, to protect exceptional state waters, or to address specific existing water pollution including nutrient and sediment loadings, stream channel erosion, depleted groundwater resources, or excessive localized flooding within the watershed and that prior to adopting more stringent regulations or ordinances, a public hearing is held. Notice of such hearing shall be given by publication once a week for two consecutive weeks in a newspaper of general circulation in the locality seeking to adopt the ordinance, with the first publication appearing no more than 14 days before the hearing. The VESCP authority shall report to the Board when more stringent stormwater management regulations or ordinances are determined to be necessary pursuant to this section. However, this section shall not be construed to authorize any district or locality to impose any more stringent regulations for plan approval or permit issuance than those specified in §§ 62.1-44.15:55 and 62.1-44.15:57.

B. Any provisions of an erosion and sediment control program in existence before July 1, 2012, that contains more stringent provisions than this article shall be exempt from the analysis requirements of subsection A.

History.
1973, c. 486, § 21-89.12; 1988, c. 891, § 10.1-570; 2012, cc. 785, 819; 2013, cc. 756, 793; 2023, cc. 506, 507.

Editor's note.
Acts 2016, cc. 68 and 758, cl. 9, as amended by Acts 2023, cc. 665 and 666, cl. 1, provides: "That the State Water Control Board (the

Board) shall adopt regulations to implement the requirements of this act before July 1, 2024. The adoption of such regulations shall include the reduction of regulations through consolidation of duplicative requirements and be exempt from the requirements of Article 2 (§ 2.2-4006 et seq.) of the Administrative Process Act (§ 2.2-4000 et seq.) of the Code of Virginia. However, the Department shall (i) provide a Notice of Intended Regulatory Action, (ii) form a stakeholders advisory group, (iii) provide for a 60-day public comment period prior to the Board's adoption of the regulations, and (iv) provide the Board with a written summary of comments received and responses to comments prior to the Board's adoption of the regulations. This enactment shall become effective in due course.

The regulations shall become effective on July 1, 2024, concurrent with the effective date of the remainder of this act."

Acts 2016, cc. 68 and 758, cl. 10, as amended by Acts 2017, c. 345, cl. 2 and Acts 2023, cc. 665 and 666, cl. 1, provides: "That the provisions of this act, except for the ninth enactment, shall become effective on July 1, 2024, concurrent with the effective date of the regulations required by the ninth enactment of this act."

The 2023 amendments.

The 2023 amendments by cc. 506 and 507 are identical, and deleted "after giving due notice" at the end of the first sentence of subsection A and added the second sentence.

§ 62.1-44.15:65. (Effective July 1, 2024) Authorization for more stringent ordinances.

A. As part of a VESCP, a locality is authorized to adopt more stringent soil erosion and sediment control ordinances than those necessary to ensure compliance with the Board's regulations, provided that the more stringent ordinances are based upon factual findings of local or regional comprehensive watershed management studies or findings developed through the implementation of a locally adopted watershed management study and are determined by the locality to be necessary to prevent any further degradation to water resources, to address total maximum daily load requirements, to protect exceptional state waters, or to address specific existing water pollution including nutrient and sediment loadings, stream channel erosion, depleted groundwater resources, or excessive localized flooding within the watershed and that prior to adopting more stringent ordinances, a public hearing is held. Notice of such hearing shall be given by publication once a week for two consecutive weeks in a newspaper of general circulation in the locality seeking to adopt the ordinance, with the first publication appearing no more than 14 days before the hearing. The VESCP authority shall report to the Board when more stringent erosion and sediment control ordinances are determined to be necessary pursuant to this section. This process shall not be required when a VESCP authority chooses to reduce the threshold for regulating land-disturbing activities to a smaller area of disturbed land pursuant to § 62.1-44.15:55. This section shall not be construed to authorize any VESCP authority to impose any more stringent ordinances for land-disturbance review and approval than those specified in § 62.1-44.15:55.

B. Any provisions of an erosion and sediment control program in existence before July 1, 2012, that contains more stringent provisions than this article shall be exempt from the analysis requirements of subsection A.

History.
1973, c. 486, § 21-89.12; 1988, c. 891, § 10.1- 570; 2012, cc. 785, 819; 2013, cc. 756, 793; 2016, cc. 68, 758; 2023, cc. 506, 507.

§ 62.1-44.15:66. No limitation on authority of Department of Energy.

The provisions of this article shall not limit the powers or duties of the Department of Energy as they relate to mine reclamation under Chapters 10 (§ 45.2-1000 et seq.) and 12 (§ 45.2-1200 et seq.) of Title 45.2 or oil or gas exploration under the Virginia Gas and Oil Act (§ 45.2-1600 et seq.).

History.
　1973, c. 486, § 21-89.13; 1988, c. 891, § 10.1-571; 1996, c. 688; 2012, cc. 785, 819; 2013, cc. 47, 129, 756, 793; 2021, Sp. Sess. I, c. 532.

Editor's note.
　Effective October 1, 2021, "Chapters 10 (§ 45.2-1000 et seq.) and 12 (§ 45.2-1200 et seq.)" was substituted for "Chapters 16 (§ 45.1-180 et seq.) and 19 (§ 45.1-226 et seq.) of Title 45.1" and "Virginia Gas and Oil Act (§ 45.2-1600 et seq.)" was substituted for "Virginia Gas and Oil Act (§ 45.1-361.1 et seq.)" to conform to

Acts 2021, Sp. Sess. I, c. 387, at the direction of the Virginia Code Commission.
　Acts 2021, Sp. Sess. I, c. 532, cl. 2 provides: "That the provisions of this act shall become effective on October 1, 2021."

The 2021 Sp. Sess. I amendments.
　The 2021 amendment by Sp. Sess. I, c. 532, effective October 1, 2021, substituted "Department of Energy" for "Department of Mines, Minerals and Energy" and deleted "strip" preceding "mine."

ARTICLE 2.5.

CHESAPEAKE BAY PRESERVATION ACT.

§ 62.1-44.15:67. Cooperative state-local program.

A. Healthy state and local economies and a healthy Chesapeake Bay are integrally related; balanced economic development and water quality protection are not mutually exclusive. The protection of the public interest in the Chesapeake Bay, its tributaries, and other state waters and the promotion of the general welfare of the people of the Commonwealth require that (i) the counties, cities, and towns of Tidewater Virginia incorporate general water quality protection measures into their comprehensive plans, zoning ordinances, and subdivision ordinances; (ii) the counties, cities, and towns of Tidewater Virginia establish programs, in accordance with criteria established by the Commonwealth, that define and protect certain lands, hereinafter called Chesapeake Bay Preservation Areas, which if improperly developed may result in substantial damage to the water quality of the Chesapeake Bay and its tributaries; (iii) the Commonwealth make its resources available to local governing bodies by providing financial and technical assistance, policy guidance, and oversight when requested or otherwise required to carry out and enforce the provisions of this article; and (iv) all agencies of the Commonwealth exercise their delegated authority in a manner consistent with water quality protection provisions of local comprehensive plans, zoning ordinances, and subdivision ordinances when it has been determined that they comply with the provisions of this article.
　B. Local governments have the initiative for planning and for implementing the provisions of this article, and the Commonwealth shall act primarily in a supportive role by providing oversight for local governmental programs, by establishing criteria as required by this article, and by providing those resources necessary to carry out and enforce the provisions of this article.
　C. Each local government in Tidewater Virginia shall publish on its website the elements and criteria adopted to implement its local plan as required by this article, including those elements and criteria required by 9VAC25-830-60 for local programs.

History.
　1988, cc. 608, 891, § 10.1-2100; 2013, cc. 756, 793; 2022, c. 207.

The 2022 amendments.
　The 2022 amendment by c. 207 added subsection C.

§ 62.1-44.15:68. Definitions.

For the purposes of this article, the following words shall have the meanings respectively ascribed to them:

"Chesapeake Bay Preservation Area" means an area delineated by a local government in accordance with criteria established pursuant to § 62.1-44.15:72.

"Criteria" means criteria developed by the Board pursuant to § 62.1-44.15:72 for the purpose of determining the ecological and geographic extent of Chesapeake Bay Preservation Areas and for use by local governments in permitting, denying, or modifying requests to rezone, subdivide, or use and develop land in Chesapeake Bay Preservation Areas.

"Daylighted stream" means a stream that had been previously diverted into an underground drainage system, has been redirected into an aboveground channel using natural channel design concepts as defined in § 62.1-44.15:51, and would meet the criteria for being designated as a Resource Protection Area (RPA) as defined by the Board under this article.

"Department" means the Department of Environmental Quality.

"Director" means the Director of the Department of Environmental Quality.

"Secretary" means the Secretary of Natural and Historic Resources.

"Tidewater Virginia" means the following jurisdictions:

The Counties of Accomack, Arlington, Caroline, Charles City, Chesterfield, Essex, Fairfax, Gloucester, Hanover, Henrico, Isle of Wight, James City, King and Queen, King George, King William, Lancaster, Mathews, Middlesex, New Kent, Northampton, Northumberland, Prince George, Prince William, Richmond, Spotsylvania, Stafford, Surry, Westmoreland, and York, and the Cities of Alexandria, Chesapeake, Colonial Heights, Fairfax, Falls Church, Fredericksburg, Hampton, Hopewell, Newport News, Norfolk, Petersburg, Poquoson, Portsmouth, Richmond, Suffolk, Virginia Beach, and Williamsburg.

History.
1988, cc. 608, 891, § 10.1-2101; 2005, c. 41; 2012, cc. 785, 819; 2013, cc. 756, 793; 2015, c. 674; 2021, Sp. Sess. I, c. 401.

The 2021 Sp. Sess. I amendments.
The 2021 amendment by Sp. Sess. I, c. 401, effective July 1, 2021, inserted "and Historic" in the definition for "Secretary."

§ 62.1-44.15:69. (Effective July 1, 2024) Powers and duties of the Board.

Editor's note.
Acts 2016, cc. 68 and 758, cl. 9, as amended by Acts 2023, cc. 665 and 666, cl. 1, provides: "That the State Water Control Board (the Board) shall adopt regulations to implement the requirements of this act before July 1, 2024. The adoption of such regulations shall include the reduction of regulations through consolidation of duplicative requirements and be exempt from the requirements of Article 2 (§ 2.2-4006 et seq.) of the Administrative Process Act (§ 2.2-4000 et seq.) of the Code of Virginia. However, the Department shall (i) provide a Notice of Intended Regulatory Action, (ii) form a stakeholders advisory group, (iii) provide for a 60-day public comment period prior to the Board's adoption of the regulations, and (iv) provide the Board with a written summary of comments received and responses to comments prior to the Board's adoption of the regulations. This enactment shall become effective in due course. The regulations shall become effective on July 1, 2024, concurrent with the effective date of the remainder of this act."

Acts 2016, cc. 68 and 758, cl. 10, as amended by Acts 2017, c. 345, cl. 2 and Acts 2023, cc. 665 and 666, cl. 1, provides: "That the provisions of this act, except for the ninth enactment, shall become effective on July 1, 2024, concurrent with the effective date of the regulations required by the ninth enactment of this act."

§ 62.1-44.15:71. (Repealed effective July 1, 2024) Program compliance.

Editor's note.

Acts 2016, cc. 68 and 758, cl. 9, as amended by Acts 2023, cc. 665 and 666, cl. 1, provides: "That the State Water Control Board (the Board) shall adopt regulations to implement the requirements of this act before July 1, 2024. The adoption of such regulations shall include the reduction of regulations through consolidation of duplicative requirements and be exempt from the requirements of Article 2 (§ 2.2-4006 et seq.) of the Administrative Process Act (§ 2.2-4000 et seq.) of the Code of Virginia. However, the Department shall (i) provide a Notice of Intended Regulatory Action, (ii) form a stakeholders advisory group, (iii) provide for a 60-day public comment period prior to the Board's adoption of the regulations, and (iv) provide the Board with a written summary of comments received and responses to comments prior to the Board's adoption of the regulations. This enactment shall become effective in due course. The regulations shall become effective on July 1, 2024, concurrent with the effective date of the remainder of this act."

Acts 2016, cc. 68 and 758, cl. 10, as amended by Acts 2017, c. 345, cl. 2 and Acts 2023, cc. 665 and 666, cl. 1, provides: "That the provisions of this act, except for the ninth enactment, shall become effective on July 1, 2024, concurrent with the effective date of the regulations required by the ninth enactment of this act."

§ 62.1-44.15:72. Board to develop criteria.

A. In order to implement the provisions of this article and to assist counties, cities, and towns in regulating the use and development of land and in protecting the quality of state waters, the Board shall promulgate regulations that establish criteria for use by local governments to determine the ecological and geographic extent of Chesapeake Bay Preservation Areas. The Board shall also promulgate regulations that establish criteria for use by local governments in granting, denying, or modifying requests to rezone, subdivide, or use and develop land in these areas.

B. In developing and amending the criteria, the Board shall consider all factors relevant to the protection of water quality from significant degradation as a result of the use and development of land. The criteria shall incorporate measures such as performance standards, best management practices, and various planning and zoning concepts to protect the quality of state waters while allowing use and development of land consistent with the provisions of this chapter. The criteria adopted by the Board, operating in conjunction with other state water quality programs, shall encourage and promote (i) protection of existing high quality state waters and restoration of all other state waters to a condition or quality that will permit all reasonable public uses and will support the propagation and growth of all aquatic life, including game fish, that might reasonably be expected to inhabit them; (ii) safeguarding of the clean waters of the Commonwealth from pollution; (iii) prevention of any increase in pollution; (iv) reduction of existing pollution; (v) preservation of mature trees or planting of trees as a water quality protection tool and as a means of providing other natural resource benefits; (vi) coastal resilience and adaptation to sea-level rise and climate change; and (vii) promotion of water resource conservation in order to provide for the health, safety, and welfare of the present and future citizens of the Commonwealth.

C. Prior to the development or amendment of criteria, the Board shall give due consideration to, among other things, the economic and social costs and benefits that can reasonably be expected to obtain as a result of the adoption or amendment of the criteria.

D. In developing such criteria the Board may consult with and obtain the comments of any federal, state, regional, or local agency that has jurisdiction by law or special expertise with respect to the use and development of land or the protection of water. The Board shall give due consideration to the comments submitted by such federal, state, regional, or local agencies.

E. In developing such criteria, the Board shall provide that any locality in a Chesapeake Bay Preservation Area that allows the owner of an onsite sewage treatment system not requiring a Virginia Pollutant Discharge Elimination System permit to submit documentation in lieu of proof of septic tank pump-out shall require such owner to have such documentation certified by an operator or onsite soil evaluator licensed or certified under Chapter 23 (§ 54.1-2300 et seq.) of Title 54.1 as being qualified to operate, maintain, or design onsite sewage systems.

F. In developing such criteria, the Board shall not require the designation of a Resource Protection Area (RPA) as defined according to the criteria developed by the Board, adjacent to a daylighted stream. However, a locality that elects not to designate an RPA adjacent to a daylighted stream shall use a water quality impact assessment to ensure that proposed development on properties adjacent to the daylighted stream does not result in the degradation of the stream. The water quality impact assessment shall (i) be consistent with the Board's criteria for water quality assessments in RPAs, (ii) identify the impacts of the proposed development on water quality, and (iii) determine specific measures for the mitigation of those impacts. The objective of this assessment is to ensure that practices on properties adjacent to daylighted streams are effective in retarding runoff, preventing erosion, and filtering nonpoint source pollution. The specific content for the water quality impact assessment shall be established and implemented by any locality that chooses not to designate an RPA adjacent to a daylighted stream. Nothing in this subsection shall limit a locality's authority to include a daylighted stream within the extent of an RPA.

G. Effective July 1, 2014, requirements promulgated under this article directly related to compliance with the erosion and sediment control and stormwater management provisions of this chapter and regulated under the authority of those provisions shall cease to have effect.

H. Effective July 1, 2023, requirements promulgated under this article directly related to compliance with onsite sewage system pump-outs shall be managed and enforced by the Department of Health in Accomack, Essex, Gloucester, King and Queen, King William, Lancaster, Mathews, Middlesex, Northampton, Northumberland, Richmond, and Westmoreland Counties, and the incorporated towns within those counties.

History.

1988, cc. 608, 891, § 10.1-2107; 2012, cc. 785, 819; 2013, cc. 756, 793; 2014, c. 151; 2015, c. 674; 2020, c. 1207; 2022, c. 486.

Editor's note.

Acts 2020, c. 1207, cl. 2 provides: "That the State Water Control Board (the Board) shall adopt regulations to implement the provisions of this act. The initial adoption of such regulations shall be exempt from the requirements of Article 2 (§ 2.2-4006 et seq.) of Chapter 40 of Title 2.2 of the Code of Virginia. Such proposed regulations shall be subject to a public comment period of at least 60 days prior to final adoption by the Board."

Acts 2022, c. 486, cl. 2 provides: "That the Department of Health (the Department) shall provide outreach and education to homeowners to ensure compliance with onsite sewage treatment system pump-out requirements adopted pursuant to the Chesapeake Bay Preservation Act (§ 62.1-44.15:67 et seq. of the Code of Virginia). The Department shall provide to the Chairmen of the House Committee on Health, Welfare and Institutions and the Senate Committee on Education and Health an interim report by December 1, 2024, and a final report by December 1, 2025, on compliance with such onsite sewage treatment system pump-out requirements in the localities specified in subsection L of § 32.1-164 of the Code of Virginia, as amended by this act, and subsection H of § 62.1-44.15:72 of the Code of Virginia, as amended by this act, and the incorporated towns within such localities. Such reports shall also include recommendations to improve compliance with onsite sewage treatment system pump-out requirements adopted pursuant to the Chesapeake Bay Preservation Act."

The 2020 amendments.

The 2020 amendment by c. 1207, in subsection B in the last sentence, substituted "safeguarding of the clean waters" for "safeguarding the clean waters" in clause (ii), inserted clauses (v) and (vi), and redesignated former clause (v) as clause (vii); and made stylistic changes.

The 2022 amendments.

The 2022 amendment by c. 486 added subsection H and made stylistic changes.

§ 62.1-44.15:74. Local governments to designate Chesapeake Bay Preservation Areas; incorporate into local plans and ordinances; impose civil penalties.

Editor's note.

Acts 2016, cc. 68 and 758, cl. 9, as amended by Acts 2023, cc. 665 and 666, cl. 1, provides: "That the State Water Control Board (the Board) shall adopt regulations to implement the requirements of this act before July 1, 2024. The adoption of such regulations shall include the reduction of regulations through consolidation of duplicative requirements and be exempt from the requirements of Article 2 (§ 2.2-4006 et seq.) of the Administrative Process Act (§ 2.2-4000 et seq.) of the Code of Virginia. However, the Department shall (i) provide a Notice of Intended Regulatory Action, (ii) form a stakeholders advisory group, (iii) provide for a 60-day public comment period prior to the Board's

adoption of the regulations, and (iv) provide the Board with a written summary of comments received and responses to comments prior to the Board's adoption of the regulations. This enactment shall become effective in due course. The regulations shall become effective on July 1, 2024, concurrent with the effective date of the remainder of this act."

Acts 2016, cc. 68 and 758, cl. 10, as amended by Acts 2017, c. 345, cl. 2 and Acts 2023, cc. 665 and 666, cl. 1, provides: "That the provisions of this act, except for the ninth enactment, shall become effective on July 1, 2024, concurrent with the effective date of the regulations required by the ninth enactment of this act."

ARTICLE 2.6.
ADDITIONAL UPLAND CONDITIONS FOR WATER QUALITY CERTIFICATION.

§ 62.1-44.15:81. Application and preparation of draft certification conditions.

A. Any applicant for a federal license or permit for a natural gas transmission pipeline greater than 36 inches inside diameter subject to § 7c of the federal Natural Gas Act (15 U.S.C. § 717f(c)) shall submit a separate application, at the same time the Joint Permit Application is submitted, to the Department containing a description of all activities that will occur in upland areas, including activities in or related to (i) slopes with a grade greater than 15 percent; (ii) karst geology features, including sinkholes and underground springs; (iii) proximity to sensitive streams and wetlands identified by the Department of Conservation and Recreation or the Department of Wildlife Resources; (iv) seasonally high water tables; (v) water impoundment structures and reservoirs; and (vi) areas with highly erodible soils, low pH, and acid sulfate soils. Concurrently with the Joint Permit Application, the applicant shall also submit a detailed erosion and sediment control plan and stormwater management plan subject to Department review and approval.

B. After receipt of an application in accordance with subsection A, the Department shall issue a request for information about how the erosion and sediment control plan and stormwater management plan will address activities in or related to the upland areas identified in subsection A. The response to such request shall include the specific strategies and best management practices that will be utilized by the applicant to address challenges associated with each area type and an explanation of how such strategies and best management practices will ensure compliance with water quality standards.

C. At any time during the review of the application, but prior to issuing a certification pursuant to this article, the Department may issue an information request to the applicant for any relevant additional information necessary to determine (i) if any activities related to the applicant's project in upland areas are likely to result in a discharge to state waters and (ii) how the applicant proposes to minimize water quality impacts to the maximum extent practicable to protect water quality. The information request shall provide a reasonable amount of time for the applicant to respond.

D. The Department shall review the information contained in the application, the response to the information request in subsection B, and any additional information obtained through any information requests issued pursuant to subsection C to determine if any activities described in the application or in any additional information requests (i) are likely to result in a discharge to state waters with the potential to adversely impact water quality and (ii) will not be addressed by the Virginia Water Protection Permit issued for the activity pursuant to Article 2.2 (§ 62.1-44.15:20 et seq.). The Department of Wildlife Resources, the Department of Conservation and Recreation, the Department of Health, and the Department of Agriculture and Consumer Services shall consult with the Department during the review of the application and any additional information obtained through any information requests issued pursuant to subsection B or C. Following the conclusion of its review, the Department shall develop a draft certification or denial. A draft certification, including (i) any additional conditions for activities in upland areas necessary to protect water quality and (ii) a condition that the applicant shall not commence land-disturbing activity prior to approval by the Department of the erosion and sediment control plan and stormwater management plan required pursuant to subsection E, shall be noticed for public comment and potential issuance by the Department. The Department shall make the information contained in the application and any additional information obtained through any information requests issued pursuant to subsection B or C available to the public.

E. Notwithstanding any applicable annual standards and specifications for erosion and sediment control or stormwater management pursuant to Article 2.3 (§ 62.1-44.15:24 et seq.) or 2.4 (§ 62.1-44.15:51 et seq.), the applicant shall not commence land-disturbing activity prior to resolution of any unresolved issues identified in subsection B to the satisfaction of the Department and approval by the Department of an erosion and sediment control plan and stormwater management plan in accordance with applicable regulations. The Department shall act on any plan submittal within 60 days after initial submittal of a completed plan to the Department. The Department may issue either approval or disapproval and shall provide written rationale for its decision. The Department shall act on any plan that has been previously disapproved within 30 days after the plan has been revised and resubmitted for approval.

F. No action by either the Department or the Board on a certification pursuant to this article shall alter the siting determination made through Federal Energy Regulatory Commission or State Corporation Commission approval.

G. The Department shall assess an administrative charge to the applicant to cover the direct costs of services rendered associated with its responsibilities pursuant to this section.

H. Neither the Department nor the Board shall expressly waive certification of a natural gas transmission pipeline of greater than 36 inches inside diameter under § 401 of the federal Clean Water Act (33 U.S.C. § 1341). The Department or the Board shall act on any certification request within a reasonable period of time pursuant to federal law. Nothing in this section shall be construed to prohibit the Department or the Board from taking action to deny a certification in accordance with the provisions of § 401 of the federal Clean Water Act (33 U.S.C. § 1341).

History.
2018, c. 636; 2020, c. 958; 2021, Sp. Sess. I, c. 501; 2022, c. 356.

The 2020 amendments.
The 2020 amendment by c. 958, in subsection A, clause (iii) and subsection C, second sentence, substituted "Department of Wildlife Resources" for "Department of Game and Inland Fisheries."

The 2021 Sp. Sess. I amendments.
The 2021 amendment by Sp. Sess. I, c. 501, effective July 1, 2021, added the last sentence in subsection A; inserted subsection B, and redesignated the remaining subsections accordingly; in subsection D, in the first sentence, inserted "the response to the information request in subsection B," substituted "subsection C" for "subsection B," added "or C" in the second

sentence, and rewrote the former next-to-last sentence, which read: "Following the conclusion of its review, the Department shall develop a draft certification for public comment and potential issuance by the Department or the Board pursuant to § 62.1-44.15:02 that contains any additional conditions for activities in upland areas necessary to protect water quality"; in subsection E, inserted "resolution of any unresolved issues identified in subsection B to the satisfaction of the Department and" in the first sentence, and substituted "its decision" for "any disapproval"; and added subsection H.

The 2022 amendments.
The 2022 amendment by c. 356 deleted "or the Board pursuant to § 62.1-44.15:02" following "by the Department" in subsection D in the penultimate sentence.

§ 62.1-44.15:83. Requests for public hearing, hearings, and final decisions procedures.

A. The issuance of a certification pursuant to this article shall be a permit action.

B. The Department shall assess an administrative charge to the applicant to cover the direct costs of services rendered associated with its responsibilities pursuant to this section.

History.
2018, c. 636; 2022, c. 356.

The 2022 amendments.
The 2022 amendment by c. 356 deleted "for

purposes of § 62.1-44.15:02" in subsection A at the end.

ARTICLE 4.

REGULATION OF SEWAGE DISCHARGES.

§ 62.1-44.19:1. Prohibiting sewage discharge under certain conditions in Virginia Beach.

If the Board or the State Department of Health determines that a receiving stream in the City of Virginia Beach is being polluted by the sewage discharge from a private or public sewage utility, and that it is possible to connect such utility to the sewage system of a municipality, sewage treatment authority, or sanitation district, the Board may order the utility in the City of Virginia Beach to stop such discharge into the receiving stream. The utility shall discontinue such discharge within one year of such order by providing either (i) adequate treatment as determined by the Board or the State Department of Health or (ii) a connection to central facilities.

History.
1972, c. 840; 2022, c. 235.

The 2022 amendments.
The 2022 amendment by c. 235 rewrote the

section, which read: "Whenever the State Department of Health or the State Water Control Board determines that a receiving stream in Virginia Beach is being polluted by the sewage discharge from a private or public sewage utility, and that it is possible to connect such utility to the sewage system of a municipality, sewage treatment authority, or sanitation district, the Board is hereby empowered to order the utility in Virginia Beach to stop such discharge into the receiving stream. The utility shall discontinue the said discharge either by adequate treatment as determined the State Department of Health or Water Control Board, or by a connection to central facilities, either of which is to occur within one year."

§ 62.1-44.19:2. Additional requirements on sewage discharge in the Cities of Chesapeake, Hampton, Newport News, Norfolk and Virginia Beach.

A. Beginning January 1, 1973, every sewage pumping station in the Cities of Chesapeake, Hampton, Newport News, Norfolk, and Virginia Beach shall:

1. Have adequate personnel on call at all times, each of whom may serve multiple pumping stations, as prescribed by the Chesapeake, Hampton, Newport News, Norfolk, or Virginia Beach City Council, respectively;

2. As prescribed by the Board, be inspected at such intervals and maintain such records of inspection. Such records shall be open for review by the Board or its representatives at any reasonable time it designates;

3. Have an automatic alarm system installed to give immediate warning of any pump station failure;

4. Have emergency pump connections installed and have portable pumps available to pump sewage to downstream sewer lines during any period of pump station failure;

5. Not use, except in an emergency pursuant to regulations as provided by the Board, any overflow line from any such pumping station except as provided in subdivision 4.

B. Any sewerage system within the City of Chesapeake, Hampton, Newport News, Norfolk, or Virginia Beach that complies with the requirements of this section is deemed to meet the requirements for continuous operability as set forth in regulations of the Board or the State Department of Health.

History.
1972, c. 840; 1975, c. 373; 1976, c. 188; 2022, c. 235.

The 2022 amendments.
The 2022 amendment by c. 235 added the subsection designations and made stylistic changes.

ARTICLE 4.01.
WATER QUALITY MONITORING, INFORMATION AND RESTORATION ACT.

§ 62.1-44.19:6. Citizen right-to-know provisions.

A. The Board, based on the information in the 303(d) and 305(b) reports, shall:

1. Request the Department of Wildlife Resources or the Virginia Marine Resources Commission to post notices at public access points to all toxic impaired waters. The notice shall be prepared by the Board and shall contain (i) the basis for the impaired designation and (ii) a statement of the potential health risks provided by the Virginia Department of Health. The Board shall annually notify local newspapers, and persons who request notice, of any posting and its contents. The Board shall coordinate with the Virginia Marine

Resources Commission and the Department of Wildlife Resources to assure that adequate notice of posted waters is provided to those purchasing hunting and fishing licenses.

2. Maintain a "citizen hot-line" for citizens to obtain, either telephonically or electronically, information about the condition of waterways, including information on toxics, toxic discharges, permit violations and other water quality related issues.

3. Make information regarding the presence of toxics in fish tissue and sediments available to the public on the Internet and through other reasonable means for at least five years after the information is received by the Department of Environmental Quality. The Department of Environmental Quality shall post on the Internet and in the Virginia Register on or about January 1 and July 1 of each year an announcement of any new data that has been received over the past six months and shall make a copy of the information available upon request.

B. The Department of Environmental Quality shall provide to the Virginia Department of Health and local newspapers, television stations, and radio stations, and shall disseminate via official social media accounts and email notification lists, the discharge information reported to the Director of the Department of Environmental Quality pursuant to subsection B of § 62.1-44.5, when the Virginia Department of Health determines that the discharge may be detrimental to the public health or the Department determines that the discharge may impair beneficial uses of state waters.

History.
1997, c. 519; 2000, cc. 17, 1043; 2020, cc. 958, 1182.

on the beneficial uses of state waters. The Department of Environmental Quality shall consult with the Virginia Department of Health in preparing such report."

Editor's note.
Acts 2020, c. 1182, cl. 2 provides: "That by December 1, 2020, the Department of Environmental Quality shall report to the General Assembly (i) a protocol that could be used to determine whether a discharge would have a de minimis impact on the beneficial uses of state waters and (ii) a proposed implementation procedure if subsection B of § 62.1-44.19:6 of the Code of Virginia were to be amended to require dissemination to media outlets, social media accounts, and email distribution lists of all discharges reported pursuant to subsection B of § 62.1-44.5 of the Code of Virginia except for those determined to have a de minimis impact

The 2020 amendments.
The 2020 amendment by c. 958 substituted "Department of Wildlife Resources" for "Department of Game and Inland Fisheries" in subdivision A 1 in the first and last sentences.

The 2020 amendment by c. 1182 rewrote subsection B, which read: "The Board shall provide to a local newspaper the discharge information reported to the Director of Department of Environmental Quality pursuant to § 62.1-44.5, when the Virginia Department of Health determines that the discharge may be detrimental to the public health or the Board determines that the discharge may impair beneficial uses of state waters."

ARTICLE 4.02.

CHESAPEAKE BAY WATERSHED NUTRIENT CREDIT EXCHANGE PROGRAM.

§ 62.1-44.19:13. Definitions.

As used in this article, unless the context requires a different meaning:

"Annual mass load of total nitrogen" (expressed in pounds per year) means the daily total nitrogen concentration (expressed as mg/L to the nearest 0.01 mg/L) multiplied by the flow volume of effluent discharged during the 24-hour period (expressed as MGD to the nearest 0.01 MGD), multiplied by 8.34 and

rounded to the nearest whole number to convert to pounds per day (lbs/day) units, then totaled for the calendar month to convert to pounds per month (lbs/mo) units, and then totaled for the calendar year to convert to pounds per year (lbs/yr) units.

"*Annual mass load of total phosphorus*" (expressed in pounds per year) means the daily total phosphorus concentration (expressed as mg/L to the nearest 0.01mg/L) multiplied by the flow volume of effluent discharged during the 24-hour period (expressed as MGD to the nearest 0.01 MGD) multiplied by 8.34 and rounded to the nearest whole number to convert to pounds per day (lbs/day) units, then totaled for the calendar month to convert to pounds per month (lbs/mo) units, and then totaled for the calendar year to convert to pounds per year (lbs/yr) units.

"*Association*" means the Virginia Nutrient Credit Exchange Association authorized by this article.

"*Attenuation*" means the rate at which nutrients are reduced through natural processes during transport in water.

"*Best management practice,*" "*practice,*" or "*BMP*" means a structural practice, nonstructural practice, or other management practice used to prevent or reduce nutrient loads associated with stormwater from reaching surface waters or the adverse effects thereof.

"*Biological nutrient removal technology*" means (i) technology that will achieve an annual average total nitrogen effluent concentration of eight milligrams per liter and an annual average total phosphorus effluent concentration of one milligram per liter, or (ii) equivalent reductions in loads of total nitrogen and total phosphorus through the recycle or reuse of wastewater as determined by the Department.

"*Delivered total nitrogen load*" means the discharged mass load of total nitrogen from a point source that is adjusted by the delivery factor for that point source.

"*Delivered total phosphorus load*" means the discharged mass load of total phosphorus from a point source that is adjusted by the delivery factor for that point source.

"*Delivery factor*" means an estimate of the number of pounds of total nitrogen or total phosphorus delivered to tidal waters for every pound discharged from a permitted facility, as determined by the specific geographic location of the permitted facility, to account for attenuation that occurs during riverine transport between the permitted facility and tidal waters. Delivery factors shall be calculated using the Chesapeake Bay Program watershed model.

"*Department*" means the Department of Environmental Quality.

"*Enhanced Nutrient Removal Certainty Program*" or "*ENRC Program*" means the Phase III Watershed Implementation Plan Enhanced Nutrient Removal Certainty Program established pursuant to subsection G of § 62.1-44.19:14.

"*Equivalent load*" means 2,300 pounds per year of total nitrogen and 300 pounds per year of total phosphorus at a flow volume of 40,000 gallons per day; 5,700 pounds per year of total nitrogen and 760 pounds per year of total phosphorus at a flow volume of 100,000 gallons per day; and 28,500 pounds per year of total nitrogen and 3,800 pounds per year of total phosphorus at a flow volume of 500,000 gallons per day.

"*Facility*" means a point source discharging or proposing to discharge total nitrogen or total phosphorus to the Chesapeake Bay or its tributaries. This term does not include confined animal feeding operations, discharges of stormwater, return flows from irrigated agriculture, or vessels.

"*General permit*" means the general permit authorized by this article.

"MS4" means a municipal separate storm sewer system.

"Nutrient credit" or *"credit"* means a nutrient reduction that is certified pursuant to this article and expressed in pounds of phosphorus or nitrogen either (i) delivered to tidal waters when the credit is generated within the Chesapeake Bay Watershed or (ii) as otherwise specified when generated in the Southern Rivers watersheds. "Nutrient credit" does not include point source nitrogen credits or point source phosphorus credits as defined in this section.

"Nutrient credit-generating entity" means an entity that generates nonpoint source nutrient credits.

"Permitted facility" means a facility authorized by the general permit to discharge total nitrogen or total phosphorus. For the sole purpose of generating point source nitrogen credits or point source phosphorus credits, "permitted facility" shall also mean the Blue Plains wastewater treatment facility operated by the District of Columbia Water and Sewer Authority.

"Permittee" means a person authorized by the general permit to discharge total nitrogen or total phosphorus.

"Point source nitrogen credit" means the difference between (i) the waste load allocation for a permitted facility specified as an annual mass load of total nitrogen, and (ii) the monitored annual mass load of total nitrogen discharged by that facility, where clause (ii) is less than clause (i), and where the difference is adjusted by the applicable delivery factor and expressed as pounds per year of delivered total nitrogen load.

"Point source phosphorus credit" means the difference between (i) the waste load allocation for a permitted facility specified as an annual mass load of total phosphorus, and (ii) the monitored annual mass load of total phosphorus discharged by that facility, where clause (ii) is less than clause (i), and where the difference is adjusted by the applicable delivery factor and expressed as pounds per year of delivered total phosphorus load.

"State-of-the-art nutrient removal technology" means (i) technology that will achieve an annual average total nitrogen effluent concentration of three milligrams per liter and an annual average total phosphorus effluent concentration of 0.3 milligrams per liter, or (ii) equivalent load reductions in total nitrogen and total phosphorus through recycle or reuse of wastewater as determined by the Department.

"Tributaries" means those river basins listed in the Chesapeake Bay TMDL and includes the Potomac, Rappahannock, York, and James River Basins, and the Eastern Shore, which encompasses the creeks and rivers of the Eastern Shore of Virginia that are west of Route 13 and drain into the Chesapeake Bay.

"Waste load allocation" means (i) the water quality-based annual mass load of total nitrogen or annual mass load of total phosphorus allocated to individual facilities pursuant to the Water Quality Management Planning Regulation (9VAC25-720) or its successor, or permitted capacity in the case of nonsignificant dischargers; (ii) the water quality-based annual mass load of total nitrogen or annual mass load of total phosphorus acquired pursuant to § 62.1-44.19:15 for new or expanded facilities; or (iii) applicable total nitrogen or total phosphorus waste load allocations under the Chesapeake Bay total maximum daily loads (TMDLs) to restore or protect the water quality and beneficial uses of the Chesapeake Bay or its tidal tributaries.

History.

2005, cc. 708, 710; 2012, cc. 748, 808; 2013, cc. 756, 793; 2015, c. 164; 2021, Sp. Sess. I, cc. 363, 364.

Editor's note.

Acts 2021, Sp. Sess. I, cc. 363 and 364, cl. 4 provides: "That if the Secretary of Natural and Historic Resources (the Secretary) determines on or after July 1, 2026, that the Commonwealth has not achieved, or in the event of increased nutrient loads associated with climate change will not be able to maintain, its nitrogen pollution reduction commitments in the Chesapeake Bay Total Maximum Daily Load (TMDL) Phase III Watershed Implementation Plan, the Secretary may develop an additional watershed implementation plan or plans pursuant to § 2.2-218 of the Code of Virginia. Any such plan shall take into consideration the progress made by all point and nonpoint sources toward meeting applicable load and waste load allocations, the best available science and water quality modeling, and any applicable U.S. Environmental Protection Agency guidance for Chesapeake Bay TMDL implementation. In any such plan, the Secretary may include as priority projects upgrades with nutrient removal technology of 4.0 mg/L annual average total nitrogen concentration at municipal wastewater treatment facilities with a design capacity greater than 10.0 MGD discharging to James River Segment JMSTF2 so long as (i) the scheduled date for compliance is January 1, 2036; (ii) notwithstanding the wasteload allocations specified in clause (iii), compliance requires operating the nutrient removal technology to achieve an annual average total nitrogen concentration of less than or equal to 4.0 mg/L or, until such time as the facility is upgraded to achieve such concentration, the option of achieving an equivalent discharged load based on an annual average total nitrogen concentration of 4.0 mg/L and actual annual flow treated, including the use of point source nitrogen credits; and (iii) the facilities have and retain the following total nitrogen waste load allocations: Falling Creek WWTP (182,738 lbs/year), Proctors Creek WWTP (411,151 lbs/year and, in the event that Proctors Creek WWTP is expanded in accordance with 9VAC25-40-70 and Falling Creek WWTP is upgraded to achieve 4.0 mg/L, 493,391 lbs/year), and Henrico County WWTP (1,142,085 lbs/year). If the Secretary opts to include such facilities in the plan, the State Water Control Board shall include the foregoing concentrations limits, waste load allocations, and schedules for compliance in the Water Quality Management Planning Regulation, the Watershed General Virginia Pollutant Discharge Elimination System permit, and individual VPDES permits, as applicable."

The 2021 Sp. Sess. I amendments.

The 2021 amendments by Sp. Sess. I, cc. 363 and 364, effective July 1, 2021, are identical, and inserted the definition for "Enhanced Nutrient Removal Certainty Program" or "ENRC Program."

§ 62.1-44.19:14. Watershed general permit for nutrients.

A. The Board shall issue a Watershed General Virginia Pollutant Discharge Elimination System Permit, hereafter referred to as the general permit, authorizing point source discharges of total nitrogen and total phosphorus to the waters of the Chesapeake Bay and its tributaries. Except as otherwise provided in this article, the general permit shall control in lieu of technology-based, water quality-based, and best professional judgment, interim or final effluent limitations for total nitrogen and total phosphorus in individual Virginia Pollutant Discharge Elimination System permits for facilities covered by the general permit where the effluent limitations for total nitrogen and total phosphorus in the individual permits are based upon standards, criteria, waste load allocations, policy, or guidance established to restore or protect the water quality and beneficial uses of the Chesapeake Bay or its tidal tributaries.

B. This section shall not be construed to limit or otherwise affect the Board's authority to establish and enforce more stringent water quality-based effluent limitations for total nitrogen or total phosphorus in individual permits where those limitations are necessary to protect local water quality. The exchange or acquisition of credits pursuant to this article shall not affect any requirement to comply with such local water quality-based limitations.

C. The general permit shall contain the following:

1. Waste load allocations for total nitrogen and total phosphorus for each permitted facility expressed as annual mass loads, including reduced waste load allocations where applicable under the ENRC Program. The allocations for each permitted facility shall reflect the applicable individual water quality-based total nitrogen and total phosphorus waste load allocations. An owner or operator of two or more facilities located in the same tributary may apply for

and receive an aggregated waste load allocation for total nitrogen and an aggregated waste load allocation for total phosphorus for multiple facilities reflecting the total of the water quality-based total nitrogen and total phosphorus waste load allocations established for such facilities individually;

2. A schedule requiring compliance with the combined waste load allocations for each tributary as soon as possible taking into account (i) opportunities to minimize costs to the public or facility owners by phasing in the implementation of multiple projects; (ii) the availability of required services and skilled labor; (iii) the availability of funding from the Virginia Water Quality Improvement Fund as established in § 10.1-2128, the Virginia Water Facilities Revolving Fund as established in § 62.1-225, and other financing mechanisms; (iv) water quality conditions; and (v) other relevant factors. Following receipt of the compliance plans required by subdivision C 3, the Board shall reevaluate the schedule taking into account the information in the compliance plans and the factors in this subdivision, and may modify the schedule as appropriate;

3. A requirement that the permittees shall either individually or through the Association submit compliance plans to the Department for approval. The compliance plans shall contain, at a minimum, any capital projects and implementation schedules needed to achieve total nitrogen and phosphorus reductions sufficient to comply with the individual and combined waste load allocations of all the permittees in the tributary. The compliance plans may rely on the exchange of point source credits in accordance with this article, but not the acquisition of credits through payments authorized by § 62.1-44.19:18, to achieve compliance with the individual and combined waste load allocations in each tributary. The compliance plans shall be updated annually and submitted to the Department no later than February 1 of each year. The compliance plans due beginning February 1, 2023, shall address the requirements of the ENRC Program;

4. Such monitoring and reporting requirements as the Board deems necessary to carry out the provisions of this article;

5. A procedure that requires every owner or operator of a facility authorized by a Virginia Pollutant Discharge Elimination System permit to discharge 100,000 gallons or more per day, or an equivalent load, directly into tidal waters, or 500,000 gallons or more per day, or an equivalent load, directly into nontidal waters, to secure general permit coverage by filing a registration statement with the Department within a specified period after each effective date of the general permit. The procedure shall also require any owner or operator of a facility authorized by a Virginia Pollutant Discharge Elimination System permit to discharge 40,000 gallons or more per day, or an equivalent load, directly into tidal or nontidal waters to secure general permit coverage by filing a registration statement with the Department at the time he makes application with the Department for a new discharge or expansion that is subject to an offset or technology-based requirement in § 62.1-44.19:15, and thereafter within a specified period of time after each effective date of the general permit. The procedure shall also require any owner or operator of a facility with a discharge that is subject to an offset requirement in subdivision A 5 of § 62.1-44.19:15 to secure general permit coverage by filing a registration statement with the Department prior to commencing the discharge and thereafter within a specified period of time after each effective date of the general permit. The general permit shall provide that any facility authorized by a Virginia Pollutant Discharge Elimination System permit and not required by this subdivision to file a registration statement shall be deemed to be covered under the general permit at the time it is issued, and shall file a registration statement with the Department when required by this section. Owners or operators of facilities that are deemed to be permitted under this

section shall have no other obligation under the general permit prior to filing a registration statement and securing coverage under the general permit based upon such registration statement;

6. A procedure for efficiently modifying the lists of facilities covered by the general permit where the modification does not change or otherwise alter any waste load allocation or delivery factor adopted pursuant to the Water Quality Management Planning Regulation (9VAC25-720) or its successor, or an applicable total maximum daily load. The procedure shall also provide for modifying or incorporating new waste load allocations or delivery factors, including the opportunity for public notice and comment on such modifications or incorporations; and

7. Such other conditions as the Board deems necessary to carry out the provisions of this chapter and § 402 of the federal Clean Water Act (33 U.S.C. § 1342).

D. 1. The Board shall (i) review during the year 2020 and every 10 years thereafter the basis for allocations granted in the Water Quality Management Planning Regulation (9VAC25-720) and (ii) as a result of such decennial reviews propose for inclusion in the Water Quality Management Planning Regulation (9VAC25-720) either the reallocation of unneeded allocations to other facilities registered under the general permit or the reservation of such allocations for future use.

2. For each decennial review, the Board shall determine whether a permitted facility has:

a. Changed the use of the facility in such a way as to make discharges unnecessary, ceased the discharge of nutrients, and become unlikely to resume such discharges in the foreseeable future; or

b. Changed the production processes employed in the facility in such a way as to render impossible, or significantly to diminish the likelihood of, the resumption of previous nutrient discharges.

3. Beginning in 2030, each review also shall consider the following factors for municipal wastewater facilities:

a. Substantial changes in the size or population of a service area;

b. Significant changes in land use resulting from adopted changes to zoning ordinances or comprehensive plans within a service area;

c. Significant establishment of conservation easements or other perpetual instruments that are associated with a deed and that restrict growth or development;

d. Constructed treatment facility capacity;

e. Significant changes in the understanding of the water chemistry or biology of receiving waters that would reasonably result in unused nutrient discharge allocations over an extended period of time;

f. Significant changes in treatment technologies that would reasonably result in unused nutrient discharge allocations over an extended period of time;

g. The ability of the permitted facility to accommodate projected growth under existing nutrient waste load allocations; and

h. Other similarly significant factors that the Board determines reasonably to affect the allocations granted.

The Board shall not reduce allocations based solely on voluntary improvements in nutrient removal technology.

E. The Board shall maintain and make available to the public a current listing, by tributary, of all permittees and permitted facilities under the general permit, together with each permitted facility's total nitrogen and total phosphorus waste load allocations, and total nitrogen and total phosphorus delivery factors.

F. Except as otherwise provided in this article, in the event that there are conflicting or duplicative conditions contained in the general permit and an individual Virginia Pollutant Discharge Elimination System permit, the conditions in the general permit shall control.

G. The Board shall adopt amendments to the Water Quality Management Planning Regulation and modifications to Virginia Pollutant Discharge Elimination System permits or registration lists to establish and implement the Phase III Watershed Implementation Plan Enhanced Nutrient Removal Certainty Program (ENRC Program) as provided in this subsection. The ENRC Program shall consist of the following projects and the following waste load allocation reductions and their respective schedules for compliance.

1. Priority projects for additional nitrogen and phosphorus removal (schedule for compliance):

PROJECT NAME	DESCRIPTION (COMPLIANCE SCHEDULE)
HRSD-Chesapeake/Elizabeth STP	Consolidate into regional system and close treatment facility (1/1/2023)
HRSD-Boat Harbor WWTP	Convey by subaqueous crossing to Nansemond River WWTP for nutrient removal (1/1/2026)
HRSD-Nansemond River WWTP	Upgrade and expand with nutrient removal technology of 4.0 mg/L total nitrogen (1/1/2026) and 0.30 mg/L total phosphorus (1/1/2032)
HRSD-Nassawadox WWTP	Convey to regional system for nutrient removal (1/1/2026)
Fredericksburg WWTF	Expand with nutrient removal technology of 3.0 mg/L total nitrogen and 0.22 mg/L total phosphorus (1/1/2026)
Spotsylvania Co.-FMC WWTF	Convey to Massaponax WWTF and close treatment facility (1/1/2026)
Spotsylvania Co.-Massaponax WWTF	Expand with nutrient removal technology of 4.0 mg/L total nitrogen and 0.30 mg/L total phosphorus to consolidate and close FMC WWTF (1/1/2026)
Spotsylvania Co.-Thornburg STP	Upgrade with nutrient removal technology of 4.0 mg/L total nitrogen and 0.30 mg/L total phosphorus (1/1/2026)
HRRSA-North River WWTP	Phosphorus removal tertiary filtration upgrade (1/1/2026)
South Central Wastewater Authority WWTF	Upgrade with nutrient removal technology of 4.0 mg/L total nitrogen and 0.30 mg/L total phosphorus (1/1/2026)
HRSD-Williamsburg WWTP	Upgrade with nutrient removal technology of 4.0 mg/L total nitrogen (1/1/2026) and 0.30 mg/L total phosphorus (1/1/2032)
HRSD-VIP WWTP	Upgrade with nutrient removal technology of 4.0 mg/L total nitrogen (1/1/2026) and 0.30 mg/L total phosphorus (1/1/2032)

HRSD-James River WWTP — Upgrade with nutrient removal technology of 4.0 mg/L total nitrogen (1/1/2026) and 0.30 mg/L total phosphorus (1/1/2028)

HRSD-Army Base WWTP — Convey to VIP WWTP for nutrient removal (1/1/2032) or upgrade with nutrient removal technology of 4.0 mg/L total nitrogen (1/1/2026) and 0.30 mg/L total phosphorus (1/1/2032)

Each priority project and the associated schedule of compliance shall be incorporated into the applicable Virginia Pollutant Discharge Elimination System permit or registration list. Each priority project facility shall be in compliance (i) by complying with applicable annual average total nitrogen and total phosphorus concentrations for compliance years 2026, 2028, and 2032; (ii) for the South Central Wastewater Authority WWTF, by implementing a phased construction program approved by the Department, and acquiring sufficient point source credits until its phased construction is completed as provided in this subsection; or (iii) only for a facility subject to an aggregated waste load allocation, by exercising the option of achieving an equivalent discharged load by the date set out in the schedule of compliance based on the applicable total nitrogen and total phosphorus annual average concentrations and actual annual flow treated without the acquisition and use of point source credits generated by permitted facilities not under common ownership. Noncompliance shall be enforceable in the same manner as any other condition of a Virginia Pollutant Discharge Elimination System permit.

The following requirements shall apply to the phased construction program to upgrade the South Central Wastewater Authority WWTF: (a) by August 1, 2023, the South Central Wastewater Authority (SCWWA) shall submit a phased construction program to the Department, which shall review and approve such program by September 1, 2023, or as soon as possible thereafter;(b) by December 31, 2023, or within 150 days of approval by the Department of the phased construction program, whichever is later, SCWWA shall commence construction of the initial phase of construction; (c) by February 1, 2024, and annually thereafter, SCWWA shall submit a progress report to the Department describing its progress toward completing the phased construction program; (d) within 30 days of substantial completion of each major phase of construction, SCWWA shall submit an application for a certificate to operate to the Department and promptly place the associated treatment units into operation; (e) the phased construction program for the SCWWA WWTF priority project shall be completed as soon as possible on the schedule approved by the Department but no later than January 1, 2030; and (f) for each compliance year during the phased construction program that the facility does not achieve the nutrient removal technology concentration specified in this subsection, the SCWWA WWTF shall be responsible for acquiring sufficient point source credits to comply with its total nitrogen and total phosphorus waste load allocations applicable to that compliance year.

2. Nitrogen waste load allocation reductions — HRSD-York River WWTP:

Reduce the total nitrogen waste load allocation for the HRSD-York River WWTP to 228,444 lbs/year effective January 1, 2026.

3. James River HRSD SWIFT nutrient upgrades:

Reduce total nitrogen waste load allocations for HRSD treatment works in the James River basin to the following allocations effective January 1, 2026:

FACILITY NAME	TOTAL NITROGEN WASTELOAD ALLOCATION (lbs/year)
HRSD-Army Base WWTP	219,307
HRSD-Boat Harbor STP	304,593
HRSD-James River STP	243,674
HRSD-VIP WWTP	487,348
HRSD-Nansemond STP	365,511
HRSD-Williamsburg STP	274,133

Reduce total phosphorus waste load allocations for HRSD treatment works in the James River basin to the following allocations effective January 1, 2026:

FACILITY NAME	TOTAL PHOSPHORUS WASTELOAD ALLOCATION (lbs/year)
HRSD-Army Base WWTP	27,413
HRSD-Boat Harbor STP	38,074
HRSD-James River STP	30,459
HRSD-VIP WWTP	60,919
HRSD-Nansemond STP	45,689
HRSD-Williamsburg STP	34,267

Reduce total phosphorus waste load allocations for HRSD treatment works in the James River basin to the following allocations effective January 1, 2030:

FACILITY NAME	TOTAL PHOSPHORUS WASTELOAD ALLOCATION (lbs/year)
HRSD-Army Base WWTP	21,931
HRSD-Boat Harbor STP	30,459
HRSD-James River STP	24,367
HRSD-VIP WWTP	48,735
HRSD-Nansemond STP	36,551
HRSD-Williamsburg STP	27,413

Reduce total phosphorus waste load allocations for HRSD treatment works in the James River basin to the following allocations effective January 1, 2032:

FACILITY NAME	TOTAL PHOSPHORUS WASTELOAD ALLOCATION (lbs/year)
HRSD-Army Base WWTP	16,448
HRSD-Boat Harbor STP	22,844
HRSD-James River STP	18,276
HRSD-VIP WWTP	36,551
HRSD-Nansemond STP	27,413
HRSD-Williamsburg STP	20,560

Transfer the total nitrogen (454,596 lbs/year) and total phosphorus (41,450 lbs/year) waste load allocations for the HRSD-Chesapeake/Elizabeth STP to the Nutrient Offset Fund effective January 1, 2026.

Transfer the total nitrogen (153,500 lbs/yr) and total phosphorous (17,437 lbs/yr) waste load allocations for the HRSD-J.H. Miles Facility consolidation to HRSD in accordance with the approved registration list December 21, 2015, transfer.

History.
2005, cc. 708, 710; 2010, c. 288; 2017, c. 9; 2021, Sp. Sess. I, cc. 363, 364; 2022, cc. 127, 128; 2023, cc. 177, 178.

Editor's note.

Acts 2021, Sp. Sess. I, cc. 363 and 364, cl. 2 provides: "That the Enhanced Nutrient Removal Certainty Program as established in subdivisions G 1, 2, and 3 of § 62.1-44.19:14 of the Code of Virginia, as amended by this act, shall be deemed to implement through January 1, 2026, the Commonwealth's Chesapeake Bay Phase III Watershed Implementation Plan in lieu of the floating waste load allocation concept proposed in Initiative 52 of the Commonwealth's Chesapeake Bay Phase III Watershed Implementation Plan. However, nothing in this act shall be construed to limit the State Water Control Board's authority to impose (i) additional requirements or modifications to phosphorous waste load allocations necessary to achieve compliance with the numeric chlorophyll-a criteria applicable to the James River; (ii) requirements or modifications to waste load allocations necessary to comply with changes to federal law that become effective after January 1, 2021; or (iii) requirements or modifications to waste load allocations necessary to comply with a court order issued after January 1, 2021."

Acts 2021, Sp. Sess. I, cc. 363 and 364, cl. 3 provides: "That the State Water Control Board shall modify the Virginia Pollutant Discharge Elimination System (VPDES) permits for the facilities listed in subdivision G 1 of § 62.1-44.19:14 of the Code of Virginia, as amended by this act, to include any requirements and compliance schedules established in this act."

Acts 2021, Sp. Sess. I, cc. 363 and 364, cl. 4 provides: "That if the Secretary of Natural and Historic Resources (the Secretary) determines on or after July 1, 2026, that the Commonwealth has not achieved, or in the event of increased nutrient loads associated with climate change will not be able to maintain, its nitrogen pollution reduction commitments in the Chesapeake Bay Total Maximum Daily Load (TMDL) Phase III Watershed Implementation Plan, the Secretary may develop an additional watershed implementation plan or plans pursuant to § 2.2-218 of the Code of Virginia. Any such plan shall take into consideration the progress made by all point and nonpoint sources toward meeting applicable load and waste load allocations, the best available science and water quality modeling, and any applicable U.S. Environmental Protection Agency guidance for Chesapeake Bay TMDL implementation. In any such plan, the Secretary may include as priority projects upgrades with nutrient removal technology of 4.0 mg/L annual average total nitrogen concentration at municipal wastewater treatment facilities with a design capacity greater than 10.0 MGD discharging to James River Segment JMSTF2 so long as (i) the scheduled date for compliance is January 1, 2036; (ii) notwithstanding the wasteload allocations specified in clause (iii), compliance requires operating the nutrient removal technology to achieve an annual average total nitrogen concentration of less than or equal to 4.0 mg/L or, until such time as the facility is upgraded to achieve such concentration, the option of achieving an equivalent discharged load based on an annual average total nitrogen concentration of 4.0 mg/L and actual annual flow treated, including the use of point source nitrogen credits; and (iii) the facilities have and retain the following total nitrogen waste load allocations: Falling Creek WWTP (182,738 lbs/year), Proctors Creek WWTP (411,151 lbs/year and, in the event that Proctors Creek WWTP is expanded in accordance with 9VAC25-40-70 and Falling Creek WWTP is upgraded to achieve 4.0 mg/L, 493,391 lbs/year), and Henrico County WWTP (1,142,085 lbs/year). If the Secretary opts to include such facilities in the plan, the State Water Control Board shall include the foregoing concentrations limits, waste load allocations, and schedules for compliance in the Water Quality Management Planning Regulation, the Watershed General Virginia Pollutant Discharge Elimination System permit, and individual VPDES permits, as applicable."

Acts 2022, cc. 127 and 128, cl. 2 provides: "That the nutrient technology requirements of 3.0 mg/L total nitrogen and 0.22 mg/L total phosphorus for the Fredericksburg Waste Water Treatment Facility established in the first enactment clause of this act shall take effect and apply on an annual basis when the expanded Fredericksburg Waste Water Treatment Facility receives its certificate to operate."

Acts 2023, cc. 177 and 178, cl. 2 provides: "That the Department of Environmental Quality, concurrently with its approval of the phased construction program for the upgrade of the South Central Wastewater Authority Wastewater Treatment Facility listed in subdivision G 1 of § 62.1-44.19:14 of the Code of Virginia, as amended by this act, shall execute corresponding amendments to the water quality improvement agreement pursuant to § 10.1-2131 of the Code of Virginia consistent with the scope and schedule of the approved phased construction program."

Acts 2023, cc. 177 and 178, cl. 3 provides: "That the Department of Environmental Quality, by December 31, 2023, or as soon as possible thereafter, shall modify the Virginia Pollutant Discharge Elimination System permit for the South Central Wastewater Authority Wastewater Treatment Facility as listed in subdivision G 1 of § 62.1-44.19:14 of the Code of Virginia, as amended by this act, to include the requirements and compliance schedule established in this act."

The 2021 Sp. Sess. I amendments.

The 2021 amendments by Sp. Sess. I, cc. 363 and 364, effective July 1, 2021, are identical, and substituted "The Board" for "By January 1, 2006, or as soon thereafter as possible, the board" in subsection A; inserted "including reduced waste load allocations where applicable under the ENRC Program" in subdivision C 1; in subdivision C 3, deleted "within nine months after the initial effective date of the general permit" following "A requirement that" and added the last sentence; and added subsection G.

The 2022 amendments.

The 2022 amendments by cc. 127 and 128 are identical, and inserted the entries in both columns for "Fredericksburg WWTF" in subdivision G 1 in the list after the first paragraph.

The 2023 amendments.

The 2023 amendments by cc. 177 and 178 are identical, and added clause (i) designation and (ii) in subdivision G 1 in the first paragraph after the list of projects and added the second paragraph of subdivision G 1.

§ 62.1-44.19:20. (Contingent expiration date — See Editor's note) Nutrient credit certification.

A. The Board may adopt regulations for the purpose of establishing procedures for the certification of point source nutrient credits except that no certification shall be required for point source nitrogen and point source phosphorus credits generated by point sources regulated under the Watershed General Virginia Pollutant Discharge Elimination System Permit issued pursuant to § 62.1-44.19:14. The Board shall adopt regulations for the purpose of establishing procedures for the certification of nonpoint source nutrient credits.

B. Regulations adopted pursuant to this section shall:

1. Establish procedures for the certification and registration of credits, including:

a. Certifying credits that may be generated from effective nutrient controls or removal practices, including activities associated with the types of facilities or practices historically regulated by the Board, such as water withdrawal and treatment and wastewater collection, treatment, and beneficial reuse;

b. Certifying credits that may be generated from agricultural and urban stormwater best management practices, use or management of manures, managed turf, land use conversion, stream or wetlands projects, shellfish aquaculture, algal harvesting, and other established or innovative methods of nutrient control or removal, as appropriate;

c. Establishing a process and standards for wetland or stream credits to be converted to nutrient credits. Such process and standards shall only apply to wetland or stream credits that were established after July 1, 2005, and have not been transferred or used. Under no circumstances shall such credits be used for both wetland or stream credit and nutrient credit purposes;

d. Certifying credits from multiple practices that are bundled as a package by the applicant;

e. Prohibiting the certification of credits generated from activities funded by federal or state water quality grant funds other than controls and practices under subdivision B 1 a; however, baseline levels may be achieved through the use of such grants;

f. Establishing a timely and efficient certification process including application requirements, a reasonable application fee schedule not to exceed $10,000 per application, and review and approval procedures;

g. Requiring public notification of a proposed nutrient credit-generating entity; and

h. Establishing a timeline for the consideration of certification applications for land conversion projects. The timeline shall provide that within 30 days of receipt of an application the Department shall, if warranted, conduct a site visit and that within 45 days of receipt of an application the Department shall either determine that the application is complete or request additional specific information from the applicant. A determination that an application for a land conversion project is complete shall not require the Department to issue the certification. The Department shall deny, approve, or approve with conditions an application within 15 days of the Department's determination that the application is complete. When the request for credit release is made concurrently with the application for a land conversion project certification, the concurrent release shall be processed on the same timeline. When the request for credit release is from a previously approved land conversion project, the Department shall schedule a site visit, if warranted, within 30 days of the request and shall deny, approve, or approve with conditions the release within 15 days of the site visit or determination that a site visit is not warranted. The timelines set out in this subdivision shall be implemented prior to adoption of regulations. The Department shall release credits from a land conversion project after it is satisfied that the applicant has met the criteria for release in an approved nutrient reduction implementation plan.

2. Establish credit calculation procedures for proposed credit-generating practices, including the determination of:

a. Baselines for credits certified under subdivision B 1 a in accordance with any applicable provisions of the Virginia Chesapeake Bay TMDL Watershed Implementation Plan or approved TMDLs;

b. Baselines established for agricultural practices, which shall be those actions necessary to achieve a level of reduction assigned in the Virginia Chesapeake Bay TMDL Watershed Implementation Plan or approved TMDLs as implemented on the tract, field, or other land area under consideration;

c. Baselines for urban practices from new development and redevelopment, which shall be in compliance with postconstruction nutrient loading requirements of the Virginia Stormwater Management Program regulations. Baselines for all other existing development shall be at a level necessary to achieve the reductions assigned in the urban sector in the Virginia Chesapeake Bay TMDL Watershed Implementation Plan or approved TMDLs;

d. Baselines for land use conversion, which shall be based on the preconversion land use and the level of reductions assigned in the Virginia Chesapeake Bay TMDL Watershed Implementation Plan or approved TMDLs applicable to that land use;

e. Baselines for other nonpoint source credit-generating practices, which shall be based on the Virginia Chesapeake Bay TMDL Watershed Implementation Plan or approved TMDLs using the best available scientific and technical information;

f. Unless otherwise established by the Board, for certification within the Chesapeake Bay Watershed a credit-generating practice that involves land use conversion, which shall represent controls beyond those in place as of July 1, 2005. For other waters for which a TMDL has been approved, the practice shall represent controls beyond those in place at the time of TMDL approval;

g. Baseline dates for all other credit-generating practices, which shall be based on the Virginia Chesapeake Bay TMDL Watershed Implementation Plan or approved TMDLs; and

h. Credit quantities, which shall be established using the best available scientific and technical information at the time of certification;

3. Provide certification of credits on an appropriate temporal basis, such as annual, term of years, or perpetual, depending on the nature of the credit-generating practice. A credit shall be certified for a term of no less than 12 months;

4. Establish requirements to reasonably assure the generation of the credit depending on the nature of the credit-generating activity and use, such as legal

instruments for perpetual credits, operation and maintenance requirements, and associated financial assurance requirements. Financial assurance requirements may include letters of credit, escrows, surety bonds, insurance, and where the credits are used or generated by a locality, authority, utility, sanitation district, or permittee operating an MS4 or a point source permitted under this article, its existing tax or rate authority. In lieu of long-term management fund financial assurance mechanisms established or required by regulation for projects generating credits from stream restoration, a third-party long-term steward approved by the Department, such as a public agency, nongovernmental organization or private land manager, may hold long-term management funds in a separate interest-bearing account to be used only for the long-term management of the stream restoration project;

5. Establish appropriate reporting requirements;

6. Provide for the ability of the Department to inspect or audit for compliance with the requirements of such regulations;

7. Provide that the option to acquire nutrient credits for compliance purposes shall not eliminate any requirement to comply with local water quality requirements;

8. Establish a credit retirement requirement whereby five percent of non-point source credits in the Chesapeake Bay Watershed other than controls and practices under subdivision B 1 a are permanently retired at the time of certification pursuant to this section for the purposes of offsetting growth in unregulated nutrient loads; and

9. Establish such other requirements as the Board deems necessary and appropriate.

C. The Board shall certify (i) credits that may be generated from effective nutrient controls or removal practices, including activities associated with the types of facilities or practices historically regulated by the Board, such as water withdrawal and treatment and wastewater collection, treatment, and beneficial reuse, using the best available scientific and technical information and (ii) credits that are located in tributaries outside of the Chesapeake Bay watershed as defined in § 62.1-44.15:35, using an average of the nutrient removal rates for each practice identified in Appendix A of the Department's document "Trading Nutrient Reductions from Nonpoint Source Best Management Practices in the Chesapeake Bay Watershed: Guidance for Agricultural Landowners and Your Potential Trading Partners "; however, in the certification and recertification of credits under this subsection, the Department may substitute a delivery factor that is deemed by the Director to be based on the best available scientific and technical information appropriate for the tributaries located outside of the Chesapeake Bay watershed as an alternative to any delivery factor derived from the application of the Chesapeake Bay Program watershed model.

D. The Department shall establish and maintain an online Virginia Nutrient Credit Registry of credits as follows:

1. The registry shall include all nonpoint source credits certified pursuant to this article and may include point source nitrogen and point source phosphorus credits generated from point sources covered by the general permit issued pursuant to § 62.1-44.19:14 or point source nutrient credits certified pursuant to this section at the option of the owner. No other credits shall be valid for compliance purposes.

2. Registration of credits on the registry shall not preclude or restrict the right of the owner of such credits from transferring the credits on such commercial terms as may be established by and between the owner and the regulated or unregulated party acquiring the credits.

3. The Department shall establish procedures for the listing and tracking of credits on the registry, including but not limited to (i) notification of the

availability of new nutrient credits to the locality where the credit-generating practice is implemented at least five business days prior to listing on the registry to provide the locality an opportunity to acquire such credits at fair market value for compliance purposes and (ii) notification that the listing of credits on the registry does not constitute a representation by the Board or the owner that the credits will satisfy the specific regulatory requirements applicable to the prospective user's intended use and that the prospective user is encouraged to contact the Board for technical assistance to identify limitations, if any, applicable to the intended use.

4. The registry shall be publicly accessible without charge.

E. The owner or operator of a nonpoint source nutrient credit-generating entity that fails to comply with the provisions of this section shall be subject to the enforcement and penalty provisions of § 62.1-44.19:22.

F. Nutrient credits from stormwater nonpoint nutrient credit-generating facilities in receipt of a Nonpoint Nutrient Offset Authorization for Transfer letter from the Department prior to July 1, 2012, shall be considered certified nutrient credits and shall not be subject to further certification requirements or to the credit retirement requirement under subdivision B 8. However, such facilities shall be subject to the other provisions of this article, including registration, inspection, reporting, and enforcement.

History.
2012, cc. 748, 808; 2013, cc. 756, 793; 2016, c. 653; 2022, c. 422; 2023, c. 723.

Editor's note.
Acts 2020, c. 1289, Item 377 L 3, as added by Acts 2021, Sp. Sess. I, c. 552, and amended by Acts 2022, Sp. Sess. I, c. 2, Item 378 J 3, effective for the biennium ending June 30, 2023, provides: "Notwithstanding § 62.1-44.19:20, Code of Virginia, the application fee schedule adopted by the State Water Control Board pursuant to § 62.1-44.19:20, Code of Virginia, shall be set at an amount representing no less than 60 percent, not to exceed 62 percent, of the direct costs for the administration, compliance and enforcement of the nutrient credit certification program. To the extent practicable, the Board shall solicit input from affected stakeholders when establishing the new fee structure."

Acts 2022, c. 526, cl. 2 provides: "That the provisions of this act shall become effective 30 days after the Department of Environmental Quality issues guidance regarding the implementation of this act."

The 2022 amendments.
The 2022 amendment by c. 422 added the second to last sentence in subdivision B 4.
The 2022 amendment by c. 526, added the last sentence in subdivision B 4.

The 2023 amendments.
The 2023 amendment by c. 723, in subdivision C, substituted "The" for "Prior to the adoption of such regulations, the" and added "however, in the certification and recertification of credits under this subsection, the Department may substitute a delivery factor that is deemed by the Director to be based on the best available scientific and technical information appropriate for the tributaries located outside of the Chesapeake Bay watershed as an alternative to any delivery factor derived from the application of the Chesapeake Bay Program watershed model".

§ 62.1-44.19:20. (Contingent effective date — See Editor's note) Nutrient credit certification.

A. The Board may adopt regulations for the purpose of establishing procedures for the certification of point source nutrient credits except that no certification shall be required for point source nitrogen and point source phosphorus credits generated by point sources regulated under the Watershed General Virginia Pollutant Discharge Elimination System Permit issued pursuant to § 62.1-44.19:14. The Board shall adopt regulations for the purpose of establishing procedures for the certification of nonpoint source nutrient credits.

B. Regulations adopted pursuant to this section shall:

1. Establish procedures for the certification and registration of credits, including:

a. Certifying credits that may be generated from effective nutrient controls or removal practices, including activities associated with the types of facilities or practices historically regulated by the Board, such as water withdrawal and treatment and wastewater collection, treatment, and beneficial reuse;

b. Certifying credits that may be generated from agricultural and urban stormwater best management practices, use or management of manures, managed turf, land use conversion, stream or wetlands projects, shellfish aquaculture, algal harvesting, and other established or innovative methods of nutrient control or removal, as appropriate;

c. Establishing a process and standards for wetland or stream credits to be converted to nutrient credits. Such process and standards shall only apply to wetland or stream credits that were established after July 1, 2005, and have not been transferred or used. Under no circumstances shall such credits be used for both wetland or stream credit and nutrient credit purposes;

d. Certifying credits from multiple practices that are bundled as a package by the applicant;

e. Prohibiting the certification of credits generated from activities funded by federal or state water quality grant funds other than controls and practices under subdivision B 1 a; however, baseline levels may be achieved through the use of such grants;

f. Establishing a timely and efficient certification process including application requirements, a reasonable application fee schedule not to exceed $10,000 per application, and review and approval procedures;

g. Requiring public notification of a proposed nutrient credit-generating entity; and

h. Establishing a timeline for the consideration of certification applications for land conversion projects. The timeline shall provide that within 30 days of receipt of an application the Department shall, if warranted, conduct a site visit and that within 45 days of receipt of an application the Department shall either determine that the application is complete or request additional specific information from the applicant. A determination that an application for a land conversion project is complete shall not require the Department to issue the certification. The Department shall deny, approve, or approve with conditions an application within 15 days of the Department's determination that the application is complete. When the request for credit release is made concurrently with the application for a land conversion project certification, the concurrent release shall be processed on the same timeline. When the request for credit release is from a previously approved land conversion project, the Department shall schedule a site visit, if warranted, within 30 days of the request and shall deny, approve, or approve with conditions the release within 15 days of the site visit or determination that a site visit is not warranted. The timelines set out in this subdivision shall be implemented prior to adoption of regulations. The Department shall release credits from a land conversion project after it is satisfied that the applicant has met the criteria for release in an approved nutrient reduction implementation plan.

2. Establish credit calculation procedures for proposed credit-generating practices, including the determination of:

a. Baselines for credits certified under subdivision B 1 a in accordance with any applicable provisions of the Virginia Chesapeake Bay TMDL Watershed Implementation Plan or approved TMDLs;

b. Baselines established for agricultural practices, which shall be those actions necessary to achieve a level of reduction assigned in the Virginia Chesapeake Bay TMDL Watershed Implementation Plan or approved TMDLs as implemented on the tract, field, or other land area under consideration;

c. Baselines for urban practices from new development and redevelopment, which shall be in compliance with postconstruction nutrient loading requirements of the Virginia Stormwater Management Program regulations. Baselines for all other existing development shall be at a level necessary to achieve the reductions assigned in the urban sector in the Virginia Chesapeake Bay TMDL Watershed Implementation Plan or approved TMDLs;

d. Baselines for land use conversion, which shall be based on the pre-conversion land use and the level of reductions assigned in the Virginia Chesapeake Bay TMDL Watershed Implementation Plan or approved TMDLs applicable to that land use;

e. Baselines for other nonpoint source credit-generating practices, which shall be based on the Virginia Chesapeake Bay TMDL Watershed Implementation Plan or approved TMDLs using the best available scientific and technical information;

f. Unless otherwise established by the Board, for certification within the Chesapeake Bay Watershed a credit-generating practice that involves land use conversion, which shall represent controls beyond those in place as of July 1, 2005. For other waters for which a TMDL has been approved, the practice shall represent controls beyond those in place at the time of TMDL approval;

g. Baseline dates for all other credit-generating practices, which shall be based on the Virginia Chesapeake Bay TMDL Watershed Implementation Plan or approved TMDLs; and

h. Credit quantities, which shall be established using the best available scientific and technical information at the time of certification;

3. Provide certification of credits on an appropriate temporal basis, such as annual, term of years, or perpetual, depending on the nature of the credit-generating practice. A credit shall be certified for a term of no less than 12 months;

4. Establish requirements to reasonably assure the generation of the credit depending on the nature of the credit-generating activity and use, such as legal instruments for perpetual credits, operation and maintenance requirements, and associated financial assurance requirements. Financial assurance requirements may include letters of credit, escrows, surety bonds, insurance, and where the credits are used or generated by a locality, authority, utility, sanitation district, or permittee operating an MS4 or a point source permitted under this article, its existing tax or rate authority. In lieu of long-term management fund financial assurance mechanisms established or required by regulation for projects generating credits from stream restoration, a third-party long-term steward approved by the Department, such as a public agency, nongovernmental organization or private land manager, may hold long-term management funds in a separate interest-bearing account to be used only for the long-term management of the stream restoration project. Notwithstanding any release schedule set out in regulations of the Board, the Department may accelerate the release of a maximum of 50 percent of nutrient credits from a stream restoration project based on (i) a determination that the level of risk for restoration failure is low, (ii) the provision of additional financial assurance in an amount adequate to cover the cost of project repair or replacement in the event of failure, and (iii) the experience of the applicant or the applicant's agents who will implement the stream restoration project;

5. Establish appropriate reporting requirements;

6. Provide for the ability of the Department to inspect or audit for compliance with the requirements of such regulations;

7. Provide that the option to acquire nutrient credits for compliance purposes shall not eliminate any requirement to comply with local water quality requirements;

8. Establish a credit retirement requirement whereby five percent of non-point source credits in the Chesapeake Bay Watershed other than controls and practices under subdivision B 1 a are permanently retired at the time of certification pursuant to this section for the purposes of offsetting growth in unregulated nutrient loads; and

9. Establish such other requirements as the Board deems necessary and appropriate.

C. The Board shall certify (i) credits that may be generated from effective nutrient controls or removal practices, including activities associated with the types of facilities or practices historically regulated by the Board, such as water withdrawal and treatment and wastewater collection, treatment, and beneficial reuse, using the best available scientific and technical information and (ii) credits that are located in tributaries outside of the Chesapeake Bay watershed as defined in § 62.1-44.15:35, using an average of the nutrient removal rates for each practice identified in Appendix A of the Department's document "Trading Nutrient Reductions from Nonpoint Source Best Management Practices in the Chesapeake Bay Watershed: Guidance for Agricultural Landowners and Your Potential Trading Partners "; however, in the certification and recertification of credits under this subsection, the Department may substitute a delivery factor that is deemed by the Director to be based on the best available scientific and technical information appropriate for the tributaries located outside of the Chesapeake Bay watershed as an alternative to any delivery factor derived from the application of the Chesapeake Bay Program watershed model.

D. The Department shall establish and maintain an online Virginia Nutrient Credit Registry of credits as follows:

1. The registry shall include all nonpoint source credits certified pursuant to this article and may include point source nitrogen and point source phosphorus credits generated from point sources covered by the general permit issued pursuant to § 62.1-44.19:14 or point source nutrient credits certified pursuant to this section at the option of the owner. No other credits shall be valid for compliance purposes.

2. Registration of credits on the registry shall not preclude or restrict the right of the owner of such credits from transferring the credits on such commercial terms as may be established by and between the owner and the regulated or unregulated party acquiring the credits.

3. The Department shall establish procedures for the listing and tracking of credits on the registry, including but not limited to (i) notification of the availability of new nutrient credits to the locality where the credit-generating practice is implemented at least five business days prior to listing on the registry to provide the locality an opportunity to acquire such credits at fair market value for compliance purposes and (ii) notification that the listing of credits on the registry does not constitute a representation by the Board or the owner that the credits will satisfy the specific regulatory requirements applicable to the prospective user's intended use and that the prospective user is encouraged to contact the Board for technical assistance to identify limitations, if any, applicable to the intended use.

4. The registry shall be publicly accessible without charge.

E. The owner or operator of a nonpoint source nutrient credit-generating entity that fails to comply with the provisions of this section shall be subject to the enforcement and penalty provisions of § 62.1-44.19:22.

F. Nutrient credits from stormwater nonpoint nutrient credit-generating facilities in receipt of a Nonpoint Nutrient Offset Authorization for Transfer letter from the Department prior to July 1, 2012, shall be considered certified nutrient credits and shall not be subject to further certification requirements or to the credit retirement requirement under subdivision B 8. However, such facilities shall be subject to the other provisions of this article, including registration, inspection, reporting, and enforcement.

History.
2012, cc. 748, 808; 2013, cc. 756, 793; 2016, c. 653; 2022, cc. 422, 526; contingently amended by 2023, c. 723.

§ 62.1-44.19:21. Nutrient credit use by regulated entities.

A. An MS4 permittee may acquire, use, and transfer nutrient credits for purposes of compliance with any waste load allocations established as effluent limitations in an MS4 permit issued pursuant to § 62.1-44.15:25. Such method of compliance may be approved by the Department following review of a compliance plan submitted by the permittee that includes the use of nutrient credits. The permittee may use such credits for compliance purposes only if (i) the credits, whether annual, term, or perpetual, are generated and applied for purposes of compliance for the same calendar year; (ii) the credits are acquired no later than a date following the calendar year in which the credits are applied as specified by the Department consistent with the permittee's Virginia Stormwater Management Program (VSMP) permit annual report deadline under such permit; (iii) the credits are generated in the same locality or tributary, except that permittees in the Eastern Coastal Basin may also acquire credits from the Potomac and Rappahannock tributaries; and (iv) the credits either are point source nitrogen or point source phosphorus credits generated by point sources covered by the general permit issued pursuant to § 62.1-44.19:14, or are certified pursuant to § 62.1-44.19:20. An MS4 permittee may enter into an agreement with one or more other MS4 permittees within the same locality or within the same or adjacent eight-digit hydrologic unit code to collectively meet the sum of any waste load allocations in their permits. Such permittees shall submit to the Department for approval a compliance plan to achieve their aggregate permit waste load allocations.

B. An applicant required to comply with water quality requirements for land-disturbing activities operating under a General VSMP Permit for Discharges of Stormwater from Construction Activities or a Construction Individual Permit may acquire and use perpetual nutrient credits certified and registered on the Virginia Nutrient Credit Registry in accordance with § 62.1-44.15:35.

C. A confined animal feeding operation issued a permit pursuant to this chapter may acquire, use, and transfer credits for compliance with any waste load allocations contained in the provisions of a Virginia Pollutant Discharge Elimination System (VPDES) permit. Such method of compliance may be approved by the Department following review of a compliance plan submitted by the permittee that includes the use of nutrient credits.

D. A facility registered under the Industrial Stormwater General Permit issued pursuant to this chapter or issued a VPDES permit regulating stormwater discharges that requires nitrogen and phosphorus monitoring at the facility may acquire, use, and transfer credits for compliance with any waste load allocations established as effluent limitations in a VPDES permit. Such method of compliance may be approved by the Department following review of a compliance plan submitted by the permittee that includes the use of nutrient credits.

E. Public notice of each compliance plan submitted for approval pursuant to this section shall be given by the Department.

F. This section shall not be construed to limit or otherwise affect the authority of the Board to establish and enforce more stringent water quality-based effluent limitations for total nitrogen or total phosphorus in permits where those limitations are necessary to protect local water quality. The exchange or acquisition of credits pursuant to this article shall not affect any requirement to comply with such local water quality-based limitations.

History.
   2012, cc. 748, 808, § 10.1-603.15:3; 2013, cc. 756, 793; 2021, Sp. Sess. I, c. 360.

The 2021 Sp. Sess. I amendments.
   The 2021 amendment by Sp. Sess. I, c. 360,

effective July 1, 2021, made stylistic plural-to-singular changes in subsections B-D and made related stylistic changes; and inserted "or issued a VPDES permit regulating stormwater discharges that requires nitrogen and phosphorus monitoring at the facility" in subsection D.

§ 62.1-44.19:21.2. Nutrient and sediment credit generation and transfer; public body.

A. Except as provided in subsection B, the only nonpoint nutrient credits that shall be transferred pursuant to either (i) § 62.1-44.15:35 or (ii) subsections B, C, and D of § 62.1-44.19:21 are nutrient credits generated by the private sector, including credits generated by the private sector pursuant to an agreement with a public body.

B. Other than for purposes of subsection A of § 62.1-44.19:21, nutrient credits or sediment credits generated by a project undertaken by a public body, including a locality, and certified by the Department shall be used only by such public body and only for the purpose of compliance with the provisions of this chapter by such public body's project. For the purposes of this subsection, the term "public body's project" means a project for which the public body is the named permittee and for which no third party conducts any lease, sale, grant, transfer, or use of the project or its nutrient or sediment credits.

C. Any publicly owned treatment works that is permitted under the Watershed General Virginia Pollutant Discharge Elimination System (VPDES) Permit pursuant to § 62.1-44.19:14 and is constructing or expanding the treatment works, wastewater collection system, or other facility used for public wastewater utility operations may, as an alternative to acquiring and using certain perpetual nutrient credits pursuant to subsection B of § 62.1-44.19:21, permanently retire a portion of its wasteload allocation if (i) notice is given by such applicant to the Department, (ii) a ratio of 10 pounds of nitrogen allocation for each pound of phosphorous allocation retired is also permanently retired and applied toward the land-disturbing project, and (iii) the general permit registration list is modified to reflect the permanent retirement of the wasteload allocation. Except for a water reclamation and reuse project at a treatment works, no more than 10 pounds per year of phosphorous allocation may be applied toward a single project's postconstruction phosphorus control requirement.

D. Nothing in this section shall be construed to prevent any (i) public body, including a locality, from entering into an agreement with a private third party for the development of a project to generate nonpoint nutrient credits on terms and conditions upon which the public body and private third party agree or (ii) locality from operating a locality pollutant loading pro rata share program for nutrient reductions established pursuant to § 15.2-2243.

History.
   2020, cc. 1102, 1103.

ARTICLE 7.

POLLUTION FROM BOATS.

§ 62.1-44.33. Board to adopt regulations; tidal waters no discharge zones.

A. The State Water Control Board is empowered and directed to adopt all necessary regulations for the purpose of controlling the discharge of sewage and other wastes from both documented and undocumented boats and vessels on all navigable and nonnavigable waters within this Commonwealth. No such regulation shall impose restrictions that are more restrictive than the regulations applicable under federal law; provided, however, the Board may adopt such regulations as are reasonably necessary with respect to: (i) vessels regularly berthed in marinas or other places where vessels are moored, in order to limit or avoid the closing of shellfish grounds; and (ii) no discharge zones. Documented and undocumented boats and vessels are prohibited from discharging into the Chesapeake Bay and the tidal portions of its tributaries sewage that has not been treated by a Coast Guard-approved Marine Sanitation Device (MSD Type 1 or Type 2); however, the discharge of treated or untreated sewage by such boats and vessels is prohibited in areas that have been designated as no discharge zones by the United States Environmental Protection Agency. Any discharges, as defined in 9VAC25-71-10, that are incidental to the normal operation of a vessel shall not constitute a violation of this section.

B. The tidal creeks of the Commonwealth are hereby established as no discharge zones for the discharge of sewage and other wastes from documented and undocumented boats and vessels. Criteria for the establishment of no discharge zones shall be premised on the improvement of impaired tidal creeks. Nothing in this section shall be construed to discourage the proper use of Type 1 and Type 2 Marine Sanitation Devices, as defined under 33 U.S.C. § 1332, in authorized areas other than properly designated no discharge zones. The Board shall adopt regulations for designated no discharge zones requiring (i) boats and vessels without installed toilets to dispose of any collected sewage from portable toilets or other containment devices at marina facilities approved by the Department of Health for collection of sewage wastes, or otherwise dispose of sewage in a manner that complies with state law; (ii) all boats and vessels with installed toilets to have a marine sanitation device to allow sewage holding capacity unless the toilets are rendered inoperable; (iii) all houseboats having installed toilets to have a holding tank with the capability of collecting and holding sewage and disposing of collected sewage at a pump-out facility; if the houseboats lack such tank then the marine sanitation device shall comply with clause (iv); (iv) y-valves, macerator pump valves, discharge conveyances or any other through-hull fitting valves capable of allowing a discharge of sewage from marine sanitation devices shall be secured in the closed position while in a no discharge zone by use of a padlock, nonreleasable wire tie, or removal of the y-valve handle. The method chosen shall present a physical barrier to the use of the y-valve or toilet; and (v) every owner or operator of a marina within a designated no discharge zone to notify boat patrons leasing slips of the sewage discharge restriction in the no discharge zone. As a minimum, notification shall consist of no discharge zone information in the slip rental contract and a sign indicating the area is a designated no discharge zone.

In formulating regulations pursuant to this section, the Board shall consult with the State Department of Health, the Department of Wildlife Resources, and the Marine Resources Commission for the purpose of coordinating such regulations with the activities of such agencies.

For purposes of this section, "no discharge zone" means an area where the Commonwealth has received an affirmative determination from the U.S. Environmental Protection Agency that there are adequate facilities for the removal of sewage from vessels (holding tank pump-out facilities) in accordance with 33 U.S.C. § 1322 (f)(3), and where federal approval has been received allowing a complete prohibition of all treated or untreated discharges of sewage from all vessels.

C. Violation of such regulations and violations of the prohibitions created by this section on the discharge of treated and untreated sewage from documented and undocumented boats and vessels shall, upon conviction, be a Class 1 misdemeanor. Every law-enforcement officer of this Commonwealth and its subdivisions shall have the authority to enforce the regulations adopted under the provisions of this section and to enforce the prohibitions on the discharge of treated and untreated sewage created by this section.

History.
Code 1950, § 62.1-44.1; 1968, c. 659; 1970, c. 638; 1975, c. 204; 1997, c. 502; 2001, c. 42; 2004, c. 287; 2009, c. 337; 2011, c. 220; 2020, c. 958.

"Department of Wildlife Resources" for "Department of Game and Inland Fisheries" in subsection B in the second paragraph.

The 2020 amendments.
The 2020 amendment by c. 958 substituted

ARTICLE 11.

DISCHARGE OF OIL INTO WATERS.

§ 62.1-44.34:21. Administrative fees.

A. The Board is authorized to collect from any applicant for approval of an oil discharge contingency plan and from any operator seeking acceptance of evidence of financial responsibility fees sufficient to meet, but not exceed, the costs of the Board related to implementation of § 62.1-44.34:15 as to an applicant for approval of an oil discharge contingency plan and of § 62.1-44.34:16 as to an operator seeking acceptance of evidence of financial responsibility. The Board shall establish by regulation a schedule of fees that takes into account the nature and type of facility and the effect of any prior professional certification or federal review or approval on the level of review required by the Board. All such fees received by the Board shall be used exclusively to implement the provisions of this article.

B. Fees charged an applicant should reflect the average time and complexity of processing approvals in each of the various categories.

C. When adopting regulations for fees, the Board shall take into account the fees charged in neighboring states, and the importance of not placing existing or prospective industries in the Commonwealth at a competitive disadvantage. Within six months of receipt of any federal moneys that would offset the costs of implementing this article, the Board shall review the amount of fees set by regulation to determine the amount of fees which should be refunded. Such refunds shall only be required if the fees plus the federal moneys received for the implementation of the program under this article as it applies to facilities exceed the actual cost to the Board of administering the program.

D. On October 1, 1995, and every two years thereafter, the Board shall make an evaluation of the implementation of the fee programs and provide this evaluation in writing to the Senate Committees on Agriculture, Conservation and Natural Resources, and on Finance and Appropriations; and the House Committees on Appropriations, Chesapeake and Its Tributaries, and Finance.

History.
1990, c. 917; 1992, c. 345.

Editor's note.
The Virginia Code Commission authorized the substitution of "Senate Committees on Ag-

riculture, Conservation and Natural Resources, and on Finance and Appropriations" for "Senate Committees on Agriculture, Conservation and Natural Resources, and Finance" in subsection D. March 10, 2021.

ARTICLE 12.
VIRGINIA SPILL RESPONSE COUNCIL.

§ 62.1-44.34:25. Virginia Spill Response Council created; purpose; membership.

A. There is hereby created the Virginia Spill Response Council. The purpose of the Council is to (i) improve the Commonwealth's capability to respond in a timely and coordinated fashion to incidents involving the discharge of oil or hazardous materials which pose a threat to the environment, its living resources, and the health, safety, and welfare of the people of the Commonwealth and (ii) provide an ongoing forum for discussions between agencies which are charged with the prevention of, and response to, oil spills and hazardous materials incidents, and those agencies responsible for the remediation of such incidents.

B. The Secretary of Natural and Historic Resources and the Secretary of Public Safety and Homeland Security, upon the advice of the director of the agency, shall select one representative from each of the following agencies to serve as a member of the Council: Department of Emergency Management, State Water Control Board, Department of Environmental Quality, Virginia Marine Resources Commission, Department of Wildlife Resources, Department of Health, Department of Fire Programs, and the Council on the Environment.

C. The Secretary of Natural and Historic Resources or his designee shall serve as chairman of the Council.

History.
1990, c. 598; 1991, c. 66; 2014, cc. 115, 490; 2020, c. 958; 2021, Sp. Sess. I, c. 401.

The 2020 amendments.
The 2020 amendment by c. 958 substituted "Department of Wildlife Resources" for "De-

partment of Game and Inland Fisheries" in subsection B.

The 2021 Sp. Sess. I amendments.
The 2021 amendment by Sp. Sess. I, c. 401, effective July 1, 2021, inserted "and Historic" in subsections B and C.

§ 62.1-44.34:28. Council to submit annual report.

The Council shall submit a report annually to the Secretaries of Natural and Historic Resources and Transportation and Public Safety, which includes (i) an evaluation of the emergency response preparedness activities undertaken and the emergency response activities conducted during the year and (ii) a description of the activities of the Council during the year.

History.
1990, c. 598; 2021, Sp. Sess. I, c. 401.

The 2021 Sp. Sess. I amendments.
The 2021 amendment by Sp. Sess. I, c. 401,
effective July 1, 2021, inserted "and Historic."

CHAPTER 3.2.

CONSERVATION OF WATER RESOURCES; STATE WATER CONTROL BOARD.

§ 62.1-44.36. Responsibility of State Water Control Board; formulation of policy.

Being cognizant of the crucial importance of the Commonwealth's water resources to the health and welfare of the people of Virginia and of the need of a water supply to assure further industrial growth and economic prosperity for the Commonwealth, and recognizing the necessity for continuous cooperative planning and effective state-level guidance in the use of water resources, the State Water Control Board is assigned the responsibility for planning the development, conservation and utilization of Virginia's water resources.

The Board shall continue the study of existing water resources of the Commonwealth, means and methods of conserving and augmenting such water resources, and existing and contemplated uses and needs of water for all purposes. Based upon these studies and policies that have been initiated by the Division of Water Resources, and after an opportunity has been given to all concerned state agencies and political subdivisions to be heard, the Board shall formulate a coordinated policy for the use and control of all the water resources of the Commonwealth and issue a statement thereof. In formulating the Commonwealth's water resources policy, the Board shall, among other things, take into consideration the following principles and policies:

1. Existing water rights are to be protected and preserved subject to the principle that all of the state waters belong to the public for use by the people for beneficial purposes without waste.

2. Adequate and safe supplies shall be preserved and protected for human consumption, while conserving maximum supplies for other beneficial uses. When proposed uses of water are in mutually exclusive conflict or when available supplies of water are insufficient for all who desire to use them, preference shall be given to human consumption purposes over all other uses.

3. It is in the public interest that integration and coordination of uses of water, especially by localities with shared water supplies, and augmentation of existing supplies for all beneficial purposes be achieved for the maximum economic development thereof for the benefit of the Commonwealth as a whole.

4. In considering the benefits to be derived from drainage, consideration shall also be given to possible harmful effects upon ground water supplies and protection of wildlife.

5. The maintenance of stream flows sufficient to support aquatic life and to minimize pollution shall be fostered and encouraged.

6. Watershed development policies shall be favored, whenever possible, for the preservation of balanced multiple uses, and project construction and planning with those ends in view shall be encouraged.

7. Due regard shall be given in the planning and development of water recreation facilities to safeguard against pollution.

The statement of water resource policy shall be revised from time to time whenever the Board determines it to be in the public interest.

The initial statement of state water resource policy and any subsequent revisions thereof shall be furnished by the Board to all state agencies and to all political subdivisions of the Commonwealth.

History.

Code 1950, § 10-17.1; 1966, c. 561; 1972, c. 728; 2020, c. 1105.

The 2020 amendments.

The 2020 amendment by c. 1105, in the second paragraph in the first sentence, substituted "the Commonwealth" for "this Commonwealth," in the second sentence, substituted "policies that" for "such policies as," and in the last sentence, deleted "but not be limited to" following "consideration"; redesignated subdivisions (1) through (7) as 1 through 7, in subdivision 2, substituted "shall" for "should" in the first sentence; in subdivision 3, inserted "especially by localities with shared water supplies"; in the next to last paragraph, substituted "determines" for "shall determine"; and made stylistic changes.

§ 62.1-44.38. Plans and programs; registration of certain data by water users; advisory committees; committee membership for federal, state, and local agencies; water supply planning assistance.

A. The Board shall prepare plans and programs for the management of the water resources of the Commonwealth in such a manner as to encourage, promote, and secure the maximum beneficial use and control thereof. These plans and programs shall be prepared for each major river basin of the Commonwealth, and appropriate subbasins therein, including specifically the Potomac-Shenandoah River Basin, the Rappahannock River Basin, the York River Basin, the James River Basin, the Chowan River Basin, the Roanoke River Basin, the New River Basin, and the Tennessee-Big Sandy River Basin, and for those areas in the Tidewater and elsewhere in the Commonwealth not within these major river basins. Reports for each basin shall be published by the Board.

B. 1. In preparing river basin plan and program reports enumerated in subsection A, the Board shall (i) estimate current water withdrawals and use for agriculture, industry, domestic use, and other significant categories of water users; (ii) project water withdrawals and use by agriculture, industry, domestic use, and other significant categories of water users; (iii) estimate, for each major river and stream, the minimum instream flows necessary during drought conditions to maintain water quality and avoid permanent damage to aquatic life in streams, bays, and estuaries; (iv) evaluate, to the extent practicable, the ability of existing subsurface and surface waters to meet current and future water uses, including minimum instream flows, during drought conditions; (v) evaluate, in cooperation with the Virginia Department of Health and local water supply managers, the current and future capability of public water systems to provide adequate quantity and quality of water; (vi) estimate, using a data-driven method that includes multiple reasonable assumptions about supply and demand over varying time frames, the risk that each locality and region will experience water supply shortfalls; and (vii) evaluate hydrologic, environmental, economic, social, legal, jurisdictional, and other aspects of each alternative management strategy identified.

301

2. The Board shall direct the Department of Environmental Quality (the Department) in its facilitation of regional water planning efforts. The Department shall (i) ensure that localities coordinate sufficiently in the development of regional water plans; (ii) provide planning, policy, and technical assistance to each regional planning area, differentiated according to each area's water supply challenges, existing resources, and other factors; and (iii) ensure that each regional plan clearly identifies the region's water supply risks and proposes strategies to address those risks.

3. When preparing drought evaluation and response plans pursuant to subdivision 1, the Board shall recognize the localities that include any portion of the service area of a water supply utility in the Commonwealth that uses the Potomac River as a water supply source as a distinct drought evaluation region. Such plans shall incorporate the provisions of the Metropolitan Washington Water Supply and Drought Awareness Response Plan: Potomac River System (2000), including provisions related to triggers, actions, and messages for the Potomac River drought evaluation region. Nothing in this subdivision regarding the incorporation of such provisions shall be construed to limit the authority of the Governor during a declared drought emergency.

C. The Board may, by regulation, require each water user withdrawing surface or subsurface water or both during each year to register, by a date to be established by the Board, water withdrawal and use data for the previous year including the estimated average daily withdrawal, maximum daily withdrawal, sources of water withdrawn, and volume of wastewater discharge, provided that the withdrawal exceeds one million gallons in any single month for use for crop irrigation, or that the daily average during any single month exceeds 10,000 gallons per day for any other user. Location data shall be provided by each user in a coordinate system specified by the Board.

D. The Board shall establish advisory committees to assist it in the formulation of such plans or programs and in formulating recommendations called for in subsection E. In this connection, the Board may include committee membership for branches or agencies of the federal government, branches or agencies of the Commonwealth, branches or agencies of the government of any state in a river basin located within that state and Virginia, the political subdivisions of the Commonwealth, and all persons and corporations interested in or directly affected by any proposed or existing plan or program.

E. The Board shall prepare plans or programs and shall include in reports prepared under subsection A recommended actions to be considered by the General Assembly, the agencies of the Commonwealth and local political subdivisions, the agencies of the federal government, or any other persons that the Board may deem necessary or desirable for the accomplishment of plans or programs prepared under subsection B.

F. In addition to the preparation of plans called for in subsection A, the Board, upon written request of a political subdivision of the Commonwealth, shall provide water supply planning assistance to such political subdivision, including assistance in preparing drought management strategies, water conservation programs, evaluation of alternative water sources, state enabling legislation to facilitate a specific situation, applications for federal grants or permits, or other such planning activities to facilitate intergovernmental cooperation and coordination.

History.

Code 1950, § 10-17.4; 1966, c. 561; 1972, c. 728; 1981, c. 633; 1989, c. 219; 2020, c. 1105; 2023, cc. 36, 37.

The 2020 amendments.

The 2020 amendment by c. 1105 added subdivision B 2; in subdivision B 1 and in subsections D through F, deleted "of this section" five times, after three instances of "subsection A" and after one instance of "subsection E" and "subsection B"; in subdivision B 1, substituted "domestic use" for "domestic water use" in clause (ii), and rewrote clause (vi), which read: "identify water management problems and alternative water management plans to address such problems"; in subsection C, substituted "any other user" for "all other users" in the first sentence, and added the last sentence; and in subsection F, substituted "including" for "to include."

The 2023 amendments.

The 2023 amendment by cc. 36 and 37 are identical, and added subdivision B 3.

§ 62.1-44.38:1. Comprehensive water supply planning process; state, regional, and local water supply plans.

A. The Board, with advice and guidance from the Commissioner of Health, local governments, public service authorities, and other interested parties, shall establish a comprehensive water supply planning process for the development of local, regional, and state water supply plans consistent with the provisions of this chapter. This process shall be designed to (i) ensure that adequate and safe drinking water is available to all citizens of the Commonwealth; (ii) encourage, promote, and protect all other beneficial uses of the Commonwealth's water resources; (iii) encourage, promote, and develop incentives for alternative water sources, including desalinization; and (iv) encourage the development of cross-jurisdictional water supply projects.

B. The Board shall adopt regulations designating regional planning areas based primarily on river basins as appropriate based on water supply sources. The Board shall consider existing interjurisdictional arrangements in designating regional planning areas. The Board may, as appropriate, designate multiple regional planning areas within a single river basin in order to enhance the manageability of planning within such basin. The regulations shall identify the particular regional planning area in which each locality shall participate and shall state which local stakeholder groups, including local governments, industrial and agricultural water users, public water suppliers, developers and economic development organizations, and conservation and environmental organizations, shall or may participate in coordinated water resource planning. The regulations shall provide a mechanism for a locality to request a change of its designated regional planning area to an adjoining planning area that is based on water supply source, river basin, or existing or planned cross-jurisdictional relationship, which change shall be effective upon approval of the Department, notwithstanding the provisions of Article 2 (§ 2.2-4006 et seq.) of Chapter 40 of Title 2.2. The regulations shall further recognize the localities that include any portion of the service area of a water supply utility in the Commonwealth that uses the Potomac River as a water supply source as a distinct regional planning area. Such plan shall incorporate the provisions of the Metropolitan Washington Water Supply and Drought Awareness Response Plan: Potomac River System (2000), including provisions related to triggers, actions, and messages for the Potomac River drought evaluation region. Nothing in this subsection regarding the incorporation of such provisions shall be construed to limit the authority of the Governor during a declared drought emergency.

C. 1. Each locality in a regional planning area shall participate in cross-jurisdictional, coordinated water resource planning. Such local coordination shall accommodate existing regional groups that have already developed water supply plans, including planning district commissions, and other regional planning entities as appropriate.

2. Each locality in a regional planning area shall develop and submit, with the other localities in that planning area, a single jointly produced regional water supply plan to the Department of Environmental Quality (the Department). Such regional water supply plan shall (i) clearly identify the region's water supply risks and (ii) propose regional strategies to address those water supply risks.

3. Each regional water supply plan also shall comply with applicable criteria and guidelines developed by the Board. Such criteria and guidelines shall take into account existing local and regional water supply planning efforts and requirements imposed under other state or federal laws. The criteria and guidelines established by the Board shall not prohibit a town from entering into a regional water supply plan with an adjacent county in the same regional planning area.

4. This section is intended to inform any regional water resource planning being done in the Commonwealth pursuant to interstate compacts.

D. The Board and the Department shall prioritize the allocation of planning funds and other funds to localities that sufficiently participate in regional planning.

E. In accordance with subdivision B 2 of § 62.1-44.38, the Department shall facilitate regional planning and provide assistance to each regional planning area as needed.

History.

2003, c. 227; 2006, c. 18; 2020, c. 1105; 2022, c. 331; 2023, cc. 36, 37.

The 2020 amendments.

The 2020 amendment by c. 1105, in subsection A, deleted "the" preceding "advice and guidance" in the first sentence, and "but not limited to" preceding "desalinization" in clause (iii), added clause (iv), and made stylistic changes; added subsection B, subdivisions C 1, 2, and 4, and subsections D and E; redesignated former subsection B as subdivision C 3, and therein substituted "Each regional water supply plan also shall comply with applicable" for "Local or regional water supply plans shall be prepared and submitted to the Department of Environmental Quality in accordance with" in the first sentence, and added "in the same regional planning area" in the last sentence.

The 2022 amendments.

The 2022 amendment by c. 331 in subsection B in the first sentence, added "as appropriate based on water supply sources" at the end; and added the second and last sentences.

The 2023 amendments.

The 2023 amendment by cc. 36 and 37 are identical, in subsection B, deleted "further" following "regulations shall" in the fifth sentence and added the last two sentences.

CHAPTER 3.7.

CHESAPEAKE BAY AND VIRGINIA WATERS CLEAN-UP AND OVERSIGHT ACT.

§ 62.1-44.117. Development of an impaired waters clean-up plan; strategies; objectives.

A. The Secretary of Natural and Historic Resources shall develop a plan for the cleanup of the Chesapeake Bay and Virginia's waters designated as impaired by the U.S. Environmental Protection Agency. The plan shall be revised and amended as needed to reflect changes in strategies, timetables, and milestones. Upon the request of the Secretary of Natural and Historic Resources, state agencies shall participate in the development of the plan.

B. The plan shall address both point and nonpoint sources of pollution and shall include, but not be limited to the following:

1. Measurable and attainable objectives for cleaning up the Chesapeake Bay and other impaired Virginia waters;

2. A description of the strategies to be implemented to meet specific and attainable objectives outlined in the plan;

3. Time frames or phasing to accomplish plan objectives and the expected dates of completion;

4. A clearly defined, prioritized, and sufficiently funded program of work within the plan both for point and nonpoint source clean-up projects;

5. A disbursement projection plan detailing the expenditures for point and nonpoint projects and whenever possible, a listing of the specific projects to which the funds are to be allocated;

6. Potential problem areas where delays in the implementation of the plan may occur;

7. A risk mitigation strategy designed to reduce the potential problems that might delay plan implementation;

8. A description of the extent of coordination between state and local governments in developing and achieving the plan's objectives;

9. Assessments of alternative funding mechanisms, that shall include but not be limited to the feasibility of utilizing the Virginia Resources Authority, that would address the needs of the Commonwealth to handle and appropriate state funds prudently and efficiently and address the needs of localities to achieve their goals in a timely and affordable manner; and

10. Recommendations to the oversight committees, as defined in § 62.1-44.118, for legislative action.

C. In reporting and documenting progress being made in clean-up efforts to the oversight committees, the plan shall include measures to assess the progress in accomplishing the program of work outlined in the plan. Special emphasis shall be given to the identification of trends that are either positively or negatively impacting plan accomplishment. These shall include, but are not limited to:

1. Stream miles added and removed from the 303(d) list under the federal Clean Water Act; waters meeting water quality standards; and total reductions of nitrogen, phosphorus, and sediment by tributary basin from point and nonpoint sources of pollution;

2. Scope of water quality monitoring of rivers, streams, estuaries, and lakes and the cumulative number of miles or acres assessed to evaluate the effectiveness of the efforts to restore impaired waters;

3. Number of best management practices (BMP) implemented; participation level in BMP cost-share programs; number of Total Maximum Daily Loads developed and implemented; local compliance levels with nonpoint programs, such as erosion and sediment control, stormwater management, and the Chesapeake Bay Preservation Act; number of wastewater treatment upgrades underway and number completed; and levels of compliance with nutrient-based permit limits; and

4. Updated or new strategies that would permit the optimal use of resources to meet plan objectives as the plan is revised over time.

For the purposes of this chapter "impaired waters" means those waters as defined in § 62.1-44.19:4.

History.
2006, c. 204; 2021, Sp. Sess. I, c. 401.

The 2021 Sp. Sess. I amendments.
The 2021 amendment by Sp. Sess. I, c. 401,

effective July 1, 2021, twice inserted "and Historic" in subsection A.

§ 62.1-44.118. Status reports on progress; legislative oversight.

The Secretary of Natural and Historic Resources shall submit the impaired waters clean-up plan as described in § 62.1-44.117 no later than January 1, 2007, to the House Committee on Agriculture, Chesapeake and Natural Resources, the House Committee on Appropriations, the Senate Committee on Agriculture, Conservation and Natural Resources, and the Senate Committee on Finance and Appropriations. Thereafter, a progress report on the implementation of the plan shall be submitted annually to these committees of oversight. The report shall be due on November 1 of each year. Water quality reporting requirements in subsection D of § 10.1-2127, subsection C of § 10.1-2128.1, and § 10.1-2134 shall be annually consolidated in the November 1 report. If there are questions as to the status of the clean-up effort, the chairman of any of these committees may convene his committee for the purpose of receiving testimony. The executive branch departments and the Secretary of Natural and Historic Resources may request a meeting of any of the committees to inform them as to the progress of the clean-up or to propose specific initiatives that may require legislative action.

History.
2006, c. 204; 2007, c. 637; 2011, c. 245; 2016, c. 127; 2021, Sp. Sess. I, c. 401.

effective July 1, 2021, inserted "and Historic" twice and "and Appropriations."

The 2021 Sp. Sess. I amendments.
The 2021 amendment by Sp. Sess. I, c. 401,

CHAPTER 3.8.
CHESAPEAKE BAY WATERSHED IMPLEMENTATION PLAN INITIATIVES.

Article 1. Chesapeake Bay Watershed Implementation Plan.

Article 2. Nutrient Management Plans for Chesapeake Bay Cropland.

Article 3. Chesapeake Bay Watershed Livestock Stream Exclusion.

ARTICLE 1.
CHESAPEAKE BAY WATERSHED IMPLEMENTATION PLAN.

§ 62.1-44.119. (For contingent effective date, see § 62.1-44.119:1) Target date.

In recognition of the ecological, cultural, economic, historical, and recreational value of the Chesapeake Bay, as well as the Commonwealth's commitment to the Chesapeake Bay Partnership and the 2014 Chesapeake Bay Agreement, the target date to achieve the water quality goals contained in Virginia's final Chesapeake Bay Total Maximum Daily Load Phase III Watershed Implementation Plan shall be December 31, 2025.

History.
2020, cc. 1185, 1186.

Editor's note.
Acts 2020, cc. 1185 and 1186, cl. 3 provides: "That the Secretary of Natural Resources and the Secretary of Agriculture (the Secretaries) shall convene a stakeholder advisory group (the Group) to review annual progress toward the implementation of the Commonwealth's agricultural commitments in the Chesapeake Bay Total Maximum Daily Load Phase III Watershed Implementation Plan. The Group shall (i) develop a process to assist any operator of 50 or more acres of Chesapeake Bay cropland in developing a nutrient management plan that meets the requirements of the goals to be achieved by the target date and (ii) develop a plan for the stream exclusion program in the Chesapeake Bay watershed. Such plans and progress reports shall include identification of priority regions, operators affected within each region, initiatives to enhance progress, an accounting of funding received toward the agricultural commitments, shortfalls remaining, and the consequences of such funding shortfalls. The Group shall make recommendations to the Governor regarding necessary revisions to Chapter 3.8 (§ 62.1-44.119 et seq.) of Title 62.1 of the Code of Virginia, as created by this act, to ensure that the Commonwealth's commitments are achieved by December 31, 2025. The Group shall include representatives from the Department of Conservation and Recreation, soil and water conservation districts, the Virginia Farm Bureau Federation, the Virginia Agribusiness Council, the Chesapeake Bay Commission, the Chesapeake Bay Foundation, the Virginia Cooperative Extension, the Virginia Cattlemen's Association, the Virginia Association of the Commissioners of the Revenue, and the Virginia Association of Counties. The Group shall also include two legislative members, one each from the Senate and the House of Delegates. Such legislative members shall be members of the Virginia delegation of the Chesapeake Bay Commission."

Acts 2020, cc. 1185 and 1186, cl. 4 provides: "That the Department of Conservation and Recreation shall, no later than July 1, 2021, establish through the Soil and Water Conservation Technical Advisory Committee and with stakeholder input a portable stream fencing practice for inclusion in the Virginia Agricultural Best Management Practice Cost-Share Program."

Acts 2020, cc. 1185 and 1186, c. 5 provides: "That the Virginia Soil and Water Conservation Board, as established pursuant to § 10.1-502 of the Code of Virginia, shall establish, no later than December 31, 2020, the methodology for identifying perennial streams, as defined in § 62.1-44.122 of the Code of Virginia, as created by this act."

Acts 2021, Sp. Sess. I, cc. 363 and 364, cl. 2 provides: "That the Enhanced Nutrient Removal Certainty Program as established in subdivisions G 1, 2, and 3 of § 62.1-44.19:14 of the Code of Virginia, as amended by this act, shall be deemed to implement through January 1, 2026, the Commonwealth's Chesapeake Bay Phase III Watershed Implementation Plan in lieu of the floating waste load allocation concept proposed in Initiative 52 of the Commonwealth's Chesapeake Bay Phase III Watershed Implementation Plan. However, nothing in this act shall be construed to limit the State Water Control Board's authority to impose (i) additional requirements or modifications to phosphorous waste load allocations necessary to achieve compliance with the numeric chlorophyll-a criteria applicable to the James River; (ii) requirements or modifications to waste load allocations necessary to comply with changes to federal law that become effective after January 1, 2021; or (iii) requirements or modifications to waste load allocations necessary to comply with a court order issued after January 1, 2021."

Acts 2021, Sp. Sess. I, cc. 363 and 364, cl. 4 provides: "That if the Secretary of Natural and Historic Resources (the Secretary) determines on or after July 1, 2026, that the Commonwealth has not achieved, or in the event of increased nutrient loads associated with climate change will not be able to maintain, its nitrogen pollution reduction commitments in the Chesapeake Bay Total Maximum Daily Load (TMDL) Phase III Watershed Implementation Plan, the Secretary may develop an additional watershed implementation plan or plans pursuant to § 2.2-218 of the Code of Virginia. Any such plan shall take into consideration the progress made by all point and nonpoint sources toward meeting applicable load and waste load allocations, the best available science and water quality modeling, and any applicable U.S. Environmental Protection Agency guidance for Chesapeake Bay TMDL implementation. In any such plan, the Secretary may include as priority projects upgrades with nutrient removal technology of 4.0 mg/L annual average total nitrogen concentration at municipal wastewater treatment facilities with a design capacity greater than 10.0 MGD discharging to James River Segment JMSTF2 so long as (i) the scheduled date for compliance is January 1, 2036; (ii) notwithstanding wasteload allocations specified in clause (iii), compliance requires operating the nutrient removal technology to achieve an annual average total nitrogen concentration of less than or equal to 4.0 mg/L or, until such time as the facility is upgraded to achieve such concentration, the option of achieving an equivalent discharged load based on an annual average total nitrogen concentration of 4.0 mg/L and actual annual flow treated, including the use of point source nitrogen credits; and (iii) the facilities have and retain the following total nitrogen waste load allocations: Falling Creek WWTP (182,738 lbs/year), Proctors Creek WWTP (411,151 lbs/year and, in the event that Proctors Creek WWTP is expanded in accordance with 9VAC25-40-70 and Falling Creek WWTP is upgraded to achieve 4.0 mg/L, 493,391 lbs/year), and Henrico County WWTP (1,142,085 lbs/year). If the Secretary opts to include such facilities in the plan, the State Water Control Board shall include the foregoing concentrations limits, waste load allocations, and schedules for compliance in the Water Quality Management Planning Regulation, the Watershed General Virginia Pollutant Discharge Elimination System permit, and individual VPDES permits, as applicable."

§ 62.1-44.119:1. Effective date.

A. The provisions of this chapter shall not become effective unless, on or after July 1, 2028, the Secretary of Agriculture and Forestry and the Secretary of Natural and Historic Resources jointly determine that the Commonwealth's commitments in the Chesapeake Bay Total Maximum Daily Load Phase III Watershed Implementation Plan have not been satisfied by a combination of (i) agricultural best management conservation practices, including the coverage of a sufficient portion of Chesapeake Bay cropland by nutrient management plans or the installation of a sufficient number of livestock stream exclusion practices, and (ii) other point or nonpoint source pollution reduction commitments.

B. In making the determination required in subsection A, the effective date of the provisions of this chapter shall be extended for a period of one calendar year for each calendar year that the Commonwealth has not fully funded the amount calculated pursuant to § 10.1-2128.1 for effective Soil and Water Conservation District technical assistance and implementation of agricultural best management practices pursuant to § 10.1-546.1 from July 1, 2023, through the end of the biennial period in which the Secretary of Agriculture and Forestry and the Secretary of Natural and Historic Resources have made the joint determination required in subsection A. Nothing in this subsection shall prohibit adding funding to the Virginia Natural Resources Commitment Fund as established in § 10.1-2128.1 in any year from July 1, 2023, to the year the joint determination is made pursuant to subsection A for distribution in another program year in order to achieve full funding.

C. In no case shall the effective date of the provisions of this chapter be extended beyond July 1, 2030, unless sufficient funding for effective Soil and Water Conservation District technical assistance and implementation of agricultural best management practices has not been provided pursuant to § 10.1-2128.1 in any calendar year.

History.
2020, cc. 1185, 1186; 2021, Sp. Sess. I, c. 401; 2023, cc. 735, 736.

Editor's note.
Acts 2020, cc. 1185 and 1186, cl. 2 was codified as this section at the direction of the Virginia Code Commission.

Acts 2020, cc. 1185 and 1186, cl. 3 provides: "That the Secretary of Natural Resources and the Secretary of Agriculture (the Secretaries) shall convene a stakeholder advisory group (the Group) to review annual progress toward the implementation of the Commonwealth's agricultural commitments in the Chesapeake Bay Total Maximum Daily Load Phase III Watershed Implementation Plan. The Group shall (i) develop a process to assist any operator of 50 or more acres of Chesapeake Bay cropland in developing a nutrient management plan that meets the requirements of the goals to be achieved by the target date and (ii) develop a plan for the stream exclusion program in the Chesapeake Bay watershed. Such plans and progress reports shall include identification of priority regions, operators affected within each region, initiatives to enhance progress, an accounting of funding received toward the agricultural commitments, shortfalls remaining, and the consequences of such funding shortfalls. The Group shall make recommendations to the Governor regarding necessary revisions to Chapter 3.8 (§ 62.1-44.119 et seq.) of Title 62.1 of the Code of Virginia, as created by this act, to ensure that the Commonwealth's commitments are achieved by December 31, 2025. The Group shall include representatives from the Department of Conservation and Recreation, soil and water conservation districts, the Virginia Farm Bureau Federation, the Virginia Agribusiness Council, the Chesapeake Bay Commission, the Chesapeake Bay Foundation, the Virginia Cooperative Extension, the Virginia Cattlemen's Association, the Virginia Association of the Commissioners of the Revenue, and the Virginia Association of Counties. The Group shall also include two legislative members, one each from the Senate and the House of Delegates. Such legislative members shall be members of the Virginia delegation of the Chesapeake Bay Commission."

Acts 2020, cc. 1185 and 1186, cl. 4 provides: "That the Department of Conservation and Recreation shall, no later than July 1, 2021, establish through the Soil and Water Conservation Technical Advisory Committee and with stakeholder input a portable stream fencing practice for inclusion in the Virginia Agricultural Best Management Practice Cost-Share Program."

Acts 2020, cc. 1185 and 1186, cl. 5 provides: "That the Virginia Soil and Water Conservation Board, as established pursuant to § 10.1-502 of the Code of Virginia, shall establish, no later than December 31, 2020, the methodology for identifying perennial streams, as defined in § 62.1-44.122 of the Code of Virginia, as created by this act."

Acts 2021, Sp. Sess. I, cc. 363 and 364, cl. 2 provides: "That the Enhanced Nutrient Removal Certainty Program as established in subdivisions G 1, 2, and 3 of § 62.1-44.19:14 of the Code of Virginia, as amended by this act, shall be deemed to implement through January 1, 2026, the Commonwealth's Chesapeake Bay Phase III Watershed Implementation Plan in lieu of the floating waste load allocation concept proposed in Initiative 52 of the Commonwealth's Chesapeake Bay Phase III Watershed Implementation Plan. However, nothing in this act shall be construed to limit the State Water Control Board's authority to impose (i) additional requirements or modifications to phosphorous waste load allocations necessary to achieve compliance with the numeric chlorophyll-a criteria applicable to the James River; (ii) requirements or modifications to waste load allocations necessary to comply with changes to federal law that become effective after January 1, 2021; or (iii) requirements or modifications to waste load allocations necessary to comply with a court order issued after January 1, 2021."

Acts 2021, Sp. Sess. I, cc. 363 and 364, cl. 4 provides: "That if the Secretary of Natural and Historic Resources (the Secretary) determines on or after July 1, 2026, that the Commonwealth has not achieved, or in the event of increased nutrient loads associated with climate change will not be able to maintain, its nitrogen pollution reduction commitments in the Chesapeake Bay Total Maximum Daily Load (TMDL) Phase III Watershed Implementation Plan, the Secretary may develop an additional watershed implementation plan or plans pursuant to § 2.2-218 of the Code of Virginia. Any such plan shall take into consideration the progress made by all point and nonpoint sources toward meeting applicable load and waste load allocations, the best available science and water quality modeling, and any applicable U.S. Environmental Protection Agency guidance for Chesapeake Bay TMDL implementation. In any such plan, the Secretary may include as priority projects upgrades with nutrient removal technology of 4.0 mg/L annual average total nitrogen concentration at municipal wastewater treatment facilities with a design capacity greater than 10.0 MGD discharging to James River Segment JMSTF2 so long as (i) the scheduled date for compliance is January 1, 2036; (ii) notwithstanding the wasteload allocations specified in clause (iii), compliance requires operating the nutrient removal technology to achieve an annual average total nitrogen concentration of less than or equal to 4.0 mg/L or, until such time as the facility is upgraded to achieve such concentration, the option of achieving an equivalent discharged load based on an annual average total nitrogen concentration of 4.0 mg/L and actual annual flow treated, including the use of point source nitrogen credits; and (iii) the facilities have and retain the following total nitrogen waste load allocations: Falling Creek WWTP (182,738 lbs/year), Proctors Creek WWTP (411,151 lbs/year and, in the event that Proctors Creek WWTP is expanded in accordance with 9VAC25-40-70 and Falling Creek WWTP is upgraded to achieve 4.0 mg/L, 493,391 lbs/year), and Henrico County WWTP (1,142,085 lbs/year). If the Secretary opts to include such facilities in the plan, the State Water Control Board shall include the foregoing concentrations limits, waste load allocations, and schedules for compliance in the Water Quality Management Planning Regulation, the Watershed General Virginia Pollutant Discharge Elimination System permit, and individual VPDES permits, as applicable."

Acts 2023, cc. 735 and 736, cl. 4 provides: "That the determination made pursuant to subsection A of § 62.1-44.119:1 of the Code of Virginia, as amended by this act, shall consider that municipal wastewater point source reduction should be consistent only with the applicable point source plan for Watershed Implementation Plan Phase III as adopted pursuant to § 62.1-44.19:14 of the Code of Virginia."

The 2021 Sp. Sess. I amendments.
The 2021 amendment by Sp. Sess. I, c. 401, effective July 1, 2021, inserted "and Historic."

The 2023 amendments.
The 2023 amendment by cc. 735 and 736, redesignated and revised former section as subdivision A from text which read: "The provi-

sions of this chapter shall not become effective unless, on or after July 1, 2026, the Secretary of Agriculture and Forestry and the Secretary of Natural and Historic Resources jointly determine that the Commonwealth's commitments in the Chesapeake Bay Total Maximum Daily Load Phase III Watershed Implementation Plan have not been satisfied by a combination of (i) agricultural best management conservation practices, including the coverage of a sufficient portion of Chesapeake Bay cropland by nutrient management plans or the installation of a sufficient number of livestock stream exclusion practices"; and added subdivisions B and C.

§ 62.1-44.119:2. Agricultural commitments; work group.

The Secretary of Natural and Historic Resources and the Secretary of Agriculture and Forestry shall convene a stakeholder advisory group, hereinafter referred to as the Group, to review annual progress and make recommendations toward the implementation of the Commonwealth's agricultural commitments in the Chesapeake Bay Total Maximum Daily Load Phase III Watershed Implementation Plan. The Group shall develop (i) a process to assist any operator of 50 or more acres of Chesapeake Bay cropland in developing a nutrient management plan that meets the requirements of the goals to be achieved by the target date and (ii) a plan for the stream exclusion program in the Chesapeake Bay watershed. Such plans and progress reports shall include the number of practices completed by river basin in the prior program year and practices needed to complete the agriculture sector nutrient load reductions, including sediment reductions by river basin, identification of priority regions, the number of operators affected within each region, initiatives to enhance progress, an accounting of funding received toward the agricultural commitments, shortfalls remaining, and the consequences of such funding shortfalls. Such progress reports shall also include specific percentages relating to nutrient management plan and stream exclusion adoption compared to the requirements of the Phase III Watershed Implementation Plan.

History.
2023, cc. 735, 736.

Editor's note.
Acts 2023, cc. 735 and 736, cl. 2 provides: "That the stakeholder advisory group (the Group) created by the Secretary of Agriculture and Forestry and the Secretary of Natural and Historic Resources pursuant to § 62.1-44.119:2 of the Code of Virginia, as created by this act, shall make recommendations to the Governor and the Chairmen of the House Committee on Agriculture, Chesapeake and Natural Resources and the Senate Committee on Agriculture, Conservation and Natural Resources to ensure that all of the Commonwealth's agricultural sector commitments are achieved in accordance with the Chesapeake Bay Total Maximum Daily Load Phase III Watershed

Implementation Plan. The Group shall develop a year-to-year timeline for achieving specific metrics for the achievement of the Commonwealth's agricultural sector commitments, including the coverage of a sufficient portion of Chesapeake Bay cropland by nutrient management plans or the installation of a sufficient number of livestock stream exclusion practices, in the Chesapeake Bay Total Maximum Daily Load Phase III Watershed Implementation Plan. Such timeline shall include specific annual percentages for nutrient management plan and stream exclusion adoption to meet the requirements of the Phase III Watershed Implementation Plan. The year-to-year timeline for achieving specific metrics shall be used to determine reasonable progress per § 62.1-44.119:4 of the Code of Virginia, as created by this act. The Group shall include representatives from the Department of Conservation and Recreation, soil and water conservation districts, the Virginia Farm Bureau Federation, the Virginia Agribusiness Council, the Shenandoah Riverkeepers, the Chesapeake Bay Commission, the Chesapeake Bay Foundation, the James River Association, the Virginia Cooperative Extension, the Virginia Cattlemen's Association, the Virginia Association of the Commissioners of the Revenue, and the Virginia Association of Counties. The Group shall also include two legislative members, one each from the Senate and the House of Delegates appointed by the Senate Committee on Rules and the Speaker of the House of Delegates, respectively. Such legislative members shall be members of the Virginia delegation of the Chesapeake Bay Commission. A preliminary report from the Group shall be due on December 1, 2023. The first annual report for the Group shall be due on July 1, 2024, and include the timeline with specific metrics. Thereafter, the progress report shall be due on an annual schedule to be determined by the Group."

Acts 2023, cc. 735 and 736, cl. 3 provides: "That the Secretary of Agriculture and Forestry and the Secretary of Natural and Historic Resources shall, no later than August 1, 2025, jointly review the July 1, 2025, report of the Group established by the second enactment of this act as well as other relevant information at their disposal and together determine in their judgment whether work accomplished to date as well as planning and resource allocation are sufficient to substantially reach the allocated goals by July 1, 2028, and whether additional initiatives or resources or both will be necessary to continue an incentive-based effort."

§ 62.1-44.119:3. Virginia Natural Resources Commitment Fund reporting requirements.

Each soil and water conservation district shall report to the Department of Conservation and Recreation recommendations for improving the disbursement of funding and for program efficiencies that would expedite disbursal of funds provided through the Virginia Natural Resources Commitment Fund established under § 10.1-2128.1.

History.
2023, cc. 735, 736.

§ 62.1-44.119:4. Regulatory format on agricultural practices before effective date.

Notwithstanding the provisions of this chapter, no regulatory action pursuant to §§ 62.1-44.121 and 62.1-44.123 shall be imposed on agricultural practices prior to July 1, 2028, provided that reasonable progress is being achieved and a detailed plan to include full funding, as provided under subsection C of § 10.1-2128.1, for reaching the needed number of voluntary incentivized practices has been developed.

History.
2023, cc. 735, 736.

ARTICLE 2.
NUTRIENT MANAGEMENT PLANS FOR CHESAPEAKE BAY CROPLAND.

§ 62.1-44.120. (For contingent effective date, see § 62.1-44.119:1) Definitions.

As used in this article, unless the context requires a different meaning:

"Chesapeake Bay cropland" means cropland in the Commonwealth located in the Chesapeake Bay watershed on which fertilizer, manure, sewage sludge, or another compound containing nitrogen or phosphorous is applied. "Chesapeake Bay cropland" does not include lands on which bovines are pastured.

"*Department*" means the Department of Conservation and Recreation.

"*Nutrient management plan*" means a plan prepared by a certified nutrient management planner pursuant to § 10.1-104.2 and regulations adopted thereunder.

"*Operator*" means any person who exercises managerial control over Chesapeake Bay cropland.

History.
2020, cc. 1185, 1186.

§ 62.1-44.121. (For contingent effective date, see § 62.1-44.119:1) Chesapeake Bay cropland; nutrient management plans.

A. Any operator of 50 or more acres of Chesapeake Bay cropland shall maintain and implement an approved nutrient management plan.

B. The Department shall review any nutrient management plan submitted pursuant to subsection A within 30 days of submission and shall determine whether such nutrient management plan was prepared by a certified nutrient management planner. If the Department determines that such plan was prepared by a certified nutrient management planner, the Department shall approve such plan. An approved nutrient management plan shall be revised and resubmitted for approval to the Department every five years thereafter. If the Department determines that such nutrient management plan was not prepared by a certified nutrient management planner, the Department shall provide to the person who is required to submit the nutrient management plan a list of items required to be corrected, and such person shall have 30 days to resubmit the plan.

C. Any nutrient management plan required pursuant to subsection A shall be made available to the Department upon request.

D. Any information collected by the Department pursuant to subsection B or C is excluded from the mandatory disclosure provisions of the Virginia Freedom of Information Act (§ 2.2-3700 et seq.).

History.
2020, cc. 1185, 1186.

ARTICLE 3.

CHESAPEAKE BAY WATERSHED LIVESTOCK STREAM EXCLUSION.

§ 62.1-44.122. (For contingent effective date, see § 62.1-44.119:1) Definitions.

As used in this article, unless the context requires a different meaning:

"*Department*" means the Department of Conservation and Recreation.

"*Perennial stream*" means a body of water depicted as perennial on the most recent U.S. Geological Survey 7-1/2-minute topographic quadrangle map (scale 1:24,000) or identified by a method, established in guidelines approved by the Department, that does not require field verification.

"*Stream exclusion practice*" means protection of a body of water by fencing, including temporary fencing, or another physical means sufficient to exclude livestock from such body of water. A stream exclusion practice may include designated livestock stream crossings that satisfy criteria established in guidelines adopted by the Department.

History.
2020, cc. 1185, 1186.

Editor's note.
Acts 2020, cc. 1185 and 1186, cl. 4 provides: "That the Department of Conservation and Recreation shall, no later than July 1, 2021, establish through the Soil and Water Conservation Technical Advisory Committee and with stakeholder input a portable stream fencing practice for inclusion in the Virginia Agricul-

tural Best Management Practice Cost-Share Program."
Acts 2020, cc. 1185 and 1186, c. 5 provides: "That the Virginia Soil and Water Conservation Board, as established pursuant to § 10.1-502 of the Code of Virginia, shall establish, no later than December 31, 2020, the methodology for identifying perennial streams, as defined in § 62.1-44.122 of the Code of Virginia, as created by this act."

§ 62.1-44.123. (For contingent effective date, see § 62.1-44.119:1) Bovine livestock stream exclusion.

Any person who owns property in the Chesapeake Bay watershed on which 20 or more bovines are pastured shall install and maintain stream exclusion practices sufficient to exclude all such bovines from any perennial stream in the watershed.

History.
2020, cc. 1185, 1186.

CHAPTER 5.3.

RAPPAHANNOCK RIVER BASIN COMMISSION.

§ 62.1-69.25. (Effective January 1, 2024) Definitions.

As used in this chapter, unless the context requires a different meaning:
"*Rappahannock River Basin*" means that land area designated as the Rappahannock River Basin by the State Water Control Board pursuant to § 62.1-44.38 and which is also found in the Twenty-fifth, Twenty-seventh, Twenty-eighth, and Thirty-first Senatorial Districts or the Thirtieth, Sixty-first, Sixty-second, Sixty-third, Sixty-fourth, Sixty-fifth, Sixty-sixth, Sixty-seventh, and Sixty-eighth House of Delegates Districts, as those districts exist on January 1, 2024.

History.
1998, c. 553; 2000, cc. 386, 456; 2002, cc. 496, 523; 2013, c. 173; 2023, c. 98.

Editor's note.
Acts 2023, c. 98, cl. 2 provides: "That the provisions of this act shall become effective on January 1, 2024."

The 2023 amendments.
The 2023 amendment by c. 98, effective January 1, 2024, rewrote the section, which formerly read: "As used in this chapter, unless the context requires a different meaning: 'Rappahannock River Basin' means that land area designated as the Rappahannock River Basin by the State Water Control Board pursuant to § 62.1-44.38 and which is also found in the Fourth, Seventeenth, Twenty-fourth, Twenty-sixth, Twenty-seventh, and Twenty-eighth Senatorial Districts or the Eighteenth, Twenty-eighth, Thirtieth, Thirty-first, Fifty-fourth,

Fifty-eighth, Eighty-eighth, Ninety-eighth, and Ninety-ninth House of Delegates Districts, as those districts exist on January 1, 2012."

§ 62.1-69.29. (Effective January 1, 2024) Membership; terms; vacancies.

The membership of the Commission shall consist of 30 members, which includes 13 legislative members and 17 nonlegislative citizen members, to be appointed as follows: nine members of the House of Delegates, one member each of the Thirtieth, Sixty-first, Sixty-second, Sixty-third, Sixty-fourth, Sixty-fifth, Sixty-sixth, Sixty-seventh, and Sixty-eighth House of Delegates Districts, as those districts exist on January 1, 2024; four members of the Senate, one member each of the Twenty-fifth, Twenty-seventh, Twenty-eighth, and Thirty-first Senatorial Districts, as those districts exist on January 1, 2024; one member or designee of each of the 16 governing bodies of the jurisdictions in which not less than two percent of the jurisdiction is found wholly or partially within the Rappahannock River Basin, that at any time pass a resolution containing the language required by § 62.1-69.26, to be appointed by the respective local governing body; and one member or designee of a Soil and Water Conservation District found wholly or partially within the Rappahannock River Basin, to be appointed jointly by the Soil and Water Conservation Districts found wholly or partially within the Rappahannock River Basin. Nonlegislative citizen members of the Commission shall be citizens of the Commonwealth of Virginia.

All members of the Commission shall serve terms coincident with their terms of office. Appointments to fill vacancies, other than by expiration of a term, shall be for the unexpired terms. All members may be reappointed. Vacancies shall be filled in the same manner as the original appointments.

For the purposes of this section, "nonlegislative citizen member" means a member of one of the local governing bodies or the Soil and Water Conservation Districts of the jurisdictions found wholly or partially within the Rappahannock River Basin.

History.
1998, c. 553; 2000, cc. 386, 456; 2004, c. 471; 2009, c. 601; 2013, c. 173; 2023, c. 98.

Editor's note.
Acts 2023, c. 98, cl. 2 provides: "That the provisions of this act shall become effective on January 1, 2024."

The 2023 amendments.
The 2023 amendment by c. 98, effective January 1, 2024, rewrote the first paragraph.

§ 62.1-69.30. (Effective January 1, 2024) Chairman and vice-chairman; quorum; meetings.

The Commission shall elect annually a chairman and vice-chairman from among its membership. Nine members of the Commission shall constitute a quorum. The Commission shall meet no more than four times each year. The meetings of the Commission shall be held at the call of the chairman or whenever the majority of the members so request. Each member of the Commission shall have an equal vote.

History.
1998, c. 553; 2000, cc. 386, 456; 2004, c. 471; 2013, c. 173; 2023, c. 98.

Editor's note.
Acts 2023, c. 98, cl. 2 provides: "That the provisions of this act shall become effective on January 1, 2024."

The 2023 amendments.
The 2023 amendment by c. 98, effective January 1, 2024, added "annually" in the first

sentence; and substituted "Nine" for "Eleven"
in the second sentence.

§ 62.1-69.31. Staffing and support.

The local governing bodies and Planning District Commissions found wholly or partially in the Rappahannock River Basin shall provide staff support for the Commission as the localities determine appropriate. Additional staff support may be hired or contracted for by the Commission through funds raised by or provided to it. The Commission is authorized to determine the duties of such staff and fix staff compensation within available resources.

All agencies of the Commonwealth shall cooperate with the Commission and, upon request, shall assist the Commission in fulfilling its purposes and mission. The Secretary of Natural and Historic Resources or his designee shall act as the chief liaison between the administrative agencies and the Commission.

History.
1998, c. 553; 2000, cc. 386, 456; 2021, Sp. Sess. I, c. 401.

The 2021 Sp. Sess. I amendments.
The 2021 amendment by Sp. Sess. I, c. 401, effective July 1, 2021, inserted "and Historic."

§ 62.1-69.32. Withdrawal; dissolution.

A. A locality may withdraw from the Commission one year after providing a written notice to the Commission of its intent to do so.

B. The Commission may dissolve itself upon a two-thirds vote of all members.

C. The Commission may be dissolved by repeal or expiration of this chapter.

D. The Commission shall be dissolved if the membership of the Commission falls below two-thirds of those eligible.

E. Upon the Commission's dissolution, all funds and assets of the Commission shall be divided on a pro rata basis. The Commonwealth's share of the funds and assets shall be transferred to the Office of the Secretary of Natural and Historic Resources for appropriate distribution.

History.
1998, c. 553; 2000, cc. 386, 456; 2021, Sp. Sess. I, c. 401.

The 2021 Sp. Sess. I amendments.
The 2021 amendment by Sp. Sess. I, c. 401, effective July 1, 2021, inserted "and Historic."

§ 62.1-69.33. Funding.

A. The Commission shall annually adopt a budget, which shall include the Commission's estimated expenses. The funding of the Commission shall be a shared responsibility of state and local governments. The Commonwealth's contribution shall be set through the normal state appropriations process. The Commission's local government members shall determine a process for distribution of costs among the local government members.

B. The Commission shall annually designate a fiscal agent.

C. The accounts and records of the Commission showing the receipt and disbursement of funds from whatever source derived shall be in such form as the Auditor of Public Accounts prescribes, provided that such accounts shall correspond as nearly as possible to the accounts and records for such matters maintained by similar enterprises. The accounts and records of the Commission shall be subject to an annual audit by the Auditor of Public Accounts or his legal representative, and the costs of such audit services shall be borne by the Commission. The results of the audits shall be delivered to the chief elected officer in each of the Commission's member jurisdictions, the members of the

House of Delegates and the Senate who serve on the Commission, the chairmen of the House Committee on Appropriations and the Senate Committee on Finance and Appropriations, and the Secretary of Natural and Historic Resources. The Commission's fiscal year shall be the same as the Commonwealth's.

History.
1998, c. 553; 2000, cc. 386, 456; 2021, Sp. Sess. I, c. 401.

Editor's note.
The Virginia Code Commission authorized the substitution of "the Chairmen of the House Committee on Appropriations and the Senate Committee on Finance and Appropriations" for "the chairmen of the House Appropriations Committee and the Senate Finance Committee" in subsection C. March 10, 2021.

The 2021 Sp. Sess. I amendments.
The 2021 amendment by Sp. Sess. I, c. 401, effective July 1, 2021, in subsection C, inserted "and Appropriations" and "and Historic,"

CHAPTER 5.5.
ROANOKE RIVER BASIN BI-STATE COMMISSION.

Section
62.1-69.41. Staffing and support.

§ 62.1-69.41. Staffing and support.

The Virginia Department of Environmental Quality and the North Carolina Department of Environment and Natural Resources shall provide staff support to the Commission. Additional staff may be hired or contracted by the Commission through funds raised by or provided to it. The duties and compensation of such additional staff shall be determined and fixed by the Commission, within available resources.

All agencies of the Commonwealth of Virginia and the State of North Carolina shall cooperate with the Commission and, upon request, shall assist the Commission in fulfilling its responsibilities. The Virginia Secretary of Natural and Historic Resources and the North Carolina Secretary of the Department of Environment and Natural Resources or their designees shall each serve as the liaison between their respective state agencies and the Commission.

History.
2002, cc. 657, 843; 2003, c. 885; 2021, Sp. Sess. I, c. 401.

The 2021 Sp. Sess. I amendments.
The 2021 amendment by Sp. Sess. I, c. 401, effective July 1, 2021, inserted "and Historic."

CHAPTER 5.6.
RIVANNA RIVER BASIN COMMISSION.

Section
62.1-69.52. Withdrawal; dissolution.

§ 62.1-69.52. Withdrawal; dissolution.

A. A locality may withdraw from the Commission one year after providing written notice to the Commission of its intent to do so.

B. The Commission may be dissolved (i) upon three-fourths vote of its members, (ii) if the membership falls below three-fourths of the number of localities eligible for membership in the Commission, or (iii) by repeal or expiration of this chapter.

C. Upon the Commission's dissolution, all funds and assets of the Commission, including funds received from private sources, shall be divided and distributed on a pro rata basis to the member local governing bodies. All state funds and assets, if any, shall be transferred to the Office of the Secretary of Natural and Historic Resources for appropriate distribution.

History.
2004, c. 394; 2021, Sp. Sess. I, c. 401.

The 2021 Sp. Sess. I amendments.
The 2021 amendment by Sp. Sess. I, c. 401,

effective July 1, 2021, inserted "and Historic" in subsection C.

CHAPTER 8.

IMPOUNDMENT OF SURFACE WATERS.

Section
62.1-104. Definitions.

§ 62.1-104. Definitions.

(1) Except as modified below, the definitions contained in Title 1 shall apply in this chapter.

(2) *"Board"* means the State Water Control Board. However, when used outside the context of the promulgation of regulations, including regulations to establish general permits, pursuant to this chapter, "Board" means the Department of Environmental Quality.

(3) *"Impounding structure"* means a man-made device, whether a dam across a watercourse or other structure outside a watercourse, used or to be used for the authorized storage of flood waters for subsequent beneficial use.

(4) *"Watercourse"* means a natural channel having a well-defined bed and banks and in which water flows when it normally does flow. For the purposes hereof they shall be limited to rivers, creeks, streams, branches, and other watercourses which are nonnavigable in fact and which are wholly within the jurisdiction of the Commonwealth.

(5) *"Riparian land"* is land which is contiguous to and touches a watercourse. It does not include land outside the watershed of the watercourse. Real property under common ownership and which is not separated from riparian land by land of any other ownership shall likewise be deemed riparian land, notwithstanding that such real property is divided into tracts and parcels which may not bound upon the watercourse.

(6) *"Riparian owner"* is an owner of riparian land.

(7) *"Average flow"* means the average discharge of a stream at a particular point and normally is expressed in cubic feet per second. It may be determined from actual measurements or computed from the most accurate information available.

(8) *"Diffused surface waters"* are those which, resulting from precipitation, flow down across the surface of the land until they reach a watercourse, after which they become parts of streams.

(9) *"Floodwaters"* means water in a stream which is over and above the average flow.

(10) *"Court"* means the circuit court of the county or city in which an impoundment is located or proposed to be located.

317

History.
  Code 1950, § 62-94.1; 1956, c. 632; 1958, c. 638; 1968, c. 659; 1977, c. 26; 2022, c. 356.

The 2022 amendments.
  The 2022 amendment by c. 356 added the second sentence in subdivision (2).

CHAPTER 10.

VIRGINIA PORT AUTHORITY.

§ 62.1-129.1. Employees; employment; personnel rules; health insurance; retirement plans.

A. Employees of the Authority shall be employed on such terms and conditions as established by the Authority. The Board of Commissioners of the Authority shall develop and adopt personnel rules, policies, and procedures to give its employees grievance rights, ensure that employment decisions shall be based upon the merit and fitness of applicants, and prohibit discrimination because of race, religion, color, sex, sexual orientation, gender identity, or national origin.

B. The Authority shall issue a written notice to its employees regarding the Authority's status. The date upon which such written notice is issued shall be referred to herein as the "option date." Each employee may, by written request made within 180 days of the option date, elect not to become employed by the Authority. Any employee of the Virginia Port Authority who: (i) elects not to become employed by the Authority and who is not reemployed by any other department, institution, board, commission or agency of the Commonwealth; (ii) is not offered the opportunity to remain employed by the Authority; or (iii) is not offered a position with the Authority for which the employee is qualified or is offered a position that requires relocation or a reduction in salary, shall be eligible for the severance benefits conferred by the provisions of the Workforce Transition Act (§ 2.2-3200 et seq.). Any employee who accepts employment with the Authority shall not be considered to be involuntarily separated from state employment and shall not be eligible for the severance benefits conferred by the Workforce Transition Act.

C. Any employee of the Authority who is a member of any plan providing health insurance coverage pursuant to Chapter 28 (§ 2.2-2800 et seq.) of Title 2.2, shall continue to be a member of such health insurance plan under the same terms and conditions. Notwithstanding subsection A of § 2.2-2818, the costs of providing health insurance coverage to such employees who elect to continue to be members of the state employees' health insurance plan shall be paid by the Authority. Alternatively, an employee may elect to become a member of any health insurance plan established by the Authority. The Authority is authorized to: (i) establish a health insurance plan for the benefit of its employees and (ii) enter into agreements with the Department of Human Resource Management providing for the coverage of its employees under the state employees' health insurance plan, provided that such agreement requires the Authority to pay the costs of providing health insurance coverage under such plan.

D. Any retired employee of the Authority shall be eligible to receive the health insurance credit set forth in § 51.1-1400 provided the retired employee meets the eligibility criteria set forth in that section.

E. Any Authority employee who is a member of the Virginia Retirement System or other retirement plan as authorized by Article 4 (§ 51.1-125 et seq.) of Chapter 1 of Title 51.1, shall continue to be a member of the Virginia Retirement System or other authorized retirement plan under the same terms and conditions. Alternatively, such employee may elect to become a member of the retirement program established by the Authority for the benefit of its employees pursuant to § 51.1-126.4. The following rules shall apply:

1. The Authority shall collect and pay all employee and employer contributions to the Virginia Retirement System or other such authorized retirement plan for retirement and group life insurance in accordance with the provisions of Chapter 1 (§ 51.1-124.1 et seq.) of Title 51.1 for any employee who elects to remain a member of the Virginia Retirement System or other such authorized retirement plan.

2. Employees who elect to become members of the alternative retirement plan established by the Authority pursuant to § 51.1-126.4 shall be given full credit for their creditable service as defined in § 51.1-124.3, and vesting and benefit accrual under the retirement plan. For any such employee, employment with the Authority shall be treated as employment with any nonparticipating employer for purposes of the Virginia Retirement System or other retirement plan authorized pursuant to Article 4 (§ 51.1-125 et seq.) of Chapter 1 of Title 51.1.

3. For employees who elect to become members of the alternative retirement plan established by the Authority, the Virginia Retirement System or other such authorized plan shall transfer to the alternative retirement plan established by the Authority, assets equal to the actuarially determined present value of the accrued basic benefits as of the transfer date. For purposes hereof, the "basic benefits" means the benefits accrued under the Virginia Retirement System or other such authorized retirement plan based on creditable service and average final compensation as defined in § 51.1-124.3. The actuarial present value shall be determined by using the same actuarial factors and assumptions used in determining the funding needs of the Virginia Retirement System or other such authorized retirement plan so that the transfer of assets to the alternative retirement plan established by the Authority will have no effect on the funded status and financial stability of the Virginia Retirement System or other such authorized retirement plan. The Authority shall reimburse the Virginia Retirement System for the cost of actuarial services necessary to determine the present value of the accrued basic benefit of employees who transfer to an Authority retirement plan.

4. The Authority may provide that employees of the Authority who are eligible to participate in the deferred compensation plan sponsored by the Authority shall be enrolled automatically in such plan, unless such employee elects, in a manner prescribed by the Board, not to participate. The amount of the deferral under the automatic enrollment and the group of employees to which the automatic enrollment shall apply shall be set by the Board; provided however, that such employees are provided the opportunity to increase or decrease the amount of the deferral in accordance with the Internal Revenue Code of 1986, as amended.

History.
  1997, c. 232; 2000, cc. 66, 657; 2008, cc. 325, 621; 2020, c. 1137.

The 2020 amendments.
  The 2020 amendment by c. 1137 inserted "sexual orientation, gender identity" in the last sentence of subsection A.

§ 62.1-132.1. General powers.

A. Except as provided in subsection B, the Authority is vested with the powers of a body corporate, including, without limitation, to:

1. Sue and be sued;
2. Make contracts;
3. Adopt and use a common seal, and alter such seal at its pleasure;
4. Procure insurance, participate in insurance plans, and provide self-insurance. The purchase of insurance, participation in an insurance plan, or the creation of a self-insurance plan by the Authority shall not be deemed a waiver or relinquishment of any sovereign immunity to which the Authority or its officers, directors, employees, or agents are otherwise entitled;
5. Develop policies and procedures generally applicable to the procurement of goods, services and construction based on competitive principles; and
6. Exercise all the powers that are conferred upon industrial development authorities created pursuant to Chapter 49 (§ 15.2-4900 et seq.) of Title 15.2, except that the power to effect a change in ownership or operation of the Port of Virginia shall be subject to the provisions of § 62.1-132.19.

B. Expenditures by the Authority for capital projects are restricted to projects located on real property that is owned, leased, or operated by the Virginia Port Authority, except those expenditures (i) as provided in § 62.1-132.13 or 62.1-132.14, (ii) on grants to local government for financial assistance for port facilities as approved by the Board in policies posted on the Authority's website, or (iii) to provide support for the types of projects eligible for funding under subsection A of § 33.2-1509, subsection A of § 33.2-1600, or § 33.2-1526.4.

History.
  1981, c. 589; 1997, c. 232; 2013, cc. 762, 794; 2015, c. 609; 2020, cc. 1230, 1275. are identical and substituted "§ 33.2-1526.4" for "subsection A of § 33.2-1601" in clause (iii) of subsection B.

The 2020 amendments.
  The 2020 amendments by cc. 1230 and 1275

§ 62.1-132.3:2. Port of Virginia Economic and Infrastructure Development Grant Fund and Program.

A. From such funds as may be appropriated by the General Assembly and any gifts, grants, or donations from public or private sources, and any funds transferred at the request of the Executive Director from the Port Opportunity Fund created pursuant to § 62.1-132.3:1, there is hereby created in the state treasury a special nonreverting, permanent fund to be known as the Port of Virginia Economic and Infrastructure Development Grant Fund (the Fund), to be administered by the Virginia Port Authority. The Fund shall be established on the books of the Comptroller. Any moneys remaining in the Fund at the end of each fiscal year, including interest thereon, shall not revert to the general fund but shall remain in the Fund. Expenditures and disbursements from the Fund, which shall be in the form of grants, shall be made by the State Treasurer on warrants issued by the Comptroller upon written request signed by the Executive Director. Moneys in the Fund shall be used solely for the purpose of grants to qualified applicants to the Port of Virginia Economic and Infrastructure Development Grant Program.

B. As used in this section, unless the context requires a different meaning:

"New, permanent full-time position" means a job of an indefinite duration, created by a qualified company as a result of operations within the Commonwealth, requiring a minimum of 35 hours of an employee's time per week for the entire normal year of the company's operations, which normal year shall consist of at least 48 weeks, or a position of indefinite duration that requires a minimum of 35 hours of an employee's time per week for the portion of the taxable year in which the employee was initially hired for the qualified company's location within the Commonwealth. "New, permanent full-time position" includes security positions as required within a foreign trade zone, established pursuant to Foreign Trade Zones Act of 1934, as amended (19 U.S.C. §§ 81a through 81u). "New, permanent full-time position" does not include seasonal or temporary positions, jobs created when a position is shifted from an existing location in the Commonwealth to the qualified company's new or expanded location, or positions in building and grounds maintenance or other positions that are ancillary to the principal activities performed by the employees at the qualified company's location within the Commonwealth.

"Qualified company" means a corporation, limited liability company, partnership, joint venture, or other business entity that (i) locates or expands a facility within the Commonwealth; (ii) creates at least 25 new, permanent full-time positions for qualified full-time employees at a facility within the Commonwealth during its first year of operation or during the year when the expansion occurs; (iii) is involved in maritime commerce or exports or imports manufactured goods through the Port of Virginia; and (iv) is engaged in one or more of the following: the distribution, freight forwarding, freight handling, goods processing, manufacturing, warehousing, crossdocking, transloading, or wholesaling of goods exported and imported through the Port of Virginia; ship building and ship repair; dredging; marine construction; or offshore energy exploration or extraction.

"Qualified full-time employee" means an employee filling a new, permanent full-time position in the qualified company's location within the Commonwealth. A "qualified full-time employee" does not include an employee (i) for whom a tax credit was previously earned pursuant to § 58.1-439 or 58.1-439.12:06 by a related party as listed in § 267(b) of the Internal Revenue Code or by a trade or business under common control as defined in regulations issued pursuant to § 52(b) of the Internal Revenue Code; (ii) who was previously employed in the same job function at an existing location in the Commonwealth by a related party as listed in § 267(b) of the Internal Revenue Code; or (iii) whose job function was previously performed at a different location in the Commonwealth by an employee of a related party as listed in § 267(b) of the Internal Revenue Code or a trade or business under common control as defined in regulations issued pursuant to § 52(b) of the Internal Revenue Code.

C. Beginning January 1, 2014, but not later than December 31, 2024, and subject to appropriation, any qualified company that locates or expands a facility within the Commonwealth shall be eligible to apply for a one-time grant from the Fund, in an amount determined as follows:

1. One thousand dollars per new, permanent full-time position if the qualified company creates at least 25 new, permanent full-time positions for qualified full-time employees during its first year of operation or during the year in which the expansion occurs;

2. Fifteen hundred dollars per new, permanent full-time position if the qualified company creates at least 50 new, permanent full-time positions for

qualified full-time employees during its first year of operation or during the year in which the expansion occurs;

3. Two thousand dollars per new, permanent full-time position if the qualified company creates at least 75 new, permanent full-time positions for qualified full-time employees during its first year of operation or during the year in which the expansion occurs; and

4. Three thousand dollars per new, permanent full-time position if the qualified company creates at least 100 new, permanent full-time positions for qualified full-time employees during its first year of operation or during the year in which the expansion occurs.

D. The maximum amount of grant allowable per qualified company in any given fiscal year is $500,000. The maximum amount of grants allowable among all qualified companies in any given fiscal year is $5 million.

E. To qualify for a grant pursuant to this section, a qualified company must apply for the grant not later than March 31 in the year immediately following the location or expansion of a facility within the Commonwealth pursuant to an application process developed by the Virginia Port Authority. Within 90 days after the filing deadline, the Executive Director shall certify to the Comptroller and the qualified company the amount of grant to which the qualified company is entitled under this section. Payment of each grant shall be made by check issued by the State Treasurer on warrant of the Comptroller within 60 days of such certification and in the order that each completed eligible application is received. In the event that the amount of eligible grants requested in a fiscal year exceeds the funds available in the Fund or $5 million, such grants shall be paid in the next fiscal year in which funds are available.

F. A qualified company that has received a grant in accordance with the requirements provided in this section shall be eligible for a second grant from the Fund if it (i) locates or expands an additional facility in a separate location, as determined by the Virginia Port Authority, within the Commonwealth; (ii) creates at least 300 new, permanent full-time positions at the additional facility over and above those agreed upon in the qualified company's original memorandum of understanding with the Virginia Port Authority; and (iii) increases cargo volumes through the Port of Virginia by at least five percent, not including any volume increase resulting from the original grant, from the additional facility. If the qualified company satisfies the requirements provided in this subsection and receives a grant consistent with the requirements of this section, then the qualified company shall enter into another separate memorandum of understanding with the Virginia Port Authority as provided in subsection G.

G. Prior to receipt of a grant, the qualified company shall enter into a memorandum of understanding with the Virginia Port Authority establishing the requirements for maintaining the number of new, permanent full-time positions for qualified employees at the qualified company's location within the Commonwealth. If the number of new, permanent full-time positions for any of the three years immediately following receipt of a grant falls below the number of new, permanent full-time positions created during the year for which the grant is claimed, the amount of the grant must be recalculated using the decreased number of new, permanent full-time positions and the qualified company shall repay the difference.

H. No qualified company shall apply for a grant nor shall one be awarded under this section to an otherwise qualified company if (i) a credit pursuant to § 58.1-439 or 58.1-439.12:06 is claimed for the same employees or for capital expenditures at the same facility by the qualified company, by a related party as listed in § 267(b) of the Internal Revenue Code, or by a trade or business under common control as defined in regulations issued pursuant to § 52(b) of the Internal Revenue Code or (ii) the qualified company was a party to a reorganization as defined in § 368(b) of the Internal Revenue Code, and any corporation involved in the reorganization as defined in § 368(a) of the Internal Revenue Code previously received a grant under this section for the same facility or operations.

I. The Virginia Port Authority, with the assistance of the Virginia Economic Development Partnership, shall develop guidelines establishing procedures and requirements for qualifying for the grant, including the affirmative determination that each applicant is a qualified company, as defined above, engaged in a port-related business. The guidelines shall be exempt from the Administrative Process Act (§ 2.2-4000 et seq.). For the purposes of administering this grant program, the Virginia Port Authority and the Department of Taxation shall exchange information regarding whether a qualified company, a related party as listed in § 267(b) of the Internal Revenue Code, or a trade or business under common control as defined in regulations issued pursuant to § 52(b) of the Internal Revenue Code has claimed a credit pursuant to § 58.1-439 or 58.1-439.12:06 for the same employees or for capital expenditures at the same facility.

History.
2012, Sp. Sess. I, c. 3; 2013, cc. 549, 806; 2014, c. 470; 2015, c. 246; 2019, c. 565; 2023, cc. 238, 239.

The 2023 amendments.
The 2023 amendment by cc. 238 and 239 are identical, substituted "December 31, 2024" for "June 30, 2025" in the introductory language of subsection C.

§ 62.1-132.3:2.1. Port of Virginia Economic Development Grant Program and Fund.

A. There is hereby created in the state treasury a special nonreverting fund to be known as the Port of Virginia Economic Development Grant Fund (the Fund), to be administered by the Virginia Port Authority. The Fund shall be established on the books of the Comptroller. All funds appropriated for such purpose and any gifts, donations, grants, bequests, and other funds received on its behalf shall be paid into the state treasury and credited to the Fund. Interest earned on moneys in the Fund shall remain in the Fund and be credited to it. Any moneys remaining in the Fund, including interest thereon, at the end of each fiscal year shall not revert to the general fund but shall remain in the Fund. Moneys in the Fund shall be used solely for the purpose of providing grants to qualified applicants to the Program. Expenditures and disbursements from the Fund, which shall be in the form of grants, shall be made by the State Treasurer on warrants issued by the Comptroller upon written request signed by the Executive Director.

B. There is hereby created the Port of Virginia Economic Development Grant Program (the Program). The Program shall consist of the following component programs:

1. The Economic and Infrastructure Development Grant Program established by § 62.1-132.3:2.2.

2. The International Trade Facility Grant Program established by § 62.1-132.3:2.3.

C. 1. Except as provided in subdivision 3, for the Economic and Infrastructure Development Grant Program, the maximum amount of grants allowable among all qualified companies, as that term is defined in § 62.1-132.3:2.2, in any fiscal year shall be $5 million plus any amounts carried over from a prior fiscal year.

2. Except as provided in subdivision 3, for the International Trade Facility Grant Program, the maximum amount of grants allowable among all international trade facilities, as that term is defined in § 62.1-132.3:2.3, in any fiscal year shall be $1.25 million plus any amounts carried over from a prior fiscal year.

3. In the event that the amount of grants claimed for either of the programs described in subdivision 1 or 2 in any fiscal year is less than the maximum allowable amount, the excess amount may (i) be used to provide grants by the other program if that program is oversubscribed or (ii) be carried over to the next fiscal year.

History.
2023, cc. 238, 239.

§ 62.1-132.3:2.2. Economic and Infrastructure Development Grant Program.

A. As used in this section, unless the context requires a different meaning:

"*Fund*" means the Port of Virginia Economic Development Grant Fund established by § 62.1-132.3:2.1.

"*New, permanent full-time position*" means a job of an indefinite duration, created by a qualified company as a result of operations within the Commonwealth, requiring a minimum of 35 hours of an employee's time per week for the entire normal year of the company's operations, which normal year shall consist of at least 48 weeks, or a position of indefinite duration that requires a minimum of 35 hours of an employee's time per week for the portion of the taxable year in which the employee was initially hired for the qualified company's location within the Commonwealth. "New, permanent full-time position" includes security positions as required within a foreign trade zone, established pursuant to the Foreign Trade Zones Act of 1934, as amended (19 U.S.C. §§ 81a through 81u). "New, permanent full-time position" does not include seasonal or temporary positions, jobs created when a position is shifted from an existing location in the Commonwealth to the qualified company's new or expanded location, or positions in building and grounds maintenance or other positions that are ancillary to the principal activities performed by the employees at the qualified company's location within the Commonwealth.

"*Qualified company*" means a corporation, limited liability company, partnership, joint venture, or other business entity that (i) locates or expands a facility within the Commonwealth; (ii) creates at least 25 new, permanent full-time positions for qualified full-time employees at a facility within the Commonwealth during its first year of operation or during the year when the expansion occurs; (iii) is involved in maritime commerce or exports or imports manufactured goods through the Port of Virginia; (iv) is engaged in the distribution, freight forwarding, freight handling, goods processing, manufacturing, warehousing, crossdocking, transloading, or wholesaling of goods exported and imported through the Port of Virginia; ship building and ship repair; dredging; marine construction; or offshore energy exploration or extraction; and (v) pays a minimum entry-level wage rate per hour of at least 1.2 times the federal minimum wage or the Virginia minimum wage, as required by the Virginia Minimum Wage Act (§ 40.1-28.8 et seq.), whichever is higher. In areas that have an unemployment rate of one and one-half times the statewide average unemployment rate, the wage rate minimum may be waived by the Authority. Only full-time positions that qualify for benefits shall be eligible for assistance.

"*Qualified full-time employee*" means an employee filling a new, permanent full-time position in the qualified company's location within the Commonwealth. "Qualified full-time employee" does not include an employee (i) for whom a tax credit was previously earned pursuant to § 58.1-439 or 58.1-439.12:06 by a related party as listed in § 267(b) of the Internal Revenue Code or by a trade or business under common control as defined in regulations issued pursuant to § 52(b) of the Internal Revenue Code; (ii) who was previously employed in the same job function at an existing location in the Commonwealth by a related party as listed in § 267(b) of the Internal Revenue Code; or (iii) whose job function was previously performed at a different location in the Commonwealth by an employee of a related party as listed in § 267(b) of the Internal Revenue Code or a trade or business under common control as defined in regulations issued pursuant to § 52(b) of the Internal Revenue Code.

B. The Port of Virginia shall develop as a component of the Port of Virginia Economic Development Program the Economic and Infrastructure Development Grant Program.

C. Beginning January 1, 2025, and subject to appropriation, any qualified company that locates or expands a facility within the Commonwealth shall be eligible to apply for a one-time grant from the Fund, in an amount determined as follows:

1. If the qualified company creates at least 25 new, permanent full-time positions for qualified full-time employees during its first year of operation or during the year in which the expansion occurs, $1,000 per new, permanent full-time position;

2. If the qualified company creates at least 50 new, permanent full-time positions for qualified full-time employees during its first year of operation or during the year in which the expansion occurs, $1,500 per new, permanent full-time position;

3. If the qualified company creates at least 75 new, permanent full-time positions for qualified full-time employees during its first year of operation or during the year in which the expansion occurs, $2,000 per new, permanent full-time position; and

4. If the qualified company creates at least 100 new, permanent full-time positions for qualified full-time employees during its first year of operation or during the year in which the expansion occurs, $3,000 per new, permanent full-time position.

E. To qualify for a grant pursuant to this section, a qualified company must apply for the grant not later than March 31 in the year immediately following the location or expansion of a facility within the Commonwealth pursuant to an application process developed by the Virginia Port Authority. Within 90 days after the filing deadline, the Executive Director shall certify to the Comptroller and the qualified company the amount of grant to which the qualified company is entitled under this section. Payment of each grant shall be made by check issued by the State Treasurer on warrant of the Comptroller within 60 days of such certification and in the order that each completed eligible application is received.

F. A qualified company that has received a grant in accordance with the requirements provided in this section shall be eligible for a second grant from the Fund if it (i) locates or expands an additional facility in a separate location, as determined by the Virginia Port Authority, within the Commonwealth; (ii) creates at least 300 new, permanent full-time positions at the additional facility over and above those agreed upon in the qualified company's original memorandum of understanding with the Virginia Port Authority; and (iii) increases cargo volumes through the Port of Virginia by at least five percent, not including any volume increase resulting from the original grant, from the additional facility. If the qualified company satisfies the requirements provided in this subsection and receives a grant consistent with the requirements of this section, then the qualified company shall enter into another separate memorandum of understanding with the Virginia Port Authority as provided in subsection G.

G. Prior to receipt of a grant, the qualified company shall enter into a memorandum of understanding with the Virginia Port Authority establishing the requirements for maintaining the number of new, permanent full-time positions for qualified employees at the qualified company's location within the Commonwealth. If the number of new, permanent full-time positions for any of the three years immediately following receipt of a grant falls below the number of new, permanent full-time positions created during the year for which the grant is claimed, the amount of the grant shall be recalculated using the decreased number of new, permanent full-time positions, and the qualified company shall repay the difference.

H. No qualified company shall apply for a grant, nor shall one be awarded under this section to an otherwise qualified company, if (i) a credit pursuant to § 58.1-439 or 58.1-439.12:06 or a grant pursuant to Section § 62.1-132.3:2.3 is claimed for the same employees or for capital expenditures at the same facility by the qualified company, by a related party as listed in § 267(b) of the Internal Revenue Code, or by a trade or business under common control as defined in regulations issued pursuant to § 52(b) of the Internal Revenue Code or (ii) the qualified company was a party to a reorganization as defined in § 368(b) of the Internal Revenue Code, and any corporation involved in the reorganization as defined in § 368(a) of the Internal Revenue Code previously received a grant under this section for the same facility or operations.

I. The Virginia Port Authority, with the assistance of the Virginia Economic Development Partnership, shall develop guidelines establishing procedures and requirements for qualifying for the grant, including the affirmative determination that each applicant is a qualified company, as defined above, engaged in a port-related business. The guidelines shall be exempt from the Administrative Process Act (§ 2.2-4000 et seq.). For the purposes of administering this grant program, the Virginia Port Authority and the Department of Taxation shall exchange information regarding whether a qualified company, a related party as listed in § 267(b) of the Internal Revenue Code, or a trade or business under common control as defined in regulations issued pursuant to § 52(b) of the Internal Revenue Code has claimed a credit pursuant to § 58.1-439 or 58.1-439.12:06 or a grant pursuant to § 62.1-132.3:2.3 for the same employees or for capital expenditures at the same facility.

History.
2023, cc. 238, 239.

§ 62.1-132.3:2.3. International Trade Facility Grant Program.

A. As used in this section, unless the context requires a different meaning:

"Affiliated companies" means two or more companies related to each other so that (i) one company owns at least 80 percent of the voting power of the other or others or (ii) the same interest owns at least 80 percent of the voting power of two or more companies.

"Capital investment" means the amount properly chargeable to a capital account for improvements to rehabilitate or expand depreciable real property placed in service during the taxable year and the cost of machinery, tools, and equipment used in an international trade facility directly related to the movement of cargo. "Capital investment" includes expenditures associated with any exterior, structural, mechanical, or electrical improvements necessary to expand or rehabilitate a building for commercial or industrial use and

excavations, grading, paving, driveways, roads, sidewalks, landscaping, or other land improvements. For purposes of this section, machinery, tools, and equipment shall be deemed to include only that property placed in service by the international trade facility on and after January 1, 2025. Machinery, tools, and equipment excludes property (i) for which a credit under this section was previously granted; (ii) placed in service by the taxpayer, by a related party as defined in § 267(b) of the Internal Revenue Code, as amended, or by a trade or business under common control as defined in § 52(b) of the Internal Revenue Code, as amended; or (iii) previously in service in the Commonwealth that has a basis in the hands of the person acquiring it, determined in whole or in part by reference to the basis of such property in the hands of the person from whom acquired or § 1014(a) of the Internal Revenue Code, as amended.

"Capital investment" does not include:

1. The cost of acquiring any real property or building;

2. The cost of furnishings;

3. Any expenditure associated with appraisal, architectural, engineering, or interior design fees;

4. Loan fees, points, or capitalized interest;

5. Legal, accounting, realtor, sales and marketing, or other professional fees;

6. Closing costs, permit fees, user fees, zoning fees, impact fees, or inspection fees;

7. Bids, insurance, signage, utilities, bonding, copying, rent loss, or temporary facilities costs incurred during construction;

8. Utility hook-up or access fees;

9. Outbuildings; or

10. The cost of any well or septic system.

"*Fund*" means the Port of Virginia Economic Development Grant Fund established by § 62.1-132.3:2.1.

"*Indexing ratio*" means the greater of (i) the change in the United States Average Consumer Price Index for all items, all urban consumers (CPI-U), as published by the Bureau of Labor Statistics for the U.S. Department of Labor for the previous year, or (ii) zero.

"*International trade facility*" means a company that:

1. Is engaged in port-related activities, including, warehousing, distribution, freight forwarding and handling, and goods processing;

2. Uses maritime port facilities located in the Commonwealth;

3. Transports at least five percent more cargo through maritime port facilities in the Commonwealth during the calendar year than was transported by the company through such facilities during the preceding calendar year; and

4. Pays a minimum entry-level wage rate per hour of at least 1.2 times the federal minimum wage or the Virginia minimum wage, as required by the Virginia Minimum Wage Act (§ 40.1- 28.8 et seq.), whichever is higher. In areas that have an unemployment rate of one and one-half times the statewide average unemployment rate, the wage rate minimum may be waived by the Authority. Only full-time positions that qualify for benefits shall be eligible for assistance.

"*New, permanent full-time position*" means a job of an indefinite duration, created by a qualified company as a result of operations within the Commonwealth, requiring a minimum of 35 hours of an employee's time per week for the entire normal year of the company's operations, which normal year shall consist of at least 48 weeks, or a position of indefinite duration that requires a minimum of 35 hours of an employee's time per week for the portion of the taxable year in which the employee was initially hired for the qualified company's location within the Commonwealth. "New, permanent full-time position" includes security positions as required within a foreign trade zone, established pursuant to Foreign Trade Zones Act of 1934, as amended (19 U.S.C. §§ 81a through 81u). "New, permanent full-time position" does not include seasonal or temporary positions, jobs created when a position is shifted from an existing location in the Commonwealth to the qualified company's new or expanded location, or positions in building and grounds maintenance or other positions that are ancillary to the principal activities performed by the employees at the qualified company's location within the Commonwealth.

"*Qualified full-time employee*" means an employee filling a new, permanent full-time position in the qualified company's location within the Commonwealth. "Qualified full-time employee" does not include an employee (i) for whom a tax credit was previously earned pursuant to § 58.1-439 or 58.1-439.12:06 by a related party as listed in § 267(b) of the Internal Revenue Code or by a trade or business under common control as defined in regulations issued pursuant to § 52(b) of the Internal Revenue Code; (ii) who was previously employed in the same job function at an existing location in the Commonwealth by a related party as listed in § 267(b) of the Internal Revenue Code; or (iii) whose job function was previously performed at a different location in the Commonwealth by an employee of a related party as listed in § 267(b) of the Internal Revenue Code or a trade or business under common control as defined in regulations issued pursuant to § 52(b) of the Internal Revenue Code.

B. The Port of Virginia shall develop as a component of the Port of Virginia Economic Development Program the International Trade Facility Grant Program.

C. Beginning January 1, 2025, and subject to appropriation, an international trade facility that increases its qualified trade activities shall be eligible to receive a grant from the Fund. The amount of such grant shall be equal to either (i) $3,500, adjusted each year by the indexing ratio, per qualified full-time employee that results from increased qualified trade activities by the applicant or (ii) an amount equal to two percent of the capital investment made by the applicant to facilitate the increased qualified trade activities. The election of which award to apply for shall be the responsibility of the applicant. Both awards shall not be granted for the same activities that occur in a calendar year. The portion of such grant earned under clause (i) with respect to any qualified full-time employee who works in the Commonwealth for less than 12 full months during the credit year shall be determined by multiplying the credit amount by a fraction the numerator of which is the number of full months such employee worked for the international trade facility in the Commonwealth during the credit year and the denominator of which is 12.

D. Prior to receipt of a grant, the international trade facility shall enter into a memorandum of understanding with the Virginia Port Authority establishing the requirements for either a schedule of capital investment or maintaining the number of new, permanent full-time positions for qualified employees at the international trade facility's location within the Commonwealth. If the number of new, permanent full-time positions for any of the three years immediately following receipt of a grant falls below the number of new, permanent full-time positions created during the year for which the grant is claimed, the amount of the grant shall be recalculated using the decreased number of new, permanent full-time positions, and the international trade facility shall repay the difference.

E. No international trade facility shall apply for a grant, nor shall one be awarded under this section to an otherwise qualified international trade facility, if (i) a credit pursuant to § 58.1-439 or 58.1-439.12:06 or a grant pursuant to §§ 62.1-132.3:2.2 is claimed for the same employees or for capital expenditures at the same facility by the international trade facility, by a related party as listed in § 267(b) of the Internal Revenue Code, or by a trade or business under common control as defined in regulations issued pursuant to § 52(b) of the Internal Revenue Code or (ii) the international trade facility was a party to a reorganization as defined in § 368(b) of the Internal Revenue Code, and any corporation involved in the reorganization as defined in § 368(a) of the Internal Revenue Code previously received a grant under this section for the same facility or operations.

F. The Virginia Port Authority, with the assistance of the Virginia Economic Development Partnership, shall develop guidelines establishing procedures and requirements for qualifying for the grant, including the affirmative determination that each applicant is an international trade facility, engaged in a port-related business. The guidelines shall be exempt from the Administrative Process Act (§ 2.2-4000 et seq.).

History.
2023, cc. 238, 239.

§ 62.1-132.3:4. Virginia Waterway Maintenance Grant Program.

A. Once each fiscal year, the Authority shall award a grant of funds to a qualified applicant or applicants to support a dredging project or projects that have been approved by the Authority. The source of the grant funds shall be the Virginia Waterway Maintenance Fund created pursuant to § 62.1-132.3:3. Applicants shall be limited to political subdivisions and the governing bodies of Virginia localities.

B. The Authority shall develop guidelines establishing an application process, procedures for evaluating the feasibility of a proposed dredging project, and procedures for awarding grants. The guidelines and procedures shall be exempt from the Administrative Process Act (§ 2.2-4000 et seq.). The guidelines and procedures shall provide that:

1. The Authority shall evaluate each application to determine its completeness, the sufficiency of its justification for the proposed project, the status of any necessary permits, the adequacy of its project management organization, and the potential beneficial use of dredged materials for the purpose of mitigation of coastal erosion, flooding, or other purposes for the common good.

2. The Authority shall not require any level of matching contributions from the applicant.

3. No award of a grant shall support any dredging project for a solely privately owned marina or dock. However, the Authority may award a grant to a political subdivision or governing body for the dredging of a waterway channel with a bottom that is privately owned if such political subdivision or governing body holds a lease of such bottom with a term of 25 years or more.

4. Prior to receipt of a grant, the applicant shall enter into a memorandum of understanding with the Authority establishing the requirements for the use of the grant funds.

C. Projects for which the Authority may award grant funding include (i) feasibility and cost evaluations, pre-project engineering studies, and project permitting and contracting costs for a waterway project conducted by the Commonwealth; (ii) the state portion of a nonfederal sponsor funding requirement for a federal project, which may include the beneficial use of dredged materials that are not covered by federal funding; (iii) the Commonwealth's maintenance of shallow-draft navigable waterway channel maintenance dredging and the construction and management of areas for the placement of dredged material; and (iv) the beneficial use, for environmental restoration and the mitigation of coastal erosion or flooding, of dredged materials from waterway projects conducted by the Commonwealth.

History.
2018, c. 642; 2022, c. 282.

The 2022 amendments.
The 2022 amendment by c. 282, added the second sentence of subdivision B 3.

§ 62.1-132.3:5. Virginia Port Volume Increase Grant Program and Fund.

A. As used in this section:

"*Agricultural entity*" means a person engaged in growing or producing wheat, grains, fruits, nuts, or crops; tobacco, nursery, or floral products; forestry products, excluding raw wood fiber or wood fiber processed or manufactured for use as fuel for the generation of electricity; or seafood, meat, dairy, or poultry products.

"*Base year port cargo volume*" means the total amount of (i) net tons of noncontainerized cargo, (ii) TEUs of cargo, or (iii) units of roll-on/roll-off cargo actually transported by way of a waterborne ship or vehicle through a port facility during the period from January 1, 2023, through December 31, 2024. Base year port cargo volume must be at least 75 net tons of noncontainerized cargo, 10 loaded TEUs, or 10 units of roll-on/roll-off cargo for an eligible entity to be eligible for the grants provided in this section. For an eligible entity that did not ship that amount in the year ending December 31, 2023, including an eligible entity that locates in Virginia after such periods, its base cargo volume shall be measured by the initial January 1 through December 31 calendar year in which it meets the requirements of 75 net tons of noncontainerized cargo, 10 loaded TEUs, or 10 units of roll-on/roll-off cargo. Base year port cargo volume shall be recalculated each calendar year after the initial base year.

"*Eligible entity*" means an agricultural entity, manufacturing-related entity, or mineral and gas entity.

"*Major facility*" means a new facility to be located in Virginia that is projected to import or export cargo through a port in excess of 25,000 TEUs in its first calendar year.

"*Manufacturing-related entity*" means a person engaged in the manufacturing of goods or the distribution of manufactured goods.

"*Mineral and gas entity*" means a person engaged in severing minerals or gases from the earth.

"*Port cargo volume*" means the total amount of net tons of noncontainerized cargo, net units of roll-on/roll-off cargo, or containers measured in TEUs of cargo transported by way of a waterborne ship or vehicle through a port facility.

"*Port facility*" means any publicly or privately owned facility located within the Commonwealth through which cargo is transported by way of a waterborne ship or vehicle to or from destinations outside the Commonwealth and that handles cargo owned by third parties in addition to cargo owned by the port facility's owner.

"*TEU*" or "*20-foot equivalent unit*" means a volumetric measure based on the size of a container that is 20 feet long by eight feet wide by eight feet, six inches high.

B. There is hereby created in the state treasury a special nonreverting fund to be known as the Virginia Port Volume Increase Grant Fund, referred to in this section as "the Fund." The Fund shall be established on the books of the Comptroller. All funds appropriated for such purpose and any gifts, donations, grants, bequests, and other funds received on its behalf shall be paid into the state treasury and credited to the Fund. Interest earned on moneys in the Fund shall remain in the Fund and be credited to it. Any moneys remaining in the Fund, including interest thereon, at the end of each fiscal year shall not revert to the general fund but shall remain in the Fund. Moneys in the Fund shall be used solely for the purpose of providing grants to eligible entities pursuant to subsections C and D. Expenditures and disbursements from the Fund, which shall be in the form of grants, shall be made by the State Treasurer on warrants issued by the Comptroller upon written request signed by the Executive Director.

C. 1. Beginning January 1, 2025, an eligible entity that uses port facilities in the Commonwealth and increases its port cargo volume at these facilities by a minimum of five percent in a single calendar year over its base year port cargo volume shall be eligible to receive a grant from the Fund in an amount determined by the Virginia Port Authority in accordance with subdivisions 2 and 3. The Virginia Port Authority may waive the requirement that port cargo volume be increased by a minimum of five percent over base year port cargo volume for any eligible entity that qualifies as a major facility.

2. Eligible entities that increase their port cargo volume by a minimum of five percent in a calendar year shall be eligible to receive a grant in the amount of $50 for each TEU, unit of roll-on/roll-off cargo, or 16 net tons of noncontainerized cargo, as applicable, above the base year port cargo volume. An eligible entity that is a major facility as defined in this section shall be eligible to receive a grant in the amount of $50 for each TEU, unit of roll-on/roll-off cargo, or 16 net tons of noncontainerized cargo, as applicable, transported through a port facility during the major facility's first calendar year. An eligible entity may not receive more than $250,000 for each calendar year. The maximum amount of grants allowed for all eligible entities pursuant to this section shall not exceed $3.8 million for each calendar year. In the event that the amount of eligible grants requested in a fiscal year exceeds the funds available in the Fund or $3.8 million, such grants shall be paid in the next fiscal year in which funds are available. The Virginia Port Authority shall allocate the grants pursuant to the provisions of subdivision D.

3. An eligible entity shall be eligible for a grant pursuant to this section only if the eligible entity owns the cargo at the time the port facilities are used.

D. For every year in which an eligible entity is applies for a grant, the eligible entity shall submit an application to the Virginia Port Authority by March 1 of the calendar year after the calendar year in which the increase in port cargo volume occurs. The eligible entity shall attach a schedule to its application with the following information and any other information requested by the Virginia Port Authority:

1. A description of how the base year port cargo volume and the increase in port cargo volume were determined;

2. The amount of the base year port cargo volume; and

3. The amount of the increase in port cargo volume for the calendar year stated both as a percentage increase and as a total increase in net tons of noncontainerized cargo, TEUs of cargo, and units of roll-on/roll-off cargo, as applicable, including information that demonstrates an increase in port cargo volume in excess of the minimum amount required to claim the grants awarded pursuant to this section.

E. The Virginia Port Authority shall not make awards under this section to applicants who are receiving tax credits for under § 58.1-439.12:10 for the same cargo.

F. The Virginia Port Authority shall develop guidelines establishing procedures and requirements for qualifying for grants under this section. The guidelines shall be exempt from the Administrative Process Act (§ 2.2-4000 et seq.).

History.
  2023, cc. 238, 239.

§ 62.1-132.3:6. Virginia Barge and Rail Usage Grant Program and Fund.

A. As used in this section:

"Barge and rail cargo volume" means the total amount of (i) net tons of noncontainerized cargo, (ii) TEUs of cargo, or (iii) units of roll-on/roll-off cargo actually by barge or rail rather than by trucks or other motor vehicles on the Commonwealth's highways, measured from January 1 through December 31 of each calendar year.

"International trade facility" means a company that:

1. Does business in the Commonwealth and is engaged in port-related activities, including warehousing, distribution, freight forwarding and handling, and goods processing;

2. Has the sole discretion and authority to move cargo originating or terminating in the Commonwealth;

3. Uses maritime port facilities located in the Commonwealth; and

4. Uses barges and rail systems to move cargo through port facilities in the Commonwealth rather than trucks or other motor vehicles on the Commonwealth's highways.

B. There is hereby created in the state treasury a special nonreverting fund to be known as the Virginia Barge and Rail Usage Grant Fund, referred to in this section as "the Fund." The Fund shall be established on the books of the Comptroller. All funds appropriated for such purpose and any gifts, donations, grants, bequests, and other funds received on its behalf shall be paid into the state treasury and credited to the Fund. Interest earned on moneys in the Fund shall remain in the Fund and be credited to it. Any moneys remaining in the Fund, including interest thereon, at the end of each fiscal year shall not revert to the general fund but shall remain in the Fund. Moneys in the Fund shall be used solely for the purpose of providing grants to international trade facilities pursuant to subsections C and D. Expenditures and disbursements from the Fund, which shall be in the form of grants, shall be made by the State Treasurer on warrants issued by the Comptroller upon written request signed by the Executive Director.

C. 1. Beginning January 1, 2025, an international trade facility shall be eligible to receive a grant from the Fund in an amount determined by the Virginia Port Authority in accordance with subdivision 2.

2. The amount of the grant shall be $25 per 20-foot equivalent unit (TEU), 16 tons of noncontainerized cargo, or one unit of roll-on/roll-off cargo moved by barge or rail rather than by trucks or other motor vehicles on the Commonwealth's highways.

3. Applicants shall be required to increase their barge and rail cargo volume for a calendar year by at least five percent above the preceding calendar year's volume in order to be eligible for the grant.

D. The Virginia Port Authority shall issue the grants under this section, and in no case shall more than $1 million in grants be issued pursuant to this section in any fiscal year of the Commonwealth. In the event that the amount of eligible grants requested in a fiscal year exceeds the funds available in the

Fund or $1 million, such grants shall be paid in the next fiscal year in which funds are available. The international trade facility shall not receive any grant under this section unless it has applied to the Virginia Port Authority for the grant and the Virginia Port Authority has approved the grant. The Virginia Port Authority shall determine the grant amount allowable for the year and shall provide a written certification to the international trade facility, which certification shall report the amount of the grant approved by the Virginia Port Authority.

E. The Virginia Port Authority shall not make awards under this section to applicants who are receiving tax credits for under § 58.1-439.12:09 for the same cargo.

F. The Virginia Port Authority shall develop guidelines establishing procedures and requirements for qualifying for grants under this section. The guidelines shall be exempt from the Administrative Process Act (§ 2.2-4000 et seq.).

History.
2023, cc. 238, 239.

§ 62.1-140. Definitions; bond resolution; form and requisites of bonds; sale and disposition of proceeds; temporary bonds.

Editor's note.
Acts 2020, c. 1289, as amended by Acts 2021, Sp. Sess. I, c. 552, Item 458 A 6, and Acts 2022, Sp. Sess. I, c. 2, Item 467 A 7, effective for the biennium ending June 30, 2023, provides: "Notwithstanding § 62.1-140, Code of Virginia, the aggregate principal amount of Commonwealth Port Fund bonds, and including any other long-term commitment that utilizes the Commonwealth Port Fund, shall not exceed $440,000,000."

CHAPTER 20.

MISCELLANEOUS OFFENSES.

Section
62.1-195.1. [Repealed.]
62.1-195.3. [Repealed.]

§ 62.1-195.1. Repealed by Acts 2021, Sp. Sess. I, c. 387, cl. 11, effective October 1, 2021.

Cross references.
For this section as effective October 1, 2021, see §§ 45.2-1645 and 45.2-1646.

Editor's note.
Acts 2021, Sp. Sess. I, c. 532, amended this section effective October 1, 2021. The amendment was given effect in § 45.2-1645 at the direction of the Virginia Code Commission.

Former § 62.1-195.1, pertaining to prohibition of drilling for oil or gas in the Chesapeake Bay, derived from Acts 1989, c. 325; 1990, c. 967; 1992, cc. 480, 887; 1993, c. 239; 1994, c. 957; 2012, cc. 785, 819; 2013, cc. 756, 793; 2021, Sp. Sess. I, c. 401.

§ 62.1-195.3. Repealed by Acts 2021, Sp. Sess. I, c. 387, cl. 11, effective October 1, 2021.

Cross references.
For this section as effective October 1, 2021, see § 45.2-1647.

fracturing and groundwater management area, derived from 2020, c. 626.

Editor's note.
Former § 62.1-195.3, pertaining to hydraulic

CHAPTER 21.

VIRGINIA RESOURCES AUTHORITY.

§ 62.1-198. Legislative findings and purposes.

The General Assembly finds that there exists in the Commonwealth a critical need for additional sources of funding to finance the present and future needs of the Commonwealth for water supply; land conservation or land preservation, including land for parks and other recreational purposes; oyster restoration projects, including planting and replanting with seed oysters, oyster shells, or other material that will catch, support, and grow oysters; wastewater treatment facilities; drainage facilities; solid waste treatment, disposal, and management facilities; recycling facilities; resource recovery facilities; energy conservation and energy efficiency projects; professional sports facilities; certain heavy rail transportation facilities; public safety facilities; airport facilities; the remediation of brownfields and contaminated properties, including properties contaminated by defective drywall; the design and construction of roads, public parking garages, and other public transportation facilities, and facilities for public transportation by commuter rail; construction of local government buildings, including administrative and operations systems and other local government equipment and infrastructure; site acquisition and site development work for economic development projects; community development projects, to include projects related to the production and preservation of housing, including housing for persons and families of low and moderate income; recovered gas energy facilities; the location or retention of federal facilities in the Commonwealth and the support of the transition of former federal facilities from use by the federal government to other uses; and renewable energy projects, including solar, wind, biomass, waste-to-energy, and geothermal. This need can be alleviated in part through the creation of a resources authority. Its purpose is to encourage the investment of both public and private funds and to make loans, grants, and credit enhancements available to local governments to finance water and sewer projects; land conservation or land preservation programs or projects; oyster restoration projects; drainage projects; solid waste treatment, disposal, and management projects; recycling projects; energy conservation and energy efficiency projects; professional sports facilities; resource recovery projects; public safety facilities; airport facilities; the remediation of brownfields and contaminated properties, including properties contaminated by defective drywall; the design and construction of roads, public parking garages, and other public transportation facilities, and facilities for public transportation by commuter rail; site acquisition and site development work for the benefit of economic development projects; community development projects, to include projects related to the production and preservation of housing, including housing for persons and families of low and moderate income; technology; construction of local government buildings, including administrative and operations systems and other local government equipment and infrastructure; infrastructure for broadband services; recovered gas energy facilities; federal facilities or former federal facilities; and renewable energy projects. The General Assembly determines that the creation of an authority for this purpose is in the public interest, serves a public purpose, and will promote the health, safety, welfare, convenience, or prosperity of the people of the Commonwealth.

History.
1984, c. 699; 1989, cc. 533, 551; 1990, c. 506; 1998, c. 399; 2000, c. 790; 2001, cc. 652, 661; 2003, c. 561; 2005, cc. 727, 769; 2007, cc. 81, 649, 663; 2008, cc. 3, 24, 238, 259, 504, 605, 613; 2009, cc. 14, 246, 311, 543, 632; 2010, cc. 42, 724, 820; 2011, c. 270; 2023, cc. 440, 441.

The 2023 amendments.
The 2023 amendment by cc. 440 and 441 are identical, substituted "economic development projects; community development projects, to include projects related to the production and preservation of housing, including housing for persons and families of low and moderate income" in the first sentence; added "community development projects, to include projects related to the production and preservation of housing, including housing for persons and families of low and moderate income" in the second sentence; and made stylistic changes.

§ 62.1-199. Definitions.

As used in this chapter, unless the context requires a different meaning:

"Authority" means the Virginia Resources Authority created by this chapter.

"Board of Directors" means the Board of Directors of the Authority.

"Bonds" means any bonds, notes, debentures, interim certificates, bond, grant or revenue anticipation notes, lease and sale-leaseback transactions, or any other obligations of the Authority for the payment of money.

"Capital Reserve Fund" means the reserve fund created and established by the Authority in accordance with § 62.1-215.

"Cost," as applied to any project financed under the provisions of this chapter, means the total of all costs incurred by the local government as reasonable and necessary for carrying out all works and undertakings necessary or incident to the accomplishment of any project. It includes, without limitation, all necessary developmental, planning and feasibility studies, surveys, plans and specifications, architectural, engineering, financial, legal or other special services, the cost of acquisition of land and any buildings and improvements thereon, including the discharge of any obligations of the sellers of such land, buildings or improvements, real estate appraisals, site preparation and development, including demolition or removal of existing structures, construction and reconstruction, labor, materials, machinery and equipment, the reasonable costs of financing incurred by the local government in the course of the development of the project, including the cost of any credit enhancements, carrying charges incurred before placing the project in service, interest on local obligations issued to finance the project to a date subsequent to the estimated date the project is to be placed in service, necessary expenses incurred in connection with placing the project in service, the funding of accounts and reserves which the Authority may require, and the cost of other items which the Authority determines to be reasonable and necessary. It also includes the amount of any contribution, grant, or aid which a local government may make or give to any adjoining state, the District of Columbia or any

department, agency, or instrumentality thereof to pay the costs incident and necessary to the accomplishment of any project, including, without limitation, the items set forth above. "Cost" also includes interest and principal payments pursuant to any installment purchase agreement.

"Credit enhancements" means surety bonds, insurance policies, letters of credit, guarantees, and other forms of collateral or security.

"Defective drywall" means the same as that term is defined in § 36-156.1.

"Federal facility" means any building or infrastructure used or to be used by the federal government, including any building or infrastructure located on lands owned by the federal government.

"Federal government" means the United States of America, or any department, agency, or instrumentality, corporate or otherwise, of the United States of America.

"Former federal facility" means any federal facility formerly used by the federal government or in transition from use by the federal government to a facility all or part of which is to serve any local government.

"Local government" means any county, city, town, municipal corporation, authority, district, commission, or political subdivision created by the General Assembly or pursuant to the Constitution and laws of the Commonwealth or any combination of any two or more of the foregoing.

"Local obligations" means any bonds, notes, debentures, interim certificates, bond, grant or revenue anticipation notes, leases, credit enhancements, or any other obligations of a local government for the payment of money.

"Minimum capital reserve fund requirement" means, as of any particular date of computation, the amount of money designated as the minimum capital reserve fund requirement which may be established in the resolution of the Authority authorizing the issuance of, or the trust indenture securing, any outstanding issue of bonds or credit enhancement.

"Project" means (i) any water supply or wastewater treatment facility, including a facility for receiving and stabilizing septage or a soil drainage management facility, and any solid waste treatment, disposal, or management facility, recycling facility, federal facility or former federal facility, or resource recovery facility located or to be located in the Commonwealth, the District of Columbia, or any adjoining state, all or part of which facility serves or is to serve any local government, and (ii) any federal facility located or to be located in the Commonwealth, provided that both the Board of Directors of the Authority and the governing body of the local government receiving the benefit of the loan, grant, or credit enhancement from the Authority make a determination or finding to be embodied in a resolution or ordinance that the undertaking and financing of such facility is necessary for the location or retention of such facility and the related use by the federal government in the Commonwealth. The term includes, without limitation, water supply and intake facilities; water treatment and filtration facilities; water storage facilities; water distribution facilities; sewage and wastewater (including surface and ground water) collection, treatment, and disposal facilities; drainage facilities and projects; solid waste treatment, disposal, or management facilities; recycling facilities; resource recovery facilities; related office, administrative, storage, maintenance, and laboratory facilities; and interests in land related thereto. The term also includes energy conservation measures and facility technology infrastructure as defined in § 45.2-1702 and other energy objectives as defined in § 45.2-1706.1. The term also means any heavy rail transportation facilities operated by a transportation district created under the Transportation District Act of 1964 (§ 33.2-1900 et seq.) that operates heavy rail freight service, including rolling stock, barge loading facilities, and any related marine or rail equipment. The term also means, without limita-

tion, the design and construction of roads, the construction of local government buildings, including administrative and operations systems and other local government equipment and infrastructure, public parking garages and other public transportation facilities, and facilities for public transportation by commuter rail. In addition, the term means any project as defined in § 5.1-30.1 or 10.1-603.28 and any professional sports facility, including a major league baseball stadium as defined in § 15.2-5800, provided that the specific professional sports facility projects have been designated by the General Assembly as eligible for assistance from the Authority. The term also means any equipment, facilities, and technology infrastructure designed to provide broadband service. The term also means facilities supporting, related to, or otherwise used for public safety, including but not limited to law-enforcement training facilities and emergency response, fire, rescue, and police stations. The term also means the remediation, redevelopment, and rehabilitation of property contaminated by the release of hazardous substances, hazardous wastes, solid wastes, or petroleum, where such remediation has not clearly been mandated by the United States Environmental Protection Agency, the Department of Environmental Quality, or a court pursuant to the Comprehensive Environmental Response, Compensation and Liability Act (42 U.S.C. § 9601 et seq.), the Resource Conservation and Recovery Act (42 U.S.C. § 6901 et seq.), the Virginia Waste Management Act (§ 10.1-1400 et seq.), the State Water Control Law (§ 62.1-44.2 et seq.), or other applicable statutory or common law or where jurisdiction of those statutes has been waived. The term also means any program or project for land conservation, parks, park facilities, land for recreational purposes, or land preservation, including but not limited to any program or project involving the acquisition of rights or interests in land for the conservation or preservation of such land. The term also means any dredging program or dredging project undertaken to benefit the economic and community development goals of a local government but does not include any dredging program or dredging project undertaken for or by the Virginia Port Authority. The term also means any oyster restoration project, including planting and replanting with seed oysters, oyster shells, or other material that will catch, support, and grow oysters. The term also means any program or project to perform site acquisition or site development work for the benefit of economic and community development projects for any local government. The term also means any undertaking by a local government to build or facilitate the production or preservation of housing or a recovered gas energy facility and any local government renewable energy project, including solar, wind, biomass, waste-to-energy, and geothermal projects. The term also means any undertaking by a local government to facilitate the remediation of residential properties contaminated by the presence of defective drywall. The term also means any undertaking by a local government to provide grants, loans, financial assistance, or any other incentives pursuant to § 15.2-958.

"Recovered gas energy facility" means a facility, located at or adjacent to (i) a solid waste management facility permitted by the Department of Environmental Quality or (ii) a sewerage system or sewage treatment work described in § 62.1-44.18 that is constructed and operated for the purpose of treating sewage and wastewater for discharge to state waters, which facility or work is constructed and operated for the purpose of (a) reclaiming or collecting methane or other combustible gas from the biodegradation or decomposition of solid waste, as defined in § 10.1-1400, that has been deposited in the solid waste management facility or sewerage system or sewage treatment work and (b) either using such gas to generate electric energy or upgrading the gas to pipeline quality and transmitting it off premises for sale or delivery to commercial or industrial purchasers or to a public utility or locality.

History.

1984, c. 699; 1985, c. 67; 1986, c. 331; 1987, cc. 117, 133; 1989, cc. 533, 551; 1990, c. 506; 1998, c. 399; 1999, c. 897; 2000, c. 790; 2001, cc. 652, 661; 2005, cc. 727, 769; 2007, cc. 81, 649, 663; 2008, cc. 3, 24, 238, 259, 504, 605, 613; 2009, cc. 14, 246, 311, 543, 632; 2010, cc. 42, 724, 820; 2011, cc. 270, 616; 2018, c. 153; 2021, Sp. Sess. I, c. 327; 2022, cc. 739, 782; 2023, cc. 440, 441.

Editor's note.

Effective October 1, 2021, "§ 45.2-1702" was substituted for "§ 11-34.2" and "§ 45.2-1706.1" was substituted for "§ 67-101.1" to conform with recodification of Title 67 by Acts 2021, Sp. Sess. I, c. 387 at the direction of the Virginia Code Commission.

The 2021 Sp. Sess. I amendments.

The 2021 amendment by Sp. Sess. I, c. 327, effective July 1, 2021, substituted "§ 67-101.1" for "§ 67-101" at the end of the third sentence in the definition of "Project."

The 2022 amendments.

The 2022 amendments by cc. 739 and 782 are identical, and inserted "or 10.1-603.28" in the fifth sentence in the "Project" definition.

The 2023 amendments.

The 2023 amendment by cc. 440 and 441 are identical, substituted "the context requires a different meaning" for "a different meaning clearly appears from" in the introductory language; substituted "'Cost'" for "The term" in the last sentence in the definition of "Cost"; in the definition of "Project", substituted "production or preservation of housing or" for "building of" in the fourteenth sentence, and added the last sentence; and made stylistic changes.

§ 62.1-203. Powers of Authority.

The Authority is granted all powers necessary or appropriate to carry out and to effectuate its purposes, including the following:

1. To have perpetual succession as a public body corporate and as a political subdivision of the Commonwealth;

2. To adopt, amend and repeal bylaws, and rules and regulations, not inconsistent with this chapter for the administration and regulation of its affairs and to carry into effect the powers and purposes of the Authority and the conduct of its business;

3. To sue and be sued in its own name;

4. To have an official seal and alter it at will although the failure to affix this seal shall not affect the validity of any instrument executed on behalf of the Authority;

5. To maintain an office at any place within the Commonwealth which it designates;

6. To make and execute contracts and all other instruments and agreements necessary or convenient for the performance of its duties and the exercise of its powers and functions under this chapter;

7. To sell, convey, mortgage, pledge, lease, exchange, transfer and otherwise dispose of all or any part of its properties and assets;

8. To employ officers, employees, agents, advisers and consultants, including without limitations, attorneys, financial advisers, engineers and other technical advisers and public accountants and, the provisions of any other law to the contrary notwithstanding, to determine their duties and compensation without the approval of any other agency or instrumentality;

9. To procure insurance, in amounts and from insurers of its choice, or provide self-insurance, against any loss, cost, or expense in connection with its property, assets or activities, including insurance or self-insurance against liability for its acts or the acts of its directors, employees or agents and for the indemnification of the members of its Board of Directors and its employees and agents;

10. To procure credit enhancements from any public or private entities, including any department, agency or instrumentality of the United States of America or the Commonwealth, for the payment of any bonds issued by the Authority, including the power to pay premiums or fees on any such credit enhancements;

11. To receive and accept from any source aid, grants and contributions of money, property, labor or other things of value to be held, used and applied to carry out the purposes of this chapter subject to the conditions upon which the aid, grants or contributions are made;

12. To enter into agreements with any department, agency or instrumentality of the United States of America or, the Commonwealth, the District of Columbia or any adjoining state for the purpose of planning, regulating and providing for the financing of any projects;

13. To collect, or to authorize the trustee under any trust indenture securing any bonds or any other fiduciary to collect, amounts due under any local obligations owned or credit enhanced by the Authority, including taking the action required by § 15.2-2659 or 62.1-216.1 to obtain payment of any unpaid sums;

14. To enter into contracts or agreements for the servicing and processing of local obligations owned by the Authority;

15. To invest or reinvest its funds as provided in this chapter or permitted by applicable law;

16. Unless restricted under any agreement with holders of bonds, to consent to any modification with respect to the rate of interest, time and payment of any installment of principal or interest, or any other term of any local obligations owned by the Authority;

17. To establish and revise, amend and repeal, and to charge and collect, fees and charges in connection with any activities or services of the Authority;

18. To do any act necessary or convenient to the exercise of the powers granted or reasonably implied by this chapter; and

19. To pledge as security for the payment of any or all bonds of the Authority, all or any part of the Capital Reserve Fund or other reserve fund or account transferred to a trustee for such purpose from the Water Facilities Revolving Fund pursuant to § 62.1-231, from the Water Supply Revolving Fund pursuant to § 62.1-240, from the Virginia Solid Waste or Recycling Revolving Fund pursuant to § 62.1-241.9, from the Virginia Airports Revolving Fund pursuant to § 5.1-30.6, from the Dam Safety, Flood Prevention and Protection Assistance Fund pursuant to § 10.1-603.17, from the Virginia Tobacco Region Revolving Fund pursuant to § 3.2-3117, or from the Resilient Virginia Revolving Fund pursuant to § 10.1-603.37. Notwithstanding the foregoing, any such transfer from the Virginia Tobacco Region Revolving Fund may be pledged to secure only those bonds of the Authority issued to finance or refinance projects located in the tobacco-dependent communities in the Southside and Southwest regions of Virginia.

History.
1984, c. 699; 1985, c. 67; 1986, c. 415; 1987, cc. 117, 133, 324; 1994, c. 684; 1998, c. 399; 1999, c. 897; 2003, c. 561; 2006, cc. 648, 765; 2011, c. 616; 2015, cc. 399, 433; 2022, cc. 739, 782.

The 2022 amendments.
The 2022 amendments by cc. 739 and 782 are identical, and substituted "§ 10.1-603.17, from the Virginia Tobacco Region Revolving Fund pursuant to § 3.2-3117, or from the Resilient Virginia Revolving Fund pursuant to § 10.1-603.37." for "§ 10.1-603.17, or from the Virginia Tobacco Region Revolving Fund pursuant to § 3.2-3117." in subdivision 19.

§ 62.1-216. Purchase and credit enhancements of local obligations.

The Authority shall have the power and authority, with any funds of the Authority available for such a purpose, to purchase and acquire, on terms which the Authority determines, local obligations to finance or refinance the cost of any project. The Authority may pledge to the payment of any bonds all or any portion of the local obligations so purchased. The Authority may also, subject to any such pledge, sell any local obligations so purchased and apply the proceeds of such a sale to the purchase of other local obligations for financing or refinancing the cost of any project or for any other corporate purpose of the Authority.

The Authority shall also have the power and authority to issue credit enhancements, on terms which the Authority determines, to credit enhance local obligations issued to finance or refinance the cost of any project.

The Authority may require, as a condition to the purchase or credit enhancement of any local obligations, that the local government issuing the local obligations covenant to perform any of the following:

A. Establish and collect rents, rates, fees and charges to produce revenue sufficient to pay all or a specified portion of (i) the costs of operation, maintenance, replacement, renewal and repairs of the project; (ii) any outstanding indebtedness incurred for the purposes of the project, including the principal of and premium, if any, and interest on the local obligations; and (iii) any amounts necessary to create and maintain any required reserve, including any rate stabilization fund deemed necessary or appropriate by the Authority to offset the need, in whole or part, for future increases in rents, rates, fees or charges;

B. Create and maintain a special fund or funds for the payment of the principal of and premium, if any, and interest on the local obligations and any other amounts becoming due under any agreement entered into in connection with the local obligations, or for the operation, maintenance, repair or replacement of the project or any portions thereof or other property of the local government, and deposit into any fund or funds amounts sufficient to make any payments as they become due and payable;

C. Create and maintain other special funds as required by the Authority; and

D. Perform other acts, including the conveyance of real and personal property together with all right, title and interest therein to the Authority, or take other actions as may be deemed necessary or desirable by the Authority to secure payment of the principal of and premium, if any, and interest on the local obligations or obligations to the Authority with respect to any credit enhancement and to provide for the remedies of the Authority or other holder of the local obligations in the event of any default by the local government in the payment, including, without limitation, any of the following:

1. The procurement of credit enhancements or liquidity arrangements for local obligations from any source, public or private, and the payment therefor of premiums, fees or other charges.

2. The payment of the allocable shares of the local governments, as determined by the Authority, of any costs, fees, charges or expenses attributable to liquidity arrangements incurred in connection with the issuance of bonds by the Authority to acquire local obligations of one or more local governments. The determination of such allocable shares may be made by the Authority on any reasonable basis.

3. The combination of one or more projects, or the combination of one or more projects with one or more other undertakings, facilities, utilities or systems, for the purpose of operations and financing, and the pledging of the revenues from such combined projects, undertakings, facilities, utilities and systems to secure local obligations issued in connection with such combination or any part or parts thereof.

4. The payment of the allocable shares of the local governments, as determined by the Authority on any reasonable basis, of rate stabilization funds established or required by the Authority in connection with the issuance

of bonds by the Authority to acquire or provide credit enhancement for local obligations of two or more local governments.

All local governments issuing and selling local obligations to the Authority or to be credit enhanced by the Authority are authorized to perform any acts, take any action, adopt any proceedings and make and carry out any contracts with the Authority that are contemplated by this chapter. Such contracts need not be identical among all participants in financings of the Authority, but may be structured as determined by the Authority according to the needs of the contracting local governments and the Authority.

To the extent permitted by law for local obligations issued after July 1, 2003, local governments may enter into agreements with the Authority that provide for a local government to consider and make appropriations from the following: (i) funds or revenues from service districts created under Chapter 24 (§ 15.2-2400 et seq.) of Title 15.2, (ii) funds or revenues accumulated and held by the local government, or (iii) any funds or revenues to be received or generated by the local government in amounts sufficient to pay all or a specified portion of the amounts set forth in subsection A or to make deposits into the special fund or funds provided for in subsections B and C and to pledge and apply the amounts so appropriated for such purposes.

History.
1984, c. 699; 1985, c. 67; 1998, c. 399; 2003, c. 561; 2023, cc. 440, 441.

The 2023 amendments.
The 2023 amendment by cc. 440 and 441 are identical, rewrote the third paragraph of subdivision D 4.

§ 62.1-218. Grants to local governments.

The Authority shall have the power and authority, with any funds of the Authority available for this purpose, to make grants to local governments. In determining which local governments are to receive grants, the Department of Environmental Quality, the Department of Health, the Department of Housing and Community Development, and the Virginia Waste Management Board shall assist the Authority in determining needs for wastewater treatment facilities; water supply facilities; solid waste treatment, disposal, or management facilities; housing, including housing for persons and families of low and moderate income; or recycling facilities, and the method and form of such grants.

History.
1984, c. 699; 1992, cc. 378, 887; 2023, cc. 440, 441.

The 2023 amendments.
The 2023 amendment by cc. 440 and 441 are identical, in the second sentence, added "the Department of Housing and Community Development" and "housing, including housing for persons and families of low and moderate income"; and made stylistic changes.

CHAPTER 21.1.

WASTEWATER INFRASTRUCTURE POLICY.

§ 62.1-223.1. State policy as to community and onsite wastewater treatment.

It is the policy of the Commonwealth to prioritize universal access to wastewater treatment that protects public health and the environment and supports local economic growth and stability. To further this policy, the Commonwealth endorses (i) public education about the importance of adequate wastewater treatment; (ii) collaboration among local, state, and federal government entities, including consistent collaboration and coordination of grant requirements and timelines; (iii) the prioritized, focused, and innovative use of state and federal funding to address needs determined pursuant to § 62.1-223.3; (iv) a preference for community-based and regional projects as opposed to cumulative and repetitive site-by-site individual solutions; (v) the use of integrated solutions across sewer and onsite wastewater treatment systems; and (vi) the incorporation of the effects of climate change into wastewater treatment regulatory and funding programs.

History.
2021, Sp. Sess. I, c. 382.

Effective date.
This chapter is effective July 1, 2021.

§ 62.1-223.2. (Expires July 1, 2030) Wastewater Infrastructure Policy Working Group.

A. The Wastewater Infrastructure Policy Working Group (the Working Group) is established as an advisory board within the meaning of § 2.2-2100 in the executive branch of state government. The purpose of the Working Group is to continually assess wastewater infrastructure needs in the Commonwealth and develop policy recommendations.

B. The Working Group shall have a total membership of four ex officio members. The Director of the Department of Environmental Quality, the State Health Commissioner, the Director of the Department of Housing and Community Development, and the Executive Director of the Virginia Resources Authority, or their designees, shall serve ex officio with voting privileges. Members of the Working Group shall serve terms coincident with their terms of office. A majority of the members shall constitute a quorum.

C. The Working Group shall invite participation in its meetings by the Virginia Association of Counties, the Virginia Association of Planning District Commissions, the U.S. Department of Agriculture Rural Development, the Virginia Onsite Wastewater Recycling Association, the Virginia Association of Municipal Wastewater Agencies, the Virginia Rural Water Association, and SERCAP, Inc.

D. The Working Group shall have the following powers and duties:

1. Assess wastewater infrastructure needs in the Commonwealth and develop policy recommendations.

2. Promote public education about the importance of adequate wastewater treatment.

3. Encourage collaboration among local, state, and federal government entities, including consistent collaboration and coordination of grant requirements and timelines.

4. Endorse community-based and regional projects as opposed to cumulative and repetitive site-by-site individual solutions and integrated solutions across sewer and onsite wastewater treatment systems.

5. Support prioritized, focused, and innovative use of state and federal funding to address needs determined pursuant to § 62.1-223.3.

6. Prioritize universal access to wastewater treatment that protects public health and the environment and supports local economic growth and stability.

7. Support the incorporation of the effects of climate change into wastewater treatment regulatory and funding programs.

8. Submit an annual report to the Governor and the General Assembly for publication as a report document as provided in the procedures of the Division of Legislative Automated Systems for the processing of legislative documents and reports. The Secretary of Natural and Historic Resources shall submit to the Governor and the General Assembly an annual executive summary of the interim activity and work of the Working Group no later than the first day of each regular session of the General Assembly. The executive summary shall be submitted as a report document as provided in the procedures of the Division of Legislative Automated Systems for the processing of legislative documents and reports and shall be posted on the General Assembly's website.

E. The Secretaries of Natural and Historic Resources, Commerce and Trade, and Health and Human Resources shall provide staff support to the Working Group. The Center for Coastal Resources Management at the Virginia Institute of Marine Science and the Virginia Coastal Policy Center at William and Mary Law School shall advise the Working Group. All agencies of the Commonwealth shall provide assistance to the Working Group upon request.

F. Notwithstanding the provisions of § 30-19.1:9, the provisions of this section shall expire on July 1, 2030.

History.
2021, Sp. Sess. I, c. 382.

Editor's note.
At the direction of the Virginia Code Commission, "Secretary of Natural and Historic Resources" was substituted for "Secretary of Natural Resources" and "Secretaries of Natural

and Historic Resources" was substituted for "Secretaries of Natural Resources" to conform to the name change by Acts 2021, Sp. Sess. I, c. 401.

Effective date.
This section is effective July 1, 2021.

§ 62.1-223.3. Wastewater infrastructure needs assessment.

The Department of Environmental Quality (the Department), in partnership with the Virginia Department of Health and in consultation with stakeholders, including representatives of the Department of Housing and Community Development, the Virginia Resources Authority, the U.S. Department of Agriculture Rural Development, the Virginia Onsite Wastewater Recycling Association, the Center for Coastal Resources Management at the Virginia Institute of Marine Science, the Virginia Association of Municipal Wastewater Agencies, the Virginia Rural Water Association, SERCAP, Inc., local governments, and conservation organizations, shall determine every four years an estimate of the amount of wastewater infrastructure funding that is (i) necessary to implement the policy of the Commonwealth articulated in § 62.1-223.1 and (ii) not eligible to be covered by grant funding pursuant to the Virginia Water Quality Improvement Act of 1997 (§ 10.1-2117 et seq.). The Department shall report such estimate to the Governor and the General Assembly no later than July 1, 2023, and no later than July 1 every four years thereafter.

History.
2021, Sp. Sess. I, c. 382.

Effective date.
This section is effective July 1, 2021.

CHAPTER 22.

VIRGINIA WATER FACILITIES REVOLVING FUND.

Section
62.1-229. Loans to local governments or other entities.

§ 62.1-229. Loans to local governments or other entities.

Except as otherwise provided in this chapter, money in the Fund shall be used solely to make loans to local governments or other entities as permitted by federal law to finance or refinance the cost of any project. The local governments or other entities to which loans are to be made, the purposes of the loan, the amount of each such loan, the interest rate thereon and the repayment terms thereof, which may vary between loan recipients, shall be designated in writing by the Board to the Authority following consultation with the Authority. No loan from the Fund shall exceed the total cost of the project to be financed or the outstanding principal amount of the indebtedness to be refinanced plus reasonable financing expenses. Loans may also be made from the Fund, in the Board's discretion, to a local government (i) for the purpose of correcting onsite sewage disposal problems (small water facility projects) to protect or improve water quality and prevent the pollution of state waters or (ii) which has developed a funding program to provide low-interest loans or other incentives to facilitate the correction of onsite sewage disposal problems (small water facility projects), provided that the moneys may be used only for the program and that the onsite sewage disposal systems to be repaired or upgraded are owned by eligible businesses or individual citizens of the Commonwealth where (a) public health or water quality concerns are present and (b) connection to a public sewer system is not feasible because of location or cost. To be eligible for loan funding, a business shall be located within a locality that is in the Rural Coastal Virginia Community Enhancement Authority, as defined in § 15.2-7600. Eligible businesses include bed-and-breakfast operations, campgrounds, and restaurants, as those terms are defined in § 35.1-1, and businesses that use working waterfronts, as defined in § 15.2-2201.

Except as set forth above, the Authority shall determine the terms and conditions of any loan from the Fund, which may vary between loan recipients. Each loan shall be evidenced by appropriate bonds or notes of the local government or other entity payable to the Fund. The bonds or notes shall have been duly authorized by the local government or other entity and executed by its authorized legal representatives. The Authority is authorized to require in connection with any loan from the Fund such documents, instruments, certificates, legal opinions and other information as it may deem necessary or convenient. In addition to any other terms or conditions which the Authority may establish, the Authority may require, as a condition to making any loan from the Fund, that the local government or other entity receiving the loan covenant to perform any of the following:

A. Establish and collect rents, rates, fees and charges to produce revenue sufficient to pay all or a specified portion of (i) the costs of operation, maintenance, replacement, renewal and repairs of the project; (ii) any outstanding indebtedness incurred for the purposes of the project, including the principal of and premium, if any, and interest on the loan from the Fund to the local government or other entity; and (iii) any amounts necessary to create and maintain any required reserve, including any rate stabilization fund deemed necessary or appropriate by the Authority to offset the need, in whole or part, for future increases in rents, rates, fees or charges;

B. With respect to local governments, levy and collect ad valorem taxes on all property within the jurisdiction of the local government subject to local taxation sufficient to pay the principal of and premium, if any, and interest on the loan from the Fund to the local government;

C. Create and maintain a special fund or funds for the payment of the principal of and premium, if any, and interest on the loan from the Fund to the local government or other entity and any other amounts becoming due under any agreement entered into in connection with the loan, or for the operation, maintenance, repair or replacement of the project or any portions thereof or other property of the local government or other entity, and deposit into any fund or funds amounts sufficient to make any payments on the loan as they become due and payable;

D. Create and maintain other special funds as required by the Authority; and

E. Perform other acts, including the conveyance of, or the granting of liens on or security interests in, real and personal property, together with all rights, title and interest therein, to the Fund, or take other actions as may be deemed necessary or desirable by the Authority to secure payment of the principal of and premium, if any, and interest on the loan from the Fund and to provide for the remedies of the Fund in the event of any default in the payment of the loan, including, without limitation, any of the following:

1. The procurement of insurance, guarantees, letters of credit and other forms of collateral, security, liquidity arrangements or credit supports for the loan from any source, public or private, and the payment therefor of premiums, fees or other charges;

2. The combination of one or more projects, or the combination of one or more projects with one or more other undertakings, facilities, utilities or systems, for the purpose of operations and financing, and the pledging of the revenues from such combined projects, undertakings, facilities, utilities and systems to secure the loan from the Fund made in connection with such combination or any part or parts thereof;

3. The maintenance, replacement, renewal and repair of the project; and

4. The procurement of casualty and liability insurance.

All local governments or other entities borrowing money from the Fund are authorized to perform any acts, take any action, adopt any proceedings and make and carry out any contracts that are contemplated by this chapter. Such contracts need not be identical among all local governments or other entities, but may be structured as determined by the Authority according to the needs of the contracting local governments or other entities and the Fund.

Subject to the rights, if any, of the registered owners of any of the bonds of the Authority, the Authority may consent to and approve any modification in the terms of any loan subject to guidelines adopted by the Board.

History.

1986, c. 415; 1996, c. 20; 1999, c. 1012; 2023, c. 97.

The 2023 amendments.

The 2023 amendment by c. 97, in the fourth sentence of the first paragraph, added "(i) for the purpose of correcting onsite sewage disposal problems (small water facility projects) to protect or improve water quality and prevent the pollution of state waters or (ii)," substituted "funding program to provide low-interest" for "low-interest loan program to provide," and added "eligible businesses or"; added the last sentence of the first paragraph; and made stylistic changes.

CHAPTER 23.2.
COMBINED SEWER OVERFLOW MATCHING FUND.

§ 62.1-241.11. Definitions.

Editor's note.

Acts 2020, c. 634 provides: "§ 1. That the owner or operator of any combined sewer overflow (CSO) system east of Charlottesville that discharges into the James River watershed shall submit to the Department of Environmental Quality (the Department) the following:

"A. By July 1, 2021, an interim plan detailing all known actions the owner or operator can initiate by July 1, 2022, to address the requirements of any consent special order issued by the State Water Control Board (the Board) to the owner or operator regarding the CSO system; and

"B. By July 1, 2024, a final plan updating the interim plan and detailing all actions the owner or operator will take to satisfy all requirements of any consent special order issued by the Board to the owner or operator regarding the CSO system.

"Both the interim plan and the final plan shall be divided into discrete projects or phases that may be planned or constructed individually or in combination and shall include for each project or phase (i) an estimated timeline from the start of detailed planning to completion of construction, (ii) an estimated cost, (iii) the projected resultant water quality improvements, and (iv) proposed funding sources. The owner or operator, subject to Department approval, may substitute for any proposed action in either the interim or final plan an alternative action or actions to address the requirements of any consent special order issued by the Board to the owner or operator regarding the CSO system, provided that such alternative is at least as cost-effective as the original proposed action. The Department shall assist the owner or operator in developing both the interim plan and the final plan and in identifying available sources of funding and financing.

"§ 2. Any such owner or operator of a CSO system shall:

"A. By July 1, 2022, initiate construction and related activities pursuant to the interim plan required in subsection A of § 1;

"B. By July 1, 2025, initiate construction and related activities pursuant to the final plan required in subsection B of § 1;

"C. By July 1, 2027, complete construction and related activities pursuant to the interim plan required in subsection A of § 1;

"D. By July 1, 2030, identify any additional action that is applicable to the owner or opera-

tor of a CSO system and is necessary to meet, by 2036, the requirements of the total maximum daily load (TMDL) for bacterial impairments of the James River and its tributaries in the Richmond area, as described in the implementation plan for such TMDL issued by the Department in 2011; and

"E. By July 1, 2035, complete construction and related activities pursuant to the final plan required in subsection B of § 1.

"§ 3. Any such owner or operator of a CSO system shall report annually to the Department on its progress pursuant to § 1 and § 2, with the first annual report due no later than December 1, 2020, and the final annual report due after completion of (i) the construction activities pursuant to the final plan required in subsection B of § 1 and (ii) additional actions identified in subsection D of § 2. The report, which may be included as part of any annual report required under a consent special order issued by the Department to the owner or operator regarding the CSO system, shall include information on the level and sources of funding and financing such owner or operator has applied to the CSO system in each of the past five fiscal years, as well as an assessment of funding needs in future years with a request that appropriation amounts sufficient to carry out the purposes of this act be included in the budget bill. No later than January 1 of each year, the Department shall transmit, with any additional information the Director of the Department determines to be appropriate, the CSO system progress reports to the Chairmen of the Senate Committee on Finance and Appropriations, the Senate Committee on Agriculture, Conservation and Natural Resources, the House Committee on Appropriations, and the House Committee on Agriculture, Chesapeake and Natural Resources; the Virginia delegation to the Chesapeake Bay Commission; the Secretary of Natural Resources; and the Governor. The Department may recommend extending the deadlines in § 2 to allow adaptive management by the owner or operator due to a natural disaster or other act of God, or because of a lack of available funding and financing.

"§ 4. The Governor shall take into account the reports required in § 3 during the preparation of the biennial budget bill and subsequent amendments thereto. The General Assembly may take such reports into account in enacting the general appropriation act and may evaluate the feasibility of the deadlines in § 2 on a biennial basis beginning in 2022 and modify such deadlines as necessary, taking into account any potential adverse effects on (i) the owner's or operator's bond rating; (ii) the utility rates, fees, or charges assessed by the owner or operator; (iii) any environmental justice community, or owner's or operator's customers living below the federal poverty level; or (iv) any other relevant aspect of the owner's or operator's operations. No sooner than July 1, 2025, and no more frequently than every two years thereafter, the owner or operator may petition the Board for, and the Board may grant, an extension to one or more of the deadlines in § 2 if the Board determines that (a) the General Assembly has not extended such deadline and (b) funding sufficient to meet such deadline has not been secured and the owner or operator has exhausted all reasonable options for securing such funding.

"§ 5. Notwithstanding the provisions of § 1 or § 2, no such owner or operator of a CSO system shall be prohibited from seeking modifications to a consent special order with the concurrence of the Department and the Board if alternative actions for protecting water quality are determined to be more cost-effective."

CHAPTER 24.

SURFACE WATER MANAGEMENT AREAS.

§ 62.1-242. Definitions.

As used in this chapter, unless the context requires otherwise:

"Beneficial use" means both instream and offstream uses. Instream beneficial uses include but are not limited to protection of fish and wildlife habitat, maintenance of waste assimilation, recreation, navigation, and cultural and aesthetic values. Offstream beneficial uses include but are not limited to domestic (including public water supply), agricultural, electric power generation, commercial, and industrial uses. Domestic and other existing beneficial uses shall be considered the highest priority beneficial uses.

"Board" means the State Water Control Board. However, when used outside the context of the promulgation of regulations, including regulations to establish general permits, pursuant to this chapter, "Board" means the Department of Environmental Quality.

"Nonconsumptive use" means the use of water withdrawn from a stream in such a manner that it is returned to the stream without substantial diminution in quantity at or near the point from which it was taken and would not result in or exacerbate low flow conditions.

"Surface water withdrawal permit" means a document issued by the Board evidencing the right to withdraw surface water.

"Surface water management area" means a geographically defined surface water area in which the Board has deemed the levels or supply of surface water to be potentially adverse to public welfare, health and safety.

"Surface water" means any water in the Commonwealth, except ground water, as defined in § 62.1-255.

History.
1989, c. 721; 1992, c. 812; 2022, c. 356.

The 2022 amendments.
The 2022 amendment by c. 356 added the second sentence in the definition of "Board."

§ 62.1-243. Withdrawals for which surface water withdrawal permit not required.

A. No surface water withdrawal permit shall be required for (i) any nonconsumptive use, (ii) any water withdrawal of less than 300,000 gallons in any single month, (iii) any water withdrawal from a farm pond collecting diffuse surface water and not situated on a perennial stream as defined in the United States Geological Survey 7.5-minute series topographic maps, (iv) any withdrawal in any area which has not been declared a surface water management area, or (v) any withdrawal from a wastewater treatment system permitted by the State Water Control Board or the Department of Energy.

B. No political subdivision or investor-owned water company permitted by the Department of Health shall be required to obtain a surface water withdrawal permit for:

1. Any withdrawal in existence on July 1, 1989; however, a permit shall be required in a declared surface water management area before the daily rate of any such existing withdrawal is increased beyond the maximum daily withdrawal made before July 1, 1989.

2. Any withdrawal not in existence on July 1, 1989, if the person proposing to make the withdrawal has received a § 401 certification from the State Water Control Board pursuant to the requirements of the Clean Water Act to install any necessary withdrawal structures and make such withdrawal; however, a permit shall be required in any surface water management area before any such withdrawal is increased beyond the amount authorized by the said certification.

3. Any withdrawal in existence on July 1, 1989, from an instream impoundment of water used for public water supply purposes; however, during periods when permit conditions in a surface water management area are in force under regulations adopted by the Board pursuant to § 62.1-249, and when the rate of flow of natural surface water into the impoundment is equal to or less than the average flow of natural surface water at that location, the Board may require the release of water from the impoundment at a rate not exceeding the existing rate of flow of natural surface water into the impoundment.

Withdrawals by a political subdivision or investor-owned water company permitted by the Department of Health shall be affected by subdivision 3 of subsection B only at the option of that political subdivision or investor-owned water company.

To qualify for any exemption in subsection B of this section, the political subdivision making the withdrawal, or the political subdivision served by an authority making the withdrawal, shall have instituted a water conservation program approved by the Board which includes: (i) use of water saving plumbing fixtures in new and renovated plumbing as provided under the Uniform Statewide Building Code; (ii) a water loss reduction program; (iii) a water use education program; and (iv) ordinances prohibiting waste of water generally and providing for mandatory water use restrictions, with penalties, during water shortage emergencies. The Board shall review all such water conservation programs to ensure compliance with (i) through (iv) of this paragraph.

C. No existing beneficial consumptive user shall be required to obtain a surface water withdrawal permit for:

1. Any withdrawal in existence on July 1, 1989; however, a permit shall be required in a declared surface water management area before the daily rate of any such existing withdrawal is increased beyond the maximum daily withdrawal made before July 1, 1989.

2. Any withdrawal not in existence on July 1, 1989, if the person proposing to make the withdrawal has received a § 401 certification from the State

Water Control Board pursuant to the requirements of the Clean Water Act to install any necessary withdrawal structures and make such withdrawal; however, a permit shall be required in any surface water management area before any such withdrawal is increased beyond the amount authorized by the said certification.

To qualify for either exemption in subsection C of this section, the beneficial consumptive user shall have instituted a water management program approved by the Board which includes: (i) use of water-saving plumbing; (ii) a water loss reduction program; (iii) a water use education program; and (iv) mandatory reductions during water shortage emergencies. However, these reductions shall be on an equitable basis with other uses exempted under subsection B of this section. The Board shall review all such water management programs to ensure compliance with (i) through (iv) of this paragraph.

D. The Board shall issue certificates for any withdrawals exempted pursuant to subsections B and C of this section. Such certificates shall include conservation or management programs as conditions thereof.

History.
1989, c. 721; 1993, c. 213; 2021, Sp. Sess. I, c. 532.

Editor's note.
Acts 2021, Sp. Sess. I, c. 532, cl. 2 provides: "That the provisions of this act shall become effective on October 1, 2021."

The 2021 Sp. Sess. I amendments.
The 2021 amendment by Sp. Sess. I, c. 532, effective October 1, 2021, substituted "Department of Energy" for "Department of Mines, Minerals and Energy."

§ 62.1-248.2. Permit rationale.

In granting a permit pursuant to this chapter, the Department shall provide in writing a clear and concise statement of the legal basis, scientific rationale, and justification for the decision reached. When the decision of the Department is to deny a permit pursuant to this chapter, the Department shall, in consultation with legal counsel, provide a clear and concise statement explaining the reason for the denial, the scientific justification for the same, and how the Department's decision is in compliance with applicable laws and regulations. Copies of the decision, certified by the Director, shall be mailed by certified mail to the permittee or applicant.

History.
2022, c. 356.

Editor's note.
Acts 2022, c. 356, cl. 3 provides: "That any permits or orders issued by the Air Pollution Control Board or the State Water Control Board prior to the effective date of this act shall continue in full force and are enforceable by the Department of Environmental Quality."

§ 62.1-250. State agency review.

Prior to the creation of a surface water management area, or the issuance of a permit within one, the Board shall consult and cooperate with, and give full consideration to the written recommendations of, the following agencies: the Department of Wildlife Resources, the Department of Conservation and Recreation, the Virginia Marine Resources Commission, the Department of Health, and any other interested and affected agencies. Such consultation shall include the need for development of a means in the surface water management area for balancing instream uses with offstream uses. Agencies may submit written comments on proposed permits within forty-five days after notification by the Board. The Board shall assume that if written comments are not submitted by an agency, within the time period, the agency has no comments on the proposed permits.

History.
1989, c. 721; 2020, c. 958.

The 2020 amendments.
The 2020 amendment by c. 958 substituted

"Department of Wildlife Resources" for "Department of Game and Inland Fisheries" in the first sentence.

CHAPTER 25.

GROUND WATER MANAGEMENT ACT OF 1992.

§ 62.1-255. Definitions.

As used in this chapter, unless the context requires otherwise:

"Agricultural irrigation" means irrigation that is used to support any operation devoted to the bona fide production of crops, animals, or fowl, including the production of fruits and vegetables of any kind; meat, dairy, and poultry products; nuts, tobacco, nursery, and floral products; and the production and harvest of products from silvicultural activity.

"Beneficial use" includes domestic (including public water supply), agricultural, commercial, and industrial uses.

"Board" means the State Water Control Board. However, when used outside the context of the promulgation of regulations, including regulations to establish general permits, pursuant to this chapter, "Board" means the Department of Environmental Quality.

"Department" means the Department of Environmental Quality.

"Eastern Shore Groundwater Management Area" means the ground water management area declared by the Board encompassing the Counties of Accomack and Northampton.

"Ground water" means any water, except capillary moisture, beneath the land surface in the zone of saturation or beneath the bed of any stream, lake, reservoir or other body of surface water wholly or partially within the boundaries of the Commonwealth, whatever the subsurface geologic structure in which such water stands, flows, percolates or otherwise occurs.

"Ground water withdrawal permit" means a certificate issued by the Board permitting the withdrawal of a specified quantity of ground water in a ground water management area.

"Irrigation" means the controlled application of water through man-made systems to supply water requirements not satisfied by rainfall to assist in the growing or maintenance of vegetative growth.

"Nonagricultural irrigation" means all irrigation other than agricultural irrigation.

"Person" means any and all persons, including individuals, firms, partnerships, associations, public or private institutions, municipalities or political subdivisions, governmental agencies, or private or public corporations organized under the laws of the Commonwealth or any other state or country.

"Surficial aquifer" means the upper surface of a zone of saturation, where the body of ground water is not confined by an overlying impermeable zone.

History.

1992, c. 812; 2018, c. 427; 2019, c. 755; 2020, c. 670; 2022, c. 356.

The 2020 amendments.

The 2020 amendment by c. 670 inserted the definitions for "Agricultural irrigation," "Irrigation," and "Nonagricultural irrigation."

The 2022 amendments.

The 2022 amendment by c. 356 added the second sentence in the definition of "Board."

§ 62.1-256. Duties of Board.

The Board shall have the following duties and powers:

1. To issue ground water withdrawal permits in accordance with regulations adopted by the Board;

2. To issue special orders as provided in § 62.1-268;

3. To study, investigate and assess ground water resources and all problems concerned with the quality and quantity of ground water located wholly or partially in the Commonwealth, and to make such reports and recommendations as may be necessary to carry out the provisions of this chapter;

4. To require any person withdrawing ground water for any purpose anywhere in the Commonwealth, whether or not declared to be a ground water management area, to furnish to the Board such information with regard to such ground water withdrawal and the use thereof as may be necessary to carry out the provisions of this chapter, excluding ground water withdrawals occurring in conjunction with activities related to exploration for and production of oil, gas, coal or other minerals regulated by the Department of Energy;

5. To prescribe and enforce requirements that naturally flowing wells be plugged or destroyed, or be capped or equipped with valves so that flow of ground water may be completely stopped when said ground water is not currently being applied to a beneficial use;

6. To enter at reasonable times and under reasonable circumstances, any establishment or upon any property, public or private, for the purposes of obtaining information, conducting surveys or inspections, or inspecting wells and springs, and to duly authorize agents to do the same, to ensure compliance with any permits, standards, policies, rules, regulations, rulings and special orders which it may adopt, issue or establish to carry out the provisions of this chapter;

7. To issue special exceptions pursuant to § 62.1-267;

8. To adopt such regulations as it deems necessary to administer and enforce the provisions of this chapter; and

9. To delegate to its Executive Director any of the powers and duties invested in it to administer and enforce the provisions of this chapter except the adoption and promulgation of rules, standards or regulations; the revocation of permits; and the issuance, modification, or revocation of orders except in case of an emergency as provided in subsection B of § 62.1-268.

History.

1992, c. 812; 2021, Sp. Sess. I, c. 532.

Editor's note.

Acts 2021, Sp. Sess. I, c. 532, cl. 2 provides:

"That the provisions of this act shall become effective on October 1, 2021."

The 2021 Sp. Sess. I amendments.
  The 2021 amendment by Sp. Sess. I, c. 532,

effective October 1, 2021, substituted "Department of Energy" for "Department of Mines, Minerals and Energy" in subdivision 4.

§ 62.1-256.2. (Expires July 1, 2025) Eastern Virginia Groundwater Management Advisory Committee established; sunset.

A. The Department of Environmental Quality (the Department) shall establish the Eastern Virginia Groundwater Management Advisory Committee (the Committee) as an advisory committee to assist the State Water Commission and the Department in the management of groundwater in the Eastern Virginia Groundwater Management Area. Members of the Committee shall be appointed by the Director of the Department and shall be composed of nonlegislative citizen members consisting of representatives of industrial and municipal water users; representatives of public and private water providers; developers and representatives from the economic development community; representatives of agricultural, conservation, and environmental organizations; state and federal agency officials; and university faculty and citizens with expertise in water resources-related issues. The Department shall convene the Committee at least four times each fiscal year. Members of the Committee shall receive no compensation for their service and shall not be entitled to reimbursement for expenses incurred in the performance of their duties.

B. During each meeting of the Committee, the Department shall (i) update the Committee on activities pertaining to groundwater management in the Eastern Virginia Groundwater Management Area and (ii) solicit members to present topics and analysis for examination at future meetings. The Committee may develop specific statutory, budgetary, and regulatory recommendations, as necessary, to enhance the effectiveness of groundwater management in the Eastern Virginia Groundwater Management Area.

C. The Department shall annually report the results of the Committee's examinations and related recommendations, and any responses from the Department, to the State Water Commission, the Governor, and the General Assembly no later than November 1 of each year.

D. The provisions of this section shall expire on July 1, 2025.

History.
  2020, c. 805.

§ 62.1-258.1. Irrigation wells for nonagricultural use prohibited; exceptions.

Unless the Department of Environmental Quality has determined that the quantity or quality of the ground water in the surficial aquifer is not adequate to supply the proposed beneficial use, it shall be unlawful in a ground water management area for any person to construct a well for nonagricultural irrigation purposes except in the surficial aquifer. The provisions of this section shall not apply to wells constructed prior to the effective date of regulations adopted pursuant to subsection H of § 62.1-266.

History.
  2020, c. 670.

§ 62.1-259. Certain withdrawals; permit not required.

No ground water withdrawal permit shall be required for (i) withdrawals of less than 300,000 gallons a month; (ii) temporary construction dewatering; (iii) temporary withdrawals associated with a state-approved ground water remediation; (iv) the withdrawal of ground water for use by a ground water heat pump where the discharge is reinjected into the aquifer from which it is withdrawn; (v) the withdrawal from a pond recharged by ground water without mechanical assistance; (vi) the withdrawal of water for geophysical investigations, including pump tests; (vii) the withdrawal of ground water coincident with exploration for and extraction of coal or activities associated with coal mining regulated by the Department of Energy; (viii) the withdrawal of ground water coincident with the exploration for or production of oil, gas or other minerals other than coal, unless such withdrawal adversely impacts aquifer quantity or quality or other ground water users within a ground water management area; (ix) the withdrawal of ground water in any area not declared a ground water management area; or (x) the withdrawal of ground water pursuant to a special exception issued by the Board.

History.
1992, c. 812; 2021, Sp. Sess. I, c. 532.

Editor's note.
Acts 2021, Sp. Sess. I, c. 532, cl. 2 provides: "That the provisions of this act shall become effective on October 1, 2021."

The 2021 Sp. Sess. I amendments.
The 2021 amendment by Sp. Sess. I, c. 532, effective October 1, 2021, substituted "Department of Energy" for "Department of Mines, Minerals and Energy" in clause (vii).

§ 62.1-262. (For contingent expiration date, see Acts 2021, Sp. Sess. I, c. 100) Permits for other ground water withdrawals.

Any application for a ground water withdrawal permit, except as provided in §§ 62.1-260 and 62.1-261 and subsection H of § 62.1-266, shall include a water conservation and management plan approved by the Board. A water conservation and management plan shall include: (i) use of water-saving plumbing and processes including, where appropriate, use of water-saving fixtures in new and renovated plumbing as provided under the Uniform Statewide Building Code; (ii) a water-loss reduction program; (iii) a water-use education program; and (iv) mandatory reductions during water-shortage emergencies including, where appropriate, ordinances prohibiting waste of water generally and providing for mandatory water-use restrictions, with penalties, during water-shortage emergencies. The Board shall approve all water conservation plans in compliance with clauses (i) through (iv).

History.
1992, c. 812; 2020, c. 670.

Section set out twice.
This section is effective until amendments by Acts 2021, Sp. Sess. I, c. 100 take effect pursuant to Acts 2021, Sp. Sess. I, c. 100, cl. 3. For this section as amended by Acts 2021, Sp. Sess.

I, c. 100 see the following section, also numbered 62.1-262.

The 2020 amendments.
The 2020 amendment by c. 670, in the first sentence, inserted "and subsection H of § 62.1-266" and in the second sentence, substituted "clauses (i) through (iv)" for "subdivisions (i) through (iv) of this section."

§ 62.1-262. (For contingent effective date, see Acts 2021, Sp. Sess. I, c. 100) Permits for other ground water withdrawals.

Any application for a ground water withdrawal permit, except as provided in § 62.1-260 or 62.1-261 or subsection H of § 62.1-266, shall include a water conservation and management plan approved by the Board. Such water conservation and management plan shall include (i) the use of water-saving plumbing and processes including, where appropriate, water-saving fixtures in new and renovated plumbing as provided under the Uniform Statewide Building Code; (ii) a water-loss reduction program; (iii) a water-use education program; (iv) a water auditing plan that complies with requirements established by the Board in regulations; (v) a leak detection and repair plan that complies with requirements established by the Board in regulations; and (vi) mandatory reductions during water-shortage emergencies, including, where appropriate, ordinances prohibiting waste of water generally and providing for mandatory water-use restrictions, with penalties, during water-shortage emergencies. The Board shall approve any water conservation plan that complies with clauses (i) through (vi). Once approved by the Board, such water conservation and management plan shall be incorporated by reference as a condition in the ground water withdrawal permit. The Board shall not issue a ground water withdrawal permit, except as provided in § 62.1-260 or 62.1-261 or subsection H of § 62.1-266, without an approved water conservation and management plan.

History.
1992, c. 812; 2020, c. 670; 2021, Sp. Sess. I, c. 100.

Section set out twice.
This section is set out as amended by Acts 2021, Sp. Sess. I, c. 100. For this section effective until the amendments by Acts 2021, Sp. Sess. I, c. 100 take effect see the preceding section, also numbered 62.1-262.

Editor's note.
Acts 2021, Sp. Sess. I, c. 100, cl. 2 provides: "That the State Water Control Board (the Board) shall adopt regulations to implement the provisions of this act."
Acts 2021, Sp. Sess. I, c. 100, cl. 3 provides: "That the provisions of the first enactment of this act shall become effective 30 days after the

adoption by the State Water Control Board of the regulations required by the second enactment of this act."

The 2021 Sp. Sess. I amendments.
The 2021 amendment by Sp. Sess. I, c. 100, in the first sentence, substituted "provided in § 62.1-260 or 62.1-261 or subsection H" for "provided in §§ 62.1-260 and 62.1-261 and subsection H"; in clause (i) deleted "use of" preceding "water-saving fixtures"; inserted clauses (iv) and (v) and redesignated former clause (iv) as clause (vi); in the third sentence substituted "any water conservation plan that complies" for "all water conservation plans in compliance" and "clauses (i) through (vi)" for "clauses (i) through (iv)"; and added the last two sentences. For contingent effective date, see Editor's note.

§ 62.1-263.1. Permit rationale.

In granting a permit pursuant to this chapter, the Department shall provide in writing a clear and concise statement of the legal basis, scientific rationale, and justification for the decision reached. When the decision of the Department is to deny a permit pursuant to this chapter, the Department shall, in consultation with legal counsel, provide a clear and concise statement explaining the reason for the denial, the scientific justification for the same, and how the Department's decision is in compliance with applicable laws and regulations. Copies of the decision, certified by the Director, shall be mailed by certified mail to the permittee or applicant.

History.
2022, c. 356.

Editor's note.
Acts 2022, c. 356, cl. 3 provides: "That any

permits or orders issued by the Air Pollution Control Board or the State Water Control Board prior to the effective date of this act shall continue in full force and are enforceable by the Department of Environmental Quality."

§ 62.1-266. Ground water withdrawal permits.

A. The Board may issue any ground water withdrawal permit upon terms, conditions, and limitations necessary for the protection of the public welfare, safety, and health.

B. Applications for ground water withdrawal permits shall be in a form prescribed by the Board and shall contain such information, consistent with this chapter, as the Board deems necessary.

C. All ground water withdrawal permits issued by the Board under this chapter shall have a fixed term not to exceed 15 years. The term of a ground water withdrawal permit issued by the Board shall not be extended by modification beyond the maximum duration, and the permit shall expire at the end of the term unless a complete application for a new permit has been filed in a timely manner as required by the regulations of the Board, and the Board is unable, through no fault of the permittee, to issue a new permit before the expiration date of the previous permit.

D. Renewed ground water withdrawal permits shall be for a withdrawal amount that includes such savings as can be demonstrated to have been achieved through water conservation, provided that a beneficial use of the permitted ground water can be demonstrated for the following permit term.

E. Any permit issued by the Board under this chapter may, after notice and opportunity for a hearing, be amended or revoked on any of the following grounds or for good cause as may be provided by the regulations of the Board:

1. The permittee has violated any regulation or order of the Board pertaining to ground water, any condition of a ground water withdrawal permit, any provision of this chapter, or any order of a court, where such violation presents a hazard or potential hazard to human health or the environment or is representative of a pattern of serious or repeated violations that, in the opinion of the Board, demonstrates the permittee's disregard for or inability to comply with applicable laws, regulations, or requirements;

2. The permittee has failed to disclose fully all relevant material facts or has misrepresented a material fact in applying for a permit, or in any other report or document required under this chapter or under the ground water withdrawal regulations of the Board;

3. The activity for which the permit was issued endangers human health or the environment and can be regulated to acceptable levels by amendment or revocation of the permit; or

4. There exists a material change in the basis on which the permit was issued that requires either a temporary or a permanent reduction or elimination of the withdrawal controlled by the permit necessary to protect human health or the environment.

F. No application for a ground water withdrawal permit shall be considered complete unless the applicant has provided the Executive Director of the Board with notification from the governing body of the locality in which the withdrawal is to occur that the location and operation of the withdrawing facility is in compliance with all ordinances adopted pursuant to Chapter 22 (§ 15.2-2200 et seq.) of Title 15.2. The provisions of this subsection shall not apply to any applicant exempt from compliance under Chapter 22 (§ 15.2-2200 et seq.) of Title 15.2.

G. A ground water withdrawal permit shall authorize withdrawal of a specific amount of ground water through a single well or system of wells, including a backup well or wells, or such other means as the withdrawer specifies.

H. The Board may adopt regulations to develop a general permit for the regulation of irrigation withdrawals from the surficial aquifer greater than

355

300,000 gallons in any one month. Regulations adopted pursuant to this subsection shall provide that withdrawals from the surficial aquifer may be permitted under either a general permit developed pursuant to this subsection or another ground water withdrawal permit.

I. The Board shall promulgate regulations establishing criteria for determining whether the quantity or quality of the ground water in a surficial aquifer is adequate to meet a proposed beneficial use. Such regulations shall specify the information required to be submitted to the Department by a golf course or any other person seeking a determination from the Department that either the quantity or quality of the ground water in a surficial aquifer is not adequate to meet a proposed beneficial use. Such regulations shall require the Department, within 30 days of receipt of a complete request, to make a determination as to the adequacy of the quantity or quality of the ground water in a surficial aquifer.

History.

1992, c. 812; 2018, c. 424; 2020, c. 670.

Editor's note.

Acts 2020, c. 670, cl. 2 was codified as sub-

section I of this section at the direction of the Virginia Code Commission.

The 2020 amendments.

The 2020 amendment by c. 670 added subsection H.